...turned
...loan may be re...

Also by James Bland

CRIME STRANGE BUT TRUE
THE BOOK OF EXECUTIONS

The Complete
True Crime Diaries

JAMES BLAND

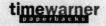

A *Time Warner* Paperback

First published in Great Britain in 2002 by Time Warner Paperbacks

True Crime Diary: Volume 1 Copyright © 1986 James Bland
True Crime Diary: Volume 2 Copyright © 1989 James Bland
The Complete True Crime Diaries Omnibus copyright © 2002 James Bland

The moral right of the author has been asserted.

A CIP catalogue record for this book
is available from the British Library.

ISBN 0 7515 3292 4

Printed and bound in Great Britain by
Clays Ltd, St Ives plc

Time Warner Paperbacks
An imprint of
Time Warner Books UK
Brettenham House
Lancaster Place
London WC2E 7EN

www.TimeWarnerBooks.co.uk

PREFACE

True Crime Diary recounts a large number of modern murder stories, many of them already famous. The subjects have been chosen according to my own preferences, with due regard for variety, oddities of character and quirks of fate. It is, as far as I know, the first time that such a collection has been arranged as a book of anniversaries, though about a third of the contents were originally published as a series with the same title in *True Crime Monthly*.

I have no doubt that some readers will notice discrepancies between my own accounts of certain cases and those currently available by other authors. This is always irritating to anyone with a keen interest in the subject, and it must be admitted that some authors in this field are not above presenting fiction as fact. As I do not wish to be regarded as one of them, I feel obliged to say that I have confined myself to using information which I believe to be accurate and that if I have erred at all, I have done so in good faith.

I make no apology for the fact that some of the stories are shocking, for nobody acquainted with the subject would expect otherwise. It is not only the cases of mass murder to which I am referring; many others, such as those of the Papin Sisters or Dr Geza de Kaplany, were so horrifying as to be incomprehensible to any normal person. I have no fresh insights or theories to offer in respect of such crimes; as with all the other cases, I have been content to describe them in a concise and, I hope, interesting manner. If the reader finds them absorbing, then the book is as J intended it to be.

True Crime Diary

Volume 1

Inquest on Margaret Lofty, 1915

JANUARY 1

On 1 January 1915, a man calling himself John Lloyd and claiming to be an estate agent told a London coroner's court of the tragic death of his wife, Margaret Elizabeth Lloyd, formerly Lofty, in a house in Highgate fourteen days earlier.

Weeping copiously, he said that on the day before her death he and his wife had moved into rooms at 14, Bismarck Road after travelling from Bath, where they had just been married. He had found her lying dead in the bathroom when he returned to the house after going out to buy some tomatoes.

A local doctor, who had been called to the house, told the court that Mrs Lloyd's death had been caused by drowning, and suggested that she had fainted as a result of getting into a hot bath while she was suffering from influenza.

The coroner's jury, having no reason to suspect foul play, accepted this explanation and brought in a verdict of death by misadventure. But that was not the end of the matter.

A report of the inquest, published in the *News of the World*, was read by a Buckinghamshire fruit-grower, Charles Burnham, whose daughter Alice had died in similar circumstances in Blackpool a year earlier, after marrying a man named George Smith. This George Smith, who claimed to be a bachelor of independent means, had insured Alice Burnham's life for £500 on the day before the marriage. Burnham informed the police that he suspected that George Smith and John Lloyd were the same person. As a result, an extensive investigation was started, and Charles Burnham's suspicions soon proved to be justified.

Moreover, a third case came to light — that of Beatrice

9

Williams, formerly Mundy, who had died in almost identical circumstances in Herne Bay in July 1912. Her husband, who called himself Henry Williams and claimed to be a picture-restorer, had gained £2500 by her death. Henry Williams was now also found to have been George Smith.

Margaret Lloyd's life had been insured for £700, and she had made a will in her husband's favour just a few hours before her death

On 23 March 1915, following police inquiries in many towns, George Joseph Smith, aged forty-three, was charged with three murders. At his trial on one of those charges, which began at the Old Bailey on 22 June, 112 witnesses and 264 exhibits were produced. Smith was shown to be a callous, predatory individual, who had committed bigamy several times in order to deprive lonely or unhappy women of their savings, and no one was left in any doubt that he was also a murderer.

In a demonstration of how he could have drowned his victims without leaving any signs of a struggle, a nurse was placed in a bath and pulled under the water by her feet. The rushing of water into her nasal passages produced immediate unconsciousness, and she had to be revived by artificial respiration.

Despite frequent outbursts, Smith was convicted and sentenced to death. He was hanged at Maidstone Prison on 13 August 1915.

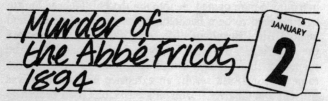

Murder of the Abbé Fricot, 1894

JANUARY 2

On the evening of 2 January 1894, the Abbé Fricot, rector of the parish of Entrammes, near Laval, sat down to make up his accounts in the company of his curate, the Abbé Albert Bruneau. What passed between the two priests is not known for certain, but it was clearly of some importance. At half past six a choir practice was cancelled without notice, the choir having already turned up at the rectory. Half an hour later, on being told that supper was ready, Bruneau said that Fricot had gone out. He then began playing the organ before going to have supper on his own. Though he appeared shaken at this point, it was also noticed that he had a good appetite. Later, when Fricot had still not appeared, a search of the premises was started, with neighbours being called in to help.

The search went on all night to no avail. In the morning Bruneau suggested that Fricot might have committed suicide and led his neighbour, a man named Chelle, to a well in the garden. There, under thirty feet of water, and concealed by logs, lay the body of the missing rector; his head had been battered with a heavy instrument. There were bloodstains on the edge of the well.

Bruneau was immediately suspected of the murder. His hand had been cut, but he claimed this had happened as he looked into the well at three o'clock in the morning, before leading Chelle to it. But there were also bloodstains on the keys of the organ, which Bruneau had played the previous evening. In his desk were found 1300 francs, which he appeared to have stolen from the rector's strong-box. A nun who visited the rectory had been told by Bruneau that Fricot had committed suicide — a mortal sin — and that his death had been made to look like murder in order to avoid a scandal.

Bruneau's character could hardly have helped to allay suspicion. A man of peasant origin, he was found to be a liar, a thief and a frequenter of brothels — at one of which he had contracted gonorrhoea. He had been a curate in Astillé, in the same province, for some years and during that time had used a bequest of 16,000 francs, intended for charity, for his own purposes. It was also while he was there that the rectory was burgled four times. He had

11

taken up his post in Entrammes at the age of thirty-one in November 1892, his arrival being quickly followed by the theft of 500 francs from a strong-box. It is likely that Fricot knew Bruneau to be the thief.

Neighbours claimed that on the night of the rector's death they heard groans coming from the rectory garden. It was supposed that Fricot, in making up his accounts, had decided that something had to be done about his curate's criminal activities, and that Bruneau had killed him after hearing what Fricot had to say on the matter.

Bruneau was brought to trial on 9 July. His sordid past was exposed, with prostitutes telling the court that he was a regular customer, and a brothel-keeper stating that he was not the only priest to turn up at her premises wearing his cassock. He was found guilty and sentenced to death, his execution on 29 August 1894, being attended by 16000 people. He died with dignity, declaring his innocence to the last.

Last murder by the Boston Strangler, 1964

JANUARY 4

On 4 January 1964, the man known as the Boston Strangler committed his last murder. The body of the victim, Mary Sullivan, aged nineteen, was found in a Boston apartment. She had been stripped naked, tied up, raped and strangled; finally, a broom handle had been thrust into her body and, as a cruel act of mockery, a New Year greetings card placed against her right foot. Albert DeSalvo, a non-drinking, non-smoking schizophrenic with uncontrollable sexual urges, later confessed to being the Strangler. He was to remember that as Mary Sullivan lay dead 'she was looking like she was surprised and even disappointed with the way I had treated her'.

It was his thirteenth murder in just over eighteen months, though at the time it was believed to be only his eleventh, the other two not having been attributed to him. His victims had all been women and, though several were either elderly or middle-aged, all had been raped or sexually abused. He gained admission to their homes by posing as a workman, and invariably managed to avoid leaving fingerprints. Generally, the weapon he used was a ligature made from stockings, its ends being left in a bow under the victim's chin. Some of the victims were also found to have been beaten over the head, stabbed or bitten.

As the pattern became familiar, public tension mounted. The police searched their records for known sexual deviants and questioned many suspects, but they received only false confessions. One woman, in February 1963, had successfully fought off the Strangler, but was suffering from a partial loss of memory as a result of her ordeal. After the death of Mary Sullivan, when the murders suddenly stopped, it was feared that the culprit would never be caught.

Then, on 27 October the same year, a young married woman in Cambridge, Massachusetts, was tied up and sexually assaulted by an intruder. The description she gave of him led police to DeSalvo, who had a record for breaking and entering. This, in turn, led to his photograph being circulated to neighbouring states, with the result that scores of women, all victims of sex attacks, identified him as their assailant. But DeSalvo, even then, was not suspected of being the Strangler. Held on rape charges, he was sent to the Boston State Hospital at Bridgewater for observation. On 4 February 1965, after confessing to a great many crimes, he was judged to be not competent to stand trial and committed to the hospital by court order. It was only then that he confessed to being the Strangler.

He gave details of the murders, in some cases making a sketch of the victim's home. He demonstrated the knot he

13

had used when strangling his victims. But the police, while convinced that he was telling them the truth, could not find any evidence to support his confessions. The state therefore reached an agreement with DeSalvo's attorney that no charges would be brought in connection with the murders, but that DeSalvo would be brought to trial for some of his other crimes instead.

The hearing began on 30 June 1966, with reporters and other observers from all over the world present. At the end of it DeSalvo, pleading for medical treatment, was sent to prison for life. In 1973, at the age of forty-two, he was stabbed to death by a fellow prisoner in Walpole State Prison.

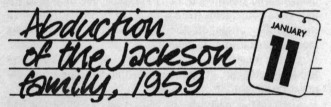

Abduction of the Jackson family, 1959

JANUARY 11

On 11 January 1959, Carrol Jackson, driving along a road near Apple Grove, Eastern Virginia, with his wife and two little daughters — one aged five, the other eighteen months — was forced to a halt by the driver of an old blue Chevrolet who had pulled over in front of them and stopped suddenly. Before Jackson could reverse and drive away, the other driver jumped out into the road and, threatening them with a gun, made the whole family get into the trunk of his own car. Later, when Jackson's car was found abandoned, a police search started, but no member of the missing family was to be seen alive again.

The bodies of Jackson and the younger girl were found in a ditch near Fredericksburg seven weeks later; Jackson had been shot in the head, the child had died of suffocation lying underneath him. Seventeen days after that the other

14

two members of the family were found in a shallow grave near Annapolis, Maryland; the mother had been raped and murdered, the child beaten to death with a blunt instrument. The grave was not far from the place where another woman had been shot dead and then sexually assaulted in June 1957, and police were quick to suspect that the same person was responsible for both crimes.

During the investigation that followed, an anonymous letter was received from Norfolk, Virginia, accusing Melvin Rees, a jazz musician, of the crimes, but police searched for Rees without success. The following January the letter-writer contacted them again, this time giving his name as Glenn L. Moser and informing them that Rees was working as a salesman in a music shop in West Memphis, Arkansas. Rees was immediately arrested and identified by a witness to the 1957 murder; a search of his parents' home in Hyattsville resulted in the discovery of the gun used to kill Jackson, together with detailed notes about this and other crimes.

Melvin Rees, a former university student, was known to his friends to be a mild-mannered, intelligent man. He played the piano, the guitar, the saxophone and the clarinet, taking work wherever he could find it. But he had an unusual 'philosophy' of murder: 'You can't say it's wrong to kill,' he had once remarked. 'Only individual standards make it right or wrong.'

Glenn Moser, who knew Rees well, had had cause to ask him outright if he had murdered the Jacksons, and had received an evasive answer. It now became clear that he was a sadist, responsible not only for these and the Annapolis murder, but also for the sex-murders of two teenage girls abducted near the University of Maryland, and two others whose bodies had been recovered from Maryland rivers.

The 'Sex Beast', as he was to be called, was tried for murder, firstly in Maryland, where he was given a life sentence, then in Virginia, where he was sentenced to death. He was executed in 1961, at the age of twenty-eight.

Trial of Clifford Olson concluded, 1982

In the Supreme Court of Vancouver, British Columbia, on 12 January 1982, the trial of Clifford Olson, an ex-convict accused of the murder of eleven young people, was brought to a swift conclusion when the defence counsel informed the court that his client, who had earlier denied the offences, wished to change all of his pleas to guilty. When the judge asked the reason for this, he explained that the accused wanted to spare the families of his victims the ordeal of listening to details of the crimes. The pleas were formally registered and a sentence of life imprisonment passed on each charge. The judge recommended that Olson should never be released on parole.

Olson, who was forty-two years old, already had a long record of violent crimes and had, in fact, spent almost all his adult life in jail. Since his release two years earlier, there had been many reports of the disappearance of children and young people in the Vancouver area, and the discovery of three bodies — two boys and a girl — at Weaver Lake, fifty miles east of the city, led to intensive police action.

Olson, living on the outskirts of Vancouver with his wife and baby son, was kept under surveillance. He was arrested in August 1981, after being identified by an eighteen-year-old girl who had been raped while she was out hitch-hiking two months previously. Searching his apartment, police discovered a number of articles belonging to one of the Weaver Lake victims.

Confronted with this evidence, Olson confessed that he was guilty of all three of the murders, and many others, too. He offered to show police where another eight victims had been buried, but only if he was paid $10,000 for each

16

corpse, together with an extra $30,000 for the three which had already been found.

The police refused the offer outright, pointing out that they already had enough evidence to convict him of murder. But, to their astonishment, the Attorney-General, Alan Williams, accepted it, insisting only that $90,000 of the proceeds should be placed in trust for Olson's son. When the money had been paid, and his lawyer was satisfied that it could not be recovered, Olson led police to the sites of eight different graves.

Olson's crimes caused widespread revulsion. His victims, aged between nine and eighteen, had been picked up at random and beaten, stabbed, strangled or mutilated. The revelation, at the end of his trial, that he had been paid $100,000 out of public funds, despite protests from the police, caused much anger. The unprecedented offer was, however, defended by the Solicitor-General, Robert Kaplan, on the grounds that the parents of the victims were entitled to give their children Christian burials.

Two weeks after the payment had been made known to the public, Olson offered the police a 'bargain deal': in return for a further $100,000, he would take them to the graves of twenty other victims. But this time, though he was suspected of many other murders, the offer was not taken up.

A year later, in January 1983, the man who, according to his counsel, had wanted to spare the feelings of his victims' parents, caused further anger by announcing that, in collaboration with a freelance writer, he intended to write a book about his crimes for publication. This led to demands for the law to be changed in order to prevent anyone making a profit out of crime.

Trial of Richard Prince, 1898

At the Old Bailey on 13 January 1898, Richard Prince, an out-of-work actor, was brought to trial for the murder of William Terriss, an immensely popular member of the same profession, at a rear entrance of the Adelphi Theatre, London, on 16 December previously.

Prince, aged thirty-nine, had been born on a farm near Dundee, where his father was a ploughman; his real name was Richard Millar Archer. He was neither a good actor nor a lucky one, and had never been anywhere near the heights to which he aspired; he had made, at best, a meagre living out of occasional small parts.

Of late he had been maintained by payments from the Actors' Benevolent Fund, pawning all but one set of his clothes and existing on meals of bread and milk; his landlady, out of sympathy, had reduced his rent from 4s (20p) to 3s (15p) a week. When his grant was suddenly terminated he became desperate.

He saw Terriss, who had once had him thrown out of a play for making an offensive remark, as the cause of his misfortune. 'He had kept me out of employment for ten years, and I had either to die in the street or kill him,' he was afterwards to declare.

On the evening of his death Terriss, aged fifty, arrived at the theatre where he was appearing in a play called *Secret Service*, in the company of a friend. He intended to enter by a pass-door in Maiden Lane, in order to avoid his fans. But as he inserted his key in the lock, Prince, who had been watching for him, rushed across the street and thrust a kitchen knife into his back with great force.

Terriss turned and fell, a second blow slashing his side and a third inflicting a wound in his chest. He died inside

18

the theatre a little while afterwards. The evening's performance had to be cancelled.

Prince, who had offered no resistance, was handed over to a policeman and taken to Bow Street Police Station. There, having admitted responsibility for the crime, he asked for something to eat. At the committal proceedings the following morning he was subjected to shouts and jeers from the crowds that filled the court.

At his trial Prince wore an Inverness cape. He made a plea of 'guilty with provocation' at first, but changed this on the advice of his counsel to one of not guilty by reason of insanity. Members of his own family and others told the court that his behaviour was unusual, his mother stating that he was 'soft in the head', and medical evidence was given of his 'insane delusions'.

The accused conducted himself throughout in a theatrical manner, as if pleased at having suddenly obtained in real life the leading part which had for so long escaped him on the stage.

The trial lasted one day, the jury deliberating for half an hour before informing the court that they found the accused guilty of the crime but not responsible for his actions. He was committed to the criminal lunatic asylum at Broadmoor and hastily removed from the courtroom after attempting to make a speech of thanks.

He was happier in the asylum than he had been outside and took a keen interest in the entertainments put on by the inmates.

Kidnapping of Lesley Whittle, 1975

On 14 January 1975, Lesley Whittle, aged seventeen, was found to be missing from her home in the village of Highley, in Shropshire. She had not appeared for breakfast that morning and was not in her bedroom. A ransom note, demanding £50,000 for her return, was found on a piece of tape with embossed lettering; it ordered the family not to contact the police and said that a telephone call would be made to a shopping centre in Kidderminster that evening.

Ronald Whittle, the victim's brother, informed the police and later went to the shopping centre to take the call. In the meantime, however, the kidnapping had been reported on television and, as a result, the call was not made.

Two days later, at 11.45 p.m., Ronald Whittle received a telephone call at home, telling him to take the ransom money to a telephone kiosk in Kidsgrove, near Stoke-on-Trent, where he would find another message. He arrived there early in the morning and found the message on a piece of Dynotape, telling him to drive to the nearby Bathpool Park and make contact with the kidnapper by flashing the lights of his car. He followed the instruction, but the kidnapper did not appear.

A further telephone call gave Ronald an opportunity to ask the kidnapper for proof that Lesley was with him. The man agreed to get him the proof — the answer to a certain question — and call back, but he never did so.

By this time the kidnapper was known to have committed other serious crimes. On the night of 15 January a security guard at a transport depot in Dudley, Worcestershire, had seen a shabby little man hanging around the premises and asked him what he wanted. Receiving an unsatisfactory answer, he turned away from the man, intending to call the police, but was shot six times in the back. A stolen car which had been parked nearby was found to contain Lesley's slippers, more messages from the kidnapper, and a tape-recording made by Lesley asking her family to co-operate with him.

Moreover, an examination of the cartridge cases found at the depot showed that the same gun had been used by a notorious criminal called the 'Black Panther', who specialized in sub-post office burglaries and was known to have committed three murders.

An intensive police search led to the discovery, on 7 March 1975, of Lesley Whittle's body in the network of sewage tunnels underneath Bathpool Park; it was hanging, naked, by a wire rope below a narrow ledge. The sewage system had been the kidnapper's hide-out and his victim's place of captivity.

On 11 December the same year two policemen driving through Mansfield Woodhouse, Nottinghamshire, late at night noticed a suspicious-looking man loitering near the post office and stopped to speak to him. The man produced a sawn-off shotgun and ordered them to drive him to Blidworth, six miles away. But they managed, with the help of two members of the public, to overpower him, and found in his possession two hoods of the sort known to have been used by the Black Panther.

The man turned out to be Donald Neilson, aged thirty-nine, of Grangefield Avenue, Thornaby, Bradford, a married man with a teenage daughter. Neilson, who had changed his name from Nappey, was a joiner and occasional taxi-driver. But in his attic police found more guns and hoods, together with burglary equipment.

Neilson was tried in Oxford in June 1976 for the kidnapping and murder of Lesley Whittle, for which he was sentenced to twenty-one years' imprisonment. He was then tried for the murders of three sub-postmasters and sentenced to life imprisonment for each offence. No charge was brought against him in connection with the shooting of the security guard in Dudley, as the victim in this case had lived for fourteen months after the offence had been committed.

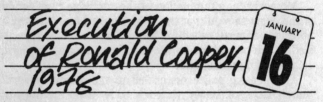

Execution of Ronald Cooper, 1978

JANUARY 16

Ronald Frank Cooper, who was hanged in South Africa on 16 January 1978, was a fantasist who wanted to become a mass murderer. Fortunately for the rest of society, he was assailed by doubt and misfortune in his attempts to put his ideas into practice.

Cooper had a troubled childhood: he is known to have hated his father and to have tried, at the age of eleven, to strangle a girl. Early in 1976 he was an unemployed labourer living in a hotel in Berea, Johannesburg. It was then that he committed his first-known crime as an adult.

Following a ten-year-old boy into an apartment block in a different district of Johannesburg, he pulled out a gun and forced the child to accompany him to a nearby park. There, however, he suddenly gave up whatever he had in mind and allowed his victim to go home. The boy, Tresslin Pohl, was later taken out in a police car to look for him, but without success.

A month later, on 17 March 1976, Ronald Cooper made a long entry in his diary, no doubt to convince himself that he was now more resolute than he had been before. He began, falteringly enough: 'I have decided that I think I should become a homosexual murderer ...' Then, taking the bull by the horns, he continued: '... and shall get hold of young boys and bring them here where I am staying and I shall rape them and then kill them.'

Soon his imagination was running wild: 'I shall not kill all the boys in the same way. Some I shall strangle with my hands. Other boys I shall strangle with a piece of cord or rope. Others again I shall stab to death, and others I shall cut their throats. I can also suffocate or smother other boys …'

He went on and on, listing different ways in which he would dispose of his victims, finally stating that after killing thirty boys, he would turn his attention to the opposite sex and kill at least six girls or women. Yet, in spite of this, he remained as half-hearted as ever in practice.

Four days after making this entry Cooper followed another ten-year-old boy into a block of flats. Pushing him against a wall, he pressed a knife against his chest, inflicting two minor wounds, but ran off when the boy screamed. At his next attempt, in a block in his own district, he pulled a boy out of the lift and tried to strangle him, but once again took to his heels when the victim screamed.

On 16 May, in yet another apartment block, he grasped Mark Garnet, aged twelve, by the throat. When the boy lost consciousness Cooper tied a rope round his neck and made an unsuccessful attempt at sodomy. Afterwards he loosened the rope, hoping that the boy was still alive. But this time the attack had been fatal.

Overcome with remorse, Cooper described the murder in three different diaries — a clear sign of mental conflict. 'I only wish I can undo what I did,' he wrote in one of them. 'It's a really dreadful thing that I did. I never want to do such a thing again.'

He was not to have any more opportunities, for Tresslin Pohl, a schoolfriend of Mark Garnet's, had discovered where Cooper was living: he had followed him home after seeing him in a cinema and, surprisingly, kept this information to himself. But now, hearing of Mark's death, he decided to go to the police.

Police officers went immediately to the hotel and waited in a car near the entrance. When Cooper emerged he took fright at the sight of them, and after a brief chase, was

taken into custody. The diaries found in his room left no
doubt about his guilt.

Cooper was twenty-six years old at the time of his
execution.

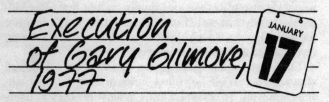

Execution of Gary Gilmore, 1977

JANUARY 17

On 17 January 1977, Gary Gilmore, a double murderer,
was executed by firing squad in the State of Utah, at his
own insistence. It was the outcome of a successful legal
battle over what he called 'the right to die' and brought an
end to a ten-year moratorium on the death penalty in the
United States. The case was, of course, highly publicized
and provided Norman Mailer with a subject for a very
successful book, *The Executioner's Song*.

Nine months earlier Gilmore, aged thirty-five, had been
released on parole from the federal penitentiary in Marion,
Illinois, after serving over eleven years. A violent and
dangerous man, he had, in fact, spent more than half of his
life in detention, and during his last term, he and a friend
had beaten and knifed a fellow-convict so badly that he had
almost died.

He had, it seems, no intention of making good. He
drank heavily and began stealing from stores, the thefts
being the result of habit rather than need. The two
murders were committed in July 1976, robbery being the
motive in each case.

The first murder was that of Max Jensen, a law student
working at a service station in Orem, Utah; Gilmore held
him up, forced him into the men's room, and shot him in
the back of the head while he lay on the floor The second

24

which took place the following evening, was that of Ben Bushnell, the manager of the City Centre Motel in Provo, a few miles away; the victim was shot dead in the same way. In each case Gilmore stole about $125 in cash.

On the latter occasion he was seen by the victim's wife and a guest at the motel. Afterwards, in disposing of the gun, he accidentally shot himself in the hand. The wound was noticed at a nearby garage when he went to collect his truck, which had been left for servicing, and was later reported to the police. Gilmore was arrested without difficulty while trying to leave the state by road.

His determination to avoid a commutation of sentence was due not to remorse, but to a fear of further long-term imprisonment. He told his brother, who intended to apply for a stay of execution on his behalf: 'I've spent too much time in jail. I don't have anything left in me.'

At one point he persuaded a girl with whom he was in love to smuggle drugs in to him, so that they could both commit suicide at a pre-arranged time. But the attempt failed and the girl was removed to a mental hospital for treatment.

As a result of his demand to be executed, Gilmore became a celebrity, selling the rights to his life story for about $50,000. On the night before his death he gave a farewell party inside the prison for his relatives and friends. Early the following morning he instructed his lawyers to appeal against a last-minute stay of execution; they did so, and the order was set aside.

The execution was carried out in a local cannery to which Gilmore had been taken by van. He was strapped down in an old office chair, with a dirty mattress behind the backboard to prevent ricochets. A light was shone on to him, while everyone else was in semi-darkness. When a hood had been pulled over his face, the members of the firing squad took aim from behind a screen, training their guns on a white ring pinned above his heart.

25

Murder of Julia Wallace, 1931

JANUARY 20

On the evening of 20 January 1931, Julia Wallace, the fifty-year-old wife of an insurance agent, was found battered to death in the sitting-room of her home in Wolverton Street, Liverpool. She had been struck over the head eleven times — many of the blows being dealt when she was already dead — and the walls, furniture and carpet of the room were drenched with blood. An iron bar which the couple had kept for cleaning the fireplace was missing from the house, and it appeared that about £4 in cash had also been taken. The iron bar, which was never found, was almost certainly the murder weapon.

Her husband, William Herbert Wallace, aged fifty-two, informed the police that a telephone message had been left for him at his chess club the previous evening by an unknown man calling himself Qualtrough. The message was that Qualtrough wanted to speak to him on a matter of business and that the insurance agent should call at his home in Menlove Gardens East, Mossley Hill, at 7.30 p.m. the following day. Wallace had accordingly left his own home about 6.50 p.m. and travelled by tramcar to the Menlove Gardens area of Liverpool, only to discover that Menlove Gardens East did not exist.

Arriving back at his own home about 8.45 p.m., Wallace had called for assistance from his neighbours, Mr and Mrs Johnston, saying that he was unable to get into his house because the doors wouldn't open. But when they went to help him they found that his back door, at least, opened without difficulty. The body was discovered a moment later, Wallace being strangely calm at the sight of it.

The police were suspicious of Wallace's account of his movements, especially as they could find no sign of a forced entry. It also seemed, from the pathologist's report, that Mrs Wallace had been killed before her husband left the house that evening. As for the telephone call to his chess club, that was found to have been made from a telephone box less than a quarter of a mile from Wolverton Street. So Wallace could easily have made it himself.

After continuing their investigation for two weeks, the police arrested Wallace and charged him with the crime. He was brought to trial at St George's Hall, Liverpool, on 22 April. But the case proved not to be very strong, and the judge, in his summing-up, suggested to the jury that it was insufficient to justify a conviction.

Wallace had had no motive for killing his wife. They had been a devoted couple, leading conventional lives, and he had stood to gain nothing from her death. Mrs Wallace, according to the evidence of a milk delivery boy, had still been alive at 6.30 that evening; her husband had boarded a tramcar at Smithdown Junction, a ten-minute walk from the house, at 7.10. Later, when the murder was reported, no bloodstains had been found on any of his clothes, except a macintosh on which his dead wife's body had actually been lying.

Yet, incredibly, the jury disregarded the judge's advice and returned a verdict of guilty. Wallace, under sentence of death, appealed against the conviction, and won his case before the Court of Criminal Appeal. He died two years later, claiming to the end that he knew the real identity of his wife's murderer.

The case is still the subject of much speculation.

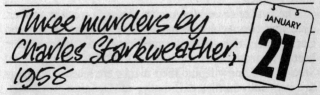

Three murders by Charles Starkweather, 1958

On 21 January 1958, Charles Starkweather, a nineteen-year-old garbage collector of Lincoln, Nebraska, called at the home of his girlfriend, Caril Ann Fugate, aged fourteen. She was not there at the time, so her mother and stepfather, Velda and Marion Bartlett, allowed him into the house to await her return. He was carrying a hunting rifle, and began to play with it while he was waiting.

Being only 5 feet 2 inches tall, and having red hair, Starkweather was known as 'Little Red'. He drove a hot-rod and read comics; the film star James Dean was his personal hero. But his girlfriend's mother was evidently uneasy in his presence, for she shouted at him, telling him to stop fiddling with his gun. At this, Starkweather shot both Mrs Bartlett and her husband dead. He then went on waiting until Caril returned.

Caril Fugate knew what Starkweather was like, for a few weeks earlier she had joined him in carrying out a robbery at a gas station, during the course of which the attendant had been murdered. She was not distressed when she arrived home and found that he had killed her mother and stepfather, and apparently raised no objection when he went into one of the bedrooms and choked her two-year-old stepsister to death. The couple calmly put a notice on the front door, stating: 'Every Body is Sick with the Flu'. They then made some sandwiches and sat down to watch television, as if oblivious of the corpses lying around.

A few days later the two teenagers drove off in Stark-weather's hot-rod, making their way across America. The police broke into the house in Lincoln and raised an alert, but it was several days before the couple were arrested and during that time the former garbage collector killed seven more people.

The first of these was August Meyer, a wealthy farmer. The next two were a teenage couple, Robert Jensen and Carol King; the girl was raped repeatedly before being beaten to death. Then C. Lauer Ward, head of the Capital Steel Works, his wife and their maid were killed after being tied up and mutilated. Finally, in Douglas, Wyoming, Merle Collison, a shoe salesman, was shot dead.

Attempting to get away from the scene of this last

crime, Starkweather found that his car would not start, and tried to force a passer-by to help him. The passer-by, an oil agent named Joseph Sprinkle, grabbed his rifle and held on to it until the police arrived. There were, by this time, 1200 police and members of the National Guard in pursuit of the couple, and they were quickly arrested, Starkweather surrendering after being grazed by a bullet.

Starkweather at first tried to protect the girl by telling the police that he had taken her hostage, but he stopped doing so when she called him a killer. He made a confession, declaring his hatred of the society he knew, which seemed to him to be made up entirely of 'Goddam sons of bitches looking for somebody to make fun of'. He was executed in the electric chair at the Nebraska State Penitentiary on 25 June 1959.

Caril Fugate, who claimed to be innocent of the crimes to which Starkweather had confessed, was sentenced to life imprisonment. She was released on parole in 1977.

Murder of David Graham Phillips, 1911

JANUARY 23

The murder of David Graham Phillips, on 23 January 1911, was a ludicrous crime, committed as a result of a false assumption on the part of his killer, Fitzhugh Coyle Goldsborough, who killed himself immediately afterwards.

Phillips, aged forty-three, was a popular author whose novel, *The Fashionable Adventures of Joshua Craig*, was among the best-sellers of the time. He had an apartment in Gramercy Park, Manhattan.

Goldsborough, aged thirty, was a member of a rich Philadelphia family. He had no occupation and no apparent aim; much of his time was spent lying in bed, either reading love stories or turning neurotic ideas over in his mind. He did not know Phillips personally.

Somehow, Goldsborough had conceived the notion that his unmarried sister, whom he adored, had been used as a real-life model for a flippant society girl in Phillips' novel, and this he regarded as a slight which had to be avenged.

The murder took place just after Phillips left his apartment on the day in question. Goldsborough, according to witnesses, confronted him with a pistol, shouting, 'Here you go!' He then shot Phillips five times before turning the gun on himself. As he fired his last shot he screamed, 'Here I go!'

Phillips was taken to hospital, where he lived for some hours. As he died he remarked, 'I can fight one bullet, but not five.'

When Goldsborough's parents were told what had happened they revealed the reason for his astonishing conduct.

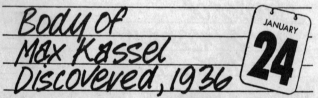

Body of Max Kassel Discovered, 1936

JANUARY 24

About ten o'clock on the morning of 24 January 1936, a man's body was discovered in a country lane near St Albans, Hertfordshire. He had died from gunshot wounds a few hours earlier, having been beaten up beforehand. There was nothing in his pockets to reveal his identity, and all marks had been removed from his clothes. It was speculated in the press that he had been the victim of a gang killing.

Three days later he was identified as Émile Allard, a

dealer in cheap jewellery. Émile Allard, however, turned out to be one of many aliases of an international crook named Max Kassel, generally known as 'Red Max'.

Kassel was a Latvian, born in 1879. He had a criminal record in France, where he had been imprisoned in 1922 for drug-trafficking, and was also known to have been involved in a vice racket in South America. More recently he had lived in Soho, arranging marriages — or, at least, marriage ceremonies — for Frenchwomen who wanted to obtain British nationality. He had been seen in Soho about 7.30 p.m. on 23 January.

During the course of their inquiries police officers learnt that Kassel had been accustomed to using the car-hire services of a Frenchman named Alexandre, who, on being interviewed, gave the impression of knowing more about the affair than he was willing to divulge.

Investigating his background, they found that he held the lease of a two-floor flat in Little Newport Street, occupied by Suzanne Naylor, a Frenchwoman married to an Englishman. Mrs Naylor was known to have a lover named Georges Lacroix, who normally lived with her at the Little Newport Street address. But neither of them were to be found there when the police went to see them.

Suspicious, the police broke in and searched the place, finding some broken window-panes and specks of blood in the bathroom. But there were no fingerprints anywhere and no clothes in the cupboards. The couple had cleaned the flat as thoroughly as possible and fled.

From a Ministry of Health insurance card, found behind a chest of drawers, the police traced a second Frenchwoman, Marcelle Aubin, who had been employed as Suzanne Naylor's maid. Marcelle Aubin informed them that her employer had left for France on 25 January.

Alexandre was questioned further and obliged to surrender his American car for examination. When bloodstains were found in it he decided to tell the police what had happened.

He said that Lacroix had telephoned him late at night

on 23 January and told him to go to the flat in Little Newport Street. When he arrived there he was shown Kassel's body and told to return at 4 a.m. to help dispose of it, Lacroix threatening him with a gun. At 4 a.m. he and Lacroix had taken the body, wrapped in a blanket, out to his car. They had then driven to St Albans together.

Kassel, he explained, had owed Suzanne Naylor £25. Lacroix had started to beat him up because he had failed to pay it back, and had shot him when Kassel resisted. The victim had broken the window in an attempt to call for help.

This account was confirmed by Marcelle Aubin, who now admitted that she had been present and that she had heard the fighting, the shots and a constant groaning from another room. She had stayed in the flat all night, helping Suzanne to remove traces of the crime, she said.

Suzanne Naylor was located in France, where she was known to the police as Paulette Bernard. She had been legally married in France before coming to England, and so was still a French citizen. Georges Lacroix proved to be an alias of Robert Vernon, a Frenchman with a record of larceny with violence, who had escaped from Devil's Island in 1927.

As extradition was impossible, it was arranged that they would both be tried in Paris, Vernon for murder and his mistress for being an accessory after the fact. Chief Inspector F.D. Sharpe of the Flying Squad had therefore to give evidence against them before a French court.

In April 1937 Robert Vernon was convicted of the murder and sentenced to ten years' hard labour and twenty years' banishment to French Guiana. Paulette Bernard, who claimed to have been an unwilling participant, was acquitted.

Mass Poisoning in Tokyo, 1948

Just before closing time on 26 January 1948, a man entered a branch of the Imperial Bank in north Tokyo, claiming to be one of the city's public health officials. Announcing that there had been an outbreak of dysentery in the area, he induced all sixteen of the bank's employees to drink a solution of potassium cyanide. He then proceeded to rob the tills as his victims collapsed around him, and made off with a large amount of money in cash and cheques. Only four members of the staff survived.

Seven months later Sadamichi Hirasawa, a fifty-six-year-old artist of Otaru, Hokkaido, was arrested in connection with the murders. Normally a poor man, Hirasawa was unable to explain a comparatively large sum of money found in his possession, and eventually confessed to the crime. He afterwards retracted the confession, saying that it had been obtained after thirty-seven days of intensive questioning, but he was convicted and sentenced to death.

The sentence was confirmed in 1955 but never carried out, as successive Justice Ministers, for some undisclosed reason, refused to give their approval to the execution order. Sadamichi Hirasawa has remained in prison ever since and his sentence has never been commuted. He is said to have been on Death Row longer than anyone else in the world.

But many doubts have been expressed about his guilt, and there have been many demands for a retrial. Of the four surviving members of the bank staff, three said only that he bore a resemblance to the person responsible for the crime, while the fourth could see no resemblance at all. Moreover, it is now known that the Japanese police did not believe him to be guilty, either.

33

Following his retirement in 1963, Hideo Noruchi, the police officer in charge of the investigation, revealed that his team of detectives had believed the culprit to be experienced in the use of poisons, and had suspected a member of the 731st Regiment of the Imperial Japanese Army. This regiment had been involved in chemical warfare research during the Second World War, using Chinese prisoners in its experiments. But its war record had been ignored by General MacArthur's Occupation Force in return for the information which had been gained.

It appears from contemporary documents which have recently been discovered in the United States that MacArthur's General Headquarters also believed the poisoner to have been a member of the 731st Regiment, but forced the Japanese police to frame an innocent man rather than allow the connection to be exposed. Japanese newspapers which tried to investigate the case at the time were censored — also on orders from MacArthur's GHQ. And an American soldier with whom Hirasawa claimed to have been playing cards on the afternoon in question was recalled from Japan before the trial started in 1949.

In February 1984 Hirasawa, then aged ninety-two, was reported to be confined to bed and going blind in Sendai Jail. A plea for clemency was made on his behalf by a group of supporters called the Save Hirasawa Committee, whose members include Takeshiko Hirasawa, the artist's adopted son. The plea was unsuccessful.

In May 1985 an attempt was made to get him released under Japan's Statute of Limitations, as thirty years had elapsed since his death sentence had been confirmed. But this also failed because the thirty-year rule was interpreted as applying only to accused persons who had not been captured or who had escaped from custody.

It seems likely that the fight to clear Hirasawa's name will continue long after his death.

Murder of Frieda Rösner, 1943

On 29 January 1943, a woman's body was found in a wood near the village of Köpenick, near Berlin. Frieda Rösner, aged fifty-one, had been out collecting firewood; her death was caused by strangulation. There were no obvious suspects, so the police officer in charge of the case began questioning known criminals from the village. One of these was Bruno Lüdke, a laundry roundsman who had earlier been sterilized after being arrested for sexual assault.

Lüdke, who was mentally defective, admitted that he had known the victim and that he had seen her in the woods. On being asked if he had killed her, he became violent and had to be restrained. He then admitted the crime and went on to confess that he was guilty of eighty-four other murders in different parts of Germany. Some of these murders were found to be on record as unsolved crimes; others were found to be offences for which innocent men had been arrested. At any rate, after an investigation lasting a year, it was concluded that Lüdke's confession was true.

Born in 1909, Lüdke had committed his first murder in 1928. His victims had all been women, rape being his usual motive, although he also robbed them; their deaths were normally caused either by strangulation or by stabbing. On another occasion he had derived pleasure from running a woman down with his horse-drawn delivery van. In addition to all this, he had been in the habit of torturing animals.

Instead of being brought to trial, Lüdke was removed to a hospital in Vienna, where he was used for experiments. He was finally put to death by means of an injection on 8 April 1944.

The Nazis treated the case as a state secret.

Execution of Kenneth Neu, 1935

Kenneth Neu, who was hanged in New Orleans on 1 February 1935, was an aspiring night-club singer with a record of mental illness. On 2 September 1933, while he was out of work in New York, he met Lawrence Shead, a homosexual theatre-owner. Shead took him for a drink, offered him a job, and invited him back to his apartment. There, however, it became clear that his real interest in him was a sexual one. Neu smashed in Shead's skull with an electric iron, put on one of his suits, and made off with his watch and wallet.

Two weeks later, in New Orleans, he met Eunice Hotter, a young waitress with whom he spent the next three nights. Eunice wanted to go to New York and Neu promised to take her there, but by now he was out of money again and decided to try blackmail.

In the lobby of the Jung Hotel, he became acquainted with Sheffield Clark, a Nashville store-owner aged sixty-three. Calling on Clark later in his room, he demanded money from him, threatening to accuse him of making homosexual advances. When Clark reached for the telephone to call the police, Neu hit him with a blackjack and strangled him. He took $300 and Clark's car keys and went to the car park to get his car, telling the attendant that he was the owner's son. He then set out for New York with Eunice Hotter, having first replaced the number plate of the stolen car with a notice chalked on a piece of cardboard: 'New Car in Transit'.

Driving through New Jersey, he was stopped by the police, who asked what the notice meant. Unable to give a satisfactory explanation, he spent the night in jail — as did Eunice Hotter and a hitch-hiker who had been in the car with them. It was then noticed that he fitted the description of a man wanted in connection with Shead's murder.

Asked if he knew Shead, Neu replied, 'Sure ... I killed him. This is his suit I'm wearing now.' He went on to confess that he had also killed Sheffield Clark. 'He seemed like a nice old man,' he said. 'But I was desperate for money.' In view of Shead's homosexuality, it was decided that Neu should be sent back to New Orleans to be tried for Clark's murder.

Neu, aged twenty-five, was a handsome man with an engaging manner. It was partly because of this that his trial, which opened on 12 December 1933, attracted a lot of attention. He appeared in court wearing Shead's suit and pleaded insanity, evidence being given that he had suffered mental deterioration as a result of syphilis. As if to emphasize the point, Neu sang on his way to and from the courtroom. He was, however, convicted, and an appeal was turned down.

On Death Row he remained cheerful, singing and tap-dancing in his cell, and receiving visits from a young woman who had apparently fallen in love with him. At the gallows he sang a verse which he had composed himself, beginning, 'I'm fit as a fiddle and ready to hang'.

While under sentence of death he had also become a Roman Catholic.

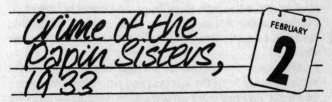

Crime of the Papin Sisters, 1933

FEBRUARY 2

On the evening of 2 February 1933, René Lancelin, a French attorney living in Le Mans, arrived for dinner at the home of a friend. He had been away all day on business and expected that his wife and twenty-seven-year-old daughter Geneviève, who had also been invited, would meet him there. But they had not turned up and his friend had had no word from them.

M. Lancelin waited for a little while, then tried to telephone his home. He received no reply. Becoming worried, he excused himself and went to find out what had happened. He found his own house in darkness, except for a faint glow from an upstairs room occupied by their maids, the sisters Christine and Lea Papin. Moreover, he was unable to get into the house as the front door had been locked from the inside. He therefore called the police.

An inspector came to his assistance, forcing his way into the house. He found the ground floor to be deserted. But on the first floor landing lay the bodies of the attorney's wife and daughter, revoltingly mutilated: the walls and doors had been splashed with blood to a height of over seven feet. The police officer immediately went in search of the maids and, finding their room locked, broke down the door. Inside, the two women lay huddled together, naked, in a bed.

They both confessed to the crime, which appeared to have been committed because Madame Lancelin had rebuked them over a blown fuse. 'When I saw that Madame Lancelin was going to jump on me I leapt at her face and scratched out her eyes with my fingers,' said Christine Papin. She then realized that she had made a mistake and quickly corrected herself: 'No ... it was on Mademoiselle Lancelin that I leapt, and it was her eyes that I scratched out. Meanwhile, my sister Lea had jumped on Madame Lancelin and scratched her eyes out in the same way.'

After this, she continued, she had brought up a knife and a hammer from the kitchen, and with these two instruments she and her sister attacked their victims afresh. 'We struck at the head with the knife, hacked at the bodies and legs, and also struck with a pewter pot, which was standing on a little table on the landing. We exchanged one instrument for another several times. By that I mean that I would pass the hammer over to my sister so that she could hit with it, while she handed me the knife — and we did the same with the pewter pot.'

She said that she had locked the attorney out because she wanted the police to be the first to arrive on the scene, and that they had taken their clothes off because they were stained with blood. 'I have no regrets — or, rather, I can't tell you whether I have any or not ... I did not plan my crime and I didn't feel any hatred towards them (the victims), but I don't put up with the sort of gesture that Madame Lancelin was making at me that evening.'

Lea corroborated Christine's account. 'Like my sister, I affirm that we had not planned to kill our mistresses,' she said. 'The idea came suddenly, when we heard Madame Lancelin scolding us.'

Christine Papin, aged twenty-eight, and her sister Lea, twenty-one, were brought to trial in Le Mans in September 1933. They were already regarded as notorious criminals by this time, and the newspapers referred to them as 'the diabolical sisters', and 'the lambs who had become wolves'. As the details of their crime were given in the courtroom, there were murmurs of horror and demands for their execution from the spectators. The prisoners listened impassively.

The judge questioned them about their motive, finding it impossible to believe that they could have made such ferocious attacks on their victims just because they were being scolded over a blown fuse. They had, after all, both agreed that they had been well paid and well treated by the family, and bore no resentment as a result of being their servants.

Observing that the prisoners had led unusually isolated lives for young people, with no social activities and no contact with members of the opposite sex, the judge asked whether they had had a sexual relationship with each other. But Christine replied, with a shrug, that they were just sisters; there was nothing else between them.

As no satisfactory explanation of the crime emerged, the defence naturally pleaded that the prisoners were not of sound mind. The jury, however, returned verdicts of guilty against both of them, though with extenuating circumstances in Lea's case, as she had been dominated by Christine. The judge then sentenced Christine to death and Lea to ten years' hard labour.

Christine's sentence was afterwards commuted to hard labour for life, but she began to show signs of insanity not long afterwards and died in a psychiatric hospital in 1937. Lea was released after serving her term.

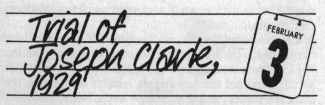

Trial of Joseph Clark, 1929

FEBRUARY 3

On 3 February 1929, Joseph Clark, aged twenty-one, was brought to trial at the Liverpool Assize Court, charged with the murder of Alice Fontaine, his former landlady. He pleaded guilty, against the advice of his counsel, and was sentenced to death. It was one of the shortest murder trials on record, lasting just four and a half minutes. He was afterwards hanged.

Clark was an amateur hypnotist who lived off his many girlfriends. He had been brought up by relatives in the United States, but worked his passage back to England in 1927. He seems to have had little difficulty inducing girls to part with their money; one of them said later, 'I could not resist him, and would do anything he suggested ... I gave him money whenever he wanted it ...'

In Birkenhead he tried to marry a girl who was under twenty-one by presenting her older sister's birth certificate at the registrar's office. When the attempt was discovered he became enraged and tried to strangle the girl with a pyjama cord, shouting, 'If I can't have you nobody else shall!' No charge was brought against him over this, as the girl was afraid of the publicity which would result from it.

Clark became a lodger at Mrs Fontaine's house in Northbrook Street, Liverpool, after meeting her daughter whose name was also Alice; he was now calling himself Kennedy. He failed to pay for his keep and constantly borrowed money. When he was finally turned out — after the discovery of a letter from one of his other victims — he sent obscene letters to both mother and daughter.

Shortly afterwards, in October 1928, Clark suddenly appeared in the daughter's bedroom as she was getting ready to go to church. He tried to strangle her, again using a pyjama cord, and after a struggle she lost consciousness. She recovered a little later and found that he had also attempted to cut her throat. Her mother's body was found downstairs, Clark's attempt to strangle Mrs Fontaine having been more successful.

After being arrested Clark made a confession. He claimed that in her last moments, after he had relaxed his grip on her throat, Mrs Fontaine had smiled at him and asked him to take care of her daughter.

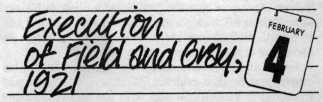

Execution of Field and Gray, 1921

FEBRUARY 4

On 4 February 1921, Jack Alfred Field, aged nineteen, and William Thomas Gray, twenty-nine, were hanged at Wandsworth Prison for a brutal murder committed on a stretch of shingle near Eastbourne on 19 August the previous year.

41

Their victim, Irene Munro, a Scottish-born typist from London, was seventeen years old. She had been spending a week's holiday at an Eastbourne boarding-house, and on the afternoon of the day in question was known to have been carrying her holiday money in her handbag.

A number of people noticed her in the company of two men, one of whom wore a herring-bone suit. Her body was afterwards found in a shallow grave; she had been battered to death with a stone, and her money had been stolen. It was the landlady of the boarding-house who identified the body.

Field and Gray were local residents, both out of work. They were initially questioned by police as a result of Gray's herring-bone suit, but were not regarded as suspects at this stage. Later, however, it was learnt from a barmaid at the Albemarle Hotel that they had been out of money on the morning of 19 August, but apparently affluent a few hours afterwards.

Then, during a house-to-house inquiry, a labourer stated that he had seen Gray, whom he knew personally, walking towards the shingle that afternoon with another man and a girl. The two culprits were arrested and charged with the crime.

They appeared for trial at the Lewes Assizes on 13 December 1920, denying the offence. Though witnesses had seen them in the girl's company, Field told the court that on the day in question he had had a drink with Gray after drawing his unemployment benefit, and that they had afterwards walked together to Pevensey — a distance of about four miles — meeting nobody on the way.

Gray, an unsavoury character, was advised by his counsel not to give evidence. While in custody he had attempted to establish an alibi with the help of a fellow-prisoner; during the course of the trial he fell asleep and was rebuked by the judge. His counsel suggested to the jury that an educated and refined girl like Irene Munro was unlikely to have associated with down-and-out men like the prisoners.

While under sentence of death the two ruffians both accused each other of the girl's murder. We do not know which of them was telling the truth.

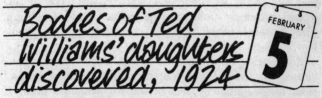

Bodies of Ted Williams' daughters discovered, 1924

On the morning of 5 February 1924, Edward Williams, a poor music teacher living in a suburb of Sydney, was returning from Mass when he stopped to speak to a crossing-sweeper named Tonkin, and offered to buy him a drink. Tonkin was surprised, for Williams did not normally drink and was known to be having a very hard time. However, he went with him to a working-men's bar where the music teacher ordered two glasses of stout.

During the course of their conversation Williams said that he was taking his three daughters to Brisbane, where he had been offered a position as choirmaster. Tonkin, he said, could have his furniture in settlement of a debt; he could go and collect it from his lodgings. The crossing-sweeper was impressed and gave Williams enough money to get the four of them to Brisbane. Later, after parting company with him, he took a handcart to the music teacher's lodgings to move the furniture.

His arrival threw Williams' landlady, Florence Mahon, into a state of confusion. She rushed upstairs to Williams' room, to see what he had to say about it. But Williams wasn't there. Instead, she found his three little girls lying together in bed, all with their throats cut. Their blood had soaked through the mattress on to some newspaper which had been spread underneath it.

The police started a search for Williams, but he was

nowhere to be found. He was still at large when the bodies of the children were buried.

Among those who knew him, the crime caused dismay as well as horror, for Ted Williams had loved his children: they had been a source of great pleasure to him, in spite of his otherwise troubled existence. A neighbour who had seen him on the afternoon of 4 February was to recall: 'He looked extremely tired until he smiled at his daughters. Then his whole face lit up and the tiredness seemed to leave him.'

After being on the run for several days Williams gave himself up and made a confession. He said that he had killed his daughters because he was frightened for them. 'I knew what I was doing,' he said. 'I was doing it for the best, because I loved them.' He was charged with murder.

Ted Williams, aged fifty-two, was a man prone to misfortune. His income had never been high and he had always found it difficult to make ends meet. For the last two years his wife, Florence Mahon's sister-in-law, had been confined in an asylum, and he and his three daughters, the eldest of whom was five and a half, had lived and slept in one room. While he went hungry to ensure that they had an adequate amount of food, he was treated with contempt by his brother-in-law who regarded him as 'a bum'. By 4 February he was close to the end of his tether.

On that day, Florence Mahon, who looked after the children for him while he went out to give lessons, said that she would do it no more: he would have to find somebody else. Later the same day her husband suggested that he should send them to an institution because they were now too old to sleep in the same room as him.

To Ted Williams, Mahon's remark was a shattering blow. When he came up for trial at the Central Court in Sydney, he told the jury: 'I saw if my girls went to an institution they would be separated. They would not be able to sit at the same table together, and when they came out they would be tools for the first smooth-tongued person who came along. I know — and you know, gentlemen — that

44

the majority of prostitutes are the women who were raised in public institutions such as my girls would have been sent to had I been agreeable. I saw it all, and saw beyond it.' Rather than allow that to happen, he had murdered them in their sleep.

He denied that he was insane; he denied that he had tried to escape justice. 'I intended to give myself up, but decided not to do so until the Monday, in order that I might learn that my children were properly buried,' he explained.

Ted Williams was convicted and sentenced to death. Many thousands of letters were sent to the Minister of Justice, Thomas Ley, asking for the sentence to be commuted. But they were brushed aside, the execution being carried out at Long Bay Jail.

Thomas Ley was later convicted of murder himself and died in Broadmoor. An account of his crime also appears in this book (see 30 November).

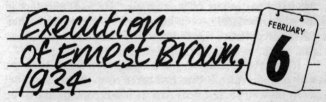

Execution of Ernest Brown, 1934

FEBRUARY 6

Ernest Brown, who was hanged on 6 February 1934, at the age of thirty-five, had been employed as a groom by Frederick Morton, a wealthy cattle-dealer of Saxton Grange, an isolated farmhouse near the village of Towton, in Yorkshire. While working in that capacity he had been having an affair with Dorothy Morton, the cattle-dealer's wife. But he proved to be a possessive man with a violent temper, and Mrs Morton found this irksome.

In June 1933 he became indignant at being asked to mow the lawn, which he did not consider to be one of his duties; he promptly left Morton's employment. A little while afterwards he sought, with Mrs Morton's help, to get the job back, but found that his former employer would now only accept him as an odd-job man. Brown therefore returned to Saxton Grange seething with resentment and promising himself revenge.

On the evening of 5 September, while his employer was away, he started an argument with Dorothy Morton because she had been out swimming with another man; he struck her and she fell to the ground. The same evening the telephone was found to be out of order and Brown began firing a shotgun outside the house, saying that he was shooting at rats. Dorothy Morton became frightened, having only her baby and her young help, Ann Houseman, for company, and soon the two women took the child and locked themselves in upstairs rooms.

At 3.30 a.m. there was an explosion outside and they saw that the garage was on fire. They left the house in terror, running into the nearby fields. In the morning the ruins of the garage, which had been completely destroyed, were examined, and the cattle-dealer's body was found in the wreckage of one of his two cars. He had been shot in the chest, evidently some hours before the explosion had taken place. Petrol was found to have been used to fuel the fire, and it was this which had caused the explosion.

It was also found that the telephone wires had been cut with a knife which Brown had taken from the kitchen.

At his trial at the Leeds Assizes it was contended that he had cut the wires after killing Frederick Morton about 9.30 p.m., and then frightened the women to prevent them leaving the house. His own claim, that Morton had caused the fire himself as a result of being drunk, was not taken seriously.

Ernest Brown's execution took place at Armley Prison in Leeds. While on the scaffold he was asked by the chaplain if he wanted to confess any other crimes before being hanged. His reply, 'Ought to burn!' or 'Otterburn!' has given rise to the idea that he may have been the

murderer of Evelyn Foster. Unfortunately, the trap opened
before he could make himself clear on this point.

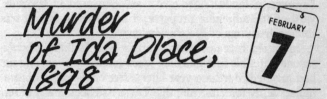

Murder of Ida Place, 1898

Just after 6.30 p.m. on 7 February 1898, a New York City
policeman arrived at the Brooklyn home of William Place,
a prosperous forty-seven-year-old insurance adjuster,
accompanied by a neighbour who had reported hearing
screams and cries for help from inside. He rang the bell
and waited for a moment, then, hearing a moan himself, got
the neighbour to help him force an entry.

Inside the house, a few feet from the front door, the two
men found Place lying unconscious on the floor. He had
serious head injuries and his face was smeared with blood.
There was a smell of gas about the place.

Sending the neighbour to summon an ambulance, the
patrolman tended the injured man. The precinct commander and two detectives arrived soon afterwards and began
to search the premises, leaving Place in the hands of the
ambulance crew. There appeared at first to be nobody else
in the house, but tracing the smell of gas to one of the front
bedrooms, the police officers found Place's wife Martha,
also unconscious, wrapped in a quilt on the floor. She too,
was taken to hospital, to be treated for gas poisoning.

But with the windows open and the gas cleared, another
smell — that of carbolic acid — caused the police to force
open the locked door of one of the other bedrooms. There,
under the mattress of a disordered bed, they found the
body of Place's daughter Ida, aged seventeen.

Ida Place had been dead for several hours. Her face had

been disfigured with acid burns while she was still alive; she had also received a heavy blow on the left temple. But her death had been caused by strangulation.

The police found no sign of a forced entry, and were unable to find the acid container. The following morning, however, a bloodstained axe was discovered in the side yard of the adjoining property; it appeared to have been thrown from one of Place's windows.

Inquiries revealed that Martha was William Place's second wife; his first had died when Ida was eleven, and he had married Martha a year later, after employing her as a housekeeper for some months. There had been many bitter quarrels between them, Martha behaving so aggressively that her husband, a year earlier, had brought charges against her, though without success.

The police also learnt from Hilda Jans, who had been a servant in the house, that she had been dismissed from her position on the day of the murder, being given a month's wages in lieu of notice, together with a bonus of $5 for having packed in readiness to leave by 5 p.m.

Asked about the smell of carbolic acid, Hilda said that she had been out in the back yard after breakfast and had first noticed it when she returned to the house around 9.15 a.m. She had not seen Ida Place afterwards, and had later found her bedroom door locked.

As soon as he regained consciousness William Place, not realizing that Ida was dead or that his wife was a patient in the same hospital, told police that Martha had tried to kill him and begged them to protect his daughter.

When he was well enough to speak to them at greater length he said that Martha had complained of Ida showing her neither affection nor respect, and resented the way in which he indulged her; that was one of their differences. Another was Martha's practice of hoarding money in her own bank account and, at the same time, running up excessive bills for him to pay.

On the day that she attacked him, he said, he had arrived home from his office to find the house in darkness.

He let himself in, calling out to his wife, his daughter and the servant — for he did not know that Hilda had been dismissed, and then, hearing nothing, went to look in the kitchen. He was going back towards the front door when he heard somebody creeping down the stairs, and, turning round, saw that it was Martha. He spoke to her, unaware that she had an axe in her hand, but she suddenly rushed forward and began to strike him with it.

The police, after listening to his account, had the unpleasant duty of informing him that his daughter had been murdered.

They were now satisfied that Martha had planned to kill both her husband and her stepdaughter, and that she had tried to kill herself when she realized that William's cries for help had been loud enough to be heard by the neighbours. She was therefore charged and taken into custody.

On 5 July she was brought to trial, dressed entirely in black. She admitted the attacks, pleading intense provocation in each case, but refused to say where she had obtained the acid or how long it had been in her possession. She was found guilty, with no recommendation of mercy, and on 20 March 1899, she was executed in Sing Sing Prison.

She was the first woman ever to die in the electric chair.

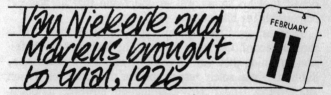

Van Niekerk and Markus brought to trial, 1926

FEBRUARY 11

On 11 February 1926, two ex-convicts, Andries Van Niekerk and Edward Markus, were brought to trial in Pretoria, accused of murdering the two occupants of a Transvaal farmhouse on the night of 2 December previously. The crime had been a callous one, and the farm-house had been set on fire afterwards. The trial, which lasted eight days, was therefore followed with much interest.

Waterval Farm, in the Transvaal's Potgietersrust district, had been managed by sixty-year-old Bill Nelson for its absent owner; Nelson's companion, Tom Denton, a fifty-five-year-old former soldier, had run a small general store on the property, selling goods to its native workers. Both were evidently kind and friendly men, for when the two ex-convicts appeared at the farm in search of work they were treated with sympathy and generosity.

Nelson hired them to decorate the outside walls of the farm and gave them food and beds. He did not expect them to start work on the day of their arrival, and the next day he and Denton took them on a shooting trip, providing them with guns. On the evening of the second day they all dined together and retired early. Then, just after midnight, the sound of shots was heard, but nobody went to the scene until it was realized that the buildings were on fire. Two men were then seen running away from the premises.

Van Niekerk, aged thirty-four, was a habitual criminal with a long history of housebreaking, theft and violence: he had spent nearly half his life in prison and had been whipped on a number of occasions. A man of low mentality, he had delusions of persecution and superiority, and was given to outbursts of fury. It was contended on his behalf that his sanity was in doubt and that he was not responsible for his actions.

Markus, aged twenty-four, was a weaker man with a shorter record. On being arrested, he had made a confession, claiming that Van Niekerk — who had threatened to kill him — was solely responsible for the deaths of Nelson and Denton. Under cross-examination, however, he began to contradict himself, and it soon appeared that a confession which Van Niekerk had made in revenge — 'both Markus and I committed the crime' — was more credible.

Towards the close the question of whether Van Niekerk

was in such a condition that he would not know the nature and quality of his actions was put to a medical expert. The witness replied, 'I have seen an imbecile of the mental age of three or four years commit an act and know it was wrong. Therefore a person of higher age must know it.'

After an absence of just over two hours the jury found both defendants guilty and they were sentenced to death. Van Niekerk, pleased that Markus was to suffer the same fate as him, then waved his handkerchief towards relatives in the courtroom. The prisoners were both hanged on 14 April 1926.

Henry Smith found murdered, 1896

On the morning of 14 February 1896, Henry Smith, a seventy-nine-year-old widower, was found dead in the kitchen of his neglected mansion in Muswell Hill, north London. He had been struck on the head twelve times during the course of a struggle and had afterwards been bound and gagged, his attackers evidently not realizing that they had killed him. His bedroom had been ransacked and money had been taken from his safe.

The culprits had entered the house through a kitchen window after trying unsuccessfully to open two other windows with a jemmy, and Mr Smith, awakened by the noise, had come downstairs in his nightshirt to investigate. Two penknives, which had been used to cut strips from a tablecloth, were found beside the body; the intruders had also left behind a toy lantern. Mr Smith's body had been found by his gardener.

Police investigating the crime soon learnt that two

strange men had been seen in the neighbourhood during the previous two days, and these were seen as the most likely suspects. Further inquiries revealed that they were Henry Fowler, aged thirty-one, and Albert Milsom, thirty-three, two known criminals from Kentish Town who were both missing from their homes. The toy lantern found at the scene of the crime was identified by Milsom's fifteen-year-old brother-in-law as his own. A warrant was then obtained for the arrest of both men, and they were apprehended in Bath on 12 April.

Fowler, an ex-convict who had been released on licence on 16 January previously, was a tough individual; he resisted arrest and was not overpowered until he had been struck several times over the head with a police revolver. But his companion, a shifty little man, gave no trouble and afterwards made a statement in which he admitted the robbery and accused Fowler of the murder. Fowler, he said, had killed the old man while he (Milsom) was outside the house. He also revealed that he and Fowler had buried their burglary tools in the grounds of the mansion.

Infuriated by what he saw as an act of betrayal, Fowler claimed that the murder had been committed by Milsom; the 'dirty dog' had put his foot on the old man's neck and made sure that he was dead, he declared. Besides the evidence of the toy lantern and their own statements, they were both identified as the men who had been seen in the neighbourhood two days before the discovery of the crime, and a £10 note found in Fowler's possession was known to have been stolen from the victim's home.

Their trial began at the Old Bailey on 19 May and lasted three days, the judge remarking in his summing up that the evidence of the two penknives indicated that two people had been engaged in tying up Mr Smith. When the jury retired to consider their verdict, Fowler fell upon Milsom and tried to strangle him. He had to be forcibly restrained by warders and policemen, the struggle continuing for twelve minutes. The jury returned a verdict of guilty against each of them and they were sentenced to death.

Henry Fowler and Albert Milsom were hanged at Newgate Prison on 9 June 1896, together with another murderer named Seaman, who was placed between them on the scaffold. An accident occurred at the execution, the hangman's assistant falling through the trap with the condemned. But he escaped unhurt, having instinctively grapped the legs of the prisoner in front of him.

It was the last triple execution to be carried out at Newgate.

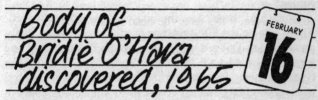

Body of Bridie O'Hara discovered, 1965
FEBRUARY 16

On 16 February 1965, the body of a naked woman was found in a patch of bracken on the Heron Trading Estate in Acton, west London. Bridie O'Hara, a twenty-seven-year-old prostitute of Agate Road, Hammersmith, had died of suffocation after an unsuccessful attempt at strangling; some of her teeth were missing and sperm was found in her throat. It appeared that she had died in a kneeling position, and also that her body had been kept somewhere cool before being taken to the place where it was found. Bridie O'Hara, a native of Dublin, had last been seen alive five weeks earlier.

At the time of this discovery police were investigating the cases of seven other prostitutes who had died mysteriously in the London area during the previous six years. The first of these, Elizabeth Figg, aged twenty-one, had been found strangled beside the Thames between Barnes and Chiswick on 17 June 1959; the skeleton of the second, Gwynneth Rees, aged twenty-two, during the clearing of a rubbish dump at Mortlake, also beside the Thames, on 8

November 1963. In the case of Gwynneth Rees the cause of death had not been established with certainty, but the fact that she too, had been a prostitute caused police to wonder whether the two cases were connected.

The other five bodies had all be found in 1964: Hannah Tailford, thirty, in the Thames at Hammersmith on 2 February; Irene Lockwood, twenty-six, also in the Thames (about 300 yards from the same place) on 9 April; Helene Barthelemy, twenty-two, near a sports ground in Brentford on 24 April; Mary Fleming, thirty, outside a garage near Chiswick High Road on 14 July, and Margaret McGowan, twenty-one, behind a car park in Kensington on 25 November.

In each of these cases the body had been found naked. There was no specific evidence of murder in two of them, for Hannah Tailford may have committed suicide, and Irene Lockwood had died from drowning. But the police regarded them as probable murder cases just the same, and when a caretaker named Kenneth Archibald confessed to having killed Irene Lockwood, he was arrested and brought to trial. He was found not guilty, having retracted his confession in the meantime.

In the case of Mary Fleming the body had been found in a sitting position in a cul-de-sac, close to a site where painters had been working the previous night. The painters had seen a man standing near a van, and when he became aware of their presence he had driven away hurriedly, almost colliding with a car. Though the driver of the car had reported the matter to the police, he had failed to make a note of the van's registration number, so the suspect could not be traced.

The deaths of Helene Barthelemy, Mary Fleming, and Margaret McGowan were all similar to that of Bridie O'Hara: teeth were missing from the bodies — false teeth in the case of Mary Fleming — and sperm was found in each of their throats. Traces of paint of a type used for spraying cars were found on the body in each case, leading police to speculate that they had been left in a garage or factory at some stage.

It seemed that the killer was a pervert who enjoyed strangling or choking his victims during oral sex, then repeating the sexual act later after forcing out some of their teeth. The fact that he removed all articles of clothing from the dead bodies led to him being called 'Jack the Stripper'.

The police were already engaged in a large-scale operation aimed at catching him, but it was not until the death of Bridie O'Hara that they located the place where the bodies had been kept — a transformer building near a paint-spray shop on the estate where Bridie O'Hara had been discovered.

The police then concentrated their efforts on the estate itself, taking note of all the vans seen in the area and paying particular attention to any which appeared there more than once. It was hinted on television that they were very near to bringing the culprit to justice. But, in fact, they never did so.

It was later claimed that one of the three main suspects, a forty-five-year-old security guard whose rounds included the paint-spray shop, had committed suicide while inquiries at the Heron Trading Estate were in progress. The man, who was unmarried, was not named, and his identity has not been made known to the public since. It is known, however, that he left a note saying he was 'unable to stand the strain any longer'.

With his death this shocking series of murders came to an end.

Murder of Mrs Durand-Deacon, 1949

On 18 February 1949, John George Haigh, aged thirty-nine, a resident at the Onslow Court Hotel in South Kensington, London, committed the crime for which he was to be hanged. It was by no means his first offence, for Haigh was a professional criminal who lived by fraud and theft and had resorted to murder several times before. To the other residents at the hotel, however, he was a man of charm and good manners who appeared to have made a success of running his own engineering business. They had no reason to suspect him of any wrong-doing.

His victim, Mrs Olive Durand-Deacon, was a rich widow of sixty-nine. She and Haigh were on friendly terms as a result of having adjacent tables in the dining-room, and when she told him of a scheme to manufacture artificial finger-nails of her own design he suggested that she visit his factory in Crawley, Sussex, where she could chose the necessary materials. This idea appealed to Mrs Durand-Deacon, and she agreed to go with him.

On the day in question they left London about 2.30 p.m., travelling in Haigh's Alvis car. About 4.15 p.m. they were seen together at the George Hotel in Crawley. But that was the last time that Mrs Durand-Deacon was seen by anyone except Haigh.

Haigh's 'factory', in Leopold Road, was actually a building which he did not own, but was occasionally allowed to use as a storeroom in connection with his 'experimental engineering' work. It contained various articles, including three carboys of sulphuric acid, a forty-five gallon drum which had been specially lined to hold corrosive chemicals, a stirrup pump, a pair of gloves and a rubber apron. If Mrs Durand-Deacon found any of these things suspicious, it did not prevent her turning her back on him, for Haigh, taking a revolver from his pocket, was able to kill her with a single shot in the back of the neck. He then removed all her valuables — a Persian lamb coat, rings, a necklace, earrings and a cruciform — before putting the body into the drum. The sulphuric acid was put in afterwards with the use of the stirrup pump.

Haigh immediately set about disposing of the valuables and paying off debts, returning to Crawley several times in the next few days in order to make sure that the body was dissolving in the acid. In the meantime he was obliged to go to the police, in the company of another resident, to report his victim's disappearance.

The police were suspicious of Haigh from the start, and were not surprised to learn that he had served three terms of imprisonment. Searching the 'factory' in Crawley, they found his revolver, some ammunition and a receipt for a Persian lamb coat which had been left at a cleaners' in Reigate. They also traced the victim's jewellery, which had been sold to a jeweller in Horsham, a few miles away.

On being taken to Chelsea police station for questioning, Haigh told the police how he had dissolved Mrs Durand-Deacon's body, evidently in the mistaken belief that if the body could not be found a murder charge could not be brought against him. An examination of the sludge outside the storeroom then led to the discovery of a human gallstone and some fragments of bone, showing that the disintegration had not been complete. These remains were later identified as those of Mrs Durand-Deacon.

Charged with the murder, Haigh confessed that he had also killed a Mr William Donald McSwann in London in 1944, Mr McSwann's parents, also in London, in 1945, and a Dr Archibald Henderson and his wife in Crawley in 1948. He claimed that he had committed these murders, like that of Mrs Durand-Deacon, because he wanted to drink the blood of the victims, but it was found that his real motive in each case had been financial gain.

He later claimed to have killed three other people, all of

whom were strangers to him, but the existence of these people was never proved.

At his trial in Lewes, in July 1949, for the murder of Mrs Durand-Deacon, Haigh pleaded that he was insane. The jury, however, took only fifteen minutes to reject this defence and returned a verdict of guilty. Haigh's execution took place at Wandsworth Prison on 6 August.

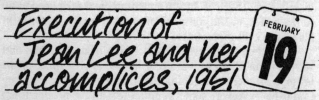

Execution of Jean Lee and her accomplices, 1951
FEBRUARY 19

On 19 February 1951, Jean Lee, a thirty-three-year-old Australian murderess, and her two accomplices, Robert David Clayton and Norman Andrews, were hanged for the murder of William Kent, a bookmaker aged seventy-three, in his hotel room in Carlton, New South Wales, in November 1949.

Jean Lee, an attractive woman, had taken to prostitution during the Second World War after the failure of her marriage; Clayton, her lover, was a petty criminal who lived off her earnings from the servicemen of various nations who were stationed in Australia at the time.

After the war they turned to blackmail, Jean Lee enticing men into compromising situations, and Clayton, pretending to be her irate husband, bursting in on them to demand compensation. Andrews, a thug, did not join them in their criminal activities until 1949.

The murder of William Kent took place on the night of 7 November. Jean Lee and her companions met him in the bar of his hotel and later she retired to his room with him and got him drunk so that she could pick his pockets. However, the old man kept a tight grip on his money and she was unable to get it away from him until she hit him on the head with a bottle. She then tied him up and let Clayton and Andrews into the room.

The two ruffians tied the old man's thumbs together with a bootlace, kicked him repeatedly and slashed him several times with a broken bottle before he finally died. The room was ransacked.

After the discovery of the body, members of the hotel staff gave descriptions of the three culprits to the police and they were soon identified and arrested in Sydney. They all made confessions and were brought to trial in March 1950, a retrial being granted as a result of the manner in which two of the confessions had been obtained. The second trial had the same result as the first, and the High Court confirmed the death sentences passed on each of them.

Their executions took place at Pentridge Jail.

Attempted execution of John Lee, 1885

FEBRUARY
23

On 23 February 1885, John Lee, a prisoner in Exeter Jail, was due to be hanged for the murder of Emma Keyse, an elderly spinster of Babbacombe, near Torquay, by whom he had been employed as a footman. The body of his victim had been discovered during the course of a fire at her home in the early hours of 15 November previously. Her throat had been cut so deeply that the vertebrae of her neck were notched; she had also been beaten over the head with a hatchet. Lee, a young man with a prison record for theft, had killed her because she had found fault with his conduct and reduced his wages from 2s 6d (12½p) to 2s (10p) a week. He had afterwards set fire to the house, probably in the hope of concealing the crime.

As the time appointed for his execution approached, Lee showed no sign of fear; the strain which the imminence of such an event always produced among the prison staff did not affect him at all. Just before 8 a.m. he was taken from his cell and the solemn procession to the scaffold began, the chief warder leading the way. Lee, accompanied by two other warders, walked behind the prison chaplain, the Reverend John Pitkin. Various officials, including the hangman, the prison governor and the under-sheriff, together with several more warders followed.

At the place of execution Lee's legs were strapped together and the white cap pulled over his face. James Berry, the hangman, then adjusted the rope round his neck and asked if he had anything to say. Lee replied that he had not. As the chaplain concluded his service the hangman pulled the lever which operated the two trap-doors. To everyone's amazement, they failed to open. The prisoner remained motionless.

Berry moved the lever to and fro, but the trap-doors still would not open. John Lee was removed from the scaffold to an adjoining room while an examination of the drop was carried out, and certain adjustments were made. Then the condemned was brought back and placed on the scaffold again. But when the hangman pulled the lever, the result was the same as it had been before: the trap-doors would not budge.

Once again the culprit was taken from the scaffold, this time to the prison basement. Further adjustments were made. After a few more minutes the prisoner was brought back for a third attempt, the drop having been tested and found to be in working order. The chaplain started the service for the third time. James Berry pulled the lever. But the trap-doors still remained closed. The third attempt had failed, too.

Everyone concerned, except the condemned, was now in a state of consternation. They had no idea what to do for the best. Finally, the chaplain told the under-sheriff that he would have nothing more to do with the execution. It had therefore to be postponed, as it could not be carried out without the chaplain being present. Mr Pitkin accompanied the prisoner as he was taken back to his cell.

Outside the prison, there was much surprise when the black flag did not appear, and this was followed by great excitement when it was heard that there had been three unsuccessful attempts to hang the prisoner. Newspaper offices were afterwards besieged by people wanting to know the latest news of the affair, and it was said that there was a general feeling that the prisoner's life should be spared after the ordeal which he had suffered. It was announced later the same day that John Lee had been reprieved and that his sentence would be commuted to life imprisonment.

The failure of the scaffold has never been satisfactorily explained. Some said it was caused by damp, others that it was due to faulty construction.

John Lee remained in prison for the next twenty-two years, and was released on 18 December 1907. The following year he published a book about his life, making himself out to be innocent of the murder of which he had been convicted. It sold well, but was not taken seriously by people acquainted with the case. His guilt had been too firmly established by the evidence.

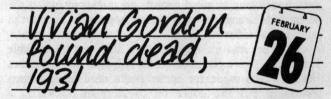

Vivian Gordon found dead, 1931

FEBRUARY 26

On the morning of 26 February 1931, Vivian Gordon, an attractive divorcée with expensive tastes, was found dead in a ravine in New York City's Van Cortlandt Park, having been strangled with a piece of clothes-line some hours earlier. Her mink coat, diamond ring and $665 wrist-watch were all missing, giving the impression that robbery had been the motive for the murder. However, the discovery of a five-volume diary in her Manhattan apartment, together with other pieces of evidence obtained elsewhere, caused police to suspect that this was not the case at all.

Vivian Gordon, who had once been convicted on a vice charge and sent to a reformatory, was found to have been both a blackmailer and a money-lender. It was also found that a few days before her murder she had given information to a committee investigating police corruption in New York City, claiming that her conviction eight years earlier had been the result of fabricated evidence. It therefore appeared that any one of a good many people could have had cause to want her out of the way.

The crime proved to be New York's most sensational murder for five years, with several well-known figures being regarded as suspects and many lurid details of the victim's life published. At one point the lawyer Bernard Gervase and a thief known as 'Knucklehead' Kaufman were arrested on suspicion, only to be released later. All this became too much for Vivian's sixteen-year-old daughter in New Jersey, and drove her to suicide.

Eventually it was discovered that in July 1929 Vivian Gordon had made a loan of $1500 to an ex-convict named Howie Schramm — known to her as Charles Reuben — and that this had never been repaid. Schramm, aged thirty-two, had a long criminal record, his crimes including the attempted strangling of a Bronx housewife during the course of a robbery in 1921.

Schramm and an associate — a thief named Dutchie Ginsman — were placed under surveillance, but no further headway was made for some weeks until an unknown informant put the police on to Herman Schwartz, a garment jobber, who said that Schramm had tried to sell him a mink coat, and had also had a diamond ring and an expensive wrist-watch for sale, on the morning of 26 February. Turning down the offer because the pelts were marked on the inside, Schwartz had taken Schramm to meet a diamond dealer and a Broadway dressmaker. The police officers investigating the crime had no doubt that the valuables in question had been those stolen from Vivian Gordon.

Another associate of Schramm's was found to be Harvey Sawyer, a young man with no criminal record. It was learnt that he had hired a Cadillac on the night of 25 February and returned it the following morning, and also that Schramm had been giving him occasional sums of money. When Schramm and Ginsman were finally interrogated in connection with the murder, they denied all knowledge of it. But Sawyer made a confession.

He revealed that the murder of Vivian Gordon had been planned beforehand, and that Schramm had taken her to Van Cortlandt Park — where Ginsman and Sawyer were waiting in the hired car — believing that she was to meet a potential victim of her own. Having introduced her to Ginsman, Schramm had got into the back of the car with her and strangled her there as they drove towards the ravine where her body was found.

Sawyer, whose own part in the affair had been confined to hiring and driving the car, believed that the murder had been carried out on behalf of 'Knucklehead' Kaufman. He also revealed that Schramm had been unable to sell the mink coat and had therefore burnt it.

Schramm and Ginsman were charged with murder and brought to trial in June 1931. Sawyer, Schwartz, the diamond dealer and the dressmaker all gave evidence, and it appeared that the prosecution's case was overwhelming. But then Howie Schramm's twenty-two-year-old sister appeared for the defence, stating that her brother had taken her out on the night of the murder and had remained in her company until daylight the following morning.

Ginsman's sister then gave *him* an alibi, testifying that he had spent the night at her home in the East Bronx. In this, she was supported by her sixteen-year-old son and a neighbouring shopkeeper.

To the amazement and disgust of the district attorney and the police officers concerned, the jury found both defendants not guilty. The case therefore remains officially unsolved.

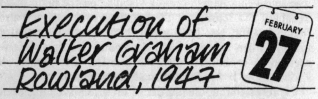

Execution of Walter Graham Rowland, 1947

On 27 February 1947, Walter Graham Rowland, a thirty-nine-year-old labourer, was hanged at Strangeways Prison for the murder of Olive Balchin, a prostitute aged about forty, whose body had been found on a bomb-site in Cumberland Street, near Deansgate, Manchester, on 20 October previously. The crime had been committed with a cobbler's hammer, which the culprit had left a few feet from the body, and had evidently taken place because Rowland was suffering from venereal disease and believed he had contracted it from the victim.

Rowland had been in trouble before and had, in fact, occupied the condemned cell at Strangeways on an earlier occasion. At the age of nineteen he had been sent to Borstal for three years for attempting to strangle sixteen-year-old Annie Schofield whom he married after being released; then, in 1934, he had strangled their daughter Mavis, aged two, with a stocking, and been sentenced to death. This latter sentence had been commuted to life imprisonment, and Rowland remained in jail until 1940, when he was freed after volunteering to serve in the army.

Demobilized from the Royal Artillery in June 1946, Rowland went to stay at the Services Transit Dormitory in

Manchester, and it was there that police went to find him after learning that he had been behaving suspiciously. 'You don't want me for murdering that woman, do you?' he asked, on being woken up. He admitted knowing Olive Balchin and said he suspected that she had given him venereal disease, but denied having killed her.

However, he was identified by a dealer in second-hand goods from whom he had bought the hammer, and also by two people who had seen him in the company of Olive Balchin on the night of 19 October. Two hairs found on Rowland's jacket matched the victim's own hair; a blood-stain on one of his shoes proved to be of the same group as Olive Balchin's blood. Moreover, samples of brick-dust, cement, charcoal and clinker from the turn-ups of his trousers matched other samples taken from the site where the body had been found.

While Rowland was awaiting trial on this occasion his wife divorced him on the grounds of cruelty. The divorce court had to sit *in camera* so that the jury at the forth-coming murder trial would not be prejudiced by disclosure of the prisoner's criminal record.

Rowland appeared for trial at the Manchester Assizes in December 1946, the case lasting five days. When the jury returned a verdict of guilty, he made a speech from the dock, claiming that he was innocent. 'The killing of this woman was a terrible crime, but there is a worse crime being committed now because someone with the knowledge of this murder is seeing me sentenced today for a crime which I did not commit,' he declared.

The case was made all the more extraordinary on 22 January 1947, when somebody else confessed to the murder of Olive Balchin. David John Ware, a thirty-nine-year-old man with a history of mental illness, was serving a sentence for theft at the time of Rowland's trial and sent his confession to the prison governor. He later retracted it, admitting that he had lied for the sake of publicity. In the meantime an inquiry had been held to discover whether there were grounds for thinking that Rowland's conviction had been a miscarriage of justice. It concluded that there were no such grounds. Rowland nonetheless persisted in denying his guilt to the end.

Four years later David John Ware was tried for the attempted murder of another woman and found guilty but insane. He was sent to Broadmoor, where he committed suicide in April 1954.

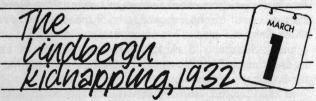

The Lindbergh kidnapping, 1932

MARCH 1

Between 8 p.m. and 10 p.m. on 1 March 1932, Charles A. Lindbergh Jr, twenty-month-old son of the famous aviator, was abducted from his nursery at the Lindbergh Estate in the Sourland Mountains of Hunterdon County, New Jersey. The nursery was on the second floor of the house, and the child's disappearance was discovered by his Scots nurse, Betty Gow; a ransom note, demanding $50,000, was found on the window-sill.

The kidnapper had used a crudely-made ladder to gain access to the nursery, and had left no fingerprints. The ransom note — which was followed by another on 6 March increasing the demand to $70,000 — contained spelling mistakes, and was believed to have been written by a German of little education.

Colonel Lindbergh appealed to the kidnapper to start negotiations, and appointed Dr John F. Condon of the Bronx, New York, to act as an intermediary. The kidnapper sent Condon a note saying that he was agreeable to this, and later, at a meeting, gave his name as John. He sent Condon the missing child's night clothes as proof that he was the person concerned.

At a second meeting, in a cemetery in the Bronx in April, Condon offered 'John' $50,000 for the child's return. The offer was accepted and the money handed over, 'John' giving Condon a note informing him that the child was to be found on a boat called *Nellie* anchored off Martha's Vineyard, Massachusetts. He then hurried away in the darkness.

Colonel Lindbergh set off immediately, and the following day a search was carried out in the area indicated. But there was no sign of either the child or the boat. On 12 May the child's body was found in a shallow grave about five miles from the Lindbergh Estate. He had been killed by a blow on the head about two months earlier.

On 18 September 1934, a cashier at a petrol station in the Bronx received a note from a customer which he recognized as part of the ransom money. He informed the police, and the following day Bruno Richard Hauptmann, a former machine-gunner in the German army who had entered the United States illegally in 1923, was arrested. More of the ransom money was found in his possession, and his handwriting was found to be the same as that on the ransom notes. It was also discovered that he had a criminal record in Germany, his known offences including robbery and burglary.

Hauptmann was brought to trial for murder and kidnapping in January 1935. The proceedings lasted six weeks, and on 13 February he was found guilty on both charges. He was executed in the electric chair at Trenton State Prison, New Jersey, at the age of thirty-six, on 3 April 1936.

In January 1983 it was reported that his widow, Anna Hauptmann, aged eighty-four, was seeking damages for his death, and had accused the State of New Jersey and several former state and federal officials of conspiring to wrongfully convict an innocent man.

Klaus Grabowski brought to trial, 1981

On 3 March 1981, Klaus Grabowski, a thirty-five-year-old butcher with a history of child-molesting, was brought to trial in Lübeck, West Germany, charged with the murder of seven-year-old Anna Bachmeier. The child had failed to return home after going out to play in the morning of 5 May the previous year, and Grabowski, who lived only a block away, was later held for questioning in connection with her disappearance. He eventually confessed to having killed Anna, and led police to a piece of waste ground where her body was found. She had been strangled with her own tights.

Grabowski denied that the crime had been a sex murder and his counsel demanded that the charge be reduced to one of manslaughter. It was stated in court that following an earlier offence — his second — he had agreed to be castrated, but later had his sex drive restored by means of hormone injections. Omitting to explain why he had taken off Anna's tights, he claimed that he had had no sexual feelings towards her. He had invited her to his apartment because he loved children, and had killed her in a panic because she tried to blackmail him, he said.

All this was too much for Marianne Bachmeier, the child's mother. After listening to the case for three days in an apparently calm collected manner, she suddenly crossed the courtroom on 6 March, pulled out a Beretta pistol and fired seven bullets into the prisoner, killing him instantly. Frau Bachmeier, a former barmaid, then lowered the gun and waited passively to be arrested. The scene was witnessed by schoolgirls on an educational visit to the court, who began to cry hysterically. Later the same day the public prosecutor announced that Marianne Bachmeier was to be charged with murder.

Frau Bachmeier's life had not been a happy one even before Anna's death. The daughter of a former SS officer, she had been sexually assaulted at the age of nine and thrown out of home when she became pregnant at sixteen. Two years later she was raped while pregnant for the second time, the father in this case being a different man. Of the two children, one had been adopted, the other placed in an orphanage.

When these facts were reported, public sympathy, which was already strongly in her favour, became overwhelming, and large sums of money were donated to the defence fund started on her behalf. However, this sympathy began to wane when it was learnt that her fellow prisoners found her arrogant and suspected that she did not really care about Anna at all. Even so, when her trial began in November 1982, it was followed with intense interest.

Marianne Bachmeier — 'the Avenging Mother', as the press called her — was convicted of manslaughter on 2 March 1983, and sentenced to six years' imprisonment. The trial judge, in an hour-long account of his findings, said that she had not planned to kill Grabowski but decided to do so when she saw him sitting in the dock. The defence had earlier claimed that she had bought the pistol with the intention of committing suicide.

She was released on parole in June 1985.

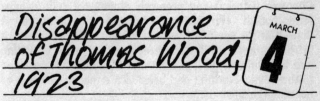

Disappearance of Thomas Wood, 1923

MARCH 4

On 4 March 1923, Thomas Wood, aged three, was reported missing from his home in Glossop, a coal-mining

69

town in Derbyshire. The report led to a search of the town and surrounding countryside, but no trace of the missing child was found. The circulation of his description to other districts, in the hope that he might be found wandering further afield, brought no results; likewise, the dragging of the River Goyt, which runs through Glossop, revealed nothing. After the search had been going on for nine days, a local man went to the police and told them that he knew something about the boy's disappearance.

Albert Edward Burrows, a farm labourer, said that on the day in question, a Sunday, he had taken Thomas Wood for a walk to Simmondley, a village about a mile from Glossop. He had left him on his own for a few minutes near a disused mineshaft on Symmondley Moor and then been unable to find him, he continued. He gave no satisfactory reason for having failed to report this earlier.

Burrows was already known to the police in connection with other offences. Four years earlier he had been sent to prison for bigamy after going through a ceremony of marriage with a woman from Nantwich, Cheshire, by whom he had had an illegitimate child. After returning to his lawful wife on release, he had been sent to prison again, this time for failing to pay maintenance to the child's mother.

The woman, Hannah Calladine, had another child, besides the one which Burrows had fathered. In December 1919, fourteen months after her second confinement, she suddenly turned up in Glossop with both children and all her belongings, and moved into Burrows' home. At this, Burrows' wife left and promptly obtained a maintenance order herself. Her husband, being a poor man, found himself at the age of fifty-seven in danger of being sent to prison yet again. But after three weeks Hannah Calladine and her children disappeared, and Mrs Burrows returned to the house. Nothing had been seen either of Hannah or her children since then.

With great difficulty, the police searched the mineshaft which Burrows had indicated, and eventually they recovered the body of Thomas Wood. He had been sexually assaulted and then murdered, probably by strangulation, before being thrown into the shaft.

The police, going to interview Burrows again, found him about to leave the house, perhaps for good. He stuck to the story he had told them before, but could not convince them he was telling the truth. On 28 March he was charged with murder.

While he was awaiting trial the police began to investigate the disappearance of Hannah Calladine and her children. It was learnt that on 11 January 1920, Burrows had taken Hannah and the younger child for a walk, and that this was the last time anyone else had seen them. Early the following morning he had taken the older child, a girl of four, for a walk — and that had been the last time anyone had seen her.

Six weeks after Burrows had been arrested the police began searching the mineshaft on Symmondley Moor again, and a fortnight later the remains of Hannah and her children were discovered there. They, too, had been murdered, probably by strangulation, though this could not be established with certainty. Burrows, who for three years had kept up a pretence that they were all still alive, was then charged with their murders.

He was brought to trial for the murder of Hannah and the younger child at the Derby Assizes in July 1923. The case against him included the evidence of another prisoner, whom Burrows had tried to persuade to forge a letter from Hannah, saying that she was still alive. The defence called no witnesses, but contended that Hannah had committed suicide. But Burrows was convicted and sentenced to death.

He was hanged in Nottingham, at the age of sixty-two, on 8 August 1923.

Murder of Gertrude Yates, 1922

On the morning of 6 March 1922, Gertrude Yates, a prostitute aged twenty-five, was found dead in the bathroom of her basement flat in Fulham, London. She had died of asphyxia, a towel having been rammed down her throat and a dressing-gown cord tied around her neck; she had also been beaten over the head with a blunt instrument. The body was naked.

In her bedroom, there was blood everywhere; a rolling-pin, with which the blows to her head had been inflicted, lay under the eiderdown. The dressing-table had been ransacked and some jewellery stolen. The body had been discovered by the victim's daily help, Miss Emily Steel, who knew Mrs Yates as Olive Young.

Miss Steel had arrived at the flat about 9.15 a.m., letting herself in with her own key. She had gone to the kitchen and started to cook sausages for her own breakfast, tidying the sitting-room as she did so. While she was thus occupied a man known to her as Major True entered the room and told her that Miss Young was still asleep and should not be disturbed, as they had had a late night together; he would send round his car for her at midday. He then put on his coat, with Miss Steel's help, and gave her half-a-crown (12$\frac{1}{2}$p) before leaving to get a taxi. Miss Steel found the body shortly afterwards and ran out to get help.

The man Miss Steel had seen in the flat was, in fact, Ronald True, a mentally-ill man of thirty who was not a major at all. He was already known to the police, his wife — who was alarmed at his deteriorating state of mind — having reported him missing only three days earlier. He was arrested at the Palace of Varieties in Hammersmith within twelve hours of the body being discovered; the police found a loaded revolver in his hip pocket.

True, a former pupil at Bedford Grammar School, was a compulsive liar and a morphia addict. His stepfather, a wealthy man, had several times sent him abroad to learn work of some sort, but he was incapable of holding any job for long. In 1915 he joined the Royal Flying Corps, but on his solo flight he crashed the plane, suffering severe concussion. A month later he was involved in another crash. After his second spell in hospital he had a nervous breakdown, and was discharged from the service. He then worked briefly at one thing after another, in various countries, but finally his stepfather reconciled himself to giving him a regular allowance for doing nothing.

He was always popular with young women, and invariably managed to impress them with lies about himself. One such woman was an actress named Frances Roberts, whom he married soon after leaving the Royal Flying Corps. She, however, could not have been taken in for very long, for he was becoming increasingly abnormal and was regularly seeking treatment for his drug-addiction — treatment which never worked. In September 1921, he was fined in Portsmouth for using forged prescriptions to obtain morphia.

He began to talk about another Ronald True, an imaginary figure whom he believed to be his enemy. This 'other' Ronald True, he said, had been impersonating him and forging his signature on cheques which bounced. At the same time he was becoming violent towards his wife and hostile towards their two-year-old son. Suddenly, early in 1922, he decided to leave home.

For the next few weeks he stayed in hotels in London, frequenting clubs and bars in the West End and committing a variety of thefts. Though apparently having a good time, he was increasingly preoccupied with the 'other' Ronald True, and bought the gun that was later found in his possession in order to protect himself against this imaginary figure.

On the night of 5 March, just before midnight, he arrived at Gertrude Yates' flat in a chauffeur-driven car which he had been using for four days. He sent the driver away and stayed the night with Mrs Yates, from whom he had earlier stolen £5. In the morning he made tea for them both, then took Mrs Yates' cup into the bedroom; it was as she sat up to drink it that he attacked her with the rolling-pin. He afterwards drank his own cup of tea and ate some biscuits.

True was brought to trial at the Old Bailey in May 1922. He pleaded insanity, producing two psychiatrists to give evidence that he was suffering from a congenital mental disorder, aggravated by his addiction to morphia. But he was found guilty and sentenced to death.

Though his appeal was dismissed by the Lord Chief Justice, he was examined by three specialists on the orders of the Home Secretary and found to be insane. He was therefore reprieved and sent to Broadmoor.

He remained there for the rest of his life, a cheerful man who took part in the social activities and was popular with the other inmates. He died, at the age of sixty, in 1951.

Bodies of Dr. Petiot's victims found, 1944

MARCH
11

On 11 March 1944, a resident of the Rue Lesueur in Paris complained to the police about greasy black smoke coming from the chimney of a neighbouring house owned by Dr Marcel Petiot. The police arrived at the house to investigate and found a card pinned to the door, directing callers to an address in the Rue Caumartin where Dr Petiot lived and also had a consulting room. They contacted him by telephone.

Dr Petiot said that he would come to the Rue Lesueur immediately, but before he appeared the chimney caught fire and the fire brigade was called to the scene. Breaking into the house, the firemen entered the cellar, where a fire had been left to burn in a stove. There they found a large number of corpses, most of which had been dismembered.

When Petiot finally turned up he was told that he would be taken into custody. Unperturbed, he said that the bodies were those of pro-Nazis and collaborators killed by the French Resistance. The police were taken in by this, and made the mistake of letting Petiot go free. Petiot, his wife and their seventeen-year-old son promptly left their home in the Rue Caumartin and went into hiding. His wife was later found in Auxerre but Petiot managed to avoid being arrested for several months.

After the fall of Paris the newspapers gave a lot of publicity to the case, and Petiot wrote to one of them, stating that he was an officer of the Resistance and that the corpses found in his cellar had been placed there by the Gestapo. The handwriting of the letter was found to correspond with that of a Captain Henri Valéry, who had joined the Free French Forces just six weeks earlier and was serving in Reuilly. Petiot was thus discovered and arrested on 2 November.

On being taken to the Quai des Orfèvres for questioning, he said that as a member of the Resistance he had killed sixty-three people, and that the twenty-seven bodies in his cellar had been mostly those of German soldiers. He also said that he had helped many Frenchmen to escape from France. This time, however, nobody was taken in.

Marcel Petiot, a qualified doctor and former Mayor of Villeneuve, was a man with marked criminal tendencies. As a schoolboy he had stolen from his classmates; as an army conscript during the First World War he had stolen drugs from a casualty clearing station, and as Mayor of Villeneuve he had robbed his electric light meter and stolen from a municipal store. Later, in Paris, he was convicted of drug-trafficking and also of stealing a book.

The bodies discovered in his cellar were found to be the remains of people who had gone to his house with all their money and valuables, thinking that he would help them to escape from the Germans. They had each been given a lethal injection, then left in a sound-proofed room built specially for the purpose. Petiot had made himself a fortune out of all these murders; in all likelihood, he had also derived enjoyment from watching through a spyhole as his victims died in agony.

After seventeen months in custody, Petiot was brought to trial at the Seine Assize Court on twenty-seven charges of murder. The trial lasted three weeks and, on 4 April 1946, the jury returned verdicts of guilty on twenty-four of those charges. Petiot, aged forty-nine, was executed by guillotine on the morning of 26 May.

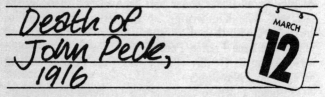

Death of John Peck, 1916

MARCH
12

On 12 March 1916, John Peck, a seventy-two-year-old timber millionaire of Grand Rapids, Michigan, died at the home of his son-in-law, Dr Arthur Warren Waite, a New York dentist. The cause of his death was diagnosed as a kidney disease and arrangements were made for the body to be cremated. But Peck's son Percy, whose mother had also died in Waite's home only a few weeks earlier, demanded its return to Michigan for burial, and afterwards requested an autopsy. When this was carried out, the body was found to contain arsenic.

Waite, aged twenty-seven, had studied at Glasgow University and worked in South Africa for some years before his marriage to Clara Peck in September 1915. In addition to having a dental practice in New York's fashionable Riverside Drive, he worked on germ-culture research at Cornell University. However, he lived extravagantly, having affairs with other women, and as his wife now inherited half of her father's fortune, he was suspected of having murdered both of her parents.

On 23 March the fashionable dentist was found suffering from an overdose of drugs, having apparently tried to take his own life. When he recovered he was charged with the murders of John and Hannah Peck and later brought to trial. Having pleaded not guilty, he then made an extraordinary confession, stating not only that he had murdered both of his wife's parents, but also that he had intended to murder his wife as well.

He had murdered his mother-in-law by putting diphtheria, tuberculosis and influenza germs in her food, he explained. He had then used the same methods in an attempt to kill his father-in-law, even using a nasal spray containing tuberculosis bacteria in his case. When these and other attempts proved unsuccessful, he had finally disposed of John Peck with the use of arsenic.

Waite revealed that it was for the sake of their money that he had murdered Clara's parents, and said that he would have murdered Clara next because he intended to have a more beautiful wife. Asked if he was crazy, he replied, 'I think not — unless it is crazy to want money'.

It was nonetheless on grounds of insanity that appeals were made on his behalf when he was convicted and sentenced to death. But these were unsuccessful and his execution in the electric chair was carried out at Sing Sing Prison on the night of 24 May 1917.

Four poisoned in Lund, 1949

On 13 March 1949, two medical students and two children in Lund, Sweden, were taken ill as a result of eating chocolate which had been poisoned with arsenic. The two students, Odvar Eiken and Anders Muren, and one of the children recovered after receiving hospital treatment, but the other child died. The investigation which followed involved the police of Norway and Denmark, as well as Sweden.

Eiken and Muren, both Norwegians in their late twenties, were room-mates lodging with a family named Svendson, and Eiken was engaged to Muren's sister Randi — a student at a teachers' training college in Kristiansand, Norway — though their engagement had not yet been formally announced. The chocolate, which had been sent to Eiken through the post, appeared to have been a gift from Randi.

Odvar Eiken had given a little of the chocolate to Muren and eaten some of it himself; the rest had been given to his landlady's eight-year-old daughter Marianne who, in turn, had given some to her friend Barbro Jakobson. It was Marianne Svendson who failed to recover from its effects.

Randi Muren denied sending the chocolate to Eiken, but agreed that handwriting on the gift card which had accompanied it was similar to her own. She revealed that since making her engagement known to friends she had received a number of anonymous letters suggesting that her fiancé was having affairs with girls in Sweden, and a further letter from a woman named Signe Lundgren claiming that she was expecting Eiken's child. At the same time Eiken, who said that he did not know anybody named Signe Lundgren, had been receiving anonymous letters of the same type about her.

The investigating officers, both Swedish and Norwegian became convinced that these letters and the poisoned chocolate were connected, and — observing that Randi Muren was an extremely attractive girl — suggested that they might have been the work of a jealous rival. Further questions elicited the information that a young Dane named Flemming Rosbörg, who had worked in Norway for a year, had recently threatened to commit suicide after failing to persuade her to marry him. As his present whereabouts were unknown, the Copenhagen police were asked to make inquiries about him.

He was soon arrested and handed over to the Swedish police for questioning, but then released after giving a satisfactory account of his movements. In the meantime, it had been learnt that shortly before the arrival of the poisoned chocolate, Odvar Eiken had received (also through the post) a small bottle of whisky inside a cigar-box. He had been ill after drinking some of it, but had not realized that the illness was connected with the whisky. When the rest of the whisky was handed to the police, together with the cigar-box, it was found to contain arsenic.

Several women named Signe Lundgren had been traced, but none of them knew Odvar Eiken or Randi Muren. Nor could any other woman be found in Sweden to substantiate the accusations which had been made against Eiken. But then another case of arsenic poisoning was reported, this time in Kristiansand.

Carstein Brekke, a friend of Randi Muren and her fiancé who was also a student at the teachers' training college, claimed that he, too, had received chocolate through the post and been ill after eating some of it. He produced a box containing several pieces which were found to have been poisoned, though with smaller amounts of arsenic than the chocolate sent to Eiken. Brekke could think of no reason why anyone should want to poison him, other than the fact that he was a friend of the other victims, he said.

The matter was further complicated by the discovery of a paid advertisement which had appeared in a Stavanger newspaper, announcing that Carstein Brekke and Randi Muren had become engaged — which both parties said they were unable to explain. However, when a police officer showed Randi the cigar-box in which the poisoned whisky had been sent to Eiken, she said that it was Brekke who owned it.

Brekke, though a close friend of Randi's, also turned out to be another of her rejected suitors. A letter which he had sent to his mother on 13 March contained information about Eiken's poisoned chocolate, though this was not known by Randi until the following day. Moreover, a note-book which he had discarded was found to have been used for imitations of Randi's handwriting. After being questioned intensively for some hours, he admitted having sent Eiken the poisoned chocolate. However, he refused to allow a police officer to take down his confession, saying that he wanted to write it himself in a more intellectual manner.

The written statement which he then made gave details of an unsuccessful attempt to get Randi Muren — the only woman in his life, he claimed — to break off her engagement, followed by an equally unsuccessful attempt to poison his rival.

Charged on a number of counts, Carstein Brekke was brought to trial in Kristiansand in October 1949, and convicted of manslaughter and attempted murder. He was then sentenced to twelve years' imprisonment and ten years' loss of rights as a citizen. The sentence of imprisonment was later increased to fifteen years when the case was taken to the Norwegian Supreme Court.

Shooting of Gaston Calmette, 1914

On the afternoon of 16 March 1914, Henriette Caillaux, the wife of the French Finance Minister, entered the offices of the daily newspaper *Le Figaro* and asked to see Gaston Calmette, the editor-in-chief. That very morning *Le Figaro* had published a facsimile of an indiscreet love letter which Madame Caillaux had received from her husband before their marriage, and Calmette assumed that she would try to come to an arrangement with him to prevent the publication of other such letters which she knew to be in his possession. He therefore agreed to see her.

A moment later the sound of shots was heard, and other members of staff rushed into Calmette's office to see what had happened. They found him lying on the floor, covered with blood. Madame Caillaux made no attempt to escape. 'I shot Calmette deliberately because he wanted to destroy my husband and me,' she confessed to the police. The following day Calmette died of his wounds. Henriette Caillaux, one of the best-known women in Paris, was charged with his murder; she was brought to trial four months later.

Joseph Caillaux, a former Prime Minister, was a very unpopular man. The rich had hated him for years because, during an earlier period as Finance Minister, he had introduced an income tax. More recently he had become widely despised as a result of his opposition to the impending war with Germany.

Gaston Calmette had been the most implacable of his opponents. He had repeatedly accused Caillaux of betraying his country and, on acquiring some of the Finance Minister's private letters written during the course of his previous marriage, had been determined to use them to

81

bring about his downfall.

At her trial Henriette Caillaux said that the attacks on her husband had caused both of them much unhappiness. Joseph Caillaux, on learning that the letters were in Calmette's hands, had bought a pistol, saying that he would kill Calmette if they were published. She had been unable to get him to part with it.

On the day of the shooting, she claimed, she had found the newspaper on the breakfast table, her husband having left without waking her. She went to his desk, where she knew that the pistol was normally kept in a locked drawer, but found the drawer open and the gun missing. After two unsuccessful attempts to see him at his ministry she decided to confront Calmette, and bought a gun herself for the purpose of threatening him. She claimed — in spite of her original confession — that she had not intended to kill him.

The trial took place during the week preceding the declaration of war between Austria–Hungary and Serbia, and its outcome depended less on the events of 16 March than on the motives of Joseph Caillaux and Gaston Calmette. There were some sensational developments in this respect, and soon the case became — for a few days, at least — the main preoccupation of the whole country.

One of Calmette's editors told the court that documents proving that Caillaux had betrayed France had been placed in the hands of the President of the Republic. This was to be refuted the following day by a statement, authorized by the Government, that the President had received no such papers. In the meantime, Caillaux was called as a witness and caused much indignation.

'Calmette has accused me of betraying my country to the Germans,' he said. 'Therefore, I am forced to tell the truth. I state here and now that *Le Figaro* has accepted German money!'

The publisher of the newspaper, called to deny the allegation, was forced to concede that *Le Figaro* had German shareholders. The admission was made with the utmost reluctance.

Later, just before the closing speeches, Caillaux re-appeared with a copy of Calmette's will, revealing that the victim of the shooting had avoided paying taxes on a very large inheritance. He also produced a contract which had been drawn up between Calmette and the Government of Austria–Hungary, by which Calmette pledged himself to write articles serving the interests of that government in return for money. The presiding judge read the contract aloud, remarking that there could be no doubt about its authenticity.

These revelations caused an uproar in the court, with spectators leaping to their feet, crying out that Calmette had been a traitor and that shooting had been too good for him. The jury considered the case for only a quarter of an hour before returning a unanimous verdict of not guilty. Caillaux and his wife did not leave the court in triumph, however, for the verdict was immediately overshadowed by the news that Austria–Hungary and Serbia were at war.

Caillaux returned to his political life after an enforced withdrawal. He was later to be imprisoned by Clemenceau for corresponding with the enemy.

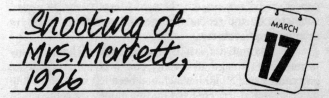

Shooting of Mrs. Merrett, 1926

MARCH 17

On the morning of 17 March 1926, Mrs Bertha Merrett, a woman of private means, was rushed to hospital from her furnished rooms in Buckingham Terrace, Edinburgh, with a bullet wound in her right ear; she was alive but unconscious. The wound appeared to have been self-inflicted, and when her son, John Donald Merrett, aged seventeen, informed the police that she had tried to kill herself because she was in financial difficulties, they saw no cause to disbelieve him.

Mrs Merrett was kept in isolation at the Royal Infirmary. When she recovered consciousness she was asked no questions about the bullet wound, but made a statement of her own accord to one of the doctors. 'I was sitting down, writing letters, and my son Donald was standing beside me,' she said. 'I said, "Go away, Donald, and don't annoy me." And the next thing I heard was a kind of explosion, and I don't remember anything more.' She died on 1 April.

Despite her statement, her death was regarded as suicide, until the discovery of one of her cheque-books in Donald Merrett's bedroom caused police officers to suspect otherwise. During the investigation which followed it was found that the signatures on many of Mrs Merrett's cheques had been forged. At the same time tests were carried out on the pistol that killed her.

Eventually, on 1 February 1927, Donald Merrett, now aged eighteen, was brought to trial in Edinburgh. He was charged with his mother's murder, and also with forging twenty-nine cheques on her account. The prosecution claimed that the absence of powder-blackening round the bullet wound proved that the gun had not been fired closely enough to be consistent with suicide, but the jury found the charge to be not proven. Donald Merrett was, however, convicted on the second charge and sentenced to twelve months' imprisonment.

This was not the last that was heard of him, by any means. At the age of twenty-one Merrett received an inheritance of £50,000, which had been left in trust for him by his grandfather. He lived on this money for some years, then, having spent most of it, returned to a life of crime. Now known as Ronald John Chesney, he committed a variety of offences — blackmail, fraud, theft and smuggling — before going into the Royal Naval Volunteer Reserve during the Second World War. After the war he lived in Germany, and was mainly engaged in black-market activities. Then, in 1954, he decided to murder his wife.

Merrett had married Vera Bonnar, the daughter of one of his mother's friends, in 1928. At the time of his inheritance he had made a settlement of £8400 on her, the money to revert to him in the event of her death. They had long since separated, and Vera Merrett, known as Vera Chesney, ran an old people's home in Ealing with her mother, who called herself Lady Menzies.

Merrett came to England in disguise, using a false passport. He visited his wife, got her hopelessly drunk, and drowned her in a few inches of water in her own bath, intending to make her death appear to have been the result of an accident. But as he was leaving the house he was seen by his mother-in-law, and realized that he would have to kill her too. After a desperate struggle he managed to overpower and strangle her. He then escaped from the house and flew back to Germany.

But he had been seen in the neighbourhood, and it was not long before the police were after him. On 16 February 1954, less than a week after the double murder, he was found dead in a wood near Cologne; he had shot himself. His arms were scratched and bruised from the struggle with his mother-in-law, and pink fibres from her scarf were found on his clothing. His German mistress, Gerda Schaller, said that Merrett had confided to her that he was guilty of the murder of his mother twenty-eight years earlier.

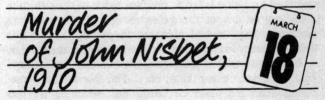

Murder of John Nisbet, 1910

MARCH 18

On the morning of 18 March 1910, John Nisbet, a forty-four-year-old cashier working for the Stobswood Colliery

Company, left his employers' Newcastle office to deliver £370 in wages to a colliery at Widdrington, thirty-five miles away. It was a journey he made every Friday, leaving Newcastle by train at 10.27 a.m. and carrying the money in a black leather bag. On this occasion, however, he did not alight at Widdrington because he was dead by the time the train arrived there. His body was discovered by a porter when the train reached Alnmouth.

Nisbet had been shot five times, his body hidden under a seat and the bag of money stolen. It was established that John Alexander Dickman, a former secretary of a colliery syndicate, had travelled in the same compartment, leaving the train at Morpeth. The post-mortem examination revealed that the bullets found in Nisbet's body had been fired from two different guns.

Dickman, a married man with two children, lived in Jesmond. He made his living out of betting on horses and was often in financial difficulties. It was also found that he had recently owned a revolver. He was therefore an obvious suspect.

On the day of the murder Dickman had had to pay excess fare at Morpeth, as he had only bought a ticket to Stannington, the previous stop. Asked to explain this, he told police that he had intended getting out at Stannington, in order to attend an interview for a job with the overseer at the Dovecot Moor colliery, but had gone on to Morpeth by mistake. This proved to be a lie, the overseer at Dovecot telling police that no such interview had been arranged.

Dickman was arrested and charged with murder. A search of his home failed to produce either of the guns, the black bag or any of the stolen money. But it was soon discovered that he had managed to pay off one or two debts to money-lenders almost immediately after the murder.

Brought to trial at the Newcastle Summer Assizes on 4 July, Dickman denied the offence. The case for the prosecution depended upon circumstantial evidence, but was strong enough to convince the jury of his guilt. He was sentenced to death.

On 9 July the black leather bag which had contained the stolen money was found in a disused mine-shaft between Morpeth and Stannington; it had been cut open — the key having been left in the victim's pocket — and all the money removed. Its discovery convinced the police that they had made no mistake in arresting Dickman. But the guns which had been used were never found.

There were many other people who felt that the evidence against Dickman was insufficient to warrant a conviction, and attempts were made to get him reprieved. But these were unsuccessful, and he was hanged at Newcastle Prison on 10 August 1910.

Albert Snyder found murdered, 1927

MARCH **20**

Getting up on the morning of 20 March 1927, Lorraine Snyder, aged ten, of Queen's Village, Long Island, came out of her bedroom and found her mother lying bound and gagged at the top of the stairs. She let out a scream, then telephoned some neighbours, who immediately came to her assistance. On being untied, Ruth Snyder, aged thirty-two, said that she had been attacked and knocked unconscious by an intruder — a big man with a moustache, looking 'like an Italian' — who had entered her bedroom while she was asleep. She supposed that she must have been dragged out of the bedroom while she was still unconscious.

Entering the bedroom themselves, the neighbours found that Mrs Snyder's husband had been murdered. Albert Snyder, forty-four-year-old art editor of *Motor Boating* magazine, lay on the bed, his head having been so savagely battered that he was almost unrecognizable. When the police were called to the scene, it was also discovered that a piece of picture wire had been tied tightly round his neck and pieces of cotton wool, soaked in chloroform, stuffed into his mouth and nostrils. Clearly, it was a case of premeditated murder, and it was not long before the police began to have doubts about Ruth Snyder's story.

Searching the house for clues, they found pots and pans scattered about the kitchen and the contents of a bureau strewn about the living-room floor. But there was no sign of a forced entry. Jewels which Mrs Snyder claimed had been stolen were found hidden under her mattress, and some scraps of paper, pieced together, turned out to be a love letter which she had received from somebody signing himself 'Judd'. Ruth Snyder, on being questioned at length, then confessed that she had been having an affair with a salesman named Henry Judd Gray, who was an employee of the Bien Jolie Corset Company.

Gray, a timid man of thirty-five, was questioned about the murder, but denied having had anything to do with it. However, the police told Ruth Snyder that he had broken down and made a confession, blaming her for what had happened. She then made a statement, admitting that she had conspired with Gray to kill her husband but claiming that she had taken no part in the crime itself.

On being confronted with this, Gray made a statement, saying that they had committed the murder together, but that he had been under her influence at the time. 'She had this power over me,' he said. 'She told me what to do and I just did it.' Thus, the truth about what had happened gradually emerged.

Ruth Snyder and Judd Gray, both unhappily married, had begun to have an affair in 1925. Mrs Snyder disliked her husband, who often compared her unfavourably with a former fiancée, and had made a number of unsuccessful attempts to kill him on her own before finally getting Gray to help her. She had also taken out life insurance policies by which she stood to gain $96,000 after the murder had been carried out.

On the night of 19 March Gray entered the house while his mistress and her husband were out at a party. When they returned he kept himself concealed until after they had gone to bed. He then entered the bedroom and, taking Snyder by surprise, struck him over the head with a sash weight. After the murder Ruth Snyder helped to disarrange the room and allowed herself to be tied up and gagged before Gray left the house.

On 25 April the two prisoners were brought to trial for murder, the case being given a tremendous amount of publicity. As the sordid details were made known, Ruth Snyder was seen to be a callous schemer who had turned a weak man into a murderer by means of 'drink, veiled threats and intensive love'. As such, she became an object of fascination among ordinary people, and received 164 proposals of marriage.

The trial ended on 9 May with both defendants being found guilty; they were sentenced to death. Both were executed in the electric chair at Sing Sing Prison in January 1928.

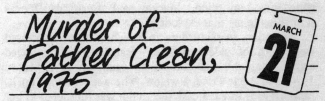

Murder of Father Crean, 1975

MARCH 21

On 21 March 1975, Father Anthony Crean, a Catholic priest, was brutally murdered at his home in Gravesend, Kent, his assailant striking him over the head with an axe and also stabbing him several times with a knife. The police suspected a twenty-two-year-old psychopath named Patrick Mackay, whose mother lived locally, and arrested him two days later. Mackay soon confessed, not only to that crime, but to two other murders as well, and was brought to trial for all three in November the same year. He was sentenced to life imprisonment.

Mackay, the son of a drunken clerk, had a long record of theft and violence. As a schoolboy, besides being a bully, a liar and a thief, he had taken to torturing animals and on one occasion had been put on probation for setting fire to a church. At thirteen he was admitted to a mental hospital after attacking his mother and sisters, and at fifteen — by which time he had committed a number of other violent crimes — he was described by a Home Office psychiatrist as 'a cold psychopathic killer'. Thereafter he became an admirer of the Nazis, drank heavily, took drugs and committed a great many burglaries and muggings.

In 1973 Father Crean, then aged sixty-three, befriended him, but not long afterwards Mackay broke into his house and stole a cheque. When he was arrested for this the priest tried to prevent him being prosecuted, and Mackay was merely fined £20 and set free.

On the day of the murder Mackay entered the house, which had been left open in Father Crean's absence. The victim, on returning, became nervous and tried to leave again, but Mackay attacked him and chased him into the bathroom, where further blows were struck. 'I must have gone out of my mind,' Mackay said afterwards. 'It was something in me that exploded.'

The other two murders to which Mackay confessed were both of elderly women: Isabella Griffiths, aged eighty-four, who was stabbed to death on 14 February 1974, and Adele Price, a widow, who was strangled on 10 March 1975. In each case the victim was murdered in her own home for no particular reason. 'I felt hellish and very peculiar inside,' said Mackay, referring to the murder of Adele Price.

Besides the three murders for which he was sent to prison, Mackay was believed to have committed eight others, but no charges were brought against him in connection with any of them.

Double murder in West Shelby, 1915

On the morning of 22 March 1915, Margaret Wolcott, a housekeeper, was found dead on her employer's farm at West Shelby, in Orleans County, New York; she had been shot with a revolver and was lying in her nightgown outside the door of a cottage occupied by Charles E. Stielow, a hired man. The farm-owner, Charles B. Phelps, aged seventy, lay in his nightshirt in the farmhouse kitchen, fatally injured, also by shooting; he died in hospital later, having been unable to speak from the time of his discovery. His desk had been broken open and all his money stolen.

Stielow, a thirty-seven-year-old German immigrant, lived with his wife, child, mother-in-law and brother-in-law; he was a strong but simple-minded man. Discovering what had happened, he had sent his brother-in-law, Nelson Green — who was equally simple minded — to inform the Orleans County Sheriff, Chester D. Bartlett. But he also got Green to hide his revolver, rifle and shotgun, as he was afraid that he might otherwise be accused of the murders himself.

The county had had no other serious crime within living memory, and the sheriff, having no idea how to conduct a murder investigation, hired an unscrupulous private detective named Newton, from Buffalo, to do it for him. Newton promptly had Green arrested, terrified him into revealing the whereabouts of his brother-in-law's guns, then forced him to make a confession that he and Stielow had killed Phelps and his housekeeper. Newton and Bartlett then arrested Stielow and had him interrogated for two days without food or sleep until he, too, confessed to the murders.

On 12 July Stielow was brought to trial. The stolen

money had not been recovered and the prisoner's confession, which he retracted, was regarded with suspicion by the judge. However, the prosecution introduced the evidence of a charlatan named Albert Hamilton, who purported to be a ballistics expert, as well as an expert in nearly every other branch of forensic science. He told the court that the bullets removed from Phelps' body had been fired from Stielow's revolver; they could not have been fired from any other weapon, he declared. Stielow was convicted and sentenced to death.

His case was taken up by members of a penal reform society and several reprieves followed, one of them arriving after he had been strapped in the electric chair at Sing Sing Prison. A tramp named King confessed that he and his companion, both of whom were now serving prison sentences for other crimes, were guilty of the West Shelby murders — but retracted the confession after being taken away for questioning by Newton and Bartlett. By this time, however, the case was causing much disquiet, and Governor Whitman of New York appointed an independent commission to look into it.

During the course of their inquiry Stielow's revolver was examined by a New York City detective, Captain Jones, who said that it had not been fired for three or four years. When test shots were fired the bullets — unlike those from Phelps' body — were found to be covered with dirt from the barrel, and when the two sets of bullets were compared it was found that their markings were entirely different. It was then clear that Stielow was innocent, and eventually, after three years in jail, he was pardoned and set free.

Though King once more confessed to the murder of Phelps and his housekeeper — and there was evidence to show that he and his friend had known about the crime before it became general knowledge — a grand jury refused to indict him. The county's one serious crime in a whole generation was thus left officially unsolved, saving the cost of a fresh trial.

Murder of William Munday, 1905

On 23 March 1905, William Munday, an elderly gentleman, was held up by a tramp with a gun between Tooringa and Toowong, in Queensland. He resisted and was shot in the stomach, but managed to give a description of his attacker before dying in hospital the same evening. Later that night the tramp was arrested after trying unsuccessfully to draw a gun on the police officer concerned. The tramp was Robert Butler, a man with a long criminal record, who had spent most of his life in jail. He was charged with murder.

Butler, a native of Kilkenny, in Ireland, was an intelligent and literate man, but bitter and destructive. Arriving in Australia at the age of fourteen, he had spent thirteen of the next sixteen years in jail for crimes which included highway robbery and burglary. He then went to New Zealand, where he was given four years' hard labour for burglary, and later eighteen years' imprisonment, of which he served sixteen, for burning down the home of a solicitor. He was also tried for the murder of a young couple and their baby, but in this case he was acquitted; he had conducted his own defence.

Returning to Australia in 1896, he was given fifteen years, later reduced to ten, for burglary. At the same time he was acquitted on a charge of highway robbery, again after defending himself. He was released in 1904.

Brought to trial for the murder of Mr Munday, he was convicted and sentenced to death. While awaiting execution, he declared that he could not have the consolation of religion at his death, as there was 'an impassable bar' between himself and any religious organization. This incorrigible criminal was about sixty years old when the sentence was carried out.

93

Murder of Mr. and Mrs. Farrow, 1905

About 7.30 a.m. on 27 March 1905, Thomas Farrow, an elderly tradesman, was found dead in the back parlour of his chandler's store in Deptford, south-east London; he had been battered over the head, and his body was covered with blood. His wife, Ann, was found unconscious in her bed upstairs, having been similarly attacked; she died in hospital three days later. The crime was discovered when a boy employed as an assistant in the store turned up for work.

It had taken place only half an hour earlier, the culprits knocking on the door of the shop and forcing their way in when Mr Farrow opened it. An empty cash-box, which had been broken open, showed that robbery had been the motive: it had earlier contained a few pounds. The main clues to the identities of those responsible were two black masks, made from silk stockings, and a thumbprint, in blood, on the cash-box tray. The masks suggested to the police that the crime had been committed by local men, afraid of being recognized.

The police questioned known criminals in the Deptford area and checked their alibis, and before long suspicion fell on Alfred Stratton, aged twenty-two, and his brother Albert, aged twenty, both of whom had convictions for house-breaking and burglary. Though both had disappeared, the police were able to speak to Alfred's girlfriend who had a black eye and was frightened. She informed them that the two brothers had both been out all night prior to the murder and that Alfred had afterwards destroyed his coat and dyed his brown shoes black.

On the Sunday following the murder a police officer found Alfred Stratton in a public house full of seamen, criminals and prostitutes; asking him to step outside, he promptly arrested him. Albert was found in a lodging-house in Stepney, and he, too, was arrested. Both were questioned and fingerprinted at Tower Bridge police station, and it was found that Alfred Stratton's right thumbprint matched the one found at the scene of the crime. They were charged with murder.

At their trial at the Old Bailey in May 1905, the thumb-print was an important part of the evidence, but its value was disputed by the defence. The jury, however, were impressed by a demonstration given by Inspector Collins of the newly-formed Finger-Print Branch at Scotland Yard and found both of the defendants guilty. Both blamed the other for the murders, and both were hanged. It was the first time that a conviction for murder had been obtained by fingerprint evidence in a British court.

Death of Mientje Manders, 1971

APRIL 2

On 2 April 1971, a girl named Mientje Manders died in Utrecht, Holland, after suffering from stomach pains for some days. It appeared that food poisoning was the cause of her death, but three months earlier another girl, Willy Maas, had also died in Utrecht after suffering from the same symptoms. Both girls had been engaged to a young man named Sjef Rijke, who was apparently grief-stricken on each occasion, but nonetheless married a third girl, eighteen-year-old Maria Haas, three weeks after the death of the second. Six weeks after that Rijke's wife left him and began divorce proceedings, having found him to be abnor-mally jealous.

Since the death of Mientje Manders the Utrecht police had been taking an interest in Rijke, and his wife was now interviewed. On being asked whether she had experienced any stomach pains, she revealed that she *had* had such pains from the time of her marriage but that they had stopped when she left her husband. Not long afterwards it was learnt that another girl, who had moved into Rijke's home in his wife's place, and begun to suffer similarly, had had a jar of peanut butter analysed at the local health department's laboratory where it was found to contain rat poison.

Even so, the police were not certain that Rijke was responsible, for he seemed to have no motive for poisoning any of these girls: they therefore arrested his middle-aged cleaning woman as well as him, releasing the cleaner only when a local store-owner informed them that Rijke had bought rat poison from him on a number of occasions.

Rijke then admitted that he had been responsible for the deaths of Willy Maas and Mientje Manders, and also that he had poisoned his wife and the girl who had lived with him after his wife had left. He denied that he had intended to murder anyone, saying that the poisonings had only taken place because he enjoyed watching women suffer.

Brought to trial in January 1972, Sjef Rijke was convicted of the murders of Willy Maas and Mientje Manders and sentenced to life imprisonment for each crime.

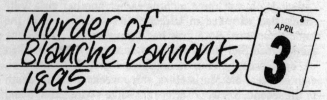

Murder of Blanche Lamont, 1895

On 3 April 1895, Blanche Lamont, a twenty-one-year-old student teacher and regular church-goer, was murdered in

San Francisco's Bartlett Street Emmanuel Baptist Church, where her body lay in the belfry for the next eleven days. Before its discovery Miss Lamont's friend Marion Williams, known as 'Minnie', was also killed in the same building. It was the body of Miss Williams, whose murder had taken place on 12 April, which was found first.

Blanche Lamont, who lived with her uncle and aunt, Mr and Mrs Noble, had been seen entering the church in the company of William Durrant, a twenty-four-year-old medical student and church official, on the afternoon of her death. Durrant afterwards offered to help Mrs Noble to find her, but cautioned her against telling others about the girl's disappearance. Three rings belonging to Miss Lamont were received by her aunt on the morning of 13 April, having been sent through the post anonymously.

Minnie Williams left a friend's house to go to church about eight o'clock on the evening of 12 April. The following morning the new pastor, J. George Gibson, reported finding that a door of the church had been forced, and later a female volunteer worker found Miss Williams' body in the library; she had been strangled, then mutilated with a table-knife. It was afterwards alleged that the police were not informed of this discovery until after Gibson had made an unsuccessful attempt to get the body removed secretly by a local undertaker.

On 14 April a patrolman on duty at the church climbed to the belfry and found the naked body of Blanche Lamont, who lay with her hands crossed on her breasts. She, too, had been strangled, but not mutilated, and nobody doubted that the two murders had been committed by the same person.

Durrant was arrested and brought to trial on 22 July. The case lasted until 1 November, but the jury took only twenty minutes to find him guilty of first-degree murder; he was sentenced to death. The trial received much publicity, the 'Demon in the Belfry' making news in Europe as well as the United States. After four stays of execution, he was hanged at San Quentin Prison on 7

January, 1898, protesting his innocence to the end.

The execution was followed by a number of false confessions, and the idea that Gibson rather than Durrant had murdered the two girls gained a certain amount of support.

Horrifying murder in Barking, 1968

On the morning of 4 April, 1968, Suchnam Singh Sandhu, a thirty-nine-year-old Punjab Sikh living in Barking, Essex, murdered his teenage daughter Sarabjit in a horrifying manner. Sarabjit, who lived away from home, had been staying with her family for a few days and had been left in her father's company while her mother was out and her two younger sisters were at school. Following a bitter argument — over a married man living in India — Sarabjit told her father that she had taken poison and written a letter blaming him for her impending death. Suchnam Singh, who was still in his pyjamas, then lost his temper and struck her twice with a hammer.

Having done so, he dressed quickly and went out, returning to the house half an hour later with a high-tensile hacksaw which he had just bought for the purpose of dismembering his daughter's body. Sarabjit, at this stage, was not dead and when he started to cut her neck she tried to grasp the saw, cutting her thumb in the attempt. But Suchnam Singh, now wearing his pyjamas again, went on sawing until he had cut off her head, then cut through her body at the waist and severed her legs at the knees. The dismemberment was carried out with the body in a large plastic bag, so that Sarabjit's blood could afterwards be poured into the bath.

With this frightful task accomplished, Suchnam Singh put the upper part of his daughter's body into one suitcase, the lower part, together with the severed legs, into another, and her head into a duffel bag, ready for disposal. The blood-stained pyjamas and the hacksaw were put into his dustbin.

That night the first suitcase was taken by public trans-port to Euston Station, London, where it was placed on the 10.40 p.m. train to Wolverhampton; the other was thrown into the River Roding from a bridge at Ilford. The follow-ing morning — by which time the first suitcase had been opened at Wolverhampton — the duffel bag was left near a roadside on Wanstead Flats, in Essex.

After the discovery of part of Sarabjit's remains, the police made a public appeal for information about a young Asian woman who might recently have left home or dis-appeared from a boarding-house. They later issued a photofit picture of a coloured man whom a ticket-collector at Euston remembered seeing with a suitcase before the departure of the Wolverhampton train.

When the second suitcase was found, also on 5 April, it was quickly established that the contents of both were parts of the same body. From an examination of the stomach contents it was learnt that the young woman had taken a fatal dose of phenobarbitone but that she had died before this had been absorbed into her system. It also ap-peared, from a scar on the inside of one of her legs and the fact that her pubic hair had been shaved off three or four months earlier, that she had received gynaecological treatment.

Detectives then began checking on Indian and Pakistani women who had received such treatment, and eventually the corpse — the head of which was discovered by a cyclist on 8 May — was identified by a doctor whom Sarabjit had been to see in Ilford in November 1967. Sarabjit, who had been pregnant at the time, had been sent to a consultant gynaecologist at Barking Hospital, where she had after-wards failed to keep an appointment for ante-natal treat-ment. It appeared that she had had an abortion during the next few weeks, though the police never discovered who had performed it.

On 11 May Suchnam Singh, a machine-minder, was questioned by police about his missing daughter. He said that Sarabjit had left home in February 1968, and that he did not know her whereabouts. He also denied knowing that she had been pregnant and refused to identify the suit-cases or items of clothing found with her remains. Two days later, however, he made a full confession. He was then charged with murder.

Sarabjit, it was learnt, had been Suchnam Singh's favourite child, and he — an educated man who had formerly been a schoolmaster — had wanted her to become a doctor. But then she had become pregnant, thus bringing the family into disgrace, and had further angered her father by saying that she was in love with a man who was already married, and wanted him to divorce or kill his wife so that he could marry her.

At the time of the murder Suchnam Singh, having struck his daughter with the hammer, had done his best to follow an old Sikh custom — that of dismembering one who had disgraced the family and sending parts of the body on trains going in different directions.

He was later brought to trial at the Old Bailey, where the evidence against him was shown to be overwhelming, and after retiring for ninety minutes the jury found him guilty of murder. He was sent to prison for life.

Jeanne Weber suspected of attempted murder, 1905

APRIL
5

On the afternoon of 5 April 1905, Maurice Weber, aged six months, was taken to the Bretonneau Hospital in Paris suffering from acute asphyxia. He had been left in the care of an aunt, Jeanne Weber, who lived in a slum in the Passage Goutte d'Or, and shortly afterwards had been found blue in the face and choking. Jeanne Weber, aged thirty, had been sitting beside him with her hands under his vest.

The resident physician examined the child and found a reddish mark on his neck which made the doctor suspect that an attempt had been made to choke him. Later, when the child had recovered, the doctor questioned the mother at length and learnt of the deaths of four other children, all related, in the previous few weeks. All had died mysteriously after being left in Jeanne Weber's charge.

The first had been Georgette Weber, a niece aged eighteen months, who had died on 2 March while her mother was working in the public laundry; the cause had been diagnosed as 'convulsions'. Georgette's sister Suzanne, a year older, had died in similar circumstances on 11 March; her death had also been put down to 'convulsions'. On 26 March a third niece, Germaine Weber, seven-month-old daughter of another brother-in-law, had died while her mother was out shopping, and this, too, had been put down to the same cause. Finally, on 27 March, the day on which Germaine was buried, Jeanne Weber's own seven-year-old son, Marcel, had fallen ill and died, the diagnosis in this case being diphtheria.

The doctor found all this information disturbing. The following morning, after examining the child again, he consulted the doctor in charge of the children's ward, who made his own examination and came to the same conclusion. As a result, the police were informed and Jeanne Weber taken into custody. It was then discovered that she had had two other children besides Marcel, both of whom had died, and that two others had died while in her care in 1902.

The interviewing of witnesses produced other startling pieces of information. On the day that Georgette died the child's mother had been called away from the laundry by a neighbour, who had entered the apartment after hearing screams; she had arrived home to find Georgette's tongue hanging out and foam on her lips, but had then gone back to the laundry after holding her in front of an open window for a while. A similar thing had happened *twice* on consecutive days before Germaine's death, except that in this case a doctor had been called each time.

Though Dr Léon Thoinot, the pathologist appointed to examine the exhumed bodies of the four children, found no signs of strangulation or choking, the examining magistrate was convinced of Jeanne Weber's guilt and determined to have her brought to trial. But when the trial took place, in January 1906, Thoinot's evidence proved to be devastating and the accused was acquitted. Soon afterwards she disappeared.

The following year, using a different name, she appeared in the village of Chambon, near Villedieu, where she became the housekeeper and mistress of a peasant named Bavouzet, who had three children. A few weeks later one of the children, a boy of nine, died suddenly, his death being put down to 'convulsions resulting from an irritation of the meninges'. The case was investigated when Jeanne Weber's identity was discovered; the child was then found to have died of strangulation. Jeanne Weber was arrested and brought to trial again, but with the same result as before.

The year after that she arrived in Commercy with a lime-burner named Émile Bouchery, who introduced her as his wife. The couple rented a room at an inn, but Bouchery had to go out that evening and said he would return late at night; the innkeeper and his wife therefore allowed their seven-year-old son to sleep in the room, to keep Jeanne company. They were later summoned by another lodger who had heard the child screaming.

Breaking into the room, the innkeeper and his wife found their son lying on the bed with his face discoloured and blood streaming from his mouth. Jeanne Weber lay beside him, her hands and her petticoat bloodstained. The boy died soon afterwards, his death having been caused by strangulation. The bleeding had been caused by his biting his tongue.

When the case was reported in the newspapers there was a storm of indignation. Jeanne Weber, however, was not brought to trial this time; instead, she was declared insane and committed to a mental hospital. She remained there until she committed suicide two years later.

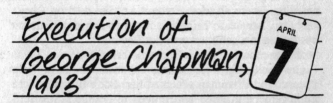

Execution of George Chapman, 1903

APRIL 7

George Chapman, who was hanged on 7 April 1903, was a philanderer and bigamist who poisoned three women with antimony, probably because he had grown tired of them. It has been suggested that he was also responsible for the 'Jack the Ripper' murders.

Chapman was a native of Poland, his real name being Severin Antoniovitch Klosovski. The son of a carpenter, he had been apprenticed to a surgeon at the age of fifteen, but failed to get a degree. After his arrival in London in 1888 he worked as a barber's assistant in the East End.

He was already married by this time, but had left his wife in Poland. Later, when she joined him in England, she found him living with another Polish woman, Lucy Baderski, whom he had also married. The two women lived in the same house with him for a short while, until the legal wife left.

Klosovski and Lucy Baderski went to America together in 1890, but parted company the following year, Klosovski coming back to England in 1892. He changed his name to George Chapman after living for a year with a girl named Annie Chapman.

In 1895 he took up with a married woman, Mary Spink, who had been deserted by her husband. They lived together, claiming to be married, and Mrs Spink — who had private means — allowed him to use some of her money to open a hairdressing shop in Hastings in 1897.

Though this proved popular, with Mrs Spink playing the piano for the benefit of customers, they gave it up six months later and moved back to London, taking the lease of the Prince of Wales Tavern, off City Road.

Towards the end of the year Mrs Spink became ill, suffering severe attacks of vomiting. She died on Christmas Day, her death being put down to consumption, and was buried in a common grave at Leyton.

A few months later a domestic servant named Bessie Taylor applied for a job as barmaid at the Prince of Wales Tavern, and Chapman accepted her. Soon they were pretending to be married and moved to Bishop's Stortford, but then returned to London, where Chapman set himself up in the Monument Tavern, in Borough.

Bessie's health was deteriorating by this time and Chapman treated her violently. When she died, in February 1901, 'exhaustion from vomiting and diarrhoea' was stated to be the cause.

After another few months Chapman met Maud Marsh, whom he also employed as a barmaid. The daughter of a labourer in Croydon, she soon became his mistress, though only after he had threatened to dismiss her. They began to live as man and wife not long afterwards.

The following year, 1902, they moved to a new pub, the Crown, which was in the same road as the Monument Tavern. Maud had also begun to suffer from vomiting and diarrhoea and, although she recovered in hospital, she became ill again after being discharged.

Her mother, who was nursing her, became ill herself after drinking a glass of brandy and soda which Chapman had prepared for Maud. This made her suspicious enough to ask her own doctor to examine Maud, and he, having done so, warned Chapman's doctor that she was being poisoned. When Maud died, on 22 October 1902, Chapman's doctor refused to issue a death certificate.

Chapman was arrested three days later and charged with her murder; he was later charged with the murders of Mary Spink and Bessie Taylor, too. His trial began at the Old Bailey on 16 March 1903, and lasted four days. He was hanged at Wandsworth Prison, at the age of thirty-seven.

Superintendent of Milford Sanatorium poisoned, 1949

APRIL
9

During the late afternoon of 9 April 1949, the superintendent of the Milford Sanatorium at Godalming, in Surrey, found a brown-paper parcel containing part of a fruit pie in his office. His secretary was not there, as it was Saturday, and there was no message to tell him who had sent it. He therefore assumed that it was from one of his friends and, taking it home with him, started to eat it. Before long he was seized with pain and began to be violently sick.

He spent the rest of the weekend in bed, feeling very ill and unable to eat anything else, and on Monday, when he returned to work, he was still weak and suffering from a stomach ache. He was then given a letter which had been left in his secretary's in-tray two days earlier. It was from a Mrs Formby, and explained the arrival of the fruit pie, which the superintendent already suspected to have been the cause of his illness.

Mrs Formby was a friend of Mrs Margery Radford, an inmate of the sanatorium, who had received the pie from her husband and been ill herself after eating some of it. Fearing it to be poisoned, she had asked Mrs Formby to have its contents analysed, informing her that she had been ill on several other occasions after receiving food or drink sent by her husband. But Mrs Formby, after consulting her own husband, had decided not to send it to Scotland Yard, as her friend had requested, but to the superintendent instead.

Having read the letter and spoken to Margery Radford, who was now close to death, the superintendent called the Surrey police. The following day the remains of the fruit pie were sent to the laboratories at Scotland Yard, where they were found to contain arsenic. Margery Radford, having suffered from tuberculosis for seven years, died on the very day that this discovery was made. It was then found that she had been systematically poisoned over a period of three months.

Her husband, Frederick Gordon Radford, was a laboratory technician at a hospital about a mile from the sanatorium. He had not been attentive to his ailing wife and was believed to have a mistress; the pies and mineral drinks which Mrs Radford had received, though bought by her husband, were delivered by her father, a Mr Kite. On being told that arsenic had been found in one of the pies and also in his wife's body, Radford held his face in his hands, denying all knowledge of the matter.

'Why should I want to kill my wife?' he asked. 'I knew she was going to die anyway. I would not be such a fool as to use arsenic with my experience, as I know the police could find it easily enough.' He then challenged Detective Superintendent Roberts, head of the Surrey CID, to charge him 'and let a judge and jury decide'.

Superintendent Roberts was not yet ready to make an arrest, as it was just possible that the suspect was telling the truth. Frederick Radford was therefore driven home by police officers after agreeing to attend the inquest the following day. In the morning, however, he was found dead, his body already cold. He had poisoned himself with cyanide.

106

Murder of David Blakely, 1955

APRIL 10

On the night of 10 April 1955, Ruth Ellis, a twenty-eight-year-old divorcée and night-club hostess, peered through a window of a public house in Hampstead, London, and saw her former lover inside. She waited outside for him, and when he emerged she produced a gun and fired at him six times in quick succession. David Blakely, a twenty-five-year-old racing driver, was killed instantly, and a passer-by was wounded in the hand.

Ruth Ellis was immediately apprehended and taken to Hampstead police station, where she admitted the shooting. 'I am guilty,' she said, adding: 'I am rather confused.' At her trial at the Old Bailey in June she was asked what her intention had been when she fired the shots. 'I intended to kill him,' she replied.

Blakely and Ruth Ellis had been lovers for the previous two years, and a few weeks earlier had set up home together in Egerton Gardens, Kensington. However, neither of them had been faithful to the other and both had resented the other's affairs. After many bitter quarrels, Blakely left without telling her where he was going. At the beginning of April she had a miscarriage.

On Good Friday — 8 April — she tried to see him at a house in Tanza Road, Hampstead, where she knew that he was spending Easter in the company of friends. But he refused to see her, and when she became noisy the police were called. It was from the same house that Blakely went out to the pub on the evening of 10 April.

Ruth Ellis was convicted and sentenced to death. Despite many petitions for a commutation, she was hanged at Holloway Prison on 13 July 1955, the execution causing much astonishment and disgust. It was the last time that a woman was hanged in Britain.

In July 1983, Ruth's daughter, then aged thirty-one, gave a newspaper interview to the *Sunday Mirror*, in which she spoke of the anguish which she had suffered as a result of knowing that her mother had been hanged.

'For most of my life I have tried to face up to the image of the hangman peering through the peephole into her cell, trying to work out how much rope he should use to make sure that frail little neck was broken,' she said. 'As for the scene on the gallows, I just blank it out.'

Her half-brother, born in 1944, had had similar problems, though he had been brought up separately. He took his own life in 1982, after years of depression.

Beginning of Adelaide Bartlett's trial, 1886

APRIL 12

On 12 April 1886, the trial of Adelaide Bartlett, aged thirty, for the murder of her husband, began at the Old Bailey. Edwin Bartlett, a forty-year-old grocer, had been found dead at the couple's lodgings in the Pimlico district of London on 1 January the same year. He had died as a result of taking a large dose of liquid chloroform.

The accused was the illegitimate daughter of a well-born Frenchwoman; she had been brought up in France and had come to England to complete her education. Her marriage had taken place in 1875.

Edwin Bartlett was an ambitious businessman and a staunch Wesleyan. Though good-humoured, he gave his wife less attention than she would have liked, with the result that she was often bored. For a period of five years her father-in-law lived with them, her husband having invited him to do so without consulting her. However, they gave the impression of being a contented couple.

In 1885 they became acquainted with a young Wesleyan minister, the Reverend George Dyson, who visited them frequently. Dyson and Adelaide were attracted to each other and began to have an affair — with Bartlett's knowledge and approval. Bartlett made a will, leaving everything to his wife and naming her lover as the executor. He also made it clear that he wanted Dyson to have Adelaide in the event of his own death.

In December Bartlett was seriously ill, but recovered well enough to celebrate Christmas. On the day before his death he visited his dentist and appeared to be in good health. It was afterwards revealed that on 29 December Dyson had given Adelaide a large amount of chloroform which he had bought in small amounts from three different chemists.

Though Dyson had also been charged with the murder, no evidence was offered against him when the case came to court. Adelaide claimed that she used chloroform in order to resist her husband's sexual demands — by getting him to inhale it. As no traces of it were found in the dead man's mouth or windpipe, the jury, at the end of the six-day trial, concluded that while grave suspicion attached to the defendant, there was insufficient evidence to show how or by whom the chloroform had been administered. She was therefore acquitted.

A study of the case by Yseult Bridges, entitled *Poison and Adelaide Bartlett*, puts forward the theory that Edwin Bartlett was induced to drink the chloroform while under the influence of hypnotic suggestion.

Death of Sarah Ricketts, 1953

On 14 April 1953, Sarah Ricketts, a seventy-nine-year-old widow of Devonshire Road, Blackpool, died of phosphorus poisoning, her death occurring at 3.15 a.m. in the presence of Louisa Merrifield, her housekeeper. Mrs Merrifield, aged forty-six, did not call in a doctor until nearly eleven hours later, but tried unsuccessfully to get an undertaker to cremate the body 'at once'. Later, when the bungalow and garden were being searched by police, she made arrangements for members of the Salvation Army to play *Abide With Me* outside.

Louisa Merrifield and her third husband Alfred, aged seventy-one, had moved into Mrs Ricketts' home only a few weeks earlier, Mrs Merrifield having obtained the job after seeing it advertised in a newspaper. Mrs Merrifield had had twenty similar jobs in the previous three years; she also had a criminal record, having served a prison sentence for ration-book frauds. Mrs Ricketts, despite feeling that she was not being properly looked after — she complained that she was not given enough food — had since changed her will in the couple's favour.

'We are landed', Mrs Merrifield told an acquaintance a few days before Mrs Ricketts' death. 'We went living with an old lady and she died and left me a bungalow worth £4000.' When asked which old lady she was talking about, she replied, 'She's not dead yet, but she soon will be'.

During a medical examination on the day before her death Mrs Ricketts was found to be in reasonably good health.

The search of the bungalow failed to reveal any trace of the poison, but a substance attached to a teaspoon in Mrs Merrifield's handbag was found to be the residue which resulted from phosphorus being mixed with rum. Alfred Merrifield was identified by a Blackpool chemist's assistant from whom he had purchased a tin of rat poison which contained phosphorus.

Louisa and Alfred Merrifield were brought to trial in Manchester in July, both pleading not guilty to the murder; the case lasted eleven days. Louisa stated that she had found Mrs Ricketts on the floor of her bedroom at 3.15 a.m. on the day of her death, and went on to tell the court: 'I picked her up and put her into bed. She said she was thankful to me. Those were the last words she spoke.' On being asked why she had not immediately gone for help, she replied, 'Well, it was not such a nice time in the morning to go out on the streets and call a doctor.'

Though the defence contended that Mrs Ricketts had died from cirrhosis of the liver, the jury found Louisa Merrifield guilty of murder and she was sentenced to death. In the case of her husband they were unable to reach agreement; the judge therefore ordered that he should be retried at the following assizes, but the case against him was finally dropped. Louisa Merrifield was hanged at Manchester's Strangeways Prison on 18 September 1953.

Alfred Merrifield, on being released, received his half-share of Mrs Ricketts' bungalow, and later appeared in sideshows in Blackpool. He died, aged eighty, in 1962.

Payroll murder in South Braintree, 1920

APRIL 15

On the afternoon of 15 April 1920, two employees of the Slater and Morrill Shoe Company were shot and fatally wounded by two other men while delivering the $16,000 weekly payroll to the company's factory in South Braintree, Massachusetts. The two killers, having grabbed the money, escaped in a car with a third gunman who had taken no active part in the crime; another two men were also seen in the car with them. The two victims were Frederick A. Parmenter, the paymaster, and Alexander Berardelli, an armed guard.

The two men who had fired the shots were both described as 'foreign-looking', one of them being clean-shaven and the other having a moustache. It was as a result of these descriptions that a police officer boarded a streetcar in the same district on 5 May and arrested two Italian immigrants, Nicola Sacco, a shoemaker aged twenty-nine, and Bartolomeo Vanzetti, a fish-pedlar aged thirty-two. Both were found to be armed with guns, Sacco having a .32 Colt automatic and Venzetti a .38 revolver; both were also found to be anarchists.

Though each was initially charged with possessing a firearm without a permit, Sacco was later brought to trial for taking part in an attempted payroll robbery in Bridgewater, near Boston, the previous Christmas. On being convicted of this offence, he was sentenced to ten to fifteen years' imprisonment. By this time he and Vanzetti had been charged with the South Braintree murders.

Their trial, which began in Dedham, Massachusetts, on 31 May 1921, made headline news in many countries. Some sixty witnesses appeared for the prosecution, and nearly 100 for the defence. The prosecution produced ballistics evidence, seeking to prove that bullets recovered from the bodies of both victims had been fired from Sacco's gun. While the value of this evidence was challenged by defence witnesses, the political sympathies of the defendants made bias inevitable. The conduct of the trial judge, who privately regarded them as 'anarchist bastards', was afterwards to be the subject of much criticism. Sacco and Vanzetti were both found guilty of first-degree murder and sentenced to death.

There were immediate demands for another trial. Organizations were set up to raise funds for their defence and a campaign of agitation began. During the next six years many petitions for clemency were presented and many protests staged. In legal circles disquiet was expressed at the verdict and the means by which it had been reached. But, on 9 April 1927, after no fewer than seven motions for a new trial had been heard and dismissed, the death sentences were confirmed. Sacco and Vanzetti were executed in the electric chair on 23 August 1927.

The controversy to which the case had given rise continued long after their deaths, and has never been forgotten. In 1977 their names were cleared in a special proclamation issued by the Governor of Massachusetts.

Six killed in Glasgow arson attack, 1984

APRIL 16

During the early hours of 16 April 1984, an arson attack was made on a Glasgow council flat, resulting in the deaths of six people. The flat, which was the home of a family named Doyle, was on the top floor of a block in Backend Street, Ruchazie. As the front door was its only exit, and petrol had been poured through the letter-box and ignited, the people inside were trapped. One of the survivors, twenty-one-year-old Stephen Doyle, only managed to escape the blaze by jumping fifty feet to the concrete below, injuring his back and legs in the process.

Stephen's brother Anthony, aged fourteen, and his twenty-five-year-old sister, Mrs Christine Halleron, both died in the flames; his father, James Doyle, aged fifty-

113

three, his brothers James and Andrew, aged twenty-three and eighteen respectively, and Mrs Halleron's eighteen-month-old son Mark all died later. James Doyle's grief-stricken widow Lilian, aged fifty-two, who was rescued by firemen after perching on a window-ledge, said later that she wished that she, too, had died in the fire which claimed the lives of her husband, sons, daughter and grandson.

The attack had been the work of Thomas Campbell, a thirty-one-year-old gangster determined to take control of Glasgow's lucrative ice-cream trade, and one of his henchmen, a twenty-two-year-old petty thief named Joseph Steele. Campbell, who had already served a ten-year prison sentence, had been responsible for many attacks on drivers working for Marchetti Brothers, a well-established rival company, and was believed to have taken part in an attempt to burn down that company's premises.

Andrew Doyle, one of the drivers concerned, had actually been hired by Marchetti Brothers to protect two of their other vans rather than sell ice-cream. On one occasion he had been threatened and his van had been damaged with pickaxe handles; on another a man with a shotgun had fired through his windscreen. Then, a week after the second attack, a group of men had beaten him up in the street. But Andrew Doyle had refused to be intimidated by Campbell's men. It was because of this that the arson attack had taken place.

Though the police officers investigating the crime had little difficulty finding out what had happened, they hesitated to make arrests for fear that they would prove to be premature. A twenty-four-year-old man, William Love, was charged in connection with the shotgun attack and, while denying that he had committed the offence, agreed that he had been at the scene on the day in question; he afterwards made a statement claiming to have overheard Campbell and others planning to set fire to the Doyles' front door, as 'a frightener'. However, it was 12 May before the police took Campbell into custody and 1 June before they arrested Joseph Steele.

114

Eventually, on 3 September 1984, the case described as 'Scotland's biggest multiple murder trial' began in Glasgow, with Campbell, Steele and five other men appearing, each charged with offences in connection with the gang's activities. It lasted twenty-seven days, with one of the accused being released when the prosecution withdrew charges against him, and others being cleared on some charges because the judge found insufficient evidence against them.

But at the end of the trial Thomas Campbell and Joseph Steele were both given sentences of life imprisonment for murdering the six members of the Doyle family, the judge recommending that Campbell should serve twenty years, but making no recommendation in Steele's case. Campbell was also given ten years, to run concurrently, for taking part in the shotgun attack, and Steele received two shorter sentences, also to run concurrently, for conspiracy and damaging an ice-cream van.

Of the other accused, Thomas Gray, aged thirty-one, was sentenced to fourteen years for attempted murder; Thomas Lafferty, forty, was given three years for taking part in the shotgun attack; George Reid, thirty-three, received a total of three years for a knife assault and for damaging an ice-cream van, and John Campbell, twenty-one, was given a year for taking part in the attack on the ice-cream van and three years for taking part in the shotgun attack.

The jailing of Campbell and his fellow-accused did not bring Glasgow's 'ice-cream war' to an end, for others associated with them have continued to operate vans on the city's council estates and many further cases of assault and damage have been reported by drivers working for Marchetti Brothers. It is believed that, in spite of the length of his sentence, Campbell is still directing the activities of gang members who were not arrested from his prison cell.

Execution of Frederick Seddon, 1912

On 18 April 1912, Frederick Seddon, a forty-year-old insurance agent, was hanged at Pentonville Prison for the murder of Eliza Barrow, a lodger at his three-storey house in Tollington Park, north London. Miss Barrow, aged forty-nine, had died from arsenic poisoning on 14 September previously.

Seddon was a mean and calculating man, obsessed with making and saving money. He had worked for the same insurance company for over twenty years, but was constantly dealing in other things — anything which enabled him to make a profit, in fact — and even managed to make 2s 6d (12$\frac{1}{2}$p) commission out of his victim's funeral. He owned various properties in addition to the house at Tollington Park, where he and his family occupied the lower floors. His crime, needless to say, was committed for gain.

Eliza Barrow, who had moved into the house in July 1910, was shabby and dirty, and every bit as miserly as Seddon himself. She occupied the top floor, and had an orphan boy, the son of an earlier landlord and landlady, living with her.

At the beginning of her tenancy she had both property and money, but gradually her fortune passed into Seddon's hands, as she was impressed by his financial astuteness and thought he was helping her to take care of it. After her death he took over £400 in gold coins from her cash-box, and then arranged a pauper's burial for her, haggling with the undertaker over the cost of it.

Eliza Barrow's doctor, without seeing the body, made out a death certificate, giving the cause as 'epidemic diarrhoea'. But after complaints from her relatives, who were

116

suspicious of Seddon's evasive answers to their questions, an exhumation was authorized and a post-mortem carried out. On 4 December Seddon was arrested and charged with murder. His wife was similarly charged a few weeks later.

Frederick and Margaret Seddon were brought to trial at the Old Bailey on 4 March 1912, both pleading not guilty. The case lasted ten days, three of them being taken up by Seddon's own evidence; this was given in such an arrogant and self-assured manner that it served only to antagonize everyone. So, while his wife was acquitted, Seddon — against whom the case was no stronger — was convicted. When asked if he had anything to say before sentence was passed, he made a long speech protesting his innocence, during the course of which he raised his hand as though taking an oath of freemasonry.

The judge, who, like Seddon, was a freemason, said in reply: 'You and I know we belong to one brotherhood ... But our brotherhood does not encourage crime; on the contrary, it condemns it. I pray you again to make your peace with the Great Architect of the Universe. Mercy — pray for it, ask for it'. He was in tears as he pronounced sentence.

Seddon was the father of five children, the youngest of which had been born just a few months before the murder. Margaret Seddon remarried and moved to Liverpool a few months after her husband's execution. She made herself a lot of money out of a newspaper confession, stating that she had seen Frederick Seddon giving poison to Eliza Barrow on the night before her death. However, she published a second statement a fortnight afterwards, claiming that the first had been a lie. Eventually she emigrated to America.

On 24 April 1918, David Greenwood, a twenty-one-year-old turner, was brought to trial at the Old Bailey, charged with the murder of Nellie Trew, aged sixteen, on 9 February previously. He denied the offence.

On the day of the murder the victim, a junior clerk working at Woolwich Arsenal, had left her home at Juno Terrace, Eltham Well Hall, to change a book at Plumstead Library. The following morning she was found raped and strangled on Eltham Common, about a quarter of a mile away. Her father had reported her missing when she failed to return home by midnight.

A replica of the badge of the Leicestershire Regiment and an overcoat button, which had been threaded with a piece of wire, were found trodden into the mud near the scene of the crime. The police had a photograph of both articles published in all the popular newspapers on the day after the body had been found.

David Greenwood, who worked for the Hewson Manufacturing Company near Oxford Street, normally wore a badge on the lapel of his overcoat. One of his workmates noticed that it was missing and remarked, pointing to the newspaper photograph, 'That looks uncommonly like the badge you were wearing.' Greenwood agreed, explaining that he had sold his badge two days earlier to a man he had met on a tram. It was then suggested to him that he should go to the police and 'clear the matter up'.

The same day, at lunch time, Greenwood went to the police station in Tottenham Court Road and told the same story. The police, learning that he lived in Eltham, took a particular interest in him, and the next day an inspector went to his place of work and took him back to Scotland Yard.

It was noticed that all the buttons had been removed from his overcoat, and that there was a little tear where one of them had been. The piece of wire which had been attached to the button discovered on Eltham Common was found to be part of a spring; the same type of spring was used at the Hewson works.

At his trial Greenwood's war record was revealed. Having enlisted at the beginning of the First World War, he had fought in the trenches and been buried alive at Ypres. He had then been discharged, suffering from neurasthenia, shell-shock and a weak heart. The defence suggested that he was not physically capable of committing the crime of which he stood accused.

The jury found the defendant guilty, adding a recommendation of mercy. His death sentence was commuted just before he was due to be executed, and he spent the next fifteen years in prison. At his release, in 1933, he was thirty-six years old.

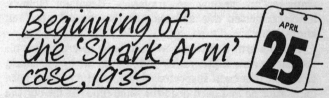

Beginning of the 'Shark Arm' case, 1935

APRIL 25

On 25 April 1935, a shark in an Australian aquarium began to vomit and, to the disgust of spectators, brought up a man's arm. When this was removed from the pool by police it was found to be so well preserved that a tattoo depicting two boxers was clearly visible on it. As there was also a length of rope tied tightly round the wrist, the police immediately suspected that a murder or suicide had taken place.

The shark had been caught by two fishermen off the beaches near Sydney a week earlier, when it became entangled in their lines. Not knowing what else to do with it, they had given it to the Coogee Beach aquarium. But it had not taken to captivity and its digestive system had failed to function normally. It died shortly afterwards.

No trace of any other part of the man's body was found in the shark's stomach or intestines, so an extensive search of the beaches and sea-bed was started in the area in which it had been caught. Though this was to be in vain, a study of missing-persons lists led to the man's identification. He was found to be James Smith, a forty-year-old former boxer who had worked as a marker in a billiard hall owned by Reginald Holmes, a wealthy boat-builder, prior to his disappearance. His wife and brother both identified the arm from its tattoo marks.

Smith had left his home on 8 April, telling his wife that he was going on a fishing holiday with a man named Patrick Brady, and that they would be staying in a rented cottage on the coast; she had heard nothing from him since. The police already knew Brady, a forty-two-year-old forger, and though he denied all knowledge of Smith's death, he was taken into custody. He then accused Smith's employer of dealing in forgeries. Reginald Holmes, however, denied this and claimed that he did not even know Brady.

Smith's arm was found to have been severed from his shoulder with a knife, rather than bitten off by the shark, as had at first been suspected; this appeared to have been done after he had been dead for some time. At the cottage on the coast a tin trunk, a mattress, three mats and a length of rope were found to be missing. It was therefore supposed that the body had been cut up there and pushed into the trunk, those parts for which there was insufficient room being tied to the outside. The trunk had then been taken out to sea and dumped, together with the mattress and mats, which were presumably bloodstained.

Three days after Brady's arrest Reginald Holmes, steering his speedboat in an erratic manner in Sydney Harbour, was pursued by a police launch. When the police caught up with him after a four-hour chase he was found to be suffering from a superficial bullet wound in his head and claimed that somebody had tried to kill him. He then admitted knowing Brady, and accused him of killing Smith and disposing of the body. On 17 May Brady was charged with murder.

However, on the night before the coroner's inquest Holmes, by now the most important witness, was shot dead in his car under Sydney Harbour Bridge, the sound of the shot being drowned by the noise of overhead traffic. Brady's lawyers then obtained an order from the Supreme Court to stop the inquest — after forty witnesses had been heard — on the grounds that Smith's severed arm was no proof of his death. Brady was released on bail, and at his trial in September for Smith's murder was acquitted for lack of evidence.

It was understood that both Smith and Brady had been involved in drug-trafficking and underworld intimidation, and that Holmes had been murdered in order to ensure his silence. But Brady, who died in 1965, maintained his innocence of Smith's murder to the end, and two other men who were tried for Holmes' murder were both acquitted.

Probable death of Belle Gunness, 1908

APRIL 28

On 28 April 1908, a farm on the outskirts of La Porte, in Indiana, owned by a widow named Belle Gunness, was burnt to the ground. The fire, which had been started deliberately, led to the discovery of four bodies among the debris, and fourteen others which had been dismembered and buried. The four recovered from the debris were believed to be those of the widow and her three children. The other fourteen were found to be the remains of men who had been murdered by the widow for their money.

Belle Gunness, who was born in Norway in 1859, had had two husbands, both of whom had died; the death of the second had occurred in suspicious circumstances in La Porte in 1904. She had since managed the farm with the help of a local handyman, Ray Lamphere, who was also her lover. It was believed that Lamphere had killed her and then set fire to the farm in order to prevent the crime being discovered. However, the body believed to be hers was inexplicably headless. Those involved in the investigation had to point to the finding of her denture in order to prove that it *was* hers.

Almost immediately after Lamphere's arrest a stranger arrived in La Porte in search of his missing brother. Andrew Hegelein, of South Dakota, was known to have visited the farm, taking $1000 in cash, but nothing had been heard from him since; his brother, having written to Mrs Gunness, had now come to see her about it. Before long it was discovered that Andrew Hegelein was one of the men who had been murdered.

Mrs Gunness was found to have been in the practice of placing newspaper advertisements in other parts of America, each of them worded in the same way: 'Rich, good-looking woman, owner of a big farm, desires to correspond with a gentleman of wealth and refinement. Object matrimony.' All of the men whose bodies had been found had replied to one of these advertisements, and each had been duped into taking a large sum of money to the farm, thinking that he was about to meet his future wife. The widow had killed and butchered all of them herself.

Ray Lamphere was brought to trial for the widow's murder, but acquitted. At the same time, however, he was convicted of setting fire to her property and given a sentence of two to twenty-one years' imprisonment. He died of tuberculosis in the Indiana State Penitentiary.

He had, at some stage, made a claim that the widow's death had been faked, the headless corpse found after the fire being that of a drunken female tramp from Chicago. But, while this might explain why the head was missing, it also suggests that Mrs Gunness was responsible for the deaths of her own children, of whom she was very fond. It is therefore unlikely to be true.

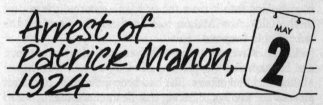

Arrest of Patrick Mahon, 1924

MAY 2

On the evening of 2 May 1924, Patrick Mahon, aged thirty-four, went to retrieve a Gladstone bag from the cloakroom at Waterloo Station, London. As he tried to leave the station afterwards he was approached by a police officer, who asked to be shown the bag's contents. Mahon said that he had not got the key, and was then taken to Kennington police station, where keys were found in his possession. Later, at Scotland Yard, the bag was opened and found to contain a cook's knife, a brown canvas bag with the initials E.B.K. and some bloodstained items of clothing.

Unable to account for these articles satisfactorily, Mahon was told that he would be held while inquiries were made. After much hesitation he finally made a statement which led to the discovery of human remains in a bungalow near Eastbourne the following morning. They were the remains of Mahon's mistress, Emily Kaye, who had been dead for over a fortnight and whose body had been dismembered. She had been pregnant at the time of her death.

Mahon, a soda-fountain salesman of Richmond, Surrey,

was a married man with one child. He had a criminal record, having been in trouble on one occasion for forgery, on another for embezzlement and on a third for robbery with violence; the third of these charges had been brought against him in 1916, when he was sent to prison for five years.

A day or two earlier Mahon's wife had found a cloak-room ticket in one of his pockets and asked a friend — a former railway policeman — to find out what had been left at Waterloo Station. The ex-policeman had inspected the bag, looking into it from the side, and reported the matter to the CID. Mrs Mahon had been asked to replace the ticket in her husband's suit.

Emily Kaye, a thirty-eight-year-old shorthand-typist and bookkeeper, was just one of many women with whom Mahon had had affairs. She had been induced to part with most of her savings, thinking that he intended taking her to South Africa — where he would set up home with her — and had joined Mahon in Eastbourne on 12 April, the bungalow having been rented for eight weeks. The exact date of her death was never established.

According to Mahon, who gave several different accounts during the course of the investigation, Emily Kaye had been accidentally killed as a result of a violent quarrel. Having dismembered her body, he had pushed the torso into a trunk — where the police found it — and burnt her head, legs and feet on the sitting-room fire; other parts were cut into small pieces and boiled in a pot or thrown from the window of a train. He had left the bag at Water-loo Station before going back to his home in Richmond.

While some parts of his story were undoubtedly true, others were clearly not — especially as he was found to have bought a cook's knife and a meat-saw in London before going to join the victim in Eastbourne. He was accordingly brought to trial in Lewes in July, with crowds of people mobbing the court-house.

Mahon denied the offence. He said that the victim had demanded that he should leave his wife in order to set up home with her, and that he had rented the bungalow as an 'experiment', in order to show her that this would be unwise. She had been killed, he said, when she hit her head against a coal-scuttle while he was defending himself against her. He was not believed.

On being found guilty, he protested about 'the bitterness and unfairness' of the judge's summing-up. He was, however, hanged at Wandsworth Prison on 9 September 1924.

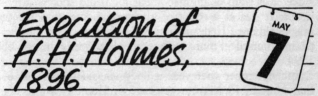

Execution of H. H. Holmes, 1896

MAY 7

H.H. Holmes, who was hanged at Philadelphia's Moyamensing Prison on 7 May 1896, was a mass murderer. His victims included mistresses, employees and acquaintances, but how many of them there were altogether is not known. He was also an insurance swindler and a bigamist.

A native of Gilmanton, New Hampshire, Holmes was born on 16 May 1860; his real name was Hermann Webster Mudgett. He practised medicine in New York for a short while after obtaining a degree at the age of twenty-four, then moved to Chicago, where he worked in a drug-store owned by a Mrs Holden. Later he became the owner of the store, Mrs Holden having mysteriously disappeared.

Holmes had married at eighteen, but deserted his wife and son in 1886, changing his name when he went to Chicago. There he soon married again — it was the first of several such marriages — and he began to swindle one of his new 'wife's' uncles, causing a family quarrel in the process. He also had a succession of mistresses, some of whom disappeared as mysteriously as Mrs Holden.

With his business thriving, Holmes bought a vacant lot and began to build a hotel, with turrets, battlements and secret passages, which became known as 'Holmes's Castle'. When this was later investigated by police, it was found that there were air-tight rooms which could be filled with gas from hidden pipes operated from the office, and that the basement contained a kiln large enough to hold a human body.

Holmes sold the drugstore in 1892, after the completion of his hotel. During the following year he had a good many guests to accommodate as a result of the Chicago Exposition. But he was involved in petty crime as well, and received a term of imprisonment for fraud shortly afterwards. It was as a result of a conversation with a fellow prisoner named Hedgspeth in St Louis Prison that he was to find himself in more serious trouble towards the end of 1894.

In September that year a body alleged to be that of Benjamin F. Pitezel, an associate of Holmes' whose life had been insured for $10,000, was found in Philadelphia; he had evidently died as a result of an explosion. Holmes, among others, went to identify the body, and the insurance company paid the $10,000 to Pitezel's wife. On hearing of this, however, Hedgspeth wrote to the company, saying that Holmes had told him about a 'foolproof method' of insurance fraud, and warning them that the body was not that of Pitezel at all.

The company investigated the case and obtained evidence which appeared to substantiate Hedgspeth's allegation. Holmes, on being questioned, agreed that he had defrauded the company using a body which had been provided by a doctor; the real Pitezel, he said, had gone abroad, taking his three children. Mrs Pitezel also admitted fraud, but did not know her husband's whereabouts; she said that Holmes had taken her children to stay with a widow in Kentucky and that she had not seen them since.

Later, however, Holmes confessed that the body in Philadelphia *was* Pitezel's, and said that the dead man had committed suicide; the children were safe in England. But the bodies of two of the children were then found in a cellar in Toronto, and the remains of the third were recovered from a chimney in Irvington.

Holmes was eventually brought to trial on 28 October 1895, for the murder of Benjamin Pitezel, but the case against him included evidence that he had committed other murders, too. The witnesses included a Chicago car mechanic, who told the court that he had been employed by Holmes at the 'castle' to strip the flesh from three corpses which he believed to have been brought from the city mortuary. Holmes, he said, had paid him $36 for each of the bodies so treated.

While under sentence of death Holmes wrote his memoirs for a newspaper, claiming that he had killed twenty-seven people. He afterwards said that the confession was entirely false, and had been written for the sake of sensationalism. On the scaffold he said that he had been responsible for only two deaths and that these were both of women on whom he had performed illegal operations.

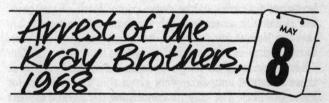

Arrest of the Kray Brothers, 1968

MAY 8

At 6 a.m. on 8 May 1968, teams of detectives raided homes in the East End of London and arrested seventeen members of a criminal gang led by the twin brothers Ronald and Reginald Kray. The gang ran a protection business and was responsible for many acts of brutality, including murder, and the arrests followed a long investigation which had been greatly hampered by the fear of witnesses to give information about them. But once the downfall of the gang seemed certain, these witnesses began to come forward of their own accord, and some of its members agreed to give evidence in return for their own freedom. It thus became possible to bring various charges against the gang leaders and nine other people.

These were all brought to trial together at the Old Bailey in January 1969, the most serious charges concerning the murder of George Cornell, a member of the rival Richardson Gang from south London, the murder of Jack McVitie, a small-time crook known as 'Jack the Hat', and the alleged murder of Frank Mitchell, a well-known escaped convict popularly called 'the Mad Axeman'. Among the witnesses called by the prosecution were the barmaid of a public house in which Cornell had been shot dead in March 1966, and Ronald Hart, a cousin of the Krays, who had been present when McVitie was stabbed to death in a basement flat in Stoke Newington in October 1967.

The trial lasted thirty-nine days, with many sensational disclosures being made, and ten of the prisoners were convicted. Ronald Kray and a henchman named John Barrie were both sentenced to life imprisonment for Cornell's murder, Reggie Kray being given ten years for being an accessory to the same crime. Both of the twins were given life sentences, with a recommendation that they serve at least thirty years, for the murder of Jack McVitie. Other members of the gang, including their older brother Charles, were given long sentences for crimes related to these murders, and some were given shorter sentences for lesser offences. The charges concerning the alleged murder of Frank Mitchell, whose body was never found, were not proved.

The Kray twins, aged thirty-five, were both former professional boxers. Outwardly they were respectable businessmen, owning clubs and restaurants, and had many celebrities among their friends. But, in fact, they enjoyed their reputation for violence and the power which it gave them. 'I saw beatings that were unnecessary even by

128

underworld standards and witnessed people slashed with a razor just for the hell of it,' said Ronald Hart, who had worked for them. On one occasion, after shooting somebody, Reggie Kray had said to him, 'You want to try it some time. It's a nice feeling.'

'We were well aware that many people thought we had bitten off more than we could chew in arresting a large number of known criminals without, at that time, having sufficient evidence to secure conviction,' Commander John du Rose later recorded. 'But we were convinced that once the Gang was in custody evidence would be forthcoming. Events proved us right but there was still a lot of work to be done verifying statements and digging up fresh facts. Nothing was left to chance and a vast team of detectives worked day and night.'

While serving an earlier sentence for grievous bodily harm Ronald Kray, a homosexual, was certified insane and transferred to a mental hospital in Surrey. In 1979 he was again found to be insane, and this time he was committed to Broadmoor.

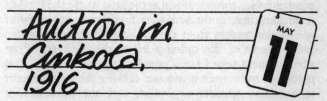

Auction in Cinkota, 1916

On 11 May 1916, a house with an adjoining workshop in the village of Cinkota, near Budapest, was sold by public auction. The owner was not present and his whereabouts were unknown; the sale had been ordered by the district court so that unpaid taxes on the property could be collected. It was bought by Istvan Molnar, a middle-aged blacksmith, who intended turning it into a smithy and general repair shop.

A week or so after Molnar and his family had moved into the house seven large tin barrels were discovered behind sheets of corrugated iron in the workshop; they were sealed and unexpectedly heavy. At first Molnar paid no attention to them, but when they were eventually opened each was found to contain the body of a naked woman.

The women, whose ages varied between thirty and fifty, had all been strangled, their deaths taking place over a period of two or three years; there was no means by which any of the bodies could be identified. Moreover, the property had previously been occupied by an unknown tenant who had rarely been seen by neighbours and who had left no personal belongings or papers which would have enabled the police to trace him.

After the investigation had dragged on for about three weeks without progress, Geza Bialokurszky, one of Budapest's most experienced detectives, was put in charge of it. Searching lists of missing persons, he came across an entry concerning a thirty-six-year-old spinster named Anna Novak who had disappeared five years earlier while employed as a cook by the widow of a Hussar colonel.

Bialokurszky questioned the widow and learnt that the missing cook's trunk was still in the attic where she had left it. Fingerprints on the lock were found to match those of one of the corpses from the Cinkota 'House of Horror', and a search of the contents led to the discovery of an advertisement torn from a popular daily newspaper. This purported to be from a widower seeking the acquaintance of a mature spinster or widow, with the possibility of marriage in mind. A post office box number was given for replies.

Bialokurszky made inquiries at the central post office in Budapest and found that the box-holder had given his name as Elemer Nagy; the address he gave was that of an empty plot of land in one of the suburbs. A search of back numbers of the newspaper revealed that the same box number had been used in over twenty advertisements of the same type during a period of less than two years. One of these had been paid for with a postal order, the advertiser using the same name but giving a false address in Cinkota. The others had been paid for in cash.

A facsimile of the signature on the postal order was published in the newspapers, and two days later a domestic servant named Rosa Diosi informed Bialokurszky that it was the handwriting of her former lover, Bela Kiss, who had been called up on the outbreak of war. She produced a postcard which he had sent her from a prisoner-of-war camp in October 1914, asking her to forward some underwear which had been left in her care; the handwriting had the same characteristics as the postal order signature, and Bialokurszky was certain that Bela Kiss was the 'Monster of Cinkota'.

Other women who had known him as a result of his advertisements came forward to provide further information, and finally a photograph was obtained. From this he was recognized as a frequent visitor to Budapest's red-light district.

Towards the end of the year five more bodies, all of naked women, were found under flowerbeds in Istvan Molnar's garden.

By this time it was known that, prior to committing his first murder Bela Kiss, a plumber by trade, had been in the practice of seducing middle-aged women, mainly servants, and coaxing them into parting with their savings. He had used the money to pay for the services of prostitutes, for which he appeared to have an almost insatiable need. He had started killing his victims after one of them had become too demanding for him.

Bela Kiss was never brought to justice, and what became of him is not known. Bialokurszky, who tried for years to trace him, became convinced that he had died in captivity after being wounded in battle. But his disappearance inevitably gave rise to a variety of legends, and some people claimed to have seen him in America long after the war ended.

MAY
12

On 12th May 1958, thirty-one-year-old Peter Manuel was brought to trial in Glasgow, charged with eight murders. The case lasted fourteen days, during the course of which the defendant dismissed his counsel and took over the defence himself. The evidence for the prosecution included Manuel's own confession, but he claimed that this had been made as a result of police threats to charge other members of his family in connection with the offences. The defendant was found guilty on all but one of the charges and sentenced to death. While awaiting execution he confessed to three other murders.

Manuel, a habitual criminal with a record of theft and rape, had been arrested following the discovery of a triple murder in Uddingston, south of Glasgow, at the beginning of the year. Peter Smart, a self-made businessman, his wife and their eleven-year-old son had been shot dead during a burglary at their home on 1 January, their bodies being found some days afterwards. Manuel, who lived with his parents, was suspected and housebreaking tools were found at his home. He and his father were both detained.

While in custody Manuel said that he would give the information which the police wanted on condition that his father was released. Later he admitted being responsible for the triple murder, and also said that he had killed seventeen-year-old Anne Kneilands in East Kilbride two years earlier, three members of a family living just outside East Kilbride in September 1956, and another seventeen-year-old girl, Isabelle Cooke, near her home in Mount Vernon a few days before the murder of Peter Smart and his family.

In the first triple murder case, as in the second, the

132

victims had all been shot during the course of a burglary. The two seventeen-year-old girls had both been the victims of sex murders, Anne Kneilands being found on a golf course with some items of clothing missing. Isabelle Cooke in a shallow grave, almost naked. It was in the case of Anne Kneilands that Manuel was acquitted for lack of evidence. In the case of Isabelle Cooke it was the murderer himself who showed police where the victim had been buried.

'This is the place,' he said. 'In fact, I think I'm standing on her now.'

Born in 1927, Manuel had been almost constantly in trouble from 1939 onwards. His first conviction was for burglary, for which he was put on probation. Soon afterwards he was sent to an approved school, from which he escaped eleven times, for housebreaking. He was then sent to Borstal for robbery and indecent assault — his first known sexual offence. Then, in 1946, he was jailed for housebreaking and rape, and served seven years before being released in 1953. He was again in prison between October 1956 and November 1957.

The three murders to which he confessed while under sentence of death were those of Helen Carlin, a prostitute found strangled in Pimlico in September 1954, Anne Steele, a fifty-five-year-old spinster who was battered to death in Glasgow in January 1956, and Ellen Petrie, who was stabbed, also in Glasgow, in June 1956.

On 8 December 1957, Sydney Dunn, a Newcastle taxi-driver, was found dead on the moors at Edmondbyers, County Durham; he had been shot in the head and his throat had been cut. A coroner's inquest found that he, too, had been killed by Peter Manuel.

Following the dismissal of his appeal, Manuel was hanged at Glasgow's Barlinnie Prison on 11 July 1958.

Discovery of ancient skull, 1983

MAY 13

On 13 May 1983, workers digging in a Cheshire peat bog found a woman's skull which, though over 1500 years old, was so well preserved that it still contained parts of the brain, hair and ligaments. Because of its good condition, nobody at the time suspected its age, and a pathologist who examined it said that it was part of the body of a woman who had allegedly been murdered in the same area in 1960 or 1961. This mistake led to the conviction of Peter Reyn-Bardt, a fifty-seven-year-old former airline official, a few months later.

Reyn-Bardt, a homosexual, had married Malika Maria de Fernandez, a thirty-two-year-old part-time waitress, on 28 March 1959. At the time he was a BOAC executive at Manchester Ringway airport, fearing that discovery of his homosexuality would lead to prosecution and the loss of his job. He saw marriage as a means of acquiring an appearance of respectability. But when his wife realized this her attitude towards him changed, and she started to leave him for months at a time.

Reyn-Bardt set up home on his own in a cottage in Wilmslow, a suburb of Manchester, where his wife suddenly appeared some months later. After a bitter quarrel over money he strangled her, then hacked her body to pieces with an axe and buried the remains in his large wooded garden. In 1963 he moved to Portsmouth.

Twelve years later, still in Portsmouth, he met Paul Russell Corrigan, with whom he was arrested and sent to prison for abducting boys for sexual purposes. When Corrigan, following his release in January 1981, fell foul of the law again — this time he had tortured and killed a boy in Birmingham — he told the police how Reyn-Bardt had murdered his wife.

Now living in Knightsbridge, London, Reyn-Bardt was questioned about his wife's disappearance but denied having killed her. However, the discovery of the ancient skull 300 yards from the cottage in Wilmslow led to further questioning, and Reyn-Bardt, confronted with the 'evidence', then made a confession. In December 1983, after a three-day trial at Chester Crown Court, he was sentenced to life imprisonment.

By this time tests carried out at the radio-carbon dating laboratory at Oxford University had shown the skull from the peat bog to be that of a woman who had died, aged between thirty and fifty, about AD 410.

Maria Budlick's encounter with Peter Kürten, 1930

MAY
14

On 14 May 1930, Maria Budlick, a twenty-one-year-old domestic servant, left her home in Cologne to look for work in Düsseldorf, twenty miles away. Arriving at Düsseldorf station, she met a man who offered to show her the way to a hostel, and set off through the streets in his company. But when he tried to persuade her to go into the Volksgarten Park with him she refused.

At this time the city was being terrorized by the 'Monster of Düsseldorf', a brutal sadist responsible for many shocking crimes, and Maria Budlick was unwilling to go into the park with a stranger who, for all she knew, may have been 'the Monster' himself. However, her refusal led to an argument which continued until a second man intervened, asking 'Is everything all right?' The first man then took himself off.

The servant girl's rescuer was a soft-spoken, courteous man — the sort she could trust. Grateful for his help, she went with him to his one-room flat in Mettmännerstrasse, where he gave her a glass of milk and a sandwich. Afterwards they went by tram together to the edge of the city, Maria believing that she was being taken to a hostel, then got out to walk in the Grafenburg Woods. Suddenly the man stopped.

'Do you know now where you are?' he asked. 'I can tell you. You are alone with me in the middle of the woods. Now you scream as much as you like and nobody will hear you!'

At this, he seized her by the throat and tried to rape her. The terrified girl put up a struggle, but had almost lost consciousness when the man unexpectedly loosened his grip. 'Do you remember where I live, in case you're ever in need and want my help?' he asked. Maria, though she *did* remember, had the good sense to say that she did not. The man then released her and showed her the way out of the woods.

Maria Budlick did not report the attack, but when it came to the attention of the police (as a result of a letter of hers which had been misdirected) she showed them the building where she had been taken by her attacker. While they were there the man appeared; he entered his room after seeing the servant girl outside, then left a few minutes later. He was found to be Peter Kürten, a forty-seven-year-old married man with convictions for theft and assault, who had spent a total of over twenty years in prison. He was a factory worker and a keen trade unionist.

Though not questioned at the time, Kürten was arrested a week later after his wife had informed the police that he had confessed to being the 'Monster of Düsseldorf'. He admitted sixty-eight crimes, including the nine murders and seven attempted murders for which he was brought to trial in April the following year. It seems that after seeing Maria Budlick at the building in Mettmännerstrasse he had told his wife about his crimes so that she could claim a reward for his capture, knowing that he would soon be arrested anyway.

Kürten, described at his trial as 'the king of sexual delinquents', was stimulated to the point of orgasm by the sight of blood or fire. Unlike most other known sadists, he killed both men and women — and also children and animals. Moreover, to the spectators in the Düsseldorf courtroom it was evident that he derived pleasure from describing his crimes in detail.

Though a defence of insanity was made on his behalf, he was found guilty on all counts, and sentence of death was pronounced nine times. He was calm and courteous to the end, and before being executed by guillotine on 2 July 1931, said that it would give him much pleasure to hear the sound of his own blood gushing from his neck after the sentence had been carried out.

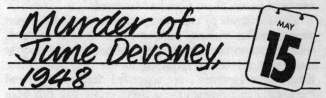

Murder of June Devaney, 1948

During the early hours of 15 May 1948, June Anne Devaney, aged three years and eleven months, was found to be missing from a ground-floor children's ward of the Queen's Park Hospital in Blackburn, Lancashire. The discovery was made by Staff Nurse Gwendoline Humphreys, who found the child's cot empty when she entered the ward just before 1 a.m. It appeared from a trail of footprints on the polished floor that she had been removed by an intruder.

Nurse Humphreys raised the alarm and a search of the hospital and its grounds was started. Just under two and a half hours later the missing child was found dead about

100 yards from the ward. She had been raped and then brutally murdered, her assailant holding her by the leg and dashing her head against one of the boundary walls.

The crime was such an atrocious one that the Chief Constable of Blackburn feared an outbreak of public disorder. He called on Scotland Yard for assistance without delay, hoping to bring the culprit to justice quickly, and within a few hours Detective Chief Inspector John Capstick and Detective Sergeant John Stoneman arrived to take charge of the investigation. But it was to take them three months to find the person responsible.

June Devaney, the daughter of a miner, had been admitted to hospital on 5 May suffering from mild pneumonia, but had made a good recovery and was due to be discharged on the morning of her murder. Though under four years of age, she was the oldest child in the ward and the only one who could talk. It would therefore not have been possible for any of the other five children, even if they had been awake at the time, to give the police any information about what had occurred.

The footprints in the ward had been made by a man wearing socks, who had entered by the door at one end, walked over to the cots, then moved towards the door at the other end before returning to the first door; those beside June Devaney's cot suggested that he had stood there for some moments. As these prints had not been made by any member of the hospital staff, it was assumed that they had been made by the murderer.

It seemed, too, that the person concerned had taken a Winchester bottle containing sterile water from a nearby trolley and placed it under June's cot, for Nurse Humphreys remembered that it had been in its usual place when she went into the ward prior to the child's disappearance. An examination of this bottle by a finger-print expert resulted in the discovery of several fresh prints which had also not been left by any of the staff. But when photographs of these were sent to Scotland Yard they were found not to match those of any known criminal.

Capstick believed that the murderer was a local man with a knowledge of the hospital; he therefore proposed that every male person in Blackburn between the ages of fourteen and ninety who was not bedridden should be fingerprinted. The Mayor of Blackburn made a public announcement about this, calling for co-operation from the town's 110,000 inhabitants and promising that all the fingerprints would be destroyed after they had been compared with those of June Devaney's murderer. He then set an example by becoming Capstick's first volunteer.

It was a tremendous undertaking, but Capstick was certain that it would eventually lead to the solution of the crime. Suddenly, on the afternoon of 12 August after 46,000 sets of prints had been checked, one of the experts scrutinizing the latest batch exclaimed, 'I've got him! It's here!'

That evening Peter Griffiths, a twenty-two-year-old former Guardsman working as a flour-mill packer, was arrested as he left his home in Birley Street, in one of the town's poorest districts. On being charged and cautioned, he admitted the offence, saying that he had had a number of drinks beforehand. He had abducted the child from the ward after removing his shoes, and had later beaten her head against the wall to stop her crying, he said.

The suit which he had worn on the night in question was examined and found to have been stained with June Devaney's blood; fibres taken from it were identical to others found on the dead girl's body. Though police suspected that Griffiths had also murdered an eleven-year-old boy in Farnworth earlier the same year, they were not able to obtain a second confession.

At his trial at the Lancashire Assizes, it was suggested that Griffiths, a solitary person who drank heavily, was suffering from a form of mental illness and was not responsible for his actions. But the jury took only twenty-three minutes to find him guilty and he was sentenced to death. He was hanged at Walton Prison on 19 November 1948.

139

Disappearance of Camille Holland, 1899

During the early evening of 19 May 1899, Miss Camille Holland, aged fifty-six, left her farmhouse near Saffron Walden in the company of her lover, fifty-three-year-old Samuel Dougal, telling their maid that she was going shopping and would not be long. Two hours later Dougal returned alone, saying that she had gone to London and would be back shortly. However, she did not return at all that day, and the following morning Dougal informed the maid that he had received a letter from Miss Holland, saying that she was going on a holiday. In fact, she was dead, but four years were to elapse before her body was discovered.

Miss Holland, a wealthy woman, had been living with Dougal as his wife for several months. She had bought the farm, which Dougal renamed Moat House Farm, in January, and they had moved into it on 27 April after staying in lodgings in Saffron Walden in the meantime. The day after her disappearance a younger woman moved in to take her place, bringing a little girl. Though Dougal began introducing this newcomer as his widowed daughter, it later turned out that she was his legal wife.

Dougal, an ex-soldier with a prison record for forgery, had been married three times; his first two wives had died in Nova Scotia, where he had served for ten years, and his third marriage had taken place in Dublin in 1892. He had had four children by his first wife and two by his third, in addition to an unknown number by other women. His third marriage ended in divorce in 1902 after Mrs Dougal had run away with an engine-driver. Dougal himself, whatever his marital state, was rarely without a mistress for long, and sometimes had several at the same time.

140

Soon after Miss Holland's disappearance he began to transfer money from her bank account to his own by means of forgery; he managed to become the owner of Moat House Farm in the same way. He was thus able to buy himself a car and spend much of his time hunting, shooting and drinking, as well as having affairs, without any financial difficulties. But Miss Holland's continued absence gave rise to rumours, and eventually one of the forgeries was discovered. A police investigation then became inevitable.

In March 1903 Dougal fled. He was arrested in London, with £563 in banknotes and gold and many valuables in his possession, and charged with forging a cheque. The following day he was taken to the police station in Saffron Walden, and a search of Moat House Farm was started.

Five weeks later Miss Holland's body was recovered from an old drainage ditch. She had been shot in the back of the head at close range, the bullet having been fired from a revolver owned by Dougal. The ex-soldier was charged with her murder on 30 April.

He was brought to trial in Chelmsford on 22 June. The following day, having given no evidence, he was convicted and sentenced to death. After an appeal had been dismissed, he wrote a long letter to the Home Secretary, claiming that he had shot Miss Holland by accident, but this was to no avail and he was hanged at Chelmsford Prison on 8 July 1903.

He admitted his guilt on the scaffold.

Murder of Bobby Franks, 1924

On 21 May 1924, Bobby Franks, fourteen-year-old son of a millionaire businessman, was abducted outside his school in the Chicago suburb of South Side Kenwood. The boy's mother received a telephone call, informing her that he had been kidnapped and that a ransom note would be sent through the post. The caller gave his name as Mr Johnson.

The following day a demand for $10,000 was received, the note stating that the missing boy was 'at present well and safe'. But before anything could be done about it the police informed Bobby Franks' father that a boy's body had been found in a culvert by the Pennsylvania railroad tracks.

In spite of facial disfiguration caused by hydrochloric acid, the body was quickly identified as Bobby Franks. His skull was fractured and he had been strangled.

A week later a pair of spectacles which had been found near the body were traced to Nathan Leopold Jr, a nineteen-year-old law student at Chicago University. Leopold, an amateur ornithologist, agreed that the spectacles were his and said that he must have dropped them in the culvert while bird-watching in the area some time previous to the murder. However, there were no weather marks on them, and this suggested that he was lying, as there had been a lot of rain prior to the date of the murder. Leopold was therefore regarded as a suspect.

Asked what he had been doing on the afternoon of 21 May, he said that he and his friend Richard Loeb, an eighteen-year-old fellow student, had been out with two girls, whose names were Mae and Edna. But, while Loeb corroborated this, neither he nor Leopold could give any information which enabled the police to trace these girls.

Moreover, specimens of Leopold's typing were found to match that of the ransom note. Leopold and Loeb who both, like Bobby Franks, had extremely wealthy parents and were accordingly questioned at length. Loeb eventually confessed; then Leopold confessed, too. They were brought to trial for murder and kidnapping in July the same year.

Besides being accustomed to wealth and luxury, the two defendants were both intellectually gifted, Leopold having an I.Q. of 200. But they were bored and had decided to commit a 'perfect' murder after failing to derive sufficient excitement from a series of petty thefts. Bobby Franks, a friend of Loeb's younger brother, had not been chosen as their victim because they disliked him; he had merely been an easy person to entice into a hired car. The crime, in the words of their lawyer, Clarence Darrow, had been a 'senseless, useless, purposeless, motiveless act of two boys'.

A plea that both defendants were mentally ill — Leopold being a paranoiac and Loeb a schizophrenic — probably saved their lives, for at the end of the trial each was sentenced to life imprisonment for murder and ninety-nine years for kidnapping. The failure of the judge to impose the death penalty, however, caused grave public disquiet and continued to be a contentious matter for years afterwards.

The case was brought back into the headlines in January 1936, when Richard Loeb was murdered by a fellow convict.

Nathan Leopold served thirty-three years, during which he ran educational rehabilitation courses for other prisoners and volunteered to take part in anti-malaria experiments. Following his release in 1958, he went to Puerto Rico, where he married in 1961. He died ten years later.

Questioning of Wayne Williams, 1981

During the early hours of 22 May 1981, a police surveillance team on patrol near the Chattahoochee River in Atlanta, Georgia, heard the sound of a splash and saw a young black man driving away from the scene in a station-wagon. They stopped the man for questioning but afterwards let him go, as they appeared to have no cause to arrest him. However, they remained suspicious, and the man — Wayne Williams, a twenty-three-year-old music-talent promoter and freelance photographer — was placed under observation. Two days later, when the body of Nathaniel Cater, aged twenty-seven, was found floating in the river, Williams was suspected of murder.

Cater had been seen leaving a theatre with Williams just before his disappearance, the witness informing police that the two men had been holding hands. It was found, too, that dog hairs on Cater's body were similar to others found at Williams' home and inside his station-wagon. But by this time Williams was suspected not only of Cater's murder but also of twenty-seven others.

The twenty-seven other people who had been murdered were all young blacks, teenagers and children of both sexes whose bodies had been found in Atlanta during the previous two years. The crimes had been committed without apparent motive — except in the case of a girl who had been raped — and by a variety of means, including suffocation, strangulation, shooting and stabbing. They were believed by blacks to be the work of a white racist, and the police had been subjected to much criticism over their failure to catch him.

Their inquiries now established that Williams had been seen in the company of two of these other victims, and laboratory tests on fibres, as well as dog hairs, from his home showed that he had been connected with another eight. Though he was charged only with the murder of Nathaniel Cater and one other person — Jimmy Payne, the twenty-sixth victim — his arrest brought this long series of crimes to an end.

Wayne Williams, an intelligent and resourceful man, was a homosexual with a hatred of other blacks and a frustrated desire for instant personal success. The evidence against him was entirely circumstantial but at his trial, which began in January 1982, the prosecution was allowed to produce evidence relating to other murders besides those with which he was charged. This, together with the sudden cessation of the murders, weighed heavily against him, and he was convicted on both counts.

He was sentenced to two consecutive terms of life imprisonment.

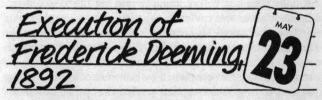

Execution of Frederick Deeming, 1892

MAY 23

On 23 May 1892, Frederick Deeming, a multiple murderer and confidence trickster aged about fifty, was hanged in Melbourne, Australia. A large number of officials and newspaper reporters were present, and the hangman and his assistant both wore false beards to prevent themselves being identified. A crowd of 10,000 people waited outside the prison while the execution was carried out.

Deeming, the youngest of seven children, had been born in Liverpool. A flamboyant and charming man, he travelled a great deal, committing many thefts and frauds with ease; women were generally fascinated by him. He married an English girl who bore him four children, but abandoned her twice — once in Australia and once in South Africa. It was because she pursued him that she was finally murdered.

In 1891 Deeming took up residence in Rainhill, to the east of Liverpool, claiming to be Mr Albert Williams, an Inspector of Regiments. He let it be known that he was looking for a house on behalf of Baron Brook, a personal friend, and went to look over a nearby villa which the owner, Mrs Mather, wanted to let furnished to a suitable tenant. Having reached an agreement with Mrs Mather, he was allowed to move into the property without paying any rent in advance, in order to prepare for the Baron's arrival. He then began to court Mrs Mather's daughter Emily, aged twenty-five, who believed him to be a bachelor.

Before long, however, Deeming's wife arrived unexpectedly, bringing their four children, and insisted on moving into the villa with him. When Emily Mather heard about this, Deeming told her that Mrs Deeming was his sister, and that she had brought her children to spend a short holiday with him before going to join her husband abroad. Emily Mather was evidently satisfied with this explanation.

Deeming asked Mrs Mather's permission to cement the ground under the floor of the villa so that the floorboards would lie more evenly and provide surfaces suitable for some valuable carpets owned by Baron Brook. Mrs Mather agreed to this, and Deeming started the work himself. By the time he had finished his wife and four children had been murdered and their bodies buried in the cement. He employed a local carpenter to re-lay the floorboards.

A short while after this Deeming told Mrs Mather that he had to go to Australia and that Baron Brook would not be moving into the villa after all. He then married Emily, and they set sail together, arriving in Melbourne in December 1891.

'Mrs Williams', however, was soon to be disposed of in the same way as Mrs Deeming and her children: about 20 December her body was buried in cement under the dining-

146

room hearth of a small furnished house which the couple had rented in Andrew Street, Windsor. She had been struck on the head six times and her throat had been cut. But this time Deeming was more careless and the body was discovered by the owner of the house.

Deeming was arrested in Perth in March 1892, just in time to prevent him marrying an heiress named Kate Rounsevell. By the time he appeared for trial, charged with the murder of Emily Mather, the remains of his wife and children had been discovered and he had been accused in newspaper articles of both crimes, as well as many others.

He pleaded that he was insane, then, towards the end of the trial, made a long speech denying the allegations which had been made against him and describing the spectators in the courtroom as 'the ugliest race of people I have ever seen'.

He died unrepentant, smoking a cigar as he walked to the place of execution.

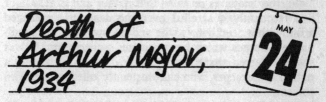

Death of Arthur Major, 1934

On 24 May 1934, Arthur Major, a forty-four-year-old lorry-driver of Kirkby-on-Bain, Lincolnshire, died in agony after a short illness. His wife Ethel, who was two years younger, told their doctor that her husband had died during the night after having 'another of his fits'. The doctor therefore put Major's death down to 'status epilepticus', and arrangements were made for the funeral. But the following day the local police received a remarkable anonymous letter, signed 'Fairplay'. It read:

'Have you ever heard of a wife poisoning her husband?

Look further into the death of Mr Major of Kirkby-on-Bain. Why did he complain of his food tasting nasty and throw it away to a neighbour's dog, which has since died? Ask the undertaker if he looked natural after death. Why did he stiffen so quickly? Why was he so jerky when dying? I myself have heard her threaten to poison him years ago. In the name of the law, I beg you to analyse the contents of his stomach.'

The police discovered that Arthur Major had been a drunken bully, whose fourteen-year-old son regularly slept at his grandfather's house, a mile away, to avoid him. Ethel Major, after being questioned, suddenly turned to the police officer concerned and asked: 'I'm not under suspicion, am I? I haven't done anything wrong!' The police officer gave a non-committal answer, then went to see the neighbour whose dog had died; the body was dug up so that its stomach contents could be examined. The next day Arthur Major's funeral was called off by order of the coroner, so that the contents of *his* stomach could be examined, too. Both the dog and the lorry-driver were found to have died from strychnine poisoning.

Further inquiries revealed that Arthur and Ethel Major had frequently quarrelled over the dead man's alleged affair with a neighbour's wife and his own wife's expenditure on clothes which he considered unnecessary. It was also discovered that Ethel's father, Tom Brown, was a retired gamekeeper, who had frequently killed vermin with poison.

When Ethel Major was asked if she knew about this, she replied, 'I didn't know where he kept his poisons. I never at any time had any poison in the house.' She then revealed that she knew more about the cause of her husband's death than had so far been made known to anyone except the police, for she added, 'I didn't know that my husband died of strychnine.'

Tom Brown showed the police a locked box which he kept in his bedroom; it contained a bottle of strychnine crystals. He informed them that his daughter knew the contents, but would not have been able to use them as the key to the box had been lost more than ten years previously and had not been replaced. The key was later found in Ethel Major's possession.

Ethel Major was brought to trial for her husband's murder at the Lincoln Assizes in November 1934, convicted and sentenced to death. Despite a strong recommendation of mercy from the jury, she was hanged at Hull Prison on 19 December the same year.

Death of 'Pigsticker' Ayres, 1931

MAY 30

On the night of 30 May 1931, Herbert Ayres, a forty-five-year-old casual labourer known as 'Pigsticker', was attacked and killed in an area of woodland and makeshift huts near Elstree, in Hertfordshire. The crime was committed by two other labourers and witnessed by a third, but nothing was reported until three days later, when the victim's charred body was found in a smouldering refuse tip at Scratchwood Sidings, half a mile away. It was then found that he had died as a result of a heavy blow on the head which had fractured his skull.

There were a large number of navvies in the area, all living in shacks and known to each other by nicknames. When the police began making inquiries, the one who had witnessed the crime — a fellow named Armstrong — told them what had happened, identifying the culprits as 'Moosh' and 'Tiggy', two men who shared a hut and kept three dogs to protect it. According to his account, Armstrong had been staying the night in this hut, and had been dozing on the floor when he heard a quarrel going on outside. He had then looked out and seen 'Moosh' and 'Tiggy' beating up 'Pigsticker'. Afterwards, he said, they took the body away in a sack, carrying it over a pole.

'Moosh' and 'Tiggy' were found to be William Shelley, aged fifty-seven, and Oliver Newman, sixty-one, both of whom had the reputation of being tough and disagreeable. To the police officers who went to arrest them, their dogs seemed tough and disagreeable as well, and the officers concerned waited outside the shack for some hours until its occupants gave themselves up. The arrests were followed by the discovery of a bloodstained axe under the floor of the hut.

Shelley and Newman admitted having caused Ayres' death, but claimed that they had only used their fists. They said that the dead man had been in the habit of stealing from them, and that on the night in question they had found some bacon and bread to be missing from their hut. They had therefore beaten him up and, on realizing that they had killed him, buried his body in the tip.

The two men were brought to trial at the Old Bailey, the case lasting two days. Both were convicted and sentenced to death, Shelley afterwards commenting that the sentence was twenty years late. They were hanged on 5 August 1931.

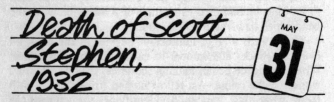

Death of Scott Stephen, 1932

During the early hours of 31 May 1932, Elvira Barney, a wealthy twenty-seven-year-old socialite, telephoned her doctor in a hysterical state and told him that there had been 'a terrible accident' at her home in Knightsbridge,

London. The doctor hurried to her address, 21, William's Mews, and found Michael Scott Stephen, her twenty-four-year-old lover, lying dead on the stairs. He had been shot in the chest at close range.

The police were called, and a Smith and Wesson revolver with two empty chambers was found near the body. Mrs Barney, who was separated from her husband, had been out to a party with Stephen earlier and, on returning, they had started to quarrel over another woman. According to her own statement, Mrs Barney had then threatened to commit suicide, using the gun which she kept at her bedside, and Stephen had been accidentally killed when he tried to take it away from her.

But neighbours who had been woken up by the quarrel told the police that Mrs Barney had actually threatened to shoot *him*, and that the threat had been followed by the shot or shots. On 3 June Mrs Barney was arrested and charged with murder.

At her trial at the Old Bailey the following month witnesses gave evidence that the accused and her lover had often quarrelled, and one — a chauffeur's wife — claimed that on an earlier occasion Mrs Barney had leant out of the window and fired at him while he was in the mews below.

The firearms expert, Robert Churchill, stated that the gun which had been used was one of the safest types in existence and that considerable pressure was needed to fire it. This evidence, however, was challenged by the defence counsel, Sir Patrick Hastings, who pointed out that there was no safety catch and proceeded to press the trigger several times without apparent difficulty. 'It doesn't seem to require any terrific muscular strength,' he remarked as he did so.

Mrs Barney stuck to her story that Stephen had been killed by accident. Her counsel, after asking for the gun to be placed on the edge of the witness-box, suddenly ordered her to pick it up. The fact that she automatically picked it up with her right hand served to cast doubt on the evidence of the chauffeur's wife, who had said that Mrs Barney had fired with her left hand on the earlier occasion.

The jury deliberated for an hour and fifty minutes before returning a verdict of not guilty. Mrs Barney then left the court and found herself applauded by a large crowd outside.

Four years later she was found dead in a hotel in Paris.

Mrs. Freeman Lee found murdered, 1948

JUNE
1

On 1 June 1948, a milkman on his delivery round in Maidenhead, Berkshire, called at the home of Mrs Freeman Lee, a ninety-four-year-old recluse, and found two full bottles still standing on the doorstep from previous days. He told a neighbour, who looked through the window of the downstairs room to which Mrs Lee normally confined herself night and day. As she was not there, the neighbour then peered through the letter-box.

He saw cushions lying on the floor of the hall and, beyond them, a black trunk with a woman's shoe beside it. As his eyes became accustomed to the light, he also saw a punch of keys lying on the floor. He decided to inform the police.

A constable arrived soon afterwards, accompanied by a local solicitor who was a friend of the old lady. Unable to summon her to the door, they forced an entry and began to search the house. There were seventeen rooms altogether, and Mrs Lee was not in any of them; a search of the garden revealed that she was not there either. Finally, as the constable telephoned the police station to make a report, it occurred to the solicitor to open the trunk in the hall.

There, under a lot of old clothes, he found the body of

Mrs Lee. She had been battered over the head and also bound and gagged. It was later established that she had died from suffocation.

Mrs Lee had lived in the same house for about forty years, and was well-known in Maidenhead. It was generally believed that she was rich as, indeed, she had been in the distant past, but she had been very poor in recent years, existing on a small allowance from a legal benevolent society. Besides that, she had suffered a stroke which left her partially paralysed on one side. Her house was in a shocking state of disrepair and disorder; every part of it had been neglected.

Though the pathologist was unable to state with certainty when her death had occurred, it was found that the last person to see her alive — other than her murderer — had been an electrician who called at the house to install an electric boiling-ring during the early evening of 29 May. Clearly, she had been killed sometime between then and the following morning.

Two parts of a single fingerprint, discovered on the lid of a cardboard box, were identified at Scotland Yard; they had been left by George Russell, a housebreaker with a criminal record. When Russell was located in St Albans five days later a scarf which had belonged to the victim was found in his possession.

Russell denied ever having been inside the house, but when confronted with the fingerprint evidence he began to cry and said that he wanted to make a statement. In this, he inadvertently revealed that he knew Mrs Lee's true circumstances. He was therefore arrested and charged with her murder.

George Russell was brought to trial at the Berkshire Assizes, denying the offence. His counsel sought to discredit the prosecution witnesses, but to no avail; he was convicted and sentenced to death. Showing no emotion at this, the prisoner looked round the hushed courtroom, then tweaked his left ear before leaving the dock. His life of crime, which had lasted over twenty years, was brought to an abrupt end when he was hanged at Oxford Prison on 2 December 1948.

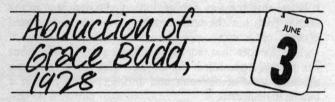

Abduction of Grace Budd, 1928

JUNE 3

On 3 June 1928, twelve-year-old Grace Budd left her home in New York City in the company of a harmless-looking old man who said that he was taking her to a children's party which was being given by his sister. When she had not returned by 10 p.m. her anxious parents reported the matter to the police. But it was six and a half years before they found out what had become of her — and then they were informed of it in a particularly cruel manner.

The harmless-looking old man, calling himself Frank Howard, had turned up at the home of Edward Budd and his wife on 1 June after seeing an advertisement asking for farm work which their son Paul, aged eighteen, had placed in a newspaper. He said that he owned a large farm in Farmingdale, Long Island, and promised the youth a job there. On the day of the abduction he had lunch with the family at noon, and said that he would take Paul back to Long Island with him when he and Grace returned from the party. The address at which he claimed that the party was being held proved to be non-existent, as did the old man's farm in Long Island.

The police obtained a sample of the man's handwriting from a telegram which he had sent to Paul from Yorkville, Manhattan, on 2 June. They also had an agate container in which he had given the family some cottage cheese; this was found to have been bought from a pedlar in the same vicinity, but provided no distinct fingerprints. There were

154

no other clues to the real identity of 'Frank Howard', and it was not until the morning of 11 November 1934, when Mrs Budd unexpectedly received a letter from him, that any further progress on the case was made.

In this letter, written solely for the purpose of causing further suffering to the missing girl's family, 'Frank Howard' stated that he had murdered Grace and 'feasted on her flesh for nine days'.

'I learned to like the taste of human flesh many years ago during a famine in China,' he said. 'I can't exactly describe the taste. It is something like veal, then again it resembles chicken, only it is tastier than either. The best flesh, that which is most tender, is to be had from children. Little girls have more flavour than little boys.'

The handwriting was identical to the sample which the police had obtained earlier, and the letter had been sent in an envelope which they were able to trace. On 13 December the culprit, whose real name was now known to be Albert Fish, was arrested in a shabby New York City boarding-house. He immediately made a confession, stating that he had originally intended to kill and eat Paul but had changed his mind after seeing Grace. Some hours later he led police to a patch of woodland in Westchester County, where the missing girl's remains had been buried.

The police dug into the frozen earth, working far into the night. Before daylight Grace Budd's skull and bones, together with her clothes, had been recovered.

Albert Fish, then aged sixty-four, was a house painter by trade and the father of six children. He had been arrested many times, and had been sent to prison for writing obscene letters, among other things. But while in custody he admitted to being responsible for numerous other crimes, and is now thought to have criminally assaulted over 100 girls and murdered at least fifteen of them.

He derived sexual pleasure from receiving pain as well as from inflicting it, and an X-ray photograph showed the presence of a large number of needles which he had inserted into his own body.

'There was no known perversion that he did not practise, and practise frequently,' a prison psychiatrist recorded.

Fish was brought to trial for the murder of Grace Budd in White Plains, New York, on 12 March 1935, the judge refusing to allow female spectators into the courtroom in view of the nature of the case. A plea of insanity was made on his behalf, but he was convicted and sentenced to death on 22 March.

'I thought he was insane, but I figured he should be electrocuted anyway,' one of the jurors said later.

Unperturbed by the prospect of his own death, Albert Fish was executed at Sing Sing Prison on 16 January 1936.

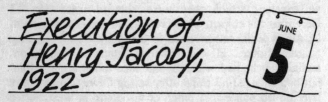

Execution of Henry Jacoby, 1922

JUNE 5

On 5 June 1922, Henry Jacoby, an eighteen-year-old pantry boy, was hanged at Pentonville Prison for the murder of Lady White, sixty-five-year-old widow of a former chairman of the London County Council. Though the crime had been a brutal one, the jury at his trial had made a recommendation of mercy on account of the prisoner's youth, and there had been a lot of agitation in favour of the sentence being commuted. When the execution was carried out within a few days of Ronald True being reprieved (See 6 March), the two cases together were seen by many people as proof of the existence of class privilege.

Lady White, on the morning of 14 March previously, had been found dying from head injuries in her bedroom at the Spencer Hotel in Portman Street, London. There were no signs of a struggle or a forced entry; the murder weapon had not been left at the scene, and nothing appeared to have been stolen. Jacoby, who had only been employed at the hotel for three weeks, was questioned by police and gave information about his background which was found to be false. He was searched and found to have two blood-stained handkerchiefs in his pockets. He finally made a confession of his own accord.

Jacoby said that while lying in bed in the early hours he had been aware of being in a hotel full of rich people, and suddenly decided to steal something from one of the rooms. He got up and took a hammer from a tool bag which some workmen had left in the basement — to 'use if necessary' — then started trying the doors. Finding one unlocked, he entered the room and shone a torch around.

When Lady White woke up and screamed he began to panic and struck her several times with the hammer. He later washed the hammer and wiped it dry with the handkerchiefs before returning it to the tool bag.

Jacoby was held on remand in Brixton Prison, where Ronald True greeted him with his customary joviality. 'Here's another for our Murderers' Club!' he said, slapping him on the back. 'We only accept those who kill them outright!'

Brought to trial at the Old Bailey on 28 April 1922, the prisoner pleaded not guilty. He said in his defence that he thought the person in Lady White's bedroom was an intruder and was afterwards frightened when he realized what he had done. The judge advised the jury that if blows were struck with the intention of inflicting grievous bodily harm and the victim died as a result of them, the assailant was guilty of murder.

When appeals for mercy were dismissed, requests were made for Henry Jacoby to be given a Christian burial. But these were similarly unsuccessful, and his body was interred inside the prison where the hanging took place.

Murder of Mrs. Paterson, 1927

On the evening of 9 June 1927, William Paterson, of Riverton Avenue, Winnipeg, arrived home to find his wife missing. She had left no message for him and their two children did not know what had become of her. Some hours later, when she had still not appeared, he finished putting the children to bed and called the police to find out if any accidents had been reported. They were unable to help him.

Then, suddenly discovering that his suitcase had been forced open and some money stolen, Mr Paterson knelt at his bedside to pray. As he did so, he found his wife's body underneath the bed. Emily Paterson had been beaten to death with a hammer and then raped, her death occurring at approximately eleven o'clock in the morning. Some clothes had also been stolen from the house.

The crime led to the arrest, trial and execution of Earle Nelson, 'the Gorilla Murderer', who, at the age of thirty, had been responsible for many sex killings, mainly in the United States.

Nelson, a strange-looking man with a receding forehead and protruding lips, had hitch-hiked into Winnipeg on 8 June, taking a room in a boarding-house in Smith Street, where he told the landlady that he was 'a religious man of high ideals'. The same day he murdered a fourteen-year-old girl living in the same house and hid her body under the bed of an unoccupied room, where it was found four days later.

After the murder of Mrs Paterson he sold the stolen clothes to a second-hand shop, then went to a barber's to have a shave; the barber noticed that he had blood in his hair. He left Winnipeg in a hurry two days later, after his

158

description had been circulated by the police, and was arrested while hitch-hiking between Wakopa and Bannerman. His trial took place in Winnipeg in November 1927.

Nelson was born in America and brought up by an aunt, his mother having died of venereal disease contracted from his father, when he was nine months old. At the age of ten he was knocked down by a streetcar, receiving injuries which were to cause bouts of pain and dizziness for the rest of his life. In 1918 he was committed to an asylum after an assault on a child, but escaped several times and got married in 1919. His aunt and his wife both gave evidence at his trial, the defence being one of insanity.

Nelson's interest in religion was a genuine one; he had read the Bible avidly as a child, both before and after his accident, and is known to have talked about the subject a lot. But he was also an intensely jealous man — so much so that when his wife was in hospital he immediately began to accuse her of having affairs with the doctors. His marriage lasted only six months.

Of his twenty-two known victims, all but two were killed in America, the first in San Francisco in February 1926. Most were boarding-house landladies, some of them in their fifties or sixties; most were strangled and afterwards raped. The 'Gorilla Murderer' kept on the move and used false names in order to avoid capture. He showed no remorse for his crimes except at the place of execution, when he begged for forgiveness.

He was hanged in Winnipeg on 13 January 1928.

During the early morning of 10 June 1971, an estate house in St Lucia, in the West Indies, was found to be on fire. The alarm was raised by neighbours, but by the time the fire was extinguished the building had been destroyed. The bodies of its two occupants, James and Majorie Etherington, who had been in the banana business, were then found among the debris of a ground-floor bedroom. They were buried on the neighbouring island of Barbados after being viewed, though hardly examined, by the Caribbean Government pathologist.

It was assumed that the fire had been started by accident, and the police at first gave it little attention. But a day or two later an insurance company investigator went to the site and found evidence of arson. A louvred window of the rear scullery, which the fire had not reached, had been broken from the outside, and footprints were found on the floor beneath it. A piece of plastic hose, smelling of petrol, led from the house to the garage, where a car was found with its petrol tank open.

When these discoveries were reported the police took the matter more seriously, and asked Scotland Yard to provide assistance. The local police commissioner, learning that a number of men had been seen hanging about near the Etheringtons' home on the evening before the fire, had three known criminals named Florius, Faucher and Charles held for questioning. 'If I get any real trouble on the island, I bring these three in,' he explained to Professor Keith Simpson, the Home Office Pathologist. 'If they haven't done it, they always know who has!'

Florius, the ringleader, had burn marks on his neck and arm, and he and Anthony Charles — 'who just does what he's told' — both had scratches which suggested that they had been involved in a struggle. The three men admitted having robbed the Etheringtons, and said that the couple had been tied up during the course of the crime. But they denied having used violence or starting the fire.

When the bodies were exhumed for a more thorough examination James Etherington's skull was found to have been smashed in with a blunt instrument, though he was still alive when the fire started. His wife had been gagged as well as bound, and she, too, had died in the fire.

Florius, Faucher and Charles were charged with murder, and brought to trial in Castries, the capital of St Lucia, three months later. The result was a foregone conclusion, and during a speech from the dock Faucher told the court that the victims had been burnt to death deliberately, as Florius had believed that electronic records could otherwise be made of their thoughts. All three were found guilty and subsequently hanged.

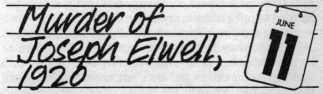

Murder of Joseph Elwell, 1920

JUNE
11

On the morning of 11 June 1920, Joseph Elwell, a well-known bridge expert, was found slumped in a chair in his New York home, with a bullet wound in his forehead. The discovery was made by his housekeeper when she arrived at the house about 8 a.m., at which time Elwell was still alive. He was immediately rushed to hospital, where he died a little while afterwards. The revelations which followed provided much entertainment for the general public, but did not help the New York police in their attempts to solve the crime.

Elwell, aged forty-five, was a rich man and a known philanderer. His two books, *Elwell on Bridge* and *Elwell's Advanced Bridge*, were widely read in the United States, and enabled him to move in high society. He was also thought to be handsome and young-looking, though this impression was due to his wigs and false teeth. At the time of the shooting he was not wearing either, so when his housekeeper arrived she saw him as a bald and toothless man whom she did not recognize. Joseph Elwell had been shot as he sat in his pyjamas, reading letters which had arrived in the morning's post.

Though married in 1904, Elwell had been separated from his wife for some years. Among his possessions police found a list of women's names and addresses, which the newspapers described as a 'love index'. A pile of women's underwear was also found, though the dead man was known to have been living on his own. His companion of the previous evening had been Viola Kraus, who had just been divorced; they had dined together and then been to a show before Elwell returned home in the early hours of the morning. He had afterwards made a number of telephone calls from his bedroom, including one about 6 a.m., when he tried to call a number in Garden City.

As the weapon with which Elwell had been shot was a .45 calibre army revolver, the culprit was thought to be almost certainly a man — and the fact that $400 in cash and items of jewellery had been left untouched suggested that theft had not been the motive. Police officers interviewed all of his known acquaintances, both male and female, and heard various rumours about lovers, husbands and fellow bridge-players, all motivated by jealousy. Yet no real suspect emerged, and nobody has since been able to provide us with one.

The murder of Joseph Elwell remains one of New York's most famous unsolved crimes.

Human remains left in the Bois de Boulogne, 1981

On the evening of 13 June 1981, a man of Oriental appearance was seen leaving two large suitcases in the Bois de Boulogne before taking to his heels. The witnesses were suspicious and the police were immediately called to the scene. The suitcases were found to contain most of the remains of a young woman, whose body had been cut into pieces and wrapped in plastic rubbish sacks. A bullet was recovered from the base of her skull and traces of semen were found in her sex organs. There was, however, no evidence that she had been raped.

The remains were identified as those of Renée Hartevelt, a twenty-five-year-old Dutch student who had been doing post-graduate work at the Université Censier in Paris. They were found to have been left by Issei Sagawa, a Japanese student at the same college, who lived in the Rue Erlanger, in the sixteenth arrondissement. He had taken the two suitcases to the Bois de Boulogne by taxi on the evening in question, and when police searched his studio apartment they found not only the .22 calibre rifle with which the victim had been shot, but also some other parts of her body, which he had been keeping in his refrigerator.

Sagawa, aged thirty-two, made a confession. He said that Renée Hartevelt, with whom he shared an interest in literature, had visited his apartment on the afternoon of 11 June to help him with some difficult translations, as her French was better than his own. While she was there he asked her to have sexual intercourse with him, but she refused. It was as a result of this rebuff that the murder had taken place.

Sagawa explained, without remorse, that he had killed his fellow-student with a single shot in the back of the neck, and had afterwards pulled off her clothes and had intercourse with the corpse. He had then cut the body into pieces, stopping every now and then to take photographs of it. Those parts which were not put into the suitcases for disposal were kept so that he could eat them, and some had already been consumed. He said that he had wanted to eat a girl's flesh for a long time.

Though all the known facts indicated that this account was true, Sagawa was not tried for the crime. He was, instead, placed under psychiatric observation and later declared to be unfit to stand trial by reason of insanity. He remained in a mental hospital in Paris until May 1984, when he returned to Japan as a result of an agreement between the two countries concerned. This agreement was reached about the same time as the Japanese company Kurita Water Industries, of which Sagawa's father was the president, signed a business deal with a French chemical conglomerate, Elf-Aquitaine.

In Japan, Issei Sagawa entered a mental hospital, where he remained until August 1985. He was then discharged on the hospital superintendent's orders because his 'examination and treatment were finished'. His discharge, however, had been opposed by the hospital's deputy superintendent, Dr Tsuguo Kaneko, who expressed the view that Sagawa was an untreatable psychotic who should have been in prison.

Sagawa, in the meantime, had written a book about the murder of Renée Hartevelt which quickly became a best-seller. Following his discharge from the hospital, he gave a magazine interview, saying that his act of cannibalism had been 'an expression of love', and that he still dreamed of eating a woman's flesh, though without murdering her and only with her consent. He was reported to be staying with his parents in Yokohama.

Housekeeper found dead in Belgravia, 1946

JUNE 14

On 14 June 1946, Detective Inspector James Ball arrived at a house in the Belgravia district of London after being informed that the housekeeper, Miss Elizabeth McLindon, was missing. The house, in Chester Square, was shortly to become the home of the exiled King of Greece, and Miss McLindon, an attractive woman aged forty, had taken up residence there on her own some weeks earlier. It was the king's secretary who had reported her missing.

Miss McLindon's clothes and other belongings were still in the house, but it seemed from the supply of milk outside the back door that she had not been there for six days. However, the door of the library was locked and the key missing; it was therefore necessary for Ball to force it open. When he did so he found the housekeeper's dead body. Miss McLindon had been shot through the back of the neck as she sat at the telephone, evidently about to make a call — and from the condition of the body it appeared that she had been dead for five or six days.

A bullet recovered from the wall and a used cartridge found on the floor had both been fired from a Browning automatic pistol. But the door key was not found there, and there were no signs of a forced entry or a struggle. It seemed that the dead woman had let the culprit into the house herself, and that he had afterwards locked the library door and taken the key away with him.

A search of the housekeeper's bedroom resulted in the discovery of valuable jewellery and a box of letters from various men, all of whom appeared to have been her lovers — and generous ones at that. Two of the letters, both signed 'Arthur', were of particular interest: they had both been posted in Brighton — the first on 11 June, the second the following day — and asked her why she had not been answering the telephone.

As they had both arrived after her death and yet been opened and placed in the bedroom with the others, it was suspected that the murderer had returned to the house in the hope of causing confusion over the date on which the crime had been committed.

Miss McLindon's sister Veronica told the police that 'Arthur' was the dead woman's fiancé, Arthur Boyce, a painter working on Brighton pier. On being questioned, Boyce claimed that he knew nothing of Miss McLindon's death — even though it had been reported in all the newspapers — and that he had been trying to contact her by telephone for several days. But it was learnt from his workmates that he had recently been in possession of a pistol, which he had told them he was going to throw into the sea.

It was also discovered that Arthur Boyce was a convicted bigamist who had served an eighteen-month prison sentence, and that he was wanted for passing dud cheques. One of these cheques — for £135 — had been used to pay for an engagement ring, which the jeweller concerned had recovered from Miss McLindon on 8 June, after the cheque had been returned to him. Boyce was arrested in connection with these offences.

Though Detective Inspector Ball was unable to find the gun with which the murder had been committed, he managed to trace a man named John Rowland, of Caernarvon, who had had a Browning automatic stolen from him while he was sharing lodgings with Boyce in Fulham some months previously.

Rowland was certain that Boyce had taken the gun, and had written to him to ask for it back, but received no reply. An empty cartridge case which had been fired from this gun was produced at Ball's request, and found to have markings indentical to those of the one which had been left in the house in Chester Square.

Arthur Boyce was then charged with murder and brought to trial shortly afterwards. It was believed that he had killed Miss McLindon because she was about to telephone the police after learning that he had paid for her engagement ring with a dud cheque, and that he had afterwards gone to great lengths to conceal his guilt. The jury was much impressed by the ballistics evidence, presented by the famous gunsmith, Robert Churchill, and the prisoner was convicted.

He was hanged on 12 November 1946.

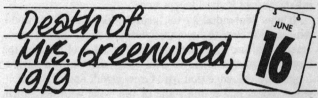

Death of Mrs. Greenwood, 1919

During the early hours of 16 June 1919, Mabel Greenwood, the wife of a solicitor, died at her home in Kidwelly, Carmarthenshire, after an agonizing illness which had started the previous afternoon. Her health had not been good beforehand and her doctor gave the cause of her death as valvular heart disease. But many people suspected that she had been poisoned.

Harold Greenwood, her forty-five-year-old husband, had a practice in nearby Llanelly, but relied upon his wife's private income for the comfort in which they and their four children lived. Unlike his wife, he was not liked in Kidwelly, and a nurse who had attended Mrs Greenwood maintained that there should have been a post-mortem.

Greenwood's marriage, four months later, to Gladys Jones, thirty-one-year-old daughter of one of the proprietors of the *Llanelly Mercury*, gave rise to further rumour and speculation, and the police informed him that they would probably want to have his first wife's body exhumed. He replied that he was agreeable to this, and on 16 April 1920, the exhumation took place.

A post-mortem then revealed that the rumours were justified, for there was no evidence of disease. Instead, arsenic was found in various parts of the body.

A coroner's jury in June found that the deceased had died of arsenic poisoning, and named her husband as the person who had administered the poison. This verdict was applauded by the spectators, and the following day Harold Greenwood was formally charged with murder.

He spent the next four and a half months in prison, and was brought to trial in Carmarthen on 2 November 1920. The case against him then proved to be weaker than the inhabitants of Kidwelly expected.

It was contended by the prosecution that Greenwood, who was known to have purchased a product containing arsenic in June 1917, had poisoned a bottle of wine on the day his wife was taken ill. But while the family's parlour maid gave evidence that Mrs Greenwood, and Mrs Greenwood alone, had drunk some of this wine with her lunch, Irene Greenwood, the defendant's twenty-one-year-old daughter, stated that she, too, had drunk some of it, not only at lunch, but also at supper.

Though another witness claimed that there had been no wine on the table at supper, Irene Greenwood's evidence was enough to raise doubts about the prisoner's guilt. Moreover, these doubts were reinforced by the defence counsel's suggestion that Mrs Greenwood's doctor, an extremely vague person, might have accidentally poisoned her himself.

Harold Greenwood, who had remained calm throughout the trial, was acquitted and left the court a free man. But his legal practice was ruined by the case and he was broken in spirit. He died nine years later, at the age of fifty-five.

Policeman murdered by Barry Prudom, 1982

On 17 June 1982, a policeman was shot dead by a motorist during the course of a routine traffic check near Harrogate in Yorkshire. There were no witnesses to the crime, and there was no apparent motive for it. But as he lay dying, PC David Haigh managed to write the registration number of the culprit's car in his notebook. The killer was then found to be Barry Peter Prudom, a thirty-seven-year-old man already wanted on a wounding charge. His car, a green Citroen, was found abandoned in a field near Leeds.

Prudom, formerly a stable and hard-working man, had had domestic problems for some years, and it seems that they had finally become too much for him. Towards the end of the seventeen-day manhunt which followed he told members of a family which he had taken prisoner: 'I told him (PC Haigh) I'd been sleeping out in the car, and that I didn't think that was an offence. But he said he was going to take me in and got stroppy, so I shot him.' He had, however, given a false name, probably because he feared being arrested for the earlier offence.

After abandoning the car Prudom made his way to Lincolnshire where he broke into a bungalow and robbed an elderly woman of £5, leaving her tied up but unharmed. He then went to Girton, near Newark-on-Trent, where he broke into the home of George Luckett and his wife Sylvia, in search of food and money. George Luckett was shot dead when he tried to defend himself with his own gun; his wife was shot in the head, but survived.

Prudom stole the Luckett's car and drove towards Dalby Forest in north Yorkshire, intending to lie low. But after another shooting, in which a policeman was injured, an intensive search for him was begun. Before long there was a third encounter; this time an unarmed police sergeant was shot three times, the last shot being fired as he lay helpless on the ground.

The search received a great deal of publicity, with much being made of the large number of policemen who were armed and the fact that Prudom had once had SAS training. Another unusual feature of the manhunt was the part played by Eddie McGee, a survival expert called in by the police to track the fugitive.

The taking of the prisoners occurred on the evening of 3 July when Prudom broke into a house in Malton; the victims were Maurice Johnson and his wife, both in their seventies, and their son Brian, aged forty-three. They were held at gunpoint at first, then tied up until Prudom felt that it was safe for him to release them.

He ate and rested in their house, threatening to kill them unless they did as they were told; he also watched television news bulletins and made a voluntary confession of his crimes. When they tried to persuade him to give himself up he refused.

'I'll never let the police take me,' he said. 'I'll kill myself first.'

Early the following morning he left the house and hid in a shelter which he had made by putting wooden boards against a wall. A few hours later Eddie McGee found him and the police started to close in. Prudom immediately began shooting at them. 'Come and get me, you bastards!' he shouted. 'I'll take some of you to hell with me!'

He remained in the shelter as police armed with a variety of weapons took up positions nearby. At 9.30 that Sunday morning an assault was made, with stun-grenades being hurled and rifle-shots fired. Just before 9.40 a.m. Prudom was killed by a bullet which, according to evidence given at the subsequent inquest, was 'almost certainly' fired from his own gun.

He was later found to have sustained twenty-two other injuries during that short series of exchanges which brought Britain's biggest manhunt to an end.

Murder of Mrs. Chung, 1928

On the afternoon of 19 June 1928, a Chinese couple spending part of their honeymoon in the Lake District village of Grange-in-Borrowdale, left their hotel to go for a walk. Chung Yi Miao, a twenty-eight-year-old doctor of law, and his wealthy twenty-nine-year-old wife had arrived in Grange the previous day after being married in New York a little over a month earlier. They seemed to be happy together.

Some hours later Chung returned for dinner alone, saying that his wife had gone shopping in the nearby town of Keswick. He then remained at the hotel, keeping himself to himself, until finally he began to express anxiety about the lateness of the hour. His wife had still not returned when he decided to go to bed.

Suddenly, at eleven o'clock that night, a police officer called to tell him that his wife was dead.

Mrs Chung's body had been discovered beside a bathing pool a short distance from the hotel; she had been strangled. Her skirt had been pushed up round her waist, and she was lying in such a way as to give the impression that she had been raped or sexually assaulted, though this was later found to have been simulated. Articles of jewellery which had apparently been stolen were discovered — without Chung's knowledge — during a search of the couple's bedroom. They had been deliberately concealed.

Chung Yi Miao was taken into custody on suspicion of murder. At Keswick police station the following morning, having been told nothing about the apparent sex offence and robbery, he convinced the police of his guilt by remarking, 'It is terrible — my wife assaulted, robbed and murdered!' Despite uncertainty about his motive for the crime, he was formally charged and brought to trial at the Carlisle Assizes in November the same year.

Chung denied the offence, and the trial lasted three days. The evidence offered by the prosecution was entirely circumstantial — the defendant's knowledge of the state in which the body had been found, the jewellery hidden in the hotel bedroom, the fact that the cord used to murder Mrs Chung was of the same type as used in the hotel, and so on. The motive now suggested was thwarted sexual desire.

In his defence it was stated that two unknown men of Oriental appearance had been following the couple, the suggestion being that *they* could have murdered Mrs Chung after the defendant had left her. An attempt was also made to show that Chung's accent had caused misunderstandings. For example, he denied that in referring to his wife's body, on the night that he was informed of her death, he had asked, 'Had she knickers on?' What he had really asked, he said, was, 'Had she necklace on?'

The jury was not impressed by all this and found the case proved; Chung was sentenced to death. Following an unsuccessful appeal, which he conducted himself, he was hanged at Strangeways Prison, Manchester, on 6 December 1928.

It was afterwards suggested that the real reason for the murder was Chung's discovery, just after their marriage, that his wife would not be able to have children.

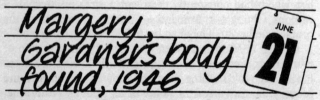

Margery Gardner's body found, 1946

JUNE 21

During the early afternoon of 21 June 1946, the body of Margery Gardner, aged thirty-two, was found in a hotel bedroom in the Notting Hill district of London. She had died from suffocation, though only after being subjected to a number of sadistic acts: while alive, she had been whipped, her nipples almost bitten off and a rough instrument rotated in her vagina, causing much bleeding. After washing blood from her face, her murderer had covered her body up to the neck with bedclothes. He had left the curtains drawn.

Margery Gardner was a married woman, separated from her husband; she spent much of her time drinking and dancing and occasionally worked as a film extra. On the night of 20 June she had been to the Panama Club in South Kensington in the company of Neville Heath, a twenty-nine-year-old former RAF officer with a criminal record for housebreaking, theft and fraud. He had afterwards taken her to the hotel by taxi.

The police were certain that Heath was the person responsible for the murder, and released his name and description to the press, saying that they wanted him 'to assist them with their inquiries'. On 24 June they received a letter from him, posted in Worthing, in which he claimed to be innocent of the crime.

'I booked in at the hotel last Sunday, but not with Mrs Gardner, whom I met for the first time during the week,' he wrote. 'I had drinks with her on Friday evening, and whilst I was with her she met an acquaintance with whom she was obliged to sleep. The reasons, as I understand them, were mainly financial.

'It was then that Mrs Gardner asked if she could use my hotel room until two o'clock and intimated that, if I returned after that, I might spend the remainder of the night with her. I gave her my keys and told her to leave the hotel door open.

'It must have been almost 3 a.m. when I returned to the hotel and found her in the condition of which you are aware. I realised I was in an invidious position, and rather than notify the police I packed my belongings and left.'

He said that he was using a false name, but could be

contacted through the personal column of the *Daily Telegraph*. He also said that he had the instrument with which Mrs Gardner had been beaten and would be forwarding it to them. It never arrived.

The police continued their search for him, circulating copies of a photograph to every force in the country. On 6 July he went to Bournemouth police station, calling himself Group Captain Rupert Brooke, in connection with the disappearance of twenty-one-year-old Doreen Marshall, who was believed to have had dinner with him on the evening of 3 July. He was recognized and held for questioning by officers of the Metropolitan Police. On 8 July he was taken by car to London, where he was later charged with the murder of Margery Gardner.

About the time the charge was made the body of Doreen Marshall was found in Branksome Chine, a wooded valley about a mile from the hotel in which Heath had been staying in Bournemouth. Like Margery Gardner, she was naked and had various injuries. In this case, however, the victim had died as a result of deep knife-wounds in her throat, and had been mutilated afterwards.

Though Heath was charged with this second murder, his trial, which began at the Old Bailey on 24 September, concerned only the first. A defence of insanity was made on his behalf, his counsel seeking to establish that his long history of petty crime was proof of instability. Heath, however, appeared indifferent to it all. On being found guilty, he had nothing to say; on being sentenced to death, he made no appeal. He showed no sign of remorse and made no confession.

'My only regret at leaving the world is that I have been damned unworthy of you both,' he wrote to his parents.

Neville Heath was hanged at Pentonville Prison on 26 October 1946.

Murder of Mrs. Parker, 1954

On the afternoon of 22 June 1954, Mrs Honora Parker, a middle-aged woman, was beaten to death in a park in Canterbury, New Zealand, by two teenage girls, one of whom was her own daughter. The girls attacked her with a brick wrapped in a stocking, striking forty-five blows — twenty-four of them to their victim's head and face — before running to a nearby teashop to raise the alarm. But nobody was taken in by their story that Mrs Parker had been killed when she slipped and fell on the pavement, and soon they admitted the truth. Pauline Parker, aged sixteen, and her friend Juliet Hulme, fifteen, were therefore charged with murder.

The two girls were found to have had a lesbian relationship which had been a matter of concern to the parents of both. Mrs Parker had been determined to put a stop to it, but had failed to do so. Then, early in 1954, Mr Hulme decided to take Juliet to South Africa. Pauline declared that she would go, too, regardless of the opposition of her own parents. The idea of murdering her mother seems to have occurred to her about the same time. 'Why could not mother die?' she wrote in her diary on 13 February. 'Dozens of people, thousands of people, are dying every day. So why not mother, and father too?'

A later entry, written two days before the crime took place, showed that both girls had given the idea a lot of thought. 'We discussed our plans for moidering mother and made them a little clearer,' Pauline recorded. 'I want it to appear either a natural or an accidental death.'

Pauline Parker and Juliet Hulme were brought to trial in Christchurch, both apparently unrepentant. The court was given details of their sex life and various fantasies in which they had jointly indulged, the defence contending that their crime had been the result of 'paranoia of the exalted type', and that they were both certifiably mad. To the prosecution, however, they were 'highly intelligent and perfectly sane, but precocious and dirty-minded girls', who had committed a 'callously planned and premeditated murder'.

The jury agreed with the prosecution, and the prisoners were found guilty and sentenced to be detained during Her Majesty's pleasure. But this proved not to be a very harsh sentence, for they were both released in 1958.

Shooting of Stanford White, 1906

JUNE 25

On 25 June 1906, Stanford White, a distinguished architect aged fifty-two, became the victim of a sensational shooting during the first performance of a new farce at the Madison Square Roof Garden Theatre in New York. In the middle of the play he was suddenly shot dead by Harry Thaw, a thirty-four-year-old millionaire playboy. He fell to the floor and died instantly, one of Thaw's three bullets having entered his brain.

Thaw, on being arrested, admitted responsibility for White's death, but claimed that it had been a justified act. He said that his wife, a former model and chorus girl, had been seduced by the victim some years earlier, and that in such a case an 'unwritten law' allowed the husband to avenge the wrong which his wife had suffered. He was charged with murder.

Thaw was the son of a railroad magnate. Born in Pennsylvania, he had inherited his father's wealth while still in his twenties, and was well-known for his extravagance and gambling. In April 1905 he married twenty-year-old Evelyn Nesbit, with whom he had been in love for the previous four years. But he was a jealous man and, on learning that his wife had been Stanford White's mistress, became enraged and decided upon the shooting.

He was brought to trial in January 1907, his wife appearing as a witness in support of his claim that he had a moral right to kill Stanford White. His lawyers pleaded that he had suffered a temporary aberration which absolved him of responsibility for what had happened. The District Attorney, however, claimed that the shooting had been a 'cruel, deliberate, malicious, premeditated taking of human life', and that the concept of the 'unwritten law' had been devised solely to prevent his conviction. The jury deliberated for two days, but was unable to reach agreement.

The prisoner was brought to trial again in January 1908, his lawyers this time making a plea of insanity and producing evidence to show that he was a manic-depressive. The plea was successful and Thaw, on being found guilty but insane, was committed to an asylum in Matteawan.

During the next four years a number of appeals were made for his release, but all were dismissed. Then, in August 1913, he escaped from the asylum and went to Canada. Though deported and taken back to New York, he managed to obtain a retrial which resulted in his acquittal; he was accordingly set free in June 1915. He then began divorce proceedings, his wife having given birth to a child which could not have been his in 1913.

As a result of the murder case many disclosures had been made about Thaw's private life: he had been revealed not only as a libertine but also as a sadist who enjoyed whipping members of the opposite sex, including his wife. But eighteen months after his release he was indicted for kidnapping and whipping a nineteen-year-old youth. Once again he was declared insane and committed to Matteawan, where he remained until 1922, when the verdict was reversed.

After that he roamed the world, always living in style. He managed to keep out of further trouble for the rest of his life, but sometimes showed signs of madness. He died, aged seventy-four, in 1947.

Execution of Frederick Field, 1936

On 30 June 1936, Frederick Field, a thirty-two-year-old deserter from the Royal Air Force, was hanged for the murder of Beatrice Sutton, a middle-aged widow and prostitute, in her flat in Clapham, London, the previous April. The crime had been committed for no real reason. Field, in a confession which he later retracted, stating; 'I was just browned off. I don't even know who the woman was.'

It was not the first time he had been involved in a murder case; he had been 'browned off' before. On the morning of 2 October 1931, the body of another prostitute, twenty-year-old Norah Upchurch, was found in an empty building in Shaftesbury Avenue, where Field, then employed by a signfitter, had been working. She, too, had been strangled, and on that occasion Field aroused suspicion by claiming to have given the key to the premises to a person he believed to be a prospective purchaser; as a result, the door had to be forced.

His conduct at the inquest on Norah Upchurch was also suspicious for, having described the person to whom he had given the key as a 'man in plus fours, with gold fillings', he identified one of the other men present as the person concerned. The coroner and his jury together inspected the man's teeth and found that 'there was not a gold tooth in his head'. Field was afterwards said by the coroner to be a compulsive liar.

Though no charge had been made against him in connection with that crime, Field approached a newspaper in July 1933 and offered the editor an exclusive confession on the understanding that his defence costs would be paid in the event of him being brought to trial. He was then serving in the RAF.

As a result of this confession, Field was charged with the murder and brought to trial at the Old Bailey. He had by now retracted the confession, and said that he had wanted to be tried in order to prove his innocence. As his account of the murder differed from the findings of the police, the jury was directed to acquit him. But in view of what subsequently occurred, it is accepted that he was, in fact, guilty.

Three years later, after being arrested as an RAF deserter, Field confessed to the murder of Beatrice Sutton — expecting, no doubt, that if he withdrew *this* confession his second trial would have the same result as the first. But this time he made the mistake of including information which only the murderer could have known. The jury took only fifteen minutes to find him guilty.

Mrs Phennie Perry found murdered, 1937

JULY 2

On the morning of 2 July 1937, Mrs Phennie Perry, aged twenty, was found murdered on a pathway in the Jamaica district of Queens County, New York, with her two-year-old daughter lying unhurt beside her. The crime had been committed about 10.30 the previous night, and the victim's screams had been heard by a night-watchman at a nearby junk-yard. But the watchman had been drunk at the time and the police had not taken his report seriously. They had therefore failed to make a proper investigation.

Mrs Perry, of 153rd Street, Jamaica, was the wife of an employee of a steel construction corporation. She had been battered over the head with a piece of concrete which the person responsible had left at the scene. Besides the murder weapon, the police found a number of other items, including a man's shoe, a strip of material torn from a shirt, and some letters and bills addressed to Ulysses Palm, a Deacon of the Amity Baptist Church, who lived in a flat below the one occupied by Mrs Perry and her husband.

Palm, a married man aged thirty-nine, worked in a chain store. The police went to his flat in his absence and found a shoe from the same pair as the one left at the scene of the crime, and also the shirt from which the strip of material had been torn. When Palm was questioned he admitted owning some of the articles found near the body, but said that he had given the pair of shoes to Arthur Perry, the dead woman's husband.

Perry, aged twenty-two, said that Palm had written a suggestive letter to his wife and had tried to break into her bedroom the previous morning, as a result of which there had been a confrontation between the two men later in the day. He agreed that Palm had given him the pair of shoes, but said that he had afterwards returned them.

Palm denied all this. He was able to prove that he had been some miles away at work at the time Perry claimed to have spoken to him, and that he had not left early enough to have been back in Jamaica at the time of the murder. It was also discovered that the letter to Mrs Perry was not in his handwriting, and that the tear in the shirt had been started with a cut.

When police made inquiries at a theatre where Mrs Perry had played bingo on the evening in question they learnt that Perry had been seen there, in the company of a woman and a child, about 10 p.m. Moreover, an examination of Perry's clothes revealed a bloodstain on one of his socks, corresponding with a hole in the shoe found at the scene of the crime. It was therefore clear that Perry was the culprit, and that in murdering his wife he had sought to divert suspicion from himself to Ulysses Palm.

While in jail awaiting trial, Arthur Perry admitted his guilt to a detective who was posing as one of his fellow prisoners. 'I don't know why I did it,' he said.

Perry was tried in November 1937, found guilty and sentenced to death. The conviction was quashed on appeal, as the judge had allowed hearsay evidence to be introduced. But a second trial in 1938 had the same result as the first, and the condemned man was executed in the electric chair on 3 August 1939.

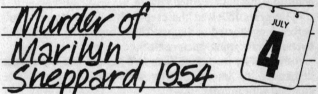

Murder of Marilyn Sheppard, 1954

JULY 4

During the early hours of 4 July 1954, a brutal murder was committed in one of the bedrooms of a luxurious house overlooking Lake Erie, in Cuyhoga County, Ohio. Marilyn Sheppard, the wife of a young neuro-surgeon working at Cleveland's Bay View Hospital, had gone to bed alone two or three hours earlier, her husband having fallen asleep on a couch downstairs. She was later found to have been struck thirty-five times over the head with a blunt instrument.

Dr Samuel Sheppard, aged thirty, claimed that he had been woken up by his wife's screams and that he was knocked unconcious from behind when he rushed up to the bedroom. On regaining his senses, he heard a noise down-

181

stairs and went down in time to see an unknown man leaving the house. Pursuing him in the direction of the lake, he managed to catch hold of him, only to be knocked unconscious again. This time, when he came to, he was lying on the edge of the lake, his body partly in the water. He then struggled back to the house and telephoned a neighbour to ask for help.

The police were sceptical about Sheppard's story. So, too, was Dr Samuel Gerber, the coroner, who arrived on the scene soon after them. A burglary appeared to have been simulated. There was no sand in Sheppard's hair, as there should have been if he had really been lying unconscious on the edge of the lake. A bloody imprint, which the coroner believed to be that of a surgical instrument, was found on the victim's pillow. And Sheppard's wrist-watch, speckled with blood, was found among other items in a canvas bag near the house. Later, when it was discovered that he had been having an affair with a young female colleague, his guilt seemed certain.

The press followed the case with a keen interest, and before long started to suggest that Sheppard's family and friends were using their influence to prevent his being arrested. 'Why isn't Sam Sheppard in jail?' one newspaper demanded to know. Shortly after this Sheppard was charged with murder.

His highly-publicized trial at the Cuyhoga County criminal court lasted from 18 October to 21 December 1954. At the end of it he was found guilty and sentenced to life imprisonment.

Despite several attempts to secure a retrial, Sheppard spent the next twelve years in jail. But a retrial was eventually granted, and began at the same court on 24 October 1966. The course which this one took was very different from that of the first trial.

In the first place, the police officer who had originally accused him of the crime had to admit that he had not made inquiries to ascertain whether injuries which the prisoner had received could have been self-inflicted; he had merely assumed that they *had* been.

Dr Gerber, whose evidence about the bloodstained imprint of a 'surgical instrument' had made such an impression at the first trial, had to admit that he had never seen an instrument of the sort he had in mind, though he had since looked for one all over the United States.

The speckles found on Sheppard's wrist-watch, according to the prosecution, could only have been caused by 'flying blood' during the course of the attack. However, Sheppard's lawyer drew attention to blood particles on the inside of the watch band, arguing that this proved that his client's watch had been removed from his wrist *before* the attack had taken place.

The trial ended on 16 November 1966, the prisoner being found not guilty of the murder for which he had already spent so long in prison; he was therefore released. Although he managed to get himself reinstated on the medical register, Sheppard was widely mistrusted and eventually forced out of the profession. He then turned to professional wrestling as a means of earning a living.

His private life gave him further cause for unhappiness. His second wife, a German divorcée whom he had married while still a prisoner, sued him for divorce, claiming that he carried offensive weapons and had threatened her with violence. A third marriage followed, but his health began to deteriorate soon afterwards.

A sad, rejected figure, Dr Samuel Sheppard died on 6 April 1970. His few remaining friends believed that his death had been caused by his failure to regain his position in society.

Death of Bella Wright, 1919

On the evening of 5 July 1919, Bella Wright, a twenty-one-year-old factory worker, left her home in the village of Stoughton, in Leicestershire, by bicycle to visit her uncle in the nearby hamlet of Gaulby. She arrived at her uncle's home in the company of another cyclist, a man whom she described as a stranger, but who waited outside the house until it was time for her to return home. Bella then joined him again, and after stopping to speak briefly to her uncle and his son-in-law at the garden gate, they rode off together. It was the last time that Bella was seen alive.

Later the same evening her body was discovered on the Gartree road, about two miles from Gaulby. Her head was covered in blood, but she was fully dressed and her bicycle lay beside her. It therefore seemed that she had died from injuries received as a result of falling off the bicycle. However, the following morning the local policeman found a bullet embedded in the surface of the road about seventeen feet from the place where the body had lain. An examination of the body then revealed that Bella Wright had been shot in the face.

The bullet had struck her below the left eye, then — according to the doctor who carried out the post-mortem — travelled 'upwards, inwards and backwards', finally leaving an exit wound which had been hidden by her hair. A gunsmith who examined the bullet was unable to say for certain whether it had been fired from a revolver or a rifle. And as there was no evidence of robbery or sexual assault, there was no apparent motive for her murder.

From Bella's relatives in Gaulby the police obtained a description of the stranger who had accompanied her to and from the house, and also learnt that he had been riding a green bicycle. All attempts to trace him, however, were unsuccessful until suddenly, on 23 February 1920, the frame of a green bicycle with the front wheel still attached to it was brought to the surface of the Leicester Canal after becoming entangled with the tow-rope of a barge.

Dredging of the canal bed then resulted in the discovery of a revolver holster containing live cartridges of the type which had caused the death of Bella Wright, together with other parts of the same bicycle.

Though the frame number of the bicycle had been removed by filing, a secret identification number on the handlebar bracket enabled police to trace it to Ronald Light, a thirty-four-year-old Leicester man now employed as mathematics master at a school in Cheltenham, Gloucestershire. Light, a former Army officer, had been living with his widowed mother in Leicester at the time of the girl's death. On being questioned about his bicycle, he at first denied having owned one and then claimed to have sold it to somebody whose name he could not remember. He was arrested and charged with Bella Wright's murder.

At his trial, which began at the Leicester Castle Courthouse on 10 June 1920, the evidence against him appeared to be overwhelming. But Light, who had been educated at Rugby, proved to be an impressive witness. He admitted having met Bella while cycling in the Leicestershire countryside and again outside her uncle's house, but claimed that he had not gone as far as the Gartree road with her.

Afterwards, on reading newspaper reports of her death, he had realized that he was suspected and feared that he might be accused of her murder. The disposal of the bicycle, and also the holster and ammunition for his old service revolver, had resulted from this fear, he told the court. The revolver itself had been taken from him when he left the Army, suffering from shell-shock.

Sir Edward Marshall Hall, defending, suggested that Bella Wright had not, in fact, been murdered, but accidentally hit by a stray rifle bullet fired from a distance. He then went on to stress that the prisoner, who had not known her before the day of her death, had had no motive for killing her. After considering the case for three hours, the jury returned a verdict of not guilty, and Light was released to the cheers of the spectators and the crowds outside.

What became of him afterwards is not known.

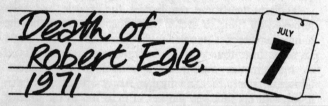

Death of Robert Egle, 1971

JULY 7

On 7 July 1971, Robert Egle, aged fifty-nine, died in hospital in St Albans, Hertfordshire, after eight days of intense pain. His death was put down to broncho-pneumonia and polyneuritis, and no inquest was thought necessary. His body was cremated.

Egle had worked for a firm which produced photographic equipment in the village of Bovingdon, near Hemel Hempstead; he was the head of its storeroom. He had been taken ill at the beginning of June with a severe attack of diarrhoea, but after three days at home was well enough to return to work. At the end of the month, when he became ill again, he suffered from nausea, a violent backache and numbness at the tips of his fingers.

In the meantime another of the firm's employees, forty-one-year-old Ronald Hewitt, had been repeatedly ill with diarrhoea, vomiting and stomach pains over a period of four weeks. He continued to feel 'a bit shaky' until he left the job two days after Egle's death.

Two months earlier, on 10 May, a smart young man named Graham Young had started working for the firm as an assistant storeman. As such, he had been in close contact with the dead man and had been in the practice of fetching tea for the storeroom employees. Ron Hewitt was later to recall that he had often left his tea after just a sip or two because it tasted bitter, and that on those occasions Bob Egle had finished it for him after drinking his own.

Young was absent-minded and unpredictable. He had a keen interest in chemistry and pharmacy; he also talked about Hitler a lot. At Bob Egle's funeral he impressed his managing director by showing a detailed knowledge of the illness from which the deceased had suffered. He was afterwards put in charge of the storeroom for a probationary period.

In September the same year another of the firm's employees, Frederick Biggs, sixty-year-old head of the Work-In-Progress department, was taken ill with stomach pains and vomiting. Later the same month Peter Buck, the import-export manager, was similarly ill.

Then, in October, David Tilson, a clerk in Buck's department, and Jethro Batt, assistant storeman, both began to suffer from a variety of symptoms, including stomach pains, vomiting and pains or numbness in their legs. Both became worse, Tilson being admitted to hospital; both started losing their hair. Another employee, Mrs Diana Smart, also began suffering from stomach and leg pains, vomiting and other symptoms.

Tilson, having been discharged from hospital on 28 October, was readmitted four days later; he was by then almost bald and completely impotent. Fred Biggs was admitted to hospital on 4 November with pains in his chest and feet. Batt was admitted on 5 November, by which time he was completely bald, impotent and suicidal. Mrs Smart, after returning to work, became ill again.

These illnesses alarmed the rest of the firm's staff, and gave rise to rumours that the water supply had been contaminated. The area medical officer carried out a thorough examination of the premises, but could find no explanation. Then, on 19 November, Fred Biggs died. At this, several members of the staff announced that they were leaving.

A local doctor was called in to give a talk to the entire staff at a meeting in the firm's canteen, to assure them that there was no cause for alarm. Graham Young, as if determined to draw attention to himself, questioned him at length. It was as a result of this that he was suddenly suspected of being responsible for what had happened, and a police investigation was instigated.

Young was then found to have been released from Broadmoor only six months earlier, having spent nine years there for poisoning his father, his sister and a schoolfriend.

He was immediately arrested on suspicion, and a search of his bedsitter in Hemel Hempstead resulted in the discovery of various poisons, together with a diary containing incriminating evidence.

Fred Biggs was found to have died of thallium poisoning; Bob Egle, whose ashes were exhumed for analysis, was then found to have died from the same cause.

While in custody Young boasted that he had poisoned his stepmother, whose death in 1962 — when he was fourteen years old — had been put down to natural causes. A further case of administering poison was also revealed. In July 1972 he was brought to trial at St Albans for the murders of Robert Egle and Frederick Biggs and several lesser crimes. He pleaded not guilty.

Throughout the trial he conducted himself with remarkable calmness. He claimed that a partial confession had been made in return for food, clothes, access to a solicitor and an opportunity to sleep, and that his diary entries were merely notes for a novel which he had intended to write.

To the jury, however, it was clear that he was a psychopath who had used his victims for the purpose of scientific experiment. He was found guilty on both charges of murder, two of attempted murder and two of administering poison.

After sentencing Graham Young, aged twenty-four, to life imprisonment, the judge allowed the foreman of the jury to read a statement expressing concern about the sale of poisons to the public.

Sir Harry Oakes found murdered 1943

On the morning of 8 July 1943, Sir Harry Oakes, a self-made millionaire, was found brutally murdered at his home in the Bahamas. He had been struck four times over the head with a blunt instrument and his body had been doused with insecticide and set on fire while he was still alive. This horrifying crime had been committed in the victim's bedroom during the course of the previous night, while his wife and son were away from home. As nothing had been stolen, it was assumed that robbery had not been the motive for it.

Sir Harry Oakes, aged sixty-nine, was American by birth, but had become a Canadian citizen in 1939; he had made his fortune out of Canadian gold mines. He lived in style in the Bahamas, but there were many people there who disliked him, and it was clear that narrowing down the list of suspects was not going to be easy. The Duke of Windsor, who was governor of the islands and a friend of Sir Harry's, took personal charge of the investigation, calling in two Miami police captains to find the culprit. Within a few days the victim's son-in-law, Count Alfred de Marigny, was charged with the murder.

De Marigny, an adventurer from Mauritius, had married the victim's daughter Nancy in secret in May 1942, a few days after her eighteenth birthday; the ceremony had taken place in New York. While some members of the family found the Count a likeable man, Sir Harry was convinced that he had only married Nancy for the sake of her inheritance, and repeatedly told him that she would be left nothing; there had been frequent quarrels between the two men, some of them in public. By the time the thirty-three-year-old de Marigny was brought to trial in

October few doubted that he was guilty, and there were even suggestions that a lynch mob might be formed.

But Nancy de Marigny was certain of her husband's innocence, and hired a New York private detective named Raymond Campbell Schindler to collect evidence for his defence. Schindler, finding that the prosecution's case depended on the evidence of a single fingerprint which had allegedly been found on a Chinese screen beside Sir Harry's bed, brought in Maurice O'Neill, a fingerprint expert from the New Orleans Police Department, to examine it. His findings led to a courtroom sensation.

The fingerprint had not been photographed on the screen: it had, according to the prosecution, been dusted with fingerprint powder, then removed from the surface with a piece of transparent tape, so that its outline remained intact. As this was not in accordance with established police procedure, O'Neill viewed it with suspicion and photographed the screen himself, using highly sensitive equipment. He found no evidence of the fingerprint ever having been there.

Moreover, the fingerprint produced by the prosecution was found to have a background of circles, which appeared to be moisture marks. There was nothing on the Chinese screen which could have caused these; the only possible explanation for them was that the fingerprint had not been taken from the screen at all, but from a wet glass. As one of the investigating officers was known to have asked de Marigny at the beginning of the investigation to pour him a glass of water, it was claimed by the defence that the evidence had been fabricated.

Alfred de Marigny was found not guilty and carried from the courthouse in triumph. His marriage ended six years later.

Schindler one of the greatest of America's private detectives, was not entirely satisfied with the outcome of his investigation: he wanted to bring the real culprit to justice. However, he was denied the co-operation of the Bahamas authorities, and so was unable to make any further progress. The following year, when he asked for the case to be reopened, the Duke of Windsor would not hear of it.

Attempts by other investigators to solve the mystery were similarly thwarted.

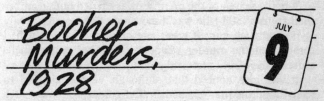

Booher Murders, 1928

JULY 9

On the evening of 9 July 1928, Henry Booher's farm near the village of Mannville, in Alberta, was the scene of a multiple murder. Henry was some miles away, working on another farm, when it took place, and his two teenage daughters had gone into Mannville to watch a game of basketball. The other members of the family — his wife, Eunice, and his two sons, Fred, aged twenty-four, and Vernon, twenty — had remained at home.

Between 8 and 9 p.m. Vernon ran to the home of their nearest neighbour to raise the alarm. He had been getting the cows in from the pasture for the night, he said breathlessly, and on returning to the house had found his mother and brother dead. He had to telephone Mannville for a doctor.

An examination revealed that Mrs Booher had been shot in the back of the head while she sat at the living-room table. Fred was lying on the kitchen floor, having been shot through the mouth and neck; he had apparently rushed into the kitchen on hearing the shot which killed his mother. There was another body, that of Gabriel Goromby, a Hungarian hired hand, in the nearby bunkhouse; he had been shot twice through the head and once through the breast. Dr J.D. Heaslip, who was also the coroner, insisted that nothing should be disturbed until the police arrived.

Soon afterwards Henry Booher arrived home and learnt what had happened. He and Vernon went outside together, Vernon returning a few minutes later to say that a fourth person had been killed. Wasyl Rosyak, another hired hand, had been shot in the face and stomach as he was about to feed some pigs which the family kept in a barn.

When a search of the premises was carried out an empty shell from a .303 rifle was discovered. The Booher family owned no such gun; it was therefore assumed that it had come from the murder weapon. The other empty shells must all have been removed by the murderer.

It was also noticed that, although Vernon claimed to have found the first two bodies after getting the cows in for the night, there were no cows in the corral until the following morning, when they brought themselves back from the pasture. So while the 'Mannville tragedy' was generally supposed to have been the work of an unknown maniac, Vernon Booher was, in fact, regarded by the police as a suspect right from the start.

Charles Stevenson, another neighbour, informed the police that *he* owned a .303 sporting rifle and that it had been taken from his house, together with a box of shells, without his knowledge; he had last seen it on 8 July, a Sunday, before he and his family went to church. This rifle had often been lent to members of the Booher family. Moreover, it was discovered that on that Sunday morning Vernon Booher had been seen riding towards Stevenson's farm.

By 17 July it was considered that there was enough circumstantial evidence to bring charges against Vernon, who was already being held as a 'material witness'. The preliminary hearing was held in Mannville the following day, the proceedings being watched by Dr Adolph Maximilian Langsner, a Viennese criminologist with psychic powers, who had been asked to assist the police in their search for the murder weapon. On 20 July Langsner

Right: George Joseph Smith, the Brides in the Bath murderer.
(SYNDICATION INTERNATIONAL)

Below: Eight of the Boston Strangler's victims.
(POPPERFOTO)

Right: Lesley Whittle's killer Donald Neilson after his arrest. He was attacked by members of the public as police struggled with him. (SYNDICATION INTERNATIONAL)

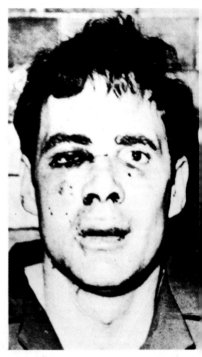

Below: Lesley Whittle's body is carried in a coffin from the drain where it was found. (SYNDICATION INTERNATIONAL)

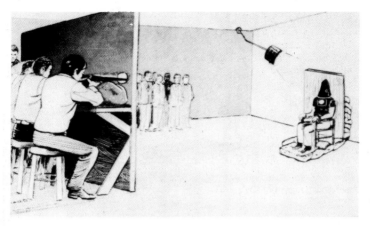

Above: Artist's impression based on eye-witness accounts of the execution of Gary Gilmore. (POPPERFOTO)

Below: A group of newsmen examine and photograph the chair in which Gary Gilmore faced the firing squad. (POPPERFOTO)

Above: A reconstruction of the place where Marcel Pétiot's victims met their death. (POPPERFOTO)

Below: Police search the grounds of the 'factory' at Crawley, Sussex, scene of the acid bath murders committed by John George Haigh. (SYNDICATION INTERNATIONAL)

R

In replying to this letter, please write on the envelope:—

Number 9656 Name R. Ellis

H.M. PRISON HOLLOWAY. N.7. Prison

2. 6. 55

Dear Alex, Sorry to be so long in answering your letter of April 24. Thank you for offering to help me, but there is not a thing any one can do.

So you are once again at Studios. How are things going with you. I hope your son is well, give him my best regards.

I am quite well, just waiting patiently to get into court. This place is not half as bad as you may think, on the outside.

You should come and do some sketching here?

Well Alex, if you see Jackie tell her I am sorry I could not see her when she came.

By for now, and than

Yours
Ruth Ellis

No. 244   (21441 – 3-11-42)

A letter to 'Alex' from Ruth Ellis while she was in Holloway Prison. (inset) Ruth Ellis.
(SYNDICATION INTERNATIONAL)

Special Notice

MURDER

M.P. (FH). It is desired to trace the after-described for interview respecting the death of **MARGERY GARDNER**, during the night of 20th-21st inst. **NEVILLE GEORGE CLEVELY HEATH**, alias **ARMSTRONG, BLYTH, DENVERS** and **GRAHAM**, C.R.O. No. 28142-37, b. 1917, 5ft. 11½in., c. fresh, e. blue, believed small fair moustache, h. and eyebrows fair, square face, broad forehead and nose, firm chin, good teeth, military gait ; dress, lt. grey d.b. suit with pin stripe, dk. brown trilby, brown suede shoes, cream shirt with collar attached or fawn and white check sports jacket and grey flannel trousers. Nat. Reg. No. **CNP** 2147191.

Has recent conviction for posing as Lt.-Col. of South African Air Force. A pilot and believed to possess an " A " licence, has stated his intention of going abroad and may endeavour to secure passage on ship or plane as passenger or pilot. May stay at hotels accompanied by woman.

Enquiries are also requested to trace the owner of gent's white handkerchief with brown check border, bearing " L. Kearns " in black ink on hem and stitched with large " K " in blue cotton in centre.

The poster issued by the police during their search for Neville Heath.
(SYNDICATION INTERNATIONAL)

Above: The burnt-out car in the Rouse murder case. (SYNDICATION INTERNATIONAL)
Below: The car belonging to the Drummond family, murdered while on holiday in France, being prepared to go on show at Blackpool in a reconstruction of the crime for holidaymakers. (POPPERFOTO)

Above: Police searching Norman Thorn's farm for the body of his victim.
(SYNDICATION INTERNATIONAL)

Police dogs on Wimbledon Common hunting
for clues to the disappearance of Muriel
McKay (POPPERFOTO) (inset) Muriel McKay.
(SYNDICATION INTERNATIONAL)

located the missing gun in a patch of brush 135 yards from the Boohers' house.

Two days later Vernon made a confession. He had been in love with a nurse whom his mother and brother had tried to prevent him seeing, he explained; that was why he had killed them. The two hired hands had been killed a little while afterwards in order to mislead the police.

When Vernon Booher was brought to trial in Edmonton on 24 September he surprised the spectators by pleading not guilty to the charges when everybody knew that he had confessed. The judge ruled that the confession should not be admitted as evidence after a defence claim that it had been obtained as a result of hypnotic influence exercised by Langsner. However, the crown was able to present evidence of three partial confessions, as well as a good deal of circumstantial evidence, and the accused was convicted on all four charges. He was sentenced to death.

On 4 December the conviction was quashed on appeal, a second trial beginning on 21 January the following year. By this time Vernon Booher was unwell; he was suffering from nervous strain and close to a breakdown. Convicted again on all charges, he was hanged at Fort Saskatchewan jail on 24 April 1929.

None of his surviving relatives was at the jail when the execution took place, and there was nobody to claim his remains. His body was buried in the prison grounds.

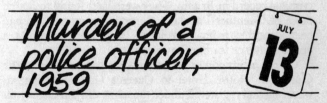

Murder of a police officer, 1959

On the afternoon of 13 July 1959, Mrs Verne Schiffman, a thirty-year-old model occupying a flat in South Kensington, London, received a telephone call from a man who was trying to blackmail her. It was not the first time that he had been in contact with her, and Mrs Schiffman's telephone was being tapped by the police; the call was quickly traced to a kiosk at South Kensington underground station. Mrs Schiffman kept the man talking for fifteen minutes while Detective Sergeant Raymond Purdy and Detective Sergeant John Sandford went to arrest him.

Pulling the culprit from the telephone box, the two police officers took him up the stairs towards the exit, but he managed to break away from them. Chasing him along Sydney Place, they cornered him in a block of flats in Onslow Square, about 100 yards from the station, and questioned him briefly before Sandford went to ring the caretaker's bell, to ask him to assist them. Purdy was thus left to guard the prisoner on his own.

The ringing of the bell brought no response, and Sandford called out to his colleague across the hall, saying that the caretaker must have gone out. At that moment the prisoner suddenly pulled out a gun and shot Purdy through the heart. He then ran out into the street and made good his escape while Sandford hesitated to leave his dying colleague.

The gunman, who had called himself Mr Fisher when he spoke to Mrs Schiffman, was described by Sandford as being about thirty years old and 5 feet 10 inches tall, with a slim build and brown hair; he spoke with an American accent. His fingerprints, taken from the scene of the murder, enabled the police to discover that he had no criminal record in Britain. They were later found to match those of Guenther Podola, a German immigrant who had been deported from Canada in 1958, after receiving a prison sentence for burglary and theft.

On the afternoon of 16 July Podola was arrested at the Claremont House Hotel in Queen's Gate, Kensington, where he had registered under the name of Paul Camay on 25 June. The manager, having reported that 'Mr Camay' was acting 'very strangely' — he had been hiding in his room ever since the shooting — was shown a photograph of Podola provided by the Royal Canadian Mounted Police, and said he believed it to be the same man. A small party of police officers then broke into the room and overpowered him, Podola being struck in the face by the door handle as the door flew open. His gun was found hidden in the hotel attic.

At Chelsea police station Podola was found to be 'dazed, frightened and exhausted', and suffering from a number of minor injuries, the worst of which was a bruise under his left eye. The following day he was taken to St Stephen's Hospital, where he was handcuffed to a bed in a public ward and kept under guard by two policemen. He appeared to be in a state of shock and seemed hardly aware of his surroundings. He was later to claim that he could remember little of what had happened to him before his arrival at the hospital.

On 20 July he was charged with the murder of Detective Sergeant Purdy, then taken to Brixton Prison to await trial. During the weeks that followed he continued to maintain that he was suffering from loss of memory, and several doctors examined him to try to determine whether this was really true. When he appeared at the Old Bailey on 10 September with the bruise under his eye still visible, a jury was empanelled to decide the matter, his counsel arguing that he was unfit to stand trial.

The jury, having listened to the evidence for nine days, decided that Podola was *not* suffering from a genuine loss of memory. He was therefore brought to trial before a different jury, but the same judge, on 24 September. The main prosecution witness was Detective Sergeant Sandford.

In his own defence, Podola made a statement from the dock, declaring that he did not know whether he was guilty or not because he could not remember the crime. However, the jury took only a little over half an hour to find the charge proved, and he was sentenced to death.

Guenther Podola was hanged at Wandsworth Prison on 5 November 1959.

Eight Chicago nurses found murdered, 1966

Just after 6 a.m. on 14 July 1966, two patrolmen arrived at a nurses' residence in Chicago's South Side and found a young woman standing on a window ledge above the sidewalk, screaming hysterically. Corazon Amurao, a twenty-three-year-old Filipino, was the sole survivor of a massacre which had taken place during the course of the preceding night. The eight other nurses in the building had all been strangled or stabbed to death.

All these murders were the work of a man who had forced his way into the residence, armed with a gun and a knife, about seven hours earlier, telling the nurses that he wanted their money. Miss Amurao said that he was about twenty-five years old, with short, brownish hair, and had worn a dark jacket and trousers with a white T-shirt. He had smelled of alcohol.

He made all the nurses lie on the floor of one of the bedrooms while he tied and gagged them with strips of bed linen, then went through the house searching for money. He then took them out of the room one at a time, at intervals of about twenty minutes, and murdered them in other parts of the building.

Though he had told them repeatedly that he would not harm them, Miss Amurao had not believed this, and had taken advantage of one of his absences to conceal herself under a bunk bed, where she remained unnoticed. Having thus saved her own life, she had gone on lying there until she felt it was safe to move.

An examination of the bodies revealed that several of the victims had been strangled *and* stabbed, but that none had been sexually assaulted. It also revealed that the culprit was skilled at tying knots, which led police to suspect that he was a seaman. They therefore made inquiries at a nearby branch of the National Maritime Union, and found that a man answering the killer's description had been there to seek work during the previous few days.

The man had filled in an application form, giving his name as Richard F. Speck and providing the statutory photograph to accompany it. As no work had been found for him so far, he was expected to call at the union again. A trap was set to ensure that he was arrested when he did so.

At the same time copies of the photograph were distributed to all the detectives in Chicago's South Side, and visits were made to bars and boarding-houses during an intensive search for him. He was soon found to be registered at a flop-house called the Raleigh Hotel, where freshly-laundered clothes fitting Miss Amurao's description of those which the killer had been wearing were discovered in his room.

Though Speck failed to return to the Raleigh that night, fingerprints found in the room matched those left at the nurses' residence, and police were left in no doubt that he was the killer. On the morning of 16 July a press conference was called, Speck being named as the main suspect in the case and his photograph released for publication. Late at night on the same day an ambulance was called to the Starr Hotel, in Chicago's North Side, where a man who had registered under a different name had slashed his wrists with a broken bottle. It was found to be Richard Speck.

The suspect was identified by Corazon Amurao, and brought to trial for first-degree murder in April 1967. Found guilty, he was sentenced to death, the sentence being later commuted to terms of imprisonment totalling 400 years.

Chicago's worst case of multiple murder, described as the 'most bestial crime in the city's history', had effectively been solved in a record sixty-seven hours.

Execution of Charlotte Bryant 1936

On 15 July 1936, Charlotte Bryant, a thirty-three-year-old Irish woman with five children, was hanged at Exeter Prison for the murder of her husband. The crime had been committed at the couple's home near Sherborne, Dorset, the previous December, the victim being poisoned with weed-killer. It was not the first time that an attempt had been made on his life.

Frederick Bryant, aged thirty-nine was a former corporal in the military police. He had met his wife while serving in Ireland during 'the Troubles' of 1920-1 and brought her back to England with him. He had since worked as a farm labourer, living with his family in tied cottages. One of the farms on which he had been employed was at Over Compton, near Yeovil. He had remained there for eight or nine years before moving to the Sherborne area early in 1934.

Charlotte, an illiterate woman, was unkempt and almost toothless. She had had a long succession of affairs with other men, taking money in return for her favours whenever it was forthcoming. Her reputation in Over Compton was so bad that her husband had lost his job over it. However, Frederick Bryant made no complaint about his wife's behaviour, and was even pleased that she was able to bring home money to supplement his wages.

'Four pound a week is better than thirty bob,' he said to a neighbour. 'I don't care a damn what she does.'

Shortly before Bryant lost his job Leonard Parsons, a gypsy pedlar and horse-dealer, began staying with them as an occasional lodger, sleeping on a couch in the kitchen. He and Charlotte became lovers, resuming their affair each time he returned to the cottage. But she became more attached to him than he was to her, and it was as a result of this attachment that she started trying to poison her husband.

In October 1935, after two unsuccessful attempts had been made on Bryant's life — his illness, in each case, was diagnosed as gastro-enteritis — Parsons left, saying that he would not be coming back. A few weeks afterwards Charlotte set out in pursuit of him, having made a third unsuccessful attempt to kill her husband in the meantime, but returned home after an encounter with his 'natural wife', Priscilla Loveridge, at a gypsy camp near Weston-super-Mare. Three days after that, on 22 December, Frederick Bryant died in agony.

Arsenic was found not only in his body but also in household dust taken from the cottage. An empty tin, containing traces of the poison, was found among some rubbish a short distance away.

At Charlotte's trial at the Dorset Assizes in May 1936, Parsons gave evidence against her, telling the court that some months before her husband's death the prisoner had told him that she would soon be a widow and that he and she could then get married. An elderly woman, who had also been a lodger at the cottage, said that on the night of 21 December Charlotte had coaxed her husband into drinking some Oxo, and that on another occasion she had disposed of a tin of weed-killer. Charlotte ate caramels in the dock and appeared to be unaware of the gravity of her situation.

While in the condemned cell she refused to see her children, saying that she did not want to cause them any further distress, and on the day of the execution she went to the scaffold bravely.

'Her last moments were truly edifying,' said the priest who attended her.

Murder of Herman Rosenthal, 1912

During the early hours of 16 July 1912, Herman Rosenthal, a professional gambler, was shot dead outside the Hotel Metropole in New York by a number of men who left the scene in a car. The murder was followed by the arrest of Lieutenant Charles Becker, forty-two-year-old head of New York City's Gambling Squad, whose subsequent conviction was hailed by the press as a blow against organized crime.

Prior to his downfall Becker had run a protection racket, taking a percentage of the profits of New York's gambling salons in return for allowing them to operate without hindrance from his own men. Rosenthal had accepted him as a business partner following the enforced closure of one establishment and frequent police raids on another, but when a dispute about money led to further interference he swore an affidavit giving details of Becker's activities.

On the evening of 15 July District Attorney Charles Whitman, who was determined to bring police corruption in the city to an end, interviewed Rosenthal at length. Later, on hearing of the murder, he was convinced that the police chief had instigated it. He then offered immunity from prosecution to anyone who helped him to bring Becker to justice.

Before long the offer was accepted by Jack Rose, the man who had hired the killers on Becker's behalf. Rose made a thirty-eight-page confession and agreed to appear as a prosecution witness. Becker was therefore brought to trial, with six others, in October the same year, Rose's evidence helping to ensure his conviction. He was sentenced to death for first-degree murder.

A fresh trial was granted in April 1914, the defence suggesting that prosecution witnesses had been offered rewards for giving evidence against him. He was nonetheless found guilty again, and once more sentenced to death.

An appeal for clemency was made to Charles Whitman, who had since been elected State Governor, but this was turned down and Becker was executed in the electric chair on 30 July 1915. A silver plate was attached to his coffin, stating that he had been murdered by Governor Whitman, but this was removed when Becker's widow realized that she could be prosecuted for criminal libel.

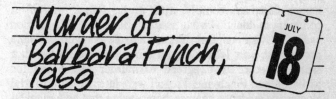

Murder of Barbara Finch, 1959

JULY 18

On the night of 18 July 1959, Mrs Barbara Finch, the second wife of a rich medical practitioner, was shot dead in the driveway of her home in a Los Angeles suburb. Her estranged husband, Dr Raymond Bernard Finch, and his young mistress, Carole Tregoff, were both involved in the incident, and to the police officers who investigated the affair it appeared to be a clear case of premeditated murder.

Dr Finch and his wife, who were both members of the Los Angeles Tennis Club, had married in 1951, each having been divorced by previous partners as a result of their association. Mrs Finch, then aged twenty-six, already had a daughter from her first marriage and bore her new husband a son two years later. By 1957, however, their marriage was merely a façade that they kept up for the sake of the children.

Finch, who was seven years older than his wife, rented

an apartment in the name of George Evans. Carole Tregoff, a twenty-year-old model who worked as his secretary, regularly met him there, and later divorced her own husband. She then moved into another apartment, calling herself Mrs George Evans. But not long afterwards Mrs Finch announced that she was going to begin divorce proceedings, citing Carole as co-respondent. The financial settlement which she sought would be so great that her husband would be left almost penniless.

Bitter quarrels, acts of violence and threats of murder followed, Finch becoming desperate. But eventually, in May 1959, Mrs Finch filed for divorce and her lawyer obtained a court order for her husband's income to be turned over to her. When Finch, who had by this time left home, failed to comply with it, he found himself in contempt of court.

On a visit to Las Vegas, Carole Tregoff became acquainted with John Cody, a thirty-year-old man with a criminal record who agreed to murder Mrs Finch for $1400. When Finch and Tregoff were later brought to trial Cody gave evidence against them, saying that he had taken their money but made no attempt on Mrs Finch's life. He even quoted Finch as saying on one occasion, 'When you shoot her, let her know what she's getting it for. Tell her, "This is from Bernie!"'

On the night of 18 July Marie Anne Lidholm, a Swedish *au pair* who lived in the doctor's house, was watching television in the company of Mrs Finch's twelve-year-old daughter. Mrs Finch was out at the time, but her car was heard in the garage shortly before midnight. A few seconds later she was heard screaming for help, and the *au pair* ran out to see what was happening.

Mrs Finch, who had been lying on the floor of the garage in her husband's presence, managed to get away and ran out across the lawn. Marie Anne then ran back to the house to call the police, hearing the sound of a shot as she did so. Barbara Finch was afterwards found with a bullet in her back and two skull fractures which could have been caused by the butt of a gun.

A leather dispatch-case, identified as the property of 'Bernie' Finch, had been left in the garage. It contained an assortment of articles, including drugs, hypodermic syringes, a large carving knife and two coils of clothes-line, later described as a 'do-it-yourself murder kit'. The gun, a .38 revolver, was not found.

Finch claimed that he had been trying to obtain evidence which he could use against his wife at the divorce hearing, and that it was for this purpose that he had hired Cody. He said that he and Carole Tregoff had confronted her in the garage, and that it was Mrs Finch who had produced the gun. Carole had fled at the sight of it, but he, during the course of a struggle, had managed to get hold of it and throw it into some bushes. The gun had discharged the shot which killed his wife as it hit the ground.

Carole Tregoff likewise declared that they were innocent, denying that she had been involved in a conspiracy to kill Mrs Finch or that she had intended her any harm on the night in question. However, they were both charged with murder and conspiracy to murder, and brought to trial in December the same year.

The case was sensational, and various well-known people, including film actresses, attended as 'guest reporters'. But on 12 March 1960, after deliberating for nine days, the jury was unable to reach agreement and the judge declared a mistrial. Three months later, on 27 June, a second trial started before a different judge. This lasted until 7 November, making it the longest murder trial in Californian history, but ended the same way. Finally, on 27 March 1961, the jury at a third trial found Finch guilty of first-degree murder, Tregoff of second-degree murder and both of conspiracy to murder. They were both given sentences of life imprisonment.

Carole Tregoff remained in jail until 1969, when she was released on parole, having refused to answer any letters from Finch in the meantime. Her lover served another two years before he, too, was released.

Murder of Adele Kohr, 1970

On the night of 20 July 1970, Adele Kohr, a nurse in her early twenties, was driving towards her home in the village of East Islip, Long Island, when she found herself being followed by the driver of another car. Sensing that she was in danger, she tried to pull away from him, but could not do so. The man brought his car up alongside hers and appeared determined to force her to stop.

Fearing for her safety, Adele drove on, but used only her left hand to steer the car. With her other hand she scrawled notes haphazardly across the pages of a spiral-bound notebook which she normally used to record gasoline purchases and mileages. She wrote:

'A man in a car pulled alongside me ... on the Sagtikos ... he wants me to stop ... he is following me in the same lane and I can't pull away ... doing 65 ... he is alongside again ... beard ... glasses ... long hair ... hippy type ... blue shirt ... the car is a Tempest ... light green ... T-37 ...'

The man finally forced her to a halt within a quarter of a mile of her home, then quickly reversed his own car up to hers so that she could not drive off again. As he got out of the car and came towards her, she noted one last detail — 'dark pants ...' Then the man smashed her windscreen with a jack and reached in to open the door.

Adele Kohr's car was found abandoned by a patrolman not long afterwards, its headlights still switched on, its engine turning over in neutral — and the spiral-bound notebook lying on one of the seats. Her naked body was found the following morning in a small wood about twenty miles away; she had been savagely beaten, raped, murdered and then run over by her killer's car. Her death had been caused by strangulation.

Detectives of the Suffolk County Homicide Squad found Adele's notes to be of very great assistance to them in their search for the person responsible. Checking the county automobile records, they made a list of eighteen people owning Pontiac Tempests which were either green or might have appeared green in the sodium vapour light of the Sagtikos State Parkway, along which the frightened nurse had been driving. They then started to interview them in the hope that one would be found to match the dead girl's description of the killer.

One of the car-owners was found to be Linda Meyer, of Hawthorne Street, Central Islip, whose husband, a tall young man, had long hair, a beard and glasses. When asked by police officers to accompany them to head-quarters, he walked out to their waiting car without a word. By the time they arrived at the Suffolk County Police Headquarters he was utterly despondent. 'I'm sick,' he said helplessly. 'I'm very sick. I need help . . .'

It was found that he had already been tried three times for attacks on women, and that each charge had been more serious than the one before. He was also found to have kidnapped, robbed and raped a twenty-three-year-old woman from Huntingdon, Long Island, just a few weeks previously.

Brought to trial on a number of serious charges, Robert Meyer pleaded temporary insanity. He was found guilty of second-degree murder and sentenced to twenty-five years' or life imprisonment. His wife afterwards thanked the Homicide Squad detectives for the way in which they had dealt with the case. 'My husband is a sick man, and I don't believe he has any business being free,' she said.

Murder of Archibald Brown, 1943

On the afternoon of 23 July 1943, Archibald Brown, a forty-seven-year-old invalid of Rayleigh in Essex, was taken out in his wheelchair, as usual, by Nurse Mitchell, his family's resident help. After they had gone some distance along one of his favourite walks they stopped so that he could have a cigarette and the nurse could tidy his blankets. Suddenly there was a loud explosion, the invalid being blown to pieces and Nurse Mitchell thrown to the ground. An anti-tank mine, known as a Hawkins No. 75 Grenade Mine, had been attached to the seat of the wheelchair.

Nurse Mitchell, who suffered only minor injuries, told the police that the wheelchair was kept in an airraid shelter next to the victim's house in London Road when it was not in use, and that Mr Brown's nineteen-year-old son Eric had been busy inside the shelter, with the door bolted, earlier in the day. Eric, a bank clerk, was currently serving in the army, and was found to have attended lectures on the type of mine which had been used. It was also found that a store of these mines was kept at his company headquarters.

Archibald Brown had been a constant bully, and had made life difficult for the whole family. Some years earlier he had been involved in a motor-cycle accident, as a result of which he had gradually developed paralysis of the spine; since then his conduct towards his wife had been insufferable. When Eric, the elder of two sons, was questioned he admitted attaching the mine to the wheelchair, saying that he had resented the way in which his mother was treated.

'My father is now out of his suffering, and I earnestly hope that my mother will now live a much happier and normal life,' he said.

Eric Brown had difficulty accepting the fact that he was a murderer, and while in custody made an unsuccessful attempt to take his own life. At his trial in Chelmsford, in November 1943, the defence produced evidence that he was suffering from schizophrenia and the jury returned a verdict of guilty but insane.

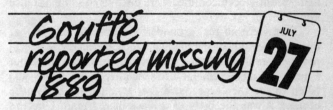

Gouffé
reported missing
1889

JULY
27

On 27 July 1889, a Paris court bailiff named Gouffé was reported missing by his brother-in-law. The police did not take the matter too seriously at first, for the forty-nine-year-old widower was known to have had affairs with at least twenty women and may well have started another. But three days later, when there was still no sign of him, Marie-François Goron, Chief of the Sûreté, decided to look into the matter himself. He had a feeling that Gouffé was in trouble.

Going to the bailiff's office in the Rue Montmartre, he found eighteen used matches on the floor near the safe. He also learnt from the concierge that on the night of 26 July an unknown man had let himself into the office, leaving shortly afterwards. It therefore seemed that this man had obtained Gouffé's keys and attempted to open the safe. Though nothing was known to have been stolen, Goron was sure that the case was important enough to justify a full-scale investigation.

He examined the bailiff's financial affairs and sent detectives to interview his mistresses. At the same time he circulated Gouffé's description to all the police forces in France, and set several clerks the task of checking provincial newspapers for reports of bodies found anywhere in the country. It was thus that he found out about the discovery of an unidentified male corpse in the village of Millery, near Lyons.

The corpse had been found in a sack on the bank of the Rhône on 13 August after villagers had reported noticing an unpleasant smell in the vicinity. The man had been strangled, and the remains of a wooden trunk in which he had evidently been confined were discovered some distance away.

There were no real grounds for Goron to believe that this was the body of the missing bailiff, especially as a local physician estimated that the man had been dead for about a year. In any case, Gouffé's brother-in-law, who was taken to see the corpse, said that it could not be Gouffé because it was the body of a black-haired man; Gouffé's hair was chestnut, he said. But Goron's instinct told him that it *was* Gouffé, and he refused to believe otherwise.

Some months afterwards, when he wrote to the Lyons police to ask what progress had been made on the case, Goron was sent some labels which had been removed from the broken trunk. Taking these to the Gare de Lyon, he found that the trunk had been transported from Paris by train on the very day that Gouffé had been reported missing.

This discovery led to an exhumation of the body, a fresh post-mortem being carried out by Professor Alexandre Lacassagne at the University of Lyons. Lacassagne found that the earlier examination had been carried out incompetently and that many of its reported findings were incorrect. The body *was* that of the missing bailiff; the hair had changed colour as a result of confinement in the trunk. To prove his point, Lacassagne washed the hair and beard with soap and water until their colour changed back to chestnut.

Goron had already discovered that a couple named Michel Eyraud and Gabrielle Bompard had disappeared from Paris on 27 July. Eyraud, a middle-aged professional swindler, and his companion, a young woman from a middle-class home who was known to have resorted to prostitution, had both been seen in Gouffé's company two days earlier, and further inquiries revealed that they had purchased a wooden trunk in London on 11 June.

Determined to trace them, Goron circulated their descriptions, together with a photograph of Eyraud, and these were published in French, British and American newspapers. As a result, on 16 January 1890, he received the first of three letters from Eyraud, all protesting his innocence and all posted in New York. Then, on 22 January Gabrielle Bompard arrived at Goron's office in the company of another man, to blame Eyraud and a stranger for the murder and claim that she had personally had no part in it. She was arrested and interrogated unmercifully for a fortnight before she finally made a confession.

She then revealed that on the night of 26 July previously she had received Gouffé in her apartment in the Rue Tronson-Ducoudray, ostensibly for the purpose of making love, while Eyraud was concealed in an alcove behind the divan. Eyraud had strangled Gouffé by hand after an elaborate attempt to hang him had failed. He had then taken the bailiff's keys and tried, also unsuccessfully, to open his safe by the light of matches. The following day the couple had taken the body to Millery and disposed of it.

Michel Eyraud remained at large until 20 May 1890, when he was arrested as he left a brothel in Havana. He was then returned to Paris where he and Gabrielle Bompard stood trial at the Seine Assize Court in December.

He was executed by guillotine in February 1891, his former companion receiving twenty years' imprisonment.

Besides being a personal triumph for Goron, the case is nowadays seen as a milestone in the history of forensic science.

Murder of Hella Christofi, 1954

On the evening of 29 July 1954, Hella Christofi, a thirty-six-year-old German woman married to a Cypriot waiter, was murdered at the couple's home in South Hill Park, Hampstead. The crime was committed by the victim's mother-in-law, Styllou Christofi, a fifty-three-year-old peasant who could speak little English, and appears to have been motivated by obsessive jealousy.

Hella and her husband Stavros had been married for fifteen years and had three children. Stavros worked at a West End restaurant, and Hella in a fashion shop. Styllou Christofi had lived with them since her arrival in London a year earlier, but it had been decided that she should return to Cyprus as she and her daughter-in-law could not get on together.

On the evening in question Styllou Christofi struck Hella with an ash-plate, fracturing her skull, and then strangled her. Shortly before midnight a neighbour walking his dog saw her trying to burn the body with newspaper in the backyard. But as the body was almost naked he assumed that it was a tailor's dummy and took no further notice.

An hour later Mrs Christofi spoke to a couple in a car near Hampstead station. 'Please come!' she said excitedly. 'Fire burning! Children sleeping!'

When the police were called the body was found to be charred and smelling of paraffin. The victim's wedding ring was discovered in her mother-in-law's bedroom.

Styllou Christofi was brought to trial at the Old Bailey. Though the prison doctor at Holloway believed her to be insane, she refused to allow a plea of insanity to be made on her behalf and so, on being found guilty, was sentenced to death. Three other doctors examined her afterwards and found her to be sane.

It was not the first time that she had been tried for murder. A similar charge had been brought against her in Cyprus in 1925, after her own mother-in-law had died as a result of having a burning torch rammed down her throat. On that occasion she had been acquitted.

Following the dismissal of her appeal, Styllou Christofi was hanged at Holloway on 13 December 1954.

Discovery of Mrs Kempson's body, 1931

AUGUST
3

On 3 August 1931, Mrs Annie Louisa Kempson, a widow in her fifties, was found murdered at her home in St Clement's Street, Oxford. Her killer had battered her over the head with a hammer in the entrance hall and then, after moving her to the dining-room, had driven a sharp instrument through her neck, severing an artery. By the time her body was discovered Mrs Kempson had been dead for two days.

The house had been ransacked and a small sum of money stolen, but a much larger amount hidden in the bedroom had not been found. It appeared that the victim had known the person responsible, for there were no signs of a forced entry and the first blow had been struck from behind. However, there were no fingerprints and the weapons used had not been left at the scene. There were no clues to the murderer's identity at all.

The police began routine inquiries in the neighbourhood, but made no progress until nine days later, when another widow, Mrs Alice Mary Andrews, was interviewed.

Mrs Andrews, who lived about ten minutes' walk from the victim's home, revealed that on the evening of 31 July a salesman named Seymour, from whom she had earlier purchased a vacuum cleaner, had called at her own house, claiming to have been robbed of all his money while he was bathing in the Thames.

Mrs Andrews had lent him 4s 6d (22½ p), but he had returned to the house later the same day, asking if she could put him up for the night as he had missed his last bus home. She had agreed to do this and the following morning, before he left, noticed that he had a hammer and chisel wrapped in brown paper. She had afterwards received a letter from him, thanking her for her kindness and enclosing a postal order for 10s 6d (52½p). This had been posted in Hove, Sussex, on 5 August but did not give Seymour's address.

Mrs Andrews also said that Mrs Kempson had bought a vacuum cleaner of the same type as her own at about the same time, and a receipt found at the dead woman's home confirmed this. Moreover, it was soon learnt from other inquiries that the salesman in question, after borrowing the 4s 6d from Mrs Andrews, had bought the hammer and chisel at a local ironmonger's shop for 4s (20p). The remainder had been spent on a shave before he and Mrs Andrews had breakfast together the following morning.

Henry Daniel Seymour turned out to be a fifty-year-old man with a long record of serious crime. He lived by housebreaking and fraud, using his job as a salesman as a means of discovering suitable victims to rob. Only a year earlier he had been in trouble for assaulting a woman during the course of one of his demonstrations.

It was learnt, too, that Seymour had left a hotel in Aylesbury, Buckinghamshire, on 31 July without paying his bill and returned surreptitiously the following afternoon (after the murder) to collect his personal belongings. On being seen by the landlord, he had then promised to pay the bill later. But the landlord had insisted on keeping his suitcase until he did so — and still had it, as Seymour had

212

not been back since.

Inside the suitcase the police found a hammer which matched the indentations in Mrs Kempson's skull. It had been soaked, and the maker's label had been removed — only to be discovered in tiny fragments when the case was subjected to closer examination.

Seymour was traced to Brighton, where he was living in lodgings. He admitted having bought the hammer and chisel on 31 July, saying that he had hoped to get a job as a carpenter, but denied all knowledge of the crime. He was unable to give a satisfactory account of his movements on the morning of 1 August, as the witnesses he named could not corroborate his story. He was charged with murder.

Brought to trial in Oxford in October the same year, he pleaded not guilty. Though there was no proof that he had been to the victim's house on the morning of the crime, there was a considerable amount of circumstantial evidence against him, and he gave a poor impression of himself when he entered the witness box. He was accordingly found guilty and sentenced to death.

His execution took place at Oxford Prison on 10 December 1931.

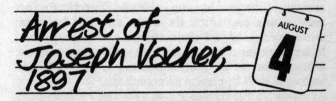

Arrest of Joseph Vacher, 1897

AUGUST 4

On 4 August 1897, a tramp attacked a woman gathering pine cones in a wood near Tournon, in southern France. The woman called to her husband, who was close at hand, and between them they overpowered the offender and took him to a nearby inn where he was forced to await the arrival of the police. Joseph Vacher, a man with a history of mental instability, was later sentenced to three months' imprisonment for an offence against public decency. But he was also questioned in connection with a series of far more serious crimes.

During the previous three and a half years no fewer than eleven sex murders had been committed in country regions in the south-east of France. The victims — seven women and four youths — had all died from strangulation or stabbing, and had afterwards been raped, mutilated or disembowelled. Though witnesses failed to identify Vacher as the person responsible for these crimes, he eventually confessed to all of them. He had committed them 'in moments of frenzy', he declared.

Born in 1869, Vacher was a member of a large peasant family; his parents had fourteen other children. While serving in the army he tried to commit suicide by cutting his throat with a razor because his expected promotion was delayed. On another occasion he shot himself with a pistol after shooting a girl in a fit of jealousy. This second attempt on his own life left him scarred and partially paralysed in the face as well as damaging one of his eyes.

After periods of confinement in two different lunatic asylums he was discharged on 1 April 1894, and began roaming the countryside, begging food from farms. He carried a large sack, a cudgel and an accordion, the contents of the sack including a set of knives. His first sex murder was committed six weeks after he had been pronounced cured, the victim being a twenty-one-year-old factory girl; his other victims were mainly farm workers. While at the inn at Tournon, waiting for the police, he amused himself by playing his accordion.

Joseph Vacher claimed that as a child he had been bitten by a mad dog, and said that he believed this to be the cause of his own madness. However, he was examined by Professor Alexandre Lacassagne and other doctors, who declared him sane. He was brought to trial at the Ain Assizes in October 1898, charged with the murder of a shepherd three years earlier, and found guilty after further speculation about his sanity.

The 'Ripper of the South-East' was executed by guillotine, at the age of twenty-nine, on 31 December 1898.

Drummond family found murdered, 1952

AUGUST
5

On the morning of 5 August 1952, French police were called to the scene of a triple murder on a riverbank near the village of Lurs in Provence. The victims — Sir Jack Drummond, a distinguished British biochemist aged sixty-one, his forty-six-year-old wife and their eleven-year-old daughter Elizabeth — had been on holiday in France and had camped at the site the previous evening. Sir Jack and Lady Drummond had both been shot; their daughter had been battered to death. The nearest house was about 150 yards away, on a farm owned by a seventy-five-year-old peasant named Gaston Dominici.

It was Dominici's thirty-three-year-old son Gustave, who lived and worked on the farm, who had raised the alarm. According to his statement, he had heard shots being fired about one o'clock in the morning, but had been too frightened to go out and investigate them. The matter had been reported after his discovery of the girl's body about 5.30 a.m. The weapon with which Sir Jack and Lady Drummond had been murdered was later recovered from the river a short distance away, its position indicating that the murderer was somebody who knew the area well. It was a carbine of a type issued to American troops during the Second World War.

Though a search of the farmhouse revealed nothing, the

215

police suspected that its inhabitants — Gaston Dominici, his son and his daughter-in-law — knew more about the crime than had so far been admitted. Little progress was made for some weeks until it was learnt from a railway worker that Elizabeth Drummond had still been alive when Gustave Dominici found her. When Gustave confirmed this, he was arrested for failing to give aid to a person who was in danger of dying. He was sentenced to two months' imprisonment, but this was afterwards quashed on appeal.

For the next twelve months Commissaire Edmond Sebeille, who was in charge of the case, persisted with his inquiries, questioning not only the inhabitants of the farmhouse but also their many relatives throughout the region. He was constantly hampered by lying, the people responsible being apparently indifferent to whether their stories sounded plausible. But eventually Gustave Dominici and his brother Clovis, aged forty-nine, admitted that their father was the murderer. The old man, cursing his sons' treachery, made a confession a few days later.

Gaston Dominici, carrying his carbine, as he always did at night, had been discovered in the act of watching Sir Jack and Lady Drummond as they undressed for the night. He had shot Sir Jack during the course of a struggle and had then killed the other two members of the family to prevent them having him arrested. Elizabeth Drummond had been attacked with the butt of the carbine as she tried to escape.

The prisoner later retracted his confession and went on to make and retract several others before being brought to trial at the Digne Assize Court in November 1954. At one point he made a counter-accusation against Gustave, and Gustave withdrew his accusation against his father and accused somebody else. On another occasion, during a reconstruction of the crime, the prisoner attempted to commit suicide by jumping from a railway bridge.

After an eleven-day trial, Gaston Dominici was found guilty and sentenced to death, the sentence being commuted to life imprisonment on account of his advanced age. He was pardoned and released on 14 July 1960, at the age of eighty-three, and died five years later.

Body found in Scottish cemetery, 1967

AUGUST 7

On the morning of 7 August 1967, the body of fifteen-year-old Linda Peacock was found in a cemetery a short distance from her home in Biggar, between Edinburgh and Glasgow. She had died as a result of head injuries and strangulation and, although no attempt had been made to rape her, there were bite-marks on one of her breasts. These marks were quite distinct, indicating that they had been made a few minutes before the girl's death. Had she lived longer, their outlines would have been masked by the spread of bruising.

Linda had been reported missing from home the previous night. The autopsy report stated that she had probably died between 10 and 11 p.m., and it was learnt that screams had been heard coming from the cemetery at 10.20 p.m. Chief Superintendent William Muncie, Head of the Lanarkshire CID, soon began to suspect that a teenager at a nearby approved school was the person responsible.

Gordon Hay, aged seventeen, had been seen lying in his bed by one of the school's masters at 10.30 p.m.; another of the masters had seen him in the dining-room just over half an hour earlier. But the school was only a few minutes' walk from the scene of the crime, and it was discovered that Hay had entered the dormitory in a dirty and dishevelled state just before 10.30 p.m. He was also found to have spoken to the victim at a fair on 5 August and to have in his possession a boat hook which could have caused her head injuries.

However, the evidence against him was insufficient to justify an arrest until Dr Warren Harvey, a consultant at the Glasgow Dental Hospital, and Detective Inspector Osborne Butler of the Identification Bureau of the Glasgow Police managed to identify him from the bite-marks on his victim's breast. This took many weeks' work of a largely experimental nature, in a branch of forensic science which was relatively new. But when Hay was finally brought to trial in Edinburgh the following year the evidence was impressive enough to satisfy the court that he was guilty.

Gordon Hay thus became the first murderer to be identified by this method in Scotland and, having been under the age of eighteen when the crime was committed, was sentenced to be detained during Her Majesty's pleasure. An appeal was subsequently heard by a panel of five judges, who upheld his conviction.

Mabel Tattershaw's body revealed, 1951

AUGUST
9

On 9 August 1951, a young man telephoned the offices of the *News of the World* in London, claiming to have found the body of a woman who had been strangled. He said that he was speaking from Nottingham and had not yet informed the police of his discovery. He offered the newspaper an exclusive story about it for £250.

While one reporter tried to get further information out of the man, another telephoned the Nottingham police. It turned out that the caller was speaking from a public call-box and when his time was up he had to give its number so that he could be recalled. The number was immediately passed to the Nottingham police, with the result that an officer arrived at the kiosk while the call was still in progress. He took the man away for questioning.

Herbert Leonard Mills, an unemployed clerk aged nineteen, then informed the police that he had found a woman's body in an orchard in Sherwood Vale, on the outskirts of Nottingham, the previous day. He said that he liked to read and write poetry, and often went to the orchard for this purpose. He afterwards led police to the place in question.

The body was found to be that of Mrs. Mabel Tattershaw, aged forty-eight of Longmead Drive, Nottingham, who had disappeared from her home on 3 August. Mrs. Tattershaw at first appeared to have died as a result of being battered with a blunt instrument; it was only when a post-mortem was carried out that strangulation was established as the cause of her death. She had not been robbed or sexually assaulted.

Herbert Mills, who said that he had not known Mrs. Tattershaw, was not regarded as a suspect and so was allowed to go free. He wrote his own account of the discovery of the body for the *News of the World*, and this was published, together with his photograph. He was, however, rebuked at the coroner's inquest for failing to tell the police about the body immediately after finding it.

For a few days the police made no real progress with the case; there seemed to have been no motive for the murder, and suggestions that Mrs. Tattershaw had had a lover proved to be unfounded. Then, suddenly, certain questions were asked about Herbert Mills and his various statements. Why had he told Norman Rae, crime reporter for the *News of the World*, that he had found the body of a woman who had been strangled when the cause of her death was not apparent at a preliminary examination by a pathologist? And why had he described her face as white and pale in his newspaper article when it had not been white and pale at all?

These doubts were confided to Norman Rae, who agreed to raise them with Mills himself. When he did so Mills began to change his story, saying that he had actually discovered the body some days earlier than he had previously claimed. The victim's face *had* been white then and the marks on her neck had been apparent, he said. Even so, the questions served to unnerve him, and at a subsequent meeting, on 24 August he admitted that *he* had been Mrs. Tattershaw's murderer.

In a fresh account of what had happened, which Rae obtained from him in writing, Mills said that he had met Mrs. Tattershaw at a cinema on 2 August while he was preoccupied with the idea of committing a 'perfect' murder. He had then met her again the following day by arrangement, and taken her to the orchard where the crime was committed. He had afterwards become impatient for the body to be discovered, so that he could gloat over the inability of the police to bring him to justice.

Mills' confession was handed to the police, and he was arrested and charged with murder. He was brought to trial at the Nottingham Assizes in November, convicted and sentenced to death. He was hanged on 11 December 1951.

Death of Cecil Hambrough, 1893

AUGUST
10

On 10 August 1893, Cecil Hambrough, a twenty-year-old lieutenant in the Yorkshire Militia, was mysteriously killed while out shooting with two other men on an estate at Ardlamont in Argyllshire. It was at first accepted that he had shot himself by accident while climbing over a dyke, but later the police learnt that the same man had almost been drowned in another 'accident' the previous day. Further inquiries then resulted in one of Hambrough's companions, Alfred John Monson, being charged not only with murder but also with attempted murder. The trial which followed attracted a great deal of attention.

Monson, an undischarged bankrupt involved in crooked financial dealings, lived in style; he had rented the estate at Ardlamont, and pretended that he was about to buy it, but in fact he had no money at all. Cecil Hambrough, the son of an impoverished landowner who had mortgaged a life interest in his own estates, lived with Monson and his family; he was completely dominated by Monson, who had originally been engaged as his tutor, and his life had been insured for £20,000, with Mrs. Monson as beneficiary in the event of his death.

Edward Sweeney, the other man present at the shooting, was a bookmaker's clerk from London, also known as Edward Davis and — in this case — Edward Scott. An associate of Monson's, he had arrived at Ardlamont on 8 August, Monson having travelled to Glasgow to meet him, and was introduced to Hambrough as 'a marine engineer'. He had disappeared almost immediately after the tragedy of 10 August and as the police could not trace him and he failed to return of his own accord, he was declared an outlaw.

Monson had earlier devised a scheme to enable him to purchase the life interest which Hambrough's father had mortgaged, but had failed in this particular venture. On moving to Ardlamont, he had arranged the insurance on the young man's life himself, using money obtained by false pretences to pay a premium of nearly £200, also on 8 August.

In the first 'accident' on 9 August, he and Hambrough, who could not swim, were fishing in Ardlamont Bay when their boat sank. The boat was found to have had a plug-hole cut into it a few hours before, apparently by Sweeney, but no cork seemed to have been provided for it. Monson, in a statement about what had happened, claimed to have

221

left Hambrough sitting on a rock while he went for a second boat in order to rescue him. But local fishermen did not know of any rocks in Ardlamont Bay.

As for the shot with which Hambrough had been killed, three experts declared that this had been fired from a distance of nine feet. It was therefore impossible for him to have killed himself by accident, as Monson maintained.

When the accused man was brought to trial in Edinburgh, in December 1893, he was thought to have no chance. However, the case proved to be far from clearcut, for evidence about the shooting was contradictory, and the financial transactions in which Monson had been involved were baffling. The judge accordingly summed up in Monson's favour, remarking that it was the business of the Crown to prove the case, and not for the defence to prove innocence. The jury then adjourned for seventy-three minutes before returning a verdict of not proven.

Not long afterwards Edward Sweeney returned to Scotland to stand trial. But when the case was called nobody appeared for the prosecution; Sweeney was therefore released.

Monson went back to his old ways, and in 1898 was sentenced to five years' penal servitude for conspiring with two others to defraud the Norwich Union Life Assurance Society. He remained an undischarged bankrupt for the rest of his life.

Murder of three police officers, 1966

On the afternoon of 12 August 1966, the crew of a police patrol car stopped three men in a blue Vanguard shooting-brake in Braybrook Street, near Wormwood Scrubs Prison in London. Detective Sergeant Christopher Head and Detective Constable David Wombwell, got out to question the driver and found that he had no tax disc and that his insurance had expired. Head left Wombwell to write down the particulars while he went to inspect the rear of the car. Suddenly there was a shot and the young detective constable fell to the ground, fatally injured. He had been shot in the left eye.

Two of the three men got out of the Vanguard, both armed with guns. Head ran to the patrol car to take cover, but was shot in the back and fell in front of it. One of the gunmen then ran over and fired three shots at Police Constable Geoffrey Fox, who was still in his driving-seat with the engine running — too shocked to know what to do. As one of the bullets entered his left temple, his foot pushed down on the accelerator and the patrol car lurched forward. Head, who was dying, was trapped underneath it. Police Constable Fox lay dead at the wheel.

The two gunmen returned to the Vanguard, which was then driven in reverse along Braybrook Street. A moment later, it turned and sped away. But its licence number had already been noted by a married couple in another car, who suspected that a jail-break had just taken place. It was as a result of this that the culprits were quickly identified.

The owner of the car was found to be John Witney, a thirty-six-year-old unemployed man with ten convictions for petty theft. He lived with his wife in a basement flat in Fernhead Road, Paddington, where two police officers called to see him within six hours of the murder of their three colleagues. Witney, who was trembling and sweating, claimed that he had sold the car to a stranger for £15. The two police officers took him to Shepherd's Bush police station, where he was detained.

Though a search of his flat revealed no incriminating evidence, the Vanguard was found the following day in a garage rented by Witney in a railway arch at Vauxhall; used cartridges and car-theft equipment were found inside

223

it. On 14 August, when charged with the three murders, Witney admitted that he had been the driver on the day in question and named two other men as the gunmen. The three men, who had committed various robberies together, had been afraid that Head and Wombwell would search the Vanguard and find their guns.

The men Witney named were Harry Roberts, a thirty-year-old man with convictions for attempted store-breaking, larceny and robbery with violence, and John Duddy, aged thirty-seven, a long-distance lorry-driver who had been in trouble several times for theft in his youth. Both were found to be missing from their homes.

Duddy, a Scotsman, was arrested in Glasgow on 16 August. In a statement, which he afterwards denied having made, he said, 'It was Roberts who started the shooting. He shot two who got out of the car and shouted to me to shoot. I just grabbed a gun and ran to the police car and shot the driver through the window. I must have been mad.'

The search for Roberts intensified, with a reward of £1000 being offered for information leading to his capture. Yet he remained at large until 15 November, when he was found asleep in a barn at the edge of Nathan's Wood, in Hertfordshire. Taken to Bishop's Stortford police station, he then confessed his part in the 'Massacre of Braybrook Street'. He was committed for trial.

Witney and Duddy had already been brought to trial at the Old Bailey on 14 November, but when news of Roberts' capture was received the trial was adjourned so that the three prisoners could appear together. The following month they were all convicted of murder and possessing firearms, and the judge, in passing sentences of life imprisonment on each of them, recommended that they should serve at least thirty years.

John Duddy died in Parkhurst Prison, at the age of fifty-two, in February 1981.

Execution of Arthur Devereux, 1905

Arthur Devereux, who was hanged at Pentonville Prison on 15 August 1905, was a twenty-four-year-old chemist's assistant who had murdered his wife and their twin sons by poisoning them with morphine. The bodies of his victims had been discovered in a tin trunk in a furniture depository in Harrow, Middlesex, the previous April. The top of the trunk had been coated with a mixture of glue and boric acid to make it airtight.

Arthur and Beatrice Devereux had been living in a back street in Kilburn, London, when the twins were born. They had an older son, Stanley, of whom Devereux was extremely fond. However, his wages were low and his wife was already under-nourished; he knew that he would be unable to support a larger family. In January 1905, having decided to murder Beatrice and the two younger children, Devereux acquired a trunk and a bottle of poison.

He induced his wife to drink some of the poison, and also to give some of it to the twins, by telling her that it was cough medicine. He afterwards had the trunk — with the three bodies inside it — removed to the furniture depository, claiming that it was 'filled with domestic articles', and moved with six-year-old Stanley to another part of London. He managed to find Stanley a place in a private school.

When his mother-in-law asked what had become of Beatrice, Devereux answered evasively. She, becoming suspicious, made inquiries among the couple's former neighbours in Kilburn and learnt of the trunk being taken away in a Harrow company's van. Having located the company, she obtained authority to have the trunk opened, and then her fears were confirmed. Inspector Pollard of

225

Scotland Yard was put in charge of the case.

Devereux, in the meantime, had moved to Coventry, where he was working in a similar job to the one he had had before. When visited by Pollard, he did not even wait to be told the purpose of the inspector's visit before stammering, 'You have made a mistake. I don't know anything about a tin trunk.'

At his trial at the Old Bailey, in July 1905, he claimed that his wife had poisoned the twins and then herself, and that he, fearing that he would be suspected of murdering them all, had panicked and hidden the bodies. But it was pointed out by the prosecution that Devereux, in applying for a new job while his wife was still alive, had described himself as a widower.

This was seen as evidence of premeditated murder on his part, and he was convicted and sentenced to death.

Execution of Thomas Allaway, 1922

AUGUST 19

On 19 August 1922, Thomas Henry Allaway, a thirty-six-year-old private chauffeur, was hanged for the murder of Irene Wilkins, following a five-day-trial at Winchester the previous month. The crime had been committed on 22 December 1921, the victim's body being found on waste ground on the outskirts of Bournemouth the following morning. She had been killed by blows with a heavy car spanner after an unsuccessful attempt at rape.

Irene Wilkins, aged thirty-one, was the daughter of a barrister; she was unmarried and lived in Streatham, London. On the day of her death she had an advertisement published in the *Morning Post*, seeking employment as a cook, and within hours had received a telegram asking her to travel to Bournemouth to meet a prospective employer. She left Waterloo the same afternoon and arrived in Bournemouth about 7 p.m. The murder took place a short while afterwards.

A car designer informed police that he had seen the victim being driven from Bournemouth Central Station in a Mercedes and was even able to give the car's licence number. But for some reason his statement was overlooked during the early part of the investigation, the police believing that their only clues were tyre marks found at the scene of the crime and the telegram message in the murderer's handwriting. The investigation thus took considerably longer than necessary.

It was discovered that two other telegrams of the same type had been sent from the same area during the previous few days in reply to similar advertisements; both had been ignored by their recipients. The postal clerks concerned in each case could only vaguely remember the person who had handed in the message, though one said she believed it to have been a chauffeur 'with a rough voice'.

Eventually the police began to suspect Allaway, who was employed by one of the residents of nearby Boscombe. And it was at this point that the car designer's statement came to light, the licence number which he had given proving to be that of the car owned by Allaway's employer. The police then started trying to find a sample of Allaway's handwriting, to compare with that of the telegram messages.

Allaway, on learning that he was under suspicion, suddenly fled from Bournemouth, having stolen some of his employer's cheques and passed them off with forged signatures on local tradesmen. He was arrested at his wife's home in Reading on 28 April with betting slips in his pocket which bore the same handwriting as the telegram. Further samples of his handwriting were found at his lodgings in Boscombe, and the car designer and another witness identified him as the man who had been at

Bournemouth Central Station in a car on the evening in question.

At his trial Allaway claimed to have been alone at his lodgings reading a newspaper for part of that evening, and tried to give himself an alibi by saying that he had spoken to his landlord about the time of the murder. His landlord, however, said that Allaway had never spent the evening alone in his lodgings; he had always gone out about 6.30 p.m. and stayed out the whole evening. Allaway, in fact, gave a very poor impression of himself under cross-examination, and so was found guilty. It has since been revealed that he confessed to the crime on the night before his execution.

Arrest of Henri Girard, 1918

AUGUST 21

On 21 August 1918, Henri Girard, a French swindler, was arrested in Paris following an insurance company's investigation of the death of Mme Monin, a war widow who had collapsed and died at a Métro station. A policy had been taken out on her life by one of Girard's mistresses, and it was discovered that Mme Monin had visited Girard's apartment just before her death and been given an apéritif there. Her death was found to have been caused by bacterial poisoning.

Girard, who called himself a bookmaker, already had a criminal record as a result of a fraudulent company which he had set up nine years earlier. But he had lived by fraud ever since his dishonourable discharge from the Tenth Hussars in 1897, and his suspended prison sentence and 1000 franc fine on that occasion had not caused him to change his ways. Indeed, it was discovered that since that time he had made other attempts at poisoning as a means of financing his extravagant lifestyle, though he had only succeeded once.

In that case, in 1912, he had done well for himself. His victim, an insurance broker named Louis Pernotte, had admired Girard so much that in 1910 he had given him power of attorney over his estate. Girard had Pernotte's life insured for over 300,000 francs (using several different companies), and in August 1912, just before the broker and his family left on a trip to Royan, poured typhoid bacilli into a water carafe on their lunch table.

Pernotte, his wife and their two children were all taken ill, and when they returned to Paris some months later the broker had still not fully recovered. Girard was therefore allowed to give him a daily injection, as a result of which he died shortly afterwards. Then, having murdered her husband, Girard somehow convinced Mme Pernotte that she owed him 200,000 francs.

Whatever doubts she may have had about it, she paid him that sum, and the crime remained undetected for the next six years.

Girard had a laboratory in an apartment in the Avenue de Neuilly, where he also kept one of his other two mistresses. There, some years after the death of Pernotte, he experimented with poisonous mushrooms, having taken out insurance policies on the lives of two other unsuspecting people. However, both of these intended victims survived the attempts on their lives, neither of them realizing that Girard was responsible for the illnesses which they suffered.

Following his arrest, Girard remained in prison for nearly three years while the police made extensive inquiries about his activities, and built up a case which they hoped would send him to the guillotine. Finally, in May 1921, while still waiting to be brought to trial, he killed himself by swallowing a germ culture which he had managed to acquire. He was forty-six years old.

Christine Darby found murdered, 1967

AUGUST 22

On 22 August 1967, the body of seven-year-old Christine Darby, who had been abducted from outside her home in Walsall, Staffordshire, three days earlier, was found on Cannock Chase, fourteen miles away; she had been sexually assaulted and suffocated. Tyre marks were discovered nearby, and Identikit pictures were issued of a man who had been seen driving a grey Austin car in the area on the day of the child's disappearance. He did not come forward.

During the investigation which followed the owners of over 23,000 grey Austins were interviewed and extensive house-to-house inquiries carried out. But the suspect was not traced until November 1968, when a woman in Walsall saw a man trying to entice a girl of ten into a car.

The girl resisted and the man, realizing that he was being watched, drove off. But the witness, having made a note of his car number, reported the incident to the police.

The car-owner was found to be Raymond Leslie Morris, a thirty-nine-year-old foreman engineer who lived with his second wife in the same town. It was discovered that Morris, in 1966, had been accused of interfering with little girls, and that at the time of Christine Darby's murder he had owned a grey Austin. He was later identified as the man who had been seen on Cannock Chase on the day of Christine's disappearance. His arrest took place on 15 November 1968.

Raymond Morris was found to be a well-liked man with both charm and intelligence. But his first wife, whom he had divorced, revealed that at the time of their marriage he had been a fantasist whose sexual demands exhausted her. At his home police found pornographic films and indecent photographs of a small girl.

Morris's second wife had at first given him an alibi, claiming that he had been out shopping with her on the day of Christine Darby's abduction. However, she had afterwards changed her mind about this, saying that she had been mistaken.

At his trial at the Staffordshire Assizes, in February 1969, Raymond Morris was convicted and sentenced to life imprisonment. The murders of two other little girls, whose bodies had also been found on Cannock Chase, have never been solved.

A6 murder 1961

AUGUST 23

During the early hours of 23 August 1961, a shooting took place in a lay-by on the A6 in Bedfordshire which has since been the subject of much controversy. The victims were Michael Gregsten, a young research scientist who was shot dead, and his girlfriend Valerie Storie, who was also shot but managed to survive. The crime led to the execution of James Hanratty, a twenty-five-year-old petty criminal whose guilt has been disputed in at least three books on the case.

On the night of 22 August the two lovers, according to Valerie Storie's account, were sitting in a parked car near Windsor when they were held up by a man with a gun. The man got into the back seat of the car and forced Gregsten to drive at gunpoint until they reached the isolated stretch of the A6 known as Deadman's Hill, near Clophill. There he ordered him to pull into the lay-by, saying that he wanted to sleep but had first to tie them up.

Having tied Miss Storie's hands, he told Gregsten to

231

pass him a duffle bag. But as Gregsten moved to do so the gunman fired two bullets into his head, killing him instantly; he said the victim had moved too quickly and frightened him. A few minutes later he raped Valerie Storie, then made her help him to move the dead man's body out on to the ground. Finally, he shot her five times at close range and made off in the car on his own.

Valerie Storie lay on the ground, paralysed in both legs and semi-conscious, until a farm worker found her about 6.30 a.m. The car was found abandoned in Ilford, the murder weapon on a London bus. Two cartridge cases from the same gun were later found in a London hotel room which had been occupied by Hanratty — using a different name — on the night before the murder, and by a man named Peter Louis Alphon the following night.

The police at first suspected Alphon of the murder, and announced that they wanted to interview him in connection with it. He came forward of his own accord on 22 September and was held in custody until Valerie Storie picked out a different man at an identification parade at Guy's Hospital, where she was a patient, on 24 September. He was then released, the police turning their attention to Hanratty, who was later arrested in Blackpool.

Three weeks after the first identification parade Miss Storie was asked to attend another; this time she asked if she could hear the men speak. She was wheeled along the line several times, asking each man in turn to say, as the gunman had said after shooting Gregsten: 'Be quiet, will you? I'm thinking.' This time she identified Hanratty.

Hanratty's trial at the Bedford Assizes was the longest murder trial in English history, lasting twenty-one days. The defence made much of the fact that Valerie Storie had picked out a different man at the first identification parade, and also the Identikit picture constructed from her description, which bore a greater resemblance to the clerk of the court, who had to hold it up, than to the prisoner.

The prosecution, however, was helped when Hanratty, after claiming to have been in Liverpool at the time of the murder, suddenly changed his story and said that he was in Rhyl. Even so, it took the jury nine and a half hours to bring in a verdict of guilty.

Following Hanratty's execution, which took place at Bedford on 4 April 1962, witnesses were found who said that they thought they had seen him in Rhyl about the time of the murder, and Peter Alphon made a written statement declaring that *he* was the A6 murderer.

While these developments have helped to convince many people that Hanratty was the victim of a miscarriage of justice, many others have remained unshaken in their belief that he was guilty.

Murder of Mrs Caroline Luard, 1908

AUGUST
24

On the afternoon of 24 August 1908, Mrs. Caroline Luard, fifty-eight-year-old wife of a retired army officer, was shot dead in a summer-house close to the couple's home at Ightham, near Sevenoaks, Kent. The murder took place at 3.15 p.m., the shots being heard by others in the vicinity. The body was discovered by the victim's husband, Major-General Charles Luard, when he went to look for her during the early evening.

The Luards had left their home together at 2.30 that afternoon, the General, who was sixty-nine years old, intending to walk to his golf club at Godden Green, three miles away. Mrs. Luard accompanied him to a nearby village on her way to the unoccupied summer-house at Fish Ponds Woods. On his return to Ightham at 4.30 p.m., the General was surprised to find that she was not back because they had invited a friend to tea. Later, after entertaining the visitor, the General went to the summer-house on his own, and found his wife's body on the verandah.

Mrs. Luard had been shot twice through the head. Some valuable rings had been taken from the fingers of her left hand and her purse was also missing. Though there were no clues to the identity of the murderer, and the victim had had no known enemies, the Reverend R.B. Cotton, a friend of the Luards, told the coroner's inquest that he had seen a 'sandy-haired tramp' emerging from the woods about the time of her death. But it had been established at the post-mortem that Mrs. Luard had been dead for some time before her rings were removed.

Following the adjournment of the inquest, General Luard, already grief-stricken by the loss of his wife, became the main suspect in the case and began to receive abusive letters. Witnesses who appeared later testified that they had seen him on the day of the murder, their evidence showing clearly that he could not have been at the summer-house at the time of Mrs. Luard's death. Even the coroner saw fit to say that the General could not have committed the murder. But these statements failed to alleviate his distress.

Putting his home up for sale, General Luard went to stay with a friend. Not long afterwards he threw himself under a train, leaving a note saying that he had gone to join his wife.

Two years later, when John Alexander Dickman was convicted of the murder of John Nisbet, a colliery wages clerk, it seems to have been believed in some circles that he was also the murderer of Mrs. Luard. Dickman, it was said, had met Mrs. Luard at the summer-house after she had written to him about a cheque which he had forged on her account, and had killed her in order to conceal the crime.

However, an account of the case published by ex-Superintendent Percy Savage in 1938 states: 'It remains an unsolved mystery. All our work was in vain. The murderer was never caught, as not a scrap of evidence was forthcoming on which we could justify an arrest, and to this day, I frankly admit that I have no idea who the criminal was.'

Crime of Dr. Geza de Kaplany, 1962

On 28 August 1962, a young married woman in San José, California, was admitted to hospital with third-degree burns covering sixty per cent of her body. Her breasts and genitals had been particularly badly burnt and her eyes were in such a frightful state that the pupils could not be seen. Hajna de Kaplany, twenty-year-old wife of a hospital anaesthetist, was writhing in agony when police arrived at her apartment, and ambulance men burnt their hands on her body when they moved her. She had been soaked in acid.

The police had been called to the apartment block by other residents, who reported hearing a horrifying wail against background sounds of loud classical music and running water. They found, in the couple's apartment, disintegrating, acid-soaked bedclothes, a large hole in the bedroom carpet, a leather carrying-case containing bottles of sulphuric, hydrochloric and nitric acids — the last of these only one-third full — a pair of rubber gloves and a medical prescription form on which a note had been written.

The note read: 'If you want to live — do not shout; do what I tell you; or else you will die.'

Dr Geza de Kaplany, aged thirty-six, was a Hungarian refugee working at one of the San José hospitals; he and his wife, a former model, had been married for only five weeks. He admitted responsibility for his wife's injuries,

235

telling police that he had soaked her in acid in order to deprive her of her beauty and warn her against adultery. When his wife died, after thirty-six days of intense suffering, he was charged with her murder.

De Kaplany, the 'Acid Doctor', was brought to trial in San José on 7 January 1963. He faced the court calmly at first, but became hysterical when photographic evidence of the crime was produced. Having already pleaded not guilty and not guilty by reason of insanity, he then declared that he was guilty. The reason given for the terrible way in which he had treated his wife was that his love for her had been rejected.

The jury reached a verdict of guilty on 1 March, the trial having lasted thirty-five days, and de Kaplany was sentenced to life imprisonment. He was released on parole in 1976, and went to work in Taiwan as a missionary.

Nancy Chadwick found murdered, 1948

AUGUST
29

On 29 August 1948, the body of Nancy Chadwick, an eccentric sixty-eight-year-old widow who worked as a housekeeper, was found at a roadside in Rawtenstall, Lancashire. She appeared at first to have been the victim of a hit-and-run accident, but on examination was found to have been battered over the head. The body was found by a bus driver near a house occupied by Margaret Allen, a forty-two-year-old lesbian, early in the morning.

Margaret Allen, a former bus conductress who called herself 'Bill', took a keen interest in the investigation which followed, and it was she who drew a constable's attention to the dead woman's empty handbag, which was lying in a river behind her home. During the two days which followed the discovery of the body she spoke to newspaper reporters — as well as anyone else who was willing to listen to her — in a local public house, suggesting reasons for the murder. Mrs. Chadwick had been an old fool to sit on a roadside bench counting her money, she said on one occasion.

Margaret Allen was a short, sturdy woman with cropped hair; she wore men's clothes and was generally unkempt. The twentieth of twenty-two children, she lived alone, smoking heavily and neglecting the need for proper meals. She was known to have a violent temper, and it was not long before her interest in Mrs. Chadwick's murder began to arouse suspicion. On 31 August she was interviewed by police officers, and the following day her home was searched. When bloodstains were found there she confessed to the crime.

Mrs. Chadwick, she said, had turned up at her house and asked to be allowed inside. Margaret Allen had not wanted to let her in, but the old woman 'seemed to insist' on it. A hammer was lying in the kitchen at the time, and Allen hit her with it on the spur of the moment. At this, '. . . she gave a shout and that seemed to start me off more, and I hit her a few times — I don't know how many . . .' The body was hidden in the coal-house before being taken out and placed at the roadside after dark.

At her trial, which lasted only five hours, a plea of insanity was made on Margaret Allen's behalf, and her only close friend, Mrs. Annie Cook, gave evidence of the prisoner's history of depression and headaches. The accused did not give evidence herself, and the jury took just fifteen minutes to find her guilty. She was sentenced to death.

Mrs. Cook afterwards organized a petition in favour of a reprieve, but such was the prisoner's reputation that only 152 of the town's 26,000 inhabitants signed it. Ill-tempered to the end, Margaret Allen was hanged at Strangeways Prison on 12 January 1949. She was the first woman to be executed in Britain for twelve years.

Arrest of John and Janet Armstrong, 1956

On 1 September 1956, John Armstrong, a naval sickberth attendant, and his wife Janet were arrested for the murder of their five-month-old son Terence, who had died from barbiturate poisoning at their home in Gosport, near Portsmouth, on 22 July the previous year.

John Armstrong, at the time of the child's death, was twenty-five-years old and his wife nineteen. Their eldest child, Pamela, who was three, had been ill two months earlier, but had recovered in hospital; their second, a boy, had died at the age of three months in 1954. The illness, in each case, seemed to follow the same course.

Terence was at first thought to have died as a result of eating poisonous berries from the couple's garden, for the pathologist who carried out the postmortem found what appeared to be red skins in his stomach and throat.

But it was later found that these 'red skins' were, in fact, gelatine capsules which had contained Seconal, a powerful sleep-inducing drug. When the child's body was exhumed for re-examination, he was found to have swallowed enough of these capsules to cause his death in less than an hour.

Neither of the parents appeared grief-stricken over the loss of the child, and, though both denied that there had ever been any Seconal in the house, it was discovered that fifty capsules of it had been stolen in February 1955 from the hospital where John Armstrong worked. However, it was considered that there was not enough evidence to prove that either John or Janet Armstrong was guilty of murder, so neither was arrested at that time.

A year later, on 24 July 1956, Janet Armstrong applied to the Gosport magistrates for a separation order and maintenance, alleging that her husband had repeatedly used violence against her, but the order was refused.

As she left the court in tears, a senior police officer approached her and asked whether she had anything she wanted to tell him. She then said that her husband had had Seconal in the house at the time of Terence's death, and that she had afterwards disposed of it at his request. She made a written statement giving the same information, and this additional piece of evidence led to a reconsideration of whether murder charges could be justified.

As both parents had been in the house at the time the capsules were swallowed, and as it appeared from other evidence that an unsuccessful attempt had been made to poison the child the previous day — at a time when the father was not there — it was decided that John and Janet Armstrong should be jointly charged.

They were brought to trial together in Winchester in December 1956, both pleading not guilty and accusing each other of the crime. John Armstrong was convicted, his death sentence being afterwards commuted to life imprisonment; his wife was acquitted. A month later Janet Armstrong admitted that she had given the child a capsule of Seconal to help him sleep.

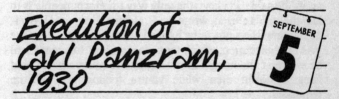

Execution of Carl Panzram, 1930

SEPTEMBER 5

The American murderer Carl Panzram, who was hanged on 5 September 1930, was a native of Warren, Minnesota; his parents were Prussian immigrants. Born in 1891, he turned to crime at an early age; he committed robberies at eleven, and was sent to a reform school, which he burnt down, at twelve. He never changed, except for the worse: he lived by robbery and burglary for the rest of his life — at least, when he was not in prison — and also committed many sex crimes, including murders.

'In my lifetime, I have murdered twenty-one human beings,' he declared in his autobiography. 'I have committed thousands of burglaries, robberies, larcenies, arsons and last but not least, I have committed sodomy on more than 1000 male human beings.'

The various accounts of his life, taken together, suggest that he actually killed rather more than twenty-one people; it is said, for example, that he killed ten people in one year alone. But it is impossible to say whether these claims are really true. Panzram was contemptuous of the rest of society and boasted about his crimes for the sake of being offensive. It is by no means inconceivable that he exaggerated for the same reason.

Panzram, at any rate, was arrested in Washington in 1928 for burglary and murder, and given a long term of imprisonment in Fort Leavenworth. 'I'll kill the first man who bothers me!' he threatened. On 20 June 1929, he killed Robert Warnke, the prison laundry superintendent. It was for this that he was sentenced to death.

He showed no remorse for his crimes and scoffed at opponents of the death penalty who tried to get him reprieved. 'I wish you all had one neck, and I had my hands on it,' he said. 'I believe the only way to reform people is to kill them.' He even wrote to President Herbert Hoover, demanding the right to be hanged without delay.

At his execution, which took place at Fort Leavenworth, he swore at the hangman, telling him to hurry up. 'I could hang a dozen men while you're fooling around!' he remarked.

His autobiography was published forty years later.

Thirteen murders in Camden, New Jersey, 1949

On the morning of 6 September 1949, Howard Unruh, a twenty-eight-year-old recluse, entered a shoemaker's shop a few doors from his home in Camden, New Jersey, armed with a Luger pistol and shot the shoemaker dead. Immediately afterwards he went to the barber's shop next door and killed the barber and a six-year-old boy whose hair he had been cutting. He then went to a drugstore next to the building in which he lived and, having shot a customer who was about to enter, killed the druggist, his wife and his mother.

Having thus murdered seven people in under six minutes, Unruh, who hated all his neighbours, began walking about outside, firing at anyone who could not take cover quickly enough. A man getting out of a delivery truck was shot dead; a youth crossing the road was wounded in the thigh and ankle; a young married woman was killed in her husband's cleaning shop, and a child of two was shot dead at the window of his parents' home.

By this time the street was almost deserted. Shopkeepers were locking and barricading their shops; urgent calls were being made for police, ambulances and doctors. The proprietor of a cafe shot the gunman from behind, causing a wound which made him limp. But he went on looking for more victims, and when a car stopped at the street corner, waiting for the traffic light to change, he killed its three occupants — a woman driver, her sixty-seven-year-old mother and her nine-year-old son. He then turned the corner and entered a house.

A woman screamed; her seventeen-year-old son tried to tackle him. But Unruh struck the youth over the head with his pistol and shot him in the arm. The woman was

241

shot in the shoulder.

When he finally ran out of ammunition the gunman returned to the flat where he and his mother lived and barricaded himself in his bedroom. Having more ammunition there, he started firing from the window. But when the police closed in on him and hurled tear-gas into the room he gave himself up. He had killed thirteen people in fifteen minutes, and was later found to have a bullet from the cafe proprietor's gun lodged in his spine.

The police found other weapons in the basement of the building, where Unruh had set up a shooting range. They also learnt that before going out into the street that morning he had attempted to kill his mother.

Howard Unruh had no criminal record. He had served as a tank machine-gunner in Italy and France during the Second World War and, on returning to the United States, started to study pharmacy. However, he was seething with resentment towards his neighbours, seeing himself as a victim of frequent insults and irritations.

'I knew that some day I would kill them all,' he told the District Attorney, showing no remorse for his crimes.

Unruh was observed for a month by four psychiatrists, who found him to be mentally ill. Instead of being brought to trial, he was committed to the Trenton State Hospital for the Insane.

Madame Fahmy brought to trial, 1923

SEPTEMBER
10

On 10 September 1923, Marie-Marguerite Fahmy, a beautiful Frenchwoman of thirty-two, was brought to trial at the Old Bailey for the murder of her playboy husband,

Prince Ali Kamel Fahmy Bey, a wealthy Egyptian ten years her junior. Prince Fahmy had been shot and fatally wounded at London's Savoy Hotel, where the couple had occupied a luxury suite, in the early hours of 10 July previously, and the coroner's inquest had concluded with a verdict of wilful murder against his wife. When Mme Fahmy pleaded not guilty to the charge, the prosecuting counsel outlined the case.

It was explained that Fahmy Bey, the son of an engineer, had inherited his wealth from his father. He had met the prisoner, a divorcée, in Paris in May the previous year, and they had married a few months later, after she had become a Muslim. However, they had not been happy together and appeared to be incompatible.

Arriving in London at the beginning of July 1923, they had had a disagreement over an operation which the prisoner was to have, and at supper in the hotel restaurant on 9 July Mme Fahmy had allegedly threatened to smash a bottle over her husband's head. Later, after they had returned to their suite, a luggage porter heard three shots and arrived in time to see Mme Fahmy throwing down a pistol. Her husband, who was lying on the floor, was bleeding from the head. He died in hospital soon afterwards.

Seid Enani, who had been Prince Fahmy's secretary, was called as a witness and gave details of his late master's life and marriage. Cross-examined by Sir Edward Marshall Hall, he denied that Fahmy Bey had treated his wife 'with persistent cruelty', but acknowledged that he had been 'a bit unkind' to her. He was then obliged to admit that on one occasion Fahmy had struck the prisoner on the chin and dislocated her jaw.

'They were always quarrelling,' said Seid Enani.

The gun which had been used on the night of Fahmy's death was a .32 Browning automatic, capable of holding eight cartridges. Though it loaded automatically, the trigger had to be pressed for each shot. However, the prosecution's expert witness, Robert Churchill, conceded that when the gun was gripped tightly little pressure was needed to fire it.

A doctor who had been called to the scene of the tragedy said that he had been shown marks on Mme Fahmy's neck which, under cross-examination, he agreed could have been caused by a hand clutching her throat. Asked about the complaint for which an operation had been thought necessary, he said that it was a painful complaint which could have been caused by her husband, whose sexual demands were alleged by the defence to have been abnormal.

Called to give evidence in her own defence, the prisoner, speaking through an interpreter, said that her husband's black valet had followed her around continually and had been in the practice of entering her room when she was dressing. When she complained to her husband, he replied that the valet had the right to do this. 'He does not count,' said Fahmy. 'He is nobody.'

She went on to say that on one occasion, in Paris, her husband had seized her by the throat and threatened her with a horse-whip, and that on another he had sworn on the Koran that he would kill her. On a further occasion, she said, he had held her prisoner aboard his yacht for three days. 'Every time I threatened to leave him, he cried and promised to mend his ways,' said Mme Fahmy.

Asked about the night of his death, she said that she had picked up the revolver, which he had given her himself, when her husband advanced on her in a threatening manner during the course of a quarrel. She claimed that, having already fired one bullet out of the window, by accident, she had not realized that it was in a condition to be fired again.

'He seized me suddenly and brutally by the throat with his left hand,' she continued. 'His thumb was on my windpipe and his fingers were pressing on my neck. I pushed him away, but he crouched to spring on me, and said, "I will kill you."

'I lifted my arm in front of me and, without looking, pulled the trigger. The next moment I saw him on the ground before me without realizing what had happened. I do not know how many times the revolver went off. I did not know what had happened.'

Under cross-examination she said that she had not wanted to kill her husband. 'I only wanted to prevent him killing me,' she maintained. 'I thought the sight of the pistol might frighten him.'

The prisoner's sister, maid and chauffeur all corroborated her claims of ill-treatment at her husband's hands, and on the fifth day of the trial, after a moving speech by Marshall Hall which held the spectators spellbound, the jury returned a verdict of not guilty. At this, there were loud cheers and the judge ordered the court to be cleared.

'Oh, I am so happy, I am so thankful,' said Mme Fahmy as she was helped from the dock. 'It is terrible to have killed Ali, but I spoke the truth. I spoke the truth.'

The trial prompted an editorial in the *Daily Mirror*, stating that marriages between Oriental men and Western women were ridiculous and unseemly.

Death of Ada Baguley, 1935

SEPTEMBER
11

During the early hours of 11 September 1935, Ada Baguley, a bedridden fifty-year-old spinster weighing seventeen stone, died at a 'nursing home for aged and chronic cases' in Devon Drive, Nottingham, run by Dorothea Waddingham, an unqualified nurse aged thirty-six, and her thirty-nine-year-old lover, Ronald Sullivan. Her death was at first thought to have been caused by a cerebral haemorrhage, but a post-mortem revealed the presence of morphine in her body. The morphine had not been prescribed by the home physician.

Miss Baguley, who suffered from disseminated sclerosis, had been placed in the home in the company of her eighty-nine-year-old mother by the County Nursing Association the previous January. There was only one other patient there at the time — a Mrs. Kemp, who died shortly afterwards. But the new arrivals were satisfied with the care they received and, after a trial period lasting three weeks, agreed to remain there.

In May 1935 Ada Baguley, who owned a small business, made a will leaving her property to 'Nurse' Waddingham and her lover, in return for a promise that she and her mother would be looked after for the rest of their lives. But her mother's health began to decline almost immediately afterwards, and she died a few days later.

When Ada Baguley died Dorothea Waddingham sent the home physician a note which her patient had evidently signed a few days earlier. The note, which had been written by Sullivan, read: 'I desire to be cremated at my death, for health's sake and it is my wish to remain with Nurse and my last wish is my Relatives shall not know of my Death.' Sullivan had signed it himself as a witness.

When this note was forwarded to the Nottingham Medical Officer of Health, whose consent was needed before the cremation could take place, a post-mortem was ordered and a police investigation began. Mrs. Baguley's body was exhumed, and this was also found to contain morphine.

Dorothea Waddingham, a former ward orderly at the Burton-on-Trent workhouse, had a criminal record for theft and fraud. She had been married to a man named Thomas Leech, but reverted to her maiden name after his death. She was brought to trial at the Nottingham Assizes in February 1936, charged with Ada Baguley's murder.

Ronald Sullivan, who had won the Military Medal for gallantry during the First World War, was also brought to trial, but he was soon released as there was no direct evidence of his involvement in the crime.

Dorothea Waddingham denied responsiblity for Ada

Baguley's death, claiming that she had only given her morphine in accordance with her doctor's instructions. But the doctor told the court that he had never prescribed the drug and the prisoner was convicted. Despite a recommendation of mercy from the jury, she was hanged at Winson Green Prison, Birmingham, on 16 April 1936, shortly after writing a letter to Sullivan in which she asked him not to be afraid for her.

Budapest-Vienna Express blown up, 1931

SEPTEMBER 12

About midnight on 12 September 1931, the Budapest-Vienna night express train was blown up by a device placed on the Bia-Torbagy Viaduct in eastern Hungary. Twenty-two people were killed and fourteen others taken to a hospital in Budapest, seriously injured. A letter found near the scene suggested that the explosion had been caused by political extremists, and the Hungarian police suspected that it was the work of the same person or group of people who had blown up the Basle-Berlin Express at Jüterbog — causing many other casualties — on 8 August the same year.

Among the journalists who hurried to the scene during the next few hours was Hans Habe who, at twenty, was chief reporter for two Viennese newspapers. Speaking to survivors, he found several of them too shocked to be able to give him any information about the disaster. So, when a burly man of about forty with a military haircut introduced himself and began to give details of his own accord, Habe naturally took an interest in him, and later gave him a lift back to Vienna.

247

The man, Sylvester Matuska, was a Hungarian businessman living in Vienna with his wife and daughter; he said that he had been staying in Budapest on business. Far from being in a state of shock, he described the accident at length and gave the impression of being pleased to be the centre of attention. Later, in Vienna, he provided Habe with drawings of the wreckage and photographs of himself. The newspaper reports which resulted from this caused a sensation.

Having drawn so much attention to himself, however, Matuska was regarded with suspicion by both the Austrian and the Hungarian police. It was found that none of the other passengers could remember seeing him on the train; it was also discovered that he had secretly acquired large quantities of explosive from two different munitions factories prior to the crime. The police officers concerned therefore suspected that, although Matuska had bought a ticket for the journey to Vienna, he had actually travelled to the viaduct by car and arrived there in time to place the explosive on the track.

Arrested in October, Matuska was questioned not only about that particular explosion, but also about the one at Jüterbog, together with an earlier attempt at a similar crime at Anzbach in Lower Austria. He made a confession, and was brought to trial in Vienna on 15 June 1932.

Matuska, a former officer in the Sixth Honved Regiment, claimed that under the influence of a man named Bergmann, or the spirit of the same man, he had decided to found a Communist party which was in favour of the Christian religion, and it was for this reason that he had started wrecking trains. But his explanation was too confused to be taken seriously as a political motive, and it was also known that he had had an orgasm at the moment the disaster occurred. He was therefore considered to be a sadist.

Having been sentenced to six years' hard labour for attempting to cause an explosion at Anzbach, Matuska was returned to Hungary, where he was sentenced to death

for the Bia-Torbagy crime. This sentence was automatically commuted to life imprisonment as the death
penalty did not exist in the country from which he had
been extradited. It appears that he remained in prison until
Hungary was overrun by the Russians, and was then set
free, but what finally became of him is unknown.

A report that he was captured by the Americans during
the Korean War is unlikely to be true.

Minister and Sexton's wife found murdered, 1922

On the morning of 16 September 1922, a courting couple
found two bodies under a crab-apple tree off a quiet road
on the outskirts of New Brunswick, a small town in New
Jersey. The Reverend Edward Hall, rector of St John's
Episcopal Church, and Mrs. Eleanor Mills, the church
sexton's wife, had been murdered about thirty-six hours
previously.

Both had been shot, the minister once and Mrs. Mills
three times; Mrs. Mills, who sang in the church choir, had
also had her throat cut and her tongue and vocal chords
removed. Some passionate love letters which the rector had
received from Mrs. Mills were found on the grass near the
bodies.

It was already well known in New Brunswick that the
couple had been having an affair, and there was even
reason to suppose that they had been planning to elope
together. So when murder charges were eventually brought
against the rector's wife and her two brothers, after a lapse
of four years, the case naturally excited much public
interest.

The trial began in Somerville, New Jersey, early in

November 1926, the prosecution alleging that Mrs. Frances Hall had overheard her husband arranging to meet Mrs. Mills on the evening of 14 September 1922, and that she and her brothers, Henry and William Stevens, had planned to catch them in a compromising situation. The murders, according to the prosecutor, had followed a quarrel witnessed by Mrs. Jane Gibson, a fifty-four year-old widow who lived nearby.

The sexton, James Mills, appeared as a prosecution witness. He told the court that Mrs. Hall had called on him before the bodies were found, and that when he suggested to her that her husband and his wife had eloped she told him that they were dead. He admitted that he had read some of the rector's letters to his wife — which he had earlier denied — before selling them to a newspaper company.

Louise Geist, a former parlourmaid employed by the Halls, was also called to give evidence but denied having any evidence to give. Her own husband, in a petition for annulment of marriage, had accused her of having taken part in, or been an accessory to, the crime; it was this which had caused the case to be reopened after a grand jury had found that there was insufficient evidence to warrant a trial. But the maid claimed to have had no part in it and said that she did not know who was responsible for the deaths of the rector and the sexton's wife.

Mrs. Gibson, who became famous as a result of this case, was suffering from a kidney complaint and had to be brought into court on a stretcher. She gave evidence from a hospital bed, attended by a doctor and a nurse; as she kept pigs, the press called her 'the Pig Woman'.

On the night of the murders, she said, she had been roused by her dog. As she had had two rows of Indian corn stolen a few nights earlier, she went outside, hoping to catch the thief returning for more. But instead she witnessed a quarrel in the lane where the bodies were afterwards found, and then a struggle, which was followed by a scream and four shots.

Mrs. Gibson identified Mrs. Hall and William Stevens as two of the people concerned. However, she did not give the impression of being a trustworthy witness, and it was suspected that she had made up the whole story for the sake of publicity. This, at any rate, was the view of her elderly mother who, sitting close to her daughter's bed, repeatedly interrupted her testimony. 'She's a liar, a liar, a liar!' the Pig Woman's mother kept saying. 'That's what she is, and what she's always been!'

Mrs. Hall denied having taken part in the crime and said that her husband's behaviour had never given her cause to be suspicious. She said that on the night of the murders she had gone to the church, in the company of her brother William, to see if he had fallen asleep there. The next morning, she telephoned the police, to find out if any accidents had been reported. William Stevens corroborated her account.

On 3 December 1926, after a trial lasting a month, the defendants were all acquitted. Mrs. Hall's cousin, Henry Carpender, who had been awaiting trial on a charge of complicity in the murders, was released at the same time. The case remains unsolved, the only plausible solution which has so far been put forward being that the murders had been carried out by the Ku Klux Klan, which was active in New Jersey at that time, as a warning against adultery.

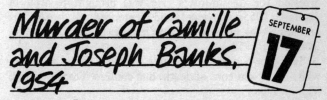

Murder of Camille and Joseph Banks, 1954

SEPTEMBER 17

On 17 September 1954, Mrs Camille Banks, a wealthy middle-aged divorcée, was found dead in her home at

Stinson Beach, California, in the company of her former husband; they had both been murdered. Mrs. Banks was in her bedroom, and had been battered over the head; her ex-husband, an alcoholic, lay on the settee in the living-room, surrounded by empty bottles.

Joseph Banks had been stabbed with a fourteen-inch kitchen knife. A suicide note left beside his body was found to be a forgery, and its wording indicated that it had been written by Mrs. Banks' Filipino houseboy, Bart Caritativo. Banks, in any case, was found to have been far too drunk to stab himself.

A typewritten will was also found. This had ostensibly been written by Mrs. Banks, and said that her entire estate was to go to Caritativo. However, it was written in broken English and contained misspellings of simple words. A letter which accompanied it had been written in the same fashion.

Bart Caritativo, aged forty-eight, had arrived in America in 1926. Mrs. Banks had been kindly disposed towards him, having found that, irrespective of his broken English and misspellings, he had literary aspirations; she had had similar aspirations herself. But following her divorce in 1954, she decided to sell her home and live abroad. The murders were discovered when a real estate agent arrived at her home to discuss the sale of the property.

Caritativo expressed shock at the murders and surprise at his apparent bequest. But handwriting experts were certain that he had forged the documents, and he was arrested for the murders. He was brought to trial in January 1955, convicted and sentenced to death. His execution took place in the gas chamber at San Quentin on 24 October 1958.

The prison psychiatrist later revealed that Caritativo, while under sentence of death, had confessed to the crimes.

Body found in Crypt, 1953

On the morning of 21 September 1953, a party of police officers and firemen equipped with arc-lights, picks and shovels began digging in the crypt of a Congregational Church in Halifax, Yorkshire. The crypt was huge, with extensive tunnels, but the work was confined to one particular corner. Before long the body of a little girl was discovered, and the men had to stop digging to await the arrival of a pathologist.

The body was that of Mary Hackett, aged six, who had been reported missing from her home in Lister Lane on 12 August after being allowed out to play in some nearby sand. She had died from head injuries caused either by blows with a blunt instrument, or through being repeatedly dashed against a wall or floor. As her face was unrecognizable, her parents had to identify her from her clothes.

The church was just across the road from Mary's home, and the crypt had been searched several times before without any trace of the missing girl being found. But the caretaker, a white-haired man named George Albert Hall, had aroused suspicion, and that corner, in which chairs and pews had been stacked and two tins of paint left open, had also been regarded with interest. To the police officers concerned, it seemed possible that the tins had been left open deliberately, so that the paint fumes would hide the smell of decomposing flesh.

Hall, who claimed to have heard 'whisperings' from the crypt on the day of Mary's disappearance, was already under constant surveillance. Now, in the light of this discovery, he was asked whether he knew anything which would assist the police in their investigation, and said that he did not.

253

But the following day he was followed to a mental hospital where he had once been a patient. There, it was afterwards learnt, he spoke to the resident medical superintendent for over an hour, during the course of which he said he had had nothing to do with Mary Hackett's death and that he had been told by a police officer, shortly after the body was found, that the little girl had died from injuries to the back of her head. This was clearly a lie, as the police officer — whom he named — had not known the cause of death at that time.

During subsequent interviews the caretaker made voluntary statements to the police which reinforced the belief that he was the murderer. He said, for example, that on the day Mary disappeared he had heard a child screaming, and that he had seen a strange man in the church grounds. He had mentioned this strange man before and even given a description of him, but had said nothing about the screaming. Eventually he was charged with the crime, and brought to trial at the Leeds Assizes.

Mary Hackett had not been sexually assaulted, and no motive could be found for her murder. The accused, however, was shown to be 'a glib liar' who had known the cause of her death before it was made public, and the jury found him guilty. He was hanged, at the age of forty-eight, at Leeds Prison in April 1954.

Body of Mary Jane Bennett discovered, 1900

SEPTEMBER 23

On the morning of 23 September 1900, a young woman's body was found on the beach at Yarmouth. She had been strangled with a bootlace during the course of the previous

254

night, the disarrangement of her clothes indicating that she had also been the victim of a sexual assault. A local landlady recognized the body as that of a Mrs. Hood, who had been spending a holiday in Yarmouth since 15 September. But laundry marks on the victim's clothes led to her being identified as Mary Jane Bennett, the wife of Herbert John Bennett, who was later found in Woolwich.

Bennett and his wife, though separated for some time, had been seen together in the town on the night of the murder, and a booking-clerk at Yarmouth Station claimed that Bennett had travelled back to London on the 7.20 train the following morning. A gold chain which, according to her landlady, Mrs. Bennett had been wearing on the evening of 22 September, was found in her husband's lodgings. It was also discovered that Bennett, who had been unfaithful to his wife many times, had entered into a liaison with a parlourmaid named Alice Meadows whom he intended to marry.

Bennett had met his wife in Northfleet, Kent, some years earlier; he was a grocer's assistant at the time and she became his music teacher. Following their marriage in 1897, they bought old violins cheaply for Mrs. Bennett to hawk from door to door, pleading near-starvation. The £400 which they made in one year by this means enabled them to set up a grocery business — the premises conveniently catching fire after being insured. Bennett later went to South Africa, from where he was soon deported on suspicion of being a spy for the Boers.

At the time of his arrest, he was working at Woolwich Arsenal, but had far more money in his possession than could have been obtained from this employment; he refused to say where it had come from and the police were unable to discover the source of it themselves. As Mrs. Bennett had given a false name and other false information to her landlady in Yarmouth, it is possible that she and her husband, despite their separation, were engaged in a further joint venture just before her death.

Brought to trial for murder at the Old Bailey, Bennett

pleaded not guilty, but the evidence against him was over-whelming. In view of his character and apparent inability to tell the truth about anything, his barrister did not dare to call him as a witness in his own defence, for fear of making the prosecution's case even stronger.

Bennett, aged twenty-two, was hanged at Norwich Prison on 21 March 1901. When the black flag was raised to show that the execution had been carried out, the flag-staff snapped. Some took this to be a sign that a mis-carriage of justice had just taken place.

Kidnapping of Charles Ross, 1937

On 25 September 1937, Charles Ross, a wealthy Chicago businessman aged seventy-two, was kidnapped at gunpoint by two men while driving with his secretary in Franklin Park, Illinois. The kidnappers forced his limousine to a halt by swerving in front of it, then ordered Ross to get into their own car. His secretary, who was left behind, reported what had happened.

Ross was taken to Wisconsin and made to write to a friend, asking him to raise a ransom of $50,000. After a second note had been received the money was delivered, Mrs. Ross inserting an advertisement in a Chicago news-paper as instructed by the kidnappers. A third note then stated that Ross would be released when the money had been spent. But he was never seen alive again.

The FBI carried out a full-scale search, with J. Edgar Hoover personally in charge of it. The ransom notes were found to have been written on a new typewriter, and inquiries were made about recent sales in Chicago. The purchaser of one model was traced to a rooming-house, and fingerprints which were discovered there matched others found on the notes.

By this time marked bills in which the ransom had been paid had started turning up at racetracks, their disposal following a definite pattern. It was this pattern which resulted in the arrest of John Henry Seadlund at a track in Los Angeles on 14 January 1938.

Seadlund, an occasional labourer with a record of petty crime, admitted his part in the kidnapping and said that he had murdered his accomplice, James Atwood Gray, as well as Charles Ross. He led the FBI to a pit in Spooner, Wisconsin, where the bodies of both men had been buried. 'Will I be hanged or fried?' he asked indifferently.

He was executed in the electric chair later the same year, at the age of twenty-eight.

Murder of a Shepherd's wife 1947

SEPTEMBER **26**

On 26 September 1947, Catherine McIntyre, forty-seven-year-old wife of a head shepherd, was found murdered at her home in Kenmore, near the small Perthshire town of Aberfeldy. She had been bound, gagged and battered over the head, and her murderer had escaped with £90 in cash — the wages of the shepherds in her husband's charge — as well as Mrs. McIntyre's wedding ring.

Though no fingerprints had been left at the scene, the police found various items in a nearby area of bracken, which had evidently been used as a hideout. These included a sawn-off shotgun, a bloodstained handkerchief, a used razor blade and the return half of a railway ticket of a special type issued to members of the Armed Forces.

Following appeals to the public for information, the gun was recognized by a farmer in Old Meldrum, Aberdeenshire, who said that he had borrowed it from a neighbour but afterwards found it to be missing from his farm. A Polish soldier named Stanislaw Myszka had been casually employed there at the time and was suspected of having stolen it, the farmer added.

A taxi-driver then revealed that he had driven a man of Myszka's description from Aberfeldy to Perth on the afternoon of 26 September and the police announced that they wished to interview this man in connection with the crime.

Myszka, a twenty-three-year-old deserter from the Polish Army in Exile, was arrested at an old RAF camp near Peterhead on 2 October, and a wedding ring similar to Mrs. McIntyre's was found hidden in one of his shoes. He had been staying with a Polish couple at Ardallie, in the same county, but fled after hearing that the police wanted to question him.

He denied having committed the crime, but hairs taken from a razor with which he had been shaved in prison appeared to be identical in structure to others found on the discarded razor blade near the scene. This, together with other incriminating pieces of evidence, led the jury at his trial to find him guilty, and he was hanged in Perth on 6 February 1948.

Murder of PC Gutteridge, 1927

SEPTEMBER **27**

On the morning of 27 September 1927, the body of PC George Gutteridge was found in a country lane between

Romford and Ongar in Essex. He had been shot four times — twice through the left cheek and once in each eye. His pencil was clutched in his hand and his pocket-book was found nearby. It was assumed from this that he had been taken by surprise as he was about to write something in the pocket-book. His death was estimated to have occurred between 4 and 5 a.m.

About 2.30 the same morning a car belonging to Dr. Edward Lovell had been stolen from a garage at the owner's house in London Road, Billericay — about ten miles away. When this was later found abandoned in Brixton, south London, there were bloodstains on the runningboard by the driver's door; there was also an empty cartridge case under one of the seats. Following these discoveries, the police began to keep known car thieves under surveillance.

One of these thieves was Frederick Guy Browne, a forty-six-year-old mechanic who had a garage near Clapham Junction. Browne, a married man with one daughter, had served several prison sentences and was known to be violent. In January 1928 he was arrested in connection with the theft of a Vauxhall two months earlier. Police searches then led to the discovery of two loaded Webley revolvers in his garage and two other guns, also loaded, in his rooms off Lavender Hill.

The police at first said nothing to him about the murder, but on finding these weapons they strongly suspected that he had been involved in it. A few days later his former accomplice, William Henry Kennedy, who was believed to have taken part in the same theft, was arrested in Liverpool.

Kennedy, a thirty-six-year-old drunkard, also had a criminal record, his offences including burglary, housebreaking, theft and indecent exposure. He had a pistol in his possession and tried to shoot the police officer who confronted him, but the safety catch was in position and the gun merely clicked. He was quickly overpowered.

Taken to New Scotland Yard, Kennedy was asked if he

had any information to give about the murder of PC Gutteridge. He asked to be allowed to think for a few minutes before answering, and then to see his wife. When Mrs. Kennedy, whom he had only married a few days previously, told him to tell the truth about what had happened, he made a long statement, admitting that he had been present at the crime but blaming Browne for it.

He and Browne, he said, had stolen Dr. Lovell's car and were driving it back to London by a route which avoided main roads when PC Gutteridge saw them and signalled to them to stop. They drove on, but stopped when they heard a police whistle and waited until he came over to speak to them.

Not satisfied with the answers to his questions, Gutteridge took out his pocket-book and was about to begin writing in it when Browne, who had been driving, fired two shots at him at close range. The two thieves then got out of the car and Browne, with Kennedy trying to restrain him, fired two more shots as his victim lay groaning on the ground.

Browne and Kennedy were both charged with murder and brought to trial at the Old Bailey on 23 April. Ballistics evidence was given with great effect, the Crown's expert, Robert Churchill, demonstrating that the cartridge case found in the stolen car had markings which matched others produced by test shots fired from one of Browne's revolvers. Powder discoloration on the victim's skin had been found to match the powder used in one of two obsolete types of ammunition found in the same gun.

Browne said that Kennedy's statement was a 'pack of wilful or imaginative lies', claiming that he had been at home in bed at the time of the murder. Kennedy stuck to his story that Browne alone was responsible for the murder, concluding, 'I can only now express my deep regret to Mrs. Gutteridge that I should have been in the car on the night of the crime.' Both men were found guilty and sentenced to death. They were hanged on 31 May 1928 — Browne at Pentonville Prison and Kennedy at Wandsworth.

Kennedy, the night before the executions, had written to his wife, urging her to join him in heaven.

Kidnapping of Bobby Greenlease, 1953

On 28 September 1953, Bobby Greenlease, the six-year-old son of a millionaire car-dealer, was taken from his convent school in Kansas City, Missouri, by a woman pretending to be his aunt. The boy's mother had suffered a heart attack and wanted to see him at once, according to the woman in question. But later, when the acting Sister Superior called Bobby's home to inquire about his mother's condition, Mrs. Greenlease answered the telephone herself. It was then realized that the boy had been abducted.

Shortly afterwards a ransom note was received, demanding $600,000 in $10 and $20 bills from each of the twelve federal reserve districts. Robert C. Greenlease Sr, the boy's father, immediately made arrangements to comply with this instruction, and during the next few days received a number of telephone calls from a man calling himself 'M', who promised that he would get Bobby back when the ransom had been paid.

Eventually the money, crammed into an army duffel bag, was thrown into a culvert outside Kansas City, and Mr. and Mrs. Greenlease waited anxiously for news that their son had been released. But they waited in vain, for Bobby was already dead.

On 6 October, two days after delivery of the ransom, police in St Louis, in the same state, learnt that a man had been parting with large sums of money in a casual manner

Carl Austin Hall, a convict on parole, was promptly arrested in a hotel suite, and found to have nearly $300,000 in cash in two suitcases. He admitted that he was one of the kidnappers, and led police to his mistress, Mrs. Bonnie Brown Heady, a forty-one-year-old alcoholic. It was Mrs. Heady who had taken Bobby from school and, though Hall said that she hadn't known the boy was being kidnapped, her fingerprints were found to match those on the ransom note.

It later emerged that Bobby had been shot and his body buried in quicklime in the backyard of Mrs. Heady's house in St. Joseph, Missouri — in a grave which had been dug beforehand. Hall had originally intended to strangle him, but the piece of rope which he had brought along for this purpose had proved to be too short, and his little victim had put up a fierce resistance. He had been dead at the time the ransom was demanded.

Hall and Mrs. Heady were quickly brought to trial and sentenced to death. They made no appeal, but likewise showed little remorse until the day of their execution drew near. They then wrote letters to Robert Greenlease Sr, begging his forgiveness for the suffering which they had caused. They were jointly executed in the gas chamber at the Missouri State Penitentiary on the night of 17 December 1953.

The rest of the ransom money was never recovered.

Human remains found near Moffat, 1935

SEPTEMBER
29

On 29 September 1935, a woman standing on a bridge near Moffat, on the Carlisle to Edinburgh road, saw a human arm lying on the bank of the stream below. When this was reported to the police a search of the area began and further human remains, including two heads and a trunk, were discovered.

Though these had been mutilated in order to hinder identification, some of them had been wrapped in a special edition of the *Sunday Graphic,* which had been distributed in Morecambe and Lancaster on 15 September.

This led police officers to suspect that the remains were those of the common-law wife of Dr. Buck Ruxton, a general practitioner in Lancaster, and their children's nursemaid, Mary Rogerson, neither of whom had been seen since 14 September.

Ruxton, aged thirty-six, was a Parsee who had qualified at the Universities of Bombay and London; his name had originally been Bukhtyar Hakim. He had acquired his practice in 1930, by which time Isabella Ruxton, then aged twenty-nine, had been living with him for two years. By 1935 they had three children.

It was known to the police that the couple often quarrelled and that Ruxton, who suspected his wife of infidelity, had several times used violence and threatened to kill her.

Prior to the discovery of the remains he had given various explanations for the absence of the two women, finally claiming that they had gone to Edinburgh together. Then, when the remains were found, he denied that they were the bodies of his wife and Mary Rogerson, and asked the police if a statement could be issued to that effect. 'All this damned nonsense is ruining my practice!' he complained.

But one of his female patients, who had been asked to scrub his staircase on 15 September, showed a police officer some carpets, felt stair-pads and a suit of clothes — all bloodstained — which Ruxton had given to her.

More bloodstained carpets were found in the possession of his charwoman, Mrs. Oxley, and a georgette blouse in which some of the remains had been wrapped was identified as having belonged to Mary Rogerson.

Following Ruxton's arrest on 13 October, fingerprints and palmprints found in his house proved to be identical to those taken from the left hand of one of the murder victims; bloodstains were found on the bathroom floor and in other parts of the house, and blood and human debris were found in his drains.

Ruxton was brought to trial at the Manchester Assizes the following March, the prosecution contending that he had strangled his wife in a fit of rage and then killed Mary Rogerson because she had witnessed or discovered the crime. Though Ruxton denied this, he was convicted and sentenced to death. His execution took place at Strangeways Prison on 12 May 1936, his confession being published the following Sunday.

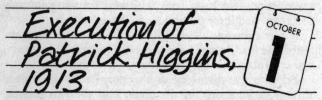

Execution of Patrick Higgins, 1913

OCTOBER 1

On 1 October 1913, Patrick Higgins, a widower, was hanged in Edinburgh for the murder of his two small sons. The crime had taken place nearly two years earlier, but had not been discovered until June 1913, when the two bodies, tied together with sash-cord, were found in a water-filled quarry near Winchburgh, in West Lothian. Higgins, a former soldier who had served in India, admitted the justice of his sentence and awaited execution with little concern. He blamed his heavy drinking for his downfall.

Some years earlier, following his discharge from the army, he had returned to Winchburgh and married a local girl; their first son, William, was born in December 1904, their second, John, in August 1907. But, though employed at the Winchburgh Brickworks, where he earned 24s

($1.20) a week, Higgins neglected his family — and later, after his wife's death in 1910, began to get into trouble with the law for failing to maintain the children.

On one occasion, in 1911, he was jailed for two months; then, when he boarded them with a widow in nearby Broxburn but failed to pay for their keep, he was warned that he would be prosecuted again. He therefore took the boys away from the widow, but was unwilling to pay for their keep elsewhere. It was then, in November 1911, that he murdered them, the children having evidently walked out to the secluded quarry with him, without any inkling of his intention.

Higgins, by this time, was spending most of his money on drink. He stayed at a lodging-house when he could afford it, but often had to sleep at the brickworks, making soup in his pail and using his spade as a frying-pan. He explained the disappearance of his sons in various ways, generally by saying that he had given them away to two women he had met on a train. He was arrested within a few days of the discovery of the bodies, the stamp of a poorhouse on one of the boy's shirts having helped the police to identify them.

Besides being a heavy drinker, Higgins had a history of epilepsy: it was for this reason that he had been discharged from the army, and several witnesses at his trial stated that they had seen him having fits. The defence counsel argued that because of this illness he had been of unsound mind at the time of the crime, but the jury found him to be sane and their recommendation of mercy proved unavailing.

Higgins's execution was carried out on a scaffold which had been erected in the well of a staircase next to the condemned cell. It was Edinburgh's first execution for many years, and caused much excitement among the inhabitants. However, the crowds outside the prison dispersed without incident as soon as the black flag appeared, many of them to go to the Musselburg Races. The prison governor later published a letter from Higgins, thanking him for the kindness which he had received during his incarceration.

Decomposed body found on Hankley Common, 1942

On 7 October 1942, troops exercising on Hankley Common, near Godalming in Surrey, found the decomposed body of a young woman lying under a mound of earth at the top of a hill. The back of her head had been smashed in with a heavy, blunt instrument and there were also stab wounds in her head and forearm. It was quickly established that the murder had taken place some weeks earlier and that the body had been dragged to the place where it was buried.

The body proved to be that of nineteen-year-old Joan Wolfe who, having run away from home several months before, had been living in a little hut made of branches, twigs and leaves in nearby woods. A search of the area resulted in the discovery of a letter which she had written to a French-Canadian soldier named August Sangret, stationed about two miles away at Witley Camp, telling him that she was pregnant and making it clear that she expected him to marry her.

The blunt instrument, a heavy stake of birch wood, was also found; it had hairs attached to its thicker end which matched those of the victim, but its surface was too rough to provide any fingerprints. The knife which had been used, which was known to have a distinctive hooked point, did not come to light until some weeks later.

August Sangret, an illiterate man with Red Indian ancestors, admitted having been intimate with Joan Wolfe and identified her clothes and belongings. He said that he had not seen her for weeks and did not know what had become of her. Finally, after making a statement running to 17,000 words — it had taken him five days, during the course of which he had not been told that she was dead —

he remarked, 'I guess you found her. I guess I shall get the blame.'

Even so, there was not enough evidence to justify a charge against him. No knife had been found among his possessions; stains found on one of his blankets and also on his battledress trousers could not be positively shown to be blood. Though strongly suspecting him of the crime, the police had no choice but to let him go free while they continued to search for the knife.

Then, on 26 November, a black, bone-handled clasp-knife with a hooked blade was found blocking a drain of the washhouse attached to the guardroom at Witley Camp. Sangret, on being questioned about it, was tricked into making statements which incriminated him. The fact that he had hidden the knife, which he said had belonged to Joan Wolfe, was regarded as evidence of his guilt because he would not have known of the victim's stabbing injuries at the time unless he had inflicted them himself.

Sangret was arrested and brought to trial for the 'Wigwam Murder' at the Kingston Assizes the following February. It was alleged by the prosecution that he had killed Joan Wolfe because she was pregnant, and had then — in keeping with a Red Indian tradition — dragged her body 400 yards in order to bury her on high ground. The jury found him guilty and, in spite of a recommendation of mercy, he was hanged at Wandsworth Prison in April 1943. He was thirty years old.

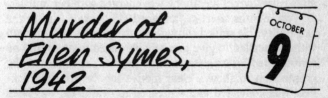

Murder of Ellen Symes, 1942

OCTOBER 9

Taking her four-year-old son home on the night of 9 October 1942, Mrs. Ellen Symes, of Strood, Kent, was

267

attacked and stabbed in the neck by a soldier in uniform. The crime took place close to her home in Brompton Farm Road, the owner of a nearby house going out to investigate after hearing screams. Mrs. Symes, who had collapsed in the road, died shortly afterwards, but her little boy was unharmed. The attacker fled from the scene.

The following morning a soldier in the Gravesend Road was seen acting suspiciously and taken to Rochester police station. He was Gunner Reginald Buckfield, a married man with three children whose constant smiling and good nature had earned him the nickname of 'Smiler'. Having deserted from an anti-aircraft unit at Gravesend, he had been working as a casual labourer on farms, his most recent job having been at Hoo, three miles from Strood, just before the murder.

Buckfield was held in custody by the police prior to being handed over to the military authorities. He spent his time writing a crime story, called *The Mystery of the Brompton Road Murders*, with a character named 'Smiler' who was presented in flattering terms. On leaving police custody under military escort, he handed the unfinished story to a detective, assuring him that he would find it very interesting.

Though he claimed that the story was fictitious, Buckfield had written into it details of the murder of Ellen Symes which only the murderer himself could have known, he was therefore regarded as a suspect. Later he was found to be the owner of a table-knife which had been discovered in a garden near the scene of the crime. So, four weeks after Ellen Symes' death, he was charged with her murder.

Two months later, in January 1943, he was tried at the Old Bailey. He smiled throughout the proceedings, though witnesses called to give him an alibi failed to do so and he contradicted his own statements. Despite the failure of the prosecution to show a clear motive for the attack, Buckfield was convicted and sentenced to death. He was later judged to be insane and committed to Broadmoor.

Murder of Mr and Mrs Goodman 1949

At ten o'clock on the night of 10 October 1949, Leopold Goodman, a wealthy forty-nine-year-old Russian Jew, and his wife Esther, aged forty-seven were found murdered in the dining-room of their home in Ashcombe Gardens, Edgware, Middlesex. They had both been battered over the head, the same weapon — the base of a television aerial — being used in each case. There were no signs of robbery; in fact, large sums of money had been left untouched in different parts of the house. The murder weapon was found in the scullery.

Earlier that evening Mr. and Mrs. Goodman had visited their daughter and her four-day-old son at a maternity home in Muswell Hill, leaving the building about 9 p.m. Their son-in-law Daniel Raven, a twenty-three-year-old advertising agent, had been there too, and had left shortly after them. Raven lived with his wife in nearby Edgwarebury Lane, their house having been bought for them by his father-in-law. On being asked by telephone to come to the Goodmans' house straight away, he arrived immaculately dressed in a light grey suit.

'Why did they tell me to go?' he asked, as he sat crying on the stairs. 'Why didn't they let me stop?'

He said that he had driven his wife's parents back from the maternity home and had wanted to stay with them as they had recently had a burglary and were worried about the possibility of another; he had only returned to his own home at their insistence, he continued. However, the police officer in charge of the case was suspicious of Daniel Raven's account, and on learning from another source that the young man had been wearing a different suit earlier, he took him to Edgware police station for further questioning.

Raven, on being asked for the keys of his house, handed them over, telling Detective Inspector J. Diller that he would find nothing there. 'I only had a bath,' he said. But on entering the house at 11.45 p.m., Diller noticed a smell of burning coming from the kitchen and managed to retrieve part of a dark blue suit from the blazing boiler. This was later found to be bloodstained, the blood being of the same rare group as the Goodmans'. In the bathroom there was no evidence of anyone having recently had a bath.

A search of the premises resulted in the discovery of a pair of shoes which had been washed and hidden in the garage; it was also found that the driver's seat of Raven's car had been scrubbed. Bloodstains of the same type were discovered on both articles.

When Daniel Raven was asked to explain the suit he admitted that it was his own, but said that he did not know how the blood had got on to it. He had left it in the bathroom, he said. On being charged with his father-in-law's murder, he protested his innocence, claiming that Leopold Goodman had made enemies by engaging in crooked business practices.

Raven was brought to trial at the Old Bailey on 22 November 1949. Despite the failure of the prosecution to show that he had a motive for the crime, he was found guilty two days later. It was afterwards contended, in support of an appeal, that he was insane, medical evidence being produced to show that he had a history of 'blackouts and brainstorms'. He was, however, hanged, the execution taking place at Pentonville Prison on 6 January 1950.

Execution of Linwood Briley, 1984

OCTOBER
13

On 13 October 1984, Linwood Earl Briley, aged thirty, was executed in the electric chair at the state penitentiary in Richmond, Virginia, for the murder of a disc jockey five years earlier. It was not his only crime, for he had also received seven life sentences for eleven other murders and robberies. Moreover, he had led the biggest escape from Death Row in the United States' history only five months before his death.

The escape had taken place at the Mecklenberg Correctional Centre in Boydton, in the same state, on 31 May, when Briley, his brother James and four other convicted murderers had overpowered six guards, stolen their uniforms and driven out of the institution in an official van, pretending that they were removing a bomb.

Though the other four were all back in custody within eight days, the two brothers remained at large until 19 June, when they surrendered to FBI agents after being discovered in a garage owned by a relative in Philadelphia.

Linwood Briley behaved calmly at his execution, maintaining that he was innocent of the crime for which he had been condemned. His brother James, who had murdered a pregnant woman and her five-year-old son during the course of a robbery, followed him to the electric chair six months later.

A third brother, Anthony, had also been convicted of murder and was serving a life sentence.

Murder of Mrs Greenhill, 1941

OCTOBER
14

On 14 October 1941, Mrs. Theodora Greenhill, sixty-five-year-old widow of an army officer, was found murdered in the drawing-room of her self-contained flat in Elsham Road, West Kensington. She had been struck on the head with a beer bottle as she sat at her writing bureau, then strangled with a ligature as she lay unconscious on the floor. On the bureau, which had been ransacked, lay a sheet of paper bearing the words: 'Received from Dr. H.D. Trevor the s ...' The writing ended abruptly with a jagged line.

Mrs. Greenhill had been trying to let the flat so that she could move out of London, and it appeared that her murderer had pretended to be a prospective tenant. After killing the old lady he had covered her face with a handkerchief; he had also gathered up some of the broken glass and put it into a waste-paper basket. The contents of a cash-box had been stolen from the victim's bedroom.

Detective Chief Superintendent Fred Cherrill, Scotland Yard's fingerprint expert, thought that the name Trevor seemed familiar, and asked the Criminal Record Office to send all files bearing it to the scene of the crime.

By the time they arrived Cherrill had found fingerprints on some of the pieces of glass, on a table near the body and on the cash-box. After spending a few minutes comparing these with the prints in the CRO files, he was able to say to the officer in charge of the investigation, 'The man we want is Harold Dorian Trevor.'

Trevor, aged sixty-two, was well known to the police. A tall, slim man with grey hair and a monocle, he had a long record of fraud and theft and had been free for a total of only forty-eight weeks during the previous forty-two years.

as the worst case of mass murder in any of the
countries in modern times.

eath of atilda Clover, 91

Octover 1891, Matilda Clover, a twenty-six-year-old
ate, was found writhing in agony in a brothel in
th Road, south-east London. She managed to say
nan named Fred had given her some white pills, but
tention was paid to this at the time, and when she
ortly afterwards, her death was put down to alcohol
ng. She was buried in a pauper's grave at Tooting.

previous week, on the evening of 13 October,
prostitute, nineteen-year-old Ellen Donworth, had
the way to hospital after collapsing on a pavement
r lodgings in Duke Street, off Westminster Bridge
Before her death she was able to say that a tall,
ed gentleman with a silk hat had given her some
stuff' to drink from a bottle earlier the same even-
this case, a post-mortem revealed that the girl had
m poisoning with strychnine.

ody seems to have suspected that 'Fred' and this
ed gentleman were the same person until the
g April, when two other young prostitutes died,
m strychnine poisoning. Emma Shrivell, aged
n, and Alice Marsh, twenty, both lived at a brothel in
d Street and claimed to have been visited by a
named Fred, who had given them some pills. It was
se deaths that Matilda Clover's body was exhumed
too, was found to have been poisoned with strych-

276

He was arrested as he left a telephone kiosk in Rhyl four
days later.

'It wasn't murder,' he said after being cautioned. 'There
was never any intent to murder. I have never used violence
to anyone in my life before. What came over me I do not
know. After I hit her my mind went completely blank and
is still like that now. Something seemed to crack in my
head.'

He was brought to trial at the Old Bailey the following
January, a plea of insanity being made on his behalf. On
being found guilty, he made a long, impassioned speech
which the spectators found very moving.

'If I am called upon to take my stand in the cold, grey
dawn of the early morning, I pray that God in His mercy
will gently turn my mother's face away as I pass into the
shadows,' he said. 'No fear touches my heart. My heart is
dead. It died when my mother left me.'

It was to be the last of many courtroom speeches made
by Harold Trevor, and could make no difference to the
sentence that was passed on him. He was hanged at Wandsworth Prison on 11 March 1942.

Disappearance of John and Phoebe Harries, 1953

On 16 October 1953, John Harries, aged sixty-three, and
his fifty-four-year-old wife Phoebe disappeared from their
farm at Llanginning, near St Clears in Carmarthenshire,
shortly after attending a local harvest thanksgiving service.
Ronald Harries, their twenty-four-year-old adopted
nephew, claimed that they had gone to London for a
holiday, leaving him to look after the place. But they were
never seen alive again, and three weeks after their dis-

273

He was arrested as he left a telephone kiosk in Rhyl four days later.

'It wasn't murder,' he said after being cautioned. 'There was never any intent to murder. I have never used violence to anyone in my life before. What came over me I do not know. After I hit her my mind went completely blank and is still like that now. Something seemed to crack in my head.'

He was brought to trial at the Old Bailey the following January, a plea of insanity being made on his behalf. On being found guilty, he made a long, impassioned speech which the spectators found very moving.

'If I am called upon to take my stand in the cold, grey dawn of the early morning, I pray that God in His mercy will gently turn my mother's face away as I pass into the shadows,' he said. 'No fear touches my heart. My heart is dead. It died when my mother left me.'

It was to be the last of many courtroom speeches made by Harold Trevor, and could make no difference to the sentence that was passed on him. He was hanged at Wandsworth Prison on 11 March 1942.

Disappearance of John and Phoebe Harries, 1953

OCTOBER
16

On 16 October 1953, John Harries, aged sixty-three, and his fifty-four-year-old wife Phoebe disappeared from their farm at Llanginning, near St Clears in Carmarthenshire, shortly after attending a local harvest thanksgiving service. Ronald Harries, their twenty-four-year-old adopted nephew, claimed that they had gone to London for a holiday, leaving him to look after the place. But they were never seen alive again, and three weeks after their disappearance the Carmarthenshire police asked Scotland Yard to help in the search for them.

Ronald Harries, who claimed to have driven the missing couple to Carmarthen railway station on the morning of 17 October, was regarded with suspicion. The discovery that Phoebe Harries had left an uncooked joint of meat in her oven suggested that she had not left the farm intentionally. Then a cheque written by John Harries was found to be fraudulent when presented for payment by his nephew: it had originally been made out for £9, but this sum had afterwards been changed to £909.

The police suspected that John and Phoebe Harries had been murdered and their bodies buried near Cadno Farm, where Ronald Harries lived. In the hope that Ronald would lead them to the bodies, they tied cotton threads across every exit, then made a lot of noise in the vicinity of the farmhouse, causing him to fear that the bodies had already been discovered.

The next morning, at dawn, they found that one of the threads had been broken. The bodies of the missing couple were then found buried in the adjoining field; they had both been battered to death. Ronald Harries was charged with their murders.

Four days after his arrest the murder weapon — a hammer which he had borrowed from a Mr. Lewis on the night of 16 October — was found buried in the undergrowth around the farm.

Ronald Harries was brought to trial at the Carmarthen Assizes in March 1954. It was clear from the evidence that he had killed his uncle and aunt for the sake of their money and property at a time when he was in financial difficulties, and that he had taken over their farm immediately afterwards. He was convicted and sentenced to death, his execution being carried out at Swansea Prison.

Arnfinn Nesset brought to trial, 1982

On 18 October 1982, Arnfinn Nesset, a forty-six-year-old former nursing-home manager, was brought to trial in Trondheim, accused of twenty-five murders and a number of other offences. It was alleged that between 1977 and November 1980, he had murdered fourteen women and eleven men, all of whom were patients at the Orkdal nursing home for the elderly, by injecting poison into their veins.

The trial lasted nearly five months, becoming the longest criminal trial in Norwegian history, with over 150 witnesses. The accused, a thin, bespectacled man, pleaded not guilty to all charges. Finally, in March 1983, the jury found him guilty of the murder of twelve women and ten men and the attempted murder of one woman.

Nesset's victims, aged between sixty-seven and ninety-four, had been killed with curacit. The court was told that after his arrest on 9 March 1981, the prisoner had admitted not only the twenty-five murders with which he was charged, but also five others. The jury of six women and four men found that in addition to the crimes of murder and attempted murder, he was guilty of forgery and embezzlement of about 13,000 kroner (£1200) from patients.

Though declared sane by medical experts, Nesset appeared to have had no real motive for the murders. Following his conviction, arguments were entered on whether they had been mercy killings, but the court found that they had not been. It was then accepted that he was suffering from permanently impaired mental faculties. The maximum sentence of twenty-one years' imprisonment and up to ten years' preventive detention was nonetheless passed on him.

It was the worst case of mass murder in any of the Nordic countries in modern times.

Death of Matilda Clover, 1891

On 20 October 1891, Matilda Clover, a twenty-six-year-old prostitute, was found writhing in agony in a brothel in Lambeth Road, south-east London. She managed to say that a man named Fred had given her some white pills, but little attention was paid to this at the time, and when she died shortly afterwards, her death was put down to alcohol poisoning. She was buried in a pauper's grave at Tooting.

The previous week, on the evening of 13 October, another prostitute, nineteen-year-old Ellen Donworth, had died on the way to hospital after collapsing on a pavement near her lodgings in Duke Street, off Westminster Bridge Road. Before her death she was able to say that a tall, cross-eyed gentleman with a silk hat had given her some 'white stuff' to drink from a bottle earlier the same evening. In this case, a post-mortem revealed that the girl had died from poisoning with strychnine.

Nobody seems to have suspected that 'Fred' and this cross-eyed gentleman were the same person until the following April, when two other young prostitutes died, also from strychnine poisoning. Emma Shrivell, aged eighteen, and Alice Marsh, twenty, both lived at a brothel in Stamford Street and claimed to have been visited by a doctor named Fred, who had given them some pills. It was after these deaths that Matilda Clover's body was exhumed and she, too, was found to have been poisoned with strychnine.

While the newspapers speculated wildly about the murderer's identity, Dr. Thomas Neill Cream, who since 9 April had been living in lodgings at 103, Lambeth Palace Road, began accusing a fellow lodger — a medical student named Walter Harper — of being responsible for the deaths.

Cream, who at this time was known as Thomas Neill, wrote to Harper's father, a doctor in Barnstaple, saying that he had evidence of his son's guilt. He offered to sell this evidence to him for £1500, but said that he would otherwise give it to the coroner concerned. The letter led to Cream's arrest on a charge of attempted extortion on 3 June.

But by this time Cream was suspected of the murders himself, and had been under police surveillance following inquiries into the rumours which he had spread in his own neighbourhood. He was later charged with the murder of Matilda Clover, and brought to trial at the Old Bailey on 17 October the same year.

The evidence against him was overwhelming, and included the testimony of Louise Harvey, a prostitute, who told the court that one evening in October 1891 the prisoner, who had spent the previous night with her, had given her some pills which she pretended to swallow but actually threw away. Other evidence was given of the doctor buying *nux vomica* — containing strychnine — and gelatine capsules from a chemist, and the finding of seven bottles of strychnine at his lodgings.

The jury was left in no doubt that the accused had murdered not only Matilda Clover, but the other three prostitutes as well, and on being found guilty he was sentenced to death.

Cream, a Scotsman who had graduated in Canada, had been in trouble before. While practising as a doctor in Chicago in 1881 he had poisoned a patient named Daniel Stott, with whose wife he had been having an affair. His other known crimes included arson, abortion, blackmail, fraud and theft.

Having received a life sentence for Stott's murder, he had been released from Joliet Prison, Illinois, in July 1891, shortly after inheriting $116,000 from his father. The murder of Ellen Donworth had taken place less than two weeks after his arrival in England.

On 15 November 1892, Neill Cream, aged forty-two, was hanged at Newgate Prison. Just before the trap opened he started to say that he was 'Jack the Ripper', but in view of his life sentence in America the claim is not generally taken seriously.

After his death his clothes and belongings were sold to Madame Tussaud's for £200.

Torso found in Essex Marsh, 1949
OCTOBER 21

On 21 October 1949, a farm labourer hunting wildfowl on the Essex marshes near Tillingham found a human torso wrapped in felt floating on the water. Horrified though he must have been by the discovery, Mr. Sidney Tiffin had the presence of mind to secure the bundle to a stake driven into the mud, before going off to inform the police. The following morning, when the tides permitted, the bundle was taken away in a boat and examined at a mortuary in Chelmsford. The post-mortem was later carried out at the London Hospital Medical School.

A bloodstained silk shirt and the remains of a pair of blue trousers clung to the torso; the head and legs were missing. There were five stab wounds in the chest, and a large number of bones had been broken after death. Fingerprints obtained by spraying glycerine under the skin enabled Scotland Yard to identify the dead man as Stanley

Setty, a second-hand car dealer of Lancaster Gate, London, who had been missing from his home since 4 October. The pathologist Francis Camps found that the broken bones were crash injuries, and suggested that the torso had been thrown out of an aeroplane into water.

Stanley Setty was a forty-six-year-old man of Turkish birth; his name had originally been Sulman Seti. He had a criminal record for fraudulent bankruptcy, and had been suspected of using his business as a cover for a variety of criminal activities. It was known that on the day of his disappearance he had sold a car and cashed a cheque at the Yorkshire Penny Bank, receiving £1000 in £5 notes.

The suggestion that his torso had been thrown from an aeroplane led to inquiries being made at airports in the east of England, and before long it was discovered that on the day following his disappearance, a former RAF pilot named Brian Donald Hume had hired a sports plane for a flight from Elstree — a private airport in Hertfordshire — to Southend, carrying two parcels.

Having said that he would return the plane before dark, Hume had left it overnight at Southend where, the following afternoon, he lifted a third bundle into it before taking off again, apparently with the intention of flying back to Elstree. This time, after three hours, he landed at Gravesend airport, claiming that he had lost his way. He finally asked officials at Elstree to send somebody to collect the plane.

Hume, aged thirty, lived with his wife and baby daughter in a maisonette in Finchley Road, Golders Green. He had a record of petty crime and was suspected of having taken part in large-scale robberies. An examination of the plane which he had hired led to the discovery of bloodstains on the floor behind the co-pilot's seat. Moreover, a £5 note which he had used to pay a taxi fare was found to have been part of the money received by Setty at the Yorkshire Penny Bank.

On being questioned by the police, Hume admitted that he had known Setty and said that he had been bribed into disposing of the bundles by three strangers, who gave him £50 in £5 notes. He had thrown them out of the plane while flying over the Channel, he explained. He was held in custody while a search was made for the three men he had described, but it soon became clear that no such men existed. It was also discovered that a large quantity of blood had been spilt on his dining-room floor.

In January 1950 Hume was brought to trial at the Old Bailey, charged with murder. The prosecution, in seeking to prove that Setty had been killed and dismembered in the prisoner's maisonette, relied on Hume being unable to account for all the blood in any other way. But Hume *did* manage to account for it; he said that he had dropped the bundle containing the torso and that the blood had escaped from it when one end fell open. He was acquitted of murder, but sent to prison for twelve years for being an accessory to the crime.

Shortly after his release in 1958 Hume published a newspaper confession, stating that he *had* committed the murder. Setty, he said, had been employing him to steal cars and fly arms illegally, but often insulted him. On 4 October 1949, Setty, according to this new account, visited the maisonette to give him a new assignment, but Hume, enraged by his remarks, attacked him with a dagger and killed him. Having done so, he drove the dead man's car back to his garage, then dismembered the body with a saw and a kitchen knife.

The confession, published in the *Sunday Pictorial*, made Hume £2000, enabling him to live extravagantly in Zürich for a while. But on 30 January 1959, he shot and killed a taxi-driver there, while escaping from a bank which he had robbed. For this he was sentenced to life imprisonment.

He remained in jail in Switzerland until August 1976, when he was found to be insane. He was then returned to Britain and committed to Broadmoor.

Death of Rosaline Fox, 1929

OCTOBER
23

On the night of 23 October 1929, Mrs. Rosaline Fox, aged sixty-three, died at the Hotel Metropole in Margate following a fire in her bedroom. The fire alarm had been raised by her thirty-year-old son Sidney, who was staying at the hotel with her, and Mrs. Fox was still alive when she was dragged from the smoke-filled room by another guest. But she died almost immediately afterwards, her death being put down to shock and suffocation, and was buried in her native village of Great Fransham in Norfolk a few days later. There were, however, grounds for suspecting that her death had not been the result of an accident.

Mrs. Fox and her son had arrived at the hotel almost penniless and without luggage earlier the same month. Two accident policies on the dead woman's life, their value totalling £3000, had been due to expire on 22 October when Sidney Fox had extended them for the surprisingly short period of thirty-six hours — until midnight on the 23rd. Moreover, an investigation by the insurance company led to the discovery that the blaze had not originated in the gas fire, as had been supposed, but had almost certainly been started deliberately with the use of petrol.

A police investigation followed. The body of Mrs. Fox was exhumed eleven days after her funeral and a post-mortem was carried out by Sir Bernard Spilsbury, who gave the cause of death as manual strangulation. Sidney Fox, a homosexual with a record of petty crime, was then arrested and charged with murder. He was brought to trial at the Lewes Assizes on 12 March 1930.

During the course of the trial a serious disagreement between Spilsbury and two of his colleagues emerged; Spilsbury claimed to have found a bruise 'about the size of half a crown' at the back of the dead woman's larynx, but Professor Sydney Smith and Dr. Robert Brontë both said that no such bruise existed. However, the prisoner gave a poor impression of himself, telling the court that after finding his mother's room on fire he had gone out and closed the door so that 'the smoke should not spread into the hotel'.

Though the judge's summing-up was largely in the prisoner's favour as far as the forensic evidence was concerned, the circumstantial evidence against him was very strong and the jury found him guilty. He was hanged at Maidstone Prison on 8 April 1930.

Mrs Phoebe Hogg murdered, 1890

OCTOBER 24

On 24 October 1890, Mrs. Phoebe Hogg, thirty-one-year-old wife of a furniture remover living in Prince of Wales Road, Kentish Town, received a note inviting her to visit Mrs. Mary Eleanor Pearcey, a twenty-four-year-old friend of the family, in her rooms in Priory Street in the same district of London.

She went to the house, taking her eighteen-month-old daughter — also named Phoebe — whose pram she left in the hall. But not long after her arrival she was savagely murdered, her skull being fractured with a poker and her throat cut so deeply that her head was almost severed from her body.

Her child was also killed — by suffocation — though it is not known at what stage this happened, or whether it was done deliberately or by accident.

At any rate, Mrs. Pearcey, having done her best to

remove bloodstains from her top-skirt, an apron, her kitchen curtains and a rug, took the two bodies from the house in the little girl's pram and wheeled them through the streets covered with an antimacassar. It was dark by this time, and she was able to push the pram for some miles without anyone stopping or reporting her.

She finally left Mrs. Hogg's body at a building site in Crossfield Road, near Swiss Cottage, where it was found by a police constable later that night. The child's body was placed on waste ground in Finchley Road, where it was not discovered until the morning of 26 October. The pram was abandoned in Hamilton Terrace, between Maida Vale and St John's Wood.

Mrs. Pearcey, whose real name was Mary Eleanor Wheeler — she had assumed that name while living with a man named Pearcey who had since left her — had committed the murder, or murders, out of jealousy. Phoebe Hogg's husband Frank had been her lover since before his marriage, and had only married Phoebe because she was pregnant.

Eleanor Pearcey, though she had another lover — a man who paid for her rooms in Priory Street — had continued to entertain Hogg in secret whenever the opportunity arose. She hoped that with Phoebe out of the way she would have him entirely to herself.

The following morning, on hearing that an unknown woman had been murdered, Frank Hogg's sister Clara, who also lived in the house in Prince of Wales Road, called on Eleanor Pearcey to ask if she knew Phoebe's whereabouts. Mrs. Pearcey said that she did not, but agreed to go with Clara to the Hampstead police, to ask to see the murdered woman's body. But when they were taken to the mortuary she became hysterical, trying to drag the sister-in-law away from the corpse.

Clara identified the dead woman and, on being shown the pram which had been found in Hamilton Terrace, said that it had belonged to Phoebe. She and Eleanor Pearcey were then taken to the house in Prince of Wales Road, where Frank Hogg and his landlady were questioned about the murder.

When Hogg was searched a key to the house in Priory Street was found in his possession.

That afternoon, while her rooms were being inspected, Eleanor Pearcey played the piano, sang and talked about her 'poor dear dead Phoebe'. The police found broken windows and blood on the walls and ceiling of the kitchen; two carving-knives were bloodstained; the poker had blood and matted hair on it; a bloodstained tablecloth was found in an outhouse, and the stained rug smelt of paraffin, with which an attempt had been made to clean it.

Mrs. Pearcey's neighbours informed them that they had heard 'banging and hammering' about 4 p.m. the previous day, but had not realized where the noise was coming from.

Mrs. Pearcey was taken to Kentish Town police station, where she was charged with murder. When she was searched it was found that her hands had cuts on them and her underclothes were heavily bloodstained; a wedding ring on one of her fingers was identified as having belonged to Phoebe. Eleanor Pearcey was brought to trial at the Old Bailey on 1 December, her trial lasting four days. She was convicted and sentenced to death.

While she waited for the date of her execution to arrive, permission was obtained for Frank Hogg to visit her but he failed to do so.

Maintaining her innocence to the end, Eleanor Pearcey was hanged at Newgate Prison on 23 December 1890, the crowd outside cheering as the black flag appeared.

Oswald Martin taken ill, 1922

OCTOBER
26

On 26 October 1921, Oswald Martin, a thirty-two-year-old solicitor of Hay-on-Wye in Brecknockshire, called at the home of Major Herbert Rowse Armstrong, an older member of the same profession, at his home in the nearby village of Cusop. The two men were involved in a professional dispute over the uncompleted sale of an estate at the time, and it seemed that Armstrong, a widower of fifty-two with three children, had invited his young rival to tea in an attempt at conciliation.

However, they found that they had little to say to each other and neither of them raised the subject of the dispute. Later, after returning to his own home, Oswald Martin began to feel ill. He retched and vomited throughout the night, his illness continuing for some days afterwards.

His family doctor, Dr. Tom Hincks, was uneasy about his patient's symptoms, and became even more so after learning from Martin's father-in-law, a local chemist, that Major Armstrong regularly bought large quantities of arsenic from his shop. It was then remembered that a month earlier Martin had received a box of chocolates through the post, apparently from an anonymous well-wisher.

These chocolates had been placed on the table at a dinner-party at Martin's home on 8 October, but were eaten only by one of his sisters-in-law, who afterwards became ill.

In view of the suspicions which had suddenly been aroused, it was thought advisable to have the remaining chocolates, as well as a sample of Martin's urine, sent to the Clinical Research Association in London to be analysed. When both were found to contain arsenic, a

285

secret police investigation began, Major Armstrong being finally arrested in his office on 31 December and charged with attempted murder.

But by this time Armstrong was also suspected of having poisoned his wife, whose death on 22 February previously had been put down to heart disease. On 2 January 1922, Mrs. Armstrong's body was exhumed and a post-mortem carried out by Dr. Bernard Spilsbury revealed arsenic in her remains. Armstrong was subsequently charged with her murder.

He was brought to trial at the Hereford Assizes on 3 April, the case lasting ten days. The prisoner, a neat little man weighing only about seven stone, was confident that he would be acquitted, but could give no satisfactory explanation for having a packet of arsenic in one of his pockets, and a further two ounces of it in his desk at the time of his arrest. He was therefore found guilty.

His execution took place at Gloucester Prison on 31 May 1922.

Last crime of an Axe-man, 1919

OCTOBER 27

On 27 October 1919, Mike Pepitone, a New Orleans grocer, was brutally murdered in his own home by an unknown intruder. The crime was discovered by his wife, who rushed into the room in time to see the murderer escaping. The man had gained entry to the couple's home by chiselling out a door panel.

It was to prove to be the last of a series of violent crimes which had begun eight years earlier, the person responsible being known as the 'Axe-man of New Orleans'. A year later the victim's widow shot and killed a man named Joseph Mumfre in a Los Angeles street, declaring that *he* was the Axe-man.

The police found that Mumfre had a criminal record, and that all of the Axe-man's crimes had been committed during his brief periods of freedom following prison sentences. But no real evidence connected him with the crimes, and the identity of the culprit remains unknown.

The first four deaths attributed to the Axe-man had occurred in 1911; the victims were an Italian grocer named Tony Schiambras, his wife and two other grocers whose names were Cruti and Rosetti. These crimes were followed by a lull lasting until 23 May 1918, when somebody murdered another couple running a grocery store. Joseph Maggio and his wife were both struck with an axe as they slept, their assailant afterwards cutting their throats with a razor. In this case, the brothers of the dead man were accused but afterwards released.

Then, in the early hours of 28 June, Louis Besumer, another grocer, and his common-law wife were both attacked with a hatchet. Mrs. Besumer died of her injuries a few days later, and on 5 August her husband who had survived the attack, was arrested for her murder. But the same night, the Axe-man attacked a pregnant woman, Mrs. Scheider, whose husband found her unconscious when he returned home from work.

Mrs. Scheider recovered from the attack and gave birth to her child a week later. By this time the Axe-man had committed a further murder — that of Joseph Romano, a barber, who died of head wounds inflicted at his home on 10 August.

Louis Besumer, on being tried for his wife's murder, was acquitted.

On 10 March 1919, the Axe-man broke into the home of a family named Cortimiglia, injuring the husband and wife and killing their baby. Rosie Cortimiglia accused two members of an Italian family, Iorlando Jordano and his son Frank — who lived opposite them and, in fact, had found

287

them after the attack — of killing her child, but Charles Cortimiglia was equally insistent that neither of the Jordanos was responsible.

They were, however, brought to trial on 21 May 1919 and convicted, Frank being sentenced to death and his father to life imprisonment. But a few days after the shooting of Joseph Mumfre, Rosie Cortimiglia, whose husband had since left her, confessed that the Jordanos had *not* committed the crime and that she had accused them falsely out of malice. The two men were then set free.

In the meantime the Axe-man had attacked and injured a man named Steve Boca on 10 August 1919, had been disturbed in the act of trying to break into the home of a chemist on 2 September, and had attacked a nineteen-year-old girl in her bed on 3 September.

The Axe-man, having entered a building by chiselling out one of the door-panels, generally attacked his victims with an axe found on the premises, and invariably left the weapon at the scene of the crime. The motive for the attacks was never discovered, and the reason for their sudden cessation is also unknown.

Mrs. Pepitone was sentenced to ten years' imprisonment for shooting Mumfre, but served only three years before being released.

Wrotham Hill murder, 1946

OCTOBER
31

During the early morning of 31 October 1946, Dagmar Peters, a poor spinster aged forty-seven, left her home — a small bungalow which was really just a hut — at Kingsdown in Kent, to visit her sister-in-law in London. She did this every week, hitching lifts on lorries, but this time did not complete the journey. Later the same day her body was found in a shrubbery on Wrotham Hill on the A20. She had been strangled.

The murder had been committed while Miss Peters was sitting upright, and scratches on her legs, sustained after death, indicated that her body had been dragged or carried to the place where it was found. There was no apparent reason for the crime, for she had not been sexually assaulted and had been too poor to rob.

However, certain items known to have been in her possession — an attaché case, a purse, a key and a yellow string handbag — were missing, and the police appealed to the public in their attempts to trace them. At the same time inquiries were made about lorry-drivers known to have driven along that stretch of road between 5 a.m. and 8 a.m. on the day of the murder.

It was soon learnt that the yellow handbag had been found in a lake some distance from the road by a fifteen-year-old boy who had given it to a neighbour. She (the neighbour) had given it to another woman who, in turn, had given it to a third. The bag had thus changed hands three times within forty-eight hours, each of the three women scrubbing it as it came into her possession. Shortly after this discovery parts of the dead woman's attaché case were found further along the A20.

From subsequent inquiries it seemed that the yellow handbag had been carried downstream from the village of East Malling, where an old mill had been turned into a cider works. While discussing this possibility with his assistant, Detective Chief Inspector Robert Fabian noticed a pile of bricks standing at the factory gates. These were found to have been delivered on 31 October by a firm of haulage contractors in Cambridge which had so far been overlooked in connection with the investigation.

The driver who had delivered them, a man calling himself Sydney Sinclair, was interviewed at Cambridge Police Station. He was a tough-looking character and

Fabian, sensing that he was an old lag, soon got him to admit that his real name was Harold Hagger. He had sixteen convictions, including one for an assault on a woman.

Hagger admitted having handled the attaché case, saying that he had found it and then thrown it away. On being driven along the route, he pointed out the place where he had thrown it and then, surprisingly, showed Fabian where he had thrown a man's woollen vest which had also been owned by the victim. Miss Peters had bought it in Maidstone two days before her death and had been using it as a scarf when she set out to visit her sister-in-law. It proved to be the murder weapon.

On being questioned further, Hagger agreed that he had given the dead woman a lift in his lorry and said that he had 'got mad at her' and killed her by accident when she tried to steal his wallet from his jacket pocket. The jacket, according to him, had been hanging on a peg in the cab of the lorry at the time, but this was not believed, as on the morning in question it had been bitterly cold.

Harold Hagger was brought to trial for murder and, in spite of his apparent lack of motive, convicted and sentenced to death. He was hanged at Wandsworth Prison on 18 March 1947.

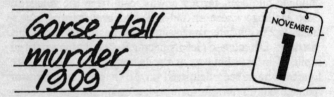

Gorse Hall murder, 1909

NOVEMBER 1

The unsolved murder of George Harry Storrs, a wealthy mill-owner and building contractor, took place at the victim's home, Gorse Hall, near Stalybridge in Cheshire, on the evening of 1 November 1909. Storrs, a generous and kindly man of forty-nine, had many friends and was liked by his employees; his coachman was so grieved by his death that he committed suicide a few days later. However, there is reason to believe that Storrs knew that he was in danger and it is generally assumed that he knew the identity of his murderer. If so, he died without revealing it.

A few weeks earlier, on 10 September, a man had broken into the grounds of Gorse Hall and fired a shot through one of the dining-room windows while the mill-owner, his wife and his wife's niece, Marion Lindley, were having dinner. Storrs, being healthy and vigorous, had gone after the intruder himself but been unable to prevent him escaping; he said afterwards — none too convincingly — that he did not know the culprit.

The incident led to the installation of an alarm bell which could be heard in Stalybridge on the roof of the hall. This was heard ringing two days before the murder, but when police arrived in response to it Storrs apologized, saying that he had rung it himself as a test. Clearly, he was apprehensive of the intruder returning.

When this happened on 1 November, the man got inside the house, armed with a revolver. Storrs once again tried to tackle him and Mrs. Storrs, managing to snatch the gun from his hand, ran upstairs to sound the alarm. But the intruder attacked the mill-owner with a knife, stabbing him repeatedly. By the time help arrived, Storrs lay dying and the man had fled.

The killer had been seen not only by Mrs. Storrs but also by Miss Lindley, the cook and the maid, and two weeks later, following their descriptions, the police arrested a young man named Cornelius Howard, living in Huddersfield, who turned out to be a cousin of the deceased.

Howard, a butcher with a record for burglary, was picked out at an identity parade and charged with the crime. But if he was guilty of it, his motive was unknown, for Mrs. Storrs and Miss Lindley both said that they had never seen him before the night of the murder and the deceased was not known to have had any contact with him.

On being brought to trial, Howard was acquitted.

Some months later a local man, Mark Wilde, was arrested after attacking another man with a knife similar to that with which Storrs had been murdered. Though Wilde was alleged to have owned the gun which had been taken from the killer's hand, and he, too, was identified by witnesses, he appeared to have had no connection at all with the inhabitants of Gorse Hall and was also acquitted.

No further arrests were ever made in connection with this baffling case, which is the subject of *The Stabbing of George Harry Storrs* by Jonathan Goodman.

Murder of PC Miles, 1952

NOVEMBER
2

On the night of 2 November 1952, two youths from south London, Christopher Craig, aged sixteen, and Derek Bentley, nineteen, attempted to break into a confectioner's warehouse in Croydon, Surrey, intent on burglary. Craig, whose older brother Niven was serving a long prison sentence for armed robbery, was carrying a revolver and a sheath knife; Bentley, who was illiterate and had a criminal record for shop-breaking, was armed with a knife and a knuckle-duster. The warehouse was in Tamworth Road.

They did not get into the premises unobserved, and ten minutes later a police van arrived at the scene, closely followed by a police car. Detective Constable Frederick Fairfax climbed on to the flat roof, twenty-five feet above the ground, where the two youths were hiding behind a lift-house. He called on them to give themselves up and, when they refused, rushed towards the lift-house and dragged Bentley out into the open.

Bentley, breaking free, shouted, 'Let him have it, Chris!' Craig then fired his gun, grazing the police officer's shoulder from a distance of six feet.

Fairfax, having fallen, got up and chased after Bentley, knocking him down with his fist. He took possession of his knife and knuckle-duster and held on to him firmly, calling out to Craig to drop his gun. 'Come and get it!' Craig called back to him from the other end of the roof.

Further shots were fired as other policemen closed in on him, and PC Sidney Miles, who had obtained the warehouse keys from the confectioner's manager, was killed as he stepped on to the roof from an interior staircase.

'Come on, you brave coppers!' shouted Craig. 'Think of your wives!' A moment later, after a truncheon, a milk-bottle and a piece of wood had been thrown at him, he continued: 'I'm Craig! You've just given my brother twelve years! Come on, you coppers! I'm only sixteen!'

By this time police reinforcements had arrived, some of the newcomers being armed. Bentley was taken from the roof, Fairfax returning with a gun. Shots were exchanged as he moved closer to Craig, taking cover behind roof-lights. Suddenly Craig found that his gun was empty. Rather than wait to be overpowered, he swung himself over the railings at the edge of the roof and jumped to the ground, fracturing his spine, breastbone and forearm. He and Fairfax spent the night in adjacent cubicles at the Croydon General Hospital.

On 9 December Bentley and Craig — the latter still using crutches — were brought to trial at the Old Bailey, charged with the murder of PC Miles. Both pleaded not guilty, Bentley on the grounds that he was under arrest at the time of the fatal shooting and had not known before-hand that his accomplice was armed, Craig on the grounds that he had not intended to kill Miles, or any of the other policemen, and had only fired shots in order to frighten them off.

After considering the cases for seventy-five minutes the jury found both prisoners guilty. Bentley was thereupon

293

sentenced to death, while Craig, as he was under eighteen years of age, was to be detained 'at Her Majesty's pleasure'. Though many pleas were made for Bentley's life to be spared, he was hanged at Wandsworth Prison on 28 January 1953.

Christopher Craig was released on licence in May 1963 and settled in Buckinghamshire. He married in 1965, at the age of twenty-eight.

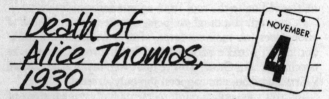

Death of Alice Thomas, 1930

NOVEMBER 4

During the early hours of 4 November 1930, Mrs. Alice Thomas, of Trenhorne Farm, Lewannick, in Cornwall, died at the Plymouth City Hospital shortly after being admitted. Her death gave rise to rumours, and when a post-mortem revealed the presence of arsenic in the body Mrs. Annie Hearn, a widow residing at Trenhorne House, 200 yards from the farm, was suspected of having poisoned her.

Mrs. Hearn, who was from the Midlands, had lived alone since the death of her sister, Lydia Everard, known as 'Minnie', on 21 July previously. Before that she and her sister had lived together at Trenhorne House, and both had been on good terms with Alice Thomas and her husband William.

On 18 October the couple had taken Mrs. Hearn for a drive to Bude, and during the course of that outing Mrs. Thomas had been ill after eating tinned-salmon sandwiches which Mrs. Hearn had prepared. Mrs. Hearn had afterwards stayed at the farm to look after her and had remained there to run the house when Mrs. Thomas' mother arrived to take over the nursing on 29 October.

However, it was said locally that Annie Hearn had been 'too friendly' with William Thomas, and this, together with the story of the salmon sandwiches, caused pointed remarks to be made by relatives attending the funeral on 8 November.

Two days later, Mrs. Hearn disappeared after writing a letter to the dead woman's husband, declaring her innocence. Her coat was found on the cliffs at Looe, on the Cornish coast, where it had apparently been left in order to give the impression that she had committed suicide.

The inquest on Alice Thomas was held on 24 November, the jury deciding on a verdict of murder by some person or persons unknown. This was followed on 9 December by the exhumation of Lydia Everard's body, in which arsenic was also found. Some weeks later Annie Hearn was discovered in Torquay, Devonshire, where she had been working as a housekeeper under a different name. She was arrested and charged with two murders.

At her trial at the Bodmin Assizes in June 1931, she faced only the charge of murdering Alice Thomas, though evidence concerning the death of her sister was introduced. But Crown witnesses had to agree that Lydia Everard's symptoms were consistent with chronic gastric catarrh, from which she had suffered for many years and which the doctor attending her had certified as the cause of her death.

It was also admitted that the organs taken for analysis had been left uncovered in the churchyard, thus exposing them to contamination by dust in an area in which the arsenic-level of the soil was exceptionally high due to the presence of tin.

The prosecution fared no better with its evidence concerning the death of Alice Thomas, for it was pointed out that, had the salmon sandwiches been poisoned with weed-killer, as alleged, they would have turned blue within a short time and nobody would have eaten them. A second dose of arsenic, from which Alice Thomas had finally died, might not have been administered during the period in which the accused was nursing her.

Annie Hearn told the court that she had not murdered anyone and denied the suggestion that she had hoped to marry William Thomas. She made a good impression, answering questions clearly and without faltering. After retiring for less than an hour the jury returned a verdict of not guilty and the prisoner was released.

The pathologist Sir Sydney Smith, who attended the trial as an adviser to Norman Birkett, the defence counsel, later described Annie Hearn as 'a foolish woman but not a murderess'. His comments on the case, in *Mostly Murder*, seem to imply that he suspected William Thomas of being the real culprit.

Body in blazing Car, 1930

NOVEMBER
6

During the early hours of 6 November 1930, two young men walking towards the village of Hardingstone in Northamptonshire after attending a Guy Fawkes' Night dance, saw a fire a short distance ahead of them. As they approached it, a respectably-dressed man climbed out of a nearby ditch and hurried past them on the opposite side of the lane, remarking, 'It looks as if someone has had a bonfire!' But the young men found that it was a car which was burning, with flames leaping to a height of fifteen feet, and ran to the village to report the matter. Later, when the flames had been extinguished, a charred corpse was found lying across the two front seats.

Though the body was unrecognizable, the ownership of the car was traced to Alfred Arthur Rouse, a thirty-six-year-old commercial traveller of Buxted Road, Finchley in north London. When the police contacted Mrs. Rouse, she said that her husband had left home on business the previous night, and also that she believed she recognized pieces of clothing retrieved from the wreckage as belonging to him. However, the police were suspicious and, following extensive publicity of the case, soon learnt that Rouse was still alive. He was apprehended at Hammersmith Bus Terminus on the night of 7 November and taken to the nearest police station for questioning.

Rouse claimed that on the night of 5 November he had given a lift to a stranger who wanted to go to Leicester. He had stopped the car in the lane near Hardingstone and asked his passenger to refill the petrol tank while he himself went into a nearby field to relieve his bowels. Shortly afterwards, he said, he had realized that the car was on fire with the man still inside it. Unable to open the door, he had then panicked and run away.

Sir Bernard Spilsbury's examination of the body had revealed that the man was still alive when the fire started. But a scrap of cloth found in the car smelled of petrol, and an expert fire-assessor found that the carburettor had been tampered with and a trail of petrol on the roadside ignited. The two young men from the village identified Rouse as the man who had climbed out of the ditch at the time of the fire.

It was discovered that Rouse had been wounded in the head with shrapnel during the First World War, and had been a compulsive womanizer ever since. He had mistresses in many towns, and his life had become increasingly complicated by maintenance orders and promises of marriage which he could not keep, though on one occasion he had committed bigamy. It seemed that he had suddenly decided to fake his own death and assume a new identity.

Charged with the murder of an unknown man, Rouse appeared for trial at the Northampton Assizes on 26 January 1931. The case lasted six days, the accused showing himself to be callous and boastful; the jury was left in no doubt that he was guilty. He was hanged at Bedford, at the age of thirty-seven, on 10 March the same year and his confession, in which he claimed to have strangled his victim after getting him drunk, was later published in the *Daily Sketch*.

The identity of his victim was never discovered.

Double murder in Cornwall, 1952

On 7 November 1952, Miles Giffard, a twenty-six-year-old unemployed man of Porthpean in Cornwall, murdered both of his parents. The crime was evidently premeditated, but so clumsily committed that it is hard to believe that he expected to get away with it. Indeed, his conduct afterwards was so careless that his arrest was inevitable, and when it happened he immediately confessed. The crime may therefore be said to have been characteristic of Giffard, for had he not been a failure in other respects it would not have taken place.

The Giffards lived in a large house on the cliffs overlooking Carlyon Bay, two miles from St. Austell, where Charles Henry Giffard was Clerk to the Magistrates. Miles Giffard had been sent to Rugby, but was afterwards removed, suffering from mental deterioration; his illness was diagnosed as a form of schizophrenia, but he was never treated for it. Later he studied law for a while, then gave it up in favour of a course in estate management; but at twenty-five, on inheriting £750, he gave that up as well, and made no further attempt to study anything.

He spent the next four months squandering his inheritance in Bournemouth, worked for a few weeks selling ice-cream, then in June 1952 returned to Porthpean to live off his parents. By now he was a constant disappointment to his father, if he had not been before, and there were some differences between them. In an attempt to assert his independence, Miles Giffard moved to London in the middle of August and rented a furnished room. But he failed in this as well, and after being reduced to living from hand to mouth, he decided to return home once again and ask his father for help.

While in London, however, he had become attached to nineteen-year-old Gabrielle Vallance, who lived in Tite Street, Chelsea; it was his desire to go on seeing her after his return to Porthpean which led to the final conflict between his father and himself. For Charles Giffard, though he gave his son the use of his car, forbade him to make trips to London. And Miles, at the age of twenty-six, was so dependent on his father that he did not dare to disobey him.

'I am dreadfully fed up as I was looking forward to seeing you,' he wrote to Gabrielle on 3 November. 'Short of doing him in, I see no future in the world at all.'

Four days later, however, he telephoned her at 5.30 p.m., saying that he would probably be travelling to London within a few hours on his father's behalf, and that he would call her again at 8.30 p.m. to confirm this. At 7.30 he found his father in the garage, working on Mrs. Giffard's car, and knocked him unconscious with an iron pipe. He then went into the kitchen and, approaching his mother from behind, struck her down with the same weapon.

At this point he telephoned Gabrielle again and said that he would be driving to London in his father's Triumph; he asked if he could have a wash and shave at her house on arrival. After the phone call, he struck both parents several more times, killing his father but not his mother. He pushed his mother to the edge of the cliff in a wheelbarrow and tipped her over, then disposed of his father's body in the same way, pushing the wheelbarrow over after him.

Before leaving Porthpean Giffard tried to clear up all the blood from the kitchen and garage; he also took pieces of jewellery from his mother's room and money from his father's coat pocket. He disposed of the murder weapon and some bloodstained articles of clothing on the way to London, and later stopped to give a lift to a couple of hitch-hikers. He rang Gabrielle's door bell at 8 a.m. on 8 November after resting for three hours in the car. He sold his mother's jewellery for £50 shortly afterwards.

On the evening of the 8th Giffard took Gabrielle to a pub and suddenly, under the influence of drink, told her that he had killed his parents. He said afterwards that 'it upset her, and we just moved on to further public houses, drinking'. The bodies, in the meantime, had been discovered; so, too, had the Triumph which had been left in Tite Street. So when Giffard took Gabrielle back to her home after closing time, he found the police waiting for him.

'I can only say that I have had a brainstorm,' he said in his statement. 'I cannot account for my actions. I had drunk about half a bottle of whisky on the Friday afternoon — before all this happened. It just seemed to me that nothing mattered as long as I got back to London.'

Miles Giffard was brought to trial at the Bodmin Assizes, a plea of insanity being made on his behalf. However, the jury deliberated for only a short while before returning a verdict of guilty. A panel of psychiatrists appointed by the Home Secretary afterwards declared him to be sane. He was therefore hanged at Bristol on 24 February 1953.

Death of Catherine Labbé, 1954

NOVEMBER
8

On the afternoon of 8 November 1954, Catherine Labbé, an illegitimate child aged two and a half, was drowned in a stone washing-basin in the courtyard of her grandmother's house at Vendôme, near Blois, in France. Denise Labbé, the child's mother, was in charge of her at the time and claimed that the drowning had been an accident. But suspicions were aroused and an examining magistrate was appointed to conduct an inquiry into the circumstances of it.

Denise Labbé, a twenty-eight-year-old secretary who worked in Paris, was arrested soon afterwards, and in January 1955 was charged with having attempted to murder her daughter on three earlier occasions. She then made a statement to the examining magistrate, admitting that she had killed her daughter and claiming that it had been a 'ritual murder'.

'I am the mistress of Jacques Algarron, Second Lieutenant in the School of Artillery at Châlons-sur-Marne,' she said. 'It was he who asked me to kill my child in order to prove my love for him ...' She went on to explain that Algarron, whom she had first met on 1 May the previous year, had cast a spell over her, saying, 'The price of our love must be the death of your daughter. Kill for me. An innocent victim must be sacrificed.' The attempts on Catherine's life had all been made since then and against Denise's own will.

Algarron, who was four years younger than Denise Labbé, denied having been in any way involved in the child's death, but was arrested and held in custody. A week later he was confronted with his accuser in the examining magistrate's chambers. He listened calmly as she repeated her allegations and, on being asked what he had to say in reply, answered, 'The girl is completely out of her head.'

The examining magistrate, however, continued his inquiry, Denise Labbé and Jacques Algarron remaining in prison in Blois. They were eventually brought to trial on 30 May 1955, the accusations and denials being repeated in court.

'He wanted our union to go from suffering to suffering until we became the ideal couple,' said Denise. 'One day, in a Paris restaurant, he asked me whether I would kill my child for him. I replied, "Yes."'

She went on to tell the court that he had told her to take sick leave from her job and throw Catherine into the river at Rennes. 'It was terrible for me because I wanted to keep my child,' she said, sobbing uncontrollably.

Algarron dismissed the whole idea as incredible. 'Doubtlessly I was at fault for not having realized what she really was — a girl without culture or finesse,' he said coldly. 'But my fault went no further than that. I would never have wanted the death of Catherine.' He described the murder as 'the most monstrous act that anyone could have committed', and said that he found it impossible to explain to himself how she could have done such a thing. Later a number of his former mistresses, of whom there were many, were called to testify that he had been a normal lover and had made no extraordinary demands on them.

But Madame Laurent, a professional foster-mother who had looked after Catherine at Agly, near Paris, told the court that Denise had been a devoted mother, and concluded her testimony by screaming at Algarron, 'Beast! Beast! Beast!' She was followed to the witness stand by Madame Thébault, who had been Denise's best friend. This witness told the court how Denise had returned to Algarron after one of the unsuccessful attempts on her daughter's life.

'She and Algarron looked at each other without saying a word when she arrived. Then she broke down in tears, throwing herself into her lover's arms. But she had exactly the attitude of a woman who was imploring her lover's pardon.'

The Advocate General described the crime as being exceptional not only for its horror but also for the absence of any easily-discernible motive. He said that Algarron, having realized Denise Labbé's 'exceptional sensuality', had inspired the crime out of a perverse desire to experiment with her and convince himself that she was in his power.

The jury deliberated for nearly three hours before returning to give their verdict. Denise Labbé, who was found guilty of murder with extenuating circumstances, was sentenced to penal servitude for life. Jacques Algarron, who was found guilty of having provoked the crime, was given twenty years' hard labour.

Denise Labbé's use of the phrase 'ritual murder' in connection with the affair was never explained.

WAAF found murdered 1944

NOVEMBER
9

During the early morning of 9 November 1944, the body of WAAF Winifred Evans, a twenty-seven-year-old wireless operator, was found in a ditch by the roadside at an aerodrome near Beccles in Suffolk. She had been suffocated, the person responsible having held her face down in the mud during the course of a brutal sexual attack. The case was investigated by Scotland Yard.

It was learnt that the previous evening Winifred Evans had been to a dance at a nearby American camp with Corporal Margaret Johns, a friend in the same unit as herself; they had returned to their station about midnight.

Winifred Evans had then visited the WAAF quarters before going off in the direction of the aerodrome where she was due to relieve another operator.

A moment or two afterwards Margaret Johns had found a man in an RAF uniform lurking in an ablution hut at the WAAF quarters; he was drunk and claimed to have lost his way back to his own camp, less than a mile away. She had given him directions and he had set off along the same road as Winifred Evans, and only a short distance behind her. It was on this road that the crime had taken place.

The police soon discovered that the airman in question was LAC Arthur Heys, a married man aged thirty-seven with a young family. He had been seen returning to his quarters after 1 a.m. on the night of the murder, and had spent a lot of time cleaning his clothes the following morning. Without Heys' knowledge, the police used his next pay parade for the purpose of identification, and Corporal Johns picked him out without difficulty.

Heys' clothing was examined by a pathologist, who found bloodstains on his tunic, rabbit hairs on his trousers — as on the clothes of the dead girl — and brickdust from the ditch on his shoes. Though Dr. Keith Simpson warned that the scientific evidence was far from conclusive, Heys was arrested and charged with the crime.

Before he was brought to trial his commanding officer received an anonymous letter, written in block letters with a blue pencil. It was a confession to the murder, stating that Heys had been wrongly accused and containing details which only the murderer could have known.

On comparing this with samples of Heys' own lettering, Superintendent Fred Cherrill, the fingerprint expert, found proof that the prisoner had written it himself. It had been written in Norwich Prison and smuggled out.

Heys was brought to trial in Bury St Edmunds in January 1945, the anonymous letter proving to be the most damning piece of evidence against him. The jury took forty minutes to find him guilty and he was afterwards hanged.

Murder of Angela Woolliscroft, 1976

On 10 November 1976, a man wearing sunglasses and armed with a sawn-off shotgun entered the branch of Barclays Bank in Upper Ham Road, Richmond, Surrey, and demanded money. After being given £2500 in notes by one of the cashiers he fired the gun at her, shattering the glass partition and wounding her in the chest and hand. He then turned and fled, dropping a woman's yellow raincoat and an empty plastic fertilizer bag in his haste to get away. The wounded cashier, Angela Woolliscroft, aged twenty, died on the way to hospital.

The owner of the raincoat, a Miss Marshall, was traced from two pieces of paper which had been left screwed up in the pocket. She told police that she had taken her sister-in-law shopping on the morning of the murder, leaving her faded maroon A40 car in a store car park in Kingston with the passenger door unlocked. On returning to it soon after 2 p.m. she had found the car in a different position with her raincoat and a pair of sunglasses missing, she explained. She had also found a lot of mud on the back of the car, some of it sticking to the number plate.

Further inquiries revealed that the car had been seen near the bank and that the driver had narrowly avoided a collision with another car immediately after the crime. It was learnt, too, that on returning the car to the car park, he had drawn attention to himself in his attempts to make other drivers give way to him. The fertilizer bag was found to have been taken from a small green opposite the bank, where it had been left by a part-time gardener who had been clearing leaves.

The police received many pieces of information from people hoping to claim a large reward offered by Barclays, one informant stating that he had seen a man named Michael George Hart taking a shotgun from one car to another in Basingstoke, Hampshire, twenty-five miles from the bank. The man in question was interviewed and his house was searched, but no evidence was found connecting him with the murder. He was, however, a known criminal, so arrangements were made for him to be kept under observation by the local police.

On 22 November the same man was recognized as the driver of a car which had just been involved in an accident. He had left the scene and, on being pursued, managed to get away. But the car was afterwards found abandoned, with an automatic pistol and seventy-two rounds of ammunition in the boot. The gun had been stolen, together with a double-barrelled shotgun and another pistol, during a burglary at a gun-shop in Reading, Berkshire, on 4 November.

Hart avoided arrest until 20 January 1977, when he tried to collect money owed to him for some work which he had carried out as a self-employed builder several months previously. He was then taken into custody and, following an unsuccessful suicide attempt, made a confession. He had driven to the car park in Kingston in a borrowed car and chosen Miss Marshall's A40 for the robbery because he had an ignition key which fitted it, he said. He had taken the yellow raincoat to hide the shotgun, and had intended to put the money into the fertilizer bag. He had afterwards covered the rear number plate of the car with mud to hinder identification.

Hart also revealed that he had blackened his face with boot polish and worn a wig as well as Miss Marshall's sunglasses. He maintained that he had shot Angela Woolliscroft by accident, though forensic evidence proved otherwise. The shotgun was later recovered from the Thames at Hampton Court.

At the time of the murder Hart was already awaiting trial on burglary charges in Basingstoke, and was wanted for attempted murder in France. He had been refused bail four times but granted it on his fifth application, on condition that he reported to the Basingstoke police twice a day. He had committed a further thirty-nine offences since the murder, including burglary, fraud, theft and receiving stolen property, some of them in association with a young woman.

On 3 November 1977, Hart, aged thirty, was convicted of murder at the Old Bailey. He was sent to prison for life, with a recommendation that he should serve at least twenty-five years. His female accomplice was sent to prison for three years for issuing worthless cheques.

Murder of Joseph Bedford, 1933

NOVEMBER
13

On the evening of 13 November 1933, Joseph Bedford, an eighty-year-old bachelor, was attacked and robbed in his dingy general store in Portslade, Sussex, receiving head injuries from which he died in hospital the following morning. The crime was committed about 8 p.m., as the old man was about to close the shop, but was not discovered until two hours later. About 9.50 a neighbour reported that the light in the shop was still on and that some of Mr. Bedford's stock was still out on the pavement. A police constable arrived to investigate the matter.

He found the door locked, but heard sounds from the dimly-lit interior — 'as if someone were stumbling against something'. Flashing his torch through the glass, he saw the shopkeeper inside with his face covered with blood. At that moment the old man staggered and fell against a showcase, and by the time the door had been forced open he was lying on the floor. His assailants had got away with about £6.

Two young men, both of them strangers to the neighbourhood, had been seen hanging about outside the shop just before the attack. They were later found to be in police custody in Worthing, where they had been arrested on a charge of loitering with intent to commit a felony.

When interviewed about the attack on Mr. Bedford, Frederick William Parker, a twenty-one-year-old labourer, admitted that he and his accomplice, Albert Probert, a fitter aged twenty-six, were the men concerned. He and Probert, he said, had held up the old man with an unloaded gun after locking the shop door, and had stolen the money from two chocolate boxes which he used as a till.

'I wish it had been a bigger job,' he said. 'It was not worth doing for £6.'

It was not until after he had admitted being involved in the crime that he learned of the old man's death, but he had blamed Probert for the violence from the outset.

Probert denied having had anything to do with it. But on 23 November, after they had each been given a nominal sentence of one day's imprisonment for the offence for which they had been arrested, the two men were jointly charged with murder.

They appeared for trial at the Sussex Assizes in Lewes on 14 March the following year. Both pleaded not guilty, a suggestion being made on their behalf that Mr. Bedford may have died of misadventure, having fallen and fractured his skull as a result of being frightened by the police constable's torch. But they were convicted of murder, the jury having retired for thirty-five minutes.

They were hanged at Wandsworth Prison on 4 May 1934.

Murder in Agra, 1912

On the night of 17 November 1912, four thugs entered the home of Henry Clark, a doctor in the Indian Subordinate Medical Service in Agra, and killed his wife with a sword. Clark was not there at the time and later told police that he had been seeing Mrs. Augusta Fullam, the widow of a military accounts examiner who had died the previous year. The police questioned Mrs. Fullam as a matter of course, and then decided to search her bungalow.

Finding a metal box which Clark had left in her care, they insisted upon having it opened. They thus discovered about 400 love letters, suggesting not only that Clark and Mrs. Fullam had been having an affair, but also that they had poisoned Mrs. Fullam's husband. Subsequent inquiries revealed that the four thugs who murdered Mrs. Clark had been hired to do so by Clark himself.

The affair had started during the summer of 1909 when Henry Clark, aged forty two, and Augusta Fullam, thirty-five, met at a ball in Meerut where they were both then living. They quickly fell in love and remained so after Clark had been posted to Agra about a year later. Following a brief reunion in April 1911, Clark began sending Mrs. Fullam supplies of arsenic — referred to as 'tonic powders' in their letters — for the purpose of disposing of her husband.

Edward Fullam, whose doctor was worried by his symptoms, was sent to the Agra Station Hospital on 8 October the same year. There, on 10 October, he died, having been given an injection of the same poison by Henry Clark, who also signed the death certificate. The true cause of Fullam's death was not discovered until nearly fourteen months late' when a court order was obtained for the body to 'e xnumed

Henry Clark and Augusta Fullam were brought to trial in two separate cases before the Allahabad High Court, the second case being against the four thugs as well as themselves. The letters found in Clark's metal box provided the prosecution with a good deal of evidence, and Mrs. Fullam sought to save herself by accusing her lover of the crime. But both were convicted, and Clark was hanged on 26 March 1913.

Mrs. Fullam, who was pregnant at the time of the trial, was sentenced to life imprisonment. She served only fifteen months before dying of heat-stroke on 29 May the following year.

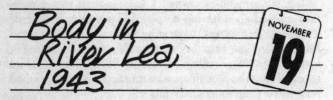

Body in River Lea, 1943

NOVEMBER 19

On the afternoon of 19 November 1943, corporation sewer men working in Luton, Bedfordshire, noticed a roughly-tied bundle wrapped in sacks in a few inches of water near the edge of the river Lea. Discovering that it contained a corpse, they informed the police; it was then found to be the body of a woman who had been dead for between twelve and twenty-four hours. She had been beaten to death with a blunt instrument, following an unsuccessful attempt to strangle her.

The woman's face had been badly battered and had to be treated in order to restore the features to their original appearance. There were no items of clothing or jewellery to help the police identify her; even her false teeth were missing. Moreover, a check on her fingerprints revealed that she had no criminal record. The police had therefore to resort to public appeals and exhaustive routine inquiries in the hope of identifying her. For three months, during the course of which they took thousands of statements, these proved unavailing.

Then, in February 1944, a large assortment of rags and pieces of clothing, collected from dustbins and rubbish dumps, was re-examined in the hope that some clue, previously overlooked, would come to light. Part of a black coat with a dyer's tag attached to it was then investigated further and found to have belonged to a Rene Manton, of Regent Street, Luton.

Detective Chief Inspector Chapman of Scotland Yard, acting upon instinct, went to Rene Manton's address personally and the door was opened to him by a little girl of eight who appeared to him to bear a strong resemblance to the dead woman. Learning from her that her mother had 'gone away', he interviewed her father, Horace William Manton — known as 'Bertie' — a lorry-driver employed by the National Fire Service.

In answer to a question regarding the whereabouts of his wife, Manton replied, 'Oh, she left me some time ago, and is working somewhere in London.' He produced a number of letters which she had apparently sent him from Hampstead during the previous three months. But Chapman did not regard these as proof that Mrs. Manton was still alive, and arranged for Superintendent Fred Cherrill to search the house for fingerprints.

Cherrill examined every object and every surface in the whole house without finding a single one of Mrs. Manton's fingerprints until he came to the very last object of all — a pickle bottle in the cellar, covered with dust. On this he found a thumbprint which corresponded with one of the dead woman's.

Bertie Manton was arrested and charged with his wife's murder. He then made a confession.

'I killed her,' he said. 'But it was only because I lost my temper. I didn't intend to. She left me about last Christmas twelvemonths, and was away for five months ... I persuaded her to mend her ways and come back to me for the

311

children's sake. She was very grumpy and quarrelsome because she thought she was going to have a baby.'

On the day of her death, he said, they had been sitting together by the fireside when a quarrel started and his wife suddenly threw a cup of hot tea in his face, saying that she hoped it would blind him.

'I lost my temper, picked up a very heavy wooden stool, and hit her about the head and face several times,' he continued. 'When I came to and got my senses again I saw what I'd done. I saw she was dead and decided I had to do something to keep her away from the children. I undressed her and got four sacks from the cellar, cut them open, and tied her up in them. I carried her down to the cellar and left her there.'

He went on to state that he had washed up all the blood and hidden the bloodstained clothing before the four children came home, and then, when they had all gone out again, wheeled his wife's body to the river on his bicycle. The next day he burnt the bloodstained clothing, together with his wife's false teeth, in the copper.

Since then he had managed to keep up the pretence that she was still alive by writing letters, ostensibly from her, and making trips to London to post them.

Bertie Manton was brought to trial at the Bedford Assizes. He pleaded not guilty to the charge of murder, claiming that he was guilty only of manslaughter, as he had had no intention of killing his wife and had been provoked into attacking her. However, the marks on her neck, which indicated that he had tried to strangle her, caused the jury to believe otherwise and he left the court under sentence of death.

His sentence was afterwards commuted to life imprisonment, but he died three years later, in November 1947, at Parkhurst Prison.

Death of Chrissie Gall, 1931

About three o'clock in the morning on 21 November 1931, Peter Queen, the son of a bookmaker, rushed into a Glasgow police station and reported that the woman he called his wife was dead. The police went to his home and found the body of Chrissie Gall with whom he had been living for almost a year: she had been strangled with a piece of clothes-line. There were no signs of a struggle. Chrissie Gall was lying in bed with the bedclothes pulled up over her chest; her false teeth were in place in her mouth. But at 5.30 that morning Peter Queen was charged with her murder.

Queen, a clerk in his father's office, had married at eighteen, but he and his wife — an alcoholic — had only lived together for two years. Chrissie Gall, who had once been employed by his father as a nursemaid, began living with Queen in December 1930, when he was thirty years old and she was twenty-seven. Chrissie, however, was tormented by the fear that others would find out about this. Drinking heavily, she began to suffer from depression, several times attempting suicide. But the two pathologists who carried out a post-mortem both said that she had been murdered.

The trial of Peter Queen began in Glasgow on 5 January 1932. It was stated by police witnesses that, on going to report Chrissie Gall's death, the accused had said, 'Go to 539, Dumbarton Road. I think you will find my wife dead. I think I have killed her.' Queen disputed this, telling the court that what he had actually said was, '*Don't* think I have killed her.' It was reluctantly admitted by the police that the statement had not been put into writing.

The medical evidence given for the prosecution was

313

challenged by Sir Bernard Spilsbury and Sir Sydney Smith, who both appeared as defence witnesses. Spilsbury declared that Chrissie Gall had committed suicide; Smith was inclined to the same view, though with less certainty. Other witnesses told the court of the prisoner's love and kindness towards her, and also of Chrissie's suicidal tendencies.

In spite of all this, the jury found the accused guilty of murder, but added a recommendation of mercy. Peter Queen was sentenced to death, the sentence afterwards being commuted to life imprisonment. He died in 1958.

Execution of Dr. Crippen, 1910

NOVEMBER
23

Dr. Hawley Harvey Crippen, who was hanged on 23 November 1910, was an American doctor who had settled in London ten years earlier, making his living from the sale of patent medicines. He was a little man with a sandy moustache and gold-rimmed glasses, polite and considerate but very discontented. His first wife had died about 1890, and his second marriage, to the ill-fated Cora Turner, had taken place two or three years later. This was the main cause of his dissatisfaction.

Cora was the daughter of a Russian Pole; her real name, prior to her marriage, had been Kunigunde Mackamotzki. She was stout and flamboyant, and sang in music halls, calling herself Belle Elmore; she had many friends and admirers in the theatrical world. But to Crippen, who was obliged to do most of the housework, she was domineering and bad-tempered. He often quarrelled with her.

For three years he found consolation in the company of

314

his typist, Ethel le Neve, a younger woman who had become his mistress. But then he lost his job and his wife threatened to go and live with another man, taking their joint savings. Crippen was thus faced with serious financial difficulties and suddenly decided upon a desperate course.

On 19 January 1910, he obtained five grains of hyoscine, a poison, from a chemist's in New Oxford Street. Less than a fortnight later his wife disappeared, and Crippen began telling friends that she had returned to America because one of her relatives was ill. But he also pawned some of her jewellery and, within a few weeks, moved Ethel le Neve into their home in Hilldrop Crescent, Holloway. Finally, towards the end of March, he announced that Mrs. Crippen had died in America.

It was not until another three months had elapsed that Scotland Yard was asked to investigate the matter, and even then a search of the house by Detective Chief Inspector Walter Dew revealed no incriminating evidence. However, the visit alarmed Crippen and his mistress, and they immediately fled the country. During a more thorough search of the premises, the police then found human remains under the floor of the cellar.

The remains, from which the head, limbs and skeleton had been removed, were those of Cora Crippen: they were identified from a piece of scar tissue, the result of abdominal surgery. The presence of hyoscine in her organs proved that she had been poisoned, and a warrant was issued for the arrest of her husband and Ethel le Neve for 'murder and mutilation'.

A few days later the captain of the SS *Montrose*, sailing from Antwerp to Quebec, recognized two of his passengers as the fugitives. Crippen had shaved off his moustache and Ethel was dressed as a boy: they were travelling as Mr. John Robinson and his sixteen-year-old son. The captain sent a wireless message to the ship's owners in Liverpool, informing them of this, and Scotland Yard was notified. Chief Inspector Dew then boarded a faster ship, the SS

Laurentic, and arrested the couple in Canadian waters on 31 July.

It was, as most accounts point out, the first time that wireless had been used during the course of a murder hunt, and it was also the first major case in which the renowned pathologist Dr. Bernard Spilsbury, was involved.

Crippen, aged forty-eight, was tried at the Old Bailey in October 1910. Shortly before he was hanged at Pentonville Prison he made a public statement, declaring his love for Ethel le Neve and maintaining that she was entirely innocent. She, in the meantime, had been tried on the charge of being an accessory after the fact, and acquitted. It is not known for certain what became of her afterwards.

John Barleycorn murder, 1943

On the morning of 29 November 1943, Mrs. Rose Ada Robinson, a sixty-three-year-old widow who managed the John Barleycorn public house in Portsmouth, was found strangled in her bedroom. The room had been ransacked and two large handbags in which she kept money from the till were empty. The crime had been committed in the early hours, the murderer having entered the premises by forcing open a window at the back. No fingerprints had been left at the scene and the only possible clue to his identity was a small black button which had been pulled from his coat as he climbed through the window. It was later ascertained that the sum of money stolen was about £450.

The police checked on all known criminals who lived locally, but made no progress on the case until three weeks later, when Harold Loughans, a man with a long record of crime, was arrested trying to sell a stolen pair of shoes in Waterloo Road, London. Loughans, apparently suffering from remorse, told the arresting officers, 'I'm wanted for things far more serious than this. The Yard wants me. It's the trap-door for me now.' He went on to confess that it was he who had killed Mrs. Robinson, after being discovered in the act of burgling the pub.

'I had to stop her screaming, but I didn't mean to kill the old girl,' he said. 'But you know what it is when a woman screams.' He went on to declare that he had since committed a dozen other burglaries — 'to get it off my mind'.

There were no buttons on his coat to match the one found on Mrs. Robinson's window-sill — he had pulled the others off and replaced them — but various fibres found on his clothes were identified as having come from the scene of the crime. Loughans, in the meantime, had dictated and signed a confession. He was therefore charged with the murder.

Brought to trial in Winchester in March 1944, he pleaded not guilty, claiming that the confession had been fabricated by the police and producing witnesses to swear that he had spent the night of the murder at a London Underground station, which was then being used as an air-raid shelter. The jury failed to agree on a verdict, so a retrial was ordered.

This took place at the Old Bailey a fortnight later, the judge refusing to allow new evidence collected by the police to rebut Loughans' alibi on the grounds that it should have been presented at the first trial. However, Sir Bernard Spilsbury, who had not given evidence in the previous trial, was allowed to appear as a defence witness and stated his belief that the accused, who had a mutilated right hand — the four fingers were merely stumps, although the thumb was intact — could not have committed the murder. This time Loughans was acquitted.

As he left the court a free man, he was immediately

arrested again, this time for another of the crimes to which he had confessed: a burglary in St. Albans, during the course of which he had almost killed a second woman by tying her up with wire. For this he was sent to prison, having been convicted of attempted murder. He later fell foul of the law again and was given fifteen years' preventive detention.

He was still in prison in December 1960 when the *People* newspaper published extracts from the autobiography of J.D. Casswell, who had appeared for the prosecution in both trials arising out of the John Barleycorn case. These, according to Loughans, suggested that he was guilty of the murder and said clearly that he had been lucky to be acquitted. He accordingly started libel proceedings, and the case was heard in 1963.

Loughans was now sixty-seven years old and suffering from cancer of the stomach; his appearance was that of a weak and tired man. But the jury, after hearing much of the evidence which had been given in the two John Barleycorn trials, *and also evidence of Loughans' crime at St. Albans a fortnight after Mrs. Robinson's murder,* found for the defendants — saying, in effect, that the plaintiff was guilty of the crime of which he had been acquitted.

Even this was not the end of the matter, for a few months later Loughans approached the *People* and offered that newspaper an article admitting that he *had* murdered Mrs. Robinson. The *People* published his story together with a photograph of him writing it.

Harold Loughans died at the age of sixty-nine in 1965.

Chalkpit murder discovered, 1946

NOVEMBER
30

On 30 November 1946, the body of John McMain Mudie, a thirty-five-year-old hotel barman, was found lying in a trench in a chalkpit near Woldingham in Surrey. He had died of asphyxia, caused by hanging, about forty-eight hours earlier, and an unsuccessful attempt had been made to cover his body with soil. There were no signs of anyone having been hanged from a tree in the vicinity, and there were several minor bruises and abrasions on the body which had not been caused by the hanging itself. A straight line round Mudie's neck, visible only in photographs, showed that the noose had been tightened before he was suspended.

Mudie had worked at the Reigate Hill Hotel, about twelve miles from the chalkpit, for the previous few months, before that he had lived in Wimbledon. He was said to have been quiet and inoffensive, and there appeared to have been no reason for his murder. However, when the police appealed to the public for information, two gardeners came forward, saying that they had seen a man behaving suspiciously at the chalkpit on 27 November — the day before Mudie's death.

He had been standing on a hill overlooking the pit until he saw them, they said, and had then run down the side of it at great speed, jumped into a parked car and driven out hastily in reverse. The car, according to these witnesses, had been a small dark saloon with the figures 101 in its registration number.

On 14 December, following further publicity, an ex-boxer named John William Buckingham went to Scotland Yard and confessed that he and another man, Lawrence Smith, had abducted Mudie, having been hired to do so by

319

Thomas Ley, the sixty-six-year-old chairman of a property company.

'Ley told me Mudie was blackmailing a young woman and her mother who lived in Wimbledon, and that he wanted to make Mudie sign a confession and leave the country,' said Buckingham.

He went on to explain that on the day of his disappearance, Mudie had been decoyed to Ley's house in Beaufort Gardens, Kensington, by means of a bogus invitation to a cocktail party, and on arrival had been pushed into the front room and held against his will. Ley had then paid Buckingham £200 for his part in the affair and Buckingham had left the house.

When Lawrence Smith, a foreman joiner, was confronted with Buckingham's statement, he agreed that the abduction had taken place, but said that Buckingham's part in it had been greater than the statement suggested. He said that when Mudie arrived at the house he and Buckingham had thrown a rug over his head and tied him up with a clothes line. They had afterwards left him bound and gagged in Ley's presence, Smith leaving the house — also with £200 — shortly after Buckingham.

Thomas Ley, an extremely fat man, was a qualified solicitor who had once been Minister of Justice in New South Wales. Mrs. Maggie Brook, one of the directors of the property company, was his former housekeeper and mistress, and was known to have stayed for a short while in the same lodging-house as Mudie in Wimbledon. It was also known that Ley, an intensely jealous man, had accused her of having sexual intercourse with Mudie, who was over thirty years her junior, and two other young men in the same house as well.

On being informed of the allegations which had been made against him, Ley denied that there was any truth in them. The police did not believe that he was a fit enough man to have moved Mudie's body on his own, and hesitated to make an arrest until more evidence came to light. Finally, they discovered that a few days before the murder, Lawrence Smith had hired a dark Ford car with the registration number FGP 101. He was afterwards identified by one of the gardeners — though not the other — as the man who had been seen at the chalkpit.

Ley and Smith were brought to trial at the Old Bailey on 19 March 1947, charged with murder. Buckingham, who had also been accused, was allowed to turn King's Evidence, as it was feared that all three would otherwise be acquitted. Both prisoners, on being found guilty, were sentenced to death, but Ley was then found to be insane and committed to Broadmoor, where he died of a stroke on 24 July the same year. Smith's sentence was commuted to life imprisonment.

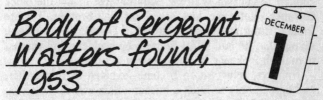

Body of Sergeant Watters found, 1953

DECEMBER
1

During the early hours of 1 December 1953, Reginald Watters, a sergeant serving with the British Occupation Forces in Germany, was found dead in his barracks in Duisburg, having apparently hanged himself. It was rumoured at the time that his German-born wife Mia was having an affair with his Irish fellow sergeant, Frederick Emmett-Dunne, and the verdict of suicide recorded at the inquest did not satisfy everyone in the unit. A few months later, when Mia and Emmett-Dunne — now stationed in England — were married, Watters' body was exhumed and a second post-mortem carried out.

This time it was found that his death had been caused not by hanging but by a blow to his throat — the sort of blow delivered with the edge of the hand in unarmed combat. The body had been hanged afterwards in order to l the true cause of death.

mett-Dunne, who had been in a commando unit
the Second World War, denied knowing anything
about Watters' death, but an investigation of his movements on the evening of 30 November led to his arrest
for murder. When committal proceedings started at Bow
Street he pleaded that as a citizen of Eire he could not
be tried before an English court for a crime which had
taken place abroad. This was accepted, and he was
returned to Germany, where he stood trial before a
military court in Düsseldorf, at the age of thirty-three, in
June 1955.

It was revealed that Emmett-Dunne had left his camp
for a short time on the evening in question, and that
following his return he had been seen cleaning his car
outside one of the barrack blocks while a bundle large
enough to contain Watters' body lay just inside the block
entrance. Later he had asked his half-brother, Private
Ronald Emmett — also stationed in Duisberg — for help,
saying that he had killed Watters by accident and wanted
to make it look as if he had committed suicide.

Emmett, reluctant to become involved in the matter,
had agreed only to fetch a bucket which was to be left on
its side below the corpse. He had then watched as Emmett-
Dunne hung the body from a bannister with a piece of
rope.

The guardroom time-sheet was found to have been
altered in order to give the impression that Emmett-Dunne
had been away from the camp for longer than he actually
had been.

Emmett-Dunne's counsel tried to show that his client
had struck Sergeant Watters in self-defence after being
threatened with a revolver, but this was not believed and
the prisoner was found guilty of murder. As there was no
death penalty in West Germany, he was given a sentence of
life imprisonment, to be served in England.

Frederick Emmett-Dunne remained in prison until July
1966, and afterwards went to work at a garage in Fulham

Road, Chelsea. In October 1969 he pleaded guilty to a charge of obtaining goods by deception having, by his own account, been blackmailed by two other ex-convicts; he asked for two similar offences to be taken into consideration. He was fined a total of £75, and advised to go to the police if anyone tried to blackmail him in future.

Haarmann and Grans brought to trial, 1924

On 4 December 1924, two depraved and predatory men were brought to trial in Hanover, charged with the murder of twenty-seven teenage boys. The trial lasted sixteen days, with nearly 200 witnesses being called, and the revelations which were made were shocking to the point of incredibility. Fritz Haarmann, aged forty-five, and his accomplice, twenty-five-year-old Hans Grans, were shown not only to have murdered a large number of refugees from other parts of Germany, but also to have cut up and sold their bodies as meat. It was one of Europe's most astonishing series of crimes for centuries.

Haarmann, a homosexual, had been a criminal since his youth. He had served prison sentences for various types of theft and fraud, and also for sex offences involving children. Following the completion of a five-year sentence in 1918, he had started to trade in smuggled meat, operating as a police spy at the same time in order to avoid prosecution for his own activities. He also started selling second-hand clothes.

The murders, for which Haarmann, at first was solely responsible, began soon afterwards. Haarmann befriended refugees arriving at Hanover's central railway station and selected individuals to take back to his lodgings at 27, Cellarstrasse. There they were killed in a frightful manner, Haarmann biting through their throats, sometimes after sexually assaulting them. Their flesh was then cut up for sale, their skulls and bones being thrown into the river Leine.

Haarmann met Grans, who was also a homosexual and a thief, in September 1919, and they took rooms together in Neuestrasse, later moving to an alley called Rothe Reihe. Grans, the son of a librarian, was emotionless and cynical; he regarded Haarmann as his inferior and often taunted him. Haarmann was to say that Grans had instigated and taken part in many of his subsequent crimes, sometimes choosing a particular victim because he wanted his clothes.

The meat-trader had some narrow escapes. In September 1918 police officers went to his rooms in Cellarstrasse at the insistence of a missing youth's parents who claimed to have seen their son in Haarmann's company, but they made such a cursory search that nothing was found to incriminate him. Haarmann, at his trial, revealed that at the time of this visit he had had the youth's head wrapped in newspaper behind his oven.

On another occasion a customer took a piece of meat which had been purchased from Haarmann to a police analyst, suspecting that it was human flesh, only to be assured that it was pork!

In spite of these and other such incidents, Haarmann and Grans became increasingly incautious: it was estimated by a police officer that during their last sixteen months of freedom they were committing two murders every week — and sometimes they sold the clothes of the victim within a day or two of acquiring them.

Many reports were made of young people disappearing on arrival in Hanover, one newspaper claiming that there had been as many as 600 such disappearances in one year. Reports were also received from suspicious acquaintances of Haarmann and Grans, stating that while many youths and boys had been seen entering their lodgings, none had ever been seen leaving. But Hanover's chief of police, knowing that Haarmann had friends in positions of authority, was reluctant to take action against him.

Then, on 17 May 1924, the first of many human skulls was found by the river. This was followed by a second skull on 29 May, and two more on 13 June. Finally, the police chief decided that something had to be done, and arranged for Haarmann to be kept under surveillance by two detectives from Berlin.

On 22 June Haarmann approached a boy named Fromm, but a quarrel started between them and then they began to fight. They were promptly arrested by the two detectives and Haarmann was held in custody, charged with indecent behaviour. The arrest was followed by a search of his rooms and the discovery of many items of clothing and personal possessions. The landlady's son was found to be wearing a coat which belonged to a boy who had been reported missing. Haarmann, on being questioned, confessed to several murders, implicating Grans, who was then arrested too.

Further human remains were discovered by boys playing in a meadow on 24 July, and later, when the river-bed was dredged, an assortment of 500 bones was recovered.

At the trial there were many scenes which were painful to watch, with grief-stricken parents identifying items which had belonged to the victims. Haarmann was allowed to interrupt the proceedings almost as he pleased, and did so frequently — sometimes jocularly, sometimes with indignation. At one point he was even allowed to smoke a cigar. As for Grans, he denied everything, though with little chance of being believed.

Fritz Haarmann, fearing that he might be sent to an asylum, insisted that he was sane and demanded to be executed. Having heard the evidence of two psychiatrists, both of whom declared that he was sane, the court decided that death was the appropriate punishment in his case. But Hans Grans was dealt with more leniently, being given a sentence of life imprisonment, which was later reduced to twelve years.

Haarmann's execution, by beheading, was carried out without delay, perhaps because it was feared that an attempt might otherwise be made to lynch him.

Disappearance of Elsie Cameron, 1924

DECEMBER 5

On 5 December 1924, Elsie Cameron, a twenty-six-year-old unemployed typist, left her parents' home in Kensal Rise, north London, to go and stay with her fiancé, Norman Thorne, on his chicken farm near the village of Crowborough in Sussex. The couple had been engaged for almost two years, and although Thorne had since fallen in love with a local girl, Elsie was determined to become his wife. However, her parents received no news from her during the next few days, and her father, on sending Thorne a telegram, received a reply saying that she had not arrived at the farm. The police were then informed that Elsie had disappeared.

Thorne, who was two years younger than Elsie, was a mechanic by trade, but had set himself up as a chicken farmer after being forced to go on the dole in the summer of 1921. His home was hardly an ideal one; he lived in squalor in one of the huts on the farm. Nor were his prospects good, for the business was not doing well and he was in financial difficulty. But Elsie, a plain and nervous woman, had been willing to tolerate this, and had even tried to convince him that she was pregnant — which she was not — in order to hurry him into marrying her. She did not realize that Thorne was equally determined to avoid doing so.

On being questioned about Elsie's disappearance, Thorne repeated his claim that she had not been to the farm that day and that he did not know her whereabouts — and he persisted in this story in spite of being told that two flower-growers had seen her in the vicinity on the day in question. But a few weeks later, when it was discovered that a neighbour had actually seen Elsie entering the farm on 5 December, he was arrested on suspicion and a search of the premises was started.

The police found Elsie's wrist-watch, which had been damaged, and some of her jewellery in a tool-shed, and the following morning unearthed an attaché case which she had been carrying when she left her parents' house for the last time. Norman Thorne then made a statement, admitting that she was dead but denying that he had killed her. Elsie's remains were afterwards discovered in the ground under a chicken-run. Her body had been dismembered with a hack-saw.

According to Thorne's statement, Elsie had arrived at the farm unexpectedly and a quarrel had taken place between them over his association with the local girl. Later he had left her alone in the hut for nearly two hours, and during that time she had hanged herself from a beam with a piece of cord. 'I was about to go to Doctor Turle and knock up someone to go for the police and I realized the position I was in,' the statement continued. He had then cut up her body and buried it.

John Norman Holmes Thorne was brought to trial at the Lewes Assizes on 4 March 1925. Sir Bernard Spilsbury, appearing as a prosecution witness, said that he had found evidence of several injuries on Elsie's head and body, and that a 'crushing blow' on her forehead could have been caused by an Indian club found outside the hut. He also said that he had found no evidence of hanging. This evidence was challenged by medical experts for the defence, but Thorne was found guilty and sentenced to death.

He was hanged at Wandsworth Prison on 22 April 1925.

Execution of Martha Marek, 1938

Martha Marek, an Austrian murderess executed on 6 December 1938, was a woman of great beauty and few scruples. Born to unknown parents about 1904, she was adopted by a poor couple named Löwenstein in Vienna and later became the ward of Moritz Fritsch, a wealthy store-owner who found her working in a dress shop in 1919. She was then sent to finishing schools in England and France and, when Fritsch died, inherited a substantial sum of money. However, she was extravagant, and soon after her marriage in 1924 to Emil Marek, an engineering student, she had nothing left.

To remedy this, she and Marek made an incredible attempt at fraud — an attempt which required a sacrifice on her husband's part and became known as the 'Case of the Chopped-off Leg'. Marek, having been insured against accident for £10,000, allowed Martha to hack one of his legs with an axe, so that he could claim to have injured himself while cutting down a tree. The wound thus inflicted was serious, and the leg had to be amputated below the knee. But the surgeon performing the operation found that it had been caused by three separate cuts, and that the angle of these was inconsistent with Marek's story.

The police investigated the matter, and the couple were charged with attempted fraud. Though they were both acquitted when the case came to court, the insurance company forced them to accept a settlement of only £3000. At the same time, they were both given short prison sentences for bribing a hospital orderly into accusing the surgeon of misconduct.

Emil and Martha Marek later went to Algiers, where they became destitute after the failure of a business venture. They returned to Vienna, where Martha, who now had two children, was reduced to selling vegetables from a street barrow. In July 1932 Marek died in a charity ward, his death being put down to tuberculosis. The following month Martha's baby daughter Ingebrog also died. But these deaths aroused no suspicion, and Martha became the companion of an elderly relative, Susanne Löwenstein.

Frau Löwenstein died after making a will in Martha Marek's favour, but again Martha spent most of her money within a short time. She began letting rooms in her house, taking in a Frau Kittenberger, who died after Martha had insured her life for £300. This time, however, poisoning was suspected, and Frau Kittenberger's son demanded an investigation. His mother's body was exhumed and found to contain thallium.

This discovery led to the bodies of Emil Marek, Ingeborg Marek and Frau Löwenstein all being exhumed, and each was found to have died of the same poison. Moreover, the police found that Martha's son Peter, who had been boarded out, was also suffering from thallium poisoning. A chemist stated that Martha had bought the poison from him. She was beheaded, her execution being carried out with an axe.

The death penalty, previously abolished in Austria, had been restored by Hitler.

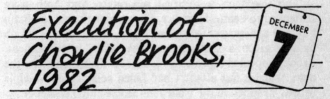

Execution of Charlie Brooks, 1982

DECEMBER 7

On 7 December 1982, Charlie Brooks, a forty-year-old black convicted of the murder of a second-hand car salesman six years earlier, was executed by lethal injection at

Huntsville Prison, Texas. As he was the first prisoner to die by this method in the United States, the execution naturally aroused much public interest and curiosity.

It was carried out in that part of the prison which had formerly been the gas chamber, the apparatus of death comprising a medical trolley, to which the prisoner was strapped, an intravenous needle inserted into his right arm and a rubber tube leading across the floor of the execution chamber to an adjacent room, where the executioner — a medical technician — was hidden.

The executioner opened a valve at his end of the rubber tube and administered a dose of sodium pentathol, causing the condemned man to lose consciousness; this was followed by quantities of pavulon and potassium chloride. Within minutes Charlie Brooks was pronounced dead, the execution having apparently been carried out efficiently and painlessly.

The crime for which Charlie Brooks was executed had taken place shortly before Christmas 1976. Brooks and another man, Woody Lourdres, had set out in the company of a prostitute with the intention of shoplifting. When their car broke down they tried to steal another from a garage by taking it for a trial run and not returning it, but the garage insisted that one of its employees should go with them. Brooks and Lourdres then took the salesman to a motel, bound him hand and foot and shot him through the head. It was never discovered which of the two actually fired the shot.

The two men were tried separately, and both were sentenced to death. However, Lourdres managed to obtain a retrial and agreed to a plea-bargain, as a result of which he was given a sentence of forty years' imprisonment. Brooks appealed repeatedly against his death sentence, the news that his last attempt had failed being received while he was strapped to the trolley in the execution chamber.

Brooks' execution was attended by a twenty-seven-year-old nurse with whom he was in love: they had both committed themselves to each other 'for the next life', and the prisoner had asked that she be allowed to be present as a witness. Having become a Muslim during the time he had spent on Death Row, he was also attended by two Islamic priests with whom he went through a brief ritual. He remained calm throughout his final ordeal.

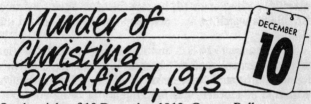

Murder of Christina Bradfield, 1913

DECEMBER 10

On the night of 10 December 1913, George Ball, a twenty-two-year-old tarpaulin packer also known as George Sumner, battered his forty-year-old employer, Christina Bradfield, to death in her shop in Old Hall Street, Liverpool. With the assistance of the shop's other employee, Samuel Angeles Elltoft, aged eighteen, he then sewed her body into a sack in readiness to dispose of it in the Leeds and Liverpool Canal. But before it could be taken from the premises a shutter from the shop window blew down, falling on to a man who was standing in the street.

The man, a ship's steward named Walter Eaves, was waiting to meet a girl and, fortunately, was wearing a bowler hat. This took the force of the blow, but was damaged by it, and when Samuel Elltoft came out to replace the shutter, Eaves told him what had happened. Elltoft told Ball, who came out to apologize and paid Eaves 2s (10p) compensation. However, when Ball and Elltoft left the shop a few minutes later, pushing a handcart covered with tarpaulin, the unlucky ship's steward was still waiting in the street and could hardly fail to notice what they were doing.

Though the sack had been weighted with pieces of iron, it was found obstructing one of the gates of a lock the following day and pulled ashore; the body was then identified without difficulty from a medallion round its neck. Elltoft was arrested at his home, but Ball, realizing that he had little chance of avoiding a murder charge, had absconded.

During the course of the ten-day search which followed Ball's photograph was shown on cinema screens all over Liverpool, and it was as a result of this that he was recognized. On being arrested, he was found to have Christina Bradfield's watch in his possession and bloodstains on his clothes.

In February 1914 Ball and Elltoft were brought to trial at the Liverpool Assizes, charged with murder. Ball was found guilty and sentenced to death; Elltoft, though acquitted of murder, was found guilty of being an accessory after the fact and sentenced to four years' imprisonment.

George Ball, having finally confessed to the murder, was hanged at Walton Prison on 26 February.

Brenda Nash found murdered, 1960

DECEMBER 11

On 11 December 1960, Brenda Nash, an eleven-year-old Girl Guide, was found dead in a ditch on Yately Common, in Hampshire, about twenty-five miles from her home in Heston, Middlesex. She had been reported missing after failing to return home on the night of 28 October previously, and it was estimated that she had been dead for about six weeks. She had been strangled during the course of a struggle, evidently while trying to resist a sexual assault.

Three months earlier, on 9 September, a Girl Guide

living in Twickenham — about three miles from Heston — had been abducted and raped by a man driving a black Vauxhall car, and police suspected that the same man was responsible for the disappearance of Brenda Nash. So far, in spite of interviewing about 5000 owners of black Vauxhalls registered in Middlesex and Surrey, they had been unable to discover his identity. They therefore began a re-examination of all the statements that had been taken.

However, the news that the body had been discovered prompted a young woman hairdresser in London's West End to tell them that a fellow employee had been asked by her uncle, who fitted the wanted man's description, to provide him with an alibi for the day of the girl's disappearance. This piece of information led to the arrest of Arthur Albert Jones, aged forty-four, a married man with a sixteen-year-old son.

Jones, who lived in Hounslow, a mile from Brenda Nash's home, was identified by the girl who had been raped in September. He was formally charged with that crime and remanded in custody.

Arthur Jones had been among the 5000 car-owners interviewed by police before the discovery of Brenda's body. On that earlier occasion he had claimed that he and his wife had been to visit his sister-in-law in Beckenham, Kent, on 28 October. But his sister-in-law, having confirmed this, now confessed to having given him a false alibi.

There was evidence to connect him directly with the murder, for green fibres found on the victim's clothes were similar to those of a rug in Jones' car, and a piece of chain found under her head matched other pieces from his house. But the police hesitated to charge him with murder in the hope of further information coming to light.

In March 1961 Jones was tried at the Old Bailey for rape, convicted, and sentenced to fourteen years' imprisonment. The publication of his photograph in the newspapers the following day led to a number of witnesses coming forward to say that they had seen him in Heston on the evening of Brenda Nash's disappearance. Then a fellow prisoner named Roberts reported that Jones had confessed the murder to him.

Jones was charged with the murder on 10 May after two witnesses had picked him out at an identity parade, and brought to trial on this charge on 17 June. The jury, after retiring for only seven minutes, returned a verdict of guilty, and he was sentenced to life imprisonment.

Beginning of the Boyle murder case, 1935

DECEMBER
13

On 13 December 1935, police in Boyle, Co. Roscommon, received a report that Patrick Henry, a sixty-seven-year-old local man, had not been seen for three months. Henry, known as 'Old Pat', was the tenant of a two-roomed cottage on the outskirts of the town — a hovel without electricity, sanitation or even running water. His landlady, who lived in another part of Boyle, had been there several times since his disappearance and found it locked on each occasion. Having received no rent from him since the end of August, she now wanted to be free to let the place to somebody else.

Two policemen accompanied the landlady to the cottage, forced the padlock by which the door was secured, and found the old man's decomposed body inside. Patrick Henry had been brutally beaten with a blunt instrument; his skull had been fractured and his jaw and other facial bones also broken. His body had been burnt in several places, some of the burns having been sustained while he was still alive. The pathologist who examined the body expressed the opinion that his death had occurred two or three months previously.

Despite the squalid conditions in which Henry had lived, the motive for his murder had clearly been robbery, for his gold watch had been stolen and the linings of his jacket and waistcoat cut open — undoubtedly in the hope that they would be found to contain money. A fifty-six-year-old man named Thomas Kelly, who had lodged with the victim for some months, had left about the time that Henry was last seen alive, and the police were certain that he was the person responsible. But they had no idea where he had gone, and it was several months before they succeeded in tracing him.

Kelly was finally apprehended in Coatbridge, near Glasgow, in June 1936, after it had been learnt that he was expected to visit a bank there. On being taken to a nearby police station, he suddenly produced a cut-throat razor, slashed the side of his neck and then put up a fierce struggle before being overpowered. He was kept under guard in a Glasgow hospital until he was well enough to be taken back to Ireland to stand trial for murder.

The trial began on 10 November, the prosecution contending that the murder had been committed on 11 September the previous year, and producing evidence that Kelly and Henry had not been on good terms. A woman living in the adjoining cottage said that she had seen Henry for the last time on 10 September, and also that she had seen Kelly the following afternoon. The manager of the local labour exchange stated that neither of the men had collected their unemployment benefit on 11 September though both had signed on the day before. But after hearing further evidence to the effect that Kelly had talked about leaving Boyle on 9 or 10 September, the prosecution obtained permission to change the date on which the murder had allegedly taken place to 10 September.

Thomas Kelly denied the offence, saying that he had left Boyle on 11 September, and that Henry had still been alive at the time of his departure. He was unable to explain satisfactorily why he had left Boyle without luggage, why he had failed to collect his dole, or why he had been using a false name and wearing spectacles which he did not need at the time of his arrest. On being found guilty, he was sentenced to death.

But later, when seven new witnesses came forward, claiming to have seen Patrick Henry alive two days after the date specified in the charge, i.e. on 12 September 1935, the Court of Criminal Appeal set aside the conviction and ordered a fresh trial. This was held in April 1937, when the defence also produced medical evidence that Henry had not been dead for as long as three months at the time the body was discovered. On this occasion the jury was unable to agree on a verdict.

On 15 November 1937, Thomas Kelly was brought to trial yet again, and this time the court heard *eleven* witnesses state that they had seen Henry alive on 12 September 1935 — but, astonishingly, the prisoner was found guilty and once more sentenced to death. It was perhaps in keeping with the character of this confusing case that the judge omitted to put on the black cap before sentence was pronounced.

Thomas Kelly was afterwards reprieved, his sentence being commuted to life imprisonment. He remained in prison for the next ten years, and was released on 17 December 1947.

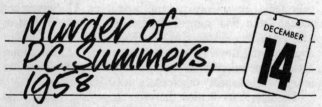

Murder of P.C. Summers, 1958

DECEMBER
14

On the night of 14 December 1958, a police constable on patrol duty in Holloway, north London, found two rival gangs of youths engaged in an affray outside a dance-hall in Seven Sisters Road. It was a frightful battle, with about twenty people, some armed with choppers, hammers or bottles, screaming and striking out at each other. PC Raymond Summers, aged twenty-three, immediately dashed in among them, ordering them to desist.

Many of them did so and took to their heels, but one man drew a ten-inch knife and thrust it into the policeman's back. Then he, too, ran off and PC Summers, tended by two teenage girls, lay dying on the pavement.

A hunt began for those who had taken part in the fighting, and before long a large number of young people were being questioned at Caledonian Road police station. Among them was Ronald Henry Marwood, a twenty-five-year-old scaffolder with cuts on his left hand, who claimed to have been involved in a fight elsewhere. Though allowed to go home after making a statement, Marwood was later found to have lied about his movements, and when police went to see him again they found him to be missing from his home.

On 20 December Scotland Yard announced that they wished to interview him in connection with the murder, but it was not until 27 January 1959 that he was seen again. He then gave himself up and made a second statement, admitting that he had struck the blow which killed PC Summers but denying that he had done so intentionally.

His story was that he and some friends had gone to the dance-hall and found a scuffle taking place outside on the pavement. Someone had aimed a blow at him with a chopper and his hand had been cut when he shielded his head with it. Afterwards, while he had his hands in his pockets, PC Summers had punched him, he said. His statement then continued:

'I must have had my hand on the knife in my right-hand pocket. I struck out, with the intention of pushing him away from me. I remember striking him with the knife and the policeman fell ... I ran away and kept on running.'

At his trial, which began at the Old Bailey on 12 March, Marwood pleaded not guilty and retracted his second state-

337

ment, saying that the police had fabricated parts of it. He had had nothing in his hand when he hit PC Summers, he said; he had merely punched him and run off. He told the court that he had drunk about ten pints of brown ale beforehand. The jury nonetheless found him guilty of murder and he was sentenced to death.

Marwood was not a habitual criminal and was not even connected with either of the gangs involved in the fighting. There was therefore widespread sympathy for him when his appeal was dismissed, and many protests were made. On the morning of his execution, 8 May 1959, hostile crowds gathered outside Pentonville Prison, and mounted police had to be called to keep order.

Murder of Marion Gilchrist, 1908

DECEMBER
21

On the evening of 21 December 1908, Helen Lambie, twenty-one-year-old servant to an elderly spinster living in Queen's Terrace, West Prince's Street, Glasgow, went out as usual to buy a newspaper. When she returned about ten minutes later, she found a neighbour, Arthur Adams, standing outside the flat; he told her that he had heard noises from inside. Helen, apparently unconcerned, unlocked the door and entered, leaving Adams standing at the threshold.

At that moment another man appeared from the spare bedroom, walked towards the door and left hurriedly, without speaking to either of them. It was only after he had made good his escape that Helen found her employer lying in front of the dining-room fireplace with a rug over her head.

Miss Marion Gilchrist, aged eighty-two, had been savagely battered, sustaining injuries from which she died shortly afterwards. A diamond crescent brooch had been stolen and a wooden box containing private papers wrenched open, but other valuables had been left untouched on Miss Gilchrist's dressing-table. In his haste to get away from the scene of the crime, the murderer had almost run into Mary Barrowman, a fourteen-year-old messenger girl walking along the street. However, the description which this third witness gave of him was markedly different from that provided by the other two.

Appealing for information, the police learnt that Oscar Slater, a German Jew in his thirties, had been offering to sell a pawn-ticket for a diamond brooch. They went to his flat in St. George's Road, a few minutes' walk from the home of the victim, but found that he had left in the company of his mistress. When further inquiries revealed that he had boarded a ship bound for the United States on 26 December, extradition proceedings were started and the three witnesses travelled to New York to give evidence against him.

Oscar Slater, whose real name was Leschziner, denied the offence. The brooch which he had pawned had *not* been Miss Gilchrist's at all and had, in fact, been in his possession some weeks before the murder took place. But, for reasons of their own, the Glasgow police were determined that he should be convicted, and Slater suddenly gave up contesting the extradition and declared himself willing to return to Scotland to face trial. He arrived back in Glasgow in the custody of a police officer on 21 February 1909, and his trial took place in Edinburgh early in May.

Various witnesses were produced by the prosecution to identify the prisoner as a man they had seen lurking near Miss Gilchrist's flat during the weeks preceding the crime. Helen Lambie and Mary Barrowman both identified him as the man they had seen on the evening of the murder, the servant more positively than she had done so in New

York and the messenger admitting that she had been shown photographs of him before making her identification. Arthur Adams could only say that Slater bore a resemblance to the man in question.

As for the medical evidence, there was disagreement among the witnesses over whether a light hammer found in the prisoner's luggage could have been the murder weapon, and none could state with certainty that clothes which he had allegedly worn at the time of the murder were blood-stained, even though the victim had been struck over fifty times.

The most important pieces of evidence produced by the prosecution were therefore far from satisfactory, and, to weaken the case still further, Slater's mistress and *their* servant both claimed that he had been at home when the murder took place. But, unfortunately for him, the prisoner was also shown to be an unsavoury character, who had lived partly by gambling and partly on immoral earnings, and the jury found him guilty by a majority verdict. He was sentenced to death.

Two days before he was due to be hanged, Slater's sentence was commuted to life imprisonment. But many believed him to be innocent and some, including Sir Arthur Conan Doyle, campaigned tirelessly for an inquiry into the case. Even so, he served over eighteen years in prison before being finally vindicated on appeal and awarded £6000 compensation.

He died twenty years later, in 1948, at the age of seventy-four.

On the evening of 23 December 1959, police went to a YWCA hostel in Birmingham to investigate a report that a young woman had been attacked by an intruder. The attack had taken place in the ground-floor laundry room, where the victim, twenty-one-year-old Margaret Brown, had been working. The intruder had entered the room, switching off the light, and struck at her in the darkness. But he had not managed to hurt her, and had run off when she screamed.

However, during a search of the premises, the police found one of the rooms locked and, forcing open the door, discovered that the occupant, twenty-nine-year-old Stephanie Baird, had been murdered in a revolting manner. Her head, which had been severed from her body, was lying on the bed. Her body, which was naked and hideously mutilated, was on the floor. And beside these gruesome remains lay a note scribbled on an envelope. It read: 'This was the thing I thought would never come.'

Stephanie Baird was found to have been strangled before her body was mutilated, but it was clear from the nature of the mutilations that her murder had been the work of a sadist. But apart from the note which had been left, there were no clues to his identity, and the police had to make extensive house-to-house inquiries in the hope of obtaining further evidence. It was after 20,000 other men had been interviewed that Patrick Byrne, a twenty-eight-year-old Irish labourer, was seen.

Byrne, who was staying with his mother in Warrington, had worked in Birmingham and lodged near the YWCA hostel at the time of the murder: it was his landlady there who had given police the address at which he could be found. But the police had no reason to suspect that he was the culprit until they asked as a matter of course, if they could take his fingerprints. He then became agitated and, following further questions, admitted that he was the person who had killed Stephanie Baird.

His handwriting was found to match that of the note left in the victim's room, and he also gave details of the crime which had not been revealed to the press. He was charged with murder.

In his confession, Byrne admitted to being a fantasist preoccupied with sadistic ideas, and also to feeling compelled to terrify women 'to get my own back on them for causing my nervous tension through sex'. On the evening in question, he said, he had peered through one of the windows of the hostel hoping to see one of the occupants undressing, and had seen Stephanie Baird, wearing an underskirt and pullover, packing a suitcase. He had then broken into the building and stood on a chair in order to watch her through the fanlight, but she had heard a noise and opened the door.

He tried to kiss her and when she resisted, pushed her back into the room and strangled her. He then took off her clothes and raped her before finding a tableknife in a drawer and mutilating her body. Having cut off her head, he held it up by the hair, watching himself in a mirror. Afterwards the sight of Margaret Brown in the laundry room excited him afresh and he tried to hit her with a stone wrapped in a brassiere from a clothes line outside.

Brought to trial at the Birmingham Assizes in March 1960, Patrick Byrne was found guilty of murder, the jury having evidently been impressed by evidence that he was sexually abnormal but not insane. This verdict was changed on appeal to one of manslaughter, but Byrne's sentence of life imprisonment was not reduced.

On 24 December 1898, Harry Cornish, sports director of New York's exclusive Knickerbocker Athletic Club, received a silver toothpick holder and a bottle of what appeared to be bromo-seltzer through the post. The package had been sent anonymously and was thought to have been a joke on the part of one of his acquaintances. A couple of days later Cornish took both articles home and gave them to his cousin who, like her mother, lived with him in his apartment on West 84th Street. The following morning his aunt, Mrs Katherine J. Adams, collapsed and died after drinking some of the 'bromo-seltzer' in a glass of water. An autopsy revealed that she had died from cyanide poisoning.

Two months earlier Henry C. Barnett, another member of the Knickerbocker Club, had received a box of Kutnow's powder — 'pleasant-tasting effervescent salts' — also sent anonymously through the post; this was analysed after he became ill and found to contain cyanide of mercury. Although Barnett had died in November, it appeared that his death had not been caused by poisoning but by diphtheria. Even so, an attempt at poisoning *had* been made, and it was remembered now that only eleven days after his death, Blanche Chesebrough, whom Barnett had been courting, had married his rival, Roland B. Molineux, the manager of a factory in Newark, New Jersey.

Molineux, a third member of the Knickerbocker Club, was the son of General Edward Leslie Molineux, a hero of the Civil War and a prominent figure in New York. He had enough knowledge of chemistry to have prepared the fatal substance; it was also known that he disliked Cornish intensely and had tried unsuccessfully to get him removed

343

from his position as sports director. Moreover, seven experts declared that his handwriting had characteristics identical to that of the package sent to Cornish which, fortunately, had not been thrown away.

When this was revealed at the inquest into Mrs. Adams' death, the jury found that Molineux had, in fact, sent the poison; the coroner then ordered his arrest. He was later alleged to have murdered Barnett as well, but the charge on which he was eventually brought to trial concerned the murder of Mrs. Adams only.

The trial took place in New York City's Central Criminal Court and lasted from 14 November 1899, to 11 February 1900. Molineux, aged thirty-two, was alleged to have murdered Mrs. Adams by mistake, having intended the poison for her nephew. The handwriting evidence proved to the most important part of the prosecution's case, and during the course of an eight-hour retirement the jury asked to be supplied with a set of the exhibits. Finally, Molineux was found guilty of murder in the first degree and sentenced to death.

In October 1901 the verdict was set aside on appeal and a fresh trial ordered. This took place in 1902, with Molineux producing an alibi for the time that the package was posted, and further handwriting experts appearing to challenge the evidence of those called by the prosecution. Another new witness claimed to have seen the package being posted and said she was 'pretty sure' that *Cornish* was the man who had posted it. This time the verdict was one of not guilty and Molineux was released.

While under sentence of death Molineux had written a book, *The Room with the Little Door*, recording his impressions of prison life. When this was published, it became quite popular, and he afterwards wrote romantic fiction for Sunday newspaper supplements. However, he was hardly romantic in real life, for he contracted syphilis and became insane, his wife having obtained a divorce in the meantime. He died in a lunatic asylum on 2 November 1917.

Murder of Harry Michaelson, 1948

During the early hours of 26 December 1948, Harry Michaelson, a lightning cartoonist known as 'One Minute Michaelson', was found fatally injured at the entrance door of his basement flat in the Paddington district of London. He had been attacked by an intruder in his bedroom but had managed to stagger outside in search of help. He was bleeding from a deep wound on his forehead and was later found to have fractured ribs as well as a fractured skull. He died in hospital without being able to give any information about the attack.

It was learnt from the porter of the block that Mr. Michaelson had been staying in his flat alone, as his wife was out of London. He had evidently been awakened by the noise of the intruder, who had entered by an open window, and had switched on the light and challenged him. His jacket and trousers were found lying on the floor, and there was no money in any of the pockets. The murder weapon, a tubular steel chair, was taken away for examination and a single fingerprint was found on it.

Though fingerprint experts tried to identify the culprit from this, they got no immediate results due to the difficulty of checking individual prints. But just over three weeks later a young man was seen acting suspiciously in the St John's Wood area and taken into custody. When his fingerprints were sent to Scotland Yard one of them was found to match the one on the steel chair. The man was found to be Harry Lewis, a twenty-one-year-old Welshman and a known thief. He had no fixed address.

On being questioned about the murder, Lewis made a full confession. He said that on the night in question he had been wandering the streets penniless when he saw the open window and decided to break into the flat. He managed to get into the victim's bedroom and had taken some money from one of the trouser pockets when Michaelson woke up and began to remonstrate with him. Lewis then panicked and began to hit him with the chair — the first object that came to hand. He afterwards left the flat by the same window as he had used before.

Harry Lewis, who had gained £5 8s 9d (£5.44) by the crime, was brought to trial at the Old Bailey on 7 March 1949. He pleaded not guilty to the murder charge, his counsel contending that Michaelson had died as a result of his hospital treatment rather than the blows struck by the prisoner. But a pathologist appearing for the prosecution said that he would have died irrespective of his operation, and Lewis was found guilty. Despite a recommendation of mercy from the jury, he was hanged at Pentonville Prison on 21 April.

Detective Chief Superintendent Peter Beveridge, who investigated the crime, later remarked that the victim had been a kindly man, and that if Lewis had asked him for money — especially at Christmas — he would almost certainly have been given some.

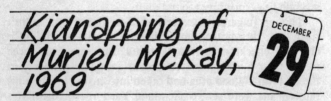

Kidnapping of Muriel McKay, 1969

On the evening of 29 December 1969, Alick McKay, deputy chairman of the *News of the World* newspaper, found his fifty-five-year-old wife Muriel missing from their home in Arthur Road, Wimbledon. No note had been left for him, the telephone in the hall had been disconnected and the contents of his wife's handbag lay scattered on the

346

stairs. Mr. McKay informed the police who, though far from convinced that it wasn't a publicity stunt, treated the disappearance as a case of possible kidnapping. Some hours later, after his telephone had been reconnected, Mr. McKay received the first of many calls from a coloured man claiming to speak for a group called 'Mafia M3'.

The man said that Mrs. McKay was in the hands of his group and would be killed unless a million pounds was paid for her return. When Mr. McKay said that he could not raise so much money the man insisted that that was the sum the group wanted, and that it should be ready in two days. He added that they had intended to kidnap the wife of Rupert Murdoch, the newspaper's millionaire chairman, but being unable to do this, had decided on Mrs. McKay instead. The call was made from a public call-box in Epping.

Two days later, following a second call, Mr. McKay received a letter from his wife which had been posted in north London. It read: 'Please do something to get me home. I am blindfolded and cold. Only blankets. Please co-operate for I cannot keep going ... I think of you constantly ... What have I done to deserve this treatment?' In further telephone calls, the kidnappers continued to insist that Mr. McKay should pay a ransom of £1 million, but it was some time before they gave instructions for its delivery.

The case was highly publicized from the start, with the result that the culprits knew the police were involved and Mr. McKay's telephone was frequently occupied with nuisance calls from other people. At one stage even the kidnappers complained, in a letter to the editor of the *News of the World*, that they had tried to contact Mr. McKay several times but found his number engaged on each occasion.

On 22 January two further letters from Mrs. McKay were received, together with a ransom note from the kidnappers giving detailed instructions about what should be done with the money. In one of the letters Mrs. McKay

347

said that she was 'deteriorating in health and spirit', and pleaded with her husband to keep the police out of the affair.

The ransom note said that half the money should be handed over to the kidnappers on 1 February. But in the meantime, following three more telephone calls, Mr. McKay received another note from them, together with two more letters from his wife which had been written in a state of despair.

On the night of 1 February a suitcase containing £500,000 — most of it in forged notes — was taken to a telephone box in Edmonton, on the A10, by a police officer pretending to be Alick McKay's son, Ian. There he received a call directing him to another call-box along the same road, where he found further instructions written in a cigarette packet. In accordance with these, the suitcase was left on a bank at High Cross. However, the kidnappers failed to collect it, and two days later Ian McKay received a telephone call in which he was accused of setting a trap for them. Police cars had been seen near the place where the money had been left, the caller said angrily.

Ian McKay denied that there had been a trap, and on 5 February fresh instructions were received for the money to be paid the following day. This time police officers impersonating Alick McKay and his married daughter Diane went to one of the A10 call-boxes and were then directed to another box in London's East End. There they received instructions to go on the Underground to Epping, where they would receive a further call. They were then told to go to Bishop's Stortford, where they were to leave the money — this time in two suitcases — beside a mini-van parked in a garage forecourt.

They arrived at the garage in a mini-cab. But before the money was left the mini-cab stopped on the other side of the road and a third police officer, who had been hiding on the floor, crawled out and disappeared behind a hedge. Other policemen later took up positions close by.

Once again the kidnappers did not collect the money,

this time because the suitcases were taken off to the local police station after being reported by a couple who thought that somebody must have lost them. But in the meantime a dark blue Volvo had been seen passing the garage several times, the driver apparently taking an interest in them. This car was afterwards found to belong to Arthur Hosein, a thirty-four-year-old Muslim from Trinidad, who lived with his family and his twenty-two-year-old brother, Nizamodeen, on a farm near Stocking Pelham in Hertfordshire.

Arthur Hosein's fingerprints were found to match those of the ransom notes, the envelopes and the cigarette packet from the call-box on the A10, and various items found in the seventeenth-century farmhouse connected the two brothers with Mrs. McKay's disappearance. But Mrs. McKay was not there and, despite a search of the farm and its surroundings lasting several weeks, no trace of her body was found.

The two brothers were brought to trial at the Old Bailey in September 1970, and found guilty of murder, kidnapping and blackmail, the jury recommending leniency in the case of Nizamodeen Hosein, as he had been dominated by Arthur. Both were given life sentences for Mrs. McKay's murder, Arthur Hosein receiving a further twenty-five years and his brother a further fifteen years on the other charges.

Though there is no certainty of what became of Mrs. McKay's body, it is generally believed that it was cut up and fed to Arthur Hosein's pigs.

Abduction of the Mosser Family, 1950

On the afternoon of 30 December 1950, Carl and Thelma Mosser, driving along Highway 66 between Tulsa and Oklahoma City, stopped to give a lift to a young man who was hitch-hiking. The family came from Atwood, Illinois, where Carl was a farmer, and were on their way to visit relatives in Albuquerque, New Mexico. However, the hitch-hiker pulled out a gun and, getting into the car, forced them to drive according to his instructions.

The gunman had nowhere in particular in mind, and during the next three days made the frightened Mossers drive from town to town in Oklahoma, New Mexico, Texas and Arkansas, until finally he shot all five members of the family and threw their bodies into a disused mineshaft near Joplin, Missouri. He then drove the car back to Tulsa himself, abandoned it and went back to hitch-hiking on the morning of 2 January.

The car was found in a ditch on 3 January by a deputy sheriff of Osage County, who afterwards examined it and found bloodstains, bullet holes and used bullets on the inside. When this became known to the inhabitants of the county, witnesses reported having seen the hitch-hiker near the car the previous morning, and roadblocks were set up in the hope that he was still in the area.

Information was received from a man running a combined filling station and grocery store in Wichita Falls, Texas, of a struggle which had taken place there on the evening of 30 December when Mosser tried to overpower the hitch-hiker after they had stopped to fill the tank.

Another man revealed that earlier the same day he had given the gunman a lift from Lubbock, Texas, to the outskirts of Oklahoma City. Then, he said, he had been forced into the trunk at gunpoint, but had later managed to escape. A receipt from a pawnshop in El Paso, made out to W.E. Cook, had been discovered in the car when it was found abandoned on Highway 66.

As a result of this last piece of information, the hitch-hiker was quickly identified as William E. Cook, a twenty-three-year-old Joplin man with a criminal record who had been released from the Missouri penitentiary in June 1950. A complaint was accordingly filed, charging Cook with the kidnapping of the motorist who had escaped.

Cook, who was of medium height and build and had a drooping eyelid, was known to have been staying at a motel in Blythe, a small town in east California, less than a fortnight earlier, and on 4 January a deputy sheriff who knew him called there to see if he had returned. To his surprise, Cook came to the door with a gun in his hand and ordered him to get back into his car. The two men then drove out into the desert, where Cook left the deputy tied up on the roadside before driving off on his own. Eleven days later he was arrested in Mexico; the bodies of the five members of the Mosser family were discovered shortly afterwards.

While in custody in San Diego William Cook confessed not only to those five murders but also to the killing of another man, whose body had been found thirty-five miles south of Mexicali, in southern California. Robert H. Dewey, aged thirty-two, of Seattle, Washington, had also been abducted and forced to drive according to Cook's instructions; he had been shot dead during the course of a struggle. It was for this murder that Cook was brought to trial and sentenced to death.

He was executed in San Quentin's gas chamber on 12 December 1951.

True Crime Diary

Volume 2

Murder of Leon Beron, 1911

On the morning of 1 January 1911, a policeman found the body of Leon Beron, a forty-eight-year-old Russian Jew, hidden among furze bushes on Clapham Common, south-west London. He had been struck on the head with a blunt instrument, then — when he was already dead — stabbed in the chest three times. There were also a number of superficial cuts on his face, including one shaped roughly like the letter S on each cheek. But it seemed that robbery had been the motive for the crime, for a gold watch and about twenty sovereigns (£20) were missing from the body.

Beron, a widower, owned nine little houses in Stepney, east London, but lived in a room above a shop in the same district. It was learnt that on the previous evening he had left a local kosher restaurant in the company of Stinie Morrison, a professional burglar aged about thirty who had served five prison sentences, totalling twelve years. Morrison, also a Russian Jew, was missing from his lodgings; he had told his landlady that he was going to Paris. He was, however, arrested at another East End restaurant on 8 January and taken to Leman Street police station.

The arrest was made ostensibly because Morrison — a convict on parole who had been out of prison only a short while — had failed to notify the police of his change of address. But he knew that this was not the only reason, and soon after his arrival at the police station he made the mistake of saying to Detective Inspector Frederick Wensley, 'You have accused me of a serious crime. You have accused me of murder!' At that stage, it was afterwards alleged, no mention had been made of Beron's death. But the police officers concerned were certain of Morrison's guilt.

Two witnesses claimed to have seen him in Beron's company during the early hours of 1 January: one of these was the driver of a hansom-cab, who said that he had driven them to Clapham from Whitechapel — a distance of six miles — after picking them up about 2 a.m. A second cab-driver said that he had picked Morrison up near the common between 2.30 and 3.00 a.m. (about the time of Beron's death), and driven him to Kennington, south London. A third cab-driver — this one had a taxi — claimed to have picked Morrison and another man up in Kennington at 3.30 a.m. Stinie Morrison, a very tall, handsome man, was brought to trial at the Old Bailey on 6 March, charged with Beron's murder.

The prosecution's case was based largely on circumstantial evidence, much of which was confused. A number of volatile East End characters, mainly aliens, appeared as witnesses, facing the court in a less than awe-struck manner. The prisoner stood throughout the nine-day trial with one hand on his hip, observing the proceedings disdainfully.

The S-shaped cuts on the dead man's cheeks were the subject of some speculation: it was suggested by the defence that Beron had been a police spy and that he had given information about the anarchists responsible for the Houndsditch Murders (see 3 January). It was also suggested that Beron's brother Solomon, who went mad during the closing speech for the defence and had to be taken away to a lunatic asylum, might have committed the murder himself. But the jury decided that Morrison was guilty and he was sentenced to death. This sentence was afterwards commuted to life imprisonment.

Accustomed though he was to being in prison, Stinie Morrison now found his existence intolerable.

He frequently protested his innocence, and in 1916, on hearing that one of the police officers responsible for his conviction had been killed in a Zeppelin raid, he smiled grimly and remarked, 'Now I believe in Providence!' However, the news proved not to be much of a consolation to him, and he finally starved himself to death in January 1921.

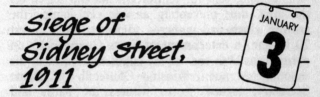

Siege of Sidney Street, 1911

JANUARY 3

Britain's most famous gun battle took place on 3 January 1911, when police officers tried to arrest two men trapped in a tenement building in Sidney Street, between Commercial Road and Whitechapel Road, in the East End of London.

The men, Fritz Svaars and Jacob Vogel, were members of a group of Russian anarchists. On 16 December previously they, in company with twelve comrades, had taken part in an attempted robbery at a jeweller's shop in Houndsditch, during the course of which three police officers had been shot dead and two others wounded. Their presence in a second-floor room occupied by Mrs Betsy Gershon had been reported by an informer on 2 January, and the building had been surrounded in the hope that they could be taken by surprise as they left. But after waiting for many hours in vain the police decided on a different course of action.

Early in the morning, with the help of the landlady, they managed to get Mrs Gershon out of the building without arousing suspicion; they then began evacuating the rest of the rooms. The anarchists remained out of sight until dawn, when police attracted their attention by throwing stones at the window. There were fifty police officers on the scene at this stage, fifteen of them armed with revolvers and four with rifles, and it was thought that such an impressive display of strength might induce the two fugitives to surrender. Instead, they opened fire, wounding a detective sergeant, and before long there were bullets ricocheting in all directions.

The police sent for reinforcements and sealed off the area, thus preventing anyone else joining the crowds which had gathered to watch the fray. At 10.15 a.m. a detachment of Scots Guards took up positions at both ends of the street and joined in the shooting. At noon, Winston Churchill, the Home Secretary, turned up to witness the battle and suggested that a cannon should be brought along, to blow in the front of the building. This proposal, unusual as it seemed to the police, was taken to the War Office and a troop of the Royal Horse Artillery was sent. Before it reached Sidney Street, however, smoke was seen coming from a top-floor window. Within half an hour the building was on fire.

The shooting continued as the blaze spread downwards, driving the anarchists before it. The fire brigade arrived but was not allowed to put out the fire. Eventually one of the men was killed by a rifle bullet; the other then fought on alone until the building collapsed around him.

The battle had lasted over six hours, with some of the spectators being hit by bullets. The firemen, when they were finally allowed to put out the fire, sustained a number of casualties before managing to get it under control. The affair led to much criticism of the government, particularly over the use of troops.

Of the others who had taken part in the Houndsditch crime, George Gardstein, the leader, had already died as a result of being accidently shot by another Russian, and several more had been arrested but were later acquited. The rest were never caught.

Disappearance of Mona Tinsley, 1937

JANUARY
5

At half past nine on the night of 5 January 1937, Nottinghamshire police were informed of the disappearance of a ten-year-old schoolgirl, Mona Tinsley, of 11, Thoresby Avenue, Newark. She had failed to arrive home after coming out of school — a twenty-minute walk away — at four o'clock that afternoon, and her parents had no idea what had become of her. The police began to investigate and the following day learnt that the missing girl had been seen with a man at Newark bus station soon after leaving the school. It was then clear that she had been abducted.

A few hours after receiving this report police officers went to see Frederick Nodder, a motor mechanic living in a semi-detached house near the village of Hayton, three and a half miles from Retford. Nodder, who had lodged with Mona's parents for three weeks in 1935, was known to them as Frederick Hudson and to their children as 'Uncle Fred'. He had been seen waiting outside Mona's school the previous afternoon, but denied knowing anything of her whereabouts.

Nodder was a married man who had left his wife. As he was wanted for non-payment of an affiliation order, he was taken into custody and charged accord-

13

ingly. It was found that he had taken Mona Tinsley by bus from Newark to Retford, a distance of about twenty miles, on 5 January, and also that the missing girl had been seen standing at the back door of his house at noon the following day.

After being identified by several witnesses, Nodder made a statement, admitting that he had seen Mona coming out of school on the day of her disappearance. He said that she had wanted to go to Sheffield to see her aunt, who had just had a baby, and that he — a friend of the aunt's — had taken her to stay overnight at his house. The next day he had taken her to Worksop and left her to travel the rest of the way to Sheffield on her own. The latter part of this statement could not be corroborated and was not believed. On 10 January Frederick Nodder was charged with abduction.

The police widened their search, going over waste ground and dumps and dragging rivers and canals, but found no trace of the missing girl. Nodder came up for trial in March at the Warwick Assizes in Birmingham and was found guilty. The judge, like everyone else, was certain that he had murdered the child and, in passing sentence, said: 'What you did with that little girl, what became of her, only you know. It may be that time will reveal the dreadful secret which you carry in your breast.' He sentenced Nodder to seven years' penal servitude — a term which he was not to complete.

Three months afterwards, on 6 June, a family boating party found Mona Tinsley's body floating on the River Idle, over twenty miles from Newark. She had been strangled. After further investigation Nodder was charged with her murder.

When he was brought to trial on this charge at the Nottingham Assizes in November, he pleaded not guilty and stuck to the story he had told earlier. But once again he was not believed, and the judge, in passing sentence of death, told him: 'Justice has slowly but surely overtaken you.'

Nodder, aged forty-four, was hanged at Lincoln Prison on 30 December 1937.

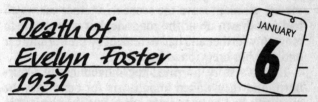

Death of Evelyn Foster 1931

JANUARY 6

During the late evening of 6 January 1931, an Otterburn bus crew making a return journey from Newcastle found a blazing car about seventy yards from the road at a desolate stretch of the Northumberland moor called Wolf's Neck. Stopping to investigate, they found Evelyn Foster, their employer's twenty-nine-year-old unmarried daughter, lying nearby with severe burns, having apparently met with an accident while driving the firm's new Hudson taxi. The bus crew took her to Otterburn at great speed, but she died shortly afterwards in the presence of her parents and family doctor. Before doing so, however, she managed to make a statement in which she claimed to be the victim of a frightful crime.

She said that she had been driving home when she was stopped at Ellishaw, not far from Otterburn, by a short, stocky man wearing an overcoat and bowler hat, who asked to be taken to Ponteland, in the direction of Newcastle. She agreed to take him, but before they reached Ponteland the man started to make advances towards her and she had to stop the car in order to fight him off. But the man then dealt her several blows, as a result of which she lost consciousness, and when she recovered she found that he had

15

taken her place in the driving-seat and was driving the car back towards Otterburn.

At Wolf's Neck, she continued, he suddenly took the car off the road, driving it over a bank with a steep drop before bringing it to a halt on the rough ground; he then got out and set fire to it while she was still inside. She managed to drag herself free of it in time to see her assailant leave the scene in another car which had just drawn up at the roadside, but was unable to move any further and had to remain by the burning car until the bus crew found her.

Evelyn's story horrified the inhabitants of Otterburn, and they waited impatiently for news that the murderer had been apprehended. But they waited in vain, for the police were unable to trace the man in the bowler hat, or anyone else who had seen him. Moreover, they soon began to doubt whether Evelyn's story was entirely true.

A pathologist, after examining the body, reported to the coroner's inquest early in February that the deceased had died of shock caused by external burns, and that she had been sitting in the car for some time after the fire had started. But he also said that he had found no bruises or cuts consistent with the blows she claimed to have received, and this, together with other findings reported at the inquest, led the coroner to raise the question of whether Evelyn Foster could have started the fire herself — perhaps for the purpose of claiming insurance money — and caused her own death by accident.

The suggestion, though bitterly resented by Evelyn's family and friends, was evidently discussed at length by the jury, for it took them two hours to arrive at a verdict of wilful murder. The police afterwards issued a statement, declaring themselves satisfied that the short, stocky man did not exist.

The case remains officially unsolved and continues to be the subject of speculation.

On the afternoon of 7 January 1974, Hans Appel, the thirty-four-year-old owner of a large construction company, and his wife's brother Dieter Poeschke, a garage mechanic aged twenty-one, were driving through the streets of Frankfurt. They were on friendly terms, and Poeschke was giving Appel a lift because his own car was out of service. Neither of them could have had any inkling of the tragedy which was about to occur.

Appel was preoccupied with his wife Renate, who was ten years younger than himself. He and she had both been married before, both had children by their earlier marriages, and Renate had since borne Appel a daughter. But then, in 1973, Renate's other brother Juergen, a former prisoner in East Germany who had been granted an amnesty, arrived in Frankfurt and moved into their home as a lodger.

Although the three adults and the children all got on well together for a while, it was not long before Appel's daughter Claudia, aged six, let him into a secret. 'Mummy and Uncle Juergen were in bed all afternoon,' she said one evening. 'They were naked!'

Hans Appel, a devoted husband, was shocked. At first he wondered whether Juergen, who had been separated from the rest of the family for sixteen years, really was Renate's brother or just a lover pretending to be. But a check with the immigration authorities was enough to dispel the suspicion, convincing him that Renate and Juergen had been committing incest.

Appel confronted them both, telling them that he

17

knew of their relationship, and when neither tried to deny it, he ordered Juergen out of the house. Juergen promptly left, taking Renate with him, and they went to live with Dieter and his wife in their two-room apartment in Sachsenhausen.

But, disgusted as he was with his wife's behaviour, Appel still loved her and wanted her back. He tried to persuade her to return with offers of jewellery and a fur coat — and when she refused he became desperate and bought himself a gun.

Suddenly, while they were in the car, he decided to confide in Dieter, and find out his opinion of what was going on. He therefore asked him if he believed that Juergen and Renate had been committing incest. Astonished by the question, Dieter then revealed that he and Juergen *both* practised incest with Renate 'all the time'!

On hearing this while he was already in a state of turmoil, Appel could stand no more. He pulled the gun from his pocket, shot and wounded Dieter, then brought the car to a halt, swerving onto the pavement. The door opened, and the wounded man fell out, but as he tried to get to his feet, Appel shot him twice more at close range and this time killed him. He then got out of the car himself and walked away from the scene.

When interviewed by the police, Appel admitted being the person responsible and the whole sordid truth emerged. He was tried in July 1974 and sent to prison for twenty-one months, but this sentence was set aside on appeal. Renate and Juergen went on living together after charges of incest against them had been dropped.

Execution of Bywaters and Thompson, 1923

On 9 January 1923, Frederick Bywaters, aged twenty, and Edith Thompson, twenty-eight, were hanged for the murder of Edith's husband in October the previous year. The case was a sensational one, and there were many protests at the executions being carried out. Reports that Edith was drugged and carried to the scaffold in a stupor provided opponents of the death penalty with a good deal of propaganda during the decades which followed.

Percy Thompson, aged thirty-two, was a shipping clerk in London, where his wife also worked as a manageress for a firm of wholesale milliners. Married in 1915, they had no children and lived uneventful lives until Edith began an affair with Bywaters, a merchant seaman, in 1921. Thereafter, though she remained with her husband and tried to keep up appearances, she saw him only as an obstacle to her happiness. Her life became one of surreptitious meetings when Bywaters was on leave and constant yearning for him when he was at sea.

On the night of the murder the Thompsons were walking towards their home in Kensington Gardens, Ilford, after visiting a London theatre, when Bywaters confronted them in the street. There was an argument between the two men, followed by a struggle, then Bywaters stabbed Percy several times with a knife before running off into the darkness. Percy Thompson died from a haemorrhage as he lay on the pavement.

Edith made a false statement to police, claiming that the crime had been committed by a stranger, but her association with Bywaters came to light and soon they were arrested. Edith then admitted that Bywaters had killed her husband, and Bywaters finally confessed his guilt. Though both of them claimed that Edith had had no part in the crime, letters found in Bywaters' possession suggested otherwise. The two prisoners were brought up for trial at the Old Bailey on 6 December 1922, both pleading not guilty.

Edith's letters, many of which were produced as evidence, contained many references to poison and innuendoes about attempts made by herself to kill her husband — on one occasion by putting powdered glass in his porridge. Though evidence was given of the complete absence both of poison and of glass from the victim's body, these references were interpreted as proof that she was guilty of collusion in a premeditated act.

Bywaters claimed that there had been no premeditation. He said that he had lain in wait for the Thompsons that night, not to kill Percy but to force him to leave Edith. He said that he had not produced his knife until Percy threatened to shoot him and appeared to be taking a gun from his pocket.

Edith Thompson gave evidence against the advice of her counsel, saying that she had not wanted to kill her husband. She explained the incriminating references in her letters by saying that she wanted Bywaters to think that she would do anything to keep him to herself.

The judge, in his summing-up, disregarded evidence in Edith's favour, laying stress upon her adultery, which disgusted him.

The case gave rise to many plays and books, F. Tennyson Jesse's novel, *A Pin to See the Peepshow*, being the most famous of them.

On the morning of 10 January 1929, the decompos-
ing body of Vivian Messiter, a representative of the
Wolfe's Head Oil Company, was discovered at the
company's depot in Southampton. He had been
beaten to death with a hammer, the attack leaving
the nearest wall and a stack of boxes spattered with
blood; he had also been robbed. The depot had been
found padlocked on the outside after his disappearance
at the end of the previous October and had remained so
until the company authorized another of its employees
to break in and take possession of it. The murder
weapon — without fingerprints — was found at the
scene of the crime.

Messiter, aged fifty-seven, had lived in lodgings and
was known never to see anyone except on business.
He had had no contact with any of his surviving relatives for months, and none of them was able to
provide any clue to the identity of his murderer.
However, a blank receipt book from which the first
nine pages had been torn was found among the dead
man's records, and pressure marks on the tenth page
showed that the ninth had acknowledged payment for
an oil sale to a company afterwards found to be fictitious. It therefore appeared that somebody had been
obtaining commission on sales which had not taken
place.

The handwriting on the receipt proved to be that of
a W.F. Thomas, whose signature had been found on a
scrap of paper left in the depot. A letter from the
same person, this time signing himself William F.
Thomas, was found at Messiter's lodgings; it had

21

been written on 23 October 1928, in reply to an advertisement in the local press for a salesman, and gave the address of a lodging house in Cranbury Avenue, Southampton.

Thomas was not to be found at the lodging house; he had left it on 3 November 1928, after staying only two weeks, and a forwarding address which he had given to the landlady proved to be non-existent. It was later discovered that he had moved to the village of Downton, about fifteen miles away, on the day of his departure, to begin working as a motor mechanic for a building contractor named Mitchell. He had remained in that employment for seven weeks, then disappeared after stealing the firm's wages, totalling £130.

William F. Thomas was found to be an alias of William Henry Podmore, a petty criminal from the Midlands who had served several short prison sentences and was wanted for car and motor-cycle frauds in Manchester. Traced to a small hotel in London, he told police that he had worked for Messiter for two days, delivering oil and repairing and testing his car, but denied having made the entry in the receipt book and claimed to know nothing about the murder.

The police did not feel that they had a strong enough case to charge him with murder; he was therefore taken to Manchester where, on 29 January, he was convicted of the car and motor-cycle frauds and sent to prison for six months. Upon his release, he was arrested at the prison gates and charged with the offence committed in Downton — for which he was given another six-month sentence.

By the time this sentence had been served, the police had enough evidence for a murder charge, Podmore having confessed the crime to two fellow-prisoners. So, when he left Wandsworth Prison on 17 December, he was again arrested.

22

Brought to trial in Winchester the following March, he continued to declare that he was innocent. He was, however, convicted, the jury being satisfied that he had murdered Vivian Messiter because his fraudulent claims had been discovered. He was hanged on 22 April 1930, at the age of twenty-nine.

Execution of John Gilbert Graham, 1957

JANUARY
11

John Gilbert Graham, who was executed in Colorado on 11 January 1957, was a mass murderer responsible for the deaths of forty-four people in a plane crash on 1 November 1955. A young married man with two small children, he had caused the accident with a time-bomb while his mother, Mrs Daisy King, was one of the plane's passengers. The crime had been committed for the sake of money.

Graham, at the time of the murders, was twenty-three years old. He and his mother ran a drive-in restaurant together in Denver, and Mrs King, who had been widowed twice, lived with him and his family. He had much to gain from his mother's death, for she was a rich woman as a result of having inherited an estate valued at $150,000 from her second husband.

He also expected to benefit from a flight insurance policy which he had taken out on her life just before she boarded the plane.

Mrs King was on the first leg of a journey to Spenard, Alaska, to visit her daughter, Helen Ruth Hablutzel (Graham's half-sister), when the time-

23

bomb, which had been placed in her luggage, went off. The plane, having left the airport in Denver only a few minutes earlier, crashed in a field, causing a second explosion. There were no survivors.

Graham had a criminal record for forgery and bootlegging; he also had experience of logging and construction jobs, from which he was thought likely to have gained a knowledge of explosives. Moreover, it was learnt that he and his mother had frequently quarrelled over money. After prolonged questioning Graham made a confession which he later retracted.

His trial, for the murder of Mrs King, began in April 1956 and was watched by millions of television viewers. The jury's verdict was returned on 4 May.

Graham later made a second confession, but showed no remorse for all the deaths which he had caused. At his execution, which took place in the gas chamber of the state penitentiary, he appeared to be as indifferent to his own fate as he had been to that of his victims.

Matricide in South Africa, 1925

JANUARY

13

During the early evening of 13 January 1925, Petrus Hauptfleisch, a drunken middle-aged slaughterer, ran from his home in Richmond, Cape Province, screaming that his sixty-seven-year-old mother had been 'burnt in the kitchen fire'. Mrs Hauptfleisch, a widow, was found dead, lying on her side on the brick-built stove in the kitchen. Her body was half naked and badly burned, and some of her clothes lay

24

scattered on the floor.

When the doctor arrived, Hauptfleisch — who had moved the body in the meantime — claimed that his mother had been cleaning the chimney by burning it out with petrol, and had accidentally burnt herself to death. But the doctor, who had known Mrs Hauptfleisch for over twenty years, did not believe this. He knew that she was far too cautious to try to clean the chimney in such a dangerous manner, and also that she was not the sort of person to walk about the house improperly dressed.

Afterwards, on examining her body, he found postmortem lividity indicating that Mrs Hauptfleisch had died while lying on her back and that she had remained in that position for an hour or more after death. This, together with the discovery of evidence of suffocation, led to Hauptfleisch being arrested and charged with his mother's murder a few days later. He was brought to trial in Cape Town in September the same year.

Hauptfleisch was an ex-farmer who had served as a soldier in the First World War. His wife had left him, taking their small son, because she could not tolerate his heavy drinking. His mother, with whom he had lived ever since, was known to have been frightened of him for the same reason. Only a month before her death she had had to take refuge with a neighbour because her son, in a drunken rage, had threatened to stone her.

At his trial it was contended that Hauptfleisch had asphyxiated his mother as she lay on her bed. Later, to make it appear that she had died in an accident, he had placed her body on the kitchen stove, doused it with petrol and set fire to it. Hauptfleisch denied all this, but did not give a good impression of himself. He was found guilty and sentenced to death.

Though a further examination of his mother's body produced the same results as the first, Hauptfleisch continued to maintain that he was innocent. However, he was hanged on 23 December 1925.

Discovery of Elizabeth Short's body, 1947

JANUARY
15

On the morning of 15 January 1947, the body of a young woman was found on a vacant lot in a suburb of Los Angeles. It had been shockingly mutilated — among other things, it had been cut into two pieces at the waist, and the letters B and D had been carved on one of the thighs. More dreadful still was the finding by pathologists that most of the victim's injuries had been inflicted while she was still alive. Her death had taken place only a short while before the gruesome discovery was made.

A fingerprint check by the FBI revealed that the body was that of Elizabeth Short, aged twenty-two, from Medford, Massachusetts, who had a record for juvenile delinquency. But Mrs Phoebe Short, Elizabeth's mother, was unable to make a positive identification because the mutilations had made the body unrecognizable.

It emerged that Elizabeth Short had been very attractive, but unhappy, drunken and promiscuous. She had left home at seventeen to go to Miami — where she was found to be in need of care and protection — and had later worked in Hollywood as a film extra. She was known in Hollywood as the 'Black Dahlia', having established an image of herself by dressing entirely in black — which was also the colour of her hair. But since then she had worked as a waitress in San Diego.

A letter produced by Phoebe Short gave her daughter's San Diego address, but the police found that she had left it, without luggage, six days before the discovery of her body. A man with whom she had been seen about the same time was interviewed, and said that on the day in question he had driven her to the Biltmore Hotel in Los Angeles, where she claimed that she was going to meet her sister; he had not seen or heard from her afterwards. It was also learnt that she had been seen in the company of another woman two or three days before her death. But what had happened to her after that nobody seemed to know.

No trace of her clothing or any other of her possessions had been found at the vacant lot, and a search of drains and sewers failed to produce a single garment which could be identified as having belonged to her.

The newspaper accounts of the case led to many false confessions — one of them from a woman who stated: 'The Black Dahlia stole my man, so I killed her and cut her up!' But these claims were easily discounted, as details of the mutilations had not been published.

A Los Angeles newspaper received through the post an envelope with a message in pasted-up letters on the outside: 'Here are Dahlia's belongings. Letter will follow.' The envelope contained Elizabeth Short's birth certificate, address book and social security card, and as the address book had one page missing, it was assumed that this had borne the name of the sender — perhaps her murderer. But no further communication was received from this person, and fingerprints found on the envelope did not match any in the FBI files.

Eventually an army corporal who claimed to have known the victim was arrested as a suspect. Bloodstains were found on his clothes and his locker contained newspaper cuttings about the crime. Moreover, he boasted: 'When I get drunk I get rough with women!' On closer examination, however, he was found to be a mentally unbalanced man who had had no connection with the murder.

No further progress was made on the case, and the crime remains unsolved. The motive for the murder has never been discovered.

Murder of Dr. Bernd Servé, 1953

JANUARY 17

On the night of 17 January 1953, Dr Bernd Servé, a lawyer, and a youth of nineteen named Adolf Hüllecremer were sitting in a stationary car in a quiet road leading north out of Düsseldorf when they were attacked by two men wearing masks, one of them armed with a gun. Servé was shot dead, the bullet entering his body below the left jaw and leaving an exit wound in his right temple; Hüllecremer was battered over the head but only lost consciousness momentarily. Both victims were then robbed, and an unsuccessful attempt was made to start the car before the attackers left the scene.

The crime was still unsolved on 28 November 1955, when Friedhelm Behre, a twenty-six-year-old baker, and his girlfriend Thea Kürmann, aged twenty-three, were found dead on the outskirts of Kalkum, a small town near Düsseldorf, four weeks after being reported missing. In this case both victims had been battered with a blunt instrument but died from drowning after their car had been driven into a gravel pit filled with water. Like Servé and Hüllecremer, the couple had been robbed, but it was not at first realized that there was a connection between the two crimes.

Ten weeks later, on 7 February 1956, another couple, Peter Falkenberg, a professional driver aged twenty-six, and Hildegard Wassing, a twenty-year-old typist, were reported missing. Falkenberg's car, with blood inside it, was found abandoned the following day, and on 9 February the couple's charred bodies were discovered in a burnt-out hayrick in the village of Ilverich, just outside Düsseldorf. Both had been battered over the head with a heavy instrument, but Falkenberg had also been shot at close range, the bullet following the same unusual path as in Dr Servé's case. The girl had been raped.

There was almost another of these 'Doubles Murders', as they were called, in a wood at Meererbusch — also near Düsseldorf — on 4 May the same year, when two men disturbed a courting couple and held them at gunpoint. On this occasion, after the man had been forced to hand over his wallet, the girl suddenly ran off, screaming for help. Although one of the gunmen caught and began to attack her, passersby arrived on the scene and the two culprits fled.

A few weeks after that, on 10 June, a man was apprehended by an armed forest ranger, who had noticed him behaving suspiciously in the same wood. Werner Boost, a twenty-eight-year-old family man who worked in a factory, admitted owning a loaded gun which had been found at the spot, saying that he used it for hunting animals. But his arrest led to the discovery of various stolen articles, including a tent, a motor-cycle, more guns and some jewellery, in the same area.

A further gun, and parts of yet another, were found in his house in Düsseldorf — together with jars of cyanide, sulphur and saltpetre — and inquiries revealed that he was an expert marksman, able to hit a target without removing the gun from a holster worn at his waist. This was regarded as significant, as Dr Servé and Peter Falkenberg were believed to have been shot in this manner.

Though suspected of having been involved in the murders, Werner was at first charged only with a trespassing offence — for which he was sent to prison for six months — but it was later found that since his arrest his wife had been receiving money from Franz Lorbach, one of his fellow factory-workers. Viewing this with suspicion, police carried out a search of Lorbach's home, and more stolen articles were discovered.

Lorbach, who had served a prison term himself for poaching, told police officers that he had received the articles in question from Boost, but had not realized that they were stolen. He was arrested and eventually, in February 1957, made a statement in which he accused Boost of the murders and admitted to having been his accomplice on the night Dr Servé was killed. Boost, he said, was a maniac who had made him commit crimes by hypnotizing him, and had also given him pep pills and a 'truth serum'. He had lived in fear of him for four years.

It was learnt that Boost, the illegitimate son of a country girl, had settled in Düsseldorf in 1950 — having previously lived in East Germany, where he had made his living by illegally escorting parties of refugees to the West. He was suspected of having committed a number of murders in the border zone at this time, but no charges were brought against him in connection with them.

Besides being able to use a gun with deadly accuracy, Boost was an expert in unarmed combat, and knew how to mix and prepare poisons. According to Lorbach, he had been experimenting with drugs and chemicals in the hope of finding new ways of killing people, and was also responsible for crimes against other courting couples, in which the men had been robbed and the women raped. On such occasions, having raped the woman himself, he would try to persuade his companion to do the same.

Brought to trial in 1959, Boost was sentenced to life imprisonment for the murders of Dr Servé and the two courting couples, and Lorbach, who had given evidence against him, was given a six-year sentence for his own part in the first of these crimes. Having served his sentence, however, Lorbach found himself a job and managed to put the past behind him. In 1965, he visited the police officer responsible for his arrest, to express his gratitude for the help which that officer had given him.

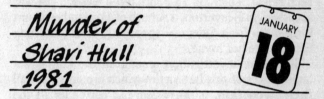

Murder of Shari Hull 1981

JANUARY 18

In a suburb of Salem, Oregon, on the evening of 18 January 1981, Shari Hull and Lisa Garcia, both aged twenty, were about to leave an office building which they had just been cleaning when a man appeared there, taking them by surprise. He forced them, at gunpoint, to undress and take part in a number of sexual acts, then made them lie face down on the floor while he shot them in the head — Shari three times and Lisa twice. Finally, he left the building, no doubt under the impression that they were dead.

Both girls were, in fact, still alive, and Lisa Garcia was conscious. Having outwitted her attacker by breathing as shallowly as possible, she dragged herself to the office telephone and called the police. Though

Shari died shortly afterwards, Lisa survived and was later to see the man responsible brought to trial. In the meantime, however, she was found to have contracted herpes from him.

The suburb in which the crimes had been committed was close to the I-5 freeway, and Lisa's description of the killer was similar to those given of a man wanted in connection with a number of robberies and sex crimes which had taken place along that freeway during the previous few weeks. Having already feared that this man would sooner or later resort to murder, police were now in no doubt that he had done so. But there were to be further murders, as well as many other attacks, along the I-5 before he was captured.

On 3 February a fireman's home near Redding, California, was broken into and his wife and stepdaughter murdered, the stepdaughter having first been raped. Then, on 15 February, a teenage girl was shot dead in Beaverton, a suburb of Portland — about forty miles from Salem — apparently after admitting the killer to her home.

It was an investigation among all the known acquaintances of this last victim which brought Randall Brent Woodfield, a thirty-year-old bartender in the same suburb, to the attention of the police. Randy Woodfield, who had only known the victim slightly, was found to have a record of minor sex offences and to have served part of a ten-year sentence for robbery before being released on parole in July 1979. A search of his home and car led to the discovery of evidence connecting him, not with the latest murder, but with the crimes against Shari Hull and Lisa Garcia. He was accordingly arrested and charged with murder and attempted murder.

At the time of his trial, in June 1981, the murder weapon had not been discovered. But there was a great deal of evidence against him, including the testimony of Lisa Garcia, who identified him with certainty as her attacker. Woodfield remained detached and unemotional throughout; he denied the offences, claiming to have been in a bar on the evening in question, but could produce nobody to corroborate this. He admitted to having purchased a gun the previous autumn but said he had got rid of it because he was afraid his parole officer would have him sent back to jail. He was nonetheless convicted and sentenced to life imprisonment.

Two months afterwards a number of charges were brought against Woodfield in connection with the murders of the fireman's wife and stepdaughter. About the same time it was announced that the gun which had been used in the Beaverton murder case had been found in a river a few miles from the place where he had lived before his arrest.

Pursuit of Lepidus and Hefeldt, 1909

On the afternoon of 25 January 1909, two young Russians, Jacob Lepidus and Paul Hefeldt, stood outside a rubber factory in Tottenham, north-east London. They had revolvers in their pockets and were awaiting the arrival of a youth carrying the firm's wages. At the same time Mr Schnurmann, the head of the firm, was standing at the factory door, also waiting for the wages to arrive — as he did every Saturday. The street was crowded, and it is unlikely that anyone took any notice of the Russians or they of Mr Schnurmann.

33

Suddenly a car drew up outside the factory, and the youth got out, carrying the money — about £80 — in a bag. He made his way towards the entrance, while the driver remained in the car and kept the engine running, but the Russians made a quick move, wrenched the bag from his hand, and ran off with it. Mr Schnurmann, who had witnessed the crime, tried to stop them, but was unable to catch either. He immediately got into the car, shouting, 'Stop thief!'

A police constable who had just appeared on the scene got in with him, and in a moment they were speeding along the road after the robbers, the driver keeping his fingers on the horn. The Russians started shooting at them, one bullet shattering the windscreen while another wounded the driver and put the engine out of action. When the policeman got out and went after them on foot, he was shot in the leg and seriously wounded. At this, Mr Schnurmann gave up the chase.

Lepidus and Hefeldt ran on, becoming desperate. A boy of ten who tried to cross the road was shot dead; so, too, was a constable who tried to apprehend them outside Tottenham police station. This second murder, however, was observed from inside the station, and reported by telephone to the divisional headquarters at Stoke Newington. Firearms were then issued to police officers in other stations, and the district was cordoned off. Those in Tottenham were ordered to pursue the murderers and drive them into an ambush.

The Russians ran on blindly and, turning a corner, saw a tramcar ahead of them. They raced towards it and jumped aboard with their guns still in their hands. The driver stopped the vehicle, ran up the stairs unnoticed, and hid on the upper deck, which was otherwise empty. The conductor was therefore forced to drive the tram at gunpoint.

The only other people on board were an elderly

man and a woman clutching her child.

Civilians armed with shotguns had joined in the pursuit, and they began firing at the tram as it gathered speed. Lepidus stood on the rear platform, shooting back at them, while Hefeldt kept his gun pointed at the conductor. When the elderly man tried to remonstrate with them, he was shot in the neck. The woman cried hysterically; the driver continued to crouch on the upper deck. Finally, the conductor tricked the gunmen into thinking that they were approaching another police station, and they jumped off the tram and ran along a side turning. The conductor drove on to the depot, to get help for the wounded man.

In the side turning the desperadoes stole a milk-cart after shooting the driver, but overturned it at the next corner. They then stole another cart and drove towards Chingford. The police behind them commandeered private cars in order to continue the pursuit. But, finding themselves in open country, the fugitives stopped the cart and made off across the fields. In doing so, they avoided a police ambush.

As the chase continued on foot, Lepidus and Hefeldt suddenly found a high fence in front of them. Lepidus, the taller man, climbed over it, but Hefeldt could not. He stood facing his pursuers for a moment, then called out to Lepidus that he was running out of ammunition. Suddenly he turned the gun on himself and fired.

Lepidus ran on alone, managing to stay ahead of the police for a little longer. But he, too, was running short of ammunition and, trying to hide in a nearby farm labourer's cottage, found himself trapped. He watched helplessly from a bedrooom window as the place was surrounded.

Two armed police officers entered the cottage and called on him to surrender. When he failed to do so shots were fired through the bedroom door, one of them hitting him above the left eye. With blood pouring down his face, he opened the door, then shot himself in the head as one of the police officers fired again. He died instantly.

Paul Hefeldt, in the meantime, had been taken off to hospital, where he remained until his own death almost three weeks later.

Execution of Harry Dobkin, 1943

On 27 January 1943, Harry Dobkin, aged forty-nine, was hanged at Wandsworth Prison for the murder of his wife Rachel. The couple had been separated for some years and Dobkin had been in trouble for failing to comply with a maintenance order which had been made against him. It seems that the murder was an act of desperation rather than callousness.

As far as the police were concerned, the case began in July 1942, when workmen clearing a bombed chapel in Lambeth, south London, discovered a skull and a number of bones. When these were examined by Dr Keith Simpson in his laboratory at Guy's Hospital they were found to be the remains of a woman who had died between twelve and eighteen months previously. The head and limbs had been severed from the rest of the body, and there were signs of strangulation.

The police searched lists of missing persons and discovered that Rachel Dobkin, whose husband had been a fire-watcher at the chapel, had been reported missing fifteen months earlier. By checking the teeth of the skull against her dental records, Dr Simpson was able to identify the remains with certainty. He then provided additional proof of identity by superimposing a photograph of the skull on a snapshot of the missing woman, showing that it matched her features exactly.

Dobkin was found to be living a few miles from Lambeth. He was a strong, heavily-built man, who made his living working in the building trade. It was discovered that the differences between his wife and himself over the payment of maintenance had continued after his release from prison, and that on one occasion he had failed to report a fire at the chapel where the remains had been buried.

On being brought to trial at the Old Bailey, Dobkin denied the offence. He gripped the spikes round the dock, sweating profusely as he heard the evidence being given against him, and collapsed when the verdict was delivered. After he had been hanged Dr Simpson carried out the routine autopsy on his body.

Death of Juliette Deitsh, 1889

JANUARY 30

On 30 January 1889, Juliette Deitsh, a girl of twelve, died from an overdose of chloroform at the home of Dr Etienne Deschamps in St Peter Street, New Orleans. She had gone there to take part in what Deschamps, aged fifty-eight, called 'an experiment', the chloroform being given to her on a handkerchief while she and the doctor were lying on a bed together, both of them naked. Her death was followed by an apparent suicide attempt by the doctor.

Deschamps, who had been born in Rennes, was actually a skilled dentist. Since his arrival in New Orleans in 1884 he had set himself up as a doctor, giving 'magnetizing' treatment. He also claimed to have occult powers, and was not above trickery.

In 1888 he became friendly with Juliette's father, a gullible widower living with his two daughters in the Rue Chartres, and informed him that he needed a young virgin as a medium, to help him to find buried treasure in the swamps of Barataria by psychic means. Deitsh, a carpenter, was sufficiently impressed by this idea to allow Juliette to be used for the purpose, and for the next six months she made regular trips to the doctor's home, accompanied by her sister Laurence, who was three years younger than herself. It was Laurence who, on the day of the tragedy, ran to tell her father what had happened.

Jules Deitsh, on arrival at the house, found Deschamps lying on the bed, covered in blood, beside Juliette's body; he had stabbed himself in the chest several times with a dental instrument.

The doctor's wounds proved to be superficial, and after being questioned by the police he was held in custody. He apparently made a second suicide attempt in his cell a few days later, but, if so, it was also unsuccessful, and he was brought to trial for murder on 29 April.

The police investigation had revealed that Juliette had been the doctor's mistress, and that he had generally, if not invariably, given her chloroform before making love to her. He would make Juliette and her sister both promise to tell nobody what had occurred, saying that he had cast a spell which would not work if anyone else knew about it.

Though Deschamps claimed that the girl had given her consent to what had taken place between them, and that the chloroform had been used for her comfort, it was only to be expected that such an affair, if it became known, would cause a scandal.

There were also a number of other things which were hardly in the doctor's favour. Deschamps claimed falsely that Juliette had been seduced by a local jeweller, and letters found in his possession, ostensibly from the dead girl to himself, were shown to be forgeries. It was known, too, that after stabbing himself, Deschamps had sent Laurence to tell her father, not that Juliette was dead, but that he (the doctor) was dying.

The prosecution contended that Deschamps had killed the girl on purpose because he was afraid that she would reveal their affair to others, and after a short trial he was convicted and sentenced to death. While in jail, awaiting the outcome of an appeal, he became disorderly and violent; he tried repeatedly to escape by making a run for it when his cell door was opened, and threatened to cause a war between France and the United States.

His appeal was unsuccessful and, in spite of being declared insane by a self-appointed commission of doctors, he was hanged on 12 May 1892.

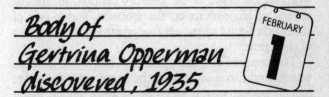

Body of Gertrina Opperman discovered, 1935

FEBRUARY 1

On 1 February 1935, the body of Gertrina Petrusina Opperman, an unmarried South African girl, was found near a railway line nineteen miles outside Pretoria. She had been savagely battered and shot through the head, but had given birth to a child shortly before her death. The child, though born alive, had died soon afterwards.

The girl was identified by M.J. Van der Bergh, a farmer of Northam, for whom she had worked as a nurse and general help. Mr Van der Bergh told a police officer that Miss Opperman had left Northam for Pretoria, 126 miles away, by train on the evening of 30 January, and produced a letter which had arrived for her from Pretoria, dated 29 January. The letter, which was signed 'J.H. Coetzee', read:

'I have just received your two letters. I was away from the second until yesterday. I will meet you on Thursday morning at about nine o'clock at the Pretoria Railway Station. Everything is still arranged. We will then talk.'

The letter had, in fact, been written by a young detective sergeant attached to the Railway Police — one of the first police officers to arrive at the scene of the crime.

Jacobus Hendrik Coetzee, who was engaged to the daughter of his chief officer, was found to have been on intimate terms with the dead girl, though he had at first pretended that he did not know her. He was arrested on the morning of 3 February, and bullets of the type recovered from the girl's body were found in his possession. An examination of the clothes he had worn on the night of 31 January resulted in the discovery of bloodstains on the trousers, and a pair of shoes was found to match footprints left at the scene of the crime.

The case aroused great interest, and when Coetzee was brought to trial in May the same year, the judge had to appeal to the jury not to allow public indignation to influence them in their consideration of the evidence.

It was contended by the prosecution that Coetzee had murdered Miss Opperman because he was afraid that she would ruin his career and marriage prospects. He had tried at first to kill her with his hands, and had left her for dead on the railway line, so that her body would be mutilated by the first train that came along. But later, on returning to the scene, he found that she was still alive, having managed to drag herself away from the line. He therefore shot her.

Coetzee denied having killed Gertrina Opperman. He admitted that he had been intimate with her and that he had offered to help her financially, but claimed that he was not the father of her child. He said that on the night in question he had gone to meet her at the railway station in Pretoria, but was unable to find her there.

The jury found the prisoner guilty, but added a recommendation of mercy because he had been 'wrongly saddled with the paternity of the unborn child of the deceased'. Coetzee was accordingly sentenced to life imprisonment with hard labour.

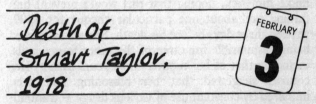

Death of Stuart Taylor, 1978

FEBRUARY 3

On 3 February 1978, Stuart Taylor, a fifty-three-year-old tobacco farmer of St Pauls, North Carolina, died in hospital in the nearby town of Lumberton. He had been admitted twice in two days, each time suffering from severe stomach pains, vomiting and diarrhoea, but on the first occasion had seemed well enough to go home after just a few hours. By the time he was re-admitted, however, his symptoms were so bad that he died while doctors were attending him. A

41

post-mortem examination then revealed that his death had been caused by arsenic poisoning.

The police investigation which followed led to the arrest of Taylor's fiancée, a twice-widowed woman of forty-five named Margie Velma Barfield, with whom he had been living at the time of his death. It also led to the discovery of lethal amounts of arsenic in the exhumed bodies of four other people who had been closely associated with the same woman — her second husband, Jennings L. Barfield, her mother, Lillie McMillan Bullard, and two people she had known as a result of working in a Lumberton nursing home or serving as a part-time home help for the elderly.

Velma Barfield was brought to trial in Elizabethtown, in the same state, towards the end of November 1978. The prosecution produced evidence of several cheques forged on Stuart Taylor's account, and also of the deaths of the other four people with whom the prisoner had been associated, though no charges had been brought against her in connection with these.

Mrs Barfield admitted forging cheques on Taylor's account and said that she had given him poison to make him sick, hoping that this would prevent him finding out about one particular cheque for $300, written three days before his death. She also admitted being responsible for three of the other four deaths, including that of her mother three years earlier. Her counsel suggested that her reasoning had been impaired by constant use of various drugs — tranquillisers, anti-depressants and sedatives — over a long period, but she was found guilty of first-degree murder and sentenced to death.

She remained on Death Row for the next six years, while one attempt after another was made to save her life. Towards the end of that time she was frequently in the news, and television viewers watched the 'killer grandmother' giving interviews, walking along prison corridors, knitting, and so on. During the last days of her life, she chose her coffin and funeral clothes and agreed to donate her organs for transplant operations. She was finally executed by lethal injection in the early hours of 2 November 1984, at the Central Prison in Raleigh, North Carolina.

Velma Barfield, then aged fifty-two, was the first woman to be executed in the United Stated for twenty-two years. She had chosen to die by lethal injection rather than in the gas chamber because she did not want to sit upright, facing a crowd of spectators, at the end. She nonetheless wore pink pyjamas for the occasion.

A prison official said afterwards that the execution had been carried out smoothly and painlessly.

Disappearance of Miss Chubb, 1958

FEBRUARY
6

On the evening of 6 February 1958, Miss Lilian Chubb, a middle-aged department-store employee, failed to arrive back at the home she shared with her brother, sister-in-law and mother-in-law in Broadstairs, Kent. This was unusual for her, for she was a creature of habit, but nothing was done about it until the following day, when she had still not returned. Her sister-in-law, Mrs Edith Daisy Chubb, then telephoned the store — which was some miles away, on the outskirts of Margate — and, on being told that Lily had not been to work for two days, reported her sister-in-law's disappearance to the police.

Shortly afterwards Lily was found dead in a hedge not far from the house. She had been strangled with a scarf about twenty-four hours previously, and her handbag was missing.

During a post-mortem carried out by Professor Francis Camps, marks were found indicating that she had been placed in a chair for some time after death. In view of this, the discovery of an invalid chair in the Chubbs' garden shed was regarded as significant. So, too, was the fact that nobody could remember seeing Lily go off to work on the morning of her death, for she was normally seen by several people at this time of the day.

Edith Chubb, aged forty-six, was a hard-working woman with five children to look after in addition to keeping house for the other members of her family. Being poor, she also worked three twelve-hour nights every week as a hospital cleaner — though she was actually a trained nurse — in the hope of making ends meet. Even then she had been unable to pay her rent prior to her sister-in-law's death, though she had afterwards had more money then usual, and had been able to pay outstanding bills.

When this was discovered by the police it was not long before she made a confession. 'You are quite right, I killed her,' she said to Chief Inspector Everitt. 'I cannot bear to think about it, but I shall feel better if I tell you.'

She then told him that on the morning of 6 February she had pulled Lily's scarf tightly round her neck and unintentionally killed her as she was going out through the front door. Then, when she realized what she had done, she brought the invalid chair from the shed, lifted the body into it, then pushed it back to the shed and left it there until she could move it from the house unobserved. It remained there until early the following morning, when, having seen her husband off to work, she covered it with a rug and pushed it to the place where it was found.

Mrs Chubb gave Everitt no real clue to her motive

for this crime, claiming that she and her sister-in-law had got on well together; she merely said that she had taken £12 from Lily's handbag before destroying it. But later, after she had been arrested, she told a woman police officer that her sister-in-law had been smug and self-centred, and that she (Mrs Chubb) had been the subject of rude letters which Lily had written to her sister in Canada. Other remarks suggested that her resentment of her sister-in-law's attitude had been partly due to her poverty and exhaustion.

Mrs Chubb was brought to trial at the Old Bailey on 30 April. She told the court that she had reached a stage at which the slightest thing her sister-in-law did upset her, and that that was why the crime had taken place. 'I felt irritated at the way she put her cup down,' said Mrs Chubb. 'I followed her downstairs and pulled her scarf. I didn't intend to hurt her, I intended to give her a shake-up. She fell backwards onto the floor and struck her head on the post of the stairs.'

The prisoner had many friends from her nursing days, and some of them appeared to give evidence on her behalf. The matron of Haine Hospital, near Broadstairs, said that Mrs Chubb, whom she had known since 1936, was a sick woman, in need of a holiday; and the family doctor said that the previous year she had been on the verge of a nervous breakdown. The jury was sympathetic towards her, and although the judge's summing-up was not in her favour, she was found guilty only of manslaughter.

She was sent to prison for four years.

Attempted execution of Will Purvis 1894

On 7 February 1894, Will Purvis, the twenty-one-year-old son of a Mississippi farmer, was due to be hanged in Columbia, Marion County, following his conviction for the murder of Will Buckley, one of his neighbours at nearby Devils Bend. The crime had been committed on 22 June the previous year, after Buckley, his brother Jim and a black farmhand named Sam Waller had made disclosures about the activities of the White Caps, a secret organization similar to the original Ku Klux Klan, which had been disbanded some years earlier. Purvis had admitted being a former member of the White Caps, but denied taking part in Buckley's murder. He claimed to have objected to the crime and left the organization because of it.

The imminence of his execution nonetheless caused much excitement. It was to be carried out in public, as was usual at this time, and crowds began to gather at the scaffold several hours beforehand. When Purvis ascended it towards noon they fell silent, waiting for him to speak, but instead of making the confession which everyone expected, he once again claimed that he was innocent, and went on to say that there were people present who could save him if they wished to. The sheriff and his three deputies then went to work, adjusting the noose round the prisoner's neck, pinioning his arms and legs and pulling a black cap down over his face. A local pastor prayed loudly.

When all was ready the sheriff took up a hatchet and severed a stay rope holding the trap in place;

the trap then opened and the condemned man fell through. But to the horror of all concerned, the knot of the halter came undone and Purvis dropped to the ground, temporarily insensible but not seriously hurt.

A second attempt to hang him was prevented by the pastor and other influential citizens, who felt that what had happened was an act of God and a sign that Purvis had been wrongly convicted. The prisoner was therefore taken back to jail, and the sheriff reported what had happened to the state governor, saying that he, too, now had serious doubts about Purvis's guilt.

Governor John M. Stone had no such doubts and refused to commute the sentence. But a fresh attempt to carry it out was delayed by three unsuccessful appeals to the State Supreme Court, the prisoner being transferred to the town of Purvis, in Lamar County, in the meantime. When the execution date was finally fixed for 12 December 1895, a party of friends broke into the jail and set him free.

Will Purvis remained at large for over a year, but gave himself up in February 1897, after a new state governor had offered to show leniency towards him. His sentence was accordingly commuted, and later, in December 1898, he was pardoned in response to public pressure.

On being released, he went back to working for his father, who now had a farm in Purvis. He later acquired a farm of his own and married the daughter of a Baptist minister. They had eleven children.

His case was resurrected in 1917, when a sixty-year-old man named Joe Beard made a death-bed confession which cleared Purvis of Buckley's murder, and on 15 March 1920, Purvis was voted $5000 compensation by the state legislature.

He later gave public lectures and radio talks, and in 1935 published his *True Life Story*. His death took place on 13 October 1938, when he was sixty-six years old.

Human remains found in manhole, 1983

FEBRUARY
8

On 8 February 1983, a drains maintenance engineer found decomposed human flesh in a manhole outside a house in north London. The discovery was reported to the police and led to the questioning of Dennis Nilsen, a thirty-seven-year-old civil servant working for the Manpower Services Commission. Nilsen confessed that he was the person responsible, and revealed the whereabouts of further remains. He said that he had killed sixteen people.

Nilsen, a tall, bespectacled Scotsman, was a bachelor and a homosexual. In his top-floor flat in Cranley Gardens, Muswell Hill, police found three human heads, each of which had been boiled, and the lower part of a body. At another house, in Melrose Avenue, Cricklewood — where he had lived previously — they discovered an assortment of human bones, weighing twenty-eight pounds.

There had, in fact, been fifteen murders — one fewer than Nilsen had originally claimed. The victims were all men — mainly homosexuals and drifters whom he had met while he was out drinking, and later strangled with ties while they were asleep or drunk. Those who had not died from strangulation had been drowned in his bath.

Nilsen was unperturbed by questions about his crimes, which had clearly given him pleasure. 'What I did seemed right at the time,' he told police officers. 'I felt that my sole reason for existence was to kill.'

The first of these murders took place on 30 December 1978, the victim being an unknown Irish youth of seventeen or eighteen. Nilsen explained that he had

48

been lonely and miserable over Christmas and wanted company for the New Year, 'even if it was only a body'. He kept the corpse in plastic bags under the floorboards for months before finally disposing of it on a bonfire in the garden. A later victim provided him with a set of steel knives, which he used to dismember subsequent ones.

Each of the first twelve murders took place while Nilsen was living in Melrose Avenue, the bodies all being hidden under the floorboards until he was ready to dissect them, and disinfectant used to mask the smell. Having dissected them, he threw some parts over the back fence, to be eaten by prowling animals, and burnt others on large bonfires, on which car tyres were also burnt to prevent the smell arousing suspicion. The bones were buried in the garden, the skulls having first been crushed with a garden-roller.

The other three murders took place at the flat in Cranley Gardens, to which Nilsen had moved in 1981. Having no access to the garden at this address, he resorted to flushing some parts down the lavatory and boiling others. The large bones were put out for the dustmen to take away.

During the course of the investigation it became clear that Nilsen had been very lucky on a number of occasions, sometimes as a result of negligence on the part of the police.

On 31 October 1979, a Chinese cook reported that Nilsen had tried to kill him, and that he had escaped only by throwing a brass candlestick at his assailant, who was thus knocked unconscious. When the police went to see Nilsen about the incident he denied all knowledge of it, and the cook was unwilling to pursue it further.

In November 1980 a Scotsman aged twenty-nine reported a similar attack, but Nilsen convinced the police that it was the result of a quarrel between two homosexual lovers, and no further action was taken at the time.

Another case of attempted murder took place in November 1981, but this was not reported until later.

On yet another occasion a microbiologist named Robert Wilson reported that he had found three carrier-bags full of human flesh in the street near Melrose Avenue. The following day he checked with police to find out what had happened, and was told that no written report had been made about the discovery.

In October 1983 Nilsen appeared at the Old Bailey on six charges of murder and two of attempted murder. He pleaded not guilty by reason of diminished responsibility, but after a trial lasting nine days he was convicted on all charges. The judge sentenced him to six terms of life imprisonment, recommending that he should serve at least twenty-five years.

The following year, in Wormwood Scrubs Prison, Nilsen's face was slashed with a razor by another prisoner. The resulting wound needed eighty-nine stitches.

Discovery of Evelyn Hamilton's body, 1942

FEBRUARY

9

On the morning of 9 February 1942, an electrician found a woman's body in an air-raid shelter in Montagu Place, west London. Evelyn Hamilton, a forty-year-old chemist's assistant, had been in London on her way from Hornchurch, Essex, where she worked, to her home in Newcastle-upon-Tyne. She had been strangled and her clothes were disarranged, though she appeared not to have been sexually assaulted. Her handbag, containing £80, had been stolen.

The following day another body was found, this time in a flat in nearby Wardour Street. Evelyn Oatley, aged thirty-five, a prostitute and former show-girl, had also been strangled, but afterwards her throat had been cut and the lower part of her body mutilated with a tin-opener. The body was found on her bed, almost naked.

Three days after that two more murders were reported. Margaret Lowe, a prostitute aged forty-three, had been strangled with a silk stocking, then mutilated with a razor in her flat in Gosfield Street, London, W1. She had been living alone and the crime was discovered when her fourteen-year-old daughter, an evacuee, went to visit her. A half-empty bottle of stout was found in the kitchen.

Shortly after this discovery, news of the fourth murder was received, the body of Doris Jouannet, the thirty-two-year-old wife of a hotel manager, having been found in the couple's flat in Sussex Gardens, near Marble Arch. She, too, had been strangled and mutilated.

These crimes, committed during the blackout, terrified the inhabitants of London, and all of Scotland Yard's resources were mobilized in an attempt to find the person responsible. But the culprit was soon to fall into the hands of the police as a result of his own carelessness.

On the evening of 12 February, the day before these two latest crimes were discovered, a Mrs Greta Heywood had met a young airman in Piccadilly. They went for a drink together, then walked down the Haymarket, where he tried to kiss her. Although she got away from him and ran off, he caught up with and attempted to strangle her in a doorway in St Alban's Street. But, luckily for her, a delivery-boy heard the scuffle, and when he went to investigate the

51

attacker took to his heels. He left behind an RAF gas-mask, which he had placed on the ground.

Later the same night Mrs Mulcahy, a prostitute, was attacked by the same man in her flat in Paddington, near the home of Mrs Jouannet. She fought back violently and screamed, and the man then gave her money and left the flat. This time he left his belt behind.

From his gas-mask and belt the airman was identified as Gordon Frederick Cummins, a twenty-eight-year-old cadet billeted in St John's Wood. A number of items stolen from the murdered women were found in his possession, and his fingerprints matched others found in the homes of Mrs Oatley and Mrs Lowe.

Cummins was a married man. He was well-educated but unreliable, and had lost a number of jobs through dishonesty. His air force colleagues found him pretentious.

Charged with all four of the murders, he was tried only for that of Evelyn Oatley, for which he was sentenced to death. He was hanged at Wandsworth Prison on 25 June 1942, an air-raid taking place as the execution was carried out. Two other murders have since been attributed to him.

Body of Georgina Hoffman discovered, 1939

FEBRUARY

12

On the night of 12 February 1939, a man walked into Vine Street police station in London's West End and reported the discovery of a woman's body in a top-floor flat in Dover Street, Piccadilly. Police officers went to the scene at once and found the dead woman lying on the floor near the door. She was naked except for an underskirt round her neck and had two stab wounds — one in her chest near the left breast and the other in her back near the top of the left shoulder. There were signs of a struggle having taken place.

The woman was Georgina Hoffman, an attractive twenty-six-year-old prostitute also known as Iris Heath; she was a married woman, separated from her husband, and had been renting the Dover Street flat for £6 a week. As she had taken off some of her clothes herself, while others had been torn from her body after being cut with a knife, it appeared that she had been murdered by one of her clients. The murder weapon had not been left at the scene.

John Roman, the man who reported the crime, had gone to the flat at the request of one of the victim's friends — another prostitute who worked in the same area. When this woman was seen by police, she informed them that she had called on Mrs Hoffman in the early hours of 10 February and found her in the company of a young man with a speech impediment, whom she then tricked into staying there on his own — after he had given her money — while she left and spent the night with the witness.

The woman went on to say that she had seen Mrs Hoffman entering the flat with the same man on the evening of 10 February, and that later — about midnight — her friend had shown her a watch that he had given her, saying that he had no money with him then but would return with some the following day and buy it back. Once again, the victim had left and spent the night with the witness.

On the 12th the witness had seen the man again — this time standing in Berkeley Street. She asked him where Mrs Hoffman was, but he replied that he had not seen her. At that moment, however, John Roman appeared, having discovered the body. The witness therefore insisted that the stranger should not be allowed to go until he'd given his name and address.

The police naturally regarded this man as the most obvious suspect and, although the name and address he had given soon proved to be false, he was identified from photographs in the Criminal Record Office as Arthur James Mahoney, a twenty-three-year-old ship's steward with a criminal record. On the morning of 13 February, he was seen by police officers at his mother's home in Brixton, and following the discovery of a bloodstained shirt in a kitchen cupboard and a bloodstained handkerchief in one of his trouser pockets, he admitted the crime and produced a sheath-knife which he said was the murder weapon. He was then taken into custody and made a full confession.

On the night of 9 February he had met the victim in the street and gone to the flat with her, he said. While they were there, she asked if he would like to stay the night with her and induced him to part with £5, saying that she needed the money badly. He afterwards gave her another £1 — almost all the money he had left — to go out and buy some cigarettes.

When she returned, another woman arrived at the flat and Mrs Hoffman went off with her, saying that she would be back in twenty minutes. But she then stayed out for the rest of the night, and by the time he left the following morning, Mahoney realized that he had been tricked.

He acquired the knife with the idea of frightening her, partly because he wanted his money back but also because he wanted to reform her, he said. But when he saw her again, he told her that he was in love with her, and gave her his wrist-watch as he had no money at the time.

Mrs Hoffman told him on this occasion that she

loved him, too, but could not give up being a prostitute.

But on the third night when he again turned up without any money, she flew into a rage and began abusing and attacking him. At this, he said, he was so incensed that he pulled out the knife and struck her with it. 'I lost my head,' he continued. 'I pushed her on the bed and we were still fighting. The bed was fully made, with the eiderdown on top. I then noticed blood coming from underneath her armpit. She was still fighting with me and screaming. I got alarmed and tried to quieten her with pillows over her face. Eventually we rolled off the bed and, as we did so, the knife fell on the floor. So I picked it up and struck her again.'

Afterwards, while she was still moaning, he tore off her clothes, wiped the knife on one of her undergarments, and took his wrist-watch from her dressing-table. Having no money, he had to walk back to Brixton.

Charged with Mrs Hoffman's murder, Arthur James Mahoney was sent for trial at the Old Bailey; he pleaded insanity but was convicted and sentenced to death, the jury, on 6 March 1939, having taken only twelve minutes to reach its verdict. He was later certified insane and committed to Broadmoor, where he died in July the following year.

FEBRUARY
13

On the morning of 13 February 1948, PC Nathaniel Edgar, aged thirty-three, was found fatally wounded in the drive of a house in Southgate, north London; he had been shot three times. There had been a recent increase in the number of burglaries in the area, and Edgar, who was patrolling in plain clothes, had been questioning a suspect when the shooting took place. Before dying in hospital, he was able to tell colleagues that the man's name and address were in his notebook, in his inside pocket.

The suspect was found to be Donald George Thomas, a twenty-three-year-old man with a criminal record, who was wanted by the military police for desertion. His address was in Cambridge Road, Enfield, but police did not find him there and appealed for information, saying that Thomas might be able to help them in their enquiries. They then learnt that a Mrs Winkless, a mother of three children, had left her home in Camberwell, south London, after falling in love with him.

A photograph of Mrs Winkless, provided by her husband, was published in the newspapers on 17 February, and seen by a Mrs Smeed, whose house in Clapham had been converted into bedsitters. Mrs Smeed told the police that she thought she recognized Mrs Winkless as one of her lodgers, and that she was occupying a room on the top floor in the company of a young man. She agreed to help police by taking up the couple's breakfast and leaving it outside their door, as usual.

When Thomas, wearing just his underpants, un-

56

locked the door, police officers rushed into the room. During the struggle which ensued, the wanted man tried to use a Luger pistol, which he had hidden under his pillow, but was quickly overpowered. Mrs Winkless was in bed when the arrest took place.

'You were lucky,' Thomas told the police officers. 'I might just as well be hanged for a sheep as a lamb.'

Seventeen rounds of ammunition, a jemmy and a rubber cosh were found in the bedroom, and bullets from the pistol matched those taken from PC Edgar's body. Mrs Winkless made a statement, saying that Thomas had admitted the murder to her.

Donald Thomas had come from a middle-class family in Edmonton and had been well educated. At sixteen he had been sent to an approved school, having previously been on probation. He had been called up for military service in January 1945, but deserted and spent the next two years on the run. Giving himself up, he had then been sentenced to 160 days' detention — only to desert again at the end of this term.

Brought to trial at the Old Bailey in April 1948, he was found guilty of PC Edgar's murder and sentenced to death. This sentence was commuted to life imprisonment, as the death penalty in Britain had been temporarily suspended. He remained in jail until April 1962, when he was released on licence.

On 14 February 1945, Charles Walton, a seventy-four-year-old hedger, was found hideously murdered in a field at the foot of Meon Hill, near the Tudor village of Lower Quinton, in Warwickshire. His throat had been slashed with a trouncing hook, which had been left in one of the wounds, and a hay-fork had been driven through his body, pinning him to the ground. It was also observed that his face was contorted with fear and that his arms were cut where he had tried to defend himself.

Walton, whose cottage was just a couple of fields away, had been a gnarled old man, suffering from rheumatism. Although his watch was missing, the nature of his injuries suggested that robbery had not been the motive for his murder, and a Warwickshire police officer drew attention to a sentence in a book of local customs and superstitions which read: 'In 1875 ... a young man killed an old woman named Ann Turner with a hay-fork because he believed she had bewitched him.'

To reinforce the idea that superstition had been the cause of the crime, Superintendent Alec Spooner then produced another book, *Warwickshire*, by Clive Holland, which states that stabbing to death with a pitchfork 'was evidently a survival of the ancient Anglo-Saxon custom of dealing with witches by means of "stacung", or sticking spikes into them'.

Though reluctant to accept such an explanation for this terrible crime, Chief Inspector Robert Fabian, the Scotland Yard officer heading the investigation, found that belief in witchcraft was very strong indeed among the inhabitants of this part of the country, and he and his assistant, Sergeant Albert Webb, were greatly hindered in their inquiries as a result.

At first they were merely received with lowered eyes and mutterings about bad crops and other misfortunes. But then, after a dog had been run over by a police car and a heifer had died in a ditch, there was more hostility, with many villagers refusing to speak to them at all and shutting doors in their faces. Some people even became ill after Fabian had questioned them.

In spite of all this, 4000 statements were taken; footprints found at the scene of the crime were traced to those who had left them, and twenty-nine samples of hair, clothing, etc., were taken from suspects to be analyzed. But no charges resulted and after a few weeks Fabian admitted defeat and returned to London. He had no idea who had committed the crime, and did not believe that anyone who *did* know would admit it to a stranger.

The murder of Charles Walton was therefore never solved.

Attempted shooting of Franklin D. Roosevelt, 1933

FEBRUARY
15

On the night of 15 February 1933, an unsuccessful attempt was made to shoot Franklin D. Roosevelt, the President-elect of the United States, in the amphitheatre at Bayfront Park, Miami. Roosevelt was sitting in the back of a Buick touring car, after making a short speech to a gathering of over ten thousand people, when five shots were fired in his direction by an unemployed Italian bricklayer named Giuseppe Zangara. Although he was unhurt, five other people were wounded; these included Anton Cermak, the Mayor of Chicago, who was so badly injured that he died nineteen days later.

The culprit, who was thirty-two years old, was only five feet tall and suffered from a chronic stomach-ache. He bore a deep resentment towards capitalist society, seeing his illness as a consequence of having been forced to work as a child in his native land and, as a result, he was in favour of murdering all presidents, kings and prime ministers — the people he saw as protecting capitalists. Even so, he was not a communist or anarchist, for he had no real interest in organized politics at all.

Zangara had lived in America since 1923, mainly in New Jersey. He had worked for most of that time, but hated cold weather, which always seemed to make his stomach-ache worse. With the decline in the construction industry, he began to live off his savings, and spent several months in Miami prior to the shooting. But as his money dwindled, his hatred of capitalists, and his desire to kill a head of state, became more intense. At one point he made up his mind to go to Washington and shoot President Herbert Hoover, whom he blamed for the Depression. But then he heard that Roosevelt was expected in Miami and decided to kill him instead. 'He is elect — that is President,' he explained after his arrest.

On 20 February, Zangara was brought to trial; he pleaded guilty to four counts of assault on others in an attempt to murder the President-elect, and was sentenced to eighty years' imprisonment. Then, on 9 March, he appeared for trial again, this time charged with the murder of Anton Cermak, who had died three days earlier. He pleaded guilty once more, and on this occasion was sentenced to death. He made no appeal, and was electrocuted at the state prison in

Raiford, Florida, on the morning of 20 March 1933 — just thirty-three days after the crime had been committed.

Following his arrest, Zangara had been elated by the publicity which he had received, and had been especially pleased to learn that items concerning him had appeared in the newsreels. Because of all this, he made the mistake of expecting cameramen to be present at his execution, and was angry when he found that there were none. 'Lousy capitalists!' he complained. 'No picture! Capitalists! No one here to take my picture! All capitalists lousy bunch of crooks!'

After the execution had been carried out his body was buried in an unmarked grave in the prison grounds.

Fire in Trinidad, 1972.

On 19 February 1972, a fire at Arima, about twenty miles from Port of Spain, destroyed the bungalow of Abdul Malik, a thirty-eight-year-old Black Power leader better known as Michael X. A racialist and a criminal with various celebrities among his friends, Malik had returned to his native Trinidad after jumping bail in Britain in 1969. The fire was later found to have been started by one of his associates after Malik had left for Guyana with his wife and four children.

On hearing what had happened, Malik sought an injunction preventing anyone visiting the scene. However, the police were already at work there, and during the next few days the bodies of two murder victims were found buried in his garden. Joseph Skerritt, a well-known local criminal, had been decapitated; Gale Benson, an attractive English girl known to have been living with one of Malik's followers, had been slashed and stabbed, then buried alive.

The dead girl's black American lover, Hakim Jamal, was located in Massachusetts, where he claimed to be looking for Gale, unaware of the fact that she was dead. Malik was later arrested in Guyana, while attempting to escape through the jungle to Brazil. He was returned to Trinidad, where, in August 1972, he was convicted of Skerritt's murder. He was sentenced to death, but not hanged until nearly three years later.

In July 1973 two of his other followers, Edward Chadee, aged twenty, and Stanley Abbott, thirty-four, were tried for the murder of Gale Benson. A third man, twenty-one-year-old Adolphus Parmasser, appeared against them, in order to avoid having to face a murder charge himself. The two defendants in this case were also convicted and they, too, were sentenced to death.

The murder of Gale Benson — the first of the two crimes — had been carried out on Malik's orders because he had begun to resent her presence in the commune in which he and his supporters lived. Joseph Skerritt had been killed because he had refused to take part in another crime — a raid on a country police post.

A fourth man involved in the murder of Gale Benson had disappeared while swimming in a nearby inlet shortly before Malik's departure for Guyana. And Hakim Jamal was murdered by gunmen in Boston in 1973, supposedly on instructions given by Malik from his death cell in Trinidad.

Malik, whose name had originally been Michael de Freitas, was well known in London, where he had spent some years living off prostitutes and harassing tenants of slum properties for the racketeer Peter Rachman before setting up an English Black Power movement. He changed his name to Malik on becoming a Muslim, and later — influenced by Malcolm X, the murdered American Black Power leader — had started calling himself Michael X.

In 1967 he was given a year's imprisonment for urging his supporters to kill any white man seen with a black woman — an offence under the new Race Relations Act — and in 1969 he was charged with robbery and demanding money with menaces. It was at this point that he jumped bail and left the country, to the relief of the British authorities, who made no attempt to get him extradited when they learnt that he was back in Trinidad.

Gale Benson was the daughter of Captain Leonard Plugge, an author, traveller and former MP for Chatham. Though Jamal's mistress, she had been dominated by Malik, who, having once described her as the prettiest woman he had ever seen, had eventually come to regard her as a 'white devil'. It seems that he suspected her of trying to make trouble of some sort between Jamal and himself.

Malik was hanged in Port of Spain on 16 May 1975, after appealing unsuccessfully several times, and Stanley Abbott remained on Death Row until his own execution on 27 April 1979. Edward Chadee's sentence was commuted.

Late at night on 20 February 1949, Marcel Hilaire, a French businessman aged forty-two, returned to his wife and three daughters in Mer, in the Loire Valley, having absconded with his twenty-year-old mistress two months earlier. His arrival prompted much gossip and speculation, for his affair with his former secretary, Christiane Page, was already common knowledge. But to Hilaire this was a matter of little or no importance.

As a rich mill-owner and a partner in a company selling American agricultural machinery, he did not see that he was answerable to anyone for his conduct — not even to Christiane's father, Jacques Page, who was also a partner in the same company — and he made no attempt to explain it. He merely took up his former way of life afresh, as though nothing out of the ordinary had happened.

Christiane Page did not return with him, and her parents and friends received no news from her. Nobody worried about this at first, for she was known to be an independent girl, well able to take care of herself: it was generally assumed that Hilaire, having grown tired of her, had given her money to go abroad. But after several months without hearing from her, Jacques Page finally asked his partner what had happened.

'We had a row over dinner at a little restaurant at Chamarande in February and she refused to get back in the car with me,' replied Hilaire. 'Roger Petit was with me. He can confirm what I'm saying. She was always talking of going to a convent, and that's probably what she did.'

Jacques Page did not doubt that Hilaire was telling him the truth. He had a high regard for his partner and, in any case, knew that Roger Petit, a former gendarme who had managed Hilaire's mill in his absence, was a man with an impeccable reputation. He therefore saw no need to make any further inquiries about his missing daughter. But by this time the matter had come to the attention of somebody else — somebody who was *not* satisfied with Hilaire's explanation.

Prior to returning home, Hilaire had been living with Christiane in a house in Sceaux, between Versailles and Paris; he had bought the house, with a sitting tenant, through an estate agent who was a friend of his. But the tenant, a schoolmaster, had heard many quarrels between them, and was aware that Hilaire had beaten Christiane unmercifully on some occasions. So when they suddenly disappeared he became suspicious and informed the estate agent, a man named Desdouets.

Desdouets, who had been to the house and heard some of the rows himself, wrote to Hilaire at his home in Mer and asked what had become of Christiane. He received no reply. Following a second letter, however, he had a personal visit from Hilaire's brother, who informed him that Christiane had left Hilaire after quarrelling with him in the restaurant in Chamarande. But when Desdouets went to the restaurant in question, he found that the proprietor remembered the couple, and learnt that they had left together in the company of Roger Petit. He informed the police, and an official investigation of the affair began.

Hilaire gave a number of different accounts of Christiane's disappearance, on one occasion claiming that she had been murdered by spies after becoming involved with a foreign secret service. But Roger Petit, on being questioned, told police that Hilaire had killed her. The following day Hilaire admitted that that was true; he had murdered Christiane because she had tried to blackmail him into divorcing his wife, he said. Her body had been dropped into a deep well on a piece of land near his mill, and the well had afterwards been filled with sand.

After their visit to the restaurant in Chamarande, he, Christiane and Roger Petit had gone to see Robert Bouguereau, a friend who owned a garage at Saint-Ay, to the south of Orléans, explained Hilaire. When they left, after drinking a bottle of wine, Bouguereau accompanied them, and they drove along the Route Nationale 20 towards the Messas crossroads. When they were almost there, Hilaire stopped the car, saying that there was something wrong with the wiring, and he and Christiane got out together. He then shot her twice in the back of the head, using Petit's pistol, while Petit and Bouguereau remained in the car. Hilaire's two companions then helped him to put Christiane's body on the back seat, and afterwards to dispose of it.

Hilaire, Petit and Bouguereau were all charged in connection with the crime, but it was not until 9 February 1953 — nearly four years after the murder had been committed — that they were brought to trial. The case was then heard at the Seine Assizes in Paris, and each of the accused admitted his own part in the affair, though with Hilaire's lawyer success-fully contesting the charge that the crime had been premeditated.

At the end of the trial Marcel Hilaire was sentenced to hard labour for life, while Petit received two years' imprisonment for complicity in the crime and Bouguereau was given a two-year suspended sentence for receiving and disposing of a body unlawfully. Petit and Bouguereau, who had both spent two years in prison awaiting trial, were then released, while Hilaire was taken back to prison in a police van.

Four and a half years later it was reported that Marcel Hilaire had been made chief accountant of Melun penitentiary.

Bryn Masterman brought to trial, 1987

FEBRUARY
23

On 23 February 1987, Bryn Masterman, a forty-seven-year-old prison officer of Gertrude Road, Nottingham, was brought to trial at Nottingham Crown Court, charged with the murder of his first wife, Janet, twenty-two years previously. Janet Masterman, aged twenty-five, had died in May 1965, apparently as a result of falling down the stairs at the couple's home, and an inquest held at that time recorded a verdict of accidental death. Masterman's arrest followed disclosures made by his second wife, Selina, after he left her in May 1986.

Selina Masterman, aged fifty-one, of North Hykeham, near Lincoln, claimed that while she and her husband were still lovers he had told her that he intended to kill Janet, and that he had later admitted having pushed her down the stairs after hitting her with a stool. She kept this secret for twenty-one years, but finally told the police about it because she was bitter at being deserted. She then agreed to draw him into a conversation on the subject, with police officers recording it.

The tape recording was produced as evidence at Masterman's trial, with the judge, jurors, barristers and solicitors being issued with headphones, to enable them to listen to it. A Home Office pathologist,

Professor Stephen Jones, afterwards told the court that Janet Masterman had died from a single blow to the side of the head.

The prisoner denied having murdered her. He said that he and Janet had argued in bed over his infidelity, and that she threatened to leave him, taking their two young sons. At this he hit her on the head with a stool, then — seeking to reason with her — pursued her to the top of the stairs and grabbed her by her nightdress. When she turned and hit him on the nose, he instinctively pushed her — as a result of which she 'flew' down the stairs and cracked her head on the floor. She died without regaining consciousness.

The trial lasted five days, and the jury, after retiring for five and a half hours, found Masterman not guilty of murder but guilty of manslaughter. The judge, Mr Justice Boreham, described this as a 'merciful' verdict.

'I know it happened twenty-two years ago, but there is no doubt in my mind it was to fulfil your own selfish sexual desires, and a young woman died,' he told the prisoner. 'I accept it was not murder — it was manslaughter, but at your own hand.'

Masterman was sent to prison for six years.

Execution of Henri Landru, 1922

FEBRUARY
25

Henri Désiré Landru, the French 'Bluebeard' executed on 25 February 1922, was a cunning and heartless criminal who specialized in the seduction and murder of middle-aged widows and spinsters for the sake of their money. A small, bald-headed, bearded man with a wife and four children, he was actually a fugitive during the four-year period in which the murders were committed, having been convicted in his absence of a different type of offence — a business fraud — in July 1914. He made the acquaintance of several of his victims by means of 'lonely hearts' advertisements in Paris newspapers.

Landru had previously committed many frauds and thefts, and had served a number of prison terms since his first conviction in 1900. The sentence which he received in 1914 was one of four years' imprisonment, to be followed by banishment to the penal settlement in New Caledonia as an habitual criminal. It was allegedly to avoid being arrested that he decided to murder his later victims instead of merely defrauding them. None of the bodies of these victims was ever found and the means by which he had killed them was never discovered, either.

The first victims were Mme Jeanne Cuchet, a widow of thirty-nine who worked in a Paris store, and her eighteen-year-old son André. Landru made their acquaintance in February 1914, while he was calling himself M. Diard and claiming to be an engineer; the deception had caused André Cuchet to apply to him for a job, and his mother attended the interview with him. Landru and Mme Cuchet began to have an affair, and on 8 December of that year moved into a villa at Vernouillet, on the outskirts of Paris, together. Mme Cuchet and her son were last seen on 4 January 1915, in the garden of the villa, and nothing more was heard of them until Landru was arrested in April 1919.

Landru, having gained some 15,000 francs in money, jewels, furniture and securities as a result of this association, was soon on the look-out for another victim. In June 1915 he met Mme Thérèse Laborde-Line, aged forty-seven, a native of Buenos Aires and the widow of a hotel-keeper. She had little money, but her furniture and other possessions had some value, and Landru persuaded her to move into the villa with him. She was seen for the last time five days afterwards.

Shortly before meeting Mme Laborde-Line Landru had begun placing the advertisements which drew further women into his clutches. The first appeared in May 1915, stating: 'Widower with two children, aged forty-three, with comfortable income, affectionate, serious, and moving in good society, desires to meet widow with a view to matrimony.' There were to be six more advertisements of this type, and altogether nearly 300 replies were received. These replies were recorded in classified sections in a black loose-leaf notebook, the discovery of which was later to ensure his conviction.

Following the murder of his next victim, Mme Désirée Guillin, a fifty-one-year-old former governess with a legacy of 22,000 francs, Landru moved to the Villa Ermitage, near the village of Gambais. There he became known as M. Fremyet, though he used other names in his dealings with the women he met through his advertisements. Mme Heon, a fifty-five-year-old widow, went to live with 'M. Petit', and was last seen at the Villa Ermitage on 8 December 1915. Mme Anna Collomb, a widow of forty-four, believed Landru to be M. Cuchet until she learnt that he was otherwise called M. Fremyet.

Mme Collomb, arriving at the villa shortly after Mme Heon's disappearance, was last seen towards the end of the same month. Her sister later wrote to both Mme Collomb and 'M. Fremyet', and, receiving no reply from either of them, wrote to ask the local mayor if he knew 'M. Fremyet's' whereabouts. By this time Landru had claimed further victims, and the mayor had already received a similar letter about a 'M. Dupont', with whom a Mme Celestine Buisson, another forty-four-year-old widow, had been staying at the Villa Ermitage. The mayor put the two letter-writers — the second being Mme Buisson's sister — in touch with each other, and after meeting to discuss the disappearances they reported the matter to the police.

Landru was arrested after Mme Buisson's sister had seen him walking with a young woman in the Rue de Rivoli in April 1919. The black notebook was found in his possession, together with various papers and identity cards which had belonged to his victims, and a search of the Villa Ermitage led to the discovery of 295 fragments of bone in the ashes from Landru's stove. In 1921 he was brought to trial for the murder of ten women and one youth — Mme Cuchet's son — and convicted on all charges.

Maintaining a complete silence to the end, the fifty-two-year-old 'Bluebeard' went to the guillotine haughtily, refusing the ministrations of the priest and also declining the usual offer of a glass of rum and a cigarette.

Over forty years later various newspapers reported the discovery of a brief confession, in Landru's handwriting, on the back of a drawing which he had done while under sentence of death. The drawing had been framed and given to one of his lawyers.

Execution of Robert Morton, 1974

FEBRUARY
27

On 27 February 1974, Robert Victor Morton, aged twenty-three, was hanged in Pretoria for a horrifying murder committed in a suburb of Cape Town just over a year earlier. The victim of the crime, fourteen-year-old Sharon Ashford, had been found dead at her home in Kensington Crescent, Oranjezicht, having been stabbed thirty-seven times — and after seeing her body one of the detectives working on the case said that he had never seen anything more gruesome. The motive for the murder was not known, but fingerprints and footprints found at the scene led to Morton's arrest soon afterwards.

Morton lived next door to his victim, at the home of a cardiac specialist who employed him to do general domestic work. He claimed that he had killed Sharon 'for the fun of it', because his whole life was a failure and he 'wanted to do something really big'. But his employer, for whom he had worked since the middle of 1971, said that he had found Morton to be pleasant and easy-going, 'with no wild fluctuations of mood or temper'. He did not seem restless or dis-contented — in fact, he appeared to be ambitionless. The reason he gave for the crime was therefore not the real one.

It was eventually learnt that on the day of the murder Morton had received a letter from a girl of fifteen with whom he had been in love for the previous two years; this had contained hurtful remarks and informed him that their relationship was at an end. That afternoon, having broken into the Ashfords' house and stolen various articles in the meantime, he telephoned the girl in question, but found her unwilling to speak to him. The murder was committed a short while after that, when Sharon arrived home from school.

Giving evidence at his trial, Morton's girlfriend, whose name was not published, intimated that she had not meant the things she said in her letter: she had seen Morton again the following afternoon and he had written to her from prison. But she was sure that he had believed them at the time and said he had since admitted to her that the letter was the cause of the crime. Even so, the court was convinced that there were no extenuating circumstances in the case, for there was evidence of premeditation but none of remorse.

Morton had given no evidence on his own behalf, and at first seemed indifferent to the prospect of being hanged. But while on Death Row he gradually sank into a state of despondency from which he never emerged.

His mother — from whom he had been parted for most of his childhood — appealed for a commutation of sentence on his behalf, arguing that he must have been insane at the time of the murder, but this was to no avail. Morton afterwards wrote to her, saying that she should not blame either herself or the girl who had pretended to reject him for the crime which he had committed.

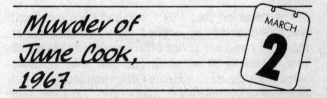

Murder of June Cook, 1967

MARCH
2

On the night of 2 March 1967, two men driving along a country lane in Oxfordshire found Mrs June Cook, a forty-one-year-old school-teacher, lying beside a damaged red Mini in a stretch of woodland; she was suffering from serious head injuries which had evidently been sustained when the car hit a tree. Her husband, Raymond Sidney Cook, a draughtsman aged thirty-two, was found inside the car — in the passenger seat — with a small abrasion on his left knee but no other injuries. The two men called an ambulance to the scene, but Mrs Cook died at Battle Hospital, Reading, shortly afterwards.

Raymond Cook said that he and his wife had dined together at a riverside hotel in Pangbourne, Berkshire. They were returning to their home at Spencers Wood, Reading, when his wife — dazzled by the headlights of another car — suddenly drove off the road and hit the tree. The doctors found nothing suspicious in this account, for it seemed to them that Mrs Cook's injuries could have been caused as a result of her head hitting the tree when she was flung through the windscreen. But PC Stephen Sherlock, a village policeman of Nettlebed, near Henley-on-Thames, was not satisfied with this explanation.

Sherlock had already been to the scene of the tragedy, and had noticed that the damage to the car had only been slight; he had also noticed that the windscreen was still intact. He therefore returned to the scene in the early hours of the morning and examined it afresh with the aid of his flashlamp. This time he found blood on the road over fifty yards from the car.

His suspicion that Mrs Cook had been murdered was soon found to be justified, for an examination of the car by another police officer revealed that it had been travelling at no more than ten miles an hour when it hit the tree. A Home Office pathologist found seven separate injuries to Mrs Cook's head and said that he did not believe they had been caused by a collision. Moreover it was known that the men who called the ambulance had seen another motorist — the driver of a blue Cortina — leave the scene quickly when they stopped to help. In view of these suspicious circumstances, Raymond Cook was arrested as he left the coroner's court on 17 March and charged with his wife's murder.

The owner of the blue Cortina was eventually

found to be Eric Jones, a forty-six-year-old plant manager and undischarged bankrupt of Wrexham, Denbighshire, who was also suspected of being an abortionist. Jones denied having been near Reading on 2 March, but when police searched his car and found that the jack was missing, they suspected that it had been used for the murder. It was later found in a yachting pool not far from Wrexham and by this time it was known that Jones had been seen in the Reading area on the night in question. He had been driving his blue Cortina, accompanied by a local girl named Valerie Newell.

Valerie Newell, known as 'Kim', was an attractive blonde aged twenty-three. Raymond Cook had recently been having an affair with her, and Eric Jones had been her lover some years earlier. The police were later informed by Mrs Janet Adams, of Thatcham, Berkshire — Kim Newell's sister — that Kim and Eric Jones had both been concerned with Cook in his wife's death; Kim had confessed this to her after Cook was arrested, said Mrs Adams. Kim Newell and Eric Jones, both of whom had already been under suspicion, were then charged in connection with the crime.

The three prisoners were brought to trial together at the Oxfordshire Assizes in June 1967. They each pleaded not guilty at first but Jones later changed his plea to guilty. Having been sentenced to life imprisonment, he appeared as a witness against the other two, and told the court that Kim Newell — for whom he had performed several abortions — had blackmailed him into taking part in the murder. He had agreed to do so, believing that he would only have to help the others to simulate an accident, he said. But when the Mini stopped at the prearranged place, Cook got out and handed him the car jack, making it clear that he was expected to kill Mrs Cook with it.

Jones went on to describe the murder, saying that

75

he struck Mrs Cook with the jack, then ran the car into the tree while she and her husband were inside it. He afterwards struck Mrs Cook again as she lay on the ground.

Raymond Cook told the court that he had lived with Miss Newell for seven weeks towards the end of 1966, but later returned to his wife, fearing that she might otherwise commit suicide after ensuring that he would inherit nothing from her. He later gave Eric Jones — to whom he had been introduced by Kim Newell — £100 to concoct grounds for a divorce, and on the night in question expected that his wife would be drugged and abducted for this purpose. He also claimed that he had tried to stop Jones killing her, and that Jones had then struck him.

Kim Newell, who was pregnant, gave evidence for two days. She said that Cook had told her that Jones was going to kidnap his wife, and that she had spoken to Jones about it herself to try to prevent Mrs Cook being harmed in the process. On 2 March Jones showed her the place where the crime was to be committed, but she told him that she did not want to be involved in it. He later told her what had happened and warned her against going to the police. Cook, in the meantime, had declined to tell her about it himself.

It was stated during the course of the trial that although Cook had had little money of his own, his wife had had assets worth about £11,000, which he stood to gain in the event of her death. The prosecution contended that Kim Newell had known this and that she was the person who had instigated the murder. She had wanted Cook to return to his wife, to make sure that she left a will in his favour, it was alleged.

At the end of the thirteen-day trial Raymond Cook was convicted of murder and Kim Newell of being an accessory before the fact; they were both given sentences of life imprisonment. When Kim Newell gave birth to a child seven weeks later, her father said that it would be adopted, so that it would never know its background.

Body of Sarah Blake discovered, 1922

MARCH
4

On the morning of 4 March 1922, a fifty-five-year-old widow was found brutally murdered in the kitchen of an Oxfordshire public house. Sarah Blake, who managed the Crown and Anchor Inn on Gallows Tree Common — between Henley-on-Thames and Pangbourne — had been so badly battered and hacked that more than sixty wounds and bruises were found on her head, face, neck, hands and arms, and blood was found on the ceiling and on her furniture. A thick iron bar used in the attack had been left beside the body, but a knife which her murderer had also used — leaving a stab-wound in her neck — had been taken away.

Mrs Blake had been seen alive at 6.30 the previous evening, but her murder had taken place not long afterwards. Police inquiries revealed that there had only been two customers in the pub that evening: a youth of fifteen named Jack Hewett, who had had some ginger beer, and a man who had left quickly after just one drink. Hewett told the police that he had returned later to get some beer for his mother but found the place closed and in darkness. Two other men had found the place closed about 7.40 p.m., and gone to drink elsewhere.

The missing knife was discovered in a hedge near the Crown and Anchor on 14 March, and three days later a man held in Reading for a minor offence made a statement confessing to the murder. Robert Alfred Shepperd was accordingly charged, but had to be released when his confession was found to be false. Then, on 4 April, Jack Hewett confessed that *he* was the murderer, saying that he had killed Mrs Blake with a flat-iron from the wall of the beer cellar. 'I'm very sorry it happened, and don't know what made me do it,' he said.

Hewett was brought to trial in Oxford in June 1922, denying the offence. He seemed to have no real motive for the crime, except possibly revenge — as Mrs Blake had rebuked him three days earlier — and after being arrested had blamed 'the pictures' for what had happened. Although he withdrew his confession, he was convicted and sentenced to be detained during His Majesty's pleasure, as he was too young to be hanged.

It was one of the earliest cases in which the influence of the cinema was blamed for a violent crime.

Murder of Gertrude Robinson, 1959

MARCH 7

On 7 March 1959, Gertrude Robinson, a seventy-two-year-old widow, was found murdered at her home in Bermuda; she had been raped and beaten to death by an unknown assailant. The crime followed a series of attacks on women during the previous twelve months, and it was suspected that the same person was responsible. But the police had no idea who he was, and when a second murder took place two months later, Scotland Yard was asked to provide assistance. Detective Superintendent William Baker and Detective Sergeant John O'Connell were sent to the island without delay.

The second murder victim was Dorothy Pearce, a fifty-nine-year-old divorcee. She was found raped and beaten to death in her bedroom on 9 May, with teeth-marks and scratches on her body, and money and jewellery left untouched in the same room. In this case fingerprints were found, but they did not corres-pond with those of any known criminal in Bermuda. The police therefore began fingerprinting every man in the locality aged between eighteen and fifty, but were still unable to identify the culprit. Six weeks after their arrival, the two Scotland Yard men abandoned the investigation and returned home.

Then, on 3 July, Rosaleen Kenny, aged forty-nine, was attacked by an intruder as she lay in bed. Her screams attracted the attention of neighbours, and the man — described as 'dark-skinned' — fled from the house. Another woman was murdered before he was finally apprehended.

Dorothy Rawlinson, a twenty-nine-year-old English office worker, was reported missing on 28 September, having left her lodgings to go swimming the previous afternoon. During a search of the beach, her blood-stained clothes were found buried in the sand; her body, partly eaten by sharks but still showing signs of a murderous attack, was later found at a coral reef two miles away.

It was learnt that Wendell Willis Lightbourne, a nineteen-year-old black youth who worked as a golf caddie, had been seen on the beach in an agitated state and wearing wet trousers on the day of Miss Rawlinson's disappearance.

Questioned about the murder, Lightbourne said that he had been fishing in the vicinity on 27 Septem-ber and admitted having seen the girl sun-bathing.

Eventually he broke down and confessed that he had killed her, saying, 'I want to get it off my mind. I can't go to Heaven now.' He then admitted the other two murders, remarking, 'I get nasty.' The crimes had been committed because he suffered from feelings of inferiority and envied the wealthier people attracted to the island.

Charged with the murder of Dorothy Rawlinson, Wendell Lightbourne was tried in December 1959 before the Bermuda Supreme Court, and on being convicted, he was sentenced to death. His sentence was afterwards commuted to one of life imprisonment, to be served in Britain.

Execution of Beck and Fernandez, 1951

MARCH **8**

Martha Beck and Raymond Fernandez, who were executed at New York's Sing Sing Prison on 8 March 1951, were heartless killers who preyed on lonely women; they had been charged with three murders and were suspected of seventeen others. The public had no sympathy for them when they were sentenced to death, and few people were horrified to learn that Martha's execution had been more protracted than usual.

The couple had met as a result of an advertisement in a 'lonely hearts' magazine towards the end of 1947. Martha, a fat, twenty-seven-year-old divorcee, was the superintendent of a home for crippled children in Pensacola, Florida: her bulky figure and craving for sex caused much amusement among those who knew her. Fernandez, already a swindler, accepted her as an accomplice when they became lovers, and she gave up her job and left her two children in order to be with him.

Fernandez was a Spaniard, six years her senior. He had been born in Hawaii, brought up in Connecticut and had then lived for some years in Spain, where he had a wife and four children who had long been abandoned. He had fought for Franco and later worked for British Intelligence in Gibraltar, but in 1945 had sustained a head injury while working his passage back to the United States. It was after this that he had begun to live by swindling.

Always a philanderer, Fernandez believed that he had a supernatural power over women which enabled him to pursue his criminal activities with ease. Having claimed over 100 victims on his own, he went on to find many others in partnership with Martha, who posed as his sister. But Martha's jealousy hampered him, for she accompanied him everywhere and did her best to prevent him sleeping with any of the women concerned. When she did not succeed in this a violent quarrel took place between them.

In December 1948 Fernandez became acquainted with Janet Fay, a sixty-six-year-old widow living in Albany, New York. He persuaded her to part with $6000 and join Martha and himself in an apartment in Long Island; she was then battered over the head with a hammer and strangled with a scarf. Having cleaned the place to prevent blood dripping through into the apartment below, Fernandez made love to Martha while the widow's corpse lay on the floor. The dead body was afterwards buried in the basement of a rented house.

Less than three weeks after Janet Fay's death, the murderous pair met Mrs Delphine Downing, a widow aged twenty-eight who lived with her twenty-one-month-old daughter Rainelle in Grand Rapids, Michigan. Before long they moved into her house, and Fernandez — having become her lover — persuaded her to sell some property which she owned and give the money to him. Then, just a few weeks after meeting her, he and Martha forced sleeping pills down her throat, shot her through the head and drowned her daughter in the bath.

They buried the two bodies in the cellar, covering them with cement, but suspicious neighbours reported the disappearances to the police and a search of the premises began. Upon being arrested, they both made confessions, admitting the murder of Janet Fay as well as those of Mrs Downing and her daughter. However, they denied having committed any of the other seventeen murders of which they were suspected, including that of Myrtle Young, a middle-aged widow whom Fernandez had bigamously married in August 1948.

The two 'lonely hearts' killers were sent back to New York, as that state still had the death penalty, whereas Michigan did not. Their trial began in July 1949 and lasted forty-four days, with Martha giving details of their sex life which made headline news. Afterwards, on Death Row, they went on declaring their love for each other to the very end. They were eventually executed in the electric chair.

Flora Gilligan found dead, 1953

MARCH
10

On 10 March 1953, Miss Flora Jane Gilligan, aged seventy-six, was found murdered outside her home in Diamond Street, York. She was naked and had died from skull injuries, having been raped, beaten and then pushed from her bedroom window in a clumsy attempt to give the impression that she had committed suicide. Nothing had been stolen during the course of the crime, even though there was money in the house. But the man responsible had tried unsuccessfully to break into the house next door before entering Miss Gilligan's home through an open window.

He had left his fingerprints at the scene of the crime, and also a footprint in a laundry basket; his shoe had recently been repaired and had a distinctive heel and sole. The police began fingerprinting soldiers at a nearby military camp and before long discovered the culprit: Philip Henry of the King's Own Yorkshire Light Infantry, a twenty-five-year-old coloured man who had been due for posting overseas on 19 March. There were other camps in the same area, and the police had been lucky to choose the right one first time.

It was found that Henry had not returned to camp on the night of the murder — though he pretended otherwise — and that he had afterwards cleaned his clothes thoroughly. Although he had disposed of the shoes which he had worn on the night in question, a cobbler was found who remembered repairing them for him. On being brought to trial at the York Assizes in June, the prisoner continued to claim that he was innocent but was found guilty and sentenced to death. He was hanged in Leeds on 30 July 1953.

Ravachol's first bomb outrage, 1892

On 11 March 1892, there was an explosion at a house in the Boulevard St Germain, in Paris, causing a lot of damage and slightly injuring one person. One of the inhabitants of the house was a judge who, the previous year, had presided at the trial of a group of anarchists, and when the remains of a bomb were found among the débris it was suspected that he had been the intended victim of the outrage. This was indeed the case, as was shortly to be proved.

The police learnt that the bomb had been planted by a man called Ravachol, who was also an anarchist and sometimes gave his name as Léger. He was described as being about five feet four inches tall, with a sallow complexion and dark hair. But attempts to trace him were unsuccessful at first, and on 27 March there was another explosion — this time in the Rue de Clichy — and on this occasion five people were gravely injured.

Three days later Ravachol was arrested by five policemen as he left a restaurant on the Boulevard Magenta. After a fierce struggle he was taken to the Sûreté, making several attempts to escape and calling out repeatedly to spectators, 'Follow me, brothers! Long live anarchy! Long live dynamite!' But by then it was known that Ravachol, whose real name was Claudius-François Koenigstein, was also wanted for several earlier crimes, including five murders.

Ravachol was the son of a Dutchman. Born in St Etienne, forty miles from Lyons, he was a dyer by trade, but had a reputation for brutality as a result of beating and threatening to kill his mother, whose maiden name he had adopted. His five known murders — all of which had taken place in the same region of France — were those of an eighty-six-year-old man and his housekeeper; a rich eccentric known as 'the hermit of Chambles', and two women (mother and daughter) who kept an ironmongery shop.

Ravachol had killed all of these people for personal gain and was also known to be guilty of smuggling, burglary, arson and stealing from a funeral vault. It was only after his second double murder that he went to Paris and became involved in revolutionary activities. But when he appeared for trial on 27 April the charges concerned only the recent bombings and Ravachol, having admitted that he was responsible for these, was allowed to read a statement declaring that anarchists were the champions of the oppressed and that it was wrong to treat them as ordinary criminals.

The casualties which had been caused by the second explosion had been serious enough to warrant the death penalty, but instead Ravachol was sentenced to life imprisonment. He was then taken to Montbrison, near St Etienne, to stand trial on other charges, and there, though he refused to answer questions about the women who kept the ironmongery shop, he admitted the murder of the 'the hermit of Chambles,' from whom he had stolen 35,000 francs. This time he was sentenced to death.

Ravachol, who was in his early forties, was executed in July 1892, singing as he went to the guillotine. Despite the unsavoury revelations which had been made about him, he was already regarded as a hero in revolutionary circles as a result of the defiant manner in which he had conducted himself at his trials. At his death he therefore became accepted as France's first great martyr of the anarchist cause.

Execution of Stephen Morin, 1985

On 13 March 1985, Stephen Peter Morin, the murderer of three women, was executed at the state prison in Huntsville, Texas, by means of a lethal injection. The thirty-seven-year-old prisoner had wanted the death sentence to be carried out, and had ordered his lawyers not to try to get him reprieved. But the execution proved to be a frightful ordeal for everyone concerned, for several attempts had to be made before a suitable vein was found, and these took no less than forty minutes. This delay, according to doctors and nurses at the prison, was due to Morin's long history of drug addiction.

'Drug abuse had made his veins brittle and almost impossible to find,' a spokesman explained.

Two years later, in the same town, the execution of Elliot Rod Johnson, another former drug addict, took almost as long. Johnson had committed a murder following a jewel robbery.

Death by lethal injection, America's newest method of execution, was first used in the case of Charlie Brooks, also in Huntsville, in 1982. On that occasion, there was no mishap: the condemned died quickly and painlessly (see vol 1, 7 December).

The following year, again in Huntsville, James David Autry, who had murdered a grocery shop assistant for three dollars' worth of beer, was injected with a saline solution in readiness for the administration of lethal drugs when a stay of execution was granted. Autry, aged twenty-nine, was eventually executed some months later, in March 1984.

On 14 March 1925, Pierre Bougrat, a Marseilles doctor in serious financial difficulties, murdered Jacques Rumèbe, an old wartime friend with whom he had fought side-by-side at Verdun. Bougrat had a luxury flat and consulting-room in the Rue Senac, where he had once received many rich patients. But by this time he had few patients at all, and his practice no longer provided him with an adequate income. His crime was an act of desperation.

Rumèbe, who was the wages clerk of a local pottery, had contracted syphilis during the First World War and was being treated by Bougrat with weekly injections of mercuric cyanide. He visited the Rue Senac for this purpose on Saturday mornings, before going to collect his firm's wages money from the bank. On this particular Saturday, however, he arrived at the bank much later than usual and afterwards went to see Bougrat again, carrying the money — 25,000 francs — in a briefcase. It was then that the murder was committed.

Bougrat, the son of a schoolmaster, had been born in Annecy in 1887. On being discharged from the army in 1919, he had married the daughter of a professor at the Marseilles Medical School, to whom he owed both his flat and his practice. But his wife had since left him — taking their one little daughter — and had started divorce proceedings as a result of an affair which Bougrat had been having with an ex-prostitute named Andrea Audibert. It was the scandal caused by this which had ruined his practice.

Bougrat had met Andrea in 1924, and was so captivated that he arranged to buy her from the man for whom she was then working, paying part of the agreed sum by monthly instalments. Later, when his wife left him, Andrea had moved into the flat in her place, but stayed only a short while before disappearing with some of his valuables. He then did not see her again until she suddenly returned, begging him to forgive her and take her back. By that time he had Rumèbe's corpse hidden in his dispensary.

The corpse had been placed in a long narrow cupboard just below the ceiling, and the doors of this had been covered with wallpaper to prevent it looking like a cupboard. Bougrat had obviously only intended to keep it there until he found a safe way of disposing of it, but with Andrea living in the flat again this would be more difficult than he had anticipated. Even so, he wanted her back, and so she remained with him until his arrest two months later. But the body remained there, too, and soon began to smell.

Towards the end of May, Bougrat was taken into custody for issuing worthless cheques. His father, now in retirement, offered to settle his debts for the sake of the family honour. But the arrest led to a search of Bougrat's premises and Rumèbe's body was soon found.

Bougrat denied having killed him, saying that Rumèbe had committed suicide in the consulting-room after being beaten up and robbed of the wages money elsewhere. He explained the hiding of the body by saying that he was afraid that he would be accused of stealing the money himself. But this explanation was not good enough to prevent him being charged with murder and theft.

At his trial, which began at Aix-en-Provence on 23 March 1927, it was contended that Bougrat had given Rumèbe a second dose of mercuric cyanide when he returned from the bank and that, having thus caused him to lose consciousness, he had killed him by forcing him to inhale prussic acid fumes.

Andrea, who had known nothing of the murder — and believed the smell in the dispensary to have been caused by a dead rat which nobody could find — was one of the witnesses who appeared against him.

Bougrat's defence was that he had given Rumèbe a second injection at his own request because he felt that the first had not been strong enough, and that his friend had collapsed and died unexpectedly a few minutes later. Bougrat had then panicked, hidden the body and stolen the 25,000 francs, it was claimed on his behalf. It was also pointed out that the prisoner had once been decorated for saving Rumèbe's life on the battlefield. He was nonetheless found guilty of premeditated murder as well as theft.

Sentenced to hard labour for life on Devil's Island, Bougrat arrived in French Guiana shortly before Christmas 1927 and, as a doctor, was set to work in the hospital on the mainland. A few months later, with a number of other convicts, he escaped to Venezuela, where he spent the rest of his life. He died, at the age of seventy-five, in 1962.

Horrifying discovery in Paris, 1887

MARCH

17

On the morning of 17 March 1887, police officers in Paris forced open the door of a third-floor luxury apartment at 17, Rue Montaigne, and found three bodies. The occupant — a courtesan named Marie Regnault — the chambermaid and the chambermaid's daughter had all been horribly murdered: Marie

Regnault had been decapitated and the other victims had had their throats cut. As valuable articles of jewellery were missing and an unsuccessful attempt had been made to open a safe in the apartment, it was obvious that robbery had been the motive for the crime.

Marie Regnault, known as 'Régine de Montille', had for a long time had three lovers, each of whom believed himself to be catering for all her needs. Since losing her favourite she had taken to drinking heavily and entertaining other men, and when a number of articles apparently belonging to a 'Gaston Geissler' were found at the scene, it seemed likely that he was the person responsible for the crime. But it was soon discovered that they had been left on purpose, in order to hinder the investigation.

On 20 March a brothel-keeper in Marseilles reported that a client had given one of her girls a watch set with diamonds and a pair of ear-rings. As these proved to be items stolen from Marie Regnault's apartment, the client, a Levantine named Pranzini, was traced and questioned. He refused to explain how the articles had come into his possession, and so was taken back to Paris. He then called on a woman who had been his mistress to give him an alibi for the night of the murder, but she refused to do so.

Pranzini, a big, powerful man, had lived in different parts of the world, including Turkey, Egypt and India, had a great variety of occupations and had affairs with many women. It was believed that he had committed 'the Crime of the Rue Montaigne' because he needed money to go back to his own country, where a rich young American woman was waiting to marry him. But, being unable to open Marie Regnault's safe, all he had gained was jewellery which he knew he could not sell without risking arrest (though he evidently thought that he could give it to other prostitutes without taking such a risk).

At his trial before the Assize Court, Pranzini claimed that he had spent the night of the murder with a married woman, whom he refused to name, and his counsel tried to convince the jury that he was a chivalrous man, putting his own life in jeopardy in order to avoid compromising the woman in question. But the jury found him guilty of murder without extenuating circumstances, and he was sentenced to death. He was executed by guillotine in the Place de la Roquette on 1 September 1887.

Death of Joan Hill, 1969

MARCH
19

On 19 March 1969, Joan Hill, the wife of a wealthy plastic surgeon of Houston, Texas, died at the Sharpstown General Hospital after being admitted the previous day. Following a brief examination of the body, her death was put down to an infection of the liver; her funeral then took place without delay. But her adoptive father, an oil millionaire named Ash Robinson, was not satisfied that the cause of her death had been properly established and accused her husband, Dr John Hill, of withholding medical treatment which could have saved her. This allegation caused Hill to threaten his father-in-law with a lawsuit for defamation.

It was known that for some years Hill's relationship with his wife had been deteriorating and that he had been having affairs with other women. When he remarried only three months after Mrs Hill's death the allegations of foul play began afresh and in

91

August 1969 the body of his first wife was exhumed for a further examination. A brain which was said to have been preserved at the hospital after the first post-mortem showed signs of meningitis, but doubt was expressed about whether this was really the brain of Mrs Hill. The second post-mortem revealed that Joan Hill had died of an acute inflammatory disease of unknown origin.

The investigation continued and eventually Dr John Hill was charged with 'murder by omission', and brought to trial in 1971. By this time he had divorced his second wife, Ann Kurth, who was called to give evidence against him.

Ann Kurth claimed that on one occasion the accused had tried to kill her by crashing his car against a bridge and also that he had confessed to having murdered his first wife. He had killed Joan Hill, it was stated, by injecting her with a bacterial culture made from 'every form of human excretion', and not taking her to hospital until she was in a state of irreversible shock. The case ended suddenly with the declaration of a mistrial, and a second trial was ordered. But before this could be heard John Hill was murdered by a gunman at his home in Houston.

The murder, which took place in September 1972, was the work of a contract killer named Vandiver, who was arrested but later killed by a policeman after jumping bail. Two women convicted of complicity in the crime stated that Ash Robinson had put out a contract for Hill's death, but a lie-detector test produced no evidence against him and he was never indicted. The case thus remains officially unsolved.

On the morning of 20 March 1985, four police
officers went to a flat in London's Earls Court to
arrest James Baigrie, a thirty-three-year-old convicted
murderer. Baigrie, who had been on the run since his
escape from an Edinburgh prison in October 1983,
had been traced to the flat in Philbeach Gardens, a
quiet crescent near Earls Court station. But when
they arrived at 6.30 a.m., the police found only his
flatmate there. Baigrie, armed with a shotgun, was
hiding in his van out in the street.

It was not long before his whereabouts were
discovered, and the police surrounded the van, calling
on Baigrie to surrender. When he refused, the police
prepared themselves for a siege, cordoning off the
road and evacuating the residents from nearby buildings. But while guns were levelled at the van from
different directions, a field telephone was provided so
that trained negotiators could keep in regular contact
with him.

The fugitive accepted the telephone, but resisted
further attempts to persuade him to give himself up,
both that day and the next. Eventually, just before
1.45 a.m. on 22 March, two CS gas cartridges were
fired through the rear windows of the van, and a final
appeal was made to him through a loudspeaker.
Seconds later the sound of a shot was heard, and
Baigrie was found dead from a bullet wound which
had left his face unrecognizable. The siege thus came
to an abrupt end over forty-three hours after it had
started.

At the inquest which followed the police were

criticized by the National Council for Civil Liberties for allegedly refusing to let Baigrie speak to friends who might have been able to influence him. But the police claimed that Baigrie had not wanted to speak to his friends, and that he had made up his mind to commit suicide a short while before they fired the gas cartridges. The jury, in recording a verdict of suicide, added a rider saying that they approved of the tactics which the police had used.

Baigrie had been given a life sentence in July 1982 for shooting an Edinburgh barman in the back, but had served only fifteen months before escaping from Saughton high-security prison. After his death two other men were charged with assisting him with intent to prevent his arrest. However, at the West London Magistrates' Court on 9 May the police offered no evidence against either of them, so the charge in each case was dismissed.

Murder of Francis Rattenbury, 1935

MARCH 24

On the night of 24 March 1935, a doctor was called to the home of Francis Rattenbury, a retired architect aged sixty-seven, of Manor Road, Bournemouth, who had been battered over the head, apparently as he sat sleeping in his armchair. He found the old man unconscious, with blood flowing from his wounds, and his thirty-eight-year-old wife Alma very drunk. 'Look at him!' cried Mrs Rattenbury. 'Look at the blood! Someone has finished him!'

The doctor telephoned for a surgeon, but by the

time he appeared Mrs Rattenbury was even more drunk and her presence made it impossible for him to carry out an examination. Rattenbury was therefore removed to a nursing home, where three wounds were found on his head and an operation was carried out.

The police were informed of what had happened, and several officers arrived at the injured man's home. They found lights switched on all over the house and the radiogram being played loudly. Mrs Rattenbury, who was incapable of answering questions coherently, laughed and cried, kissed some of them and made statements to the effect that she was responsible for the attack. She was given morphia and put into bed, but the following morning repeated her assertion that she was to blame for what had happened.

She was then taken into custody, her husband's chauffeur, eighteen-year-old George Percy Stoner, remarking as she was escorted from the house, 'You have got yourself into this mess by talking too much!'

Three days later Rattenbury died of his injuries, and on 29 March, Stoner — who by now had also been arrested — told the police that *he* was the person responsible for the crime. 'When I did the job I believe he was asleep,' he said. 'I hit him and then came upstairs and told Mrs Rattenbury.'

A bloodstained mallet which had been found was clearly the murder weapon, and Stoner, who lived in the house in Manor Road, had brought this from his grandfather's home the previous evening. Even so, the police did not altogether believe his confession, for Stoner had been Mrs Rattenbury's lover and it appeared that they were both guilty of the crime. They were therefore both charged with murder.

Stoner had entered Rattenbury's service as a handyman in September 1934, taking up residence in the house three months later, when the job of chauffeur was added to his other duties. Francis and Alma

Rattenbury, who had both been married before, had ceased to live as man and wife after the birth of their son John in 1929, and Alma later maintained that her husband knew of her affair with Stoner and did not object to it.

A few days before the murder she took Stoner to London and they stayed at the Royal Palace Hotel in Kensington, occupying separate rooms. She bought him expensive clothes and he was treated as her equal by the hotel staff. But on 24 March, on learning that she and her husband were to visit a friend in Bridport the following day, Stoner became angry and threatened her with an air-pistol. It was nonetheless contended at their trial that the murder had been the result of a conspiracy between them.

The trial opened at the Old Bailey on 27 May and lasted five days, with both defendants pleading not guilty. Alma Rattenbury now said that Stoner had been unnecessarily jealous of her husband and that on the night of the attack he had entered her bedroom and told her what had happened. 'He said that I should not go to Bridport next day, because he had hurt Rats,' she said. 'I did not understand at first. Then I heard Rats groan and my brain became alive. I ran downstairs.' She also said that she had no recollection of the statements which she had made afterwards.

Stoner, who claimed to have committed the crime under the influence of cocaine, did not give evidence.

The jury considered their verdict on 31 May, retiring for forty-seven minutes. Mrs Rattenbury was acquitted and Stoner convicted, though with a recommendation of mercy. Mrs Rattenbury was therefore released, while Stoner was sentenced to death.

But it was Mrs Rattenbury, not Stoner, who was to die, for she was ill from fear and grief over her lover's impending execution, and the constant demands of newspaper reporters made her recovery impossible.

On 4 June 1935 she took her own life, stabbing herself six times beside a stream near Christchurch, Hampshire. Stoner's sentence was later commuted to life imprisonment.

Death of Christiaan Buys, 1969

On 28 March 1969, Christiaan Buys, a forty-four-year-old South African railway labourer of Harrismith, Orange Free State, died at the Voortrekker Hospital in Kroonstad after an illness lasting several weeks. It appeared at first that the cause of his death had been lobar pneumonia, but when his kidneys, liver and stomach were sent for analysis it was found that he had been poisoned with arsenic.

His wife Maria, who was eleven years his junior, had for some months been having an affair with Gerhard Groesbeek, a shunter aged twenty who had lodged at their home for a short while at the end of the previous year, and it was known that she had been seeking a divorce at the time of her husband's death. Her sudden marriage to Groesbeek on 11 June therefore gave rise to rumour, and the couple were both arrested thirteen days later.

Maria admitted that she had given the deceased ant poison containing arsenic, and said that she had suffered much hardship, including a number of assaults, at his hands. But she denied that she had intended to kill him. 'I just wanted to avenge myself on Chris,' she said. 'I wanted to make him thoroughly sick, so that he would give me permission to divorce him.'

Other confessions followed, and in November Maria stood trial on her own before a judge and two assessors at the Bloemfontein Criminal Sessions. The evidence against her was overwhelming, and the allegations which she made against the victim of the crime were not believed, for witnesses declared that Christiaan Buys had been a quiet man, fond of his wife and children, and always kind to them. It was also claimed that Maria had said that she was tired of Buys and had threatened to 'damned well poison him' if he would not agree to divorce her. She was convicted and sentenced to death.

Gerhard Groesbeek was tried separately, also before a judge and assessors, seven months after Maria's conviction, but the case against him was not conclusive. There was no evidence that he had administered any of the poison, and though he had allegedly admitted to fellow prisoners that he was Maria's accomplice, this was not thought to be sufficient to prove him guilty beyond reasonable doubt. He was therefore acquitted.

Maria Groesbeek remained in the death cell in Pretoria while the question of a commutation of her sentence was considered. She spent much of her time praying and reading the Bible, frequently expressed sorrow for what she had done, and implored relatives to look after her children. She was finally hanged on 13 November 1970.

Poisoning of Alfred Jones, 1924

MARCH 29

On 29 March 1924, Alfred Poynter Jones, thirty-seven-year-old landlord of the Blue Anchor Hotel in Byfleet, Surrey, awoke with a hangover after a party at the hotel the previous night. He went to the bar parlour, found a bottle of bromo salts and drank part of the contents in a glass of water. But, far from feeling better, he died soon afterwards in agonizing convulsions. The bromo salts had been poisoned with strychnine.

Jean-Pierre Vaquier, a vain forty-five-year-old French inventor staying at the hotel, had been present at Mr Jones' death. Though he told police that he had loved the dead man 'like a brother', it soon became clear that his reason for staying at the hotel was his attachment to Mrs Mabel Jones, the landlord's widow, whom he had met in Biarritz a few months earlier. Later he was identified from a newspaper photograph as a man who had bought strychnine from a London chemist, signing the poison book 'J. Wanker'. He was then arrested and charged with murder.

At his trial at the Guildford Assizes in July it was revealed that Vaquier had been employed at the Victoria Hotel in Biarritz, operating a wireless set for the benefit of guests. Mabel Jones, spending a holiday there on her own, had been drawn into a passionate affair with him — an affair which involved considerable use of a French-English dictionary, as they did not speak each other's languages — with the result that when she returned to England he followed her, trying to persuade her to leave her husband. He explained his visit to England by saying that he was trying to sell the patent rights of a new type of sausage-mincer which he had invented.

The purchase of the strychnine had taken place on 1 March, 'Mr Wanker' telling the chemist that he needed it for wireless experiments. After Mr Jones' death, the bottle which had contained the bromo salts was found in the kitchen of the Blue Anchor, having been emptied and washed out, though not thoroughly enough to remove all traces of the poison. Vaquier claimed at his trial that he had bought the strychnine for Mrs Jones' solicitor, who had advised him to give a false name.

Though the prosecution's case was very strong, the prisoner was confident of being acquitted and displayed his vanity throughout the trial. But on being found guilty he shouted abuse at the judge and had to be dragged from the dock. He was hanged at Wandsworth Prison on 12 August 1924.

Child's body found in Thames, 1896

MARCH
30

On 30 March 1896, the body of a baby girl was found in the River Thames at Reading, Berkshire. She had been strangled with a piece of tape, which was still tied round her neck, and afterwards wrapped in a brown paper parcel and weighted with a brick. The brown paper bore the name Mrs Thomas and an address in Caversham, a village outside Reading, but 'Mrs Thomas' was found to be an alias of Mrs Amelia Elizabeth Dyer, a fifty-seven-year-old baby-farmer who had already moved to another address. On being identified, Mrs Dyer was arrested; the river was then dragged for further corpses.

Amelia Dyer, a native of Bristol, was separated from her husband and lived with an old woman known as Granny Smith, whom she had met in a workhouse the previous year. She took charge of unwanted children, her terms being £10 for each, and several of her charges were found at her house when she was taken into custody. Her daughter and son-in-law, who lived in rented rooms in Willesolen, Middlesex, were also arrested in connection with Mrs Dyer's activities.

The dragging of the Thames led to the recovery of six more strangled children, three of whom were never identified. Two bodies found in a weighted carpet-bag proved to be those of Doris Marmon, aged four months, who had been entrusted to Mrs Dyer's care in Cheltenham, Gloucestershire, on 31 March, and Harry Simmons, aged one year, who had been handed to Mrs Dyer and her daughter, Mrs Mary Ann Palmer, at Paddington Station, London, the following day.

At Reading police station Mrs Dyer made two attempts to take her own life: the first with a pair of scissors, the second with a boot-lace. Later, while in prison, she wrote to the Superintendent of Police, declaring that her daughter and son-in-law were innocent. 'I do know I shall have to answer before my Maker in Heaven for the awful crimes I have committed, but as God Almighty is my Judge in Heaven as on Earth, neither my daughter, Mary Ann Palmer, nor her husband, Arthur Ernest Palmer, I do most solemnly swear that neither of them had anything at all to do with it,' she said. Mary Ann Palmer, known as 'Polly', later became the prosecution's chief witness against her mother.

Though Mrs Dyer was believed to have been

101

responsible for all seven known murders — and it was suspected that she had committed others during her twenty years of baby-farming — she was tried only for that of Doris Marmon. Her trial on that charge took place at the Old Bailey in May 1896, when her daughter told the court that the victim had been taken to her rooms in Willesden on 31 March, and evidently strangled while she (the witness) was out fetching coal. Afterwards, she said, she found Mrs Dyer shoving the carpet-bag, which now contained the child's body, under her sofa. Mrs Palmer then went on to state that Harry Simmons must have been murdered in her rooms the following night, before she, her mother and her husband went out to a music-hall.

Mrs Dyer's counsel tried to save her life by introducing evidence of insanity, but two doctors appearing for the prosecution said that she was not insane; the symptoms had been feigned, they said. The jury took just five minutes to find the accused guilty, and she was sentenced to death. She was hanged at Newgate Prison on 10 June 1896.

Queensland mail train murders, 1936

APRIL

2

Shortly after 6 a.m. on 2 April 1936, two railway officials in Brisbane entered a mail train which had just arrived from Bundaberg, 180 miles to the north, in search of the conductor, Thomas Boys. They found him lying in one of the sleeping compartments, with his face so badly battered that he was unrecognizable. Two male passengers in the same compartment had also been battered: one of them, a Postal Department engineer, was already dead, the other, a businessman, was dying. Their money had been stolen and their belongings ransacked.

The person responsible had also stolen the coat and trousers of a suit belonging to the engineer, together with his departmental bag, stamped with the initials P.M.G. in gold. It was clear, too, from an examination of the wash-basin in that compartment, that he had tried to cleanse himself of bloodstains before leaving the train. But as he had left behind the waistcoat of the stolen suit, the police were able to broadcast the colour and texture of the coat and trousers he was wearing immediately after the crime.

They were thus able to discover that he had left the train at the wayside station of Wooloowin and taken a taxi from there to South Brisbane, paying his fare with bloodstained coins. From South Brisbane he had taken another taxi to Southport, and the driver of this one was able to identify him from photographs as Herbert Kopit, an incorrigible twenty-three-year-old sneak-thief who specialized in pilfering from hotel rooms.

From Southport the trail led to Murwillumbah, in New South Wales, then to Casino and finally to Sydney, where it suddenly stopped. Herbert Kopit was captured soon afterwards at a hotel in Melbourne, where he had arrived dressed as a woman and been reported as a suspected pervert.

He admitted that he was responsible for the mail train murders, saying that he had become excited when Boys looked into the sleeping compartment just before dawn and caught him picking the pockets of the other two passengers. He struck the conductor with a tyre lever which happened to be in his possession; then, as the attack woke the other passengers, he struck both of them as well. He afterwards robbed them, then tried to wash the blood from his hands and put on the engineer's coat and trousers in place of his own bloodstained suit. He threw the murder weapon out of the window before leaving the train at Wooloowin.

Kopit was brought to trial in Brisbane in June 1936 for the murder of the Postal Department engineer, Harold Steering. There was sufficient evidence to ensure his conviction, even after he had repudiated his statement to the Melbourne police, and as the death penalty had been abolished in Queensland he was sentenced to life imprisonment. He was not tried for the second murder, but stayed in jail until his death in March 1951.

Thomas Boys had suffered brain injuries which left his memory and speech impaired, and was therefore unable to give evidence against his assailant. He remained an invalid for the rest of his life, and died in July 1950.

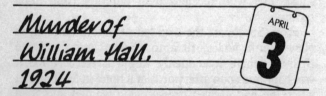

Murder of William Hall, 1924

APRIL
3

On 3 April 1924, William Hall, a twenty-eight-year-old cashier, was shot dead at his bank's sub-branch in the village of Bordon, in Hampshire. He had been working there on his own, as usual, having been sent to the village from his bank's main branch, some miles away, and as the culprit took the precaution of locking the front door after the murder had taken place, the body was not discovered until over an hour later. The murderer, in the meantime, had escaped with several hundred pounds in cash.

A bullet used in the shooting was recognized as Government ammunition, and a revolver belonging to an officer at the nearby army camp was found to be missing. A close watch was therefore kept on the camp, and for several days, during which all leave was cancelled, the place was in a state of tension. Then, on the afternoon of 8 April, Abraham Goldenberg, a young private in the East Lancashire Regiment, was seen behaving strangely. A search of one of the latrines after he had left it resulted in the discovery of a brown-paper parcel containing most of the stolen money.

Goldenberg was already known to the police officers investigating the murder. On the evening of 3 April he had volunteered information, saying that he had been to the bank to cash a cheque at 1.45 p.m. and that the cashier had been the only other person in the building at that time. Three days later he called in at the police station and said, 'No further developments have come to my knowledge. If anything does crop up, I will at once notify you.'

Two days after that, on being arrested, he confessed to being William Hall's murderer. 'I have been with my girl for some time, and I would not marry her unless I had money — and there was no chance of making any in the army,' he said. He went on to give details of the crime, and to reveal the whereabouts of the murder weapon and about a dozen bags of silver coins which he had stolen from the bank. However, he insisted that £37 which the police found in his pocket was his own money and had no connection with the crime.

At his trial, which took place in Winchester in June, an attempt was made to prove him insane, but he was found guilty and sentenced to death. As the judge finished pronouncing sentence, the silent spectators were astonished to hear the prisoner ask, 'Can I be assured that the thirty-seven pounds found upon me will be declared to be my property?'

A further plea of insanity was made at his appeal, but again without success. On 30 July 1924, Goldenberg was hanged at Winchester Prison.

Execution of Patrick Carraher, 1946

Patrick Carraher, who was hanged on 6 April 1946, was a forty-year-old criminal from the slums of Glasgow who had been regularly in trouble since his youth. He lived by theft and housebreaking, and had several convictions for crimes of violence. During his last eight years, following a prison sentence for culpable homicide, he had the reputation of being a killer — a reputation which he did his best to enhance by boasting.

The crime which led to this conviction had taken place in August 1938, when he stabbed a soldier in the neck in a Glasgow street. The soldier died on his way to hospital and Carraher, who admitted the offence, was charged with murder. It was because he had been drinking on the night in question that the jury found him guilty only on the lesser charge, and he was jailed for just three years. He received a similar sentence in 1943, after a razor-slashing incident in which the victim's jacket was ruined but no injury was caused to him.

The offence for which he was hanged took place in November 1945, when his brother-in-law, a thug named Daniel Bonnar, became involved in a fight with three brothers named Gordon. Always ready for trouble, Carraher attacked one of the brothers with a wood-carver's knife, inflicting a deep wound in his neck, and the victim, a former prisoner-of-war, died on arrival in hospital. Carraher was arrested shortly afterwards and charged with murder for the second time.

At his trial in February 1946 the prosecution's case was overwhelming and included the evidence of some of Carraher's former friends. The jury had little difficulty reaching a verdict, and the prisoner remained motionless as sentence of death was passed. Following the dismissal of his appeal, Carraher was hanged at Glasgow's Barlinnie Prison.

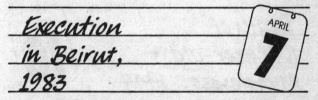

Execution in Beirut, 1983

APRIL
7

On 7 April 1983, Ibrahim Tarraf Tarraf, a thirty-six-year-old Shia Muslim and former law student from south Lebanon, was hanged in central Beirut for the murder of his landlady, Mrs Mathilde Bahout, and her son Marcel. The execution was carried out at dawn on a public gallows among the palm trees of the Sanayeh Park, where Tarraf, in 1979, had dumped the remains of his victims in rubbish bags, after murdering them and dismembering their bodies with a saw.

Following his conviction, Tarraf had been sentenced to death in March 1983, and this sentence was ratified by President Amin Gemayel and counter-signed by the

Prime Minister, Mr Chaffik el-Wazzam, the day before it was carried out. Struggling and pleading for mercy, the prisoner was dragged by policemen to the gallows, where he was handed over to two executioners, both wearing white hoods. A small group of spectators watched the proceedings in silence.

It was Lebanon's first use of the death penalty since 1972, when a blacksmith named Tewfik Itani was hanged in a Beirut prison for the murder of his brother-in-law, and the gallows stood opposite the building in which the murders had taken place. Tarraf's counsel, Mr Nimeh Nanieh, had tried unsuccessfully to obtain a stay of execution on a plea of temporary insanity.

Death of 100-year-old Murderess, 1944

On 10 April 1944, a well-known and much-respected figure died in a hospital in Strathfield, near Maitland, New South Wales, two months after celebrating her 100th birthday. Ruth Emilie Kaye, an unmarried Englishwoman, had lived in Australia for many years. She was a trained nurse and had been the matron of a nurses' home in Maitland from 1910 to 1936, when she finally retired. It was not realized at the time that 'Miss Kaye' was an assumed name and that this frail old lady had once committed a horrifying murder. She had, in fact, served a life sentence before setting foot in Australia.

Ruth Emilie Kaye's real name was Constance

Kent. She was one of the daughters of Samuel Savill Kent, an inspector of factories in the west of England, and had been born in Sidmouth, Devonshire, on 6 February 1844. Samuel Kent was married twice and had fifteen children, several of whom did not survive infancy. His second marriage — only a year after his first wife's death — was to his children's governess, who, having become his mistress, had gradually taken over the running of the household while the first Mrs Kent was still alive.

Constance was the last but one child of the first marriage. Her crime was committed on the night of 29 June 1860, at a mansion in the village of Rode, in Wiltshire, where the family was then living, and the body of the victim — her stepbrother Savill, aged three years and ten months — was found in the privy the following morning. His throat had been cut so deeply that he had almost been decapitated, and there was a four-inch stab wound in his chest. There was also a blackened area round his mouth.

An unsuccessful attempt was made to prosecute Constance — then a sullen and troublesome girl of sixteen — and this was followed by an equally un- successful attempt to prosecute Elizabeth Gough, the children's nursemaid. During the hearing against the latter it was revealed that Samuel Kent had done his best to obstruct the investigation of the crime, and this caused the villagers of Rode to suspect that he was the murderer. As a result, his life was made unbearable, and it remained so until the family moved in 1861.

The crime remained unsolved for five years, until Constance, after entering a religious home in Brigh- ton as a paying guest, suddenly travelled to London and handed a written confession to the chief magis- trate at Bow Street, stating that she was the culprit and that she had committed the murder 'alone and unaided'. Three months later, on 21 July 1865, she appeared for trial at the Wiltshire Assizes, pleaded guilty and was sentenced to death. The sentence was commuted to life imprisonment four days afterwards.

She spent the next twenty years in prison, part of the time in Millbank, where she worked in the infirmary. In one of a number of petitions for release, she explained her hatred of her stepmother who, she said, 'had taught her to despise and dislike her own mother' and 'robbed that mother of the affection both of a husband and of a daughter'. She then went on to state that it was in order to cause her stepmother 'the mental agony her own mother had endured' that she had committed her terrible crime.

Constance was forty-one years old at the time of her release — by which time her father and stepmother were both dead — and she was determined to make a new life for herself. Her brother William, a naturalist, was living in Tasmania, where he was known as William Saville-Kent; and when, the following year, he returned there after a visit to England, she accompanied him, using the name which she was to keep for the rest of her life.

She began training as a nurse in Melbourne in 1890, after responding to a call for volunteers to help deal with a typhoid crisis, and within a few months of completing the two-year course was appointed matron of a private hospital in Perth. She went on to hold posts in Sydney, Parramatta and Mittagong before settling in Maitland.

Though Constance maintained that she had acted alone on the night of the murder, she never explained how she was able to take the child from its cot without disturbing Elizabeth Gough, who slept in the same room. She likewise never explained why there was much less blood than might have been expected in the privy, where she claimed that the crime had been committed, or what had become of the weapon: a razor belonging to her father. Nor, for that matter, was any reason given for Samuel Kent's seemingly inexplicable behaviour in hindering the police investigation.

The case has therefore been the subject of much speculation, the most recent book on the subject being *Cruelly Murdered* (1979) by Bernard Taylor, in which the details of Constance's later life are to be found.

Taylor advances the theory that Samuel Kent was having an affair with Elizabeth Gough, and that they were in another room together when the murder took place. The crime, according to this theory, was committed by means of suffocation, and Samuel Kent, after the discovery of the body, inflicted the razor injuries himself and then disposed of the weapon in an attempt to divert suspicion away from the household.

It was only by doing this that he was able to avoid confessing his infidelity.

Murder of Ruby keen, 1937

On the evening of 11 April 1937, Leslie Stone, a quarry labourer aged twenty-four, met his former girl-friend, twenty-three-year-old Ruby Keen, in the saloon bar of the Golden Bell Hotel in Leighton Buzzard, Bedfordshire. He had known her since 1931, when he had courted her for some months prior to joining the Army, and on meeting her by chance the previous weekend had persuaded her to spend an evening with him 'for old times' sake'. He was hoping to resume the courtship, which had only ended when

111

he was posted to Hong Kong in 1932.

Ruby Keen, an attractive young woman who worked in a factory, had had other admirers besides Stone and was now engaged to a policeman. During the course of the evening, in two different public houses, Stone was overheard pleading with her to break off the engagement and marry him instead. Though Ruby was unwilling to do this, their exchanges were such that when they left the second pub, a few minutes before closing time, a couple of the regulars followed them at a discreet distance. They were then seen entering a coppice on the outskirts of the town, having walked past Ruby's home in Plantation Road.

The following morning Ruby's body was found in the coppice, beneath a tall fir tree. She had been raped and then strangled, her attacker kneeling beside her on the ground as he pulled her scarf tight round her neck. Her dress had been torn right down the front.

Stone was an obvious suspect. On being interviewed by police officers, he admitted having spent the evening with Ruby but claimed to have left her near her home about 10.15 p.m. The suit and shoes which he had been wearing at the time were taken for examination, and it was found that although the suit was new the surface of the cloth had been worn thin by brushing at the knees. Even so, a few grains of soil remained embedded in the trousers, and these were found to match samples taken from the ground where the murder had been committed. A small thread of artificial silk which had been brushed into the jacket was found to be identical to fibres from the slip which Ruby had been wearing on the evening in question.

Leslie Stone was charged with her murder and brought to trial at the Old Bailey in June 1937. After hearing the scientific evidence produced by the prosecution, he changed his account of what had taken place, saying that he and Ruby had quarrelled and struck each other at the scene of the crime, and that her dress had been torn as she fell to the ground. He added that he thought he had only stunned her and that he had not tried to interfere with her. He had walked away, expecting her to revive, and had brushed his clothes when he arrived back at his home.

After retiring to consider their verdict the jury sent a message to the judge, asking for his guidance on a point of law. 'If, as the result of an intention to commit rape, a girl is killed — although there is no intention to kill her — is a man guilty of murder?' they asked. The judge replied: 'Yes, undoubtedly.' A verdict of guilty was then returned and the prisoner was sentenced to death.

Following the dismissal of his appeal, Leslie Stone was hanged at Pentonville Prison on 13 August 1937.

Execution of Frederick Holt, 1920

APRIL
13

Frederick Rothwell Holt, who was hanged on 13 April 1920, was a Lancashire man from the upper middle class who had been invalided out of the army during the First World War, suffering from amnesia and depression. The victim of his crime was his mistress, Kitty Breaks, a young married woman who was separated from her husband. They had met in 1918, when Holt was thirty-one and Kitty twenty-five, and lived together for eighteen months before Kitty's body was found on sandhills at St Annes, near Blackpool, on the morning of 24 December 1919. She had insured her life for £5000 and made a will in Holt's favour just before her death.

That Holt had murdered her was never in doubt. She had been killed with shots from his service revolver, which had been left at the scene; a pair of his gloves and a set of footprints which matched the impressions of his shoes were also found there. Holt, though he had an income of £500 a year — which he had inherited — had been living beyond his means, and the prosecution contended that he had regarded the murder as a way of dealing with his financial difficulties after becoming tired of the victim.

But Sir Edward Marshall Hall, appearing for the defence, argued that his client was insane. Holt, he said, was mentally unbalanced as a result of his war experiences: the sort of man 'who might go mad at any moment'. He had been passionately devoted to Kitty and jealous of other men in her life, fearing that he might lose her. The murder had taken place as a result of an uncontrollable impulse, the perpetrator having been deprived of the will to resist it by reason of mental illness.

The fact that Holt had made no real attempt to conceal his guilt was cited as evidence of his insanity, and his love-letters to his victim were read aloud to great effect. But the prisoner's apparent indifference to the proceedings served to reinforce the prosecution's claim that he had committed a callous murder for the sake of money, and the jury found him guilty.

Holt, upon being sentenced to death, was characteristically unperturbed. 'Well, that's over,' he remarked. 'I hope my tea won't be late.'

During the following weeks he continued to show no emotion, and was pleasant to all concerned. On the morning of his execution he greeted the hangman with a friendly nod.

On the night of 15 April 1942, Edward Thomas Lee, a twenty-six-year-old able seaman in the Royal Navy, telephoned the police from a public house in Hill Lane, Southampton, and told them that there was a woman's body on the nearby common. A car was sent and he went out to meet it, but before leading police officers to the place where the dead woman lay he told them that he had killed her. He was immediately cautioned, but later repeated the statement.

The dead woman was Vera Margaret Bicknell, a clerk aged twenty-two with whom Lee had been having an affair for some time, and for whom he had left his wife and child. She had been strangled during a quarrel after telling him that she wanted to end their association, as Lee's wife had refused him a divorce. Lee was charged with her murder and brought to trial at the Hampshire Assizes in July.

He denied having killed her intentionally and, as the victim had suffered from tuberculosis, it was suggested that she had collapsed and died more quickly than a person in better health would have done; it was also stated that Lee had been suffering from a nervous condition as a result of his experiences at sea. The jury was evidently in sympathy with him, for, although the judge had told them that there were no grounds for such a verdict, they found him guilty only of manslaughter.

The judge was taken aback at this, and said that he did not know quite what to say. 'I directed the jury that it was not open to them to find manslaughter,' he continued. 'They have, in defiance of that direction and in falsity to their oaths, found that verdict. It is a verdict that I must accept, although there was no evidence, as I directed them, upon which they could act. They have chosen to do so, and that is all that I can say.'

Then, as a police officer was about to give evidence of Lee's character, Mr Justice Charles turned to the jury, which included three women, and said, 'You can leave the box now. You are not fit to be there!'

He afterwards sentenced the prisoner to fourteen years' penal servitude.

Murder of Helen Priestly, 1934

APRIL
20

On the afternoon of 20 April 1934, Helen Priestly, aged eight, who lived on the first floor of a three-storey tenement house in Urquhart Road, Aberdeen, was reported missing. She had arrived home from school for lunch at 12.15 p.m., and was sent out at half-past one to buy a loaf of bread from a co-operative bakery just along the road. But she did not return after being served, and it was quickly discovered that she had not gone back to school, either. Her mother reported her disappearance without delay.

John Priestly, a house painter, and his wife Agnes took turns to drive through the streets in a police car, looking for her, and at the same time a search was carried out in the washhouse and coal sheds of the building in which they lived. But there was no sign of the missing child, and the search continued through the cold, rainy night which followed, with neighbours taking the place of the anxious parents when they became exhausted. Suddenly, at 5 a.m., a sack containing the little girl's body was found behind the stairs on the ground floor of the tenement house. She had apparently been raped and strangled.

The bay in which the body was found contained a lavatory, which had been used regularly during the night, and it was established that the sack had been placed there after 4.30 a.m. As the sack was completely dry and rain was still falling outside, it seemed likely that one of the other tenants was responsible for the crime. Coal-ash and vomit were found round the child's mouth and cinders were found in her hair; part of the receipt which had been given to her at the bakery was still clutched in her hand. Some hours later a roofer who had been working next door told police that he had heard a child's scream coming from inside the building about 2 p.m. the previous day.

By questioning the inhabitants of the house, the police found one particular couple whose conduct struck them as being odd. Alexander Donald, a barber, and his wife Jeannie lived in a ground-floor apartment with their nine-year-old daughter. Neither of them had taken part in the search for Helen Priestly, and neither appeared to have taken any interest in what was happening in the building — except on the morning on which the body was discovered, when Donald had appeared in his doorway at 6.30, to ask whether there had been any new developments. Even then, on being told that the missing child had been found in a sack, he had gone back into his apartment without another word. Between 4 and 5 o'clock that morning a light had been seen in the Donalds' kitchen.

The Donalds kept themselves to themselves, speaking to their neighbours as little as possible. Jeannie Donald, aged thirty-eight, was a woman with a violent temper, who was known to have struck Helen Priestly on one occasion. Helen had given her a nickname, 'Coconut', which she would call out tauntingly as she went past their door.

When Alexander Donald was asked whether he had heard the commotion which followed the discovery of the body, he replied that he and his wife had heard it while they were lying in bed. Afterwards, he said, his wife had said to him, 'Do you hear? That's Mrs Joss' voice. She's screaming that the child was raped.' This surprised the police officer questioning him, because *he* had been in the hallway at the time and knew that no such thing had been said loudly enough for any of the tenants to hear. The condition of the body was known only to the police doctor, the officer in charge of the case, and himself. He did not comment on this at the time, but bore it in mind.

The autopsy revealed that the child's death had taken place at about 2 p.m., that the injuries which suggested rape had actually been inflicted with a sharp object of some sort while the child was still alive, and that the victim had had an enlarged thymus gland, which would have made her susceptible to fainting.

While Alexander Donald could prove that he had been at work at the time of the murder, his wife was unable to give a satisfactory account of her movements at the same time. Various statements of hers were found to be lies — for example, a claim that the family had no ash-can was contradicted by her daughter — and she was arrested. Forensic tests later showed that Helen Priestly's body had been in the Donalds' apartment.

It was believed that Jeannie Donald, annoyed at being taunted, had rushed out and grabbed her while she was passing the door and that the shock had caused the child to faint. Jeannie Donald, thinking that she had killed her, had then dragged her into the apartment and inflicted the injuries which suggested rape. Finally, she had panicked and strangled the child when she revived and began to scream.

Jeannie Donald was brought to trial in Edinburgh on 16 July 1934, the feeling in Aberdeen being such that she was unlikely to have a fair trial there. She did not give evidence in her own defence, and was convicted of the crime. Her death sentence was afterwards commuted to penal servitude for life, and she was released in 1944.

Body of Mary Moonen discovered, 1955

APRIL
23

On 23 April 1955, Mrs Mary Moonen, twenty-one-year-old wife of a soldier serving in Korea, was found dead in a fashionable district of Minneapolis; she had been left lying on a road after being strangled, though not robbed or sexually assaulted. A post-mortem revealed that she was three months pregnant — for which her husband could not have been responsible — and also that she had had sexual intercourse shortly before her death. However, her relatives and friends all claimed that Mrs Moonen, a Roman Catholic with a nine-month-old daughter, had been a respectable young woman with no interest in extra-marital affairs. They could not believe that she had had a lover in her husband's absence.

The police learnt that on the evening of 22 April, Mrs Moonen had had an appointment with her dentist, Dr Arnold Axilrod — and her sister, who gave them this information, went on to say that she, too, had been one of Dr Axilrod's patients but had found his conduct objectionable. On one occasion, she said, he had given her a pill which left her unconscious for several hours, and had afterwards spoken to her suggestively; on another, he had made advances towards her in his office. It was as a result of this second incident that she had stopped going to see him.

Further information about Dr Axilrod came to light as the investigation continued, the police discovering that many other female patients had lost consciousness for several hours at a time as a result of taking pills which he had given them, and that no nurse was ever present when this happened. One of the women concerned was Mrs Moonen, who had told her doctor that the dentist had raped her while she was unconscious in his surgery, and that he was the father of her unborn child.

Dr Axilrod, a former mayor, was arrested. He said that the pills which he had given to his patients were only used to deaden their reflexes and rarely caused unconsciousness. While admitting that Mrs Moonen had been to see him on the evening of 22 April and that they had quarrelled about her pregnancy, he said that he could not remember whether he had had sexual intercourse with her or not, because he had suffered a blackout. He refused to sign a statement which he was afterwards alleged to have made, confessing that he had murdered her.

He was brought to trial in September 1955, but it was not until 10 October that the court was ready to hear evidence. The newspapers then had a field-day, the dentist being accused of being a philanderer who drugged his victims so that they could not resist him. He denied having killed Mrs Moonen, and said that he had not even been intimate with her; but this was not believed and he was convicted of manslaughter. On 3 November 1955, he was sentenced to five-to-twenty years' imprisonment.

APRIL
24

Execution of Colin Ross, 1922

On 24 April 1922, Colin Campbell Ross, a former wine-bar licensee, was hanged at Melbourne Jail for the murder of a twelve-year-old girl found raped and strangled four months previously. He denied to the end that he had had anything to do with the crime, claiming that his conviction was a miscarriage of justice — and many people believed him, including the barrister T.C. Brennan, who published a book about the case later the same year.

The crime had been discovered on the morning of 31 December 1921, when a collector of empty bottles found the body of Alma Tirtschke lying on a drain-grating in Gun Alley, a cul-de-sac 115 yards from the condemned man's premises. The body was naked and had been washed and dried after death, presumably in order to remove clues to the murderer's identity. Detectives concluded that the person responsible had intended pushing it into the drain but failed to do so, perhaps because he had been disturbed.

Ross was among the first people to be interviewed in connection with the crime, but did not seem unduly worried about it, even when it was noticed that his floor had recently been scrubbed. He gave an account of his movements the previous day, saying that at one point he had seen Alma hanging about outside the home of a fortune-teller known as Madame Ghurka but had not spoken to her. He also invited the police officers questioning him to have a look round the bar, which, being unable to get his licence renewed, he was about to close for the last time.

Ross was not suspected at this stage, and the police

made no headway with the case for several days. During that time public feeling became so intense that the Victorian Government offered a reward of £1000 for information leading to the arrest and conviction of the murderer, and a further £250 was offered by a newspaper, the Melbourne *Herald*. But the people who were eventually given shares of these rewards were hardly the most reliable of witnesses.

On 9 January a woman named Ivy Matthews told police that on the afternoon of 30 December she had seen a girl she believed to be Alma — 'a little girl with auburn hair' — looking out of a curtained cubicle inside the wine-bar: a cubicle from which Ross himself had just emerged. She had afterwards challenged him and he had admitted the murder to her, vilifying the child in the process, she claimed.

This Ivy Matthews had worked for Ross as a barmaid until he sacked her a few weeks before the murder, and on 5 January had said that she knew nothing about the crime. In spite of this, she was to become the prosecution's most important witness when Ross appeared for trial.

Another prosecution witness was Sidney John Harding, a criminal with a record which included convictions for wounding, larceny, housebreaking, assault and escaping from custody. Harding was already in jail on remand when Ross was arrested on 12 January, and claimed that eleven days later Ross had told him that he was guilty of the child's murder. Harding also told police that part of this confession had been overheard by a third prisoner named Joseph Dunstan — a claim which Dunstan obligingly corroborated.

A further witness, a young prostitute named Olive Maddox, said that she, too, had seen Alma at the wine-bar on the afternoon in question, and that Ivy Matthews — to whom she had spoken about this — had told her to inform the police.

There were several discrepancies between the two confessions Ross was said to have made — for example, he had given Alma a glass of lemonade according to one of them, and three glasses of wine according to the other. The forensic evidence was also not very impressive, for blankets found in the prisoner's possession — said to have had hairs similar to those of the dead girl attached to them — apparently bore no bloodstains, even though the victim of the crime was known to have bled a good deal. No evidence of bloodstains was found during an examination of the floor of the wine-bar, either.

The trial of Colin Ross began on 20 February and lasted five days, the jury taking twenty-four hours to reach a verdict of guilty. On the morning of his execution, two months later, Ross declared, 'My life has been sworn away by desperate people. If I am hanged, I will be hanged as an innocent man.' Brennan, who was personally involved in the case, afterwards referred scathingly to the character of the chief prosecution witnesses, and claimed that Ross had been made a scapegoat in order to placate a furious public.

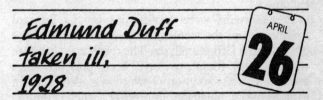

Edmund Duff taken ill, 1928

APRIL 26

On the evening of 26 April 1928, Edmund Creighton Duff, a fifty-nine-year-old retired colonial civil servant living in Croydon, Surrey, went to bed suffering from cramp in his calf muscles and nausea after eating a meal prepared by his wife. When he died the following day food poisoning was suspected, so an inquest was held and parts of his organs were removed for analysis. However, no poison was discovered, and his death was attributed to natural causes.

On 14 February the following year Duff's sister-in-law Vera Sidney, a woman of forty who lived nearby with her widowed mother, suddenly became very ill after having lunch with her mother and an aunt. She appeared to recover — as did her aunt, the cook and the cat, who were also ill — but died in pain two days later. Her death, too, was put down to natural causes.

Then, on 5 March, sixty-nine-year-old Mrs Violet Sidney — Vera's mother — complained about the taste of some medicine prescribed by her doctor. After lunch she was sick, and declared that the medicine had poisoned her. She died a few hours afterwards, and this time food poisoning was accepted as the cause of death.

Mrs Sidney's son Thomas, a married man with children of his own, was not satisfied with this, and an examination of some of his mother's organs was carried out. Although nothing abnormal was discovered, somebody drew the attention of the Home Office to these two latest deaths, and on 22 March the bodies of both Mrs Sidney and her daughter were exhumed.

Post-mortems were carried out by Sir Bernard Spilsbury, and the women's organs were sent to one of the Home Office analysts. The result was that both women were found to have been poisoned with arsenic, a strong solution of which was also found in Mrs Sidney's medicine. Moreover, when Edmund Duff's body was exhumed on 18 May, this, too, was found to contain traces of arsenic. It seems that this was not discovered earlier because organs from another body had been examined by mistake.

Inquests on the three bodies took place over a period of five months. In the case of Mrs Sidney, the coroner's jury decided that there was insufficient evidence to show whether she had committed suicide or been murdered; in those of Vera Sidney and Edmund Duff, verdicts of murder against some person or persons unknown were returned.

Suspicion centred on Grace Duff, Edmund's widow, but there was insufficient evidence to bring a charge against her — or, for that matter, against anyone else — so the case was never officially solved. However, Richard Whittington-Egan, in *The Riddle of Birdhurst Rise* (1975), claims that Grace was indeed the culprit: that she killed her husband because she was in love with a local doctor, and her mother and sister because she stood to gain from their deaths.

Grace Duff died at the age of eighty-seven in 1973.

Discovery of Mary Phagan's body, 1913

APRIL 27

On 27 April 1913, a black nightwatchman employed by the National Pencil Company at its factory in Atlanta, Georgia, found the body of a fourteen-year-old white girl, Mary Phagan, in the basement of the premises: she had been beaten about the head and strangled. Having raised the alarm, the watchman, Newt Lee, was arrested, as notes found by the body — presumed to have been written by the dead girl — suggested that he had killed her himself.

But at the inquest James Conley, another black employee, made statements which amounted to an accusation of murder against Leo Frank, the factory superintendent. He said that Frank had asked him to help carry the body into the basement, and also to write the notes found beside it. Frank, a twenty-nine-year-old American Jew from Brooklyn, was then charged with first-degree murder.

He was brought to trial on 28 July 1913, the case receiving widespread publicity. Conley, the most important of almost 200 prosecution witnesses, repeated his allegations, adding that he had also seen the accused engaged in deviant sexual acts with girls on the factory premises.

It was expected that Frank, who claimed that Conley's allegations were lies, would be acquitted, for no white man had ever been convicted on the testimony of a black. But, to the delight of the noisy crowds outside, he was convicted and sentence of death was passed on him.

Applications for a new trial were made to various courts, including the United States Supreme Court, but all were dismissed. However, in August 1915 the State Governor, with the approval of the trial judge, commuted the sentence to life imprisonment.

This led to bitter press comment and public demonstrations, and before long an armed mob calling themselves the 'Knights of Mary Phagan' broke into the prison where he was being held and abducted him.

They drove him 175 miles to Marietta, where the dead girl had been buried, and hanged him from a tree near the grave. When he was dead the crowds which had gathered began to tear off pieces of his shirt to keep as souvenirs, and photographs of his body were displayed in shops.

Leo Frank, a shy, nervous man, had been convalescing from a knife wound at the time of his abduction. One member of the lynch mob said that the hanging was 'a duty of the state'.

Murder of Alec de Antiquis, 1947

APRIL
29

On 29 April 1947, three masked gunmen raided a jeweller's shop in London's West End, leaving a stolen car parked in the crowded street outside. The firm's sixty-year-old director was beaten over the head with a revolver and a bullet was fired into the shop wall when the manager — who was seventy — threw a wooden stool at them instead of handing over the safe keys. But by this time a burglar alarm had been set off, and the three men suddenly fled from the shop empty-handed.

On reaching the stolen car, they found a lorry blocking their way; they therefore had to get out and run for it. As they did so, other people ran for cover or threw themselves onto the ground — some of them screaming — but a passing motor-cyclist, Alec de Antiquis, tried to obstruct the robbers by driving his machine across their path. He was shot in the head and fatally injured.

A moment later a further attempt was made, this time by a Mr Grimshaw, a surveyor. Mr Grimshaw tripped one of the villains up and jumped on him — but then had to let him go when he was kicked in the head and threatened with a gun. The three armed men then disappeared among the crowds.

Alec de Antiquis, the owner of a motor-cycle repair shop, was in his early thirties; he was a married man with six children. As he was lifted into an ambulance he uttered his last words: 'I'm all right. Stop them. I did my best.' He died in hospital not long afterwards.

The police officers investigating the crime made no headway for some days, for no fingerprints were found in the stolen car and widely differing descriptions of the gunmen were given by the many witnesses. But then a taxi-driver reported that on the afternoon in question he had seen two masked men enter an office block near the scene of the crime. The building was searched and a number of discarded items found. These included a raincoat from which the maker's name had been removed and a scarf which had been folded and knotted to make a mask.

A stock ticket under the lining of the raincoat enabled the police to trace it to a shop in Deptford, south-east London, and from the shop's records it was learnt that the raincoat had been sold to a man living in nearby Bermondsey on 30 December previously. The man was seen and, after some prevarication, revealed that the raincoat had been lent to his wife's brother, a twenty-three-year-old former Borstal boy named Charles Henry Jenkins, some weeks before the murder.

Jenkins, who had twice been convicted of assaulting policemen — and whose brother was in jail for manslaughter — was arrested. He refused to answer questions and had to be released when none of the twenty-seven witnesses identified him. But later he and his sister made statements claiming that the raincoat had been lent to a convict on licence named Bill Walsh. In the meantime Jenkins and two associates, Christopher James Geraghty, aged twenty-one, and Terence Peter Rolt, a youth of seventeen, had been placed under observation.

Bill Walsh, aged thirty-seven, was arrested in Plumstead, Kent, a few days later. He denied having borrowed the raincoat or taken part in the crime, but confessed that he had been involved with Geraghty and Jenkins in robbing a different jeweller's, and went on to state that he had personally absconded with all the jewellery stolen on that occasion! This proved to be true, and Walsh was charged accordingly. He was sent to jail for five years.

The murder weapon had already been found in the Thames at Wapping, in east London, and another gun — the one which had been fired in the shop the same afternoon — was discovered in the same area shortly afterwards. But no charges could be made in connection with this crime until Geraghty made a confession which implicated Rolt, and Rolt made another which implicated Jenkins. All three were then formally charged with murder and brought to trial at the Old Bailey on 21 July.

The trial lasted a week and resulted in Jenkins, Geraghty and Rolt all being convicted. Jenkins and Geraghty were both sentenced to death, their executions being carried out at Pentonville Prison on 19 September 1947. Rolt, on account of his youth, was ordered to be detained at His Majesty's pleasure for at least five years, and was not released until June 1956.

The executions caused an outcry, but, according to Sir Harold Scott, the former Metropolitan Police Commissioner, led to the disbanding of the criminal gang to which Jenkins and Geraghty had belonged. Ex-Superintendent Robert Fabian, who headed the investigation, tells us in his memoirs that they also prompted many other criminals to abandon their own guns.

Leonard Moules attacked, 1942

On 30 April 1942, Leonard Moules, a seventy-one-year-old pawnbroker, was found unconscious in his

shop in London's East End after being attacked during the course of a robbery. He was taken to Bethnal Green Hospital, where police officers waited at his bedside in the hope that he would be able to give them information about his assailants. But he died several days later, without regaining consciousness.

The old man had been beaten over the head with a blunt instrument, a single blow being struck from one angle and four more from another. It appeared from the bruising of his neck muscles that he had been held by one of his attackers while the battering took place. There was no sign of the weapon which had been used, and although a palm-print was found on the inside of the victim's safe, it could not be identified, as Scotland Yard had no index of palm-prints at this time.

The police officers concerned had therefore to resort to questioning known criminals in the area, and during the next two weeks over three hundred were seen without any further clue to the identity of the murderers being discovered. Then, on 15 May, a soldier in a Bethnal Green café was overhead remarking that he had seen two men examining a revolver in another café in the same district about the time of the murder.

One of the men was found to be George Silverosa, a twenty-three-year-old machinist, who lived at Pitsea in Essex. Upon being questioned, Silverosa, a former Borstal boy, admitted that he had taken part in the robbery at the pawnbroker's and blamed his accomplice, Sam Dashwood, for the old man's death.

Dashwood had suggested the robbery as they passed the shop on the day in question, and he (Silverosa) had agreed to take part in it on the understanding that no violence would be used, he said. As it was early closing day, the pawnbroker was putting up the shutters, and they waited until he had finished, then followed him into the shop.

130

'I closed the shop door, and as I turned round I saw the old man falling down,' said Silverosa. 'I didn't see Sam strike him, but I surmised what he had done. I said, "You silly sod, what did you do that for?" He said, "I had to. He was going to blow a whistle." I wiped some blood off the old man's head with my overcoat. I said to Sammy, "Well, we've done the damage, we had better do what we came here to do." We took some rings from the safe and off the table ...'

Sam Dashwood, aged twenty-two, also had a criminal record, and he, too, had been to Borstal. His version of what had happened was different from Silverosa's. 'George went in first,' he said. 'There was a man and a dog there. There was a scuffle, and the dog started barking. I hit the dog between the eyes. George and the old man were scuffling, and the old man went down. The old man then got up again and we both jumped on him to hold him down and he started shouting.'

He explained the violence which had been used by saying, 'I bent over the old boy to shut him up and he put his arms round my neck. I bent over him and hit him on the top of the head with the revolver ...' However, he omitted to mention the number of blows which had been struck.

When Silverosa and Dashwood were brought to trial for murder, they both avoided cross-examination by declining to give evidence. It was argued on Silverosa's behalf that there had been no common design to commit murder and that he had not used violence. But the judge dismissed this point in his summing-up, and the jury accordingly found both prisoners guilty. They were subsequently hanged.

In Pentonville Prison, a few days before the execution, Silverosa obtained permission to burn two letters in the incinerator. While they were burning, he snatched up a poker and attacked the two warders in charge of him, injuring them both. He was eventually overpowered and taken back to the condemned cell.

Disappearance of Louisa Luetgert, 1897

On 1 May 1897, Louisa Luetgert, the wife of a German immigrant, disappeared from her home in Chicago. Nothing was done about if for several days and when the police were finally informed Adolph Luetgert, a forty-nine-year-old sausage-maker with his own factory, was questioned at length. Later, following a search of the factory, he was charged with his wife's murder.

Luetgert, who weighed over seventeen stone, had lived in the United States since the 1870s. He had many mistresses, some of whom would visit him in his office — and for this reason he had had a bed installed there. Moreover, when the police emptied his steam vats they found that the sludge left in one of them contained pieces of human bone, some teeth and two gold rings. The rings were identified by relatives as having belonged to the missing woman.

The police believed that Luetgert had killed his wife, probably with one of the sharp knives used in the factory, and disposed of her body by turning it into sausages. Luetgert denied this, claiming that the rings had *not* belonged to his wife — even though her initials were engraved on one of them — and that the bone fragments were pieces of pig-bone. He maintained that he did not know his wife's whereabouts.

At his trial, which was understandably sensational,

some of Luetgert's mistresses gave evidence against him. The court heard that he had long been tired of his wife — and she of his infidelity — and that on one occasion he had said that he could take her and crush her. Though no weapon could be produced against him, and Luetgert persisted in his denials, he was found guilty of first-degree murder and sentenced to life imprisonment.

He died in the Joliet State Penitentiary in 1911, still claiming to be innocent.

Murder of Shirley Allen, 1957

MAY
4

At 8 a.m. on 4 May 1957, Mrs Doreen Dally, who lived in one of the basement flats of her own house in Bayswater, west London, was awakened by the sound of banging from the flat opposite. This noise was immediately followed by a woman crying out, 'No, Peter! No! Oh, Peter, please!' And this, in turn, was followed by a terrible scream.

Mrs Dally, aged fifty-five, went to the door in her nightdress and looked out into the passage. She saw, to her horror, that twenty-four-year-old Shirley Allen, one of the tenants who lived opposite, was at the door of her flat, with a wound in her head from which blood was streaming. She was evidently trying to leave the flat but being restrained by somebody inside. 'Oh, Mrs Dally, help me, please!' she said softly. 'Peter's gone mad!'

Mrs Dally caught hold of the woman's arm and managed to pull her into the passage. Pushing her

133

into her own flat, she told her to lock the door and went off to telephone for help. As she reached the stairs, however, she heard a sound behind her and looked round.

Ginter Wiora, the thirty-four-year-old Polish art student known as 'Peter', with whom Shirley Allen cohabited, had come out into the passage, holding a Japanese samurai sword. He stared for a moment at the door of Mrs Dally's flat, his hands crossed against his chest, then turned and looked at her. Suddenly he moved towards her, lunging with the sword, and pierced one of her breasts.

The middle-aged landlady ran up the stairs, roused another tenant and telephoned the police. As she did so, she heard more screams from the basement. She then sat down in the other tenant's flat, her night-dress stained with blood. The police arrived shortly afterwards and, on learning what had happened, went down to the basement to investigate.

The door of Mrs Dally's flat stood open, and the dead body of Shirley Allen lay behind it. She had been stabbed in the chest with the sword, and also battered over the head with a standard lamp. Both weapons lay on the floor, the blade of the sword bent and the standard lamp broken. It was the chest-wound which had caused her death.

Wiora, in the meantime, had returned to his own flat, locked the door and attempted to take his own life. When the police broke in, they found him lying on the bed, moaning. He had stabbed himself with another sword, cut his wrists with a bread-knife, and tried to gas himself. It was later discovered that he had been jealous of Shirley Allen's association with other men and had suspected her of posing for pornographic photographs.

On 25 July 1957, Ginter Wiora was brought to trial at the Old Bailey, charged with murder. Pleading diminished responsibility, he was convicted of manslaughter and sentenced to twelve years' imprisonment. The following year he was committed to Broadmoor.

Mummified corpse found in Rhyl, 1960

MAY
5

On 5 May 1960, the mummified corpse of a middle-aged woman wearing a nightdress and dressing-gown was found in a landing cupboard at the home of sixty-five-year-old Mrs Sarah Harvey, a widow living in Rhyl, north Wales. The discovery was made by Mrs Harvey's son Leslie, a taxi-driver, who was redecorating the house while his mother was in hospital. The cupboard was a large fixed one that had been locked for many years, and Mr Harvey had to force it open with a screwdriver. The corpse, which was covered in dust and cobwebs, was rigid and stuck to a piece of linoleum on the cupboard floor.

On being questioned, Mrs Harvey told police that the dead woman was Mrs Frances Knight, a semi-invalid who had died while boarding with her in 1939, and explained the hiding of the body by saying that she had not known what else to do with it. This identification was corroborated by medical evidence, and it was accepted that the body had been mummified naturally as a result of a free circulation of air currents inside the cupboard. But a groove on the left side of the neck, from which a piece of knotted stocking was taken, suggested that the dead woman had been strangled.

Mrs Harvey was therefore charged with murder. But when she appeared for trial at the next assizes in Ruthin, Denbighshire, it was admitted that the cause of death was by no means certain, and the defence claimed that the position in which the body had been found was consistent with death from disseminated sclerosis, from which Mrs Knight was known to have suffered. It was also pointed out that there could have been an innocent explanation of the piece of stocking, as there was an old custom in some parts of the country of tying a stocking or sock round one's neck when onc was ill.

The trial was brought to an end on its fifth day, when the Solicitor-General made a submission to the judge that he thought it would be wrong to invite the jury to find the prisoner guilty of murder. The judge concurred and a formal verdict of not guilty was returned. Mrs Harvey was, however, sent to prison for fifteen months for falsely obtaining £2 a week, due to Mrs Knight under a court order, by pretending — for twenty years — that she was still alive.

First of the 'Co-ed' murders, 1972

MAY 7

On 7 May 1972, Edmund Emil Kemper, a twenty-three-year-old labourer of Santa Cruz, California, committed the first of a series of shocking crimes which were later to be called the 'Co-ed Murders'. The victims were Anita Luchese and Mary Ann Pesce, two students at the Fresno State College, Berkeley, who had the misfortune to be out hitch-hiking while he was roaming the highways in his car. Kemper stopped to give them a lift, then held them at gunpoint while he drove to a wooded canyon. There he stabbed both girls to death in frenzied attacks, and afterwards violated their bodies before taking them home in the trunk of the car.

Kemper, who was 6 feet 9 inches tall and weighed twenty stone, lived with his mother, whom he hated. She was not at home when he arrived and, putting the corpses into rubbish bags, he carried them up to his room, where he again had intercourse with each of them after cutting off their heads. He then dismembered them and took the pieces out to his car in plastic sacks, his mother — who had returned in the meantime — noticing nothing unusual about his behaviour. Finally, he drove into the nearby mountains, buried the sacks and washed his car with water from a stream.

It was by no means his first offence, for Kemper, whose parents had separated when he was seven, had murdered both of his grandparents on his father's side when he was fifteen. As a result, he had spent the next five years in a hospital for the criminally insane, and had then been sent to live with his mother by the California Youth Authority, into whose care he had been released. Since then he had picked up many female hitch-hikers, mostly college students, and a number of rapes, assaults and disappearances had been reported but not solved. The disappearance of Anita Luchese and Mary Ann Pesce also remained unsolved until Kemper, a year later, revealed what had happened to them.

Four months after their murder, on 14 September 1972, Kemper picked up Aiko Koo, a fifteen-year-old Japanese high school student, and drove her, also at gunpoint, into the mountains. Stopping the car, he put tape over her mouth and, in spite of her fierce resistance, suffocated her by holding two of his fingers up her nostrils. When she was dead he had intercourse with her, then took her body home and cut off her head. He once again had intercourse with the decapitated corpse before dismembering it and burying the pieces in the mountains. Once again, the crime remained undiscovered until he confessed to it.

The next murder was that of Cynthia Schall, who was abducted and shot dead on 8 January 1973. In this case Kemper kept the body overnight in his room, waiting until his mother — a college administrative assistant — had gone to work the following morning before engaging in sexual acts with it and then dissecting it in the shower. This time parts of the body were found and identified, Kemper having thrown them over cliffs in the Carmel area, but police were unable to find the person responsible. His next crime — another double murder — took place only a month later.

Rosalind Thorpe and Alice Lui were both picked up at the local campus on the evening of 5 February 1973, Kemper offering to drive them to a nearby small town where they both lived. While he was driving he suddenly took out a gun and shot them both in the head. He then stopped the car, put both bodies into the trunk and drove to his own home. He was unable to take them up to his room, as his mother was indoors, so he cut off their heads in the trunk and left them there till the morning — when he violated at least one of them in the usual way, and afterwards cut off Alice Lui's hands. The headless corpses were found by hunters in Eden Canyon, Alameda, nine days later, but still nobody suspected Kemper of being the murderer.

On the morning of Easter Sunday, 1973, he killed his mother by hitting her on the head with a hammer, then cut off her head and hid the body. Later the same day he invited a friend of hers named Sarah Hallett to dinner, knocked her unconscious with a brick, then strangled her, cut off her head and had intercourse with the body. The next day he left the house for good, driving off in Mrs Hallett's car and later renting another with money from her handbag.

He now expected to be the subject of a manhunt and when, after a few days, there was no news of one, he telephoned the police in Pueblo, Colorado, and said that he was the 'Co-ed Killer'. To his surprise, they did not believe him, and he had to make several more such calls before he was finally taken into custody. He then made a detailed confession, claiming that he had not given himself up to the police in Santa Cruz for fear that they would 'shoot first and ask questions later'. This confession, which was so revolting that detectives interviewing him were visibly shaken by it, led to Kemper being charged with all eight murders.

Kemper was a sadist who had begun to torture animals when he was ten years old; he was also abnormally shy where women were concerned and could only satisfy himself with one who was either helpless with terror or dead. At his trial in Santa Cruz he was found to be legally sane, but his request to be executed was refused. He was sentenced to life imprisonment, without the possibility of being released on parole.

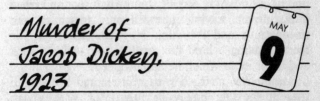

Murder of Jacob Dickey, 1923

MAY
9

On the night of 9 May 1923, Jacob Dickey, a taxi-driver, was shot dead outside his cab in a street in

Brixton, south London. The gunman escaped with a small sum of money from his victim's pocket, but left a number of articles at the scene of the crime, including his revolver and a gold-headed walking-stick. Though these offered no clue to the murderer's identity, the walking-stick was recognized from a published photograph as the property of Edward Vivian, a petty criminal who lived with a prostitute in Pimlico.

On being questioned, Vivian admitted owning the walking-stick, but denied having been involved in the murder. He said that an acquaintance named 'Scottie' Mason had been staying at his flat, and had purchased a revolver, intending to rob a taxi-driver. Vivian then went on to say that he had been suffering from food-poisoning on the evening in question, and that Mason had gone out alone, taking the walking-stick with him.

'Scottie' Mason was found to be a twenty-two-year-old deserter from the Canadian armed forces, whose real name was Alexander Campbell Mason. He was soon arrested, but denied all knowledge of the murder until confronted with evidence of his guilt. He then accused Vivian of it, saying that they had taken the taxi to Brixton together and that Vivian had shot the driver during the course of a struggle.

By this time Vivian had been questioned again and had given further information. He told police officers that Mason had arrived back at his flat about midnight on 9 May, saying that he had shot and killed a taxi-driver, having intended only to knock him unconscious and rob him. He then fled from the scene, leaving behind the revolver, the walking-stick and other items which he had dropped.

Mason was charged with murder and brought to trial at the Old Bailey in July 1923, with Vivian appearing as a prosecution witness. The prisoner was convicted and sentenced to death, but the sentence

140

was afterwards commuted to life imprisonment. He served fourteen years, and died while serving in the Merchant Navy during the Second World War.

Double murder at Aldershot, 1982

MAY
10

On the afternoon of 10 May 1982, two women walking their dogs were savagely murdered by an unknown assailant on a common at Aldershot, in Hampshire. Mrs Margaret Johnson, aged sixty-six, and Mrs Ann Lee, forty-four — both local residents who regularly went out dog-walking together — died within minutes of each other, Mrs Johnson having been stabbed five times and her friend eleven times. Their dogs, a Red Setter and a Labrador, remained with their bodies until they were found by other walkers.

There was no apparent reason for the crime, and the murder weapon was not found during a search of the common. Two anonymous telephone calls were received, the caller on each occasion saying that the murderer was a young man named Peter Fell, who lived in a nearby bedsitter. But Fell was not at home when police went to see him and, on checking with his employers, they were told that he had been at work at the time of the murders. They therefore did not regard him as a suspect.

Even so, when they released a photo-fit picture of a man who had been seen on the common on the afternoon in question, it bore such a strong resemblance to Fell that several of his acquaintances remarked upon it — and Fell went to Aldershot police station to complain that publication of the picture was an act of 'harassment'. But no further notice was taken of him, and in August 1982 he moved to Bournemouth. The crime remained unsolved for almost another year.

Then, one night, the Bournemouth police received eleven anonymous calls, all accusing Peter Fell of being the Aldershot murderer. Now married and about to become a father, Fell was immediately arrested, and the police in Aldershot approached his former employers, asking them to re-check their records. They did so, and said that the information given earlier had not been correct. They could not give Peter Fell an alibi after all.

Moreover, on questioning others who worked for the same firm, the police were told that Fell had arrived late on the afternoon of the crime, and that he had been wearing a suit — which was out of character with him, as he was normally scruffy.

At Farnborough police station, near Aldershot, Fell admitted that he had killed the two women; he said that he had done so because they laughed at him, and because one of them looked like his mother, whom he had hated. He later retracted his confession, but was charged with the two murders just the same.

Peter Fell, a twenty-three-year-old ex-soldier, was brought to trial at Winchester Crown Court in July 1984, the case lasting nineteen days. There was no forensic evidence linking him with the murders, and the prosecution depended a great deal on his tape-recorded confession, which was played in court. It took the jury over twenty-five hours to return a majority verdict of guilty on each count.

The judge, after sentencing the prisoner to life imprisonment for each murder, praised the police officer in charge of the investigation for his zeal and thoroughness. But Fell, who had made all of the thirteen anonymous telephone calls himself, could hardly have been quite as impressed.

Born in Lancashire, Peter Fell had been put into a home at the age of four, when his parents were divorced, and had not seen his mother for the next twelve years. Having joined the army as a boy soldier, he had been medically discharged from the Royal Corps of Transport just two months prior to the murders. At the time of his arrest he was working as a porter in a Brighton hotel.

Death of James Maybrick, 1889

MAY 11

On 11 May 1889, James Maybrick, an English cotton-broker aged fifty, died at his home in the Liverpool suburb of Aigburth, after an illness lasting a fortnight. The circumstances surrounding his death were suspicious and when a post-mortem revealed traces of poison his twenty-six-year-old wife Florence, an American woman, was charged with murder. It was claimed at her trial that her husband had died of natural causes, having frequently taken poisons as medicine. However, she was convicted and sentenced to death.

Besides being over twenty years older than his wife, Maybrick had been a hypochondriac, constantly taking medicines of one sort or another; he had also kept a mistress, as Florence discovered by chance in 1887. For her own part, Florence had entered into a liaison with a young bachelor named Alfred Brierley, with whom she had spent a weekend at a London hotel in March 1889. Shortly afterwards, following a scene at the Grand National, Maybrick had beaten Florence and given her a black eye. He had then made a new will, leaving her nothing.

Maybrick was sick on 27 April, and stayed in bed the next day, complaining of pains in his chest. Having received medical treatment, he was well enough to go to work on 1 May, but two days afterwards took to his bed again, suffering from pains in his legs and vomiting. During the next few days he suffered continually from vomiting and also complained of other symptoms, and though he seemed much better on 7 May, the improvement lasted only a day. Thereafter his condition worsened, and continued to do so until his death.

Living in a mansion, the Maybricks had four servants, including Alice Yapp, a nanny who looked after their two children. On or about 23 April the nanny and a maid saw arsenic-based fly-papers soaking in a basin in the couple's bedroom, and Alice Yapp mentioned this and other suspicious matters to two women who called to see Maybrick on 8 May. The same day, when Florence asked her to post a letter addressed to Alfred Brierley, the nanny found an excuse to open it instead. The letter said that Maybrick was 'sick unto death', and urged Brierley to relieve his mind of 'all fear of discovery', as the invalid was 'perfectly ignorant of everything'.

These matters were reported to Maybrick's two brothers, Edwin and Michael, who were both staying at the house at the time of his death, and because of this Florence was kept in confinement while the place was searched. The search resulted in the discovery of a sealed packet with a label which said, 'Arsenic — Poison' (to which had been added, 'for cats'), together with a number of bottles which all contained traces of arsenic.

Although the body, at a second examination, was found to contain far less than a fatal dose of this poison — and traces of strychnine, hyoscine, prussic acid and morphia were also found — much was made at Florence's trial of her buying and soaking of flypapers, which she had explained by saying that she used arsenic for cosmetic purposes. This, together with her admission that she had committed adultery, served to convince the jury that she was guilty, especially after the judge had summed up against her.

Florence Maybrick's death sentence was commuted to life imprisonment, and she was released in 1904, afterwards publishing a book about her experiences, entitled *My Fifteen Lost Years*. She died in Connecticut, at the age of seventy-eight, on 23 October 1941.

Body of John Whyte discovered, 1966

MAY 16

On 16 May 1966, the body of John Whyte, a forty-two-year-old former seaman with a record of housebreaking and theft, was found in a ditch near Nantwich, in Cheshire. He had been shot in the head and chest — though apparently not at the place where the body was discovered — and had been dead for at least three days. The Cheshire police, suspecting that he had been the victim of a gang-killing, asked Scotland Yard's help in tracing his movements during the previous few weeks.

John Whyte, a divorcee, was found to have been living for some time in hostels and lodging-houses. He had been in London at the end of March, and had hired a Morris 1100 car from a firm in Shepherd's

Bush. It was also learnt from a woman friend of his in Birkenhead — his home town — that he had said he was 'in trouble', but without explaining what he meant by this. The woman thought he had probably done something underhand.

As the investigation continued the police began to receive reports about the Morris 1100. On the evening of 3 May it had been seen parked without lights in Charing Cross, and during the following week it was seen at a caravan site in Skegness, where a man and a woman spent two hours cleaning its interior. Then, on 6 June, a woman was seen driving it near Doncaster — and finally, on 8 June, it was found burning on a piece of waste ground in south London. When bloodstains were discovered inside it the police were certain that it had been set on fire deliberately.

The couple who had been seen at the caravan site were identified as William John Clarke, aged forty-seven, and Nancy Patricia Hughes, forty, both of whom had recently finished serving eighteen-month prison sentences imposed for post office frauds. Clarke had a long record and had once been sent to Broadmoor after slashing a fellow prisoner with a broken bottle. He had spent only two of his last twenty-four years as a free man.

Clarke and Hughes, who lived together as man and wife, were traced to a hotel in Paddington, where evidence of further frauds was discovered. It was found that they had been involved with John Whyte in drawing money from post offices in various parts of the country by forging signatures on forms relating to stolen savings books. They were therefore taken into custody.

The police obtained no information from them about the death of John Whyte, Clarke suggesting that he could not tell them anything without putting his own life at risk. They were afterwards brought to trial in connection with the recent frauds and once again sent to prison. Clarke, on this occasion, was given ten years — reduced to seven on appeal — and Hughes two years.

But in the meantime the inquiries into Whyte's death went on, and the police learnt of a visit which Clarke and Hughes had made to a house in Morley, near Leeds, about a month before the crime had taken place. Clarke, during the course of this visit, had produced a gun and fired a bullet into the ceiling, from which it was now recovered by detectives. The bullet was found to have been fired from the same gun as those taken from John Whyte's body, and its discovery led to Clarke being charged with murder. It was believed that he had killed Whyte following a quarrel over the proceeds of their other crimes.

Clarke and Hughes were tried together at the Chester Assizes in November 1967. Clarke was convicted of murder and sentenced to life imprisonment; Hughes was sent to jail for three years for being an accessory after the fact. The jury's verdict in Clarke's case had been reached by a majority of ten to two.

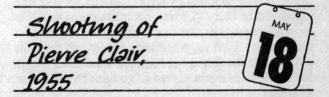

Shooting of Pierre Clair, 1955

At 8 o'clock in the morning on 18 May 1955, Pierre Clair, an accountant aged thirty-five, was approached by his former mistress as he left his hotel in the Latin Quarter of Paris to go to work. Simone Soursas, who was forty-two years old and seven months pregnant, had been waiting in the street to see him. But when she tried to speak to him he said brusquely, 'It's all over. Leave me alone!' Simone then drew an automatic pistol from under her coat and shot him four times, as a result of which Pierre Clair fell to the ground and died, begging her forgiveness.

The couple had known each other for three years, having met in a cinema one night while Simone, the wife of a radio mechanic working in the Sudan, was waiting to join her husband. Both were ugly, he having the additional misfortune of being timid and helpless while she had that of believing herself to be stupid. As soon as they became lovers she changed her mind about joining her husband and wrote to tell him that their marriage was at an end.

Richard Soursas returned to Paris as soon as he received the letter, his calmness and consideration convincing Simone that she had behaved ridiculously; she therefore went to the Sudan after all. But Pierre wrote to her frequently, flattering and cajoling her, and she, finding her new life dull, soon left her husband and rejoined Pierre in Paris. This time they went to the Côte d'Azur, where they lived together as cheaply as possible for the next two months.

Their affair had been a violent one from the beginning, for Pierre often beat her. But while the beatings were followed by reconciliations she was willing to suffer them. 'I loved his brutality as much as his tenderness,' she was to say when she was tried for his murder. Even so, when they finally left the Côte d'Azur and she found her husband waiting for her in Paris, she once again agreed to go back to the Sudan with him.

Pierre's perversity then took a new turn. Finding himself a younger and prettier mistress, he wrote to Simone, saying that he intended to commit suicide. 'I am completely possessed by a burning passion for you and I have reached the point of total despair for which there is no remedy but you,' he said. Within hours of receiving it she boarded a plane to Paris. But this time, though he agreed to resume the affair, he was less eager to be with her than before; the beatings became more frequent, the reconciliations less so. And, as luck would have it, she now found that she was pregnant.

Thereafter he behaved insufferably towards her. He taunted her over her ugliness, calling her his 'poor old woman', and made it clear that he no longer wanted her at all. During her seventh month of pregnancy, when she was suffering from low blood pressure, he gave her his jacket to repair, leaving a photograph of his other mistress in one of the pockets. Its discovery threw Simone into a state of utter despondency.

She bought the gun — or so she afterwards claimed — with the intention of taking her own life, but decided to go and see him again before doing so. It was then that the encounter which resulted in Pierre's death took place.

When Simone Soursas was brought to trial, the case for the prosecution was presented with more restraint than it might otherwise have been, the Advocate General conceding that the accused was 'worthy of commiseration'. She was found guilty only of manslaughter with extenuating circumstances and given a suspended sentence of five years' imprisonment. She was therefore set free.

While in jail she had given birth to her child — a little girl who was surprisingly pretty. The child was given to her as she left the court.

Body of Christopher Sabey discovered, 1968

MAY
20

On the morning of 20 May 1968, Christopher Sabey, the eight-year-old son of a publican, was found strangled near a disused gravel pit 200 yards from his home in the village of Buckden, in Huntingdonshire. He had left his home by bicycle early the previous afternoon, and his sister had begun to make inquiries about him when he was not back by 8.30 p.m. Later, during a search organized by the village policeman, his bicycle was found on a local building site, leaning against a pile of bricks.

Christopher had evidently been killed as he lay on the ground, his attacker kneeling on him and gripping his throat with both hands. As his body was fully dressed — apart from one shoe, which was found nearby — there was no apparent motive for the crime. The police also had difficulty obtaining information about his movements, as almost all of the village's inhabitants had been watching the F.A. Cup Final on television on the afternoon of 19 May, when the crime was committed.

However, they soon found a suspect: a youth of nineteen named Richard Nilsson, who lived in the village and worked as a labourer on the building site where the dead boy's bicycle had been found.

Nilsson, together with others employed on the site, had been interviewed on 20 May, when it was noticed that he was sweating and kept swallowing hard. It was afterwards found that he had been officially cautioned for indecent assaults on small boys and also that he had tried to strangle another boy some months earlier. He was therefore questioned again and proved unable to account for his movements on the afternoon of the 19th satisfactorily. But the police had no evidence against him and so were obliged to let him go.

Later, after he had been questioned several more times, and had changed his story repeatedly, dog hairs found on his clothes — from his own golden Labrador — and others found on Christopher Sabey's jersey were sent to the Home Office Central Research Establishment at Aldermaston to be analyzed by the new method of neutron activation. They were found to have similar trace-element characteristics.

As this was not, in itself, considered strong enough evidence to secure a conviction, detectives began collecting samples of hair from all other dogs in the village which appeared to be the same colour. Of the 144 samples thus obtained, ninety were discarded after microscopic examination and the other fifty-four, which were similar in structure as well as colour, were sent to Aldermaston for analysis. The tests proved that the hairs found on the dead boy could have come from only three dogs in the village, one of them being Nilsson's.

Nilsson had already admitted having seen Christopher on the day of the murder, saying that they had been at the building site together until 1.45 p.m. On being told the results of the tests, he said that the boy had taken some cigarettes from his pocket, suggesting that that explained the hairs on his clothes.

Certain now that Nilsson was the murderer, the police renewed their inquiries among the villagers, and this time found a witness who had seen him with the victim later than he had admitted on the afternoon in question. Mrs Colleen Harries remembered looking out of her window shortly after 4.30 p.m. and seeing Nilsson riding his moped with Christopher following on his bicycle. She later saw Nilsson walking alone near the building site.

On being questioned further on 17 July, Nilsson said that he had been on the site with Christopher between 4.30 p.m. and 5.15 p.m., and had then left him there. Though this was yet another change in his story, he persisted in denying that he was the culprit the police were seeking. He was charged with the murder.

At his trial at the Nottingham Assizes he pleaded not guilty. 'I had nothing to do with Christopher Sabey,' he told the court. 'I did not kill him. I had nothing to do with his death at all.' But the jury decided otherwise and he was sentenced to life imprisonment.

Murder of Walter Dinnivan, 1939

MAY
21

On the night of 21 May 1939, Walter Dinnivan, a retired garage proprietor, was found unconscious and bleeding in his ground-floor flat on the outskirts of Poole, in Dorset. He had been savagely battered and was suffering from multiple head wounds and a fractured skull; his attacker had also attempted to strangle him. The discovery was made when his granddaughter — who lived in the same flat — arrived home with her brother, with whom she had been to a dance. The old man was taken off to hospital, where he died from his injuries the following morning.

In the room in which the crime had been committed the police found a beer bottle — with beer in it — a tumbler and a whisky-glass, all lying on their sides on an occasional table. A woman's hair-curler, made in France, and a bloodstained brown paper bag, folded diagonally, lay on the floor nearby. And four cigarette ends were found: one on the tablecloth, two underneath the table and one on a settee cushion.

It seemed obvious that the person responsible had been drinking with Mr Dinnivan prior to the attack, and Joseph Williams, who lived about ten minutes' walk from the scene of the crime and had known the dead man for some forty years, was soon suspected. Williams, who lived in one room, was in serious financial difficulties; he had visited Mr Dinnivan frequently, and admitted to having borrowed £5 from him a few days before the murder.

Some brown paper bags similar to the one left at the scene were found in Williams' room; his right thumb-print was found on the tumbler, and his saliva was found to be of the same group as that on the four cigarette ends. Moreover, his wife was known to have had a hair-curler of the type which had been found in Mr Dinnivan's flat. Joseph Williams was accordingly brought to trial in Dorchester in October 1939.

Surprisingly, he was acquitted, and left the court a free man. But a few hours afterwards he told Norman Rae, the well-known crime reporter, 'The jury were wrong. I did it, so now I claim to be the second John Lee of Babbacombe, the man they couldn't hang.' He then insisted on returning to Poole the same night, in order to parade himself in the town where he was well known.

By the early hours of the morning, however, his nerves were in a bad state. Norman Rae, who had retired for the night, was woken up by Williams banging on his bedroom door. 'I have got to tell someone,' he sobbed over and over again. 'The jury were wrong. It was me!'

He was almost certainly telling the truth, but there was nothing that could be done about it. Having already stood trial for his life and been acquitted, he could not, under English law, be tried again for the same crime. Joseph Williams therefore remained free until his death in March 1951. The story of his confession was then published in the *News of the World*.

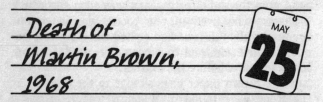

Death of Martin Brown, 1968

On 25 May 1968, the body of Martin Brown, aged four, was found in a derelict house in a slum area of Newcastle. It appeared that he had died as a result of swallowing pills from a bottle found at the scene, but on 27 May, police investigating a case of vandalism at a nearby nursery school found four scribbled notes in a child's handwriting, one of them referring to the 'murder' of Martin Brown.

Two months later Brian Howe, aged three, was found strangled on a piece of waste ground in the same area, his stomach marked with small cuts and his legs with puncture marks. The pathologist who examined his body said that little force had been needed to kill him and that the person responsible could have been another child.

The police therefore asked 1200 children in the district to fill in questionnaires about what they had done on the day of Brian Howe's murder, and interviewed those who gave evasive or unclear answers. Among the children interviewed were two girls, Norma Bell, aged thirteen, and Mary Bell, eleven, who were not related to each other but were close friends. These were questioned a number of times, changed their statements twice, and gave the impression of knowing more about the crime than they cared to admit.

Mary Bell, the more assertive of the two, was an intelligent child, but a liar and an exhibitionist. At one point, she claimed to have seen Brian in the company of an older boy, and said that she saw this boy hitting him; she also said that the boy in question had had a pair of scissors with a broken blade. This detail was to place Mary strongly under suspicion when the boy she named was found to have been elsewhere, for — unbeknown to the public — a pair of scissors with a broken blade had been found at the scene of the crime.

Norma Bell then made a statement accusing Mary of having attacked the boy in her own presence, pushing him to the ground and struggling violently with him. She denied having taken part in the crime herself, saying that she had run away when Mary asked her to help. Later, she said, they went back to the waste ground together, and Mary marked the boy's body with the scissors and a razor. Mary, however, said that the statement was a lie and that it was Norma who had killed Brian.

The two girls were both arrested, and charged with murdering Martin Brown as well as Brian Howe. At their trial, which began at the Newcastle Assizes on 5 December 1968, Norma was overawed by the proceedings but Mary remained calm and self-possessed throughout. Norma was acquitted and Mary — who was said to be suffering from an abnormality of mind 'such as substantially impaired her mental responsibility for her acts and omissions in doing or being a party to this killing' — was convicted of manslaughter on both counts.

Sentenced to detention for life, Mary Bell was sent to a special unit of an approved school, as no mental hospital would accept her. In 1970 her house-master in this institution was brought to trial, accused of indecently assaulting her, but was acquitted when the evidence against him was found to have been fabricated. Then, in September 1977, she absconded from an open prison, in the company of another inmate, and was recaptured three days later.

She was released in 1980.

Suspicious illness of Mrs Amy Clements, 1947

On the evening of 26 May 1947, Mrs Amy Clements, the wife of a doctor living in Southport, Lancashire, was admitted to the Astley Bank Nursing Home, her husband having told a local colleague by telephone that she was dying of a cerebral tumour. When she arrived there, already in a coma, she was examined by the superintendent, Dr Andrew Brown, who formed the opinion that she was suffering from morphine poisoning. She died the following morning, without regaining consciousness.

A post-mortem was carried out on Dr Brown's instructions by Dr James Houston, a young pathologist at the Southport Infirmary. Houston found no evidence of a cerebral tumour, nor did he notice any signs of morphine poisoning. His report stated that Mrs Clements had died of myeloid leukaemia, and he made out her death certificate to that effect. But Brown refused to accept this finding and informed the area coroner of his dissatisfaction.

Police inquiries followed and Mrs Clements' funeral was postponed at the last minute — after mourners had gathered at the church — so that a second post-mortem could be performed. The dead woman's husband, Dr Robert Clements, was now suspected of having murdered her.

Clements, a sixty-seven-year-old Irishman and a Fellow of the Royal College of Surgeons, had been married four times and each of his first three wives had also died. In the case of the third Mrs Clements, who died in 1939, the cause of death had been given as tuberculosis, but a woman doctor — a friend of the deceased — was suspicious of this and gave information to the Chief Constable of Southport which led to a post-mortem being ordered. But by the time the order was made the body had been cremated, so nothing more could be done.

Amy Clements had, like two of her predecessors, been a wealthy woman whose money had enabled her husband to live extravagantly. The police learnt that for several weeks her skin had been gradually turning yellow and that she had frequently lapsed into unconsciousness, with her husband apparently knowing when this was about to occur. They found, too, that Clements had had his telephone disconnected, thus preventing his wife keeping in contact with her friends. He had also been writing prescriptions for morphine sulphate tablets for patients who never received them and did not know that they had been prescribed.

After the postponement of the funeral, Clements was found unconscious in the kitchen of his flat, with a note which said: 'To whom it may concern — I can no longer tolerate this diabolical insult to me.' He died a few hours later, his death having been caused by an injection of morphine.

The second post-mortem on his wife revealed that she had also died of morphine poisoning, as Dr Brown had suspected.

Appalled at his own mistake, Dr James Houston took his own life on 2 June, with a massive dose of sodium cyanide. He left a note saying, 'I have for some time been aware that I have been making mistakes. I have not profited by my experience. I was convinced that Mrs Clements died of leukaemia, and accordingly destroyed the vital organs after completing my autopsy.' The destruction of the organs in question had made the second post-mortem an extremely difficult task to perform.

A coroner's inquest found that Mrs Clements had been murdered by her husband. The police suspected that Clements had murdered each of his other wives as well. However, they decided not to investigate these cases in view of the fact that he, too, was now dead.

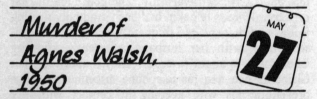

Murder of Agnes Walsh, 1950

On the morning of 27 May 1950, the body of a naked woman was found in a boarding-house in Sussex Gardens, Paddington. She had been punched six times in the face during the course of a fierce struggle — two of her injuries suggesting that her attacker had worn a ring — and had also had a handkerchief thrust into her mouth and pressed against the back of her throat. Afterwards, when she was already dead, one of her own stockings had been tied round her neck, so that it appeared at first that she had died from strangulation. The discovery was made about 10 a.m., when the rooms were being cleaned — by which time the woman had been dead for several hours.

The body was found to be that of Agnes Walsh, a known prostitute aged twenty-two, who had frequented the Piccadilly area in search of clients. She had arrived at the boarding-house the previous evening with a young man, who had entered their names in the visitors' register as 'Mr and Mrs Davidson' and given an indecipherable address in County Durham — though even this was only made out later, when the entry was subjected to close scrutiny. Her underclothes were neatly folded on a chair — showing that she had removed them herself — and although certain valuables were missing, the contents of her handbag had not been touched.

Margaret Walsh, the dead woman's sister — who was also a prostitute — told the police that she had seen Agnes in Piccadilly the previous evening, speaking to a man who was a stranger to her. She was unable to give a good description of this man, and inquiries among other prostitutes who had been in the area at the time revealed only that he had been a sad-faced, softly-spoken man with an accent. However, these details were circulated to all the main police stations in London, and printed in the *Police Gazette*, together with a sketch of a cocktail watch on a snake bracelet known to have been stolen from the dead woman. At the same time the police in County Durham were asked to make inquiries about a man named Davidson.

No further information was obtained for some days, and a search for the wanted man in London proved unavailing. But suddenly the police in Houghton-le-Spring, County Durham, sent news of the disappearance of a local man named Donald Davidson, aged twenty-nine, who had driven off in his sports car that morning, wearing bakers' clothes and a sports jacket, and had not been seen since. His departure had followed the publication of newspaper reports the same morning, stating that Scotland Yard officers were making inquiries in Durham about the murderer of Agnes Walsh.

Davidson's description was circulated to the police in neighbouring counties, but a few hours later he was found dead near Finchley Priory, just a few miles from his home. He had shot himself.

It was later learnt that Davidson and a friend had arrived in London on 25 May, while on a fortnight's motoring holiday, and had booked into a hotel in Euston. The following evening Davidson had gone out alone, returning on the morning of the 27th with his face and hands badly scratched. He explained his injuries to his friend by saying that he had been involved in a drunken brawl.

He remained in the hotel that day — though he had previously intended to go to Epsom for the Derby — but sent out several times for newspapers, claiming that he was interested in the horse-racing news. Later the two friends left London to return home, Davidson insisting that they should drive through the night.

Davidson was generally a quiet man who rarely drank, but was known to have a quick temper. It was assumed by the police that on the night in question Agnes Walsh had given offence to him in some way and that he had attacked her while he was drunk, and stolen some of her possessions to make it appear that robbery had been the motive for the crime. Then, having returned home, he had worked in his parents' bakery for a few days until his fear of arrest became so intense that he decided to take his own life.

On the day of his death he drove to an empty caravan at Finchley Priory, where he attempted to gas himself with the use of the stove but succeeded only in causing an explosion, as the gas was not poisonous. Blown out through the doorway into a field, he found himself badly burnt and bleeding, and it was only after falling into some bushes as he staggered about that he finally shot himself.

At the inquest on the body of Agnes Walsh a senior police officer, on being asked what he would have done if he had found Davidson alive, replied, 'I would have apprehended him and brought him back to London on a charge of murder.' But this was not proof that Davidson had killed her, and the jury returned a verdict of murder by some person or persons unknown.

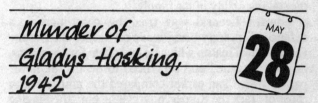

Murder of Gladys Hosking, 1942

MAY
28

On 28 May 1942, an Australian woman, Gladys Hosking, was found strangled in a street in Melbourne. There was no obvious motive for the murder, which was the third such crime in Melbourne that month. But when a serviceman who had been on sentry duty at a US army camp heard the news, he provided police with information which led to the arrest of the person responsible.

The soldier, an Australian, reported that on the night in question he had challenged a GI arriving back there in an untidy state. The GI, who was out of breath and wearing a dirty uniform, was only allowed to enter the camp after explaining that he had fallen down in a nearby park, said the sentry. His report led to all US troops in the camp being called out on parade, so that he could identify the GI concerned.

The GI was found to be Edward Joseph Leonski, a Texan, whose tent-mate gave police further inform-ation about him. Leonski, said the tent-mate, had lately become very emotional on occasions, and had told him, 'I'm a Dr Jekyll and Mr Hyde! I killed! I killed!' He was also known to have been keeping newspaper reports about the Melbourne murders.

Leonski was taken into custody and confessed that he had killed all three women, saying that he had done so because he wanted 'to get their voices'. In one case — that of the second woman, Pauline Thompson — he said that his victim had sung to him as they walked through the streets together, her voice so sweet and soft that he could feel himself 'going mad about it'. It was found that there was a history of mental instability in his family.

Edward Leonski was tried by court-martial, a defence of insanity being made on his behalf. Despite the ludicrous reason which he had given for his crimes, he was convicted and sentenced to death, the newspapers which had earlier compared the murders with those of 'Jack the Ripper' now calling him 'the Singing Strangler'. He was hanged at Pentridge Jail on 9 November 1942.

Barbara Songhurst found murdered, 1953

JUNE
1

On the morning of 1 June 1953, Barbara Songhurst, aged sixteen, of Teddington in Middlesex, was found dead in the River Thames near Richmond, Surrey; she had been battered over the head, stabbed and then raped before being thrown into the water. The discovery led to fears that eighteen-year-old Christine Reed (who, like Barbara, had been missing since the previous afternoon, when they had gone out cycling together) had also been murdered, and these fears which were confirmed when Christine's body was found in the same river at Richmond five days later. She, too, had been raped after being murdered in a similar manner.

It was learnt that on the evening of 31 May the two girls had been in the company of three youths who were camping on the river bank, and that they had been attacked shortly after leaving to cycle home. Other people camping on the bank reported hearing screams about 11 p.m., and one witness claimed to have seen a man riding a woman's bicycle along the towpath about 11.20 p.m. But no clue to the man's identity was discovered until several weeks later, when Alfred Charles Whiteway, a twenty-two-year-old building labourer, came to the attention of the police officers conducting the investigation.

Whiteway was a married man who, because of housing difficulties, had been living with his parents at Teddington while his wife stayed with hers at Kingston in Surrey. He had a criminal record for theft and was already in custody for attacking a woman and a girl on Oxshott Heath, not far from Kingston. It was for this reason that he was questioned in connection with the murders.

He denied being the person responsible, saying that he had been with his wife on the evening in question, but admitted that he had known Barbara Songhurst, as she had once lived near him in Sydney Road, Teddington. Some weeks afterwards, while being questioned at New Scotland Yard, he confessed that he had killed the two girls — only to deny the offences when he was formally charged on 20 August.

At the time of his arrest Whiteway had had an axe in his possession, but this was not realized, and he managed to conceal it under the seat of a patrol car in which he was being taken to Kingston police station. A constable cleaning the vehicle the following day found the axe, took it home and chopped wood with it, unaware of its importance until a month later. It was then found to match head injuries which the two murdered teenagers had received.

Whiteway was brought to trial at the Old Bailey in October 1953, charged with the murder of Barbara Songhurst. The axe was produced in evidence against him, his fifteen-year-old sister telling the court that it was similar to one that was missing from their home. The prosecution also produced a knife, which the prisoner — whose hobby was knife-throwing — had allegedly confessed to using during the course of the crime, together with a bloodstained shoe which he had been wearing that evening.

Though he denied having confessed to the murders, claiming that his statement had been fabricated by the police, Whiteway was found guilty and sentenced to death. He was hanged at Wandsworth Prison on 22 December 1953.

Three executed at San Quentin, 1955

JUNE
3

On 3 June 1955, Barbara Graham, a thirty-two-year-old murderess, and two male accomplices were executed in the gas chamber of San Quentin Prison, California, for the murder of an elderly woman in Burbank two years previously. The executions received much publicity, and a controversial film based loosely on Barbara Graham's life story — *I Want to Live*, starring Susan Hayward — was released a few months afterwards. This gave the impression that she was innocent of the crime for which she had been sentenced, which was not the case at all.

The crime had been committed on 9 March 1953, when Barbara Graham, her two fellow-condemned, John Albert Santo and Emmett Perkins, together with a third man named John True, forced their way into the home of sixty-two-year-old Mrs Mabel Monahan, a former vaudeville star whom they beat savagely in an attempt to discover the whereabouts of a large sum of money rumoured to be hidden there. When this got them nowhere — for there was no truth in the rumour — they ransacked the house, then killed their victim in cold blood before leaving empty-handed.

A fourth accomplice, Baxter Shorter, had at first kept watch for them outside, but fled on realizing what had happened to Mrs Monahan. He later agreed to testify against the others, but was abducted at gunpoint and killed before any charges could be brought against them. His body was never found.

Barbara Graham was an occasional prostitute and a drug-taker who already had a record for various offences; she had been married four times, each of the first three marriages ending in divorce. Though it was her involvement which attracted most of the publicity to the case, she had only been asked to take part because the others needed a woman to induce Mrs Monahan to open her door. But she did so without any qualms, and was as violent as the rest of them.

As Shorter could not be produced to give evidence against the others, Barbara was given an opportunity to do so, but scornfully refused. She was later tricked by a police officer into agreeing to pay for an alibi: a fact revealed with devastating effect during the course of the trial. In the meantime, John True, a deep-sea diver, was given the chance to appear as a prosecution witness — and he agreed to do so.

The three defendants were convicted and sentenced to death in September 1953. Santo and Perkins were afterwards convicted of the murder of a gold-mine proprietor in December 1951, and also of the murders of a supermarket owner and three of his children in October 1952.

Shortly before her death Barbara Graham confessed her guilt to the warden of San Quentin, but this was not made known to the public until several years later.

Baxter Shorter was declared legally dead in 1960, seven years after his disappearance.

Body of Albert Greenfield discovered, 1961

JUNE
4

On 4 June 1961, the body of Albert Reginald Greenfield, a blacksmith aged forty-one, was found under an old shed standing alongside the Domain Baths in Sydney; he had been stabbed over thirty times and his genitals had been hacked off in a frenzied attack during the course of the previous night. The gruesome nature of the mutilation led police officers to believe that the crime had been inspired by jealousy, and that the culprit would prove to be an outraged husband or lover. They did not anticipate difficulty in bringing him to justice.

However, they made no headway with the investigation, and the case was still unsolved on 21 November, when a second corpse, similarly mutilated and with many stab wounds, was found in a public lavatory in Moore Park. The victim this time was

Ernest William Cobbin, also aged forty-one, a married man with two children who had been living apart from his family. This second murder was clearly the work of the person who had killed Greenfield, so police officers had to abandon their original theory. This time, they decided that the killer was 'a psychopath homosexual ... killing to satisfy some twisted urge'.

But still they failed to identify him, and on 31 March the following year Frank Gladstone McLean, a war pensioner with a number of convictions for minor offences, was found lying in the gutter in Little Bourke Street, in the suburb of Darlinghurst. He had been stabbed in the neck a number of times and mutilated, and was in too bad a state to give any information about his attacker before he died. The couple who found him told the police that their baby had been crying as they arrived at the scene, and that they thought this may have warned the killer of their approach.

These 'Mutilator Murders' were by now causing much concern. As the police were still unable to catch the person responsible, the Government, which had earlier offered a reward of £1000, now offered £5000 for information leading to his arrest. But this was likewise to no avail, and it was not until May 1963 that he was finally arrested. Even then, it was only after an extraordinary sequence of events.

In November 1962 a man was found dead under a shop in Burwood Road, in the suburb of Concord. The body, which was badly decomposed, was identified as that of Alan Edward Brennan, an employee of the postal service in Alexandria, south Sydney, where he had given the shop address as his own, and it was under that name that it was buried, in spite of misgivings on the part of the coroner. But in April 1963 another post office employee reported seeing Brennan alive, and a belated examination of clothes found beside the body was carried out. This resulted in the discovery of prison markings, showing that they had been issued to Patrick Joseph Hackett, a man who had served a short sentence in October 1962 for using indecent language.

Further reports were received, confirming that Brennan was still alive, and it was now accepted that the dead man was Hackett. But a garage owner whose business was next door to the place where the body had been found said that he had seen Brennan inside the shop with another man on the evening before his disappearance. The following day there had been a notice in the shop, saying that the owner had cut his hand and would be away for three weeks.

After an extensive search the missing man was found in Melbourne, where he was working as a railway porter. On being arrested, he said that his real name was William MacDonald, and that he was an English immigrant, aged thirty-nine. He agreed to return to Sydney to stand trial, rather than face extradition proceedings, and was charged with all four murders. When he appeared for trial the Crown proceeded with the charge of murdering Patrick Hackett on 3 November 1962.

MacDonald admitted that he had killed Hackett, saying that he had met him while under the influence of drink and feeling a compulsive urge to kill. In the opinion of three psychiatrists, he was a paranoid schizophrenic, but the jury rejected their evidence and found him guilty of murder. Sentenced to life imprisonment, he was later transferred to the Morisset Hospital for the Criminally Insane.

On 6 June 1961 a man went to West Ham police station in London with a loaded pistol in his pocket after hearing that his wife had made a complaint about him. John Hall arrived in a sports car and gave a general impression of being well-off. He was seen by Inspector Philip Pawsey and Sergeant George Hutchins, who informed him that a warrant had been issued for his arrest on a charge of causing grievous bodily harm.

Hall, however, had no intention of being arrested, and when an attempt was made to search him he pulled out the pistol and forced the police officers to keep their distance while he moved towards the door. He fled from the building with Pawsey, Hutchins and PC Charles Cox in pursuit, and soon began firing at them. The inspector and the sergeant were both killed, and PC Cox was seriously injured.

The chase was taken up by other officers, some of whom had police dogs with them. Even so, it lasted for eight hours, with further shots being fired — though there were no more casualties — before the culprit finally took refuge in a telephone kiosk three miles away. He then turned the gun on himself and fired, wounding himself fatally; he died in hospital eight days later.

John Hall was a man of no settled occupation; he had been a lorry-driver, a mechanic, a commercial traveller, a book-keeper and the proprietor of a pet-shop. He was keen on activities such as surf-riding, speedboat-racing and flying, as well as pistol-shooting.

He had been married — for the second time — less

than two months earlier, his first marriage having been
dissolved two years previously.

Second life sentence for Kiernan Kelly, 1984

JUNE 7

On 7 June 1984, a fifty-four-year-old Irish tramp who
told police that he had killed nine people in thirty
years, was sentenced to life imprisonment at the Old
Bailey for the second time in a fortnight. Kiernan
Kelly, an alcoholic, had been convicted of manslaughter, having killed a fellow vagrant in a police
cell in Clapham, south-west London, the previous
August. He was said by a psychiatrist to be 'incorrigible in penal terms and incurable in medical terms' —
a description which the trial judge said was 'plainly
right'. His earlier life sentence had been for the
murder of a drinking companion — a crime committed in 1975.

Kelly, who had been living rough in England since
his arrival from the Irish Republic in 1953, had forty-
one convictions for drink-related offences. In 1977 he
was charged with killing another tramp in Kennington Park, south London, but when he appeared for
trial the jury acquitted him. Then, in the summer of
1983, he was charged with attempted murder, after
allegedly trying to push yet another tramp under an
underground train. This time the jury could not
agree, so a re-trial was ordered — and Kelly was again
acquitted. The crime in the police cell took place not
long afterwards.

The victim was fifty-five-year-old William Boyd,

who was sharing the cell with another man when Kelly was locked in with them. Kelly, who had been arrested for drunkenness and robbery, became incensed when Boyd began shouting and swearing during the course of the night and, making a ligature with his socks and shoelaces, used it to strangle him. The crime was followed by his confession that he had killed nine people, one of them being Hector Fisher, a sixty-seven-year-old retired printer who had been stabbed to death in a Clapham churchyard eight years previously.

The information contained in Kelly's fifty-two-page statement was not very detailed, and police suspected him of exaggerating the number of people he had killed. But after investigating the matter they were satisfied that he had killed at least five times, and in the case of Hector Fisher they felt justified in charging him with murder. It was for this offence that he was given his first life sentence, the judge telling Kelly that he was a dangerous man, particularly when he was drunk.

At his manslaughter trial two weeks later Kelly was said to have a violent temper and to have developed obsessions about other tramps. 'This conviction for a second killing confirms that the view of the consultant psychiatrist who says that you are incorrigible in penal terms and incurable in medical terms is plainly right,' said the judge on this occasion. In passing sentence, he went on to remark that Kelly might be considered too dangerous ever to be released.

Murder of Emily Pye, 1957

On the afternoon of 8 June 1957, Emily Pye, an eighty-year-old spinster, was beaten to death in her corner shop in Gibbet Street, Halifax, during the course of a thunderstorm. Her murderer escaped with a small amount of money from the till, leaving a much larger sum untouched in her living quarters. The crime was reported by the victim's niece and her husband, who found the body in the back room, partly covered by a rug. A few hours later the Chief Constable of Halifax requested the assistance of Scotland Yard.

Though Miss Pye's attacker had smashed her skull with a fire-iron, the pathologist who carried out a post-mortem on her body found that most of her injuries had been inflicted with fists. Detective Superintendent Herbert Hannam, the Scotland Yard officer in charge of the case, afterwards claimed that the nature of the injuries suggested that her killer suffered from mental abberation.

The police began interviewing local people, at the same time making public appeals for information from anyone who had visited the shop on the day of the murder. It was suspected that the culprit was a local man, who may even have been one of Miss Pye's customers. However, little progress was made, and before long Hannam complained at a press conference that 'vital information' was being withheld. He believed that somebody was shielding the perpetrator of the crime.

A request was made to Interpol to trace three people known to have been in Halifax on 8 June, who had since left the country. While awaiting the results of this Hannam held a conference with officers who had investigated two similar crimes in the same county: one in Bradford two years earlier, the other in Leeds seven years before that. The interviewing of local people continued.

Then in August, after 15,000 statements had been taken, a search was made for eight men whom Hannam said he wanted to interview. And on 10 August it was announced that 'considerable progress' had been made on the case. Yet no arrest followed, and some months afterwards — following several other optimistic statements to the press — the investigation was terminated. The case remains unsolved.

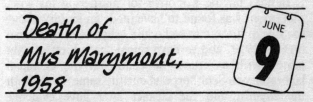

Death of Mrs Marymont, 1958

On 9 June 1958, Mrs Mary Helen Marymont, the forty-three-year-old wife of an American army sergeant stationed in Britain, was rushed to the US Air Force hospital in Sculthorpe, Norfolk. She was in a state of collapse after becoming ill the previous day, and her husband, Master Sergeant Marcus Marymont, was warned that her condition was so grave that she might not recover.

Marymont appeared to be unconcerned about this, and tried to draw the hospital's general medical officer into a discussion about his marital problems. His wife died shortly afterwards, and a post-mortem was carried out against his wishes. Her organs were then sent to Scotland Yard's Forensic Laboratory, where it was found that she had been poisoned with arsenic.

Marymont, who was six years younger than his wife, was found to have been having an affair with Cynthia Taylor, a young married woman living in Maidenhead, Berkshire, and letters found in his desk showed that he had had a motive for his wife's murder.

Mrs Taylor, who was separated from her husband, managed a local garden stores. Marymont had met her at a Maidenhead club two years earlier, and within a few months they had become deeply involved with each other. Marymont, pretending to be divorced, asked her to marry him, and she said that she would when she was free to do so. She was waiting for her own divorce with this in mind at the time of Mrs Marymont's death.

Besides having a motive for murdering his wife, Marymont was found to have made an inquiry about the sale of arsenic at a chemist's shop in Maidenhead in May 1958, and to have raised the subject of that poison with a cleaner sweeping out the chemical laboratory at Sculthorpe about the same time. Both the chemist and the cleaner later gave evidence against him.

Marymont was arrested just over a month after his wife's death, and in December 1958 he was tried by a US General Court Martial in Denham, Buckinghamshire, for murder and adultery — the latter being a punishable offence under American military law. The trial lasted ten days, with Cynthia Taylor giving evidence for seven and a half hours; it resulted in the prisoner being convicted on both charges and sentenced to hard labour for life.

Later his conviction for adultery was set aside, and his life sentence — which he was serving in Fort Leavenworth Prison, Kansas — was reduced to thirty-five years.

Murder of Zoe Wade, 1984

On 13 June 1984, firemen found the naked body of Zoe Wade, an unmarried woman aged forty-two, in the bedroom of her council flat in Bradford, Yorkshire. She had been raped and strangled, and her killer, twenty-six-year-old James Pollard had splashed cleaning solution on her body before setting fire to the place. Pollard was a known offender with a grudge against Miss Wade, and police suspected right from the start that he was the culprit. On being arrested shortly afterwards, he made a confession.

Miss Wade, a shy, nervous person who liked to keep herself to herself, had been raped and beaten by the same man after he had forced his way into her home in January 1982. A former neighbour, Pollard had warned her on that occasion, 'Don't call the police, or I will kill you!' He had afterwards been sentenced to four and a half years' imprisonment, having pleaded guilty to a charge of rape at the Leeds Crown Court, but served only sixteen months before being released on parole.

His victim, in the meantime, had suffered a great deal as a result of the crime. She was frightened to go out, and could not stand the company of men; she was also worried about what would happen when Pollard came out of jail — so worried, in fact, that she asked her local Housing Department to move her to a different address. But this request was made in vain, and when Pollard was released nobody told her about it. Miss Wade, who worked as a machinist, was therefore taken by surprise when she arrived home on the day of the murder, and her attacker was once again able to force his way into her flat without difficulty.

An examination of Pollard's clothes led to the discovery of incriminating fibres, and Miss Wade's purse — with his fingerprints on it — was found in the men's lavatory of a public house just across the road from her home. Pollard claimed that he had only gone to see her because she had failed to reply to a letter of apology which he had sent to her from prison; he also denied that he had raped her again, saying that he had killed her unintentionally while trying 'to shut her up'. He even pretended that the fire at her flat had been caused by accident.

Needless to say, he was not believed, and charges of rape and murder were brought against him. Pollard duly appeared for trial in Leeds on 5 February 1985, this time denying both offences. Under cross-examination, he admitted going to Miss Wade's flat, but denied that he had intended to kill her, saying, 'I wanted to talk to her ... I wanted to say I was sorry.'

Miss Wade had invited him in, and taken off her clothes of her own accord, he continued. At this, he had told her to get dressed again, but she, on hearing a loud noise from the direction of the front door, had looked startled, and given him the impression that she was about to scream. As a result, he had grabbed hold of her round the neck, but released her while she was still alive. 'I threw a bottle of Ajax at her because I was frightened and mad,' he said.

He admitted that he had taken off his trousers, but denied that this had been for the purpose of having sexual intercourse. 'There was no reason,' he said. 'I just took them off.'

The jury retired for an hour and twenty minutes before returning a verdict of guilty on both counts. The judge then told the prisoner that he was dangerous and vengeful, adding, 'In my view, you will remain dangerous for many years to come.' Pollard was then sentenced to life imprisonment for the murder and ten years' imprisonment for the rape, the judge informing him that he would remain in jail for at least twenty years, and perhaps a lot longer.

Even so, the news that a rapist had been released after serving only sixteen months — in spite of having threatened to kill his victim — caused much disquiet, as was only to be expected.

Murder of Countess Skarbek, 1952

JUNE
15

Late at night on 15 June 1952, a woman was stabbed to death in the foyer of the Shelbourne Hotel in London's Earls Court. The crime was witnessed by members of the hotel staff, and the police were called to the scene without delay. The killer, forty-one-year-old Dennis Muldowney, made no attempt to escape. 'I built all my dreams around her, but she was playing me for a fool!' he said self-piteously.

The victim, an attractive woman in her thirties, was Polish by birth but spoke English and several other languages fluently. Though generally known as Christine Granville, she was, in fact, the Countess Krystyna Skarbek, a wartime British Intelligence agent whose exploits in Occupied Europe had brought her fame which she did not want.

She had met Muldowney the previous year while she was working as a stewardess aboard an ocean liner, and a friendship had developed between them. They continued to see each other when Muldowney left the ship and became a night porter at the Reform Club in London. But he was possessive about her, resenting her association with other men, and when she suddenly became engaged to an old wartime colleague, Muldowney began following her.

On the day of the murder Christine had spent the evening with some Polish friends at a café not far from her hotel; one of them afterwards saw her to the hotel door, where he stood talking to her for a few minutes. Muldowney, hiding in the shadow of the basement steps, heard her say that she would soon be going to Belgium for a short holiday, and when the friend left he rushed into the hotel after her.

'You're not leaving me!' he cried. 'Not now!'

He immediately drove the dagger five inches into her chest, then sat staring at her body as it lay at his feet.

Christine's funeral was attended by wartime heroes from both sides of the Iron Curtain. Medals found in her hotel room, including the George Medal and the Croix de Guerre, were displayed beside the grave.

Brought to trial at the Old Bailey, Dennis Muldowney pleaded guilty to her murder and was sentenced to death, the proceedings lasting a mere three minutes. He was hanged at Pentonville Prison on 30 September 1952.

Double murder in Bignell Wood, 1956

JUNE
17

On 17 June 1956, a motorist driving through the New Forest near Cadnam, Hampshire, stopped to help an injured man who was leaning over the bonnet of a parked car. The man, who had a four-inch knife wound in his stomach, staggered towards him and claimed to have seen a murder — which he also described as 'a fight with two women' — in a nearby wood. The motorist summoned help, and Albert William Goozee, a thirty-three-year-old labourer and former merchant seaman, was rushed to hospital.

A policeman went into Bignell Wood to investigate and found two bodies near the remains of a picnic. Mrs Lydia Leakey, aged fifty-three, of Alexandra Road, Parkstone, near Poole in Dorset, had been stabbed and also struck with an axe; her daughter Norma, a girl of fourteen, had stab wounds in her chest and stomach. There was a wood fire still burning, tea in an aluminium teapot, and warm water in a tin kettle. The knife with which all the stab-wounds — including Goozee's — had been inflicted was later found in the injured man's car.

Goozee told the police that he had been Mrs Leakey's lover for over a year, having moved into her home as a lodger in January 1955. At that time Mrs Leakey had slept with Norma in one bedroom, while her husband, a machine operator who had lost one leg, slept in another. But as soon as she started her affair with Goozee, Mrs Leakey began to spend her nights with him, returning to the room she shared with her daughter just before her husband's alarm clock woke him up.

The situation was further complicated by the fact that Norma, who was also attracted to Goozee, went on frequent outings with the couple, and sometimes joined them in bed.

Eventually, in December 1955, Goozee joined the army, signing on for twelve years, and was sent to Catterick, in Yorkshire. Mrs Leakey wrote to him almost every day, begging him to return, but for some time he refused. She then threatened to tell the police that he had had sexual intercourse with Norma, who was still only thirteen — and who, in fact, was still a virgin at her death, as the post-mortem revealed. Not long after that, however, Goozee returned to Mrs Leakey as both lodger and lover, she having given him the money to buy himself out of the army.

This time the affair was even more complicated than before, because Norma insisted on being present when the couple made love, and threatened to tell her father of their relationship if they tried to prevent her doing so. Then Mr Leakey suddenly left home — only to move back into the house a few weeks later and order Goozee to leave. And when Goozee did this, Mrs Leakey once again persuaded him to return.

Thereafter, Goozee was frequently told to leave and just as often induced to stay, until the first week of June 1956, when he moved into other lodgings in Parkstone. Even then, Mrs Leakey continued to pursue him and persuaded him to take Norma and her for a picnic, saying that she had something she wanted to tell him.

As for what actually happened at that picnic, Goozee gave several different accounts, the last of them in December 1956, when he was on trial in Winchester. In this he stated that after sending Norma off to pick blue-bells, Mrs Leakey had asked him to make love to her, promising that it would be for the last time. But while they were lying together on a rug beside the car, Norma reappeared and, calling her mother 'a dirty rotten beast', attacked her with the axe which they had brought along to chop firewood. Mrs Leakey, whose head was bleeding, afterwards stabbed first Goozee — while he was trying to help her — and then Norma, who had managed to get between them.

But no credence could be given to this story, because most of the blood on the knife-blade matched samples of Goozee's own blood, which was of a different group from that of Mrs Leakey and her daughter and showed that he had been stabbed *after* them. It was therefore contended that he had killed them both, intending to commit suicide afterwards.

Convicted of murdering Norma Leakey, Goozee was sentenced to death. His sentence was later commuted to life imprisonment.

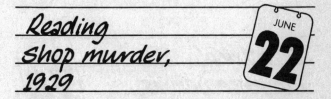

Reading Shop murder, 1929

JUNE 22

Shortly after 6 p.m. on 22 June 1929, Alfred Oliver, a sixty-year-old tobacconist, was found lying on the floor of his shop in Reading, Berkshire, suffering from head injuries. He had been attacked during the previous few minutes — while his wife was out walking their dog — and his assailant had snatched the contents of the till. Mr Oliver was unable to give a clear account of what had happened, and died of his wounds the following day.

Suspicion fell on Philip Yale Drew, an American actor in a touring company which was performing a play called *The Monster* in a local theatre that week. Drew was a man of distinctive appearance, and several witnesses claimed to have seen him near the shop about the time of the murder.

Though no charge was brought against him, Drew was subjected to a searching examination at the subsequent inquest, the coroner — a friend of the dead man — treating him almost as though he was a prisoner on trial. But the evidence was far from convincing, and after hearing about sixty witnesses the jury brought his ordeal to an end by returning a verdict of 'murder by person or persons unknown'.

This was greeted with approval by crowds thronging the streets, and the coroner's own conduct became the subject of much criticism. Even so, the affair ruined Drew's career, and he later became destitute.

The crime was never solved.

Murder of Florence Dennis, 1894

JUNE
24

On the evening of 24 June 1894, Florence Dennis, a young single woman, left her sister's home in Southend, Essex, to meet James Canham Read, a married man with eight children who worked as a clerk at the Royal Albert Docks in Woolwich. Read had formerly been her lover, and Florence had written to him five days previously, asking what 'arrangements' he had made in view of the fact that she was pregnant. He turned up to meet her with a revolver in his pocket, took her for a walk and then shot her. Florence's body was found in a ditch near the village of Prittlewell the following day.

Her sister, Mrs Ayriss, knew Read personally. He had been her lover, too, and in fact had had a child by her: it was as a result of this liaison that he had met Florence in 1892. So when her sister failed to return, Mrs Ayriss sent him a telegram, asking what had become of her. This worried Read so much that — having replied that he had not seen 'the young person' for eighteen months — he stole £160 from his employers and absconded from his home in Jamaica

Road, Stepney. Mrs Ayriss, in the meantime, had reported her sister's disappearance to the police.

Read was discovered a fortnight later at Mitcham, in Surrey, where he was living with another woman and child and known as Edgar Benson. It was then learnt that while living with his own wife — and having an affair with Florence Dennis — he had been spending almost every weekend with 'Mrs Benson', explaining his absences from this second home by pretending to be a commercial traveller. He was arrested for murder, and also charged with the theft from his employers.

Read denied having killed Florence and claimed that he was not responsible for her pregnancy; he had met Mrs Ayriss on the evening in question, and she had informed him that a soldier was the child's father, he said. However, he had been seen with Florence in the Prittlewell area, and letters had been discovered proving that he had had an affair with her. Moreover, he was known to have possessed a revolver of the type used for the crime, though this could not be found.

Convicted of murder at the Chelmsford Assizes, James Canham Read was sentenced to death, his execution taking place on 4 December 1894. His brother Harry, who had also been arrested in connection with the theft, committed suicide a few days later.

On 26 June 1926, Louie Calvert, a thirty-three-year-old petty criminal, was hanged at Strangeways Prison, Manchester, for the murder of Mrs Lily Waterhouse, a widow aged forty, three months earlier. Mrs Waterhouse — with whom the prisoner had been lodging for three weeks prior to the crime — had been battered to death at her home in Amberley Road, Leeds, on the evening of 31 March, shortly after complaining to the police that her lodger had stolen some of her possessions. During the investigation which followed it was found that the culprit's brief stay at the victim's home had been part of an extraordinary plan to dupe her own husband.

Arthur Calvert, a Leeds nightwatchman living in Railway Place — about two miles from Amberley Road — had engaged Louie as a housekeeper in 1925, and later married her after she had told him that she was pregnant. At the time he believed her to be a widow with two children — a boy who stayed with her and a girl who lived with her sister in Dewsbury, seven miles away — and must therefore have been surprised when she described herself on her wedding certificate as a spinster. During the months which followed she failed to show any signs of pregnancy, and Calvert became impatient for reassurance that a child was on the way. Eventually Louie embarked on her incredible course.

Pretending that she was going to stay with her sister for 'the confinement', she left for Dewsbury on 8 March 1926, but after sending her husband a telegram to advise him of her arrival she returned to

Leeds and went into lodgings at the home of Mrs Waterhouse. A few days later, as a result of an advertisement in a local newspaper, a seventeen-year-old unmarried mother agreed to let Louie adopt her baby daughter, and the child was given to her on 31 March. Later the same day, having murdered her landlady in the meantime, she returned to her husband and pretended to have given birth to the child herself.

Early the following morning, before the body was discovered, Louie went back to the house in Amberley Road and stole a number of articles which had belonged to her victim. She was seen leaving the house and arrested shortly afterwards, the police having discovered her identity from a letter which she had left behind. On being confronted at her home in Railway Place, she was found to be wearing Mrs Waterhouse's boots, which were several sizes too large for her. A suitcase containing crockery, cutlery and household linen stolen from the victim's home was discovered in her living-room.

Louie Calvert was known to the police as Louie Gomersal, an occasional prostitute. She was convicted at the Leeds Assizes in May 1926, and while awaiting execution confessed to another murder: that of John William Frobisher, an elderly man for whom she had also worked as a housekeeper. Frobisher's body — with his boots missing — had been recovered from the canal near his home in Leeds on 12 July 1922. An open verdict was recorded at the inquest, but the police saw no reason to investigate the matter.

Death of Michael Barber, 1981

JUNE 27

On 27 June 1981, thirty-five-year-old Michael Barber, of Westcliff-on-Sea, Essex, died in a west London hospital after an illness lasting some weeks. Though his death was at first attributed to pneumonia and kidney failure, the pathologist conducting the post-mortem suspected paraquat poisoning and sent parts of his organs to be tested by the National Poisons Units at New Cross Hospital. When his suspicions were confirmed, the police were informed, and Michael Barber's death was treated as a case of murder.

The following April Barber's twenty-nine-year-old wife Susan, who had been left £15,000 in her husband's employment insurance policy, was arrested and charged with the crime, and Richard Collins, a younger man with whom she had been having an affair at the time, was charged with a lesser offence in connection with it. The case came before Chelmsford Crown Court in November 1982, both defendants pleading not guilty.

The court heard that Michael and Susan Barber, who had three children, had been incompatible and quarrelled frequently. Susan went out to parties a lot, had a succession of lovers and twice left home; returning on each occasion because her husband begged her to do so. Then in May 1981 Michael Barber arrived back at their house in Osborne Road after cutting short a fishing trip, and found Susan and Richard Collins — his best friend and fellow darts player — making love in the bedroom. He chased Collins out of the house and gave his wife a beating.

The following day Susan made him a steak and

kidney pie but, according to the prosecution, added a spoonful of weed-killer from a can in the garden shed before giving it to him. When he became ill, she gave him more of the poison by putting it into medicine which his doctor had prescribed. Michael Barber was admitted to Southend Hospital soon afterwards, and later removed to Hammersmith after failing to respond to treatment for suspected pneumonia.

When the dead man's body was cremated Susan Barber put on a display of grief, throwing herself onto the coffin as it moved along the conveyor belt. But Richard Collins, already discarded as a lover, had begun to tell friends what had happened, and evidence of this was given to the court.

'Richard was very upset and crying,' said one witness. 'I said he did not want to believe something like that, but he said it was true. He told me that he had a photograph of Susan coming out of the garden shed, taken with a zoom lens, and it showed her with the poison. I told him he couldn't say things like that, but he told me he could prove it.'

Susan Barber told the court that she had not intended to kill her husband; she said that she gave him the poison to punish him for hurting her, without realizing that it could be fatal. She was, however, convicted of murder and sentenced to life imprisonment, while her twenty-five-year-old former lover was given two years' imprisonment for conspiracy to murder.

In July 1983 Susan Barber was allowed out of Holloway Prison briefly in order to marry a divorcee aged thirty-seven. The man had stood by her during the trial and, on hearing that the Home Office had given permission for the ceremony to take place, was reported to have said, 'I love Susan very much. I am overjoyed that we can get married.' It was also stated that he was living in her house in Osborne Road and had adopted her three children.

Body of Peter Thomas discovered, 1964

On 28 June 1964, two boys looking for fishing bait in Bracknell Woods, Berkshire, discovered a man's body in a mound of earth. The body was lying face upwards, fully clothed and with its head wrapped in towelling; it was covered in maggots and extensively decomposed. Professor Keith Simpson, the pathologist, said that the man had been dead for at least nine or ten days and that he had died as a result of a blow — perhaps a karate chop — across the throat. The body was identified from fingerprints as that of Peter Thomas, a forty-two-year-old unemployed man with a criminal record.

Peter Thomas was found to have been living alone — on unemployment benefit — in a wooden bungalow at Lydney, in Gloucestershire. Though he pretended to be poor, he had, in fact, inherited £5000 from his father three years earlier, and letters found in his home revealed that he had made a six-month loan of £2000 to a man named William Brittle, of Hook in Hampshire, at 12¹/₂ per cent interest. This loan, which had been made as a result of a newspaper advertisement, was due to be repaid about the time of Thomas' disappearance on 16 June.

Brittle was a salesman who, according to his advertisement, had wanted the loan for the sake of an 'agricultural prospect'. On being questioned by police, he said that the money had already been repaid: he had driven to Lydney with it himself on 16 June, he said. But there was no proof of this, and when asked how he had managed to raise such a large sum, Brittle said that he had won it betting on horses. The police officers then spoke to bookmakers and betting-shop employees in the district, showing them a photograph of Brittle, and found that none of them recognized him.

Brittle's car was examined and a beech leaf was found under the driver's mat. This was of interest to the investigators, as sprays of beech wood had been found over the dead man's body, though there were no beech trees in the vicinity. Bloodstains on Brittle's coat were of little value as evidence, as his blood group was the same as Thomas'. But it was also learnt that while in the army Brittle had attended a course in unarmed combat.

The police officers working on the case were sure that Brittle had visited Lydney on 16 June, and were able to trace a hitch-hiker to whom he had given a lift on the return journey. But they believed that he had gone there to kill Thomas rather than to repay the loan, and that he had afterwards concealed the body in the boot of his car.

However, no further evidence came to light to support this theory, and after the investigation had gone on for four months, a nylon-spinner named Dennis Roberts claimed to have seen Peter Thomas in Gloucester on 20 June. Though Professor Simpson insisted that this could not be true, the nylon-spinner's statement was seen as undermining the case against Brittle, and the Director of Public Prosecutions decided against having him committed for trial.

A coroner's inquest was then held in Bracknell, lasting seven days, and at the end of it the jury surprised everyone by naming Brittle as Peter Thomas' murderer. Brittle was therefore committed for trial, and appeared at the Spring 1965 Assizes in Gloucester.

The case against him was still no stronger than it had been when the Director of Public Prosecutions decided against committal proceedings, and two further witnesses had since come forward to say that they had seen Peter Thomas alive several days after the date of his disappearance. But the jury was more impressed by the evidence of Professor Simpson, who explained the various stages of development of maggots of the bluebottle fly, and insisted that those found on the body were at a stage which could not have been reached in less than nine or ten days.

William Brittle, who was not called to give evidence himself, was accordingly found guilty and sentenced to life imprisonment.

Murder of the Stubbe brothers, 1901

JULY 1

On 1 July 1901, a shocking double murder was committed on the island of Rügen, in the Rostock district of north Germany (now in the German Democratic Republic). Hermann Stubbe, aged eight, and his six-year-old brother Peter, the two sons of a carter living in the village of Göhren, had been out alone during the afternoon and failed to return home by dusk. A search was therefore started in the extensive woodland nearby, but by this time they were already dead.

Both boys had been battered over the head with a large stone discovered near the scene of the crime. Their heads, arms and legs had then been cut off, their bodies cut open and their internal organs cut out and scattered through the woods. The discovery of the bodies, on 2 July, horrified the inhabitants of Rügen and was quickly followed by the arrest of Ludwig Tessnow, a journeyman carpenter from another village who had been seen talking to the boys the previous afternoon.

Tessnow, a native of Rügen who had spent some years travelling all over Germany before returning to the village of Baabe, denied having had anything to do with the murders. But a new suit and other articles of clothing found in his wardrobe appeared to be bloodstained, and it was also learnt that Tessnow had been suspected of the unsolved murder of two girls in a village near Osnabrück in September 1898. Moreover, he was identified by a local shepherd as a man seen running away from a field near Göhren on the night of 11 June 1901, when a number of sheep were killed in a revolting manner.

Tessnow denied that he had killed either the children or the animals, and insisted that stains found on his clothes were not bloodstains but spots of a woodstain used in his work. The examining magistrate in charge of the inquiry, though convinced of his guilt, was therefore far from certain that he would be convicted if brought to trial. But the case against Tessnow was greatly strengthened when his clothes were sent to Paul Uhlenhuth, a young serologist at the University of Greifswald, for examination.

Uhlenhuth, using tests which he had only recently devised, was able to show that while Tessnow's working clothes were free of bloodstains of any sort, the better clothes from his wardrobe had been stained in various places — by both human and sheep's blood. The tests were so impressive that they ensured Tessnow's conviction and were immediately recognized as a great advance in forensic medicine. The mad carpenter of Rügen was sentenced to death, but this sentence was afterwards commuted on the grounds of his insanity. He died in the 1920s.

Execution of Dr. Robert Buchanan, 1895

JULY 2

On 2 July 1895, Dr Robert Buchanan, a New York medical practitioner, was executed in the electric chair at Sing Sing Prison for the murder of his second wife. The offence had been committed in 1892, the victim's death being caused by morphine poisoning. It had been inspired by the case of Carlyle Harris, a medical student who had been tried for a similar crime earlier the same year.

Buchanan, who had qualified as a doctor in Edinburgh, set up his practice in New York in 1886. It was initially successful and prosperous, but he was discontented with his home life and paid regular visits to brothels. When his first marriage ended in divorce in 1890, he married Anna Sutherland, the keeper of one of these establishments, who afterwards worked as his receptionist.

A wealthy woman, many years his senior, the new Mrs Buchanan had already made a will in which her husband was named as chief beneficiary. But her presence in his consulting-rooms was an embarrassment to him, and his patients began to take their ailments elsewhere.

When Carlyle Harris was brought to trial in January 1892 the case made headline news. It was the first known case in which murder had been committed with the use of morphine in New York, and the victim's death had only been properly investigated as a result of disclosures made in the *New York World*.

Buchanan, who was vain and boastful, expressed the view that Harris was a fool: the preparation of an undetectable poison could easily be accomplished, he declared. When his own wife died on 23 April, her death was thought to have been caused by a cerebral haemorrhage, but Buchanan's behaviour gave rise to suspicion and, as luck would have it, the reporter who had exposed Carlyle Harris decided to look into the matter.

Having inherited $50,000 from his second wife, Buchanan drew further attention to himself by remarrying his first less than a month later. This led to an exhumation of Anna Buchanan's body, a post-mortem being carried out by Dr Rudolph Witthaus — who had also examined the body of Harris' victim. In this case, although he found morphine in the body, the doctor also reported that the most important sign of morphine poisoning — contracted pupils — was absent.

This puzzled everyone concerned until the *New York World* reporter, questioning Buchanan in a saloon, suddenly remembered an observation which he had made during his schooldays, and realized that the contraction of the pupils could be counteracted by putting belladonna into the victim's eyes. This flash of insight caused him to request a further examination of the body, as a result of which traces of belladonna were found.

Buchanan was arrested and charged with murder, being brought to trial in March 1893. During the course of the proceedings, a cat was killed with morphine so that the effects of belladonna on its pupils could be witnessed. Even so, it was only the unconvincing answers which he gave under cross-examination that ensured Buchanan's conviction. Had he taken the advice of his counsel and declined to give evidence, he may well have been acquitted.

Kidnapping of Graeme Thorne, 1960

On the morning of 7 July 1960, eight-year-old Graeme Thorne disappeared after setting out for school from his home in the Bondi district of Sydney. A few days earlier his parents, Bazil and Freda Thorne, had won the £100,000 first prize in the Sydney Opera House Lottery, and it was immediately feared that the child had been kidnapped. Shortly afterwards a man with a foreign accent telephoned their home, saying that he had Graeme and demanding £25,000 for his return.

The call was answered by a detective, who pretended to be the boy's father but was unable to draw the man into conversation. Bazil Thorne and his wife afterwards told the police that they were willing to pay the whole of their £100,000 to get their son back safely. But they were never to be able to do so, for after a second telephone call, the kidnapper made no further contact with them.

On 16 August Graeme's body was found wrapped in a rug on a patch of waste ground in Seaforth, about ten miles from the family's home. His hands and feet were tied and a silk scarf was knotted round his neck. He had died from strangulation and a fractured skull.

It was not long before police began to suspect Stephen Leslie Bradley, a naturalized Australian who, at the time of the kidnapping, had lived in a nearby neighbourhood with his wife and their three children. Bradley, an electroplater, was Hungarian by birth: his name had originally been Istvan Baranyay, but he had changed it by deed poll. Since the crime he had altered his appearance, and he and his family had left their house. It was learnt that they were about to leave the country.

Bradley owned a car which was similar to one seen near Graeme Thorne's home on the morning of 7 July; it was also discovered that he had not been to work that day. Further evidence was provided by an examination of leaves and hairs attached to the rug in which the body had been wrapped: some of the leaves were similar to those of an unusual type of shrub growing at the house which Bradley had left, and some of the hairs were identical to those of his dog. The rug was eventually identified as one which Bradley had owned.

By the time the police were ready to arrest him, Bradley was on his way to London by sea. He was arrested in Colombo on a provisional warrant, and extradition proceedings were started against him. These resulted in his being returned to Australia, where he confessed that he had abducted Graeme Thorne and threatened to 'feed him to the sharks' unless he was paid £25,000 for his return. He denied having struck the child, and said that he had been accidentally suffocated in the boot of the car. He (Bradley) had then become frightened and hidden the body.

On being brought to trial, Bradley withdrew his confession, but the evidence against him was over-whelming. He tried to gain sympathy by telling the court that he and his wife had both been in concentration camps during the Second World War, and that he on one occasion had survived a firing squad. But this did not help him, either, and he was convicted of murder. The announcement of the jury's verdict was followed by noisy scenes in the courtroom, with one spectator shouting, 'Feed *him* to the sharks!'

As murder was no longer a capital offence in New South Wales, Bradley was sentenced to penal servi-tude for life. This was not generally considered a harsh enough punishment for what had clearly been a callous crime, and many people resented the fact that he could not be hanged.

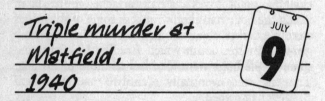

Triple murder at Matfield, 1940

JULY 9

On the afternoon of 9 July 1940, three women were murdered in the grounds of a cottage at Matfield, a village about seven miles from Tonbridge in Kent. Mrs Dorothy Fisher and her nineteen-year-old daughter Freda had both been shot in the back in an orchard screening the cottage from the Tonbridge road; their maid, Charlotte Saunders, aged about forty-eight, had been shot as she ran from the cottage after dropping a tray of crockery.

The cottage had no other occupants — for Mrs Fisher and her husband had separated in October the previous year — and the murder weapon had not been left at the scene. Although there was a great deal of disorder inside, with jewellery, money and other valuables strewn all over the different rooms, the broken crockery, when pieced together, made up four cups, four saucers and four plates — which strongly suggested that Miss Saunders had been preparing tea for four people when the murders took place. If so, the identity of the fourth person was unknown.

The police officers working on the case also discovered a lady's white hogskin glove, which could not be immediately identified, on the ground between the bodies of Mrs Fisher and her daughter. A lady's bicycle, belonging to Mrs Fisher, was found in a ditch near the entrance to the cottage.

It seemed likely that the culprit was a woman, and Detective Chief Inspector Beveridge, the Scotland Yard officer in charge of the investigation, soon learnt that a woman had been seen behaving suspiciously outside the cottage on the afternoon in question. The same woman had been seen walking along the road from Matfield to Tonbridge, where she had boarded a train to London at 4.25 p.m.

The witnesses — and there were several of them — all agreed on this woman's description, and said that she had been carrying a long, narrow object wrapped in brown paper. This was undoubtedly the murder weapon, for the pathologist Sir Bernard Spilsbury was certain that all three of the victims had been killed with a shotgun. The woman was found to be Mrs Florence Ransom, a young widow who lived with Mrs Fisher's husband Lawrence on a farm at Piddington, near Bicester in Oxfordshire.

In addition to being a farmer, Lawrence Fisher was in business, and travelled to London every day. He had remained on good terms with his wife — who had a lover of her own — and often went to Matfield to see her, as well as their daughter.

Mrs Ransom, who was known locally as 'Mrs Fisher' — and to Mr Fisher as 'Julia' — was an attractive red-haired woman, described as domineering and dictatorial by one of the servants employed at the farm. She had, according to the same man, been learning to fire a shotgun owned by the farm's cowman, and also trying — not very successfully — to learn to ride a bicycle. It was later discovered that the cowman was Mrs Ransom's brother and that an elderly housekeeper at the farm was her mother. But Mr Fisher did not know that either were related to her, and although they both admitted it to the police, Mrs Ransom strenuously denied it.

The cowman agreed that he had been teaching Mrs Ransom to fire his shotgun. He said that she had borrowed it from him on 8 July and returned it two days later, saying that it needed cleaning. Mrs Ransom was then picked out by a number of witnesses at an identification parade, and afterwards asked to try on the hogskin glove. It fitted her perfectly, though the other one of the pair could not be found. A graze on one of her knees indicated that she may have fallen off Mrs Fisher's bicycle while trying to leave the scene of the crime in a hurry.

After an investigation lasting just a few days — during the course of which desperate air battles were fought over Kent — Mrs Ransom was charged with the three murders. She was tried at the Old Bailey in November 1940, her mother and brother both telling the court that she appeared to be missing from the farm during the daytime on 9 July. Mrs Ransom denied the offence — and continued to deny that the housekeeper and cowman were related to her — but was found guilty and sentenced to death. She was later certified insane and sent to Broadmoor.

Yukio Saito declared innocent, 1984

JULY 11

On 11 July 1984, Yukio Saito, a fifty-three-year-old man who had spent nearly twenty-seven years on Japan's Death Row, was set free after a court had reviewed his case and declared him innocent of the crime for which he had been sentenced. The crime, a quadruple murder, had been committed in 1955, and Saito had confessed to it after being arrested later the same year. He afterwards retracted the confession but

TRUE CRIME DIARY

TOP
Search for clues on
wasteland near Dennis
Nilsen's home.

INSET
Dennis Nilsen

BOTTOM
 Martin Hunter-Craig, a
homosexual prostitute and
close friend of Nilsen.

TOP
Henri Désiré Landru, the French 'Bluebeard' on trial.

BOTTOM
The body of Mafia boss Albert Anastasia in the barber's shop where he was shot.

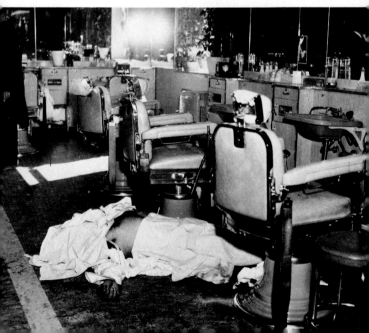

TRUE CRIME DIARY

Edward Gein, murderer
and necrophile, after
taking lie detector tests.

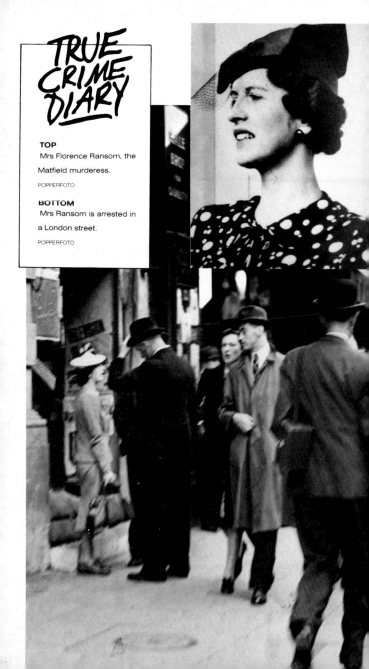

TRUE CRIME DIARY

TOP
Mrs Florence Ransom, the
Matfield murderess.

POPPERFOTO

BOTTOM
Mrs Ransom is arrested in
a London street.

POPPERFOTO

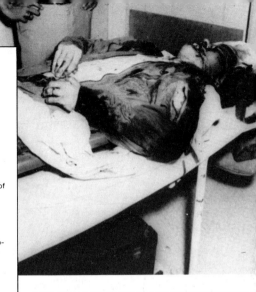

TRUE CRIME DIARY

TOP
The body of Charles Whitman, a twenty-five-year-old mass murderer of Austin, Texas.

UPI/BETTMANN NEWSPHOTOS

BOTTOM
Edmund Kemper, the 'Co-ed murderer' smoking after his appearance in court.

UPI/BETTMANN NEWSPHOTOS

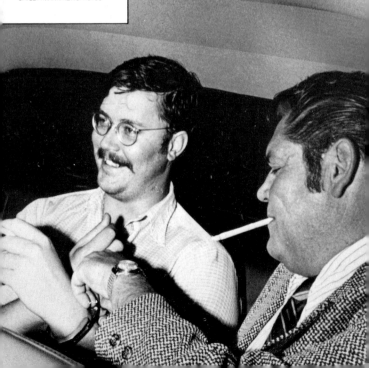

TOP
Charles Manson giving a television interview.
POPPERFOTO

BOTTOM
Manson leaving the courtroom after being convicted of seven murders.
POPPERFOTO

TRUE CRIME DIARY

TOP
Jacques Mesrine, in some
of his disguises.
THE KEYSTONE COLLECTION

BOTTOM
Mesrine took these
photos of journalist
Jacques Tillier after
knocking him unconscious
and shooting him three
times.
ASSOCIATED PRESS

Grigori Rasputin, the 'Holy Devil' whose powers of survival have been the subject of speculation.

was convicted and sentenced to death in 1957.

The crime had taken place in Matsuyama, near Sendai, the victims being a farmer and three relatives. Saito claimed that the police had forced him to confess to it after he had been arrested in connection with a different offence, and Judge Takehiko Kojima of the Sendai district court — 185 miles north of Tokyo — accepted that they had used illegal methods of interrogation in order to make him do so.

It was Japan's third such case in twelve months. On 15 July 1983, Sakae Menda, aged fifty-seven, was released from jail in south-western Japan after an appeal judge had found him innocent of two murders committed thirty-two years previously. He, too, had said that he was forced by police to confess, but previous appeals had been dismissed. Then, in March 1984, Shigeyoshi Taniguchi, who had spent thirty-four years on Death Row, was similarly released.

A year after Saito's release a Japanese woman who had died in 1979 was posthumously cleared of a murder for which she had served thirteen years in prison. Miss Shigeko Fuji had been convicted of the murder of her common-law husband, Kamesaburo Saegusa, on the evidence of two youths who worked in the victim's radio shop. The youths later retracted their evidence, saying that it had been given under pressure, but Miss Fuji withdrew an appeal against her conviction because she was afraid that the proceedings would use up the money which she needed to pay for the education of her children.

She was granted a retrial a year after her death, and her name was finally cleared thirty-two years after the crime had been committed. It was the first such retrial in Japan's history.

On 12 July 1906, the body of a young woman was
found on the shore of Big Moose Lake, a holiday
resort in the Adirondack region of New York State. It
seemed at first that she had been drowned in a boating accident, and later, when an upturned rowing-
boat was discovered in the water, with a man's straw
boater nearby, it was assumed that another death had
occurred at the same time. But an examination of the
body revealed that the woman had been pregnant and
that injuries which she had suffered were not consistent with a drowning accident. It was therefore suspected that she had been murdered.

The woman was found to be twenty-year-old Grace
Brown, from Cortland, in the same state. It was
learnt from her friends that she had been having an
affair with Chester Gillette, the superintendent of the
skirt factory where she worked, and from hoteliers in
the Adirondack lake resorts that she had been on
holiday there with a young man who sometimes
signed his name as Carl Graham and sometimes as
Charles George — registering Grace as his wife on
each occasion. It was this man, wearing a straw
boater and carrying a heavy suitcase, who had hired a
rowing-boat on 11 July and failed to return it.

Police officers went to look for Chester Gillette at
his lodgings in Cortland, but he was not there.
Instead, they found a batch of letters which he had
received from Grace Brown, telling him that she was
desperate to hide her pregnancy from her parents and
begging him to help her. A search was then started for
him in the Adirondacks, and he was apprehended at

Arrowhead on Fourth Lake. On being charged with murder, he claimed that he had accidentally over-turned the rowing-boat while leaning out to pick a water lily, and that Grace had been drowned in spite of an attempt which he had made to rescue her.

Gillette, aged twenty-three, was brought to trial in November 1906, the case lasting twenty-two days and attracting much publicity. Medical evidence was produced to show that Grace Brown had been struck in the face, probably with the prisoner's tennis racket, and that she had been drowned while unconscious. But Gillette continued to deny that she had been murdered, saying now that she had committed suicide after they had discussed their circumstances in the boat.

Found guilty of first-degree murder, Chester Gillette was sentenced to death. A number of appeals were made, but all were dismissed and he was finally executed in the electric chair at Auburn Prison on 30 March 1908. Theodore Dreiser, who had been a spec-tator at the trial, was so inspired by it that he based his famous novel, *An American Tragedy*, on the case.

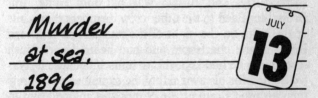

Murder at sea.
1896
JULY 13

On the night of 13 July 1896, a triple axe murder was committed aboard the *Herbert Fuller*, a sailing ship bound for Argentina carrying timber from Boston. Two of the victims, Captain Charles Nash and his wife Laura, were discovered almost immediately afterwards — while Nash was still alive — but the body of Second Mate August Blomberg was not found until later. The dying captain was on the floor of the chartroom; the body of his wife was in her bunk. They were found by Lester Monks, the ship's only passenger, who had gone to investigate after hearing screams above the sound of the wind.

Monks told the first mate, Thomas Bram, of his discovery, but Bram at first seemed unwilling to believe him. He said that he would not rouse Blomberg because the second mate had been inciting the crew to mutiny, then suddenly burst into tears and begged Monks to protect him. When Blomberg's body was eventually found in his cabin, Bram, who by this time had assumed command of the ship, drew attention to an axe which he appeared to have discovered. Saying excitedly that this was the murder weapon, he threw it into the sea before anyone could stop him.

Bram then sought to have the three bodies thrown overboard — a proposal which was resisted by the crew. Against his wishes, the crew also insisted that the *Herbert Fuller* should return to the United States. But for the six days that it took to reach port, an air of terror hung over the ship.

Bram convinced the crew that one of their number, a fellow named Charley Brown, had been acting suspiciously, and Brown was put into irons. But Brown confided to the other crew members that while at the helm on the night of the murders he had seen Bram in the chartroom and had heard Laura Nash screaming; he had kept this to himself because he was frightened for his own safety, he explained. The crew then accused Bram of the crimes and chained him to the mast.

In December 1896 Thomas Bram was brought to trial in Boston, charged with murder. The prosecution produced evidence that he had often approached fellow sailors with the idea of killing a ship's officers and stealing its cargo, and that he had also boasted of having looted other ships in which he had served: he was convicted and sentenced to death. But as a result of procedural errors, a retrial was ordered, and on being convicted for the second time in 1898, he was sentenced to life imprisonment.

Bram was pardoned in 1919, after the mystery writer Mary Roberts Rinehart had managed to convince President Woodrow Wilson that he was innocent, and he later became a successful businessman.

Crimmins children reported missing, 1965

JULY
14

On the morning of 14 July 1965, a man telephoned the police in Queens, New York City, to report the disappearance of his two children: a boy aged five and a girl a year younger. Edmund Crimmins was separated from his wife Alice, with whom the children had been living in a ground-floor apartment. He said that his wife, on finding that they were missing from their bedroom, had called to ask him whether he had taken them.

Detectives went to investigate the matter, and Alice Crimmins, an attractive woman of twenty-six, showed them the children's bedroom, where the beds were rumpled and the window stood open. She said that a latch on the door prevented it being opened from the inside — to ensure that her son did not go to the refrigerator while she was asleep — and that this had been in use the previous night. She also said that she had last seen the children before going to bed herself about 4 a.m.

That afternoon the girl, Alice Marie, was found strangled on a vacant lot, and it appeared from undigested food in her stomach that she had died about seven hours before her mother claimed to have last seen her. So Alice Crimmins — who had already given the impression of being far less distressed than might have been expected in the circumstances — now seemed not to have been telling the truth. The boy, Edmund Jr, was found dead on a piece of waste ground over a week later, his body in an advanced state of decomposition.

The police learnt that during the early hours of 14 July a neighbour looking out of her window had seen Mrs Crimmins in the company of a man; she was carrying a bundle wrapped in blankets under one arm and holding a small boy with her free hand. As she and her husband were in the process of getting divorced, it was suspected that she had killed the children herself because she feared losing custody of them. Nearly two years after the crimes had taken place Alice Crimmins was charged with her daughter's murder.

She was brought to trial in May 1968, the case attracting much attention — mainly as a result of evidence concerning the promiscuity of the accused. She was convicted of first-degree manslaughter and given a sentence of five-to-twenty years' imprisonment, but was released on bail shortly afterwards to await the outcome of an appeal. This resulted in the sentence being quashed and a fresh trial ordered.

In 1971 she was tried for the murder of her son and the manslaughter of her daughter. As at her previous trial, she screamed abuse at witnesses who appeared against her: one of these outbursts occurred when a former lover testified that during a night spent at a motel with him Alice Crimmins had confessed that she was the killer of her children. According to this witness, she had said that she preferred to see them dead rather than allow her husband to get custody of them.

Alice Crimmins was convicted on both charges and this time she was sentenced to life imprisonment. But further appeals followed, and in 1975 her conviction for murder was quashed. In January 1976 she was transferred to a residential work release establishment in Harlem.

Shooting of two police officers, 1951

During the early hours of 15 July 1951, police officers surrounding a farmhouse in Yorkshire heard the sound of shots and found two of their number fatally injured. The shooting took place at Whinney Close Farm, Kirkheaton, near Huddersfield, the home of thirty-six-year-old Alfred Moore and his family. Moore, a poultry farmer, was suspected of burglary, and the party of policemen had been awaiting his return in the hope of catching him in possession of stolen property.

The two wounded men were taken to hospital, Detective Inspector Duncan Fraser, who had been shot three times, dying before they got there. Others remaining at the scene of the crime believed that Moore was now inside the house, but no attempt was made to arrest him until armed reinforcements arrived. Moore then gave himself up, pretending to have been in bed at the time the shots were fired.

A search of the farmhouse and the adjoining yard resulted in the discovery of a pair of wet shoes, some live ammunition, discharged cartridge cases, a large assortment of keys — including skeleton keys, safe keys and car ignition keys — and certain items of value, such as gold and silver cigarette cases, which appeared to have been stolen. There were also the remains of hundreds of postage stamps and dollar bills which had been burnt in a fireplace after the shooting had occurred.

At the Huddersfield Royal Infirmary PC Arthur Jagger, the other man who had been shot, was able to make a statement. He said that he had seen Moore walking towards his home just before 2 a.m. and tried to arrest him after Moore had dived into a hedge. At this, the farmer pulled a gun from his pocket and shot him, causing him to fall to the ground. The shooting of Detective Inspector Fraser took place immediately afterwards, as Jagger lay watching but unable to move.

As Jagger was unlikely to recover, an identification parade was held at his bedside later the same day, and Moore was picked out as the culprit. A special court was then convened before a local magistrate, Jagger remaining in bed as he gave evidence. When Jagger died the following day Moore was charged with the murder of both men.

The search of the farm went on for several weeks, but the murder weapon was not discovered, even with the use of mine-detectors. Alfred Moore was nonetheless brought to trial at the Leeds Assizes in December 1951, and the jury took only fifty minutes to find him guilty. He was hanged at Armley Prison on 6 February 1952.

Murder of Alice Wiltshaw, 1952

On 16 July 1952, Mrs Alice Wiltshaw, the sixty-two-year-old wife of a pottery manufacturer, was beaten to death by an intruder at her fourteen-room house in the village of Barlaston, in Staffordshire. The person responsible got away with jewellery worth several thousand pounds, leaving the murder weapon — a heavy, old-fashioned poker — near the body. The crime was discovered by the victim's husband, Frederick Cuthbert Wiltshaw, when he arrived home from work shortly afterwards.

The property had been entered by way of an overgrown path — unlikely to have been used by a stranger — and there were no signs of a forced entry to the house. Moreover, the servants employed by Mr and Mrs Wiltshaw had all been off duty and out of the house at the time the murder took place. It therefore seemed that the culprit was somebody familiar with the building and household routine — and probably known to the victim.

Before long police began to suspect Leslie Green, the Wiltshaws' twenty-nine-year-old former chauffeur, who had been sacked two months previously for using one of the family cars for his own purposes. Green, a married man with a six-year-old daughter, had been missing from his home in nearby Longton since the beginning of July, but came forward seven days after the murder in response to a public appeal.

He denied knowing anything about the crime, saying that he had been at the Station Hotel in Stafford — twelve miles from Barlaston — during the afternoon and evening of 16 July, and had then left for Leeds by train. A number of people with whom he had been associating could give him an alibi, he said.

This at first appeared to be true, but it was later found that a train leaving Stafford at 5.10 p.m. arrived in Barlaston at 5.35, and another, leaving Barlaston half an hour later, arrived in Stafford at 6.26. If Green had caught both of those trains, he would have been in Barlaston long enough to have committed the murder — and none of his associates had seen him at the Station Hotel during that particular period of time.

It was also learnt that Green, pretending to be unmarried, had become 'engaged' to a twenty-year-old nurse in Leeds, with whom he had been in close contact since leaving his wife. But she evidently suspected him, too, for she had returned two rings which he gave her after the murder, and it was in the hope of convincing her that he was innocent that he went to the police on 23 July.

Not long afterwards an RAF macintosh which Green had worn on 16 July was located in a railway lost property office. One of the pockets contained a letter mentioning an address in Leeds, and led to the discovery of the rings which the nurse had returned. As expected, they were found to have been among the valuables stolen from Mrs Wiltshaw. The rest of the jewellery was never recovered.

Leslie Green was charged with murder and tried at the Stafford Assizes. Pleading not guilty, he then claimed that the crime had been committed by two other men, who had given him the rings the following day. But a footprint found at the scene matched the sole of one of his shoes, and a bloodstained glove which had also been found there had a hole corresponding with a recently-healed cut on one of his thumbs.

On being found guilty, he was sentenced to death. His execution took place at Winson Green Prison, Birmingham, on 23 December 1952.

Danuta Maciejowicz found dead, 1964

On 23 July 1964, the naked corpse of Danuta Maciej-owicz, a girl of seventeen, was found in a park in Olsztyn, 160 miles north of Warsaw; she had been raped and the lower part of her body had been horri-bly mutilated. The crime had taken place the previous day — one of Poland's national holidays — and Danuta's parents had reported her missing when she failed to return home after going to watch a parade in the town's main street.

The discovery of the body was followed by an unsigned letter in red ink, received by a Warsaw newspaper editor, in which the writer stated that he had 'plucked a rose in bloom in the gardens of Olsztyn' and would do it elsewhere on another occasion. The letter was in the same spidery handwriting as another which had been sent to a different newspaper three weeks earlier, in which the writer had warned that he would give 'cause for weeping'. But the police were unable to trace the person responsible.

Then, on 17 January 1965, Anna Kaliniak, a sixteen-year-old girl from a Warsaw suburb, failed to return home, also after attending a national-holiday procession. Police were still searching for her when they received a letter, again in red spidery hand-writing, telling them to go to a factory opposite Anna's home. There, in the basement, they found her body; she had been strangled with a piece of wire, stripped naked, raped and then mutilated, her killer leaving a metal spike stuck in her vagina. Once more, the police were unable to find the culprit.

Nine and a half months later, on 1 November —

All Saints' Day — there was another such murder. An eighteen-year-old hotel receptionist named Janina Popielska left her home in Poznań, 200 miles from Warsaw, and set out on foot towards a nearby village, a distance of three and a half miles. Her killer, whom she met on the way, suffocated her with a pad soaked in chloroform, then tore off her clothes and raped her three times behind a packing-shed before stabbing her to death with a screwdriver. Finally, her body was mutilated in a revolting manner and left in a packing-case at the scene of the crime.

A letter, in the now-familiar red spidery handwriting and this time containing a quotation from a Polish epic written in 1928, was received by the editor of a Poznań newspaper the following day. But the police still had no idea who the killer could be.

On May Day in 1966, when celebrations were taking place all over the country, he struck yet again. Marysia Gałązka a seventeen year-old student living in the Warsaw suburb of Zoliborz, was found dead in the tool-shed of her family's back garden after she had gone out to look for her cat; she had been stripped naked, raped and disembowelled.

This fourth outrage led to a search of records of all other unsolved murders in Poland during the previous few years, and it was learnt that a further fourteen crimes, all committed since April 1964, had features similar to those already attributed to the unknown Polish Ripper. They had all taken place within a group of towns which formed a rough circle round Warsaw, no fewer than six of them in or near Poznań. But this discovery did not prevent two further murders occurring before the culprit was arrested.

On 24 December 1966, the body of seventeen-year-old Janina Kozielska, wearing only a leather mini-skirt, was found on a late-night train in Kraków; both the mini-skirt and the lower part of her body had been slashed repeatedly, and she, too, had been raped. A letter, in the usual red spidery handwriting, was found in the mail-van, stating briefly, 'I have done it again.' The killer was not among the passengers.

Janina Kozielska was found to be the sister of Aniela Kozielska, a girl of fourteen who had been murdered while on a visit to Warsaw to see her grandmother in 1964. Her parents had no idea who had committed either of the murders, but mentioned that both girls had been associated with an academy of art in Kraków, called the Artlovers' Club — Janina as a part-time model, Aniela as a part-time student.

This was of interest to the police officers working on the case, as laboratory reports on the anonymous letters revealed that they had not been written in ordinary red ink but in a home-made solution containing artists' paint. They therefore began interviewing all 118 members of the club — people from a variety of professions, students, and even housewives — and eventually decided that Lucian Staniak, a twenty-six-year-old translator with a preoccupation with red paint and a locker full of knives, was the person they wanted.

Staniak, a native of Katowice, was not at his home when police went to see him on 31 January 1967; he was arrested at dawn the next day. In the meantime Bożena Raczkiewicz, an eighteen-year-old student, had been murdered in a railway-station shelter in Łódź. Her clothes had been cut off with a knife, then she had been raped twice and mutilated with a broken bottle.

Staniak, who had spent the night drinking, confessed to having committed twenty sex murders in less than three years. He was charged with all of them and, on being convicted, sentenced to death. Later, however, the 'Red Spider', as he had become popularly called, was declared insane and sent to an asylum in his home town.

Death of Edward Gein, 1984

On 26 July 1984, Edward Gein, a ghoulish murderer, body-snatcher and necrophile, died in an American mental institution at the age of seventy-seven. He had been in such institutions since 1957, when the remains of fifteen women were found at his farm in Plainfield, Wisconsin. It was Gein's activities which inspired the novel on which Alfred Hitchcock's famous horror film *Psycho* was based.

The events leading to Gein's arrest began on 16 November 1957, when relatives of Bernice Worden, a fifty-eight-year-old widow who ran a hardware store in Plainfield, realized that she was missing. Gein's pick-up truck had been seen near the store twice that day, and a sheriff's deputy called at his farm to see if he knew anything of her whereabouts. The farmer was not at home.

Calling again later, the deputy found that Gein was still not there. But this time he looked into a lean-to at the side of the house and saw Mrs Worden's decapitated corpse, hanging by the heels. Gein was located in the town shortly afterwards and taken into custody.

A search of the farmhouse resulted in the discovery of preserved human heads, many organs, a soup bowl made from a sawn-up skull, and lampshades and bracelets made of human skin. The relics were mainly of women whose corpses had been dug up after burial, but the remains of a woman who had been murdered three years earlier — as well as those of Mrs Worden — were also found.

Gein had a morbid interest in female corpses, particularly after the death of his mother, for whom he was said to have had an abnormal love and who had always managed to restrain him from showing a more natural interest in the opposite sex. It was because of this curiosity that he had taken initially to body-snatching and then to murder.

According to his own statements, both Mrs Worden and the woman murdered in 1954 — a middle-aged tavern keeper named Mary Hogan — had borne a resemblance to his mother, and he had killed them for this reason. He admitted acts of cannibalism as well as necrophilia, and also said that he found it sexually gratifying to drape the skin of corpses over his own body.

Though Gein was judged to be unfit to stand trial by reason of insanity, the revulsion caused by his practices was so intense that his farm was burnt to the ground by other members of the local community.

Gein was sent to the Central State Hospital at Waupon, where he remained until 1978; he was then transferred to the Mendota Mental Health Institute in Madison, where his last six years were spent. After his death, it was stated that he had not been a problem at either of these institutions, and that while at Central State he had worked as a carpenter, a mason and a hospital attendant.

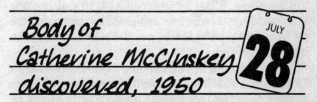

Body of Catherine McCluskey discovered, 1950

JULY 28

During the early hours of 28 July 1950, the body of Catherine McCluskey, a forty-year-old unmarried mother, was found lying in a road on the outskirts of

Glasgow, apparently the victim of a hit-and-run driver. She had, however, been run over twice by the same car — the second time when she was already dead — and a large bruise on her right temple, caused by a blow from a blunt instrument, indicated that she had been knocked unconscious beforehand. This was confirmed by the absence of any of the usual signs of a violent collision, such as broken glass and chipped paint, at the place where the body was found. It was therefore clear that Catherine McCluskey had been the victim of a murder.

The dead woman's body was identified by a friend with whom she had left her two children the previous evening. The friend, Mrs Rose O'Donnell, told police officers that the children — one aged six, the other three months — had been left with her several times when their mother went out, and that she had never before failed to collect them; she also said Miss McCluskey had told her that she was going out with a policeman. Further inquiries among the dead woman's neighbours in Nicholson Street, and at the Glasgow Assistance Board, revealed that a policeman — presumably the same one — was the father of Miss McCluskey's younger child.

PC James Robertson, a thirty-three-year-old married man with two children, soon came to the attention of the investigating officers. On the night of the murder he had left his beat at 11.15 p.m. and driven off in his black Austin car, saying that he was going to take a woman home. When he returned, at 1.10 a.m., he was in an untidy state, which he explained by saying that the car's exhaust pipe had broken and that he had had to tie it on with string.

It was found that the car had been stolen from a Lanarkshire solicitor some months earlier, while its number plates had been taken from a tractor owned by a farmer in Aberdeenshire. There were no signs of a collision on the body of the vehicle, but traces of blood, skin and hair were found on its underside. It was discovered, too, that marks on the surface of the road where the crime had taken place had been made by the broken exhaust pipe as the car went over the body.

On being questioned, Robertson said that he had found the car abandoned and had since been using it himself, having changed its number plates for those taken from the tractor. He admitted that he had killed Catherine McCluskey, but said that her death had been the result of an accident. He had agreed to drive her to the home of some friends because she said that she had been turned out of her lodgings, but on the way an argument started and he told her to get out and walk. The accident occurred when he drove towards her in reverse after relenting, he claimed.

Robertson was arrested and found to be carrying a heavy rubber truncheon which was not part of his regulation equipment. At his trial, at the Glasgow High Court, it was contended that Catherine McCluskey had been his mistress and that he had turned to murder as a means of terminating their relationship. Robertson denied that he had ever been intimate with Miss McCluskey, but was convicted and sentenced to death. His execution took place at Barlinnie Prison on 15 December 1950.

First murder of David Berkowitz, 1976

JULY
29

On 29 July 1976, two teenage girls were sitting in a stationary car in the Bronx, New York City, when a man walked over, pulled a gun out of a paper bag and fired five shots at them. Donna Lauria, an eighteen-year-old medical technician, was killed and Jody Valenti, a student nurse aged nineteen, was wounded in the thigh. There was no motive for the crime and police quickly became convinced that the culprit was a madman who killed for pleasure.

Three months later, on 23 October, Carl Denaro, aged twenty, was sitting in his sports car in front of a tavern in Queens, Long Island, in the company of his eighteen-year-old girlfriend Rosemary Keenan, when the same man fired at them through the rear wind-screen. Denaro was wounded but recovered in hospital; his girlfriend was not injured.

The connection between the two crimes was not discovered until some time afterwards, and in the meantime a third was committed. This was the shooting of another two girls — both of whom were wounded — also in Queens, on 27 November. Donna DeMasi and Joanne Lomino, who had been sitting outside a house together when the crime occurred, were found to have been shot with the same gun that had been used in both of the other cases.

Further crimes followed. On 30 January 1977, again in Queens, shots were fired at a young couple sitting in a car: the girl was fatally injured, but her companion was not hurt at all. Then, on 8 March, a female student was shot dead as she made her way home on foot in the same district. And on 17 April a couple were shot in a parked car in the Bronx: Valentina Suriani died instantly, Alexander Esau died later in hospital.

After this last attack a letter was found at the scene of the crime. It read: 'Dear Captain Joseph Borelli, I am deeply hurt by your calling me a women-hater. I am not. But I am a monster. I am the Son of Sam....' A further note, signed 'Son of Sam', was sent to a New York columnist. The killer naturally became known by this name.

There were two more shootings: the first on 26 June in Queens, when a young couple were both shot and wounded in a stationary car, the other on 31 July, when another couple were shot in similar circumstances in Brooklyn. In this last case the girl, Stacy Moskowitz, aged twenty, died in hospital; her companion, Robert Violante, who was the same age, was blinded. But after the shooting an incident occurred which led to the killer's arrest.

A parking ticket was placed on his own car, which had been left near the scene of the crime, and when he returned to it, he screwed up the ticket, got into the car and drove off. This was witnessed by a woman walking her dog, who also noticed that he was holding a gun. When the matter was reported the police were able to trace the culprit from their own records, and he gave himself up without a fight.

The killer who had terrified the inhabitants of New York City for several months turned out to be David Berkowitz, a mentally-ill postal worker aged twenty-four, who lived in a Yonkers apartment block, harbouring feelings of rejection and persecution. He was shy of women, believing that they found him ugly, and claimed to hear demons telling him to kill. He also said that after a murder he felt 'flushed with power'. He was nonetheless judged to be sane, and sentenced to 365 years' imprisonment shortly afterwards.

He later became a celebrity and made a great deal of money from the sale of his life story.

JULY
31

On 31 July 1966, Charles Whitman, a twenty-five-year-old architectural engineering student of Austin, Texas, typed a note in which he said that he intended to kill his wife. He was interrupted by friends before he could do so, and spent the next few hours in their company, giving no cause for concern. But later, about midnight, he went to see his mother in her nearby apartment, where he stabbed her and then shot her in the head. He afterwards wrote a note saying that he loved her.

It was the first of many murders, and in the early hours of the following morning he carried out his original intention by stabbing his wife to death. Just a few hours after that, heavily armed, he went to the local university campus, where he climbed the observation tower, killed the receptionist on the twenty-seventh floor with a blow of his rifle butt, then shot three other people, killing two of them. Finally, just before noon, he began firing from the top of the tower at people below.

During the next hour and a half Whitman, an ex-Marine, killed another sixteen people and wounded many more. The tower was surrounded by police, and at one point a marksman tried to shoot him from a light plane — but this attempt was called off when Whitman returned the fire. The shooting then continued until three policemen stormed the tower and killed him.

Whitman had appeared to be quite normal until some months earlier, when his mother suddenly left his father after years of ill-treatment. This disturbed

Whitman in some way, and not long afterwards he went to see the campus psychiatrist, complaining of severe headaches and manic rages, which sometimes resulted in assaults on his wife.

In his typewritten note of 31 July, he said that he could not understand his violent impulses. 'I am prepared to die,' he said. 'After my death, I wish an autopsy on me to be performed to see if there is any mental disorder.' Later he wrote a note, '12.00 a.m. — Mother already dead, 3 o'clock — both dead.' He also said that he hated his father and that life was not worth living.

Following his death, a tumour was found on Whitman's brain, but medical experts did not regard this as the cause of his violent rages. The twenty-one murders which he committed in little more than thirteen hours are therefore inexplicable.

Double Axe Murder in Fall River. 1892

AUGUST
4

About 9.30 a.m. on 4 August 1892, Mrs Abby Borden, the sixty-five-year-old second wife of a wealthy businessman, was brutally murdered as she dusted the spare bedroom of her home on Fall River, Massachusetts. Her attacker struck her over the head with an axe while she was kneeling on the floor, then went on to strike another eighteen blows when she was already dead. The body lay undiscovered until much later in the morning — and in the meantime the victim's husband was killed in the same way.

Andrew J. Borden, aged sixty-nine, had gone out

after breakfast to attend to business matters. On returning just before 11 a.m., he settled down to have a rest in the living room, unaware that he was now a widower. A few minutes afterwards he, too, was attacked and killed, the culprit in his case striking ten blows. In view of the fact that an hour and a half had elapsed between the two crimes, it was naturally suspected that the killer was another member of the household.

Before long suspicion fell upon Lizzie, Andrew Borden's second daughter by his first marriage. Lizzie, an unmarried woman of thirty-two, had been in the house all the morning, and shortly after 11 a.m. had sent for the local doctor, saying that her father had been killed. Nothing was said at this stage about her stepmother's death, and when a neighbour asked where Mrs Borden was, Lizzie replied, 'I'm sure I don't know, for she had a note from someone to go and see somebody who is sick.' However, she then made the extraordinary remark, 'But I don't know perhaps that she isn't killed also, for I thought I heard her coming in.' It was shortly after this, when the neighbour and another woman began a search of the house, that the second body was found.

Lizzie Borden had borne her stepmother a good deal of ill-will and resented her father's meanness. She was strangely calm after the discovery of the bodies, but also made statements which contradicted each other. The police learnt that members of the household, including Mr and Mrs Borden (but not Lizzie), had been ill with food poisoning during the days preceding the murder, and that Lizzie had tried unsuccessfully to buy prussic acid on 3 August. A search of the cellar led to the discovery of a recently-cleaned axe-head, which they supposed to have been part of the murder weapon.

Following the inquest, which was held in secret, Lizzie was charged with the crimes. Her trial, which took place in New Bedford in June 1893, aroused nation-wide interest, and although the case against her at first seemed very strong, some of the evidence — of the prisoner contradicting herself at the inquest, for example — was not allowed, and her elder sister and the family's maid both played down Lizzie's hatred of Mrs Borden. Lizzie gave a good impression of herself, appearing refined and modest; it did her case no harm when she fainted in the courtroom, or even when she declined to give evidence on her own behalf. At the end of the ten-day trial she was acquitted.

She returned to Fall River, where she bought herself a larger house. Her sister shared it with her for a while, but moved out after a quarrel. Lizzie then lived alone for the rest of her life, dying in 1927.

The murders for which she had been tried were never officially solved, for Lizzie was the only real suspect, and it is generally believed that she was, in fact, guilty. The case has inspired many books, as well as five stage plays and a ballet. The American authoress Victoria Lincoln argues in *A Private Disgrace* that the crimes were committed while Lizzie was suffering from an attack of temporal epilepsy.

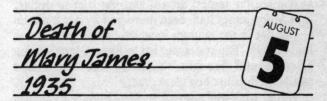

Death of Mary James, 1935

AUGUST 5

On 5 August 1935, Mary James, the fifth wife of Robert James, a barber's shop proprietor, was found dead in the lily pond at the couple's bungalow in Los Angeles. She had apparently drowned in just a few inches of water, and it was assumed that this had been the result of an accident. Little notice was taken of a grotesque swelling of her left leg, which was thought at the time to have been caused by an insect bite. But a few weeks later, when Robert James was reported for accosting a woman in the street, the police began to make further inquiries about him.

James, whose real name was Raymond Lisemba, was a native of Alabama, married for the first time in 1921. Three of his first four marriages had ended in divorce, James being a pervert who enjoyed whipping his partners as well as being whipped himself. But his third marriage had ended in circumstances which the Los Angeles police found to be of greater interest than that. Winona James had drowned in her bath only a short while after the marriage had taken place, and as a result her husband had collected $14,000 insurance money. This was particularly suspicious because James had profited in the same way — though to a lesser extent — from Mary's death.

Detectives also learnt that Charles Hope, who had worked for James in his barber's shop, had bought two rattlesnakes from a Long Beach snake farm in July 1935, returning them less than two weeks later with the comment that they 'didn't work'. When Hope was questioned about this, he said that the snakes, named Lethal and Lightning, had been purchased on James' behalf, and went on to declare that Mary James had been murdered by her husband — but not in the manner in which he had intended to murder her. The statement led to Robert James being arrested and brought to trial, with the snakes exhibited in court in a glass cage.

Hope, who was allowed to turn State's Evidence, told the court that James had offered him $100 to find two such snakes, as he wanted to have somebody bitten by them. Hope had agreed to do this, and Lethal and Lightning were actually the third pair that he had acquired on James' behalf, the first two pairs having proved unable even to kill rabbits. On the night of the murder, he said, he took the snakes to the couple's bungalow in a box, but did not produce them until Mary James, who was pregnant, had drunk so much whisky that she had become insensible, and so was unable to resist when the two men undressed her and held her down on the kitchen table.

The box was then taken into the kitchen, and the lid pushed back far enough for Mary's foot to be inserted, continued Hope. But although she was bitten several times, and her leg was badly swollen, she remained alive and began to recover from her drunken stupor. Her husband then became impatient and drowned her in bathwater, afterwards drying and dressing the body to avoid suspicion. Finally, Hope helped him to carry it out to the lily pond, where it appeared that she had accidentally fallen and drowned.

The trial, which took place during the summer of 1936, naturally attracted a great deal of attention. On being found guilty, 'Rattlesnake' James — as he became popularly called — was sentenced to death, his accomplice being given a life sentence. A series of appeals followed, but each of them was turned down, and eventually, on 1 May 1942, James became the last person to be hanged in California. Subsequent executions in that state were carried out in the gas chamber.

Execution of William Kemmler, 1890

On 6 August 1890, William Kemmler, a convicted murderer, was executed in the electric chair in New York's Auburn Prison. He was the first person to be put to death by this method, which the state had adopted in the expectation that it would prove to be more humane than hanging. The death chamber was a large room, with seats provided for officials, reporters and witnesses, but the apparatus was controlled from an adjoining room, where the executioner was hidden from view.

Kemmler, a short, black-haired man wearing a new suit, had murdered his mistress, Tillie Zeigler, with a hatchet in March the previous year. Having been ushered into the room by the warden, Charles F. Durston — who introduced him to the spectators in the manner of a master of ceremonies — he sat down calmly and made a short statement. The newspapers had been saying a lot of things about him which were untrue, he said. However, he wished everyone good luck and concluded, 'I believe I am going to a good place.'

He then had to take off his coat before he could be strapped to the chair and the electrodes fitted into place — one to his head, the other to his back, where his shirt had been torn to expose the flesh.

When all was finally ready the warden knocked twice on the door of the adjoining room, and the executioner threw the switch. The current was kept on for seventeen seconds, until the doctors present ordered it to be switched off. They then gathered round the chair, supposing Kemmler to be dead.

What happened next was described by the *New York World*'s reporter as follows:

'Suddenly the breast heaved. There was a straining at the straps which bound him ... The man was alive. Warden, physicians, everybody, lost their wits. There was a startled cry for the current to be turned on again. Signals, only half understood, were given to those in the next room at the switchboard. When they knew what had happened, they were prompt to act, and the switch-handle could be heard as it was pulled back and forth, breaking the deadly current into jets.'

Though Kemmler was unconscious, and therefore unaware of what was happening, it was accepted that the execution had been bungled, and at the second attempt the current was kept on for four minutes before the prisoner was pronounced dead.

The execution made headline news and there was much criticism for its 'unnecessary brutality': one English newspaper declared that it had 'sent a thrill of horror around the globe'. But New York was unwilling to return to 'the barbarism of hanging', and the electric chair was soon in regular use.

It is not known for certain who officiated at this first execution by electricity, but it was probably Edwin F. Davis, a wiry little electrician with a drooping black moustache, who was employed at the prison and known to have supervised the chair's construction.

Davis, at any rate, became New York's official executioner soon afterwards and later operated in New Jersey and Massachusetts, too. He carried out about 240 executions altogether before retiring in 1914.

Double execution at Darwin Jail, 1952

On 8 August 1952, two young immigrants were hanged at Darwin Jail, in Australia's Northern Territory, for murdering a taxi-driver. Jerry Koci, a twenty-year-old Czech, and his Rumanian accomplice, Jonas Nopoty, aged nineteen, had killed and robbed their victim, George Grantham, after asking him to drive them out of Darwin on the evening of 20 April previously. They left his body hidden in a patch of scrub off the Stuart Highway, and made off in his dark green Plymouth sedan.

George Grantham was a cheerful man, well known in the Darwin area. Shortly before his death he told his wife over the telephone that he had 'a job a bit out of town, with a couple of fellows', and so would not be home until after midnight. He also said that he had won over £600 at the Tennant Creek races earlier the same day.

When his disappearance was reported police started a search for him, asking aircraft pilots to report all cars seen in desolate areas and motorists to look out for car tracks leading off main roads. It was as a result of these appeals that the body was discovered by two other Northern Territory residents.

Grantham had been shot in the back of the head and stabbed in the region of the heart. The brutality of the crime shocked and angered the inhabitants of Darwin, and friends of the dead man threatened to form lynch mobs. 'You get the murderer and leave him to us,' they said to police officers. 'We'll do the hanging.'

Koci and Nopoty were apprehended while travel-

ling-

ling in the stolen Plymouth in the direction of a small town in north-west Queensland. Nopoty then revealed that it was for the sake of his vehicle that Grantham had been murdered.

Koci had earlier been involved in a car accident in which a small boy had been killed. Because of this, he was frightened of being arrested, and therefore proposed a desperate course of action. 'We'll get hold of a car and then kill the driver,' he said. 'Then we can get to Melbourne and get a ship back to Europe.'

This, at least, was Nopoty's explanation of the crime, and Koci did not deny that it was true. He refused to make a statement of any sort.

The two men were taken back to Darwin, where police officers had to guard the jail in order to prevent them being lynched. When they appeared for trial the streets outside the courthouse were full of people, and it was no secret that they intended to take the law into their own hands in the event of the prisoners being acquitted. The residents of the Northern Territory afterwards made it known that they would not tolerate commutations of sentence, either.

It was only when the executions were carried out that the danger of a lynching was averted.

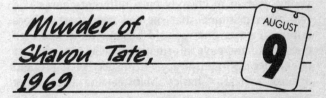

Murder of Sharon Tate, 1969

On 9 August 1969, three members of a hippie commune broke into the Los Angeles home of the film producer Roman Polanski and killed five people — including his twenty-six-year-old pregnant wife, the actress Sharon Tate. Four of the victims (Sharon Tate and three guests) were stabbed repeatedly; two of these were also shot — one in addition to being battered over the head with a blunt instrument. The fifth victim was a youth of eighteen, who was shot four times after stopping his car in the drive. Before leaving the scene the murderers daubed the slogan 'PIG' on the front door in Sharon Tate's blood.

The following night the same group, together with others — including Charles Manson, the commune leader — murdered Leno LaBianca, the forty-four-year-old president of a chain of grocery stores, and his wife Rosemary, aged thirty-five, also in Los Angeles, in a similar fashion. They broke into their victims' home, stabbed both of them many times and daubed slogans in blood on two of their walls and on the door of their refrigerator. One of the slogans on this occasion was 'HEALTER SKELTER', which was evidently a mis-spelling; the others were, 'DEATH TO PIGS' and 'RISE'. A further slogan, 'WAR', was scored on Leno LaBianca's body.

There was no known connection between the two sets of victims, and while the Los Angeles Police Department investigated the 'Sharon Tate Murders', the other crime was left to the Los Angeles Sheriff's Office. Neither was able to find out who the culprits were until many weeks later, when it was learnt that a young woman in custody on a different charge had told other prisoners that she had taken part in both crimes. Twenty-one-year-old Susan Atkins was then questioned and gave information which led to charges of murder and conspiracy to murder being brought against herself, Charles Manson and four other people.

Manson, who was thirty-five years old and only five foot two inches tall, was a violent man with a long record of crime. He lived with his hippie band in shacks on a movie ranch in the Simi Hills, thirty miles from Los Angeles, where they took hallucinogenic drugs and held sex orgies. But although his followers saw him as a Christ-like figure, and obeyed his orders without hesitation, Manson envied people who were rich and successful, and had a list of 'pigs' to be killed in a general day of reckoning which he referred to by the code-name 'Helter Skelter'.

According to Susan Atkins, he had ordered the murders of 9 August because another member of the group had been arrested in connection with a different one, and was then so pleased with the panic which they caused that he planned and personally took part in those of the following day.

Manson, Susan Atkins and two other members of the commune — Patricia Krenwinkel and Leslie Van Houten — were brought to trial in Los Angeles on 15 June 1970. Of the others who had been indicted, Linda Kasabian had been accepted as a prosecution witness, as she had not killed anybody herself — at Polanski's home, for example, she had stayed outside while the three main culprits broke in and murdered the people they found there — and Charles Watson was in Idaho, resisting extradition.

During the course of the trial, which lasted nine months, there were many sensations. On one occasion Manson hacked a cross into his forehead, and this inspired the three girls to burn similar marks onto theirs. On another he leapt ten feet over the counsel table and tried to attack the judge — which caused the judge to begin carrying a revolver. Eventually three of the prisoners were each convicted on seven counts of murder in the first degree and one of conspiracy to murder; the fourth — Leslie Van Houten — was found guilty on two counts of murder in the first degree and one of conspiracy. All four prisoners were sentenced to death.

Charles Watson was tried separately in 1971, and he, too, was sentenced to death after being convicted on seven counts of murder in the first degree and one of conspiracy. Manson, Susan Atkins and other members of the commune were subsequently convicted of other murders.

All of the death sentences passed in connection with these crimes were automatically commuted to life imprisonment when the California Supreme Court, in February 1972, voted to abolish the death penalty for murder.

Beginning of Transvaal Poisoning case, 1925

During the early hours of 10 August 1925, a middle-aged couple living in the northern Transvaal village of Koster, thirty-six miles from Rustenburg, were awakened by their son-in-law's mistress, who told them that their daughter, Anna Nortje, was ill. Mr and Mrs du Plessis accompanied the woman back to Anna's home, where they found their daughter dead and their son-in-law, Jan Christian Nortje, in tears. Nortje said that Anna, who was fully dressed except for her shoes, had died after being suddenly taken ill. She had complained of a pain in her back.

Mr and Mrs du Plessis were immediately suspicious. Anna had been to their home with her four young children the previous afternoon and had been in good health and spirits when she left. Besides that, their son Adrian — the husband of Nortje's mistress — had died mysteriously a year earlier, at the age of twenty-seven. They therefore called in the district surgeon, Dr Theodore Radloff, and insisted that this

230

second death should be investigated more thoroughly than the first.

Nortje then became evasive about the symptoms which had preceded his wife's death, protesting that he had been 'too overcome with grief to notice (them)', so a post-mortem was carried out and the dead woman's organs were sent to a medical research institute for analysis. It was thus discovered that Anna Nortje had been poisoned with strychnine.

At the inquest which followed Nortje said that his wife had suffered from pains in her chest and back for some time, and hinted that village gossip about his affair with her sister-in-law, Dirkie Cathrina du Plessis, had driven her to suicide. On 9 August, when the children had been put to bed, Anna had cooked an evening meal for the three of them — for Dirkie frequently stayed overnight at their home — then went to bed herself. Shortly afterwards he found her to be unwell, and not long after that she was dead. Nortje also claimed that a note left by Anna, saying that her heart was 'sore and full of grief', had been destroyed by the children.

Dirkie, a mother of two, gave a slightly different account, stating that she had gone to fetch Mr and Mrs du Plessis while her sister-in-law was at the point of death, and that Anna was dead by the time she returned with them. Nortje, at this point, was strangely quiet, claiming to have seen an inexplicable purple light — which he took to be a 'premonition of evil' — outside the house.

Although there was no evidence against them, Nortje and his mistress were widely suspected of having poisoned Anna and the police were criticized for failing to arrest them. A search of Nortje's home on 1 September resulted in the discovery of a broken poison bottle, and inquiries revealed that during the month of July Nortje had obtained strychnine from a chemist in the village, darting out of the shop before he could be asked to sign the poison register. The police also learnt of other occasions on which either Nortje or Dirkie had tried to acquire poison. When the two lovers were arrested in December written evidence of their liaison was found at Dirkie's home.

At their trial in Rustenburg in June 1926 the prosecution produced evidence of a confession which Nortje had allegedly made to another prisoner. Nortje, however, denied having been Dirkie's lover, or having bought or attempted to buy poison. He said that his wife had complained of being in pain during the late afternoon of 9 August and had not eaten much of the evening meal because she 'felt bad'. Under cross-examination, he admitted that Anna had been ill for about five hours before her death, and that neither he nor Dirkie had done anything to help her. Dirkie later admitted having attempted to buy poison pills, saying that she wanted them to use for killing dogs.

On being found guilty, both prisoners collapsed and the judge had to adjourn the court before passing sentence of death. Some weeks later Dirkie's sentence was commuted to a long prison term by the Executive Council, but Nortje was told that in his own case the death sentence would be carried out.

From his cell in Pretoria Central Prison, he then wrote a long letter to the Minister of Justice, once more declaring that he was innocent of his wife's murder. As this was delivered just a few hours before he was due to be hanged, a brief postponement was ordered so that the matter could be considered afresh. This time, though no credence could be given to his statement, it was decided that mercy should be shown. Nortje's sentence was accordingly commuted to life imprisonment.

Execution of William Sanchez Hepper, 1954

AUGUST
11

On 11 August 1954, William Sanchez de Pina Hepper, an artist and former BBC news translator aged sixty-two, was hanged at Wandsworth Prison, in London, for the murder of Margaret Spevick, the eleven-year-old daughter of a friend of his wife's. The crime had been committed at Hepper's flat in Hove, Sussex, where the victim was found raped and strangled six months earlier. Margaret, who attended the same London school as his own daughter, had been staying with Hepper for a few days in order to convalesce after breaking her arm.

Hepper, who had once suffered head injuries in a car accident — it was for this reason that he had resigned from the BBC — rarely saw his wife and claimed to be haunted by dreams of her infidelity. It had been his idea that Margaret should stay with him, and shortly after her arrival she had sent her mother a postcard, saying that she was having 'a splendid time'. After her death an unfinished portrait of her was found on an easel near her body.

The crime was discovered by Mrs Spevick on the evening of 7 February, when she went to the flat to see her daughter, whom she had expected to meet earlier in the day in nearby Brighton: she had to get the caretaker of the block to let her in, as nobody had opened the door to her. Hepper had already fled the country by this time, and was arrested a few days later in Spain, where he had once been a spy. The following month he was extradited to Britain.

At his trial at the Lewes Assizes in July he pleaded insanity. He told the court that he had bouts of amnesia and hallucinations, and it was suggested on his behalf that in assaulting the child he had been under the impression that he was attacking his wife.

But on being asked why he had left the country without informing Margaret's parents, the prisoner could only reply, 'I did not do things properly because I was not in a normal condition.' And a Hove psychiatrist, who told the court that the accused had regarded the crime as a hallucination, was obliged to admit that he could not explain Hepper's sudden flight.

The jury therefore rejected the plea of insanity and the prisoner was found guilty of murder.

Execution of Richard Brinkley, 1907

AUGUST
13

On 13 August 1907, Richard Brinkley, a fifty-three-year-old jobbing gardener, was hanged for the murder of a middle-aged couple at their home in Croydon, Surrey, on the night of 20 April previously. Richard and Annie Beck had both died after drinking oatmeal stout poisoned with prussic acid which Brinkley had intended for their lodger, Reginald Parker. Daisy Beck, the couple's twenty-one-year-old daughter, had also drunk some of the stout but had recovered after being rushed to hospital.

On 17 December 1906, Brinkley, who lived in Fulham, south-west London, had tricked Parker into signing a forged will, pretending that it was a list of people invited to go on a picnic outing during the spring. The will was ostensibly that of his own land-

lady, an elderly German woman named Mrs Blume
— who had also been tricked into signing it — and
stated that he was to receive her home and furniture,
together with all her stocks and cash. The second
'witness' was a man named Henry Heard, who had
presumably been tricked as well.

When Mrs Blume died on 19 December, a
coroner's jury accepted that her death was the result
of a cerebral haemorrhage. But when Brinkley
produced the will — after the inquest had taken place
— Mrs Blume's relatives decided to contest it. This
meant that both Parker and Heard would be questioned about the document at some stage, and that
Brinkley would be sent to prison.

Brinkley, keeping up the pretence of friendship,
then started visiting Parker at home almost every
evening and tried repeatedly to murder him — always
by putting poison into his food or drink after asking
him to go out and fetch a glass of water. But on each
occasion Parker — who now suspected that his was
one of the signatures on Mrs Blume's will — managed
to outwit him by declining to touch anything which
had been left in Brinkley's presence.

On the evening of 20 April Brinkley arrived with
the bottle of stout and, in spite of the fact that he was
normally a teetotaller, drank some of it himself before
offering any to Parker. There was no prussic acid in it
at that stage, but shortly afterwards Brinkley asked
Parker for the usual glass of water and poisoned the
stout while he was out of the room. Unfortunately for
him, Parker was no less suspicious than on other
occasions, and on returning refused to drink any more
of it.

The two men later took Parker's dog out for a
walk, leaving the unfinished bottle on his table. The
Becks, who had also been out for part of the evening,
found it there when they came indoors, and for some
reason thought they were entitled to help themselves

to the contents. They were thus poisoned by accident because their lodger realized that Brinkley was trying to poison him.

Surprisingly, though Parker had been in fear of his life for several months, he had made no attempt to avoid seeing Brinkley and had not sought the aid of the police. But on hearing what had happened to Mr and Mrs Beck, he revealed all that he knew of the affair. Brinkley, who had parted company with him in the street, was arrested in Fulham the following day.

He denied all knowledge of what had happened, saying that he had not seen Parker for three weeks. But a boy working in a Croydon off-licence remembered selling him the bottle of stout on the evening in question and a railway inspector who knew him by sight was certain that he had bought a rail ticket to Croydon on the same evening. It was also discovered that Brinkley had obtained prussic acid from a doctor's dispenser in Manor Road, South Norwood.

Though no evidence of poisoning was found during a second examination of Mrs Blume's body, there was enough evidence against Brinkley to ensure his conviction not only for the murder of Mr and Mrs Beck but also for the attempted murder of Daisy Beck and Reginald Parker.

His trial took place at the Guildford Assizes, and his execution at Wandsworth Prison.

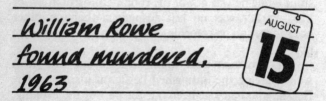

William Rowe
found murdered.
1963

AUGUST
15

On the morning of 15 August 1963, William Garfield Rowe, a sixty-four-year-old recluse, was found murdered on his farm near the village of Constantine, in Cornwall. His skull had been shattered, there was a gash in his throat, his jaw was fractured, and he had suffered many other injuries to his scalp and chest. The farmhouse had afterwards been ransacked, his killer or killers missing some £3000 which Mr Rowe had had hidden there. Mr Rowe had last been seen alive about 9.15 the previous evening.

Following the discovery of the body, road-blocks were set up in the area, and on 16 August a twenty-three-year-old man named Russell Pascoe, who had been stopped while riding a motor-cycle in the village, was questioned about his movements on the night of the murder. He said that he had been at a caravan near Truro, about fourteen miles away, with his friend Dennis Whitty and three teenage girls. But he admitted having known the victim and said that he had worked for him three or four years earlier.

Pascoe, Whitty and the three girls were taken to Falmouth police station for questioning, and the girls then told the police that on the night of the murder the two men had left the caravan on Pascoe's motor-cycle to 'do a job', taking a starting-pistol, an iron bar and a knife. They had returned in the early hours of the morning, Pascoe downcast and frightened-looking and his companion grinning. Later, after Whitty had confessed that he and Pascoe were responsible for Mr Rowe's murder, both men warned the girls that they would suffer the same fate if they revealed this to anyone else.

On being charged, Pascoe, a builder's labourer, admitted that he had been present at the crime, but said that he had 'only' hit the deceased on the head with the iron bar: it was Whitty who 'went mad with the knife', he claimed. He then gave an account of what had happened, stating:

'We went on my motor-bike and knocked on (the farmhouse) door at about 11 o'clock. Old man Rowe answered the door. Dennis was standing in front of the door and said he was a helicopter pilot and had crashed, and wanted to use the phone. I then hit Rowe on the back of the head with a small iron bar — I meant only to knock him out, that's all.

'He (Whitty) took the iron bar and went for him. I had to walk away, honest I did. I went inside and found £4 under a piano. Dennis took a watch and two big boxes of matches, and some keys from the old man's pockets. We shared the £4, and I've spent mine.'

Later, giving further details, Pascoe said, 'I didn't kill him — that was my mate. He went mad, he did. I didn't stop him in fear he would stick me. I had to walk away. I couldn't stop him. He said he finished him when he stuck the knife in his throat. I only knocked him on the head with a bar. I just knocked him out.'

Dennis John Whitty, aged twenty-two, then blamed Pascoe for what had happened. 'Pascoe made me stick him,' he said. 'I stabbed him in the chest. Pascoe was going to hit me, so I stuck him in the neck.

On 29 October the two men appeared for trial at the Bodmin Assizes, the crime being described by the prosecution as 'one of the most horrible and grue-some murders ever known in this county or this country'; both pleaded not guilty. Whitty's counsel claimed that his client had acted under 'the influence, fear and pressure of Pascoe', who three years earlier had burgled the farmhouse and stolen £200, together with jewellery which had belonged to Mr Rowe's mother; the court was also told that Whitty suffered from hysteria, black-outs and 'strange and unnatural things', such as doors opening of their own accord and a figure with wings appearing in the sky early in the morning.

However, the jury returned verdicts of guilty against both men, and they were sentenced to death.

On 17 December 1963, Pascoe was hanged at Bristol and Whitty at Winchester.

William Rowe had been a First World War deserter whose parents had hidden him for over thirty years at their farm in the fishing village of Porthleven, in Cornwall. When his father died, his mother and brother moved to Constantine, with Mr Rowe hiding under a pile of clothing in a cart. But after he had lived in secrecy for thirty-nine years — with everyone outside his immediate family believing him to be dead — an amnesty was declared and William Rowe was able to emerge as a living person.

Besides the £3000 which his murderers had missed, he had had other large sums hidden in the farm grounds — one in a safe buried in the floor of a cowshed, another in a large glass jar buried else-where. These were eventually found as a result of directions in a diary which he had left, written in Esperanto.

Execution of Santo-Geronimo Caserio, 1894

AUGUST
16

On 16 August 1894, a young Italian anarchist was executed in front of the Prison Saint-Paul in Lyons. Santo-Geronimo Caserio, who had assassinated the French President, Sadi Carnot, was far from fearless — indeed, he was terrified, and moaned inarticulately all the way from his cell to the guillotine. At the last minute, however, he managed to pull himself together for one final act of defiance. 'Courage, comrades —

and long live anarchy!' he called out in a weak voice. As he did so, the blade fell.

Caserio, a native of Motta-Visconti, near Milan, had been born in 1873, and apprenticed to a baker at the age of thirteen. He became an anarchist in 1891, and not long afterwards was given a sentence of eight months' imprisonment for distributing revolutionary literature to soldiers at a Milan barracks. He left Italy in the spring of 1893 to avoid military service, and arrived in France from Switzerland in July the same year.

For several months prior to the assassination, Caserio lived in Cette, a seaport on the Mediterranean, staying at the home of a baker named Viala, who was also his employer. He left Viala suddenly, bought himself a dagger, then made his way to Lyons, where the crime was committed. He had apparently been planning to strike 'a staggering blow' against the existing social order for quite some time.

Carnot was murdered on the evening of 24 June 1894, while he was in Lyons attending the Universal Exhibition. He was being driven to the theatre in a carriage when Caserio dashed out of the crowd lining his route and stabbed him in the chest. He died three hours later.

Caserio, who had been arrested at the scene, admitted that he was the person responsible and identified the weapon without any sign of remorse. He said that he had planned and carried out the crime on his own, without confiding his intention to anyone. At his trial at the beginning of August he described it in detail.

'When I saw the carriage approaching, I drew my dagger from my pocket, overturned two young people in front of me, threw aside the sheath, and then sprang forward,' he said. 'I grasped the carriage door with my left hand, and with my right I struck downwards with all my force.'

He went on to say that after striking the blow, he cried, 'Long live the revolution!' And he added, 'When I had stabbed the President, he looked me fixedly in the face and then sank back.'

The defence claimed that the prisoner was an epileptic and that his crime had been committed as a result of 'some mysterious and irresistible force'. It was also argued — to his own indignation — that he had been merely the 'striking arm' of others. But all this was to no avail: the jury retired for only ten minutes before finding him guilty without extenuating circumstances.

Though overcome with emotion after being sentenced to death, Caserio managed to shout a number of slogans before being taken from the courtroom.

Post Office massacre in Oklahoma 1986

AUGUST 20

On the morning of 20 August 1986, Patrick Sherrill, a forty-four-year-old part-time postman, entered the Edmond, Oklahoma, post office armed with three pistols and began shooting his fellow workers. In the space of just eight minutes, beginning at six minutes past seven, he killed fourteen people and wounded others. He then remained trapped in the building for an hour and a quarter, finally killing himself as police burst in.

Sherrill, who had been working at the post office for about eighteen months off and on, was a solitary man with a sense of grievance. He had been an object of derision for much of his life — he was reputed to be a Peeping Tom, for one thing — and had a violent temper which caused him to be known locally as 'Crazy Pat'. He appeared to have been deteriorating mentally since his discharge from the US Marine Corps over twenty years earlier.

'He was sick in the head,' one of his neighbours said afterwards. 'He should have been put away long ago. He was always angry at something — like he didn't know what he was angry about.' The same woman, whose eleven-year-old son had once been threatened by Sherrill, also remarked, 'We're black — and he didn't like blacks. He didn't like much of anything.'

But Sherrill had a keen interest in guns, and was a firearms instructor in the Oklahoma Air National Guard. A few weeks before the massacre he had been sent to Britain, to help supervise the training of US service personnel stationed at RAF Mildenhall, in Suffolk, and at the end of August he was due to take part in a national competition in Little Rock, Arkansas. His conduct while on National Guard duty had always been exemplary.

As a postman, however, he left much to be desired; his performance ratings were unfavourable and he was often in trouble; only the day before the shootings he had been threatened with dismissal. He confided his problems with his supervisors to a young female employee, telling her, 'They'll be sorry — and everyone's going to know about it. Everybody's gonna know.' Thirty-eight-year-old Richard Esser, one of the supervisors concerned, was the first person to be killed the following morning.

When police officers went to Sherrill's home they found amateur radio equipment, a computer, piles of clothes, books, paramilitary and sex magazines, two air pistols, an air rifle and boxes of ammunition. They also discovered that the hallway had been used as an indoor shooting-range, with mounted targets in one of the bedrooms. But there was only one chair in the whole house — a sure sign that visitors hadn't been welcome.

Though post office union officials in Edmond were as shocked as everyone else by what had happened, they were quick to point out that there had recently been a lot of friction between rank-and-file workers and their supervisors as a result of pressure to increase productivity. In their view, this pressure had often amounted to harassment, and it was not really surprising that a disturbed man like Sherrill should have reacted in such an extreme way.

Murder of Rose Render, 1911

During the early hours of 21 August 1911, a nineteen-year-old waitress named Rose Render was stabbed to death in the Clerkenwell district of London. A passer-by heard her cries of 'Don't, Charles! Don't!' — followed by screams — but made no attempt to help her. It was not until later in the morning, when a milkman going through Wilmington Square found her body lying on the pavement, that the crime was brought to the attention of the police.

The girl was found to have been living with a man named Charles Ellsome until shortly before her death. Ellsome, aged twenty-two, described himself as a labourer, but Rose had, in fact, been keeping him and had taken to prostitution on his account. On being confronted in a café in Soho the day after the murder, Ellsome gave his name as Brown, but told police officers, 'It's me you want.' He later claimed that all he had meant by this was that he knew he would be suspected of the crime.

Ellsome was charged with murder and appeared at the Old Bailey on 13 September, his trial lasting less than a day. A friend of the accused, a man named Fletcher, told the court that on 21 August Ellsome had woken him up between two and three o'clock in the morning and said that he had killed Rose, declaring. 'She drove me to it!' He went on to say that he had threatened her with his knife, and that Rose had thrown up her arms, saying, 'Here you are, then — do it!' He had then stabbed her eight or nine times in a fit of anger.

Fletcher was hardly the most impressive of witnesses. Under cross-examination he admitted that he suffered from epilepsy and that he had had a fit the day before the murder. Worse still, he boasted: 'I thieve for my living, and I'm proud of it!' However, it was proved that Ellsome had bought a long-bladed chef's knife a few days before the crime, and the victim's father accused him of trying to intimidate her. The jury took only half an hour to find the prisoner guilty, and on being asked whether he had anything to say before sentence was passed, Ellsome raised his eyes towards the ceiling, remarking, 'I have only got one Judge.'

The trial judge, Mr Justice Avory, was not taken in by this display of piety. 'The prisoner has been living the most degraded life that a man can live,' he said. 'I cannot doubt that he took away the life of the girl, not from jealousy that she loved another man, or that another man loved her, but from jealousy that another man should reap the benefit of her immoral life. For the crime of which he has been convicted, he must die.'

However, in his summing-up Avory had inadvertently misdirected the jury. Reminding them that they should not accept Fletcher's evidence without corroboration, he had intimated that such corroboration was provided by a statement made by that witness immediately after the murder. As the statement to which he was referring had not been introduced as evidence, the Court of Criminal Appeal was obliged to set aside the conviction — the first time it had done so in a case of murder. The prisoner had therefore to be released, as the court had no power to order a retrial.

Murder of an elephant-keeper, 1928

On the night of 24 August 1928, London Zoo's chief elephant-keeper, Sayed Ali, was battered to death by his assistant, a young Burmese named San Dwe. The two men shared rooms above the Tapir House, near the Outer Circle of Regent's Park, and it was there that the crime was committed. It was later claimed that the blows had been struck with 'a ferocity that was beyond belief'.

As far as the police were concerned, this unusual case began when two officers on patrol in the area heard groans coming from the back of the building and stopped to investigate. San Dwe, who was lying on the ground with a wounded foot, said that four men had broken into the place and killed Sayed Ali with a pick-axe. They had tried to kill him, too, but he had managed to escape, he added excitedly.

The police officers went inside the building and found

Sayed Ali's body; he had died of head injuries. His room had been ransacked and a wooden box broken open, but nothing had been taken. Two bags of copper coins were found, together with a wallet containing £36; a bloodstained pickaxe and a sledge-hammer were also found at the scene. However, the wounded man's story was not believed and, on being discharged from hospital, he was arrested.

San Dwe had arrived in London from Rangoon the previous year in charge of a white elephant. The elephant did not take to the English climate, and so was sent back to Burma not long afterwards. But San Dwe stayed on at the zoo as Sayed Ali's assistant, and deputized for him when he went for several months' holiday in his native Calcutta — as he did every year. During those months San Dwe received up to thirty shillings (£1.50) a week in tips from visitors whose children had had rides on the elephants in his care, and he was entitled to keep all this money himself.

Even so, he was not happy in England; he fretted over the loss of the animal which had been sent back to Burma, and longed to rejoin it there. Moreover, with the return of Sayed Ali from India, he had only minor duties to perform and lost his extra source of income. It seems that he killed his chief in the hope of stealing money, but then lost his nerve or suffered from feelings of guilt.

At his trial, which took place in November 1928, San Dwe was convicted of murder. His death sentence was later commuted to penal servitude for life, but he remained in jail only until 1932, when his case was considered by a special board. On his release, he was sent back to Burma.

Murder of Charles Fox, 1933

During the early hours of 27 August 1933, Charles William Fox, a twenty-four-year-old metal worker living in West Bromwich, Staffordshire, was woken up by his wife, who said that she had heard a noise coming from downstairs. He went to investigate, with Mrs Fox following, and, on looking into one of the downstairs rooms, found the window open. He immediately went to close it, unaware that the person who had opened it was in the room.

At that moment the candle which he was holding went out, and Mrs Fox heard a scuffle and a groan in the darkness. She called out to her husband, to go back upstairs with her, then returned to the bedroom alone. But a moment later, as she stood there trembling, he staggered into the room with a knife stuck in his back. Unable to speak, he threw his arms round her, then fell to the floor and died.

Mrs Fox threw open the bedroom window and screamed for help. Shortly afterwards two policemen arrived at the house, but by that time the intruder had fled. It was found that he had cut out one of the panes of the sash window by which he had entered, and left bloodstained glass both inside and outside. A doctor called to the scene found that the dead man had been stabbed seven times, one of the blows piercing his lung.

Not long after the murder had taken place a burglary was committed at the home of a butcher named Newton, half a mile away. In this case, in addition to stealing a few pounds in cash, the culprit stayed at the scene to have a shave — using the butcher's razor — and also made use of a needle and cotton which he had found in a work-basket. He eventually left, though not without leaving his fingerprints on a milk bottle. These were found to match others on file at Scotland Yard, identifying him as Stanley Eric Hobday — a man already known to the local police.

A few hours after the burglary, a farm labourer near High Legh, Cheshire, about seventy miles away, heard the sound of a crash and saw a car turn a complete somersault in a nearby lane — after which the damaged car was abandoned. The vehicle had been stolen from a private garage in West Bromwich, and one of Hobday's fingerprints was found on the starting-handle. A suitcase containing some of his belongings was also found.

In their search for Hobday, the police were assisted by the BBC, using radio for the first time to broadcast a description of somebody they wanted to interview. Three days later he was arrested near Gretna Green, in Dumfriesshire.

Hobday was a little man, whose extraordinarily small shoes — they were size four — matched plaster casts of footprints found in the soil outside Charles Fox's window. A cut in one of the sleeves of his jacket — with bloodstains round it — had been darned with black cotton identical to that found in the needle used at Mr Newton's home; it was also found to correspond with an unhealed cut on Hobday's elbow.

Hobday told the police that he had hidden the suitcase just before the murder, and afterwards found it to be missing from its hiding place. A sheath knife which he was known to have owned had been inside it at the time of its disappearance, he claimed. But his fingerprint on the starting-handle of the stolen car proved that this story was untrue; the suitcase had been in his possession at the time of the accident, and the knife had not been among the items found inside it.

Hobday was charged with all three crimes: the murder, the burglary and the car-theft. In respect of the two lesser crimes, he was clearly guilty, but this — according to the defence when he appeared for trial in Stafford — proved that he could not have been the murderer of Charles Fox.

'Is it conceivable that any man, woman or boy, after foully murdering another human being, and with his hands still bearing the stains of blood, could calmly go off to Mr Newton's house and commit a burglary, sit down and shave himself, his nerves so calm that he could thread a needle and sit down and mend his clothes, and then go off and commit another burglary — the theft of a motor-car?' Sir Reginald Coventry asked the jury. It was a fantastic story, he declared.

But Hobday's tiny shoes proved the opposite, and after a three-day trial the jury took only forty-five minutes to find him guilty. He was duly hanged at Winson Green Prison, Birmingham, on 29 December 1933.

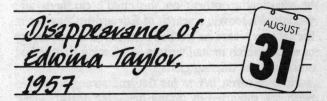

Disappearance of Edwina Taylor, 1957

AUGUST 31

On the afternoon of 31 August 1957, Edwina Taylor, a pretty girl aged four, disappeared from her home in Upper Norwood, south-east London. A search was organized by the Metropolitan Police — it proved to be one of their biggest searches ever — and various people came forward, claiming to have seen her. But none of these reported sightings led to the child's discovery, and for several days the police could find no sign of her.

Before long a second person was found to be missing from the same district: a thirty-one-year-old factory labourer named Derrick Edwardson, who lived only a quarter of a mile from Edwina's home. As Edwardson was an unstable person with a criminal record — he had indecently assaulted one little girl and threatened to murder another — it was feared that the two disappearances might be connected.

This fear was confirmed on the afternoon of 5 September, when two police officers entered the cellar beneath Edwardson's ground-floor flat and found the missing girl's body lying on a heap of coal. It was immediately clear that she had been strangled, but the post-mortem, carried out by Professor Francis Camps, revealed that she had also been sexually assaulted and struck on the head and face with a heavy blunt instrument.

Forensic evidence was found inside Edwardson's flat, linking him with the crime. Bloodstains from Edwina's group were found in his kitchen and on his suit, and fibres from her coat were found in the turn-ups of his trousers. Hairs from his dog were found to be identical to others on the child's cardigan and sandals. Moreover, a search of Edwardson's locker at the factory where he worked resulted in the discovery of a note which he had written, confessing that he had murdered the missing girl.

He had taken her to his flat and strangled her — 'with the intention of raping her after death' — but had afterwards felt ashamed of himself and thrown the body into the cellar, the note revealed. It also said that he had not interfered with the child — which the post-mortem findings showed to be untrue.

Shortly afterwards, on giving himself up, Edwardson admitted responsibility for Edwina's death. He said that he had enticed her to the flat by giving her sweets — 'just to assault her and take her home again' — but had then knocked her unconscious with the blunt end of an axe which he had bought for cutting firewood. Then, according to this account, he strangled her by accident while trying to revive her.

Haunted by the thought of the child's face, he later got up in the middle of the night to go and look at her. 'It made my hair stand on end, although I only looked at her feet,' he said.

Edwardson was charged with murder and brought to trial at the Old Bailey on 25 October 1957; he pleaded guilty and was sentenced to life imprisonment. His victim's father then wrote to the Home Secretary, asking for known sex offenders to be kept under stricter control.

beginning of the 'Pyjama Girl' case, 1934

SEPTEMBER 1

On 1 September 1934, the body of a young woman, dressed in pyjamas and partly burnt, was found in a culvert a few miles from Albury, New South Wales. Her death had been caused by savage blows to the skull with a blunt instrument — though there was also a bullet wound in her face — and had taken place anything from one to four days previously. She was apparently an Englishwoman, aged between twenty-two and twenty-eight, but her identity was unknown. Her most distinctive feature was her ears, which were an unusual shape and had no lobes.

The body was taken to Sydney University, where it

was preserved in a tank of formalin for the next ten years. Various people identified it as the body of Mrs Anna Philomena Coots, the twenty-three-year-old wife of a writer, but finally, in 1944, it was established that the 'Pyjama Girl' was Mrs Linda Agostini, an Englishwoman married to an Italian waiter. In the meantime the unsolved crime had received a good deal of publicity, and an amateur investigator — a doctor named Palmer-Benbow — had accused the New South Wales police of protecting the person responsible.

Linda Agostini, an attractive but jealous woman who drank excessively, had been living with her husband Tony in Melbourne prior to her disappearance in August 1934. When her husband was interviewed by police in July the following year he said that she had left him after a quarrel — an explanation which he had already given to friends. On being shown photographs of the dead woman at this time, he denied that she was his wife.

But in 1944 the corpse was taken out of the formalin, so that its face could be made up in a fresh attempt to solve the mystery. After that seven people said that it *was* Linda Agostini, and her husband was questioned again. Tony Agostini, who had been interned as an alien for part of the Second World War, then confessed that that was so and that he was the culprit.

He claimed that he and his wife had been unable to get on together, and that one morning she had threatened him with a gun while they were still in bed. He managed to get the gun away from her, he said, but then killed her accidentally in a struggle. The next day he drove the body to the culvert near Albury and set fire to it in order to prevent identification.

When Agostini was brought to trial in June 1944 the prosecution produced medical evidence to show that the dead woman's skull injuries had been inflicted while she was still alive, thus disproving the story that she had been shot dead by accident. The prisoner was therefore convicted of manslaughter and sentenced to a term of imprisonment with hard labour. He was eventually deported to Italy.

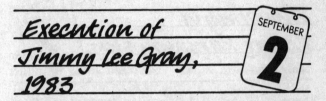

Execution of Jimmy Lee Gray, 1983

On 2 September 1983, Jimmy Lee Gray, aged thirty-four, was executed in the gas chamber of the state penitentiary in Parchman, Mississippi, for the murder of three-year-old Deressa Jean Scales. Gray, from Whittier, in California, had been convicted in 1976, but delayed the execution for almost seven years by means of a series of appeals. The last of these, to the United States Supreme Court, was rejected by a majority of six votes to three only a few hours before the sentence was carried out.

Gray entered the gas chamber just after midnight, and a few minutes afterwards the gas was released. Prison officials claimed that he was dead within two minutes, but other witnesses said that he was still convulsing and gasping for breath eight minutes later. It was the first execution in Mississippi for nineteen years.

Gray had kidnapped Deressa and taken her to a wooded area thirty miles from her home in Pascagoula. There he committed sodomy with her, then suffocated her by pressing her face into the mud. Finally, when she was dead, he threw her body off a bridge.

At the time of committing these offences, Gray was

on parole from a prison in Arizona, where he had served seven years of a twenty-year sentence. This had been imposed for the murder of his sixteen-year-old fiancée in 1968.

Shooting of Count Kamarowsky, 1907

SEPTEMBER 3

On the morning of 3 September 1907, Count Paul Kamarowsky, a Russian nobleman on holiday in Italy, was shot at his villa on the Campo Santa Maria del Giglio, in Venice, receiving wounds from which he died three days later. The crime was committed by his young fellow-countryman, Nicolas Naumoff, who had arrived at the villa a moment or two earlier, claiming to have 'important business' to discuss with him. Naumoff escaped from the scene, but was apprehended in Verona soon afterwards.

Within a few hours of his arrest three other suspects were taken into custody: a beautiful but dissolute Russian countess named Marie Tarnowska, in whose favour Kamarowsky had insured his life, her companion Elise Perrier — a Swiss girl — and Donat Prilukoff, a solicitor from Moscow who had left his wife and abandoned his practice. Prilukoff immediately made a statement in which he said that Naumoff had committed the crime, but that the Countess had planned it; he also revealed that he, too, had been involved in the conspiracy to murder the Count.

Though Marie Tarnowska denied having had anything to do with the crime, letters and telegrams discovered by the police proved that Prilukoff's allegations were true. The Countess, who was separated from her husband, had had Kamarowsky, Naumoff *and* Prilukoff as lovers all at the same time, and had used each of them to suit her own purposes. However, it was not until two and a half years later that the prisoners were brought to trial.

They eventually appeared at the Criminal Court in Venice in March 1910, the trial attracting a great deal of attention. Nicolas Naumoff told the court that he had been infatuated with Maria Tarnowska, that he had been under her 'spell', and that he had shot Kamarowsky out of jealousy, knowing that he had been intimate with the Countess. Naumoff also told the court that he believed Elsie Perrier must have known of his intention to kill the Count.

Prilukoff likewise blamed the Countess, saying that he had been happily married, prosperous and held in high esteem before he met her. 'She was too strong for me,' he declared. 'There was nothing I would not have done at her command. Because she wished it, I left my wife, I robbed my clients, I sacrificed my honour — and once I even tried to kill myself.' He went on to confess that he and Marie Tarnowska had conspired to kill Kamarowsky, stating, 'We both considered that Naumoff would be the best man to do the job.'

Marie Tarnowska — 'the Russian Vampire' — admitted that she had had affairs with many men, including Kamarowsky, Naumoff and Prilukoff, but denied being responsible for Kamarowsky's death. She agreed that she had known of Naumoff's intention to kill Kamarowsky, but said that she was unable to warn the Count that his life was in danger because she was 'acting under the orders of Prilukoff'. Shortly after this a heated argument broke out between the Countess, Naumoff and Prilukoff over who was to blame for what had happened.

Although Prilukoff and Elise Perrier were believed

to be mentally quite normal, Naumoff was shown to be a degenerate and Marie Tarnowska a drug-addict of long standing who had suffered from hysteria and convulsions.

Naumoff was found guilty of premeditated murder, though with 'responsibility lessened owing to the fact that he was suffering from a partial mental collapse'; he was therefore given a prison sentence of only three years and four months. Marie Tarnowska was found guilty of helping him, though it was accepted by the jury that 'her mental faculties were partially destroyed'; she was given a sentence of eight years and four months. Donat Prilukoff was also found guilty of helping Naumoff, and in his case a sentence of ten years' solitary confinement was passed. Elise Perrier was acquitted.

Marie Tarnowska was sent to the women's prison at Trani, on the shores of the Adriatic, to serve her sentence, but was released in 1912. She died in Paris in 1923.

Disappearance of William Lavers, 1936

SEPTEMBER
5

On the morning of 5 September 1936, William Henry Lavers, a country storekeeper of Grenfell, New South Wales, mysteriously disappeared after getting up early to serve a motorist who required petrol. Later, when his wife went outside to look for him, she found the hose of one of the hand-operated petrol pumps on the ground, with the pumping handle bloodstained and a piece of wood — also bloodstained — lying nearby. The pump gauge showed that six gallons had been taken, and a quantity of oil was also missing. Further bloodstains were found on the wrappings of a new broom at the back of the store.

It appeared that the motorist had killed Lavers and taken his body away in the car. But a search organized by the Sydney police — with hundreds of volunteers taking part — revealed no further trace of it, and no clue to the culprit's identity. The crime was still unsolved ten years later, when a car-dealer reported that he had overheard a man named Frederick McDermott admit killing the missing storekeeper. As a result of this, McDermott was arrested in Dubbo, 185 miles north-west of Sydney, on 10 October 1946, and charged with Lavers' murder.

Frederick Lincoln McDermott was a sheep-shearer and general bush-worker who had several times been in trouble for minor offences. He lived with a half-caste Maori woman named Florrie Hampton, and the admission which led to his arrest had been made during the course of a quarrel with her. On being questioned, Florrie agreed that McDermott had admitted killing Lavers, and said that he had told her so on other occasions as well. Another woman, Doretta Williams, claimed that she, too, had heard McDermott admit to having murdered the store-keeper.

'Florrie said Fred hit Lavers on the head with a pump handle,' she told police. 'He put his body in the back of the car, drove out to the old Grenfell sheep-yard, and cut up the body with an axe. Then he put it in a bag and buried it.' She added that on hearing this McDermott had said, 'Of course I killed Lavers and cut up his body with an axe.'

A fresh search for the body was as unavailing as the first, and although a woman who called herself Mrs Essie King identified McDermott as one of two men she had seen in the vicinity of Grenfell on the day of the storekeeper's disappearance, she was the only witness to do so. And when McDermott was brought to trial he denied having made certain admissions of guilt which police officers claimed that he *had* made. Even so, he was convicted of murder and sentenced to death.

The sentence was afterwards commuted to life imprisonment, but McDermott was not satisfied with this and, although appeals against his conviction failed, his vehement protestations of innocence led to the appointment of a Royal Commission to inquire into the case in 1951.

'Mrs King' died before this body's proceedings started, but Charles Garrett — the former 'Mr King', whom she had married shortly before her death — gave evidence, revealing that his wife had been paid £25 by the Sydney police for her information about the case in question. It was then suggested that she had suffered remorse and even attempted suicide as a result of having given false evidence at McDermott's trial.

Florrie Hampton, who had not been called as a witness a McDermott's trial, now denied having told police that he had said he knew the whereabouts of Lavers' body, and claimed that she had signed a statement without reading it. She said that McDermott had sometimes denied killing Lavers, and at other times had said, 'If you say I killed him, I must have.'

She also said that the police had tried to get her to give information about a second man who had been named in connection with the storekeeper's disappearance — the man 'Mrs King' claimed to have seen with McDermott in the vicinity of Grenfell.

Moreover, it was proved almost conclusively that a car which had earlier been thought to have left tracks outside the store could not have done so.

In all, ninety-nine witnesses appeared before the Royal Commission — including McDermott, who broke down under cross-examination. The Commissioner, Mr Justice Kinsella, reported his findings on 12 January 1952, saying that while there was no truth in the allegations which had been made against 'Mrs King' and the police, fresh evidence which had been produced suggested that the jury at McDermott's trial had probably been misled by erroneous evidence. This did not prove that McDermott was innocent, but the law did not require him to prove his innocence, the Commissioner declared.

McDermott was released in accordance with the Commissioner's recommendations and given £500 compensation — which was considerably less than the sum for which he had hoped.

The other man named in connection with the case was never arrested, and the storekeeper's body has never been found. The crime remains unsolved.

Assassination of President McKinley, 1901

SEPTEMBER
6

On 6 September 1901, President William McKinley was shot and fatally wounded while attending the Pan-American Exposition in Buffalo, New York. The crime took place in the Temple of Music, a building normally used for organ recitals and concerts, while McKinley was shaking hands with members of the public. His murderer was Leon F. Czolgosz, a twenty-eight-year-old man of Polish descent who claimed to be an anarchist.

Czolgosz had joined the queue of people whom the President was greeting, and had wrapped a large

259

white handkerchief round his own right hand in order to conceal the revolver that he was holding. Coming face to face with the President, he extended his left hand, as though the other had been hurt, and McKinley went to take it. But Czolgosz suddenly dashed the President's hand aside, lunged forward and fired through the handkerchief twice in quick succession.

McKinley, an affable and well-liked man, looked at Czolgosz in astonishment before slumping into the arms of those around him. One bullet had struck him in the chest, the other had passed through his abdomen. Before Czolgosz could fire again, he was knocked down by soldiers and secret service agents, who then beat him up.

The President was taken in an electric ambulance to an emergency hospital in the Exposition grounds. There surgeons operated on him for an hour and a half, but were unable to find the bullet which had caused the wound in his abdomen. McKinley died eight days later, the cause of his death — according to the autopsy report — being blood poisoning due to gangrene of the pancreas.

On being questioned at Buffalo police headquarters, Czolgosz denied having had a grudge against McKinley. He made a confession in his own handwriting, in which he stated, 'I killed President McKinley because I done my duty. I don't believe one man should have so much service and another man should have none.' He later claimed that McKinley had been 'an enemy of the good working people' and that he had been 'going around the country shouting prosperity when there was no prosperity for the poor man'.

Czolgosz, a solitary man with no close friends of either sex, had been born in Detroit a few months after his parents arrived from Poland. He generally worked in factories, but had left his last regular job in August 1898 and since then, he had lived near

Warrensville, Ohio, on a farm which he and other members of his family had bought between them. Although he regarded himself as an anarchist, he was not a member of any recognized anarchist organization, and there was no evidence that anyone else had known of his intention to kill the President.

Following McKinley's death, Czolgosz was indicted for murder in the first degree. He was brought to trial before the State Supreme Court in Buffalo shortly afterwards, refusing to discuss the case with attorneys who had been appointed to represent him, or to take the stand himself. The trial ended on its second day, the jury bringing in a verdict of guilty after thirty-four minutes. Unrepentant to the end, Czolgosz was executed at Auburn Prison on 29 October 1901 — just forty-five days after the death of his victim.

'I killed the President because he was the enemy of the good people — the good working people,' he said as he was being strapped into the electric chair. 'I am not sorry for my crime.'

It was later discovered that Czolgosz had suffered from delusions. He had no real knowledge of anarchism, and various anarchist leaders whom he had met during the summer of 1901 refused to accept him as a comrade. In fact, only five days before the shooting, one of their newspapers published a description of him, warning its readers that he was a spy.

Perhaps if they had thought better of him, the crime would not have taken place.

On 8 September 1969, Beryl Waite, the forty-five-year-old wife of a chauffeur, died at her Warwickshire home after an illness lasting several months. One of the doctors who had attended her issued a death certificate, giving the cause of her death as acute gastro-enteritis — but then began to have doubts and advised the Warwickshire coroner that she may have been poisoned. The post-mortem which followed resulted in the discovery that Mrs Waite's body contained arsenic, administered over a period of more than a year. She had received no fewer than four doses — one of them massive — during the two days which preceded her death.

William Charles Waite, the dead woman's husband, was personal chauffeur to Lord Leigh, of Stoneleigh Abbey; he was four years her junior. On being questioned about the arsenic, he said that he did not know how it could have entered his wife's body, but suggested that she might have committed suicide. He afterwards admitted that he had been having an affair with a young woman working in the estate office at Stoneleigh Abbey, but denied that this gave him a motive for his wife's murder.

Mrs Waite, who was normally a healthy woman, had begun to suffer from various symptoms — loss of weight, listlessness, insomnia and loss of appetite — during the early part of 1968. Her condition improved a little when she started to receive medical attention in July, but in January the following year she had an attack of vomiting and complained of swelling ankles and numbness in her hands and legs.

Some weeks later, after she had been admitted to hospital, her illness was diagnosed as acute polyneuritis, and during the month that she was away from home her health improved considerably. But it soon began to deteriorate again when she was discharged from hospital in April, and this time it was even worse than before.

Her husband seemed genuinely concerned about her, and began carrying her from room to room when she was unable to walk. But he destroyed articles connected with her illness as soon as her body was removed by the undertakers, and arsenic, in the form of a pesticide, was discovered at the estate garage where he worked. The police also found an empty dispenser containing traces of the same poison at the couple's home.

Six days after his wife's death Waite tried to kill himself with aspirin while staying with his parents at Home Farm, Stoneleigh Abbey. However, he recovered in hospital and was arrested for his wife's murder. In February 1970 he appeared for trial at the Birmingham Assizes, the prosecution contending that he had killed his wife in order to be free to marry his mistress, twenty-year-old Judith Regan. He denied the charge.

Called as a prosecution witness, Miss Regan told the court of her affair with the accused, saying that she and Waite had started going out together in January 1968, and had become lovers shortly afterwards. She went on to say that once, after she had become a regular visitor to the couple's flat, Mrs Waite had asked her whether there was anything going on between the prisoner and herself, and she had replied that there was not. But the witness added that on three occasions Mrs Waite had threatened to commit suicide — the last time just four days before her death.

Although Miss Regan said that she had been

alarmed by these threats, one of the doctors who had treated Mrs Waite said that she had fully co-operated in her treatment and that he was sure she had wanted to get better. And the pathologist, Dr Derek Barrow-cliff, said he thought it inconceivable that the deceased should have used such an unpleasant, distressing and at times painful method of suicide. He had never met a suicide case which resembled chronic arsenic poisoning in twenty-five years' experience, he declared.

Waite gave evidence in his own defence, claiming that his wife had spoken of ending her own life because she did not want to be a burden to him and their two children, and his counsel, Mr James Ross, maintained that there were many inexplicable features of the case. But the jury, at the end of the fifteen-day trial, found the prisoner guilty of murder. He was sentenced to life imprisonment.

Murder of Bermuda's Police Commissioner, 1972

On the night of 9 September 1972, George Duckett, Bermuda's forty-one-year-old Police Commissioner, was shot dead at his home in the Hamilton suburb of Devonshire, about half a mile from his office. He had just noticed that his back-door security light was out, and had gone to remove the bulb when he was shot from the darkness at close range. Other shots were fired into the kitchen, and Duckett's seventeen-year-old daughter Marcia was wounded in the chest.

There was no apparent motive for the crime, and

an investigation headed by Scotland Yard detectives made little headway for several months, in spite of the government offering a reward of 24,000 dollars for information about the culprits. Then, on 10 March the following year, Sir Richard Sharples, the Governor and Commander-in-Chief of Bermuda, and his aide-de-camp, Captain Hugh Sayers of the Welsh Guards, were shot dead in the garden at Government House. This time two black men were seen running away, but nobody could identify them.

Less than a month after that, on 6 April, two men who ran a shop in the Victoria Street, Hamilton, shopping centre were shot dead after being tied hand and foot with blue cord. In this case it appeared that the killers had concealed themselves on the premises before the shop closed and afterwards sawn through two iron bars at the back in order to make their escape. They also cut the telephone wires — as had happened at the home of George Duckett on the night of *his* murder.

These latest crimes caused the government to increase the reward it was offering to three million dollars, and the Metropolitan Police Commissioner to send a further team of detectives to the island. Intensive inquiries then revealed that on the night in question three black men had been seen running away from the shop in Victoria Street, one of whom had been recognized as Larry Winfield Tacklyn, a local man. Tacklyn's arrest was followed by a series of shooting incidents intended to obstruct the investigation.

Five months later a second local man, Erskine Durrant Burrows, was identified as the person responsible for two armed robberies: one at the Bank of Bermuda on 25 September, the other at a shopping complex called Pigley Wigley Plaza on 29 September. Although Burrows escaped on both occasions, a p of wire-cutters found in his room were examine the blades proved to be consistent with marks left on the cut telephone wires at George Duckett's home and the shop in Victoria Street.

Burrows was finally apprehended on 18 October, after being seen in the street carrying a sawn-off shotgun. People who had previously been frightened to give information to the police then began to do so, and both of the men in custody were found to have divulged information about the murders to associates. Before long Burrows made a written confession, claiming that he had wanted to make black people aware of the evils of colonial rule.

After much delay the two prisoners were brought to trial, both charged with each of the double murders, and Burrows alone with the murder of George Duckett. Burrows was found guilty on all charges, while Tacklyn was found guilty only of the shopping-centre murders. They were both hanged on 2 December 1977, their executions sparking off a wave of rioting and arson on the island. This led to the declaration of a state of emergency, and British troops were sent to reinforce the security forces until order was restored.

Body of Agnes Brown discovered, 1953

SEPTEMBER
11

On 11 September 1953, Mrs Agnes Irene Brown, an attractive middle-aged woman from south-east London, was found stabbed to death in a field in Chislehurst, Kent, a few hours after her husband had reported her missing. Mrs Brown, aged forty-eight, of

Passey Place, Eltham, had been to a restaurant in nearby Farnborough the previous evening in the company of twenty-seven-year-old William Pettit, her former lodger. Pettit, a labourer with a number of convictions for petty crime, was missing from his own home — also in Eltham — and a search was started for him.

Pettit was a very sick man. He suffered from tuberculosis and was mentally ill as well. He believed himself to be in love with Mrs Brown, and had threatened to kill her when her husband took him to court some months earlier; he had also threatened her on other occasions. Yet Mrs Brown had often been out with him, and at the inquest following her death a grave-digger at a Chislehurst cemetery — where Mrs Brown's parents were buried — spoke of seeing them there together.

'They used to be kissing and cuddling, and if we went anywhere near he used to call her "Auntie",' said Charles Badcock.

The same witness said that on 7 May the same year Mrs Brown had shown him a dagger which she said she had taken from Pettit.

At the restaurant where she and Pettit dined on the evening of 10 September Mrs Brown had played the piano for the benefit of other customers, while her companion watched sullenly. She afterwards told the proprietor that she was trying to help Pettit, as he was in trouble of some sort. The couple left to catch a bus about 8 p.m.

About two hours and twenty minutes later Mrs Brown's husband Arthur received an ominous telephone call.

'Hallo, old chap,' said Pettit. 'Your wife is quite all right, and everything should be all right now.'

Arthur Brown, a civil servant, asked where his wife was, and Pettit replied, 'We have had an argument or two about my future, but I am afraid it was all my fault. Everything should be all right now.'

'Where is my wife?' Mr Brown asked again.

'She has just gone across the road. She won't be five minutes.'

'Will you go and ask her to ring me up at once? She never asked you to ring me up.'

'Yes, she did — in a way.'

Pettit then rang off, and Arthur Brown stayed up all night, waiting for his wife to call him. He twice rang the restaurant in Farnborough in the hope of finding out what had happened to her, and at quarter to eight the following morning finally reported her disappearance. He did not tell the police about the telephone call from Pettit until after he had been shown his wife's body.

'One of the curious features of the whole case is that despite the summonses and threats and bindings-over, Mrs Brown still went out and was friendly with this man,' said the coroner. 'She went out with him knowing full well of the threats uttered against her over the past eight or nine months.'

The police carried on their search for Pettit for several weeks, and used the medium of television for the first time during the course of a murder hunt: photographs of the fugitive, full face and profile, were transmitted on 1 October, and a statement giving details of his description was read by John Snagge. It was thought that a man would be more suitable to read such a statement than the duty announcer, Sylvia Peters.

But by this time Pettit was dead. His body was eventually found in a bombed building in Budge Row, Cannon Street, in the City of London, and a piece of notepaper found on it bore a message to Arthur Brown: 'Forgive me for what I have done. I could have gone on living with Mr and Mrs Brown but not without Mrs Brown. I love her, I love her, I love her.'

Professor Keith Simpson, who carried out the post-mortem, found that he had had advanced tuberculosis, and concluded that his death had probably been due to natural causes.

Murder of Emily Jane Dimmock, 1907

On 12 September 1907, Emily Jane Dimmock, a twenty-three-year-old prostitute known to her friends as 'Phyllis', was found murdered in her lodgings in Camden Town, north London; she was naked and her throat had been cut. The discovery was made when Bertram Shaw, a dining-car cook with whom she had been living for the previous nine months, arrived home from work about midday. It was established by medical evidence that the crime had been committed between four and six o'clock in the morning, while Shaw was aboard a London-to-Sheffield train. He was therefore not regarded as a suspect.

It was soon learnt that, unbeknown to Shaw — who mistakenly believed that she had given up being a prostitute — Phyllis had regularly entertained men at their lodgings while he was working, generally after picking them up at a local public house called the Rising Sun. One of her last clients had been Robert Percival Roberts, a ship's cook, who admitted that he had spent the nights of 8-10 September with her and said that she had received a letter through the post just before he left on the morning of 11 September.

The letter, which she had shown to Roberts, was signed 'Bert', and asked Phyllis to meet the writer at another pub in Camden Town the same evening.

Phyllis had burnt the letter, but only after showing Roberts a picture postcard — in the same handwriting but signed 'Alice' — which she had received on an earlier occasion. This suggested a meeting at the Rising Sun at 8.15 p.m. on the day of its receipt.

The police discovered pieces of the letter in the grate in which it had been burnt, and Bertram Shaw found the postcard by accident under the lining of a drawer. Three more cards bearing the same handwriting were found in an album which Phyllis had kept, and reproductions of all four were published in the hope that the writing would be recognized.

It was, in fact, recognized by an artist's model named Ruby Young, who lived in the Earls Court district, but she did not come forward of her own accord and was only questioned as a result of a rumour reported by a journalist. In the meantime a car-man named Mac-Cowan had given a description of a man he had seen leaving the house in question shortly before 5 a.m. on 12 September.

Ruby Young identified the writing on the postcards as that of Robert Wood, an artist who had been an occasional lover of hers for three years and who had asked her to give him an alibi for the evening before Phyllis' death.

Wood was arrested and put on an identity parade. He was picked out by witnesses who had seen him with Phyllis on the evening of 11 September; he was also identified by MacCowan as the man who had left the house early the next morning. It therefore seemed that the Crown would have little difficulty proving that he was guilty and on 12 December 1907, he was brought to trial at the Old Bailey. But the case against him was then found to be not very strong at all.

Edward Marshall Hall, defending, cast doubt on MacCowan's evidence and on the character of many of the other prosecution witnesses. The prisoner's attempt to arrange a false alibi for the evening of 11 September

— which he explained by saying that he had not wanted his family to know of his association with prostitutes — was argued to be proof that he was innocent, as he would otherwise have known that the crime had taken place several hours later. Finally, the judge summed up in Wood's favour, saying that the prosecution had not 'brought the case home against him clearly enough'.

The jury retired for only seventeen minutes before returning a verdict of not guilty. This was greeted with cheers from the spectators and a roar of approval from the crowds outside. Ruby Young, who was seen as having betrayed him, had to remain in the courthouse until late at night, in order to avoid an angry mob; she eventually left disguised as a charwoman.

Robert Wood later changed his name and vanished into obscurity.

Attack on Miss Wren, 1930

SEPTEMBER
20

A strange unsolved murder case began in Ramsgate, Kent, on the evening of 20 September 1930, when a girl of twelve was sent out to buy a packet of blancmange powder from a sweet-shop across the street from her home. The shop was kept by Margery Wren, a miserly eighty-two-year-old spinster who lived in squalid conditions in spite of owning property and having money in the bank. Finding the door locked, the girl looked through the window.

Miss Wren was sitting in her back room. When she

eventually got up and came to the door, the girl saw that she had blood streaming down her face and realized that she could only speak in whispers. But she let her into the shop, went behind the counter and got out some packets of blancmange powder to show to her. The horrified child ran home and told her parents what had happened, and soon Miss Wren was taken to hospital.

It was found that she had been the victim of an assault, and that she had suffered injuries to her head and face severe enough to have caused instant death. But she lingered for five days, making various statements and then contradicting them as her mind wandered — sometimes, for example, saying that she had been attacked, sometimes that she had had an accident. Then, on one occasion, she claimed that she knew her assailant but would not name him. 'I don't wish him to suffer,' she said. 'He must bear his sins ...' And finally, just before she died, she said, 'He tried to borrow ten pounds.' But she refused to elaborate on this.

The attack was known to have taken place during the half-hour before the girl went to the shop: that is, between 5.30 p.m. and 6 p.m., when there were other people going up and down the street and children playing nearby. Miss Wren's head and face injuries had been inflicted with her own fire-tongs, to which hairs were attached. But the post-mortem revealed that an attempt had also been made to strangle her.

It seemed that the door had been locked by her murderer, who must then have escaped by the back-yard, for Miss Wren normally kept the shop open after six o'clock. It seemed, too, that the culprit had been disturbed, for, although robbery was almost certainly the motive for the crime, nothing appeared to have been stolen.

Six people were regarded as suspects, and each of these was referred to at the coroner's inquest by a letter of the alphabet. The first three, *A*, *B* and *C*, were able to clear themselves, and the police officers heading the investigation became convinced that one of the remaining three, *D*, *E* and *F*, was the murderer. But there was not enough evidence to justify charging any of them, and before long the case was abandoned.

Shooting of Count de Kerninon, 1924

On 21 September 1924, Count le Roux de Kerninon, a French nobleman, was wounded in a shooting incident at his home in Lannion, Brittany. His wife, stepson and stepson's wife all claimed that he had shot himself by accident, and this was generally believed. But the Count, who had been admitted to a nursing-home, confided to visitors — one of whom was his mistress Bernardine Nedellec — that it was his wife who had shot him. The Countess had tried to kill him, and he would 'settle with her' when he was well again, he said. Until then, he did not want her to be denounced.

After spending two days in the nursing-home, however, the Count died, the cause of his death being certified as 'a tumour on the lung, complicated by his wound'. His mistress then revealed what he had said to her about the incident, accusing the Countess of murder, and an investigation was started. But the widow's daughter-in-law, Madame Fleury, challenged the allegation, insisting that the shooting had been 'a terrible accident which has thrown us all into despair'.

'It was about 1.30 p.m., and we had just lunched,' she declared. 'My husband had gone back to his office, situated in a neighbouring house. The Count and Countess de Kerninon had gone to their room, which is on the first floor, overlooking the street. I was in the garden when I heard a shot.

'I came back to the house. I then saw Monsieur de Kerninon coming down the stairs, his hand and face covered with blood. My mother-in-law was leaning against the stair-railing in a fainting condition. "It's an accident," she said. "He had a revolver in his hand. I tried to take it away so that he should not wound himself, when suddenly it went off."'

This statement was soon followed by a fresh account given by the Countess, in which she said that her husband had committed suicide. They had quarrelled about money and she had upbraided him over his infidelity, she claimed. He had then taken a revolver and shot himself, she having tried unsuccessfully to prevent it.

But the medical evidence showed that this, like the earlier story, was untrue, for four bullet wounds had been found in the body: one in the neck, one in the cheek and two in the hands. Moreover, it was learnt that the Countess de Kerninon's son Emile, a public notary, had taken possession of the revolver, removing both the empty cartridge-cases and the unused bullets and throwing them into a cesspool.

The Countess, a domineering Algerian woman eight years older than her husband, had known of de Kerninon's affair with Bernardine Nedellec, and also of a will which he had made in Bernardine's favour. She had frequently uttered threats of violence against both of them, and had forced her husband to destroy the will just before his death. 'When he tore up the will made in my favour, the Count signed his death warrant,' Bernardine said afterwards.

On being brought to trial, Countess de Kerninon

persisted in her claim that her husband had committed suicide, in spite of the evidence against her. But the jury found her guilty of murder, though with extenuating circumstances — and on 8 May 1925 she was sentenced to eight years' penal servitude.

Suicide of Joe Ball, 1938

On the night of 24 September 1938, the owner of a tavern on the outskirts of Elmendorf, a small town in Texas, was visited by police officers investigating the disappearance of one of his waitresses. Far from trying to assist them, Joe Ball, a big, muscular man, took a revolver from his cash register and shot himself in the head. His death led to the discovery that he had murdered not only the woman in question but various others as well.

Ball, an ex-bootlegger in his forties, had been married three times and divorced twice. He had employed many young, attractive women as waitresses at the Sociable Inn and had had affairs with most of them. But none had interested him for long, and he had resorted to murder without compunction when he felt that one of them was becoming a nuisance.

In the case of twenty-two-year-old Hazel Brown — the waitress whose disappearance had prompted the investigation — the affair had lasted several months and she and Ball were often seen out together. A week after she was seen for the last time a neighbour complained to Ball about a foul smell emanating from a rain barrel in the tavern grounds. But the tavern keeper pulled a gun from his pocket and threatened to shoot the neighbour if he did not get off his property at once.

Later, when a deputy sheriff went to see him about the incident, Ball laughed it off and said that he used the rain barrel to store meat for his five pet alligators, which he kept in an outdoor pool. But it served to draw attention to him and further enquiries were made.

Lee Miller, a Texas Ranger, found that nobody in Elmendorf had seen the missing waitress leave town. He also learnt that she had opened a bank account a few days prior to her disappearance, and that none of the money which she had put into it had since been withdrawn. Miller was one of the police officers who were present at Ball's suicide.

Clifford Wheeler, Ball's handyman, was questioned at length and eventually admitted that Hazel Brown had been murdered by his employer. Wheeler had been forced to dismember the body, putting the pieces into the rain barrel, and had later buried them on a nearby river bank after Ball had cut off the head. The handyman led the police officers to Hazel Brown's shallow grave.

Ball's third wife, who had left him some months previously, was found living in California. She told detectives of another murder which her husband had committed — and in which Wheeler had also been involved — saying that she had been afraid that he would kill her, too.

Wheeler confirmed the story of this earlier murder — the victim of which was a girl of twenty named Minnie Gotthardt — and he once more helped to locate the body. It had been buried on a beach near Ingleside, on the Gulf of Mexico.

A search of Ball's home led to the discovery of letters from several former waitresses. Some of them

— including Minnie Gotthardt — had found themselves to be pregnant after leaving the Sociable Inn; others merely resented the way in which Ball had discarded them. It was learnt that some of these women had subsequently returned to Elmendorf and that none of them had been seen since.

Some months after Ball's death the former owner of a ranch adjoining his property revealed that one night in 1936 he had had the misfortune to catch the tavern keeper in the act of cutting up a woman's body and throwing the pieces to his alligators.

Terrified by Ball's violence and threats of murder, the rancher had promised to say nothing about what he had seen and had taken his family to live in California without delay. The ranch had been sold in his absence, and he had not dared to return to Elmendorf during the tavern keeper's lifetime, he explained to Lee Miller.

It was suspected that Joe Ball had fed at least four other women's bodies to his alligators, but this could not be proved. The pool had already been drained, without any human remains being found there. The alligators, which had been taken to a zoo in San Antonio, nonetheless proved to be very popular with visitors.

As for Clifford Wheeler, the reluctant accomplice, he was sent to prison for five years as an accessory to murder. He did not go back to Elmendorf after serving his sentence.

Death of Ernest Westwood, 1948

On the morning of 25 September 1948, Ernest Westwood, a seventy-year-old Yorkshireman living in the village of Southowram, near Halifax, was found unconscious in a pool of blood, having been attacked by an intruder during the hours of darkness. He was taken to hospital, where a constable waited at his bedside until later the same day, when he died without regaining consciousness.

Mr Westwood, in spite of being well over the normal age of retirement, had been working full-time at a mill in Halifax, and had also worked as a debt-collector in the evenings. He had been out debt-collecting on the evening before the crime, and the police learnt that he had had £14 in his possession when he returned home. It appeared that this money had been stolen by his murderer.

Within hours of the crime the police started a search for twenty-seven-year-old Arthur Osborne, an unemployed man who lived in Bognor Regis, Sussex, but was missing from his lodgings. It was learnt that he had arranged to marry a woman in Chichester that very day, irrespective of the fact that he was already married, but had fled on discovering that he was wanted by the police. He was later arrested on a train which had been stopped at Sutton in Surrey.

Osborne, whose thumbprint had been found on one of Mr Westwood's window sills, was charged with murder. He admitted having killed the old man with a screwdriver after breaking into the house to steal his money, but said that he had only done so because the victim threw something at him and caused him to lose his temper.

278

Arthur Osborne duly appeared for trial at the Leeds Assizes, his counsel arguing that the charge should be reduced as his client had been provoked by having something thrown at him. But the judge said that he would be sorry to see a householder's attempt to prevent a burglary being accepted as sufficient reason to reduce murder to manslaughter, and the jury followed his advice.

Although a strong recommendation of mercy was added to the jury's verdict, the Home Secretary declined to intervene on the prisoner's behalf. Osborne was accordingly hanged on 30 December 1948, his execution taking place at Armley Prison.

Remains of James Ellis discovered, 1923

SEPTEMBER 26

On 26 September 1923, the remains of a young soldier were found under some bushes in Long Valley, on the outskirts of Aldershot, in Hampshire. James Frederick Ellis, a twenty-one-year-old drummer in the Leicestershire Regiment, had been dead for four months, and little of his body was left apart from the skeleton. He had died of suffocation while tied up and gagged, with a greatcoat covering his face; the greatcoat had been held in position by a military belt fastened round his head.

Ellis, a native of Hull, had disappeared from his quarters in Aldershot towards the end of May. It was believed that he had deserted, as a close friend of his, a lance-corporal named Albert Edward Dearnley, claimed to have heard him talking about emigrating to Australia. But Dearnley also said that Ellis had been missing since 23 May, whereas everyone else who was questioned was sure that he had not disappeared until the 24th. This divergence was seen as significant when the body was discovered.

On being questioned by a police officer, Dearnley said that he had last seen Ellis at the barracks about 5.30 p.m. on the day of his disappearance. He had then asked him where he was going, and Ellis had replied, 'I may be going for a drink, or I may be going to the pictures.' Dearnley later admitted that he and Ellis, who were generally the best of friends, had often come to blows, usually over a girl. Eventually he made a written statement, withdrawing all that he had said before and admitting that he was responsible for Ellis' death.

He said that on the evening of 24 May he and Ellis had gone for a walk on the nearby common together, and played a game, using a drum-rope as a lasso. Dearnley then tied Ellis up at his own request, but left him trussed and gagged in the bushes, in order to punish him 'for his having insulted my sweetheart'. However, he denied having intended to kill him.

Sir Bernard Spilsbury, who examined the remains, believed that the tying-up *had* been done at the victim's request, and regarded it as an act of masochism on his part. But he said that Ellis had been tied and gagged in such a way that air was excluded from his lungs and he could not move or cry out. He had therefore died of suffocation, probably within ten minutes.

The girl referred to by Dearnley revealed that on one occasion during the summer, when she mentioned Ellis to him, he had told her, 'You have no need to worry any more about Ellis. He is dead, and he is not a mile from here.'

Dearnley was arrested on a coroner's warrant and appeared for trial at the Winchester Assizes in

November. Giving evidence in his own defence, he then repeated his story of the game with the drum-rope, saying that Ellis had lassoed him first, but pulled the rope so tight that it hurt him. Then, when it was his own turn to be lassoed, Ellis asked to be tied up.

'He lay down on the ground, and I put the rope round his ankles and tied them in a knot,' the prisoner stated. 'His hands were behind his back, and I tied them to the ankles. He said, "Oh, that hurts!" I said, "Oh, no, it doesn't. Shut up!" And then I suddenly thought that I would take advantage of the fact that I had tied his hands and feet together, and give him some punishment for having insulted my young lady a few nights before. I said to him, "Tot, I am going to gag you." He said, "Don't do that." I said, "I am."'

Dearnley went on to describe how, having gagged Ellis, he had pulled the greatcoat over his head, fastened it with the belt, then pushed him into the bushes where his body was found. He then went off and left him, intending to release him early in the morning, but did not wake up until later than he had expected; by that time it was too late to leave the barracks, as he had to be on duty. He afterwards assumed that Ellis had worked himself free of his bonds and deserted.

The defence contended that Dearnley was guilty only of manslaughter, as he had not intended to kill Ellis, but the judge, Mr Justice Avory, advised the jury that if a person intending to do grievous bodily harm to another caused that other person's death, then he or she was guilty of murder. The prisoner left the court under sentence of death.

Dearnley's appeal was dismissed and preparations were made for his execution. When his coffin had been made, his grave dug, and the hangman and his assistant had arrived at the prison, a last-minute respite was granted, his sentence being afterwards commuted to penal servitude for life.

The coffin was used for another soldier named Abraham Goldenberg, who had also been convicted of murder (see 3 April).

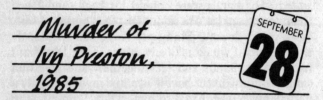

Murder of Ivy Preston, 1985

On the evening of 28 September 1985, Ivy Preston, a seventy-five-year-old spinster, was murdered in the living-room of her small terrace house in Bradford, Yorkshire. The crime was committed with much brutality, the victim being struck many times over the head with a hammer and then strangled. But there was no evidence of sexual assault and nothing seemed to be missing; the motive for the murder was therefore not immediately apparent.

Miss Preston had not been poor. She had worked for her living up to the time of her retirement ten years earlier, owned her own house and lived frugally. When police carried out a search of the premises they found almost £1000 in old, buff-coloured wage-packets which had never been opened. But there had been even more money in the house before the crime, as was soon to be discovered.

During the course of making routine enquiries police officers visited Allyson Kirk, Ivy Preston's nineteen-year-old great-niece, and her husband Ian, aged twenty-one, at their home in Todmorden, in the same county. The couple had visited Miss Preston on the evening in question, but were not at first regarded as suspects. Indeed, they seemed to be genuinely shocked by what had happened.

But the following day Detective Inspector Eddie Hemsley called at their house again and, finding them both out, went round the back and looked in their dustbin. There he found a T-shirt which had recently been washed, together with many small pieces of buff-coloured paper — torn-up wage-packets of the same type as those found at Miss Preston's house.

Shortly afterwards Allyson Kirk and her husband were arrested and £1465 was found in the glove compartment of their Volvo car. They both made confessions. 'Everyone used to laugh and say we'd all be better off if Auntie Ivy was dead,' said Allyson. 'I thought we had committed the perfect murder.'

When they appeared for trial at Leeds Crown Court in June 1986 the prosecution alleged that the couple, who had run up debts of over £8000 during the first six months of their marriage, had murdered Miss Preston for the sake of her life savings. It was Allyson Kirk who actually killed her, but her husband had driven her to the house — before going to a car-wash to establish an alibi — and had then returned to the scene of the crime to help his wife search for the dead woman's money. They found over £2000, and used £700 to pay off debts and buy food before being arrested.

Allyson Kirk pleaded guilty to the charge of murder and gave evidence against her husband; he admitted only a charge of impeding her arrest, knowing that she had committed a crime. But according to Allyson's account, the couple had taken Miss Preston away on a caravan holiday during the summer of 1985, so that Ian could return to the house in her absence, break in and steal her money. And this scheme was only abandoned when he found himself unable to force open a window — after which they decided to murder Miss Preston instead.

Ian Kirk admitted having driven his wife to her aunt's house on the night in question. Under cross-examination, he also admitted that he had helped her to dispose of the hammer afterwards. But he claimed that he was innocent of the murder itself, as he had not known what his wife intended to do.

After retiring for nearly six and a half hours the jury returned a majority verdict of guilty. Ian Kirk was therefore — like his wife — given a sentence of life imprisonment.

A police officer said afterwards that the case was 'a classic example of the dangers of falling into debt'.

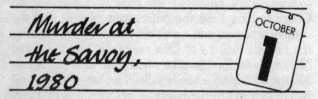

Murder at the Savoy, 1980

OCTOBER 1

On the evening of 1 October 1980, Catherine Russell, a twenty-seven-year-old prostitute, was stabbed to death in an eighth-floor room at London's Savoy Hotel. The crime was discovered by a hotel employee, who had heard screams coming from the room about 10.15 p.m., and saw a young man emerging with blood on his clothes shortly afterwards. The victim, who was only partly dressed, had been stabbed fifty-five times with a clasp-knife.

The young man had booked into the hotel just an hour and a quarter before the screams were heard, claiming to be 'D. Richards' from Birmingham; afterwards, he left without paying his bill, unnoticed by other members of the staff. But a pocket diary found at the scene — together with the murder weapon and the culprit's fingerprints — showed that his real name was Tony Marriott and give his address as Highland Avenue, Horsham, in Sussex.

A hunt was started for him and the following evening he was recognized by the landlord of a public house in Southend-on-Sea, Essex. On being taken into custody, Marriott, who was twenty-two years old, admitted the crime; he told police officers that he had invited Catherine Russell to his room at the Savoy because he wanted to murder a prostitute — and that, having stabbed her while she was getting undressed, he went on doing so, in a state of frenzy. He continued stabbing her even when she was dead.

Later, at another hotel, he made a half-hearted attempt at suicide by cutting his wrists.

'The real problem, I feel, is that I seem to develop a resentment of normal sexual relationships,' he informed the officers interviewing him.

Six months after his arrest Marriott was brought to trial at the Old Bailey, charged with murder. The defence contended that he was suffering from diminished responsibility, and evidence of 'a persistent psychopathic disorder, leading to abnormally aggressive behaviour' was produced. The plea was successful, and the prisoner was convicted only of manslaughter. He was sent to Broadmoor.

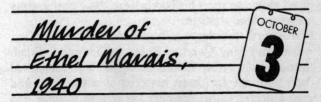

Murder of Ethel Marais, 1940

OCTOBER 3

On the evening of 3 October 1940, Mrs Ethel Marais, the wife of a South African soldier, was battered with a blunt instrument, sadistically assaulted and robbed not far from her home in Brockhurst Road, in the Cape Town suburb of Lansdowne. She was still alive when she was found behind a bush the following morning, but died of her injuries soon afterwards, without regaining consciousness. There was no clue to the identity of the person responsible, and police searched the neighbourhood for suspicious characters without success.

Nineteen days later a second murder was committed, the victim on this occasion being Mrs Dorothy Marie Tarling, of Prince George Drive, in the suburb of Wynberg. Mrs Tarling was similarly battered, abused and robbed, but in her own home, her murderer having entered the house through a window and taken her by surprise as she sat reading a newspaper. Thumb- and palm-prints found at the scene revealed only that the culprit had no criminal record, and a fresh search proved unavailing.

Then, on 11 November, the killer struck again in Wynberg, this time in Wetton Road, where Evangeline Bird, an unmarried woman of twenty-eight, was attacked and fatally injured at the front door of the house in which she lived, and dragged behind a shrubbery. In this case, unlike the others, the crime was committed in broad daylight, and the killer — a young man with a bicycle — was seen in the vicinity by two witnesses. But the police still failed to catch him, and the women of Cape Town — many of whom lived alone, as their husbands were away in the army — were panic-stricken.

A fourth murder was reported on 25 November, when Mrs May Overton Hoets, of Thornhill Road, Rondebosch, was found dead in her ransacked bedroom; she had been battered over the head and had a deep gash in her neck, as well as wounds and bruises on other parts of her body. This time both fingerprints and footprints were found, but several more weeks elapsed before the murderer was caught.

Even then, he only came to the attention of the police because he was seen in the street by the victim of a lesser offence.

Salie Linevelt, aged twenty, was arrested as he stood in a cinema queue in Wynberg. He had a ring stolen from Mrs Marais on one of the fingers of his right hand, and part of his left thumb had been cut off. It was found that he had mutilated himself with a chopper after newspapers had misleadingly reported — as part of a plan devised by the police — that the murderer's left thumb-print had been found at Mrs Tarling's home (where he had actually left a print of his other thumb). The chopper and the severed part of the thumb were among items found in a room he shared with his widowed father.

Elated at being the centre of attention, Linevelt soon confessed to all four murders. He said that he had beaten three of the women to death with a piece of piping — which he had afterwards hidden in the grounds of the house in Wetton Road — and killed the fourth with the chopper. But he denied having committed sexual acts against his victims, even though the state of the bodies indicated a sexual motive and in one case articles of underwear had been among the items taken.

'Why should I kill them to sleep with them?' he argued. 'I've been with lots of women. I'd been with a girl the night I was arrested.'

Inquiries revealed that this was not the truth: in fact, he did not seem to have associated with girls at all. But he continued to deny that the murders had been sexually motivated, saying that he had committed them because his 'boss' had ordered him to do so. It appeared from this that he was schizophrenic and had an imaginary character upon whom he could place responsibility for what had happened.

Linevelt was brought to trial before a judge and two assessors. He refused to allow a plea of insanity to be made on his behalf, and his counsel had no success in trying to prove mitigating circumstances, in spite of much attention being given to the prisoner's psychological make-up.

Mr Justice Davis, in his judgment, said that there was evidence that Linevelt 'had periods when he was moody and quiet, possibly even a little intractable', but that this — 'even taken in conjunction with his youth' — fell far short of what would be required to spare his life. He also rejected the suggestion that the number, brutality and unexplained character of the crimes were, in themselves, evidence of mitigating circumstances.

'Of course, the prisoner here is not entirely normal,' he said. 'One is thankful that normal persons do not act as he did. If he were entirely normal he could, and would, not have perpetrated these four horrible crimes. But, in saying this, I do not in the least suggest that any abnormality he may possess is such that would prove a mitigating factor in this case. In the court's view, it is rather the reverse.'

The prisoner, having continued to enjoy a great deal of attention, listened without concern as he was sentenced to death. During the last weeks of his life, in the condemned cell in Pretoria, he remained contented and cheerful; he had no wish to avoid being hanged, and seemed, if anything, relieved when the date of his execution was fixed. He died without trying to give any further explanation of his crimes.

Gruesome discovery in Essex, 1974

A long and difficult murder investigation began on 5 October 1974, when an amateur ornithologist walking along the north bank of the River Thames near Rainham, in Essex, found the upper part of a male torso at the water's edge. It was the first of a number of gruesome discoveries, several other parts of the same body being found over a ten-mile stretch of the river during the next ten days. The pathologist who examined these remains was able to state that death had probably been caused by a head injury — though the head was still missing — and that dismemberment had been carried out with a saw and a knife. The various parts had all been immersed in water about five days before the first discovery.

The police suspected that the dead man was William Henry Moseley, a thirty-seven-year-old small-time crook from north London who was missing from his home. But the remains could not be positively identified at this time, as the hands were also missing, and a whole year elapsed without any further progress being made. In the meantime, on 7 September 1975, the body of Michael Henry Cornwall, a close friend of Moseley's and a member of the same gang, was found buried in a wood near Hatfield, Hertfordshire. Cornwall had died as a result of a gunshot wound in his right temple, but had been kicked or struck a number of times beforehand.

As it seemed almost certain that the two crimes were connected, a murder squad was set up to investigate them both. On 24 October a second postmortem was carried out on the remains of the first victim, this time by Professor J.M. Cameron, who found evidence of torture: the nails of one foot had been pulled out before death, and the sole of that foot had burn marks on it. Cameron also succeeded in positively identifying the dead man as William Moseley — a task made possible by the discovery of gallstones for which Moseley had been receiving medical treatment.

Police inquiries later revealed that some days before any of the remains were found, Reginald Dudley, a fifty-four-year-old crooked jeweller, had been heard discussing Moseley's death with his fellow crook, forty-year-old Robert Maynard, and a third man at a family funeral. It was suspected that Dudley and Maynard were responsible for the murder, Dudley having been beaten up by Moseley some years earlier, after trying to thrust a broken bottle into his face during the course of a fight.

Cornwall, who was in prison at the time, had also suspected Dudley and Maynard, and it was known that he had tried to find them after his release. But on learning that Dudley and Maynard were looking for *him*, he had become frightened and gone into hiding. He was seen alive for the last time on or about 22 August 1975, and shortly afterwards it was rumoured that he had been killed.

The investigation of the two murders eventually led to the arrest of Dudley, Maynard and five other people, all of whom were committed for trial in April 1976. The trial, at the Old Bailey, lasted seven months, ending on 16 June 1977, when Dudley and Maynard were convicted of murdering both Moseley and Cornwall and sentenced to life imprisonment. Charles Clarke, a fifty-six-year-old greengrocer, was given two consecutive two-year sentences for conspiring to cause grievous bodily harm to both men, and Dudley's thirty-year-old daughter Kathleen was given a suspended prison sentence for conspiring to cause grievous bodily harm to Cornwall, who had been her lover and had actually shared a flat with her — unbeknown to her father — after Moseley's death.

Six weeks after the trial ended, Moseley's skull, which had evidently been kept in a refrigerator, was found thawing in a public convenience in Islington, north London. An examination of it confirmed the earlier opinion of both pathologists, that Moseley had died as a result of a head injury.

Double murder in Kenya, 1932

OCTOBER 6

On the evening of 6 October 1932, a youth of nineteen and two young women left the small town of Nakuru, in Kenya, in a blue Chevrolet. It appeared that they were all going to a cinema together and later, when they failed to return home, it was assumed that somebody they knew had put them up for the night. But when the next day passed without any sign of them, their parents and friends became anxious. The police were therefore informed, and an investigation began.

The youth, Charles William Ross, was found on the Eldama Ravine Road, some miles out of Nakuru, on the morning of 8 October, when his twenty-one-year-old brother Gordon went out on his motor-cycle to look for the missing party. He was dirty and untidy, as though he had been sleeping rough, and the Chevrolet was stuck in a ditch. But the two girls were not with him, and he denied knowing what had become of them: in fact, their disappearance did not seem to concern him in the least.

Ross was taken into custody and a search was started in the area in which he had been found. The body of one of the missing girls — Margaret Keppie, a qualified chemist and druggist from Leeds — was then discovered at the bottom of a ravine, below a forty-foot cliff. She had been shot in the head.

After that the search was intensified, and the following day a camp was discovered in the bush, where fresh provisions, articles of women's clothing, toilet requisites, a revolver and two empty cartridge-cases lay near the remains of a fire. But there was no trace of the second girl — twenty-year-old Winifred Stevenson, with whom the prisoner was believed to have been in love — and the search continued for several more days without success.

Eventually, on 15 October, Ross directed police officers to a secluded spot near the Menengai crater, where the decomposed body of Miss Stevenson, who had also been shot, lay covered with leaves and grass within a mile of her own home. He afterwards made a confession, stating that he had killed both girls 'for nothing'.

'It happened at 9.30 on Thursday night,' he said. 'I shot Miss Keppie near the camp. She was sitting next to me at the time and grabbed at my revolver, which I kept in my left-hand pocket. I ordered her out of the car and took her about thirty yards from the camp. She was a yard from me when I shot her. I threw her down a sort of square pit nearby.

'After that I returned for Winnie. She was sitting in the car. When I took Miss Keppie away I had ordered her to get into the car. She had not moved when I got back. She was terrified. She wanted to go home. I told her I would lead the way and she could follow. When we were near her home she said she could not go any further. She lay on the grass under a tree. She did not know what was going to happen to her. I shot her in the side of the head.'

Ross was charged with both murders, and his trial, which began in Nairobi on 28 November, lasted four days; he pleaded insanity. Defence witnesses told the court of occasions when his behaviour had not been that of a normal person — when, for example, he had slashed open the carcasses of animals he had killed, in order to cover himself with blood. It was also stated that he had been suffering from a venereal disease, and that clothes he had worn on the night of 6 October bore traces of semen. Other evidence concerned the behaviour of his father, a soldier and big-game hunter who had committed many acts of brutality — including an attempt to put one of his own children on a fire.

In addition to all this, it was shown that the prisoner was mentally deficient, having an I.Q. of only 65.7. But the prosecution argued convincingly that none of the defence evidence proved insanity in the legal sense, and after retiring for fifty-five minutes the jury returned a verdict of guilty. The prisoner was accordingly hanged in Nairobi on the morning of 11 January 1933.

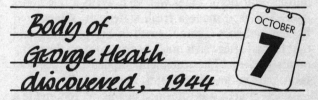

Body of George Heath discovered, 1944

OCTOBER 7

On the morning of 7 October 1944, the body of a murder victim was found in a ditch at Knowle Green, near Staines in Middlesex. George Heath, a thirty-four-year-old taxi-driver — 'the man with the cleft chin', according to the newspaper reports of the case

— had been shot in the back and robbed, and the culprits had taken his taxi-cab. The vehicle was found parked in a street in Hammersmith, west London, two days later — and a short while after its discovery an American GI was seen entering it.

Private Karl Gustav Hulten, aged twenty-two, had been absent without leave from his paratroop regiment for seven weeks. On being searched, he was found to have an automatic pistol in his left hip pocket and ammunition in one of his trouser pockets. He claimed to have found the stolen taxi abandoned near Newbury, in Berkshire, and to have spent the night of the murder in the company of a woman named Georgina Grayson, who lived in King Street, Hammersmith.

Georgina Grayson proved to be the stage-name of Elizabeth Maud Jones, an eighteen-year-old strip-tease dancer. When Hulten revealed where she lived, she was taken to Hammersmith police station to be interviewed, but was allowed to go home after making a statement, as she was not thought to have been involved in the crime. However, the same afternoon, while speaking to a War Reserve constable of her acquaintance, she made an indiscreet remark which suggested otherwise.

This was reported to detectives investigating the murder and Betty Jones was seen again a few hours later. She then made a fresh statement, saying that Hulten had shot George Heath in her presence, and that he had afterwards made her go through the dying man's pockets. The statement implied that she had taken part in the crime against her own will.

When Hulten was informed of this he, too, made a fresh statement. In this, he admitted having killed the taxi-driver, but said that he had done so by accident, and that Jones — with whom he had taken up only a few days previously — was herself to blame for the crime. 'She said she would like to do something exciting, like becoming a "gun moll", like they do back in the States,' said Hulten. He claimed that if it hadn't been for her, he wouldn't have shot Heath.

These statements also revealed that Hulten and Jones had committed other robberies, travelling at night in a stolen army truck, and that on one occasion they had attacked and almost killed a girl.

Hulten and Jones were both charged with murder. The consent of the American government had to be obtained before Hulten could be tried in a British court, but this was granted and both prisoners duly appeared at the Old Bailey on 16 January 1945. Betty Jones now claimed that she had only taken part in the crime because she was frightened by threats and violence, but at the end of the six-day trial the accused were both found guilty and sentenced to death.

Hulten was hanged at Pentonville Prison on 8 March 1945, five days after his twenty-third birthday. Betty Jones, whose sentence was commuted to life imprisonment, served nine years before being released in January 1954.

Multiple murder in New Zealand, 1941

OCTOBER
8

On 8 October 1941, Constable Edward Best, of Hokitika, New Zealand, went to visit a farmer in the bush settlement of Kowhitirangi, some miles away, after it had been reported that he had been threatening neighbours with a rifle. Eric Stanley Graham, aged forty, was a sullen man with a violent temper, and received Best in such a hostile manner that the constable left the farmstead to call for assistance.

Best later returned with a sergeant and two other constables, the sergeant intending to take Graham to the police station for questioning. But Graham, who often felt persecuted, suddenly got out his gun and shot all four of them, killing the sergeant and the two other constables outright and gravely wounding Best. Then, after shooting a local volunteer and driving off two others, he shot Best again, this time killing him.

Graham then left the farmstead with food, firearms and ammunition, and fled into the bush. A search was started for him, with police being flown in from all parts of New Zealand, and troops from Burnham Military Camp, armed Home Guardsmen and civilians also taking part.

Several times during the next few days Graham returned to his home, but on each occasion he became involved in a shooting incident with police or Home Guardsmen. One Home Guardsman was shot and fatally wounded, so that he died the following morning; another, who went to his aid, was shot from ambush and died instantly.

These two new deaths led to the evacuation of women and children from the area, and further reinforcements were flown in. The order was given that Graham should be taken 'dead or alive'.

On the twelfth day of the manhunt a police officer from Auckland, using high powered binoculars, sighted him a mile away. Closing in on him with great care, Sergeant Quirke shot him without warning from a distance of twenty-five yards. The fugitive was then captured and taken to hospital, where he died the following day.

The volunteer who had been shot on the same day as four police officers from Hokitika — a fifty-four-year-old agricultural inspector — died from his injuries seventeen months later.

On the evening of 9 October 1912, Countess Sztaray, of South Cliff Avenue, Eastbourne, set out in her brougham to meet friends for dinner at the local Burlington Hotel. After driving some distance her coachman told her that while waiting outside the house he had seen a man crouching on the roof of her porch. Assuming that a burglary was about to take place, the Countess then ordered the coachman to take her back, so that she could telephone the police. Inspector Arthur Walls, who happened to be in the neighbourhood, arrived at the house a few minutes later.

The intruder was still on the roof of the porch, unsure whether he had been seen. Walls immediately put an end to his uncertainty by ordering him to come down. But the man produced a revolver and fired two shots, wounding the police officer so seriously that he died shortly afterwards. In the confusion which followed, the murderer managed to escape, leaving a soft felt hat on the porch roof. The coachman, by this time, had driven off without seeing the man's face: he afterwards claimed that the shots had made the horse 'restless'.

The hat was traced to the shop where it had been bought, but the salesman had sold many others of the same type and had no idea who had bought that particular one. As it was the only clue to the murderer's identity, the police were not very hopeful of catching him. But then a young man named Edgar Power informed them that his friend John Williams, a professional burglar, was the person they wanted.

Williams, according to Power, had arrived in Eastbourne on 2 October in the company of his mistress, Florence Seymour, with whom he was living and who was expecting his child. He had since left for London on his own, using money which Power had given him, as he was afraid of being arrested for the crime. The murder weapon had been buried somewhere on the beach at Eastbourne.

Power, who was in love with Florence himself, agreed to take part in a plan to bring the culprit to justice. In accordance with this, he asked Florence to show him where Williams' revolver had been buried, so that it could be moved to a safer hiding place, and while she was doing so, police officers arrived on the scene and arrested them both. Florence was then terrified into making a statement about the evening of the murder, saying that Williams had left her sitting on the sea-front near South Cliff Avenue shortly before 7 p.m., and that he had later returned without his hat, saying that he had lost it. She went on to admit that the gun had been buried the following day.

John Williams, who had a criminal record, was lured into a trap in London with Power's help, arrested and charged with murder. The son of a Scottish clergyman, his real name was George Mackay, but it was under the name of Williams that he was tried — at the Lewes Assizes in December 1912 — when he was also referred to in the press as the 'Hooded Man' as a result of being hooded when he was taken to and from the courthouse. He did not have a strong defence and, although Florence changed her evidence in the hope of helping him, he was convicted and sentenced to death.

Florence gave birth while Williams was in the death cell, and was allowed to take the child to see him on the day before his execution, but a request that the couple should be allowed to marry was refused.

The execution was carried out in January 1913, when Williams was twenty-nine years old.

Execution of Susan Newell, 1923

On 10 October 1923, Susan Newell, a married woman aged thirty, was hanged at Duke Street Prison, Glasgow, for the murder of a thirteen-year old newspaper boy the previous June. The crime had been committed in the room which she and her husband rented in the nearby burgh of Coatbridge, and her husband had also been tried on the same change. He, however, had been acquitted, as it was clear that he had not been in Coatbridge when the murder took place.

Mrs Newell and her husband were a quarrelsome couple, and two days before the crime she had twice struck him on the head. The following day there was a disagreement between them when John Newell went to attend his brother's funeral, and he spent the night at his father's house. The day after that — the day of the murder — he was in Glasgow from midday till 9 p.m., and on arriving back in Coatbridge at 10.30 p.m., went to see his sister. He then went to the local police to complain about his wife assaulting him.

The murder was committed while Janet McLeod, the culprit's eight-year-old daughter by a former marriage, was playing in the street outside the house. The boy, John Johnston, came round with the evening papers, and Mrs Newell, who had been given notice to quit, called him into the room and strangled him, for no apparent reason. Janet returned to the room shortly afterwards and saw the 'little wee boy' lying on the couch, dead. She later helped her mother to put the body into a bag.

The next morning Susan Newell and her daughter set out on foot towards Glasgow, pushing the bundle on a hand-cart, covered with a bed rug. A lorry-driver stopped and offered them a lift, and Mrs Newell helped him to lift the cart onto the vehicle. But she became excited when they arrived in Glasgow, and when they lifted the cart down between them, she fell and upset it. She then became angry, told the driver that she did not need his help, and put the bundle back onto the cart. The driver went on his way, puzzled.

But a woman looking out of her kitchen window had noticed first a foot and then a head protruding from the bundle; she told her sister, and the two women began following Susan Newell and her daughter through the streets. Mrs Newell eventually left the bundle in a courtyard, but by this time a policeman had been called and she was arrested as she tried to make her escape. On being questioned, she said that the boy had been killed by her husband.

Janet McLeod also told the police that John Newell was the person responsible, but on being called to give evidence at her mother's trial she admitted that this was a lie; she had said it because her mother had told her to, she informed the court. Newell, by this time, had been able to prove that he was in Glasgow when the murder took place, and had been formally acquitted when the judge decided that he should not have been brought to trial.

Susan Newell was sentenced to death after an attempt to prove her insane had failed, and this sentence was carried out in spite of a unanimous recommendation of mercy from the jury. On the morning of her death she showed no fear, and one witness said afterwards that she was the bravest woman he had ever seen. She died without confessing her guilt, and refused to allow the hangman to pull the white cap over her face before the trap-door was opened.

Train robbery and murder in Oregon, 1923

OCTOBER
11

On 11 October 1923, three gunmen held up a Southern Pacific express train in the Siskiyou Mountains, in Oregon, killing four members of the crew. The victims included the brakeman and the fireman, who had both been ordered to uncouple the mail coach after it had been dynamited and set on fire. The murderers fled from the scene, leaving behind a revolver and a pair of overalls, in addition to their detonating equipment.

The manhunt which followed was unsuccessful, and although a garage mechanic was regarded with suspicion, the police asked Dr Edward Heinrich, a Californian criminologist, to assist them. Heinrich's microscopic examination of stains, hairs, fibres and wood dust on the overalls found at the scene of the crime provided information which not only cleared the garage mechanic but also led to the arrest of the real culprits.

The overalls belonged to a left-handed lumberjack who had worked among fir-trees of a particular type, said Heinrich. He was aged between twenty-one and twenty-five, not more than 5 feet 10 inches tall,

301

weighed about 165 pounds, and was fastidious in his personal habits. This information, together with other pieces of evidence which came to light, led police officers to the home of Hugh, Roy and Ray D'Autrement, three brothers living in rural Oregon who had all worked as lumberjacks. All three of them had disappeared, and further evidence was obtained linking them to the crime. But it then took four years to catch them.

Hugh D'Autrement was finally arrested in the Philippines, and his two brothers — who were twins — were found in Ohio. On being brought to trial, they were all convicted and sentenced to life imprisonment. Two of them were eventually released — Hugh in 1958, Ray in 1961 — but the third died in a mental institution.

The case helped to establish Heinrich as a pioneer of forensic science.

Disappearance of Arthur Johnson, 1956

OCTOBER 15

On the night of 15 October 1956, Arthur Johnson, a fifty-three-year-old unmarried farmer, was seen alive for the last time as he drove home in his van through the bleak fenlands near the village of Farcet, in Huntingdonshire, about ten o'clock. Later, when it was learnt that he had disappeared, police officers found his jacket and spectacles inside his farmhouse and bloodstains out in the yard. His van — with a lot of blood inside it — was discovered on a rough track about two and a half miles away.

Johnson, a secretive man, had had the reputation of being rich. Although his sitting-room at Crowtree Farm had a damp, musty smell caused by dry rot, police carrying out a search of the place found many small sums totalling over £80, in addition to a little under £17 in a safe. But three bands which had been used as wrappers for bundles of banknotes were also discovered, indicating that a far larger amount was missing. It therefore seemed likely that Johnson had been murdered for the sake of money.

It was clear, too, that the person responsible had driven Johnson's car to the place where it was abandoned — and, as the area was full of fields bounded by ditches and dykes, with only narrow tracks between them, it would have been almost impossible for a stranger to do this in the darkness. For this reason, the police assumed that the culprit was somebody who knew the area well, and before long they began to suspect Morris Arthur Clarke, a twenty-seven-year-old lorry driver who lived in Peterborough, about seven miles from Johnson's home.

Clarke had known the missing farmer and had actually lived at Crowtree Farm while his wife was Johnson's housekeeper. When he left in January 1954, Johnson had lent him £100 to enable him to start a business, but this was not successful. By September 1956 he had debts of over £1000 which he could not pay, and at 5.25 p.m. on the day of Johnson's disappearance he was confronted by one of his creditors over a cheque for £200 which his bank had refused to cash. But the following morning he paid £200 in notes into the bank; then, an hour later, he paid a debt of about £33 to somebody else.

When Clarke was questioned he said that he had been at work on the night in question, and that he had saved all this money without his wife knowing about it. But he had no alibi for the period between 9.55 p.m. and 1.30 a.m., and twenty ten-shilling (50p) notes taken from a bureau at his home — as well as other notes found in a pocket of his blazer — all smelt of dry rot. Even so, there was not enough evidence to justify an arrest.

Ten days after his disappearance Johnson's body was found floating in a dyke about three miles from his farm. He had been battered over the head with a blunt instrument, and his right leg had been broken. A bloodstained stick found in a barn at Crowtree Farm appeared to be the murder weapon.

Clarke continued to deny being the culprit until the police obtained a warrant to search his house, and found — in his loft — another £641 in musty-smelling notes and an old purse full of sovereigns (£1 coins) and half-sovereigns. He then confessed and was charged with murder.

On being brought to trial, Clarke was convicted and sentenced to death, the judge remarking that the circumstances of his crime were so dreadful that he should not count on 'some other sentence being substituted'. However, the sentence was commuted to life imprisonment.

Disappearance of Gay Gibson. 1947

OCTOBER
18

On the morning of 18 October 1947, one of the female passengers of the ocean liner *Durban Castle*, then off the coast of West Africa, was reported to be missing. Gay Gibson, a twenty-one-year-old actress — her real name was Eileen Isabella Ronnie Gibson — was travelling from Capetown to Southampton, but had not been seen since the previous night. As it seemed that she had fallen overboard, the captain ordered the ship to be turned back so that a search of the seas could be made. But there was no sign of her, so it was assumed that she had been eaten by sharks.

It was not long before foul play was suspected. It was already known that shortly before 3 a.m. the two bells of Miss Gibson's cabin had been rung, summoning both the steward and the stewardess. When a watchman went in response to them a man opened the door a few inches and said, 'It's all right.' He then closed the door in the watchman's face. Later, about 7.30 a.m., a stewardess found the bed in that cabin to be more disarranged than usual and also noticed some stains on the sheet and pillow case.

When James Camb, the deck steward, was belatedly named as the man who had been seen by the watchman, he denied having been in the cabin at that time. The following day he agreed to have a medical examination, and was found to have scratches on his shoulders and wrists; he claimed that these had been self-inflicted as a result of a heat-rash. When the ship reached Southampton he was held for questioning by the police.

He then admitted that he had been in Gay Gibson's cabin during the early hours of 18 October, and said that the missing actress had died after having a fit while he and she were having sexual intercourse. He had tried unsuccessfully to save her by means of artificial respiration, and then, being 'terribly frightened', had pushed her body through the porthole, he claimed. He was unable to explain the ringing of the cabin bells.

The thirty-one-year-old steward was charged with murder and brought to trial at the Winchester Assizes in March 1948. The prosecution alleged that he had strangled Miss Gibson because she resisted his advances, and in support of this produced evidence of blood and saliva on the bedclothes, as well as the scratches on the prisoner's body.

A pathologist appearing for the defence unexpectedly strengthened the case against the prisoner by admitting the presence of traces of urine, which the government pathologists had not noticed, on one of the sheets of the dead woman's bed. But perhaps Camb's failure to call for assistance on the night in question weighed most heavily against him. He was found guilty and sentenced to death.

It was later revealed that Camb had assaulted three other women — none of whom had reported him — on different occasions aboard the *Durban Castle*.

Though his appeal was dismissed by the Court of Criminal Appeal, his sentence was commuted to life imprisonment in view of the fact that the House of Commons had just voted for a five-year suspension of the death penalty.

Released on licence in September 1959, James Camb changed his name and got himself a job as a head waiter. But after a few years of freedom he began to get into trouble again — for sex offences against schoolgirls — and his licence was revoked. He therefore went back to jail to continue serving his life sentence.

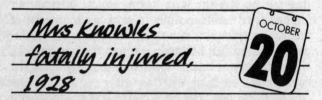

Mrs Knowles fatally injured, 1928

OCTOBER
20

One of this century's strangest cases of alleged murder began on the afternoon of 20 October 1928, when Mrs Harriet Knowles, the wife of a district medical officer in the Gold Coast territory of Ashanti (now in (now in Ghana), received a gunshot wound from which she died three days later.

Mrs Knowles and her husband were part of the territory's white community. They had given a lunch party that day at their bungalow in the Bekawi district, and afterwards retired for their usual afternoon rest. They were still in their bedroom at 4.30 p.m., when Sampson, their native houseboy, heard the sound of a shot.

Sampson, knowing that Mrs Knowles and her husband often quarrelled, ran to the home of Thortref Margin, the District Commissioner, and reported what he had heard. Margin, who had been one of the couple's lunch-party guests, promptly drove to the bungalow to find out what had happened. But Dr Benjamin Knowles, coming to the door with just a towel wrapped round him, denied that an accident had taken place and said that everything was all right. Margin therefore left, and saw no need to take any further action.

That evening, after being out for some hours, Margin returned to his house and found a message from Sampson, stating, 'Missie cry very much'. This put him in a difficult position, for he was now sure that something unfortunate had happened, but had no real grounds to justify another visit. All he was able to do was send the medical officer a brief note, saying that Sampson had 'got the wind up' and pointing out that if Knowles needed his assistance he had only to ask for it. Knowles did not reply.

The next day, after hearing Margin's story, Dr Howard Gush, the colony's surgeon, visited the couple. Knowles showed him bruises on his leg, which he said had been caused by blows with an Indian club during a 'domestic fracas' the previous afternoon. His wife, who had been shot in the left buttock, was seriously ill; the bullet had passed out of her body on the right side of the abdomen. Surprisingly — in view of what her husband had said — she told Gush that this had been the result of an accident. She had been examining her husband's revolver while he was asleep and it had gone off when she unintentionally sat on it, she said.

Gush ordered her to be taken to the hospital in Kumasi (the capital of Ashanti), where — in her husband's presence — she made a statement on oath, claiming once again that her injury had been caused by accident. But the remarks which Knowles had made to the surgeon, and other things which he said later, all suggested that he had shot her. Indeed, he and his wife had come close to quarrelling on this point as a result of Knowles telling her, on two occasions, to tell the truth. When Mrs Knowles died during the early hours of 23 October, her husband was charged with her murder.

Though Knowles was a Scotsman in a British colony, he was tried under Ashanti law, which allowed no legal representation or trial by jury. The prosecution was conducted by the Commissioner of Police; the prisoner was allowed to cross-examine witnesses and give evidence himself. It was for the judge to decide whether the prosecutor had proved his case.

Sampson gave evidence against his former employer, telling the court that just before the shot he had heard Knowles shout, 'Show me!' Other witnesses gave evidence of the prisoner's suspicious behaviour and apparently self-incriminating remarks, and experts argued that a bullet found in a wardrobe was the one which had killed Mrs Knowles, having been fired by the accused as he lay on the bed. Mrs Knowles' account of what had happened was dismissed as a false statement intended to protect her murderer.

Knowles now claimed that his wife had told the truth in saying that she had discharged the gun accidentally, and claimed that he had been treating her himself to prevent her being questioned. He challenged Sampson's evidence, saying that it was after the gun had been fired that he had shouted, 'Show me!' He also claimed that the bullet found in the wardrobe had been fired by his wife on an earlier occasion, and that a second one found on the floor was the one which had caused her death.

The judge, in his summing-up, said that he found the ballistics evidence 'very confusing'. He nonetheless concluded by saying that the evidence against the prisoner was 'overwhelming'. Knowles was therefore found guilty and sentenced to death — a sentence immediately commuted to life imprisonment by the Governor of Ashanti.

Knowles appealed to the Judicial Committee of the Privy Council on both legal and constitutional grounds, and his conviction was quashed because the trial judge had misdirected himself in failing to consider manslaughter as a possible verdict. The constitutional question which had been raised — that of whether a British citizen in a British colony was entitled to trial by jury — was left unanswered.

Following his release, Knowles made no further revelations about what had happened on the afternoon of his wife's fatal injury. He died four years later, in 1933.

Body of George Newbery discovered, 1964

OCTOBER 22

On 22 October 1964, George Newbery, a sixty-year-old taxi-driver, was found dead by the side of a farm track seven miles outside Southampton. He had suffered head injuries caused by several blows with a rusty iron pipe — which was later discovered in some nearby bushes — but had still been alive at the time of being left there. His taxi was found abandoned near a rough part of Southampton called Six Dials, not far from his home, and splashes of blood on the inside showed that he had been sitting at the driving-wheel when the attack took place. His assailant had struck him from the offside rear seat.

The police began house-to-house inquiries in the Six Dials area, and also questioned the crews of ships about to leave the country, but nobody seemed able to help them. Other taxi-drivers said that they had seen Newbery on the evening of 21 October, and a tramp came forward to say that he had seen him lying at the roadside about 11.15 p.m. — at which time, according to the pathologist, he must have been close to death. But this was all the progress that was made during the first eight days, and it looked as though the police were going to be unable to solve the crime.

It was then found that £3 had been withdrawn from the dead man's Post Office Savings Account on the afternoon following the murder, and that greasy fingerprints had been left on the withdrawal form. The fingerprints did not match those of any Post Office employee who might have touched the form, so the police were sure that they belonged to the person who had made the withdrawal. But, as that person had no criminal record in this country, they could not be identified until he was caught.

An attempt was therefore made to trace him by comparing his handwriting with the writing on various types of official documents — seamen's cards, Labour Exchange application forms, driving-licence forms, and so on — and during the weeks which ensued 100,000 such documents were checked. But this was also to no avail. By the end of the year the police still had no idea who had killed George Newbery.

But then an unemployed cable-maker named John William Stoneley was caught trying to break into a Southampton garage. Stoneley, aged twenty-one, appeared in court the following day, but was released on bail, having said that he was about to get married. However, a fingerprint check revealed that he was the person who had made the £3 withdrawal from Newbery's Post Office account, and he was quickly re-arrested.

Stoneley at first denied knowing anything about the affair, but later asked for pen and paper and wrote out a long, self-piteous statement. In this, he said that on the evening in question he and another man, George Ernest Sykes, a twenty-three-year-old dairyman, had taken the taxi to the place where the body was found, and had there attacked the driver and taken his wallet. Only one blow had been struck with the iron pipe, he claimed, and the victim's wallet had been removed from his pocket unintentionally. Moreover, he (Stoneley) and Sykes were not responsible for Newbery's death, because it 'was caused by him not getting help'.

The confession, such as it was, led to Stoneley and 'Bill' Sykes being jointly charged with murder. They were tried and convicted at the Winchester Assizes, Stoneley being sentenced to death and his companion to life imprisonment. The solving of the crime was a personal triumph for Detective Chief Superintendent Walter Jones, the Head of Hampshire's CID. It was his fortieth successful murder investigation in twelve years.

Stoneley's sentence was afterwards commuted to life imprisonment and a few months later he married a girl of nineteen in a church on Dartmoor — the bride being given away by the prison welfare officer and the groom having another prison officer as his best man. After the ceremony the couple were allowed only thirteen minutes together before Stoneley went back to jail.

Murder of Albert Anastasia, 1957

OCTOBER
25

On 25 October 1957, Albert Anastasia, a notorious New York Mafia boss, entered the basement barber's shop at the Park-Sheraton Hotel in Manhattan for a quick haircut. While he was sitting back in the chair, with his head against the rest, two other men appeared in the shop and opened fire on him with automatic pistols. He died from multiple gunshot wounds.

Anastasia, an Italian by birth, had entered the United States illegally during the First World War. In the 1920s he had been a small-time mobster in Brooklyn, but later became head of one of the five Mafia families in New York City, controlling a powerful organization of racketeers and professional killers. He was believed to be responsible for scores of murders, and for this reason was called the 'Lord High Executioner'.

In 1940 a gunman named Abe Reles, belonging to a Brooklyn gang known as 'Murder Incorporated', made a long confession, giving details of many crimes which he and his associates had committed. His information led to convictions in a number of murder cases, and Anastasia, who had strong ties with this gang, had to go into hiding.

But the 'perfect' case which had been prepared

against him by William O'Dwyer, the Brooklyn District Attorney, fell apart in November 1941, when Reles — who was supposed to be under police protection — hurtled to his death from a sixth-floor hotel window.

His death was never satisfactorily explained, and it was commonly believed that he had been murdered. O'Dwyer remarked that his case against Anastasia 'went out of the window with Reles'.

Anastasia's own murder, which caused a sensation, was clearly the work of professional killers, who had managed to take him by surprise while his bodyguard was away on an errand. Afterwards, having discarded their guns, the two men disappeared into the busy streets. They were never apprehended.

Although the crime was never officially solved, Joseph Valachi, a member of the Mafia for thirty years, later claimed that Vito Genovese, the head of another New York family, had been behind it. According to Valachi, Genovese had ordered the murder because he had discovered that Anastasia was plotting against *him*, and other Mafia leaders had tolerated this violation of the organization's rules because Anastasia was himself out of favour by this time.

Valachi's story is to be found in *The Valachi Papers* by Peter Maas, published in 1968.

Beginning of the 'Torch Murders' case 1936

Just before five o'clock on the morning of 29 October 1936, a gold-miner on his way to work near the Witwatersrand town of Brakpan found two smouldering corpses lying in a shallow water trench running alongside the road. Spiros Paizes, a thirty-one-year-old Greek café proprietor, and his assistant, Pericles Paxinos — also a Greek — had both been murdered, and their bodies had been thrown into the trench before being soaked with petrol and set on fire. A cartridge case lay in a pool of blood on the asphalt road, and signs of a desperate struggle were found near the wire fence a short distance away.

The post-mortem revealed that Paizes had been shot in the head and neck, and that Paxinos had suffered a fractured skull as a result of being struck with a heavy blunt instrument. The motive for the murders was at first not known, but it was soon discovered that both men had been involved in illicit gold-trafficking. Paizes, it was also learnt, had been one of five men who left the nearby town of Benoni by car on the night in question, travelling towards Brakpan. He had been to Benoni to see a young woman who acted as a go-between in his deals, and had had £900 in his possession at that time. The woman did not recognize any of his companions, all of whom waited for him in the car.

The police began tracing and questioning Paizes' 'clients', and became convinced that one of the people responsible for the murders — the 'Torch Murders', as they were called — was Andries Stephanus Du Plessis, a twenty-year-old criminal whose activities

314

included housebreaking and gold-running. On the night of 2 November the house in which he lived in Strubenvale, near Springs — a few miles from Brakpan, in the opposite direction — was surrounded in readiness for a raid. But by that time another three people had been killed, this time in Sandspruit, a railway siding ten miles from Volksrust, on the main line from Johannesburg to Durban. And Du Plessis was not at home.

Samuel Berman, who ran a store and filling-station, had just finished eating his evening meal in the company of his sister-in-law Essie Liebowitz and her husband Barney, who worked for him, when the front door was flung open and a masked gunman entered. Ordering Liebowitz to his feet, the man shot and killed him; he then shot Berman as he tried to escape and Mrs Liebowitz after she had locked herself in a bedroom with her baby. Finally, he forced his way into the store, opened the safe with keys taken from Liebowitz's pocket, and removed money, foreign coins, documents and a watch. Two native servants, who were washing dishes in the kitchen when the gunman entered, had by this time managed to leave the scene unharmed.

Du Plessis was arrested when he arrived home at 2 a.m., and the keys to Berman's store and safe were found in his possession. Bloodstains and a cartridge case linking him to the 'Torch Murders' were found in his car; so, too, were various items taken from Berman's safe and a helmet similar to one worn by the Sandspruit gunman. Moreover, he was identified by a native at a filling-station, who had sold petrol to him shortly after the first crime.

Du Plessis was brought to trial in Johannesburg on 15 March 1937, and elected to be tried by a judge and assessors. He admitted having been present at both crimes, but accused others of being responsible for what had happened in each case. The 'Torch Murders', he said, had been committed by two men to whom he was merely acting as chauffeur, because Paizes had caught them trying to swindle him over the sale of some gold bars. The triple murder in Sandspruit had also been the work of one of these men, and had taken place while he (Du Plessis) and a third man remained outside the store.

The trial ended on 31 March, the prisoner being found guilty of all five murders and sentenced to death; the accusations which he had made against the other three men — one a prosecution witness — were dismissed as false. Du Plessis then remained in the death cell for two and a half months while his case was considered by the Governor-General-in-Council, and was hanged on 17 June 1937 after an unsuccessful attempt to kill himself by slashing his wrists with a razor blade. He died without divulging the real names of other people known to have been involved in the murders.

Murder of Ruben Martirosoff, 1945

NOVEMBER
1

About 6.30 a.m. on 1 November 1945, the body of Ruben Martirosoff, an Armenian with a long criminal record, was found in a stationary car in Chepstow Place, Kensington, west London. He had been shot in the back of the neck as he sat at the driving-wheel, then moved to the back seat and robbed of all his valuables except a few pounds in a pocket on which he was lying. A felt hat was afterwards put over his face, concealing an exit wound above his right eye.

His death was thought to have occurred between two and four o'clock in the morning.

Martirosoff, known to his associates as 'Russian Robert', was a thief, a receiver of stolen property and a black-marketeer; he had five convictions in England and others in France and Germany. His wife, who identified his body, told police that he had gone out about eleven o'clock the previous night, intending to meet a Polish naval officer whose name she did not know. She said that her husband regularly carried large sums of money around in connection with his dealings.

It was learnt that at 1 a.m. a wartime constable had seen the car standing in Kensington Park Road, not far from Chepstow Place, and three men — one in the uniform of a foreign naval officer — walking away from it; the same witness had seen the men return and drive away in the car about twenty minutes later. Inquiries in the West End, where the same three men had been seen in a night-club between 11.15 and 11.45 p.m., revealed that one of them was Martirosoff and another a Pole named Marian, known to be in the handbag-making business.

As Marian's whereabouts were unknown, the police kept watch on a flat occupied by a Spaniard in the same line of business, with whom he was believed to be acquainted. Soon a Polish seaman called there to deliver a suitcase and, on being questioned, said that Marian had sent him. With this man's help, Marian was arrested the same afternoon on a street corner in the East End, and articles known to have been owned by the dead man — a wallet, a lighter and a wrist-watch — were found in his possession. He gave his name as Marian Grondkowski.

Further items which had belonged to Martirosoff — a signet ring and another two watches — were discovered at his lodgings in Ilford, Essex, which he shared with a friend named Henryk Malinowski; a naval officer's uniform (both men were deserters) and two automatic pistols were also found there.

Malinowski was arrested at the home of a widow whose two daughters were friendly with him. 'I saw you pick up Grondkowski,' he told police officers. Then, after being cautioned, he went on, 'I was there but I do not shoot. Grondkowski kill him.' A wallet containing four £5 notes was found in his pocket; the wallet was identified by Mrs Martirosoff as yet another of her husband's possessions.

Grondkowski and Malinowski both made written statements, each blaming the other for Martirosoff's murder but admitting to having robbed him and shared the proceeds. Later the Polish seaman who had led police to Grondkowski revealed that he had overheard the two prisoners planning not only to kill and rob Martirosoff but also to rob his wife. The case against them was further strengthened by fingerprint and ballistics evidence.

Arrested and charged within forty-eight hours of the crime, Grondkowski and Malinowski appeared for trial at the Old Bailey in February the following year. Both were convicted and sentenced to death, and on 2 April 1946 they were both hanged.

An earlier murder of which Grondkowski was suspected — that of a London taxi-driver shot dead at the wheel of his cab just a fortnight before Martirosoff's death — was never officially solved.

Death of Jacques Mesrine, 1979

Jacques Mesrine, who was killed in a police ambush in Paris on 2 November 1979, was a daring and resourceful criminal responsible for many robberies and murders. His death was a great relief to the French police, and the officers concerned were so overjoyed at it that they hugged and kissed each other, and even danced in the street. It was a fitting end to a remarkable career of crime, and one which Mesrine, who loved danger and craved publicity, would almost certainly have welcomed.

Born in Clichy in 1937, Mesrine began to associate with criminals while still a teenager and turned to burglary and safe-breaking after finishing his military service in Algeria. He was sent to prison for the first time in 1962, and by 1968 was one of the most wanted robbers in the country. He then went to Canada with a female accomplice, Jeanne Schneider, with whom he was later arrested for the kidnapping of Georges Deslauriers, a millionaire, and the murder of an elderly widow named Evelyne le Bouthillier.

Mesrine at this stage declared that he had committed several other murders but would have been incapable of the one with which he had been charged. Shortly afterwards he and his accomplice escaped from prison, Mesrine having attacked a guard and stolen his keys. They were, however, recaptured and brought to trial, when both were given prison sentences for kidnapping Deslauriers but acquitted of the murder of Mme le Bouthillier.

Mesrine served only a year of his ten-year sentence before leading a spectacular escape which made him a

319

celebrity in Canada. After a bank robbery in Montreal he and one of his accomplices intended returning to the prison to release other prisoners, but had to abandon the plan after a gun-battle with police. A few days after that two forest rangers were shot dead when they discovered Mesrine with two associates near Montreal. Mesrine went on to commit several more robberies in Canada, then went to live off the proceeds in Venezuela.

Eventually he returned to France, where he was arrested on 8 March 1973, following a dozen more armed robberies. He escaped from the courthouse in Compiègne by holding up the court — with a gun which had been left in a lavatory for him — and using the judge as a shield. He was not recaptured for several months, and in the meantime committed further robberies of banks and factories.

But he then spent three and a half years in La Santé prison before being brought to trial, and during that time wrote an autobiography, *The Killer Instinct*, published in 1977. This gave details of various murders, but also revealed that an earlier claim to have killed thirty-nine people had been a lie. Mesrine's trial finally began three months after the book's publication, and resulted in a twenty-year prison sentence. The following year he escaped yet again.

Remaining at large for the next year and a half, he on one occasion robbed a casino in Deauville and on another tried unsuccessfully to kidnap the judge who had given him his twenty-year sentence; he came close to being arrested both times. He also gave interviews to journalists and wrote an open letter to the French police, deploring the conditions which existed in top-security prisons.

At the time of his death Mesrine was living in a luxury apartment in Paris, in the Rue Belliard. The police discovered his whereabouts and, knowing that he had sworn not to be taken alive, decided against making a raid. When Mesrine came out of the building accompanied by his latest mistress they even allowed the couple to get into his BMW car, which had been parked nearby, and drive off unchallenged.

But when Mesrine stopped at a road junction, a lorry pulled up in front of his car and another behind it. Before he had time to realize what was happening, four policemen climbed out and opened fire on him, shattering his windscreen. A police car then drew up alongside him, and the officer in the passenger seat leaned out and shot him in the head, killing him instantly.

Mesrine's mistress was also found to have been shot, but later recovered from her injuries.

President Giscard d'Estaing, who regarded the Mesrine affair as an affront to national dignity, was immediately informed of what had happened.

Human remains found at Brandy Cove, 1961

NOVEMBER
5

On 5 November 1961, three pot-holers exploring a disused lead mine at Brandy Cove, on the Glamorgan coast, found the skeleton of a woman who had been murdered forty-two years previously. The woman was Mamie Stuart, a twenty-six-year-old former chorus girl whose mysterious disappearance in 1919 had led to an unsuccessful police investigation.

The body had been hidden behind a thick slab of stone fifty feet underground, after being sawn into three pieces. A wedding-ring, an engagement-ring, a black butterfly comb and a rotted sack were found in the same cavern.

The remains were identified at Cardiff's forensic science laboratory, where transparencies of the skull were projected onto photographs of the ex-chorus girl, and the rings were identified by an elderly woman who had known Mamie Stuart intimately. At the coroner's inquest which followed the jury found not only that the dead woman had been murdered, but also that the evidence pointed to a man named Everard George Shotton being the person responsible for the crime.

Mamie, who came from Sunderland, had met Shotton, a marine surveyor of Penarth, near Cardiff, in 1917. They were married the following year, and lived in furnished rooms in Swansea from February to July 1919, when Mamie went back to stay with her parents for a while. Then, in November 1919, they were together again, living in a furnished house which Shotton had rented, five and a half miles from Swansea, near the village of Newton. But when Mamie's parents wrote to her there, the letter was returned by the Post Office, marked, 'House closed'.

In March 1920 police in Swansea were shown a portmanteau which had been left unclaimed at a local hotel for some months. Inside they found a second portmanteau, containing two dresses and a pair of lady's boots — all of which had been cut to pieces — together with various other items, including a piece of paper on which the address of Mamie's parents had been written. The bag had been left by a man who had stayed at the hotel on his own, but the clothes inside it had belonged to Mamie.

During the same month Mamie's handbag, containing a ration card and about £2 in cash, was found in the front bedroom of the house which Shotton had rented.

George Shotton's marriage to Mamie Stuart was

found to have been a bigamous one, for another woman whom he had married twelve years earlier was still his legal wife. The police officers involved in the case found him living with this woman — and their little son — in a house at Caswell Bay, only a mile and a half from Newton.

On being questioned, Shotton admitted having lived with Mamie, but denied marrying her. He said that he had not seen her since early in December, when they parted after a quarrel.

The police, who suspected that Mamie had been murdered, were not satisfied with Shotton's answers. Continuing their inquiries, they found that he was a jealous and suspicious man, and that Mamie — who had a lover — had sometimes shown herself to be frightened of him. Yet they searched the house in which the couple had lived, and dug up much of the surrounding countryside, without finding any trace of her.

Finally, Shotton was arrested and brought to trial for bigamy. He pleaded not guilty, claiming that Mamie had gone through the ceremony of marriage with somebody impersonating him. But he was convicted and sentenced to eighteen months' hard labour.

Although Shotton admitted that he was the man who had left the portmanteau at the Swansea hotel, the police made no further progress on the case until the discovery of Mamie's remains in 1961.

But one of the twenty witnesses who then gave evidence at the inquest — an eighty-three-year-old retired postman — claimed that one afternoon in 1919 he had seen Shotton lift a heavy sack into his van outside the house which he had shared with Mamie, and drive off in the direction of Brandy Cove.

George Shotton was not there to deny this, as he had by this time been dead for three and a half years. He had died in a hospital in Bristol, at the age of seventy-eight, on 30 April 1958.

Horrifying murder in Camberwell, 1980

On 8 November 1980, three men and a woman — all alcoholics — lured a casual park worker named Donald Ryan to a maisonette in Camberwell, south London, where the men attacked and battered him, evidently for the sake of whatever money was to be found in his pockets. Not satisfied with knocking him 'semi-conscious', however, they went on to immerse him in a bath of scalding water, and then — while he was still alive — started to dismember him with an electric carving-knife, a saw and a machete.

Before long the remains of Donald Ryan, a former amateur boxer, were ready for disposal. The trunk and limbs were taken out and hidden in nearby streets; the head was left in the kitchen of the maisonette — in a refrigerator — and later put out in the dustbin. But when the group went to a local public house, the three men still bloodstained, their appearance gave rise to suspicion and shortly afterwards the police were informed.

The culprits were arrested on various charges, including murder, and when they were later tried at the Old Bailey the evidence was so shocking that four members of the jury were ill. The trial ended with the three men being convicted of murder and the woman of unlawful disposal of the body. The men were given life sentences, the judge recommending that John Bowden, a twenty-six-year-old Londoner, should serve at least twenty-five years, and that Michael Ward, a Camberwell grave-digger aged twenty-eight, and David Begley, a forty-one-year-old porter from Walworth, should each serve at least fifteen years.

Bowden already had a criminal record. By the time he was twenty-four he had spent a total of five years in jail for crimes which included robbery, blackmail, burglary, assault, wounding and carrying offensive weapons. Since then, in association with the other members of the group, he had regularly attacked helpless down-and-outs during the course of robbing them. But his behaviour on the evening of Ryan's murder was such that the trial judge in January 1982 remarked, 'Bowden is a man who obviously enjoyed inflicting pain, and even killing. There never was a more horrific case of murder than this!'

On being sentenced, Bowden shouted at the judge, 'You old bastard! I hope you die screaming of cancer!'

After the trial his parents described him as 'a good boy, gentle and kind', who had only become violent as a result of being kept in solitary confinement on an earlier occasion. 'He was never the same afterwards,' said his father.

A year later, at Parkhurst Prison on the Isle of Wight, Bowden and another prisoner took the assistant governor hostage at knife-point, and only released him when the Home Office agreed to investigate certain grievances of theirs.

Murder of Arthur Baker, 1902

NOVEMBER

10

On 10 November 1902, Kitty Byron, a twenty-four-year-old milliner's assistant, stabbed her lover, Arthur Reginald Baker, to death in a London street. The crime took place during the early afternoon and was witnessed by a number of bystanders. Kitty afterwards burst into tears and threw herself onto her victim's body as he lay on the ground. 'I killed him willingly, and he deserved it,' she said to the policeman who arrested her. She was later tried for murder at the Old Bailey.

Kitty had been living with Baker in lodgings in Duke Street, Portland Place, for several months prior to the crime. Baker, a stockbroker, was already married, but gave Kitty to believe that he expected a divorce and would then marry her. But he drank heavily and there were frequent quarrels between them. Finally, when their landlady asked them to leave, he said that Kitty would go if he could keep the room.

On hearing about this after Baker had left for work on the morning of 10 November, Kitty was greatly distressed. She went to the City, buying a knife on the way, then sent him an express letter from Lombard Street Post Office, saying that she wanted to see him immediately. Before long he joined her at the post office, and an argument started between them, which continued as they walked out into the street. It was then, in Post Office Court, that Kitty pulled the knife from her muff and began to stab him.

Baker was generally disliked, and his fellow Stock Exchange members provided funds for Kitty's defence. When she was tried before Mr Justice Darling in December 1902, her counsel asked for a verdict of manslaughter, appealing for sympathy on her behalf, but the prisoner seemed hardly aware of what was going on. She was found guilty of murder and sentenced to death.

But public feeling was strongly in her favour, and 15,000 people signed a petition for a reprieve. Shortly afterwards her sentence was commuted to life imprisonment, and this was eventually reduced to ten years. She served only six years before being transferred to a benevolent institution for women.

Murder in the Peak District, 1927

On the morning of 11 November 1927, a brutal murder was committed at the New Inn, a public house near the village of Hayfield, in Derbyshire's Peak District. The victim, thirty-six-year-old Mrs Amy Collinson — the landlord's wife — was alone there at the time, as her husband Arthur had a daytime job in Glossop, four miles away. It was not until he returned home at 6 p.m. that the body was discovered.

Amy Collinson had been knocked unconscious with two blows to the head, then her throat had been cut with a knife from the kitchen. This had happened in a downstairs room, and the culprit had afterwards taken £40 from a cash-box in the couple's bedroom, leaving £10 behind. He had been able to find the cash-box without difficulty and so was suspected of being a local man who had worked out its location from overhead noises while drinking there.

The Derbyshire police began interviewing the pub's regular customers, and before long George Frederick Walter Hayward, a thirty-two-year-old unemployed commercial traveller living in a nearby cottage, emerged as a suspect. 'Jerry' Hayward was heavily in debt, owing £70 to a soap firm for which he had formerly worked, £50 in rent arrears, and further sums here and there. But, although his dole money

327

was only twenty-five shillings (£1.25) a week, it was learnt that since the murder he had manged to repay £4 which he owed to a furniture firm, and that his wife had been better off than usual.

Hayward admitted that he had been to the pub on the morning of the murder. He said that he had called in there to buy some cigarettes before catching a bus to New Mills — about three miles away — to collect his dole, and that Mrs Collinson had been all right at that time. However, bloodstains were found on his hat and tie, £35 was found hidden in the chimney at his hillside cottage, and a bloodstained length of lead piping discovered on top of a disused cistern at the New Inn was found to have been cut from the outlet of his kitchen sink.

Hayward was arrested and charged with murder. At his trial in Derby in February 1928 he claimed that Amy Collinson had committed suicide because of financial difficulties which she had often told him about, but in view of the medical evidence this was impossible to believe. He was therefore convicted and sentenced to death, his execution taking place at Bagthorpe Jail, Nottingham, in April the same year.

The New Inn was later renamed The Lantern Pike.

Death of Ernest Wilson, 1957

NOVEMBER 12

On the morning of 12 November 1957, Ernest Wilson, a seventy-five-year-old retired engineer, died at his council bungalow in Windy Nook, Felling-on-Tyne, County Durham, apparently from natural causes. Only a fortnight earlier he had married a widow of sixty-six, and it was she who called his doctor to Windy Nook, saying that her husband was very ill. This was an understatement, for Mr Wilson had, in fact, died some hours previously. But the doctor knew that he had suffered for many years from myocardiao degeneration of the heart, and so recorded the cause of his death as cardio-muscular failure due to this condition.

That evening Mrs Mary Elizabeth Wilson, who was now a widow again, called on Mrs Grace Liddell, a friend living in Hebburn-on-Tyne, in the same county, and asked if she could stay the night with her. She made no mention of her husband being dead, and on being asked if she was having any trouble with him, replied that he was 'badly' and had been seen by a doctor. Mrs Liddell put her friend up for the night, and went back to Felling with her the following morning. But when they arrived at the bungalow Mrs Wilson — who seems to have been quite a humorist in her own way — gave her the door key and invited her to go in first, remarking, 'When you get in you'll get a shock!'

Mrs Liddell entered the bungalow and found Mr Wilson's body laid out on a trestle table. Mrs Wilson then said that her husband had died in hospital, and seemed not to be put out when Mrs Liddell intimated that she did not believe this. Later the same day Mrs Wilson, a dumpy, ginger-haired woman with glasses, went to the hotel where she and her late husband had had their wedding reception, and told the bar manager that Mr Wilson was ill in hospital.

Mrs Wilson had been married three times. Her first husband, a retired chimney-sweep named John Knowles, had died in August 1955, after forty-three years of marriage, and his wife afterwards went on living in the same house — this one was in Hebburn — with their lodger, John Russell, who was believed to be her lover. But Russell died only five months later, leaving her a small sum of money, and in September 1956 she married Oliver Leonard, a retired estate agent. Mr Leonard, like his successor, died only a fortnight after the wedding.

None of these deaths had been regarded with suspicion at the time, and in all likelihood that of Ernest Wilson would not have been, either. But the extraordinary behaviour of Mrs Wilson could only serve to draw attention to her, and the gossip which ensued prompted a police investigation. The bodies of Ernest Wilson and Oliver Leonard were both exhumed and found to contain phosphorus, and on 11 December Mrs Wilson was accused of murdering them.

She stood trial on these charges at the Leeds Assizes in March 1958, when she was described by the prosecution as 'a wicked woman who married in succession two men and then deliberately poisoned them in order to get the paltry benefits she hoped she might obtain'. It was alleged that the substance administered in each case had been rat or beetle poison.

The trial lasted six days, much of that time being taken up with the evidence of expert witnesses. The prisoner did not go into the witness box herself, and after retiring for just under an hour and a half the jury found her guilty of both murders. She was therefore sentenced to death, but this sentence was commuted to life imprisonment after a last-minute reprieve. She died in Holloway Prison, at the age of seventy, on 5 December 1962.

The bodies of John Knowles and John Russell had been exhumed while she was awaiting trial, and these were also found to contain phosphorus. But as no evidence could be produced to show how it came to be in either of them an open verdict was returned in each case.

NOVEMBER

13

During the early hours of 13 November 1952, the body of Patricia Curran, the nineteen-year-old daughter of an Ulster High Court judge, was found beside the drive of her home in Whiteabbey, a village near Belfast. There were a large number of wounds on her face and body — thirty-seven, in fact — and it seemed at first that she had been blasted with a shotgun. But it was later discovered that they were stab-wounds, caused by a frenzied attack with a thin-bladed knife.

The dead girl, a student at Queen's University, Belfast, had attended lectures the previous day, and had been reported missing when she was not back indoors several hours later. Her clothes were torn, indicating that her murderer had intended to rape or sexually assault her, but her college books were found neatly stacked nearby, as though she had placed them there herself. She had apparently walked home from the village bus stop on purpose, for although she normally telephoned for a car when she arrived there, she had not done so on this occasion.

The police questioned Patricia Curran's friends and fellow-villagers, and the judge appealed for information which might help to solve the crime. During a check of airmen and civilians at the nearby Edenmore RAF station suspicion fell on Leading Aircraftman Iain Hay Gordon, a twenty-one-year-old Scotsman who had tried to arrange an alibi for himself for the evening of 12 November.

Gordon was a friend of Desmond Curran, the dead girl's brother, and had been to the family's home many times. It was learnt from Desmond that he was obsessed with the murder and had expressed surprise that the victim had been stabbed so many times, as 'the fourth blow killed her'. It was also learnt that he had asked Desmond whether there was any reference to him in Patricia's diaries.

Arrested in January 1953, Iain Gordon eventually admitted the crime. He said that on the evening in question he had met Patricia by chance in White-abbey, and escorted her home at her own request. As they walked along the drive leading to the house he wanted to kiss her and she reluctantly allowed him to do so after putting her books and handbag down on the grass. But then, he said, he 'could not stop kissing her', and stabbed her with his service knife because she resisted his advances.

When Gordon appeared for trial at the Belfast Assizes in March evidence of schizophrenia was produced and the jury, after retiring for just under two hours, returned a verdict of guilty but insane. He was ordered to be detained during Her Majesty's pleasure.

Bill McCullough's body discovered, 1981

NOVEMBER 18

On the morning of 18 November 1981, Muriel McCullough, a fifty-two-year-old former beauty queen and businesswoman, telephoned her local police in the village of Ailsworth, Cambridgeshire, and said that her home appeared to have been burgled the previous night, while she was staying with a friend in Cheshire. Shortly afterwards PC Alan Gregory arrived at the house and found her in a nervous state, unwilling to go upstairs with him to investigate. He therefore went up on his own and found Mrs McCullough's husband lying dead in the master bedroom. Bill McCullough, who was four years his wife's junior, had been shot in the head.

PC Gregory was suspicious, for Mrs McCullough's behaviour in refusing to go upstairs and check her jewellery did not seem to be that of a woman who really believed that the place had been burgled. So, instead of telling her what he had discovered, he merely said that her husband was ill in bed. Even then, she remained downstairs instead of going up to see him — and afterwards, on being told the truth, she remained silent for a few moments, then finally shouted, 'Bill! Oh, my Bill! I want my Bill!'

The unimpressed constable reported his suspicions and, although Mrs McCullough was able to prove that she had been in Hale, Cheshire, 150 miles away, at the time of her husband's death, a close watch was kept on her movements. Before long the police learnt that she had had dealings with two Liverpool crooks, James Collingwood and Alan Kay, and that these two men had since been demanding money from a friend of hers named Joe Scanlon, who had helped her to make contact with them.

Scanlon later told the police that he believed Mrs McCullough had wanted to meet Collingwood so that she could arrange to have her husband beaten up. But when Collingwood was questioned he admitted that he had killed McCullough, saying that Mrs McCullough had agreed to pay him £8000 to do so, and that she had given him £1000 in advance, together with a plan of the district and details of the house. Kay had merely driven him there and waited outside while he (Collingwood) entered through an unlocked side door and shot McCullough as he slept.

Muriel McCullough had been married twice and had two children by her first marriage. Her first husband had died as a result of a heart attack and she had married his successor on 31 December 1980. But McCullough, an insurance executive, soon proved to be a heavy drinker, a debtor and a wife-beater. Moreover, he had a life insurance policy by which his wife stood to gain over £110,000 in the event of his death.

On being charged with murder, Muriel McCullough said that she had only hired Collingwood and Kay to beat her husband up. 'You have no idea what it's like when your husband beats you,' she told a senior police officer. 'I wanted him to have a taste of his own medicine, and I thought they would give him a good bashing. I wanted him to know what it's like on the receiving end.'

In November 1982 she stood trial with Collingwood and Kay at Birmingham Crown Court, the prosecution describing her as 'a tough, scheming liar' who had 'successfully kept the police at bay' for six weeks. Collingwood, having denied the offence, suddenly changed his plea to guilty, telling the court that Mrs McCullough had hired him to kill her husband but then failed to pay the bulk of his agreed fee. Muriel McCullough and Alan Kay continued to deny the offence but were both found guilty. The three prisoners were all given sentences of life imprisonment.

On the afternoon of 19 November 1924, Sir Lee
Stack, the Sirdar, or Commander-in-Chief, of the
Egyptian army and Governor-General of the Sudan,
was shot and fatally wounded by ambushers while
driving through the streets of Cairo. The attack took
place as his car slowed down at a tramway — when all
three of its occupants were injured — but the chauffeur was able to accelerate and drive away from the
scene. The culprits pursued the vehicle for fifty yards,
firing as they ran, then wounded a policeman before
making off in a taxi which they had had waiting
nearby. The Sirdar died the following day from shock
and internal haemorrhages.

The attack was immediately thought to be the
work of terrorists. Sydney Smith, a forensic scientist
then heading a department of the Egyptian Ministry
of Justice, found that the bullet which had killed the
Sirdar bore a scratched groove, which linked the
murder to several other crimes. Later it was learnt
from informers that those responsible for it were
members of a nationalist group led by Shafik
Mansour, a Member of Parliament who had been
charged in connection with the murder of a prime
minister in 1910, and the attempted murder of
another prime minister in 1914, but managed to
escape conviction each time.

As there was no evidence against any of the
members of this group, a police spy was used to trick
two brothers named Enayat into attempting to flee
the country. When they did so, they were arrested,

and four automatic pistols and a quantity of ammunition were found in their possession. These were examined by Smith, who fired test shots from two of the guns and then compared the bullets and cartridge-cases with others from the scene of the crime. He was thus able to demonstrate that both guns had been used in the attack and that one of them was the murder weapon.

On being confronted with this evidence, the Enayat brothers — one aged nineteen, the other twenty-two — made confessions which implicated six other members of their group, including Shafik Mansour and an engineer named Mahmoud Rachid. All were arrested, and tools which had evidently been used to convert ordinary bullets into dumdum, or expanding, bullets were found at the engineer's home. This discovery was regarded as an important one, as the Enayats had had dumdum bullets and others had been used in the attack.

Shafik Mansour, a lawyer by profession, at first denied having been involved in the crime. Then, after hearing that the Enayat brothers had confessed, he began to feign madness. But eventually he admitted that he had incited the other prisoners to murder Sir Lee Stack, and that he had been similarly involved in a number of earlier political murders. At the end of May 1925 he and his fellow conspirators were brought to trial in connection with the shooting.

The prosecution produced evidence of four confessions — for Mahmoud Rachid had also made one — and although Shafik retracted his, claiming that he had made it while in a trance, this made no difference to the outcome. The ballistics evidence presented by Sydney Smith was impressive enough to be accepted without question by the defence, and the prisoners were all convicted.

They were sentenced to death, and seven of them, including Shafik Mansour, were afterwards executed.

In the case of the eighth, the sentence was commuted to life imprisonment.

Disappearance of Kathleen Heathcote, 1963

NOVEMBER
21

On the night of 21 November 1963, Kathleen Heathcote, a twenty-one-year-old shop assistant, failed to arrive back at her home in Mansfield, Nottinghamshire, after going to visit her fiancé in Selston, six miles away. She had, in fact, caught the bus from Selston, and was seen to leave it at the Stockwell Gate stop in Mansfield — about 400 yards from her home — at 11 p.m. But she had then disappeared after setting off along a lane leading to Princess Street, where she lived.

When she was reported missing it was immediately suspected that she had been the victim of a crime, and police began making routine inquiries in the Mansfield area. A number of items belonging to her were found on a piece of waste ground over which she had taken a short cut, and people living nearby remembered having seen a stranger looking through their windows on the night in question.

It was also learnt that on the following day — before the girl's disappearance was reported — a policeman had given a lift in his patrol car to a frightened-looking motorist whose own vehicle was stuck in the mud at this point.

Before long Ronald Evans, a twenty-two-year-old colliery electrician living in the village of Shirebrook, four miles away, was questioned, and a search of his home resulted in the discovery of further items belonging to Kathleen, including keys from her handbag. On being confronted with this evidence, Evans, a married man, confessed that she was dead and that he was the person responsible. His story was both strange and macabre.

He had, he said, been drinking on the evening of 21 November, and saw Kathleen crossing the waste ground where he had parked his car. Although it was raining, he attacked her, threw her to the ground and raped her while she was unconscious. But afterwards, as she was coming round, she kept groaning and he became worried about her. He therefore dragged her to his car and placed her on the back seat, intending — or so he claimed — to take her to the nearest hospital.

When he found that the car was stuck in the mud, he dragged her out of it — still groaning — and pushed her into the boot before going to telephone a breakdown service. But he waited in vain for a service van to appear and eventually left the car where it was and took a taxi home.

The following day he returned and found Kathleen dead in the boot, her body stiff and cold. It was then, after Evans had closed the boot door, that the policeman arrived on the scene and offered to help him find a breakdown van. The car was pulled out of the mud shortly afterwards and Evans drove it home with the body still in the boot.

On the evening of 22 November he left his pregnant wife and his mother at a bingo hall and drove thirty miles to the Ladybower Reservoir — on the High Peak mountain range — where he stripped all the clothes from the corpse and threw it into the water, disposing of the clothes separately. He then returned to the bingo hall in time to drive his wife and mother home.

On 28 November — the day after Evans had been

charged with murder — frogmen began searching the reservoir for the missing girl's body. The following day they were joined by deep-sea divers from the Royal Navy, and finally, on 1 December, the body was found in the submerged village of Ashopton, which had been flooded when the reservoir was built nearly twenty years earlier.

In March 1964 Ronald Evans was brought to trial at the Nottingham Assizes. He admitted that he had raped Kathleen Heathcote when she was unconscious and in a serious condition, and agreed that he could have helped her instead of leaving her to die in the boot. The judge told him that he had murdered 'a decent and modest young lady', and sentenced him to life imprisonment. But that was not the last that was heard of him.

On being released on licence eleven years later, he went to live in Bristol. The police there knew that he had murdered a shop assistant, but not that it had been a sex crime. So when a series of sex offences began there shortly after his arrival, he was not regarded as a suspect. But one night in 1978 a police-woman acting as a decoy was attacked in a dark street. She fought back, calling over her radio for help, and the offender, now known as the 'Beast of Bristol', was arrested. It was Ronald Evans.

In July 1979 he appeared for trial at Bristol Crown Court, and pleaded guilty to four charges of indecent assault against women — in each case forcing the victim to take part in a sexual act by means of threats. This time he was sentenced to nine years' imprisonment, but also ordered to resume the life sentence which had been imposed on him in 1964.

NOVEMBER **22**

On 22 November 1941, the bodies of two girls were found in a wood in Buckinghamshire, during a search of the district by local police and volunteers. Doreen Hearne, aged eight, and Kathleen Trendle, six, had both died from stab wounds in the neck, each having been manually strangled to the point of unconsciousness beforehand. There was no indication that either of them had been sexually assaulted, though the skirts of both had been pulled up under their arms. The motive for the crime was therefore unknown.

The two girls had been reported missing three days earlier, after leaving their school in the village of Penn — about half a mile from their homes. Other children said that they had seen them being taken for a ride in an army lorry, and in Rough Wood, where their bodies were discovered — some four miles from the village — there were tyre marks and a large patch of oil which had been left by a vehicle. There was also a khaki handkerchief with the laundry mark 'RA 1019' among the items found at the scene.

Some of the children who had seen the lorry were able to describe it, and one boy remembered its military identification marks. The police were thus able to trace it to Yoxford, in Suffolk, where it was found to have oil leaking from its rear axle. The laundry mark 'RA 1019' was found to have been allotted to the driver of the vehicle, twenty-six-year-old Harold Hill, of the 86th Field Regiment, Royal Artillery.

The regiment had been in Hazlemere, a few miles from Penn, on the day in question, and Hill fitted descriptions of the man who had given the two girls a lift. His spare uniform — which he had been soaking — had bloodstains on it, and he was unable to explain how his handkerchief had been left at the scene of the murders. A claim that he had lost his army knife some months previously was later found to be a lie.

Harold Hill was charged with murder and brought to trial in January 1942. In spite of the absence of any discernible motive for the crime, he was convicted and sentenced to death. His execution took place in April the same year.

Murder of Edith Drew-Bear, 1934

On 25 November 1934, two men in Brighton, Sussex, reported hearing shots and screams on the East Brighton Golf Course, between Preston and Moulscombe. Police officers went to investigate, and found the body of Miss Edith Constance Drew-Bear, a twenty-one-year-old cinema attendant, in a water tank. She had been shot several times in the back and head — though none of the wounds had been fatal — and a silk scarf had then been tied tightly round her neck before she was immersed. Her death had been caused by strangulation.

Inquiries led to the arrest of Percy Charles Anderson, a motor mechanic also aged twenty-one, to whom Miss Drew-Bear had been closely attached. Anderson had been with her on the day in question, and had afterwards boarded a bus dripping wet and without his boots, jacket or waistcoat. The police found a bottle containing an irritant poison — a mixture of ammonia chloride and zinc chloride — in his pocket; they also found a number of weapons — a home-made pistol, a sheath-knife and a loaded stick — in his rooms, together with the empty container of a second pistol and bullets identical to those taken from the young woman's body.

Anderson said that he and Miss Drew-Bear had quarrelled, and that he had then gone for a swim in the sea to cool himself. He also said — or so it was later alleged — that the quarrel had started because the deceased accused him of smiling at another girl. But he could not remember what had happened after he went for a swim, as his mind had gone blank at this point.

At his trial at the Lewes Assizes in March 1935 a plea of insanity was made on his behalf. A Brighton doctor told the court that Anderson's black-out could have occurred as a result of an epileptic condition producing a state of maniacal excitement. Persons affected in this way could commit the most brutal acts of violence, being at the time perfectly oblivious of the injuries they inflicted on others and the damage that they themselves sustained, the doctor declared.

But the judge — Lord Hewart, the Lord Chief Justice — advised the jury that the onus was on the defence to prove insanity, as under the law every man was presumed to be sane until the contrary was proved. In order to meet this requirement, the defence had to show that at the time of committing the crime the prisoner had been labouring under 'such a defect of reason, from disease of the mind, as not to know the nature and quality of (his) act' — or that 'he did know it, but did not know that what he was doing was wrong'. In the case of Anderson it was difficult to see 'even a scintilla of evidence' of such a disease, the judge remarked.

Though no real motive for the crime had emerged, the jury took only forty minutes to return a verdict of guilty, and Anderson was sentenced to death. Following the dismissal of his appeal, he was hanged at Wandsworth Prison on 16 April 1935.

Murder of Colin Saunders, 1969

On 26 November 1969, Colin George Saunders, a thirty-five-year-old homosexual who worked as a chauffeur for a car-hire firm, was murdered by a young drifter from Liverpool with whom he had shared his bed-sitter in Bromley, Kent, for the previous five weeks. Stanley Wrenn, aged nineteen, attacked him in the early morning while he was still asleep, striking him twice with an iron gas-ring, then stabbing him a great many times with a knife which he had bought especially for the purpose. The crime was committed partly for the sake of money and partly out of malice, Wrenn having discovered that Saunders had infected him with gonorrhoea.

About four hours after the murder had taken place Wrenn left the house with about £12 in banknotes, some coins, Saunders' car-keys and driving licence, and a suitcase containing clean shirts and other stolen items. He got into the Humber belonging to Saunders' employers but reversed it at speed, causing a collision with another car. He then had to return to the house, pretending that he was telephoning the police, while the other driver waited in the street. A few minutes later he went out and told the other driver that the police were on their way.

But while he stood talking to him, another em-

343

ployee of Saunders' firm arrived on the scene and asked Wrenn what he was doing. Wrenn replied that he was 'taking the car round for Colin', and the newcomer helped him by moving the vehicle off the road. He then gave the keys back, telling Wrenn that he and Saunders were to go to the firm's office at eleven o'clock to see the manager. Finally, he spoke to the other driver before leaving.

Wrenn went back to the house once again, threw the keys down in the bed-sitter and shortly afterwards left for the third time, telling the driver who was still waiting that Saunders was getting up and that he (Wrenn) was going to the firm's office. This was not to the other man's liking, but he continued to wait in the expectation that the police would arrive at any moment. Wrenn, in the meantime, made his way to the nearest railway station and caught a train to London.

After waiting in the street for some hours the offended driver went to the house himself. One of the other occupants let him in, and they went into Saunders' room together. Finding the body, they called the police.

The room was in chaos, with clothes from the wardrobe strewn on the floor and splashes of blood in several places. There were two single beds, and the body lay on one of them, covered with bedclothes and a dressing-gown. The two murder weapons, both bloodstained, were found nearby; the gas-ring was later found to have been taken from another room in the same house.

There was no mystery to solve. The crime had been committed in a casual manner, and Wrenn gave himself up just as casually the following day, after he had been named in connection with it in an evening newspaper.

Appearing for trial at the Old Bailey on 24 March 1970, he pleaded guilty and was sentenced to life imprisonment. He was released in June 1980, when he was thirty years old.

Beryl Evans reported dead, 1949

On 30 November 1949, Timothy John Evans, a semi-literate van-driver aged twenty-five, walked into a police station in Wales and reported the death of his nineteen-year-old wife, whose body he claimed to have hidden in a drain at their home in the Notting Hill district of London. When police officers investigated the matter, they found that Beryl Evans was indeed dead — not in a drain but in a small wash-house — and so, too, was the couple's fourteen-month-old daughter Geraldine. Both deaths had been caused by strangulation.

Evans at first confessed to the murders, but later withdrew his confession and blamed John Reginald Halliday Christie, an older man who lived in another flat at the same address. Christie, a former wartime special constable, had known that Beryl was pregnant for the second time and offered to carry out an abortion for her, said Evans. He had afterwards said that she died during the course of this, and advised Evans to leave London for a while, saying that he would arrange for Geraldine to be unofficially adopted by a childless couple he knew. Evans, according to this account, had believed his daughter to be still alive when he reported his wife's death.

Evans was charged with both murders, and tried at the Old Bailey. Christie, who gave evidence against him, denied having had anything to do with the crimes, and seemed to have no motive for either of them. The trial was only for the murder of the child, but evidence concerning the death of Beryl Evans was admitted, as it was assumed that the two murders had been committed by the same person. On being found guilty, Evans was sentenced to death. He was hanged on 9 March 1950.

But three years later, on 24 March 1953, a West Indian tenant to whom Christie had sub-let his flat found the bodies of three other women in a kitchen cupboard which had been papered over. This shocking discovery was followed by others, the body of a fourth woman being found under floorboards in the same flat and the remains of a further two in the back garden. The four women whose bodies were found in the house — Christie's wife Ethel and three prostitutes — had all been murdered since Evans' execution. The other two had been killed and buried several years earlier.

Christie was arrested and admitted responsibility for all six of the murders, later adding that he had killed Beryl Evans as well. He already had a criminal record from many years earlier — one of his convictions being for assaulting a woman — but no importance had been attached to this when he appeared against Evans, as he had not been in trouble since 1933. At his trial at the Old Bailey — for his wife's murder — he pleaded insanity, but was found guilty. He was hanged at Pentonville Prison, at the age of fifty-five, on 15 July 1953.

Christie was a sex murderer. His last four victims — his wife and the three prostitutes — had all been strangled with ligatures, but the bodies of the three prostitutes also showed signs of carbon monoxide poisoning and sexual intercourse. Christie confessed that he had invited the women to his flat, and had used coal gas to make them lose consciousness so that he could strangle and rape them. He was, in fact, a necrophile.

But in view of his claim to have murdered Beryl Evans — though not Geraldine — and general disbelief in the possibility of two stranglers having lived in the same house at the same time, there were demands for an official inquiry into the question of whether the execution of Timothy Evans had been a miscarriage of justice. John Scott Henderson, a senior QC, was appointed by the Home Secretary to hold such an inquiry, and his report — published on the day of Christie's execution — concluded that Christie's confession to the murder of Beryl Evans had been false and that there could be no doubt that Timothy Evans had killed both Beryl and Geraldine.

In spite of this, many people believed that a miscarriage of justice *had* taken place, and during the early 1960s, following the publication of a book by Ludovic Kennedy, there were demands for a fresh inquiry. Eventually one was held under the direction of Sir Daniel Brabin, a High Court judge, who, in October 1966, reported his findings. These were that while Timothy Evans had probably not murdered his daughter — the crime for which he had been hanged — he probably *had* murdered his wife. The report led to Evans being granted a posthumous free pardon, but was received with scorn by people who had been campaigning for a review of the case.

'It took thirteen years for officialdom grudgingly to admit what was obvious in 1953 to all but the wilfully blind; that there were not two stranglers of women living in 10 Rillington Place, but one,' wrote Ludovic Kennedy in 1970.

But Professor Keith Simpson, one of the three pathologists who examined the exhumed body of Beryl Evans after Christie's arrest, tells us in his *Forty Years of Murder*, '(The) Brabin report upheld the coincidence, and it never seemed to me very far-fetched. Coincidences are far more common in life than in fiction.' He also draws attention to the lack of evidence of a sexual motive in her case and points out that — unlike the other women murdered in the same house — she was beaten up before being killed. The injuries which she received were, in his opinion, 'alien to Christie's style of murder'.

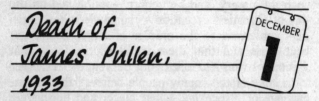

Death of James Pullen, 1933

On the evening of 1 December 1933, James Pullen, a senile old man of eighty-five, died from coal-gas poisoning at the home of his daughter and son-in-law just outside Bath, in Somerset. His son-in-law, thirty-two-year-old Reginald Ivor Hinks, was in the house with him at the time, and it was he who raised the alarm. He said that shortly after speaking to Mr Pullen in the sitting-room, he had found him lying on the kitchen floor, with his head in the oven and the gas turned on. His account suggested that his father-in-law had committed suicide.

This account was challenged at the inquest on Mr Pullen's body, initially by the dead man's own doctor, who had been called to the house on the evening in question. Dr Scott Reid, who had attended Mr Pullen for five years, said that as the dead man had suffered from senile degeneration of the brain, he would have been incapable of turning on the gas taps. Dr Reid also said that he had found a bruise on the back of the dead man's head — the result of a blow severe enough to have stunned him.

Following this sensation, two other witnesses — a pathologist and a police surgeon — both said that the bruise to which Dr Reid had referred had been caused while Mr Pullen was still alive. Then two more — a fireman and another doctor — told how they had been called to the house on the night preceding his death, when Hinks claimed that the old man had fainted or collapsed in his bath. On this occasion, according to Hinks, Mr Pullen's head had gone under the water and his face had turned black. But the old man had seemed unperturbed, and the doctor had found no evidence of inhaled water or shock. 'I thought the son-in-law must have simply got excited and was exaggerating,' the doctor said.

Hinks' wife Constance, to whom he had been married for less than a year, said that her husband had always been kind to her father and had looked after him since the end of June. She was asked about the incident which had occurred on 30 November, and told how she had helped to lift her father into a sitting position in the bath after her husband had called her to the scene. Her father had been 'practically himself' by the time the ambulance arrived, she said.

Questioned about her father's business affairs, Mrs Hinks said that he had owned four cottages, and had also owned a shop in Dorking, Surrey, until it was sold about August. He had given her £900 which he had received for the shop, and she had given it to her husband, who had used part of it to buy the house in which her father had died. Mrs Hinks also said that her father had made a will, leaving everything he owned to her.

Finally, a police constable told how he had gone to the house on the evening of 1 December and found two firemen giving Mr Pullen artificial respiration in the kitchen. The officer said that Hinks, who was wearing pyjamas and a dressing-gown, was very excited; he talked a great deal about his wife and said that he wanted Mr Pullen to be moved before she returned home. When asked what he had done when he found the old man with his head in the oven, he replied, 'I could see what had happened and I caught hold of his two feet and pulled him out. You might find a bruise on the back of his head where it hit the floor.' In a statement made later, he said that he had tried to revive the dead man by warming and massaging his heart.

The inquest, which had opened on 5 December, had already been adjourned several times, and was adjourned again after the constable had finished giving his evidence. When it was resumed on 19 January the jury returned a verdict of wilful murder against Hinks, and the coroner committed him for trial. Appearing at the Somerset Assizes, he was convicted and sentenced to death.

Hinks was a petty criminal with a record of fraud. He had married Constance after meeting her only a few weeks earlier, while he was working as a vacuum-cleaner salesman, and there could be little doubt that he had married her for the sake of the inheritance which she expected to receive at her father's death. Having done so, he had murdered her father for the same reason — and for this crime he was hanged in Bristol on 3 May 1934.

Constance, at the time of their meeting, had been a divorcée with one child, her first husband having divorced her on grounds of adultery. In January 1935 she gave birth to another child, in respect of which she later sought an affiliation order against a man living in Camberwell, south London. The man denied having been intimate with Mrs Hinks, and the order was refused.

During the early hours of 2 December 1925, Lock Ah Tam, a respected member of England's Chinese community, shot and killed his wife and two daughters at their home in Birkenhead, Cheshire. The crime was committed in a fit of rage after a family dinner party which had been held to celebrate the twentieth birthday of Tam's son Lock Ling. Tam afterwards telephoned the police and told them what he had done. The following February, at the Chester Assizes, he was convicted of murder.

Tam, a native of Canton, had settled in England after arriving as a ship's steward in 1895, at the age of twenty-three. He had afterwards risen to a position of prominence among his fellow countrymen, becoming the representative of organized Chinese dock workers in Europe and president of a Chinese Republican organization, as well as founding a seamen's club in Liverpool. At this time he was known to be prosperous, good-natured and charitable, and often helped the police to deal with problems which had arisen among Liverpool's Chinese population.

But in 1918 Tam suffered a head injury as a result of being struck with a billiard cue by a Russian sailor who had been invited to the club. He then began to drink excessively and was sometimes violent, particularly after an unsuccessful commercial venture in 1924 had led to his being declared bankrupt. His wife Catherine, a Welshwoman, stood by him loyally, but confided to a friend that she thought he was going mad.

On the night of the party Tam was in a good mood

until after the guests had left, when he suddenly began speaking angrily to his wife, stamping his feet and gesticulating. He stopped when Lock Ling intervened, but not long afterwards Margaret Sing, the maid, saw him loading a revolver. Shortly after that Tam got out his sporting-gun and shot his wife and youngest daughter; he then used the revolver to shoot his other daughter. By this time his son had run from the house in terror.

At his trial Tam was defended by Sir Edward Marshall Hall, who argued that his client had been in a state of unconscious automatism, caused by an epileptic fit, and was therefore insane at the time the murders were committed. But the jury was unconvinced by this and took only twelve minutes to reach a verdict of guilty. Tam was hanged at Walton Prison, Liverpool, on 23 March 1926.

Body of Margaret Brindley discovered, 1958

DECEMBER

3

On 3 December 1958, a lorry-driver stopped at a bridge over the River Ray, near the A41 road between Aylesbury, Buckinghamshire, and Bicester in Oxfordshire, intending to get water for his radiator. But on going down to the edge of the river, he found the body of a young pregnant woman. Margaret Brindley, a twenty-year-old prostitute, had been savagely battered, and her face was unrecognizable. However, she had been arrested for soliciting in London's Hyde Park only a few days earlier, and so could be identified from her fingerprints.

Margaret had moved to London after leaving her home in Wolverhampton, Staffordshire, when she was eighteen, and for the last ten months of her life had lived with a Turkish Cypriot named Eyyup Celal — the man who had persuaded her to go on the streets. Celal told police that he had taken Margaret to Paddington Station on 30 November so that she could go back and stay with her parents, to await the birth of her child. He also said that on 2 December — when it was believed that Margaret's murder had taken place — he had spent the whole day with another prostitute named Dorothy Johnson.

When Dorothy Johnson was questioned, she said that Celal had spent the night of 1 December with her, but not the following day. Another girl, Maureen Kelly, revealed that she and Margaret had been in Hyde Park together on the night of 1 December — and that Celal had seen them there about 9.30 p.m. It was also discovered that Celal had been seen driving along the Aylesbury to Bicester road on 2 December.

Forensic evidence linked Celal even more strongly to the crime, for a bloodstained metal bar found at the scene bore traces of paint identical to that which had been used on a door at his home, and lipstick on one of his monogrammed handkerchiefs — also found at the scene — was of the same type as a smudge left on his face by Dorothy Johnson on the morning of 2 December. Celal's car was found to be bloodstained, though he had washed it since the murder.

The twenty-one-year-old Cypriot, known as 'Tony the Turk', was therefore charged with Margaret Brindley's murder. At his trial at the Old Bailey in February 1959 it was alleged that he had committed the crime because the victim, being pregnant, had ceased to be of any use to him. Although he denied having lived off Margaret's earnings, Celal was convicted of murder and given a life sentence.

On 15 August 1960, Margaret Brindley's mother

— a woman of forty-eight, also named Margaret — was found battered to death in a house in Dunstall Hill Road, Wolverhampton, where she had been living with another man — a Jamaican — after leaving her husband. Her murderer, another West Indian living in the same house, had beaten her to death with a shoe after being insulted when he asked her for some money which she owed him. He, too, was sentenced to life imprisonment.

Murder of Mme D'Audeville, 1890

On 4 December 1890, René Sarrebourse d'Audeville, a bankrupt member of the French nobility, shot his estranged wife dead at the home of her wealthy parents, M. and Mme Heurteaux, at Nantes, in Brittany. Mme D'Audeville and her parents were having lunch at the time, and the culprit, entering suddenly, shot her in the mouth. He afterwards tried to shoot Mme Heurteaux, but her husband, a retired sardine merchant, managed to prevent this by striking his arm as he fired. Sarrebourse d'Audeville was charged with murder and brought to trial in Nantes the following March, the case exciting much public interest.

The prisoner, who was little more than thirty years of age, looked considerably older. He had led a dissipated life, spending most of his time hunting, fishing, drinking and gambling, and had married Heurteaux's daughter Félicie when he was twenty-seven for financial reasons. He then squandered the money from his marriage settlement within a short time, and finally went bankrupt as a result of speculating in stocks and shares which he could not afford. It was claimed that he had also ill-treated his wife and forced her to make a will in his favour.

In June 1890 Mme d'Audeville petitioned for a judicial separation, and was authorized to take up residence at her parents' home. The accused was left without any money at all and, being incapable of work, had to rely on friends for assistance. Then, in November, following various unsuccessful attempts to induce his wife to return to him, he bought a revolver and a double-barrelled shotgun and took rooms just a few yards from the Heurteaux residence. At the time of the shooting he also had a long, freshly-sharpened knife in his possession.

'In the room which I had taken, in the Rue Bonne-Louise, I heard roars of laughter going on between my wife and her parents,' he told the court at his trial. He said that as a result of this 'burst of merriment' he had forced his way into their presence, intending to take his own life.

But his father-in-law, on being asked whether he believed this, replied that the prisoner was 'much too great a coward' to do such a thing. 'The truth is that he was revenging himself by murdering her, because he had been deprived of the allowance I had always made her!' declared Heurteaux.

Further allegations were made by the prisoner's mother-in-law, who described him as 'a very evil man' and said that he had subjected her daughter to 'three long years of martyrdom' in his attempts to get his hands on the family fortune. Another witness, a former nurse to his children, said that the accused had dragged his wife about by the hair and beaten the children unmercifully. He had even threatened to throw the youngest one, aged four months, out of the window, this witness told the court.

Sarrebourse d'Audeville sobbed and moaned a great deal during the course of the proceedings, claiming that he had loved his wife and that the allegations of ill-treatment were all false. Three doctors testified that he was in such a condition of mind that he could not be considered responsible for his actions, and a friend's written deposition stated that the prisoner had fallen into a state of melancholy and hinted a lot about committing suicide after an attempted reconciliation with his wife had failed. By this time he had owned only a small iron bedstead and one or two chairs, and claimed that he was dying of hunger and cold.

Several other friends of the prisoner told the court that they regarded him as a scatter-brained fellow, easily excited but by no means evil, and the defence claimed that he was at the very least 'on the borderline of insanity'. But the jury took only half an hour to find him guilty, without extenuating circumstances, and he was sentenced to death. The sentence was later commuted to hard labour for life by the French President.

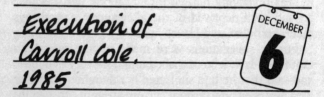

Execution of Carroll Cole, 1985

DECEMBER 6

On 6 December 1985, Carroll Edward Cole, a forty-seven-year-old drifter convicted of the murders of five women, was executed in Carson City, Nevada. The execution was carried out by means of a lethal injection, the condemned man being strapped to a table in the jail's converted gas chamber for the drugs to be administered. Cole thus became the fiftieth person to be put to death in the United States — but the first in Nevada — since the reinstatement of the death penalty nine years earlier.

Cole was a native of Sioux City, Iowa, but had been brought up near San Francisco. He had been dishonourably discharged from the navy for stealing two pistols and since then had been arrested for a variety of offences, including an unsuccessful attempt to kill his first wife by setting fire to a Dallas motel. His record also showed that he had been in mental hospitals in four different states, one of them following a suicide attempt in 1967.

Cole was arrested in December 1980 in connection with the murder of Wanda Fay Roberts, a thirty-two-year-old woman whose body had been found in a Dallas car park three weeks earlier. He then confessed that he had killed eight women during the previous nine years, and hinted that he may have killed many others as well. Some of the women he mentioned were known murder victims; others were not known to be dead or were believed to have died from natural causes. He later claimed that he had killed thirty-five women altogether.

The reason that some of these deaths had been put down to natural causes was that the victims had been hopelessly drunk at the time. 'The women had high levels of alcohol in their blood and were probably comatose or unconscious when Cole killed them,' one detective involved in the case explained. 'It doesn't take much to choke to death a person in that state and not leave any marks. Cole just might have found the way to commit the perfect murder.'

His second wife, Diana Faye, whom he had married in 1974, was one of his victims. Her body was found in their apartment in San Diego two days after Cole's arrest — by which time, according to the coroner's estimate, she had been dead for about a week. Her murder was followed by that of forty-three-year-old Sally Thompson in Dallas on the night of 30 November. Both of these women had been drinking heavily just before they died, and both were at first thought to have died of natural causes.

Carroll Cole showed little interest in the charges that were brought against him, and was unperturbed at the possibility of being executed. 'I have been in and out of institutions all my life,' he said. 'I know I'm sick. I just can't help myself. I just want the killing to stop.'

He was tried in Dallas, where he was convicted of three murders and given three life sentences, to be served concurrently. In this case he said that he had been 'repulsed' by what he called the loose morals of the victims, and said that he had killed them because they reminded him of his mother. 'I think I kill *her* through them,' he said.

Three years later Cole was brought to trial in Las Vegas for two more murders, this time pleading guilty and requesting the death penalty. When his wish was granted, he smiled and said, 'Thanks, Judge!' He later told a reporter who interviewed him on Death Row, 'I know I'll kill again if I get out of prison. So why prolong the life of a despicable person who acted as the judge, jury and executioner to the people he murdered?'

Shortly before his death Cole gave permission for his brain to be used for the purposes of research. He spent his last hours playing poker with the prison chaplain, and swallowed Valium tablets to steady his nerves before the execution was carried out.

Body of Thomas Meaney discovered, 1950

On the morning of 8 December 1950, William Donoghue, a forty-two-year-old bus conductor living in a block of flats near London's Waterloo Station, was found standing in the doorway of his own flat, staring at a body which was lying on the landing outside. The body was that of an older man, and lay face down in a pool of blood. Donoghue, who appeared dazed, kept muttering to himself, 'Is it a dummy or a body? Take it away!'

The police were informed, and a constable arrived on the scene. Donoghue, on being questioned, said, 'If that is a real man, I done it!' He then went on to say that the man had come home with him the night before. 'I thought he was joking with me,' said Donoghue. 'He was lying on the bed, making gurgling noises. I must have struck him with the bayonet and dragged him out on the landing.'

Later, at Southwark police station, Donoghue made another statement, giving more details of what had happened. The dead man was sixty-three-year-old Thomas Meaney, a friend of his who had worked as the driver of a Black Maria. Donoghue had met him at one of the local public houses the previous evening, and stayed drinking with him until closing time. Then, as they were both heavy drinkers, they went to the flat together and drank a bottle of gin which Donoghue had bought during the course of the evening. Eventually Meaney fell asleep on the bed and Donoghue dozed off leaning on a table.

Not long afterwards Donoghue woke up and tried to get into bed. He was far from sober by this time,

359

and had forgotten that Meaney was there with him. So when he found him lying asleep on the bed, he thought it was a dummy which somebody had left there for a joke.

He pulled his friend off the bed, and Meaney fell to the floor without protest, 'like a sack of coal'. While he lay there Donoghue stabbed him repeatedly with a Second World War bayonet which he normally used as a bread knife. Even then, when he saw his friend's blood, Donoghue did not realize what he had done — he merely assumed that the blood was red juice from a tube and that it had been used to trick him. He therefore dragged Meaney out onto the landing, then returned to the flat and went to bed.

It was not until he woke up several hours later and found blood all over the floor that he had any inkling of what had really happened.

Incredible though this story must have seemed, the police officers who investigated the affair could find no evidence to disprove it. Donoghue and Meaney had been friendly towards each other as they left the pub, and there was no reason to suppose that they had quarrelled afterwards. Donoghue had no injuries to suggest that there had been a struggle, and appeared to have had no other motive for killing his friend. Moreover, the dead man — who had been stabbed sixteen times in the head and neck — had no injuries to his hands, as he would have had if he had tried to protect himself.

No blood sample was taken from Donoghue at the time of his arrest, so his blood alcohol reading was not measured. But Meaney's was found to have been at a dangerously high level, at which one is ordinarily incapable of forming a felonious intent. And as Donoghue had been the drunker of the two when they left the pub together, it was possible that his blood alcohol level had been even higher than Meaney's at the time of the stabbing.

At any rate, when he was brought to trial at the Old Bailey in February 1951, the Principal Medical Officer at Brixton Prison gave his opinion that Donoghue — 'a quiet, inoffensive and respectable little man', according to his counsel — *had* been drunk enough to believe that he was stabbing a dummy rather than a human being. As a result of this, the Director of Public Prosecutions decided that there was insufficient evidence to proceed on a murder charge, and the prosecution accepted a plea of manslaughter. Donoghue was accordingly sent to prison for three years.

Execution of Alpha Otis Stephens, 1984

DECEMBER 12

On 12 December 1984, Alpha Otis Stephens, aged thirty-nine, was electrocuted at the Diagnostic and Classification Centre in Jackson, Georgia, following his conviction for murder ten years earlier. The execution took place shortly after midnight, the condemned man being strapped into the electric chair at 12.15 a.m. He declined to make a final statement, and watched intently as he was being prepared. It was noticed that he was trembling and biting his lips.

At 12.18 he was given a charge of 2000 volts — at which his head rolled slowly and his chest heaved. But when the electricity was switched off two minutes later he was seen to be breathing, and six minutes after that — when it was safe to enter the execution chamber — doctors examined him and pronounced him still alive. The warden therefore ordered that a

second jolt be given, and at 12.28 a.m. Stephens'
chest heaved once more and his head again rolled.
When the charge was cut off for the second time at
12.30 he was dead.

Stephens, known as 'Sonny Boy', had been sentenced in 1974 for the murder of a builder named
Roy Asbell during the course of a robbery. A plea for
mercy had been rejected only a few hours before the
sentence was carried out.

Though described as 'macabre' and 'disturbing' by
witnesses, the use of the second jolt when the prisoner
was found to be breathing was 'standard procedure',
according to a prison spokesman.

At an execution in Alabama in April 1983 three
charges were needed before the condemned man,
John Louis Evans, was pronounced dead. During the
first the electrode on his left leg burnt through and
fell off; then, when the second was given, a puff of
smoke and a burst of flame erupted from his left
temple and leg, but doctors said that they were still
not certain that he was dead.

Evans' lawyer afterwards complained that his
client had been 'burnt alive' and 'tortured ... in the
name of vengeance and in the disguise of justice'.

Kidnapping of Marion Parker, 1927

DECEMBER 15

On 15 December 1927, Marion Parker, one of the
twelve-year-old twin daughters of a Los Angeles bank
personnel officer, was abducted from her school by a
youth pretending that her father had met with an

accident. Her father, Perry Parker, afterwards received a number of ransom notes and telephone calls from a youth calling himself 'The Fox', and letters from his missing daughter — begging him to co-operate with the kidnapper — were also received. The ransom demanded was $1500.

Parker got the money ready in $20 gold certificates, as instructed, and drove to the place where he was to meet the kidnapper. However, he was followed by a police officer, and the culprit, realizing this, failed to appear. The next day, 17 December, he drove to a different location — having received further orders in the meantime — and waited in his car until another stopped alongside it. The driver of this second car, a youth with a handkerchief over the lower part of his face, then pointed a sawn-off shotgun at him and demanded the money.

Parker saw that the youth had a bundle which looked like a child with him, and was told that it was Marion and that she was asleep; he then handed over the money. At this, the youth said that he would leave the child further along the road, and told Parker not to move until he had done so. He then left the bundle a short distance away and drove off quickly. A moment or two later Parker was horrified to discover that his daughter was dead and that her forearms and legs had been cut off. The bundle contained the upper part of her body.

The kidnapper made good his escape, but his car, a Chrysler coupé which had been stolen in Kansas City, was found abandoned a few hours later. It was not taken away for examination for two days, as it was hoped that the culprit might return for it, but he did not. In the meantime the child's limbs, wrapped in towels and newspapers, were found in Elysian Park, in the same city.

Shortly after this somebody suggested that a youth named Hickman, a former employee of the same bank as Parker, might be the person responsible. Hickman, a messenger, had been convicted of forging cheques, and Parker had interceded on his behalf — with the result that Hickman was put on probation instead of being sent to jail. But thumb-prints found on one of the ransom notes — and also on one of the abandoned car's mirrors — were identified as his, and a search was started for him.

William Edward Hickman, aged nineteen, was arrested in Oregon on 22 December, with almost the whole of the ransom money in his possession. He was taken back to Los Angeles on Christmas Day, and soon confessed that he was guilty of the murder of Marion Parker. He had kidnapped her because he needed money to pay college expenses, then strangled her because he feared discovery, he said. He had then dissected her body so that he could put it into suitcases.

A search of the apartment which Hickman had occupied at the time resulted in the discovery of further evidence, including clotted blood in pipes in the bathroom. Shortly afterwards he made a further confession, revealing that on Christmas Eve, 1926, he and another youth named Welby Hunt had held up a Los Angeles drug-store and murdered the druggist, Ivy Toms. Welby Hunt was therefore arrested, and he also confessed, stating that he and Hickman had committed a number of other hold-ups as well.

Hickman was brought to trial for the murder of Marion Parker in January 1928, pleading not guilty by reason of insanity. But a note which he had passed to another prisoner, stating his intention of putting on an act of some sort to impress the jury, fell into the hands of the district attorney and was used against him. He was convicted and sentenced to death.

The trial of Hickman and Welby Hunt, for the murder of Ivy Toms, began the following day — 16 February — and in this case both prisoners were convicted of first-degree murder and sentenced to life imprisonment.

Hickman's execution, by hanging, had been scheduled to take place on 27 April 1928, but due to various appeals it was not carried out until 19 October the same year. During his months on Death Row he became a Catholic and spent much time reading his Bible, but was treated with contempt by many of his fellow-condemned. When the execution was finally carried out at San Quentin Prison, a mishap occurred, and he died from strangulation rather than a broken neck.

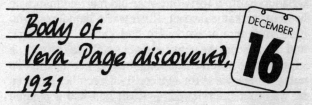

Body of Vera Page discovered, 1931

On the morning of 16 December 1931, Vera Page, a girl of eleven, was found strangled among the shrubs of a garden about a mile from her own home in London's Notting Hill district. She had been criminally assaulted and then murdered elsewhere — probably soon after her disappearance on the evening of 14 December — and the state of decomposition of the body suggested that it had been kept in a warm place, such as an inhabited room, in the meantime.

It was found, too, that although there had been rain during the night before its discovery, only the back of Vera's coat, where it had touched the ground, was damp. So the body had clearly been lying outside for only a short while.

The child had been strangled manually, and a cord had afterwards been tied loosely round her neck, perhaps to enable her murderer to carry her body over his shoulder. A finger-stall, smelling strongly of ammonia, was found in the crook of her right arm, its size indicating that it had been used by a man. There was also soot and coal-dust on her face and clothes, and candle-grease on her coat.

Inquiries in the area led to the discovery of a disused coal-cellar under the pavement of Stanley Crescent, near which Vera Page had last been seen alive, and where it was now believed that the crime had been committed; and a woman told police that during the early morning of 16 December she had seen a man pushing a bundle on a wheel-barrow near the place where the body was found.

Before long suspicion began to centre on Percy Orlando Rush, a forty-one-year-old married man who lived in the same district. Rush was a launderer, who used ammonia at work. He had known Vera Page, and had been wearing a finger-stall to protect a suppurating wound not long before her death. To make things worse for him, on 17 December — when he was first interviewed — Rush had had a pyjama cord in his pocket; this could have been the cord which was tied round Vera's neck after death.

But the evidence against him was far from conclusive. Bandages and lint from his home were not identical to those found in the finger-stall, and it could not be stated definitely that the grease on the child's coat was the same as that of candles in his possession. Moreover, the woman who had seen the man with the wheel-barrow was unable to identify him.

At the inquest which followed, Rush gave evidence, denying that he had had anything to do with Vera's death. He said that he had started to walk home from work — a journey which took him two hours — only a short while before the child was seen alive for the last time, and claimed that he had discarded his finger-stall two days earlier. The coroner, having questioned him at length, pointed out the possibilities of coincidence, and the jury returned a verdict of murder by some person or persons unknown.

The crime was never solved.

Body found in mineshaft, 1948

DECEMBER
20

On 20 December 1948, a Coal Board official looked down a disused mineshaft at Walton, near Wakefield in Yorkshire, and saw a body floating in water 130 feet below. He informed the police and it was brought to the surface with the use of grappling irons, but the head, both forearms and one leg were missing. The pathologist who carried out the post-mortem was therefore able to say only that it was the body of an elderly woman who had been five feet tall, and that it had been immersed for some years.

The missing parts were later found under the water by a mine rescue worker, and the pathologist was then able to estimate that the woman had been over seventy years of age. It was still not possible to determine the cause of her death, but it seemed unlikely that she had fallen down the shaft by accident, as the opening had been covered with heavy boards — which, in any case, had been put back into position afterwards. So the police naturally regarded her death as a possible murder, and it was not long before they discovered her identity.

A check of missing-persons lists revealed that Emma Sheard, a woman of seventy-five, had disappeared from her home in Chevet Terrace, just a hundred yards from the mineshaft, seven years earlier. The house which she had owned was still occupied by her great-niece, Winifred Hallaghan, who, on being seen by police officers, admitted not only that the body in question was that of her great-aunt, but also that she (Mrs Hallaghan) had killed her.

Mrs Hallaghan, a nursing orderly, said that she and her husband had both been living at the victim's house in 1941. There had been a great deal of tension between her great-aunt and herself at the time, and the old woman had infuriated her by saying that Mr Hallaghan was having an affair with somebody else. 'We had a row and I hit her with the flat of my hand, and she fell against the sewing machine and cracked her head,' Mrs Hallaghan told the police.

She went on to say that she had disposed of the body during the early hours of the following morning after wheeling it to the old mineshaft in a pram, and explained the old woman's disappearance to neighbours by saying that she had 'wandered away'. In 1943, however, she had forged her great-aunt's signature on a house conveyance document, transferring the property in Chevet Terrace to herself.

Although Mrs Hallaghan was arrested for murder, the charge was withdrawn during the committal proceedings. But in March 1949 she appeared for trial at the Leeds Assizes on a number of other charges — three of forgery as well as one of manslaughter — and was convicted on all of them. In passing sentence, the judge told her, 'I do not doubt that you have suffered greatly over the years, but this court must not let any such consideration interfere with the course of justice.' He sent her to prison for five years.

DECEMBER
24

On the morning of 24 December 1938, Ernest Percival Key, a jeweller aged sixty-four, was found unconscious and covered in blood in the back room of his shop in Surbiton, Surrey. He had been attacked during the course of a robbery and stabbed about thirty-one times in the head, face and neck. He died on the way to hospital.

A bowler hat which had been left at the scene of the crime was examined by the county pathologist, Dr Eric Gardner. From the evidence of its size and hairs found attached to it, he was able to give police officers some useful information about the owner's appearance before the arrival of the Home Office pathologist, Sir Bernard Spilsbury.

The hat was found to belong to William Thomas Butler, an unemployed driver aged twenty-nine who lived with his wife and two children in Teddington, about three miles from the shop. Butler had a criminal record for house-breaking, and it was discovered that shortly after the murder he had had hospital treatment for cuts on his hands, using a false name and address and claiming that he had injured himself in an accident with a wood-cutting machine. He had actually cut his hands by stabbing the old jeweller with an unguarded dagger or knife.

Charged with murder, William Butler was brought to trial at the Old Bailey on 15 February 1939. The trial lasted two days, the prisoner claiming that he had killed in self-defence and was only guilty of manslaughter. He was, however, convicted of murder and sentenced to death, his execution taking place at

Wandsworth Prison, London, on 29 March 1939.

Dr Gardner's part in the solution of this crime was exaggerated in an English newspaper article, and exaggerated even more in a German one. As a result of this publicity, Scotland Yard received a request from the German police for information about 'the clairvoyant, Erich Gardner', who could solve a murder case merely by looking at a hat.

Execution of George Loake. 1911

DECEMBER
28

On 28 December 1911, George Loake, a sixty-four-year-old unemployed engine driver, was hanged at Stafford Jail for the murder of his estranged wife Elizabeth. The crime had taken place on 7 August previously, at a house in Warwick Street, Walsall, where Elizabeth was staying with a family named Dolloway. It followed an unsuccessful attempt at reconciliation on her husband's part — the last of a number which he had made since their parting several weeks earlier.

Loake, a widower with nine children, had married Elizabeth Newitt, a divorcée eighteen years younger than himself, eight years before the tragedy occurred. At the time he had been a jovial and well-liked man, and he and Elizabeth had been happy together until the summer of 1909, when he was involved in an accident during shunting operations just outside Walsall.

As a result of this accident, he suffered internal injuries and began to complain of blinding headaches; he also became sullen, took a morbid interest in knives and started to drink heavily. Eventually, in March 1911, he was sacked for leaving his engine unattended while he went off to buy alcohol.

After working for the London and North Western Railway Company for over fifty years Loake then found himself with no prospect of obtaining work elsewhere, and no right to the pension which he would otherwise have been entitled to on reaching retirement age. As he and his wife were forced to spend their savings, they soon had nothing left, and in June 1911 they were evicted from their home in Portland Street, Walsall. It was at this point that Elizabeth left him and, taking the two children from her first marriage, went to stay with the Dolloways.

By this time Loake's behaviour was becoming progressively worse. He had repeatedly assaulted his wife during their last few months together, and now, living in a lodging house, he made frequent threats of suicide — one of them when he visited his daughter Maud the day before the murder. The effect of this was that his children were all wary of him and unwilling to offer him a home.

On 7 August — Bank Holiday Monday — Loake went to see Elizabeth about 10.30 a.m., and spoke to her in the living room of the Dolloways' house. When a quarrel started and she turned to leave the room he suddenly grabbed her from behind and began stabbing her with a knife which he had had concealed inside his coat. His wife screamed, struggled and managed to leave the house — only to die in a nearby courtyard while a doctor was examining her. A post-mortem revealed that she had six knife wounds about her face and neck, as well as others in her left hand and forearm.

Loake had been arrested after an unsuccessful attempt to cut his own throat and was brought to trial at the Staffordshire Assizes in November. One of the witnesses who appeared against him was eleven-year-old Tommy Dolloway, who had been watching the scene in the living room unobserved when the attack took place. He had afterwards run upstairs and locked himself in his bedroom until he felt that it was safe to emerge.

The defence claimed that the prisoner was guilty only of manslaughter, because he had not intended to kill his wife and had been of unsound mind at the time. But the jury took only sixteen minutes to find him guilty of murder, and the judge told them that they could not possibly have come to any other conclusion. Loake then listened in silence as he was sentenced to death.

During the next few weeks his appeal was heard and dismissed, and the Home Secretary, who had received petitions for a reprieve, decided against recommending the use of the royal prerogative to spare his life. On the morning of 28 December a small crowd of little more than a dozen people waited outside the prison for news that Loake had been hanged.

Shooting of Ruth Hadley. 1908

DECEMBER
29

On the bitterly cold night of 29 December 1908, Edward Lawrence, a rich Wolverhampton brewer, called on a Dr Galbraith, claiming to have shot a woman. Galbraith accompanied him to his home, but refused to go inside until a colleague agreed to go with him. Finally, when the two doctors entered the house together, they found a young woman lying on the dining-room floor, fatally injured. Ruth Hadley, an attractive barmaid, had been shot in the right temple and had a slight wound in her right arm. She died shortly afterwards.

Lawrence, a married man who was well known locally, had been having an affair with Ruth for some time, and had left his wife and children for her. He also had a craving for drink and, under its influence, was inclined to become violent. His wife had obtained a decree nisi on account of a brutal assault which she had suffered at his hands — as well as his adultery — but had never had the decree made absolute. More recently, Lawrence had been fined for assaulting a policeman with his teeth.

In the room in which the shooting had taken place a meal for two people was found on the table, almost untouched. Prior to the arrival of the police Lawrence, in his customary drunken state, made various remarks which appeared to be an admission of guilt, but later his attitude changed and he declared that Ruth had shot herself. Moreover, the revolver which had been used was found to contain four undischarged and only one spent cartridge, suggesting that Lawrence had reloaded it, in the hope of giving the impression that only one shot had been fired.

Lawrence was charged with murder and in March 1909 appeared for trial in Stafford, where prosecution witnesses told the court that he had shot at Ruth and threatened her on earlier occasions. It was also revealed that Ruth had left Lawrence in September 1908, returning to him just before Christmas, and that he had had another mistress in the meantime. Another witness, a servant girl who had seen the couple quarrelling on the night of Ruth's death, said that Lawrence had accused Ruth of being drunk, and that she had denied this, making as if to throw a cruet at him. The servant added that when she left the room she heard the key turn in the lock and knew that it was Ruth who had turned it.

Edward Marshall Hall, defending, produced witnesses to prove that Ruth had been as violent as his client, that she had attacked or threatened Lawrence on many occasions, and that, on returning to him in December 1908, she had been maddened by the knowledge that he had had another woman in her place. He then called the prisoner, an educated and well-spoken man, to give his own account of her death.

Lawrence told the court that on the night in question, when he accused her of being drunk, Ruth had thrown crockery and fire-irons at him, and he had told her to leave his house for ever. He had then gone to his bedroom to fetch the revolver — which he invariably kept under his pillow — and had fired it in order to frighten her. Afterwards, he said, he had gone back to the bedroom and hidden the gun under his mattress, unaware that he had wounded her slightly in the arm. But Ruth had then gone to the bedroom herself, found the gun, and returned to the dining-room, apparently intending to kill him. During the course of a struggle which took place at this point she had accidentally been shot dead.

The court listened to the prisoner's story in silence, and found it to be unexpectedly credible, even to the extent of being corroborated by minor details given by other witnesses — of the disarranged state of the bedroom, for example. The judge, who had previously been hostile to Lawrence, was suddenly won over to his side and later, following a dramatic speech by Marshall Hall, summed up in his favour.

The jury, after retiring for only twenty minutes, returned a verdict of not guilty, and the judge, in discharging the prisoner, said that he had received a 'most terrible lesson'. 'If you will turn over a new page in your life, you may yet have a happy time with your lawful wife and children, and then, perhaps,

God will forgive you for the life you have led,' Mr Justice Jelf continued. 'I earnestly trust that what I have said to you will bear fruit in your heart and in your life.'

The case thus gave Marshall Hall his greatest victory in a murder trial — at least in his own opinion. But three days later Edward Lawrence was in trouble again, this time for assaulting another man in a Wolverhampton inn.

Murder of Grigori Rasputin, 1916

DECEMBER 30

During the early hours of 30 December 1916 (or 17 December, according to the Gregorian calendar), a dissipated monk with remarkable healing powers was murdered by a group of conspirators in Petrograd (now Leningrad). The crime, which the victim had foreseen, showed the inability of the Tsar to maintain order and so was far-reaching in its effects. But it was the monk's powers of survival which made it the most famous murder in Russian history.

Grigori Efimovich Rasputin, a man of peasant origin aged about forty-five, was ungainly, drunken and lecherous, but exercised great influence at the Russian court through having several times saved the life of the Tsar's son Alexei, a haemophiliac. This influence enabled him to interfere in the affairs of both Church and State, securing appointments for his own nominees and exasperating others. He was also suspected of being the centre of a pro-German conspiracy which was undermining the war effort.

On the night of 29 December Rasputin was lured to the home of Prince Felix Yusupov, the instigator of the conspiracy. Yusupov, aged twenty-nine, was married to the Tsar's niece and had invited the 'Holy Devil' to a midnight supper on the pretext that the Princess was ill and wanted him to treat her. In fact, the Princess was not in Petrograd at the time, and Yusupov entertained Rasputin alone in an attractively-furnished room of the palace cellar, giving him cakes and wine poisoned with potassium cyanide.

The poison had no apparent effect on Rasputin, even though he consumed a large amount of it, and after an hour and a half Yusupov went to see his fellow conspirators in an upstairs room, to ask them what he should do. On being given a revolver, he returned to the dining-room and shot his guest in the back. Dr Lazovert, a Polish physician, then entered the room and pronounced Rasputin dead. But this proved to be a mistake, for shortly afterwards the victim of the crime opened his eyes, struggled to his feet and lunged at Yusupov's throat.

The terrified Yusupov ran upstairs, calling out a warning to his friends. Vladimir Purishkevich, a member of the Duma, then pursued Rasputin from the palace, firing shots at him in the snow-covered courtyard. The monk fell to the ground with bullets in his chest and shoulder, and Yusupov and Purishkevich, who were both hysterical by now, kicked and battered him as he lay there. Finally, the conspirators bound Rasputin with ropes and pushed him under the ice of the River Neva. Even so, when his body was recovered two days later, his lungs were full of water and one arm was almost free, showing that he had still been alive at the time of his immersion.

The news of Rasputin's murder was received with approval by Petrograd society and the Tsar, Nicholas II, could not punish the culprits without causing widespread offence. Yet his failure to do so served only to show that his power, which depended on fear rather than loyalty, was far from invincible. In murdering the court favourite with impunity, Prince Yusupov and his friends — one of whom was the Tsar's cousin — ensured the downfall of the Romanov dynasty.

Rasputin's powers of survival have been the subject of some speculation, and the failure of the poison — 'enough potassium cyanide to kill a monastery of monks', according to Yusupov — has naturally been seen as quite extraordinary. In this connection, however, the late Professor Keith Simpson pointed out that cyanide is more or less harmless until it comes into contact with the gastric juices, so that if the victim suffers from chronic gastritis — 'as Rasputin probably did' — he could swallow many times the fatal dose without being affected by it.

Murder of Grace Adamson. 1975

DECEMBER
31

On the evening of 31 December 1975, Mark Rowntree, a youth of nineteen with an urge to kill, was wandering round Bingley, in Yorkshire, with a long-bladed knife hidden in his shoulder-bag. He was on the look-out for a suitable victim, and before long stopped outside the home of Mrs Grace Edith Adamson in Old Main Street. Mrs Adamson, a widow of eighty-five, was knitting as she watched television, and as her curtains were undrawn, Rowntree could see her through the window.

Selecting her as the person to be killed, he rang her

doorbell and waited, holding his knife in readiness. When she came to find out who was there he induced her to open the door by saying that he was 'the police'. He then rushed into the house and stabbed her seven times, two of the wounds piercing her heart. Afterwards he left the scene of the crime, buried the weapon locally and went to a public house for a glass of beer.

Three days later Rowntree again felt the urge to kill. He bought himself another knife, and that evening made his way to the nearby village of Wastburn, where he attacked sixteen-year-old Stephen Wilson at a bus stop. The victim, with three stab wounds in his chest and stomach, ran away screaming and managed to get help. He died after being admitted to hospital, though not without giving an account of what had happened. Rowntree, in the meantime, had swum across a river — this was during a snowstorm — hitched a lift to a taxi-rank and taken a taxi back to his lodgings in Bradford Road, Shipley.

The police were now able to issue a description of the person they believed to have killed both Mrs Adamson and Stephen Wilson, saying that he was about twenty-two years old, 'with black shoulder-length hair, wearing a black jacket and carrying a shoulder-pack'. A few days later they interviewed the taxi-driver who had picked him up while he was soaked from swimming the river and thus discovered his address — but not in time to prevent him committing two more murders.

These took place on 7 January, eight days after he had killed Mrs Adamson, and the victims on this occasion were Mrs Barbara Booth, a twenty-four-year-old prostitute, and her son Alan, aged three. Rowntree had previously met Mrs Booth through a contact magazine, and on feeling once again the urge to kill, went to see her at her home in Burley, Leeds. There, having pretended that he wanted sexual intercourse, he stabbed her eighteen times, using the same knife he had used to kill Stephen Wilson. He then killed her son, who had been hiding in a corner, as he feared that the boy would be able to identify him.

Rowntree returned to his lodgings later the same day and found the officer in charge of the investigation waiting for him; he was taken into custody and admitted the four crimes. Claiming to have been driven by an insatiable desire to kill, he said that he had set himself a target of five murders, in order to beat Donald Neilson, the 'Black Panther' (see vol 1, 14 January), whom he admired.

It was learnt that Rowntree, as a baby, had been adopted by a middle-class couple. He had been sent to a public school and had qualified to go to university, but had then left home and gone to work as a bus conductor. He was found to be schizophrenic and to have been motivated by a desire for revenge as a result of being rejected by members of the opposite sex.

Rowntree appeared for trial on four charges of murder at Leeds Crown Court in June 1976. He denied murder in each case but admitted manslaughter, pleading diminished responsibility. The prosecution accepted these pleas, and the judge told the prisoner, 'It's clear from the medical evidence that at the time you committed these terrible crimes you were suffering from this severe mental illness.' He ordered that Rowntree be sent to Rampton Hospital, a top-security psychiatric establishment, for an indefinite period.